# Development Arrested

# Development Arrested

## The Blues and Plantation Power in the Mississippi Delta

CLYDE WOODS

With Introduction by
Ruth Wilson Gilmore

VERSO

London • New York

Dedicated to Lena, James, and Malik Woods, Mamie Woods,
Robert Gibson, Nathaniel Gibson, Sr., Denise Bates, and to
Willie Dixon, Fannie Lou Hamer, and Richard Wright

This paperback edition first published 2017
First published by Verso 1998
© Clyde Woods 1998, 2000, 2017
Introduction © Ruth Wilson Gilmore 2017

1 3 5 7 9 10 8 6 4 2

**Verso**
UK: 6 Meard Street, London W1F 0EG
US: 20 Jay Street, Suite 1010, Brooklyn, NY 11201
versobooks.com

Verso is the imprint of New Left Books

ISBN-13: 978-1-84467-561-6
ISBN-13: 978-1-78663-252-4 (UK EBK)
ISBN-13: 978-1-78663-253-1 (US EBK)

**British Library Cataloguing in Publication Data**
A catalogue record for this book is available from the British Library

**The Library of Congress Has Cataloged the Hardback Edition as Follows:**
Woods. Clyde Adrian.
    Development arrested : the cotton and blues empire of the
Mississippi Delta / Clyde Woods.
        p.  cm. — (The Haymarket series)
    Includes bibliographical references (p.   ) and index.
    ISBN 1–85984–811–7 (cloth)
        1. Afro-Americans—Mississippi River Valley—Economic conditions.
2. Afro–Americans—Mississippi River Valley—Politics and
government.  3. Afro–Americans—Mississippi River Valley—Social
conditions.  4. Blues (Music)—Political aspects—Mississippi River
Valley—History.  5. Plantation life—Mississippi River Valley—
History.  6. Mississippi River Valley—Economic conditions.
7. Mississippi River Valley—Race relations.  8. Mississippi River
Valley—Politics and government.  9. United States. Lower
Mississippi Delta Development Commission. I. Title.
F358.2.N4W66 1998
976.3'300496073—dc21                                98–39689
                                                                        CIP

Typeset by SetSystems Ltd, Saffron Walden, Essex
Printed and bound by CPI Group (UK) Ltd, Croydon, CR0 4YY

# Contents

In a Natchez cemetery I
learn beneath sacred grounds
that hold bones of the Who's
Who of 1800 plantation society
and remains of two Confederate
Generals. A couple of blacks
are interred with honor;
one, a musician, perhaps—
a blues singer who did
not sing rain into droughts of
his peoples' days—his people
tilling and tilling so
mansions can be erected;
the other a barber, a free Negro,
who aborted bondage and
owned slaves himself. Cut
down by a white who owed
him money. I learn Natchez
has more millionaires
than any American town
in the early 19th century.

When I visit huge mansions
I run around to the back,
looking for the house
behind the house behind
the Big house where my origins
begin in this Republic.
There: a forlorn abandoned
cabin peers from debris. My
ancestors' spirits converse
in broken accents of jimpson
weeds. Bitter winters devour
their names then rush to
confront my face. I do
not find any hints on lips
of guides that they
ever exist.

Makers of wealth
are invisible in America.
Maybe blues singers
molded tales of crimson
sorrows here and moaned them
up river to the deltas
in back stroked agony. Maybe
the crawling kingsnake,
whose head they bash—
like that of Choctaw and Chickasaw—rule
the den of truths
not revealed.

There are no monuments
to those who worked the
landscapes of reality
in this town. This painting
is incomplete. Elegant
mansions are witnesses
to crimes. They testify
with opulence. They
testify with grandeur
and extravagance. Somebody's
hands bleed so I
exist. Somebody's feet
cordoned my boundaries
from wilderness. Somebody's
shoulders hold me up.

Here is an incomplete blues
song. This Natchez I
visit. My epic is totality:
nomadic memory of the
times strolling in breezes.
And despotic hands
clapping limitations
on dawns of brown eyes.
America is my song, red
blood of native Americans
eavesdropping on the heavy
sack my mother pulls. This
land is my landscape of inherited
harvests. I excavate with
songs.

I know this land. I breathe
this land. I birth this land.
I embrace this land. Where, Architect,
James "Son" Thomas, blue
prints my song in out
stretched screams in tenderness.
He inherits from Gospel
trains rolling from prayers
and sermons. His days mothered
in Leland misery. Muddy Waters, Muralist of
the spirit, scrawls my initials
on hours in this place. His damp
metaphors of pain spread debts
inside memory. Here. Wright lifts
the anvil of articulation
to **wring meaning from meaningless
suffering**. I know.

My song, polyglot
blues singers' voyages
through words on trial. Defends
the voiceless.

In Wolf's laminated
fresco of howls on walls
of my soul. I unravel
a share
cropper's diary. A sonic
epic of landless fingers
picking cotton
mouth greed. As guardian
angels. I am the black boy,
as chattel, as sharecroppers,
as worker, as the homeless
and imprisoned.

Here. My song over
flows the gossip of grand
estates and whispers of
famished names of uprooted
from memory. Out
cast memoirs of toilers. I
balance neglect with epic
moans. I am Mississippi: frontier
landscapes of blood
letting and blood
hounds on my trails. Sagas
of the **new world**: Indians
massacred in my skull. Where
names of the lynched form
a gallery of gentle
side dishes of horror.
My song and I
are combatants on chaotic
plains of experiences.

I come from a million field
hollers and moans. The wretched
itinerary of chains.
I am the native son of
a bitch's brew hopping
a Be-Bop Express
from here to some
where and some
where. I set fires
to curtains of silence.

*Sterling D. Plumpp*
*June 17, 1998*

# Acknowledgements

In many ways this project was a lifetime in the making and, therefore, I hope to be forgiven by friends and colleagues inadvertently omitted here. First, I'd like to thank my mother, Lena Woods, who has suffered with me, and for me, over these long years. Second, my son, Malik Woods, deserves special credit for developing into a beautiful young man even though his father was not always there to guide him. Other family members were also key: Sylvia, Stephen, and Nathaniel Gibson; the Bates, Beaird, McCormick, Langley, Nelson, and Pye families; Bootsie, Vivian Wilkins, and Pauline Wilson. Additionally, many individuals in Baltimore prepared me for this journey including Beverly Boston, Eddie Conway, Rev. Vernon Dobson, Elizabeth Hurley, Twila Mohammed, Esther Redd, Andito Siwatu, and the students, staff, and faculty of the Department of Urban and Regional Planning at Morgan State University. Among my academic influences I'm especially grateful to Calvin Hernton at Oberlin College who set me on this journey twenty years ago and to my committee chairperson, Ed Soja at the University of California, Los Angeles, who helped me see it to completion. I've also been fortunate enough to receive guidance and inspiration from the following scholars to whom I'm eternally grateful: Hamza Allavi, Robert Bullard, Charles Burnett, Judith Carney, Julie Dash, Leo Estrada, Margaret FitzSimmons, John Friedmann, Teshome Gabriel, Haile Gerima, Ruth Gilmore, Eugene Grigsby, Cynthia Hamilton, Susanna Hecht, Allan Heskin, Gerald Horne, John Horton, Mel King, Yusef Lateef, Anthony Parent, Laura Pulido, Leonie Sandercock, Theressa Singleton, Michael Storper, Bonnie Thornton-Dill, Maria Varela, and Billy Woodberry; I'm eternally grateful also to the students and staff of the Department of Urban and Regional Planning, UCLA.

Additionally, numerous friends and colleagues from many disciplines were instrumental to my intellectual development: Angel Acala, Erlyene Alvarez, Lisa Brock, Anthony Browne, Shirl Buss, Yvette Galindo, Ricardo Gomes, Norma Governor, Reheema Gray, Richard Green, Secundino Guzman, Dejene Habermatian, Iyamide Hazeley, Wardell Herron, Bobbi Hodges-Betts, Tarry Hum, Maria Jackson, Florence Kabawsa, Chana Lee, Roberto Monte-Mor, Peter Ngau, Sipho Nyao, Akilah Oliver, David Organ, Steve Peck, Natasha Primo, Roxie France, Haripriya Ragan, Fatimah Rony, David Rzspenski,

Victoria Santiago, Sasha, Anthony Scott, Cheryl Sharpe, Joseph Simms, Gerald Thomas, Lisa Washington, Maliya Washington, Ron Wilkins, and Itabari Zulu. Many insights on current conditions in the Delta were gained from valuable discussions with Ronald Bailey, Owen Brooks, Ralph Cristy, Arthur Cosby, Andrew Ewing, Wilbur Hawkins, Melvin Horton, Stan Hyland, Mary Jackson, Pamela Moore, Charles Tisdale, and from the staffs of the Blues City Cultural Center in Memphis, the Federation of Southern Cooperatives, the Martin Luther King Jr Center for Social Change, the Tougaloo College Archives and the Rural Organizing and Cultural Center in Holmes County, Mississippi. Numerous individuals at Alcorn State University, Delta State University, Jackson State University, Memphis State University, Mississippi State University, Mississippi Valley State University and the University of Mississippi provided invaluable assistance. The Woodrow Wilson Rural Policy Fellowship Program deserves a note of thanks for enabling me to complete my fieldwork. I'm also extremely grateful to the many individuals and organizations in the Delta who took the time to educate me. Many thanks are due to the Verso editors, readers, and staff, particularly Mike Davis, Michael Sprinker, Colin Robinson, Jane Hindle, Gopal Balakrishnan, Pat Harper, and Adam Green. I was truly honored by Dr John Biggers's decision to allow me to use *The Upper Room* for the cover. I'd like to thank him and his representative Eugene Phony of Artcetera in Houston. Similarly, I'm deeply grateful to Memphis photographer Robert Jones for his contribution to this work. I'd like also to dedicate this work to Paul, and to all the other young people in the Delta, Baltimore, Los Angeles, and all communities who have been tragically taken from us way before their time. And I'd like to thank Carol Ahmed and the faculty, staff, and students of the Department of African and African American Studies at Pennsylvania State University. Finally, the author is solely responsible for the conclusions reached in this work.

*Clyde Woods*
*June 1998*

# Introduction

Clyde Adrian Woods left us long before anyone was ready to see him go. The last time we met face to face was outdoors in the Southern California sunshine, where the matte effect of Inland Empire smog softens wrinkles and other signs of wear. Nearly three months to the day before he died, Woods spoke mainly about his life's future purpose. He was very thin, elegant as always, smiling at the younger scholars he had just—characteristically—encouraged in their scholarship by gently demanding they explain it to him. Younger people always flocked to Woods at conferences, and if you wanted to find him, the best bet was to wander the corridors looking for crowds—eventually you would see him surrounded, guiding, talking, listening.

Our brief exchange about life's meaning took speculative twists and turns—in pursuit of what poet Claudia Rankine calls "an unknown that does not terrify." Yet, in the decades I knew him, he always lived purposefully. Indeed, it's perhaps because he never stopped wondering what he was to become that his scholarship so richly suggested possible futures.

Clyde Woods trained as an urban and regional planner at UCLA's now-defunct Graduate School of Architecture and Urban Planning (GSAUP), where Ed Soja served as his principal advisor. Early on, Soja had studied East African cities, and found his own life purpose sharply defined in the ferment that concentrated in the revolutionary and revolutionizing 1970s University of Dar es Salaam. Generations of geographers, sociologists, planners, and historians have been shaped by that time and place, even if many do not know it. While becoming an Americanist, Soja also became conversant in radical Black feminist critique, especially the works of bell hooks. In this context, and with his distinctively incisive openness, Woods developed a practice of dialectical reasoning that broke the orthodoxy of born-again Marxism so prevalent in the United States then and now. He turned his formidable thinking, meticulous research, and powerful writing toward exposing the *longue durée* of Black peasant and working-class struggle in the US South and beyond.

That *durée* itself had a history long before the Atlantic slave trade produced the fundamental conditions for the existence of a Black peasantry and working class in the Americas. It is here where Woods's work explores both domination and resistance *and* consciousness and form. Indeed, the theoretical framework for

*Development Arrested* shaped his lifelong project, which in turn connected with the indispensable creativity of Cedric Robinson—with whom he worked closely at the UCSB Department of Black Studies during the last six years of his life.

*Development Arrested* does two things. First, it details 140 years of crisis and consolidation in the Lower Mississippi Delta. How did the dominant forces of the serial historic blocs organize the relative autonomy of state, scale, capital, racism, and markets to achieve renewed regional hegemony? The dynamics argued in these chapters demonstrate not just the persistence of oppression, but also the modes and terms through which the "common" in "common sense" changes through struggle and compromise. In other words, the remarkable persistence of what Woods called the Bourbon plantocracy was not inevitable even if it can be traced across regimes of accumulation. This means, of course, the defeat and destruction of that form is possible too. But how might that be so?

Here we turn to *Development Arrested*'s second great achievement. Woods elaborated a concept he called "the blues epistemology." At a memorial in 2012, Soja told us that Woods originally intended to call his heuristic "the blues ontology." Although one might disagree with Soja's guidance, his understanding of Woods's theoretical intervention emphasized the cultural and analytical interdependencies that cohabit a single political-economic geography at any scale. Fair enough. However, what ontology might have done is draw on Robinson's insights about the entire worlds that also travelled in slave ships—via captives' consciousness and culture—and the subsequent forms of being made palpable in otherwise unendurable situations. In other words, by conceptualizing materiality as operating in excess of its own expression, Woods's work was, from the start, participating in what Robinson called the "Black Radical Tradition." His imagination, like Harriet Tubman's, enlivened through meticulous practice the work of grounding the struggle for freedom, over and over again.

The first time we met was in 1991 during my office hours when I adjuncted in African American Studies at UCLA. He arrived in his customary dapper attire, accompanied by his five-year-old son and a family friend visiting from the UK. We greeted each other formally, and after an awkward pause he made his pitch, requesting an independent study to work through whether to write his dissertation about Lower Mississippi Delta development or about the blues epistemology. By the end of the quarter I had helped him trust his scholarly sensibility to do both. He did, in a monumental dissertation.

Six years later, he asked for help finding a publisher. Then a PhD student, I was also a bookseller groupie, having long been married to an independent practitioner of the rapidly declining trade. I received the 800-page dissertation and read it nonstop while traveling from New Jersey to Los Angeles to meet up at the annual American Booksellers Association (ABA) meeting—a trade show where thousands of publishers display tens of thousands of new titles for twenty thousand or so frontline retailers.

Los Angeles's brand-new convention center hosted the ABA. The vast complex inaugurated the decades-long displacement of thousands of working-class people from the freeway-bordered edge of downtown, where not-yet-gentrified SROs and ten-story sweatshops provided shelter and income to Black, Latino, and Asian households. A few months before the center's grand opening, union personnel toured the new facility. At a time of steep union decline, the Hotel Employees and Restaurant Employees Union (HERE) had achieved prominence for its innovative Justice for Janitors anti-outsourcing campaign. One of HERE's delegates was strategist David Koff, the late documentary filmmaker whose works include *The Black Man's Land Trilogy*, as well as *Blacks Britannica*. Koff showed the group that the map of the globe carved into the vast convention center foyer was missing Africa. The trade center's management retrofitted a bit of the continent in a corner. When Clyde and I arrived I took him to the scene of forgetting and he pondered for some time the afterthought literally set in stone. It is corny but compelling that Clyde's project travels multiple obscured landscapes to lay effective guideposts through that which doesn't even figure in granite—or archival —monuments to racial capitalism's globalizing rounds.

We walked the book convention, aisle by aisle, talking with editors at many university presses. Most of them pursed their lips, distinctly dismayed by the length of the dissertation and the work's ambitious complexity. In those days both university and trade publishers readily picked up new titles in Black Studies, having turned a corner in the late 1980s thanks to the rise of oppositional studies and "diversity requirements" in university curricula. But it went better for titles that were either compensatory or devastation studies: in the former, Black people also fought in wars, or excel in math, for instance; in the latter, Black people are unemployed, or wealth-challenged, or beat up, or undereducated, or incarcerated. Clyde's book—this book—proposed thinking differently about everything, including thinking. And yet it was not a book of "theory" and therefore did not command the attention of publishers for whom that aspect of intellectual activity, especially in the United States, was pretty hot too.

Around a corner we found Colin Robinson minding the Verso booth. Clyde laid out his study to enthusiastic reception. Colin had signed a book I recommended some years earlier, and we had an easy-going, once-a-year friendship in which we talked about reading and writing, politics and theory. Colin invited a proposal that the Verso editorial board accepted. The rest is history. We are all sorry that *Development Arrested* did not enjoy the kind of editing so ambitious a work deserves—especially because in compressing 800 pages into fewer than 300, Clyde had to squeeze out too many transitions and explanations. The book is reproduced here in its original edition, without corrections. That said, a little imagination fills the gaps. I have often taught this book and marveled at how it transforms students in thought and practice—as serious scholars, as political organizers, and as humans on this planet.

Clyde Woods served on the front lines of many organizing struggles, helping people understand the underlying dynamics of systematic dispossession—in Los Angeles's Skid Row, post-flood New Orleans, post-earthquake Haiti, and beyond. He used his capacities as a researcher, analyst, writer, and listener to assist people in redefining problems such that their solutions might be forcefully imagined. In other words, his work helps to surface and focus knowledge, translating between disciplines, vernaculars, policies, and methods. Calvin Hernton, a prolific, polydisciplinary scholar, mentored Woods at Oberlin College. Hernton insisted on the rigors of partisan scholarship—the high stakes of taking a side and working to make the world better. Clyde took his purpose to heart and devoted his life to the work. He did it for happiness—for the joy he found in thinking about and through the blues epistemology.

Clyde Woods wrote many articles, edited *In the Wake of Hurricane Katrina* (Johns Hopkins University Press, 2010), and coedited with Katherine McKittrick the indispensable *Black Geographies* (Between the Lines Press, 2007). He also researched and organized a number of unfinished projects. *Development Drowned and Reborn* will appear in the University of Georgia Press Geographies of Justice Series, having been meticulously brought to completion by Jordan T. Camp and Laura Pulido, and a big group of scholars is slowly working to finish the research, outlines, and draft chapters of his magnum opus—a book on Black Los Angeles that engages 10,000 years of the region's human-environmental development, globally contextualized.

Clyde Adrian Woods's extensive archive is at the Southern California Library for Social Studies and Research in Los Angeles. The archive is enormous. I think he never met a piece of paper he didn't like. But as he demonstrates in *Development Arrested*, we might better encounter archives as proposals rather than proofs. If proposals are evidence of struggle, they indicate, as Woods consistently argues, the perpetual presence of alternatives, neither lost nor in hidden transcripts, but rather out in the open, repeatable, simultaneously syncopating other worlds. In its capaciousness, the blues epistemology employs dialectics as method without reducing consciousness to experience, even though experience matters. I was fortunate to have known this man, to have danced with him (I can't dance), sung with him (I can carry a sea lion better than I can carry a tune), and argued late into the night with him and others (like Bobby M. Wilson) for whom the purpose of what we do is to be able to depend on each other in pleasure and struggle, loss and joy. Clyde Adrian Woods, *presente.*

*Ruth Wilson Gilmore, Lisbon, 23 June 2016*

# What Happens to a Dream Arrested?

The Lower Mississippi Delta region became arrested during these changes . . . and is presently chained by the bonds of illiteracy, poverty and prejudice.
Dr Jocelyn Elders, director of the Arkansas Department of Health, 1988[1]

Dear Mr President:

The Lower Mississippi Delta Development Commission was established . . . in October 1988 as a result of legislation introduced by a bipartisan group of senators and congressmen representing the Lower Mississippi Delta region . . . 214 of the poorest and most depressed counties in Arkansas, Louisiana, Mississippi, Missouri, Illinois, Tennessee and Kentucky.

. . . Our goal is ambitious but simple—*to make the Delta and its people a full partner in America's future*. That means giving every person in the Delta the chance to be a part of the American Dream.

America as a whole faces difficult challenges as it attempts to compete in the global marketplace. By any objective economic, educational and social measurement, the 8.3 million people in the Delta region are the least prepared to participate in and to contribute to the nation's effort to succeed in the world economy.
Governor Bill Clinton of Arkansas, chairman of the Lower Mississippi Delta
Development Commission, to President George Bush, 15 October, 1989[2]

The establishment of the Lower Mississippi Delta Development Commission (LMDDC) marked the beginning of a new era for the poorest and most heavily African American region in the United States. The official goal of the commission was to design a ten-year development plan to eliminate the most profound features of economic exhaustion and human desperation. Yet the social origins, organizational practices, and public polices of the LMDDC ensured that the people of the seven-state Delta region would remain mired in a seemingly bottomless state of crisis. Led by the then Governor of Arkansas and future President, Bill Clinton, the LMDDC concerned itself with stabilizing the region's dominant plantation leadership while simultaneously silencing the century-old African American vision of human development. Consequently, a development agenda based on social justice and economic sustainability fell before one based upon the relentless expansion of social inequality.

In a larger sense, the LMDDC was part of a new international movement led by numerous regional alliances to respond to the devastating consequences of global economic restructuring. The goal of the dominant alliances or blocs is to restore and reproduce their profitability and power. Conversely, the ethnic and working-class communities still trapped in the previous structures of regional inequality are mobilizing in unprecedented numbers to create new and fundamentally transformed societies.

The intellectual traditions and the social conditions that led to the creation of the LMDDC can best be understood by examining the development history of the Mississippi Delta. In 1990, some 60 percent of the nearly half-million people living in these eighteen northwestern Mississippi counties were African Americans (see Figure 1). Although small in size this region is known nationally and internationally as a center of tragedy and schism; of extreme levels of poverty and wealth; and of historic movements of repression and freedom; and as the center of both plantation culture and the African American working-class culture known as the blues.

In order to understand the traditions of development thought that shaped the LMDDC, in this book I examine the Commission as part of the twelfth transformation of the Mississippi Delta's plantation regime. As analyzed in successive chapters, each transformation involved an economic and social crisis; a mobilization by the dominant plantation bloc; a shift in the form of social explanation; the establishment of a new stable regime of accumulation; and a new transformative crisis generated by the countermobilizations of the region's African American, Native American, and poor White communities. Successive Delta mobilizations and countermobilizations have defined and redefined the nation's identity.

The Mississippi Delta is one of the world's most prolific cultural centers. Generation after generation, the dominant regional bloc has carried the plantation banner of ethnic, class, and regional supremacy into every arena of American life, from academic scholarship to popular culture to domestic and foreign policy. Simultaneously, African Americans in the region have carried the message of Black working-class consciousness, pride, and resiliency into national and international arenas. In addition to informing their daily lives and the life of the United States as a nation, their vision of social, economic, and cultural affirmation and justice is the mother of several global languages and philosophical systems commonly known as the blues, jazz, rock and roll, and soul. Feeling powerless before the central ethnic and class conflicts present in the Lower Mississippi Valley (that is, the Delta areas of Arkansas, Louisiana, Mississippi, and Tennessee), Clinton and the other governors, congressmen, and political leaders who worked closely with the LMDDC chose to accept them, intensify them, rub them raw, and preserve them in all their horrid splendor.

In order to construct societies based on social and economic justice, a new form of consciousness must emerge. Regional planning has always held the promise of creating new social relations based on economic redistribution,

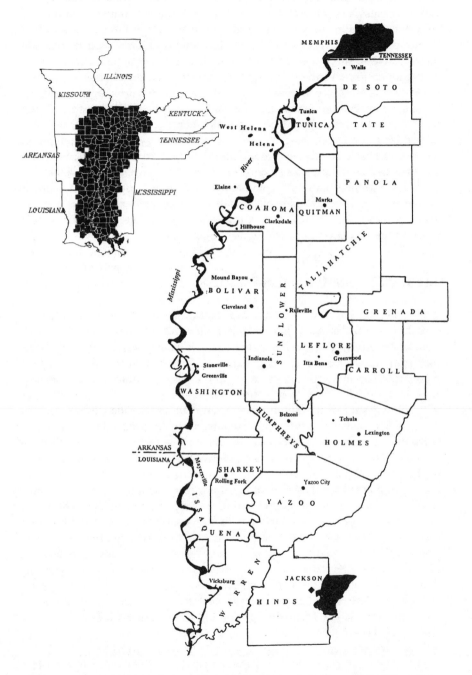

*Figure 1* The Mississippi Delta and the boundaries of the Lower Mississippi Delta Development Commission

environmental sustainability, and the full realization of basic human and
cultural rights. Yet, without a thoroughgoing critique of regional power and
culture based on indigenous conceptions of development, these efforts often
create more repressive social relations. The origins of a new form of regional
development in the Delta are to be found within the region itself among the
scattered, misplaced and often forgotten movements, projects, and agendas of
its African American communities and of other marginalized groups. Generation after generation, ethnic and class alliances arose in the region with the
aim of expanding social and economic democracy, only to be ignored, dismissed, and defeated. These defeats were followed by arrogant attempts to
purge such heroic movements from both historical texts and popular memory.
Yet even in defeat these movements transformed the policies of the plantation
bloc and informed daily life, community-building activities, and subsequent
movements. Within the unreconstructed oral and written records of these
arrested movements resides the knowledge upon which to construct new
relationships and new regional structures of equality.

## The Resilience of Plantation Relations

The plantation has always occupied a central place in US iconography. In
recent decades it has been described as a dead, yet still romanticized, aberra-
tion killed off by the inevitable march of human progress. Although the
plantation tradition has been relegated to the dustbin of history by some social
theorists, it continues to survive among those who celebrate its brutal legacy.
It is also painfully alive among those still dominated by the economic and
political dynasties of the South which preserved and reproduced themselves
through diversification and through numerous new mobilizations.

By the late 1960s, social scientists had abandoned the critical investigation
of rural relations in the predominantly African American plantation counties
of the South. When they are examined, there is a tendency to superimpose
categories created for the study of Northern manufacturing-based cities onto
the social and institutional histories of these rural regions. What is lost in the
process is not only an appreciation of the continuity of plantation-based
economic systems and power relations, but also the critique of these relations.
This lovingly cultivated theoretical blindness enabled many observers to deny
the deepening ethnic and economic crisis in the South even after African
American churches in the region began to be systematically burned in 1996.
Removing this veil is necessary before we can understand the evolution of
social relations in the Mississippi Delta and the emergence of both Clinton
and the LMDDC.

Three development traditions emerged clearly during LMDDC debates in
the late 1980s and early 1990s over the region's future. Plantation bloc leaders
asserted the superiority of the plantation system and of their leadership while
continually advocating the expansion of their monopoly over agriculture,

manufacturing, banking, land, and water. They also sought to preserve their monopoly over local, county, and state finances. Their commitment to the elimination of federal programs designed to lessen ethnic and class exploitation was, moreover, unwavering. Their control of the region forms the foundation of powerful national and international alliances which in turn guarantees that the plantation bloc's worldview will remain highly influential in the twenty-first century. This system of social domination has also guaranteed the spread of mass impoverishment, the erosion of human rights protections, and the increased deadliness of daily life; Delta rates of infant, teen, and adult mortality are among the highest in the USA.

Another tradition in the region, the New South development tradition, emerged from the predominantly White areas that after the Civil War were increasingly integrated into the sphere of Northern capital. New rail centers grew in these regions at the expense of the ports and other older urban centers that had been developed to support an economy based upon African American slavery. By the 1920s, agricultural decline and diversification led the state of Mississippi to create a program to preserve White rural areas by providing subsidies for Northern manufacturers moving into the state. Later copied by all fifty states, this program cemented the alliance between Northern capital and the expanding Southern manufacturing, commercial, financial, and utility interests. To encourage additional investment, the New South bloc launched numerous legal and illegal actions to preserve the region's "competitive advantage": a labor force disorganized through terror, and natural resources opened to uncontrolled exploitation.

The seemingly endless rounds of plant closures since the early 1980s combined with a crisis in small- and medium-sized farming to drive many rural New South communities into a state of perpetual turmoil. Unable to recruit new industries that prefer more "competitive" international locations, many of these communities now stare into the unblinking eyes of fiscal collapse. Even though they have benefited from a half-century of industrial promotion that traditionally and consciously excluded their African American neighbors, they are still seeking to blame this disaster upon them. President Clinton, Vice President Gore, the Democratic Leadership Council, and other leading members of the New South bloc increasingly look toward a receding federal government as a mechanism for their empowerment. Southern executive branch and Congressional leaders are truly reinventing government. They have moved quickly to grant the New South bloc the regulatory authority to redesign Southern state social structures so that federal funds can be used to prop up local regimes more directly. In the case of the Lower Mississippi Valley and other parts of the South, this has resulted in a plantation bloc-led restoration of White supremacist attitudes, alliances, institutions, social policies, and economic programs.

In attempting to marginalize the third tradition, the LMDDC engaged in a silencing strategy that has its roots in the mid-seventeenth century. As defined here, the third tradition of Southern political-economic explanation is centered upon resistance to plantation monopoly. It emerged from the Native American communities which experienced both genocide and exile as the plantation complex moved south and west. It emerged from the new African American communities trapped inside the boundaries of the plantation complex. It also emerged in a less consistent manner from the impoverished White farmers and workers who tried to confront plantation power. These encounters have shaped traditions of solidarity, affirmation, and resistance which view the plantation system as an evil abomination whose strength is dependent upon the repeated destruction of community after community, family after family.

These groups learned a painful lesson that many scholars have yet to learn; slavery and the plantation are not an anathema to capitalism but are pillars of it. The first school of plantation criticism was developed by those whose lives were viciously consumed by plantation slavery during its apocalyptic march across the continent. Edgar Thompson referred to the plantation as both a military form of agriculture and as a capitalist settlement institution having extensive land requirements, intensive capital and labor requirements, and internal forms of governance. In such a situation, if a worker "steals, fights, assembles unlawfully, plots, marries secretly, indulges in fornication, has illegitimate children, spends his time gambling, cock fighting or courting, the planter suffers some loss or threat of loss".[3] Slavery, sharecropping, mechanization, and prison, wage and migratory labor are just a few of the permutations possible within a plantation complex. None of these forms changes the basic features of resource monopoly and extreme ethnic and class polarization. The Mississippi Delta's plantation production complex has gone through all of these various changes and still remains the dominant feature of regional life.

After 1830, the enslaved African American community confronted a new plantation system. Exploitation increased exponentially when the Southern cotton plantation empire became the pillar of the textile-driven British industrial revolution. In the Mississippi Delta, the alluvial soils produced cotton yields double those of the rest of the South. Consequently, successful planters were able easily to buy African Americans to replace the thousands who died of exhaustion as they toiled in the receding malarial swamps. These plantations have been described as both factories in the fields and death camps. Consequently, for Blacks to be sold into the Deep South – "sold down the river" – became synonymous with a sentence of death. One observer of US capitalism during the 1850s, Karl Marx, noticed that the Deep South plantation regime was an agrarian form of capitalism that had successfully grafted the barbarism of overwork onto the horrors of slavery.

Although the United States has never experienced feudalism, many schools of economic thought hold that unfree labor systems, particularly slavery, are feudal and semifeudal throwbacks that are incompatible with capitalism. This assumption is undermined by the work of historians and political economists such as Edgar Thompson, George Beckford, and John Hebron Moore. In their studies of the United States, the Caribbean, Latin America, Asia, and Africa, they found capitalist dynamism, adaptability and innovation in plantation regimes and not the rigid and unchanging aristocracy of mythology. The drive to innovate is in many ways a product of the construction of an inherently explosive social order where supervision is never-ending and where management decisions are a matter of life and death.[4]

The value of such a perspective for understanding the Mississippi Delta is that it reorders common assumptions about the role of the Black working class. First, it reveals the daily terror and violence insultingly romanticized as "paternalism". It requires that we consider the central role of plantation agriculture in the development of capitalism in the United States. In terms of regional distinctiveness, this perspective reveals that there are several development trajectories in the South, each of which must be understood individually and relationally in order to comprehend existing alliances and to enter upon new development paths. Furthermore, many of those who proceed from the viewpoint that the plantation South was a noncapitalist semifeudal backwater from 1630 to 1965 would argue that the region needs more unregulated resource and labor exploitation to become fully capitalist. Yet, if we assume industrial capitalism emerged in the plantation South before it did in the mercantile-oriented North, we can begin to understand how the region's so-called "backwardness" and poverty may actually be the result of too much profit-oriented development. We must also revise labor history so that enslaved African Americans assume their rightful place as one of the world's first working classes, and one of its most important.

The second period of plantation criticism emerged during the Civil War and Reconstruction. The central theme of the war was land and labor reform. Both Northern Republican Free Soilers and some small farmers in the South wanted to limit competition from the plantation regimes. Based on the Southern experience, many White small farmers and laborers throughout the country believed that opportunities for them to accumulate wealth would rapidly evaporate in the face of the driving force behind plantation settlement; the monopolization of land, natural resources, infrastructure, institutions, capital, and labor. African Americans wanted to abolish and dismantle the plantation regime, to establish self-governing communities, and to become landowners, both individually and collectively. During the Civil War, African Americans attacked plantation monopolists in a number of ways. They fought gloriously in the Union army and established freedom villages and freedom towns on abandoned and confiscated plantations. After the Civil War, African American soldiers, who were known as the blues, served as the backbone of the Union Leagues movement in Mississippi that emerged to defend the land, labor, social and political reform agenda. As the Reconstruction governments were overthrown, the leaders of the Union Leagues and similar organizations were assassinated throughout the South.

By the 1880s, a mass movement of Blacks and Whites arose in the South under the banner of Populism. The Populists identified both Northern so-called Robber Barons (the extremely small group of Northern capitalists who had established monopoly control over the nation's railroad, steel, oil, banking, and agricultural industries) and Southern plantation monopolists as the enemies of cooperatively based community development. Dominated by small land-owners, this movement engaged in independent party politics while simultaneously building an economic infrastructure for a new society. Before being violently suppressed, the Colored Farmers' Alliance advocated the expansion of land ownership and the creation of cooperative stores designed to pool African American resources while boycotting stores owned by planters or allied merchants and commissaries. After luring some of the White Populist leadership into a compact to maintain White supremacy, the Delta plantation bloc provided the South with another model of how to disenfranchise both African Americans and Whites: the Mississippi Constitution of 1890. Although many of its provisions were eventually ruled unconstitutional by the Supreme Court or superseded by federal law, this document is still the foundation of state governance more than a century later. African Americans tried desperately to halt the movement to hold a constitutional convention. Once the legislature approved the proceedings, Blacks throughout the state organized to ensure some among their number would be elected as delegates. During the campaign, Black Republican F.M.B. Cook was assassinated. The only Black delegate to the convention, Isaiah Montgomery eventually made an impassioned plea for the disenfranchisement of African American voters. Dripping with fraud, subterfuge, violence, and a denial of federal authority, the full implications of the 1890 constitution were outlined by a convention delegate who was also a planter:

> In the Mississippi convention, the Delta Counties had insisted upon the poll tax ... "as their sine qua non, knowing full well that as a means of Negro dis-enfranchisement, it is worth all the rest ... It reduces the electorate and places the political control of the state in the hands not of a minority of the voters alone, but of the minority of whites ... The poll tax gets rid of most of the Negro votes there, but it gets rid of a great many whites at the same time – in fact a majority of them."[5]

The White communities bordering the plantation areas of the South continued their attack on planter monopoly, yet it was primarily restricted to the sphere of state politics. The rapid development of the Delta's 6 million acres at the turn of the century led to the creation of the most productive cotton region in the world and to the ruination of White small farmers in adjacent regions. These producers launched an attack on the Delta planters' monopolization of state offices and finances. This movement is typically referred to as "the revolt of the Rednecks" and its ideology as "Redneckism." According to Brandfon, these Delta conflicts continue to resonate throughout the region and the nation:

> Indeed, the concentration of railroads, capital, and labor into the alluvial lands to the neglect of the South's poorer cotton lands, which were unable to compete, led to the latter's too rapid deterioration ... The sharpness of the divisions between the delta and the hills made more turbulent the political reactions of the 1890s and these

in turn imprinted upon the South for generations the curious mixture of progressivism and clownishness that was the redneck political order.[6]

Although essentially voteless and increasingly segregated, African Americans still pushed their community development agenda by building schools, establishing new towns, buying land, and protesting the denial of civil and human rights. To leave the South for work and to escape persecution became more common, especially after the outbreak of World War One. Out of necessity, many of those who remained in the South focused again on the land and labor reform agenda by organizing rural unions to end peonage, to improve wages, and to end the thievery and terror associated with year-end settlements. For example, in 1919, the African American sharecroppers and tenants of the Progressive Farmers and Household Union in the Arkansas Delta staged a protest over wages and conditions. The outcome was the Elaine Massacre, an orgy of violence in which dozens of African Americans were murdered, and more than one thousand were arrested, with the assistance of "hunting parties" from the Mississippi Delta. However, this rural reform agenda reemerged in the Arkansas, Missouri, Tennessee and Mississippi Deltas during the Great Depression in the form of the multiethnic Southern Tenant Farmers' Union.

During the Depression, the critique of plantation relations also crossed ethnic, class and regional boundaries. As the plight of the Southern sharecropper gained national attention, an academic and popular literature arose in support of rural transformation. The development theories of African Americans, Southern White tenants and sharecroppers, and Northern industrial unionists began to intersect to form a broad attack on the Southern plantation bloc. Yet, the bloc's seniority in Congress was still capable of strangling social, labor, and civil rights reforms affecting every region.

Roosevelt's New Deal launched hundreds of often conflicting federal programs in a search for a social–spatial fix—a series of alliances and agreements capable of restoring long-term profitability and social peace. The Mississippi Delta presented a special problem. After a 1933 visit, investigators with the Mississippi Valley Committee of the federal Works Progress Administration concluded that the region had to change, and change fundamentally:

> Stabilization of the old social order in most of the region will accomplish little toward human betterment. The pernicious tenant system should be abolished as soon as practical through readjustment in land utilization, and ownership. Meanwhile the degrading mode of life which it tends to breed and perpetuate should not be permitted to spread.[7]

Several groups within the federal government recommended cooperative land reform efforts while, from the floor of the Mississippi legislature to the White House, the Delta planters pushed the idea of a plow-up of cotton acreage and expulsions of African Americans from the region. Under the 1933 federal Agricultural Adjustment Administration program, planters were paid for reducing acreage which guaranteed their profits even as they evicted one-third of all tenants and sharecroppers in the region. Planters created the Delta Council to coordinate production, labor, and ethnic policy in the region and then formed the National Cotton Council to influence cotton production, manufacture, and trade issues nationally and internationally. These events marked the beginning of the cotton enclosure movement. Over the next thirty years, this intervention would drive several million African Americans out of the rural South and into the cities of the South, Northeast, Midwest, and West.

In 1948, an alliance was formed between national African American organizations, unions, religious organizations, and Democratic Party officials. These forces agreed to use federal legislation and the federal courts in order slowly to dismantle the Southern system of segregation and disenfranchisement. However, this alliance did not specifically address how impoverished African Americans would be able to continue to survive in the rural South. In the minds of many African Americans, the historic Southern land, labor, and cultural reform agenda took a back seat to civil rights, the desegregation of facilities, and the urban industrial employment agenda. Simultaneously, Delta planters introduced more tractors and new mechanical cotton pickers into the fields which eliminated another one-third of the families that were living on plantations at the beginning of the Depression.

After the 1954 *Brown v. Board of Education* decision mandating desegregation of public education, a pro-segregation organization formed by the Delta plantation bloc rapidly spread from Mississippi to every state in the South and Southwest. The chapters of the Citizens' Council, whose membership was exclusively White, pushed a development agenda with four basic elements: economic retaliation against any person advocating school integration; the creation of a private White school system; the expulsion of African Americans from the rural South; and movement of White Southerners out of the Democratic Party.

The formation of the Citizens' Council in 1954 was followed in 1956 by the creation of the Sovereignty Commission, a Mississippi intelligence agency. Operating until 1973, this state-funded body actively subverted civil rights and community development organizations and individuals. Between 1954 and 1965, a final push against the Delta's African American communities came in the form of the introduction of high-yield cotton, new pesticides, and new herbicides. This movement eliminated the last one-third of the plantation residents.

This rapid chemical, biological, and genetic agricultural transformation thoroughly destroyed and reordered African American community life. Homelessness, hunger, ill health, poisoning, and violence intensified in the Delta to a degree not found in other predominantly African American areas of the South. The agricultural–social transformation conducted in the Delta had the same genealogy as the Green Revolutions launched worldwide by US firms and the federal government: high-yield corn in Mexico; high-yield rice in India, Indonesia, and the Gambia; and high-yield wheat in many nations. Often these projects were in part designed to preclude peasant rebellions and to place expanded food production under the control of a restructured and entrepreneurial rural elite. As in the Delta, these elites were directly integrated into a global complex of international research, financial, chemical, machinery, and commodity institutions.[8]

As it had quashed the rural rebellions that occurred in other countries, the Green Revolution in the South gutted the Southern freedom movement. Through mass evictions and community destruction, the Green Revolution transformed the Southern rural crisis into a non-Southern urban crisis marked by an unprecedented series of urban rebellions. African American movements of the 1950s in the South were initially organized around an urban agenda focused on eliminating state terror and segregated accommodations. Attempts by young African American students to integrate public transportation and facilities through sit-ins and freedom rides were met by chilling violence. According to presidential advisor Arthur M. Schlesinger, Jr. the Kennedy administration hoped to channel this rapidly spreading mass movement into the more acceptable area of voting rights:

> Negro voting did not incite social and sexual anxieties; and white Southerners could not argue against suffrage for their Negro fellow citizens with quite the same moral fervor they applied to the mingling of the races in schools. Concentration on the right to vote, in short, seemed the best available means of carrying the mind of the white South.[9]

A leader of the Congress of Racial Equality (CORE), James Farmer, recounted an event that led to a shift in the strategy of the civil rights movement:

> I was in jail in Mississippi. Bobby Kennedy called a meeting of CORE and SNCC [the Student Nonviolent Coordinating Committee] in his office. I could not be there, of course. I was in the clink. But several people from CORE went. And several people from SNCC went, just those two because they were the activist groups in the freedom rides. This was the Summer of '61. And at that meeting what Bobby said to them according to the reports, he said, "Why don't you guys cut out all that shit. Freedom Riding and sitting-in shit, and concentrate on voter education." Says, "If you do that I'll get you a tax exemption." ... The SNCC guy almost hit him ... "Tell us that we concentrate on voter registration when we're fighting a tiger down there in Mississippi and Alabama. You're trying to buy us off."[10]

By 1962, the Mississippi chapters of the CORE, the National Association for the Advancement of Colored People, the Southern Christian Leadership Conference, and the SNCC had formed the Council of Federated Organizations (COFO) to coordinate their actions in the Delta. With foundation funds, COFO launched a voter registration campaign that in 1964 evolved into the Mississippi Freedom Democratic Party (MFDP). The party's first objective was to challenge the legality of the Democratic Party seating convention delegates, and accepting congressional candidates, from districts where Blacks were not allowed to vote. This movement spread to other states until the Democratic Party finally yielded. Out of this movement emerged Delta resident Fannie Lou Hamer. She was a key figure in rejuvenating the historic African American land, labor, and cultural reform agenda, an agenda fully adopted by the Reverend Martin Luther King Jr, in the last year of his life.

Out of the Delta's Poor People's Committees, formed in 1967, came the national Poor People's March on Washington. In April 1968, the poor of the Delta, the South, Appalachia, the Southwest, the reservations, and the inner cities were to assemble under the leadership of King in Washington, DC, and occupy the capital until Congress and President Johnson addressed the issues of hunger, poverty, and homelessness. Two weeks before he was to lead this march, King was killed while assisting striking sanitation workers in the capital of the Mississippi Delta: Memphis, Tennessee. The march became a memorial for King; the mass encampment on the National Mall in Washington, DC, was named Resurrection City. One of the key federal institutions targeted for sit-ins and disruption by the leadership was the Department of Agriculture (USDA). In the Delta, the USDA required unemployed, incomeless, and homeless residents to pay cash for food stamps. Starvation in the Delta elicited two responses. Outraged church congregations in Africa and Europe began to send food, clothing, and money. Conversely, the USDA accelerated its financial and technical support for the Southern enclosure, the Green Revolution, regional expulsions, and planter profits. During the 1960s, USDA direct cash payments to several Delta planters exceeded $200,000 annually.

In the 1990s, the decline of rural African American life has been marked by the abandonment of both rural communities and the rural reform agenda. As early as 1968, King observed that the historic African American community-centered development agenda had been overcome by the "paralysis of analysis." The institutionalization of "paralysis" ensured that inconsequential debates and statements on race by society's elites became a permanent fixture of national life. The reemergence during the 1990s of the decades-old practice of bombing and burning rural Black churches signaled a push for greater social and political control over African American communities through violence, fear, and outmigration. Yet it is still not clear whether or not the existing African American leadership organizations are capable of launching a unified response. Both Martin Luther King and Fannie Lou Hamer suggested that this paralysis could only be overcome by first recognizing the permanent position of the rural South as the pillar of African American identity, consciousness, and morality. Any real and fundamental progress must be based on the rural development agenda carved out of a rocky and unyielding landscape by previous generations of working-class African Americans.

## The Recovery of African American and Populist Political Economy

Between the turn of the century and World War Two, a concentrated effort was launched to radically alter and reinterpret the very strong rural reform traditions existing throughout the USA. The nationally dominant alliance of regional blocs and the emerging social science disciplines anointed mass-production agriculture, manufacturing, and science as the centers and sources of modern civilization and progress. The New Dealers and their successors in the realm of national policy promised institutionally regulated prosperity, global superiority, an ever-rising standard of living, and social justice for all based upon an urban manufacturing-based civilization. Older reform traditions were abandoned and modern strategies for modern times were adopted.

Yet, in the 1960s, African American organizations that emerged from the civil rights movement had returned to the historic tasks both of building rural communities based on cooperative principles and of dismantling the plantation complex. Similarly, in the academic community, several scholars renewed the tradition of African American and populist plantation criticism by examining the bitter fruits of the New Deal. Since it is still lovingly defended by conservatives, moderates, progressives, liberals, and radicals alike, research on the New Deal gutting of rural African American communities is still marginalized.

In the preface of his 1971 work on the Southern Tenant Farmers' Union, *Cry from the Cotton*, Donald Grubbs explained the social implications of the New Deal policies:

> Through the Agricultural Adjustment Administration, Franklin Roosevelt gave southern planters the means and the incentives to substitute machines and unem-ployed casual labor for their tenants ... Particularly for black people in this country, the cry from the cotton was a shriek against white ignorance and callousness. Driven off the land as planters happily replaced them with tractors, attracted north by the hope for freedom and employment, they found that their life in America was undergoing a second major change. Hideously inhuman as slavery was, they at least had employment and security; with the switch to sharecropping, they kept employ-ment but lost security; and today on welfare they are allowed neither employment nor security ... yesterday through ignorance and greed, the propertied drove the propertyless off the land; tomorrow, Harlem and Watts and the South Side will be burning. White America could not understand the cry from the cotton; can it understand the cry for black power?[11]

In "The New Deal and the Roots of Agribusiness," a statement he made to the First National Conference on Land Reform in 1973, Grubbs drew out the political implications of the New Deal agricultural programs. He argued that the reenfranchisement of Black voters did not end planter political dominance because so many had already been expelled:

> ... the New Deal was seldom progressive and certainly not radical; it strengthened both the traditional incentives and the traditional institutions ... a positive monetary inducement was offered to Southern planters to demote their workers to the status of casual labor employed only seasonally. Eventually millions drifted out of the south all together, probably the largest government-impelled population movement in all our history ... One suspects immediately that so humane a man as Roosevelt must have felt forced into such a program by his political dependence on Southern

conservatives ... To be sure farm labor had less political muscle, but in the next decade or two, liberal southerners like Ellis Arnall, Lister Hill, and Estes Kefauver could have certainly benefitted from Roosevelt's encouragement of rural democracy. It may not have been inevitable for the Strom Thurmonds and George Wallaces to become so dominant in the South that the course of our history was wrenched to the right.[12]

During the late 1970s three works were published which challenged the notion of the withering away of the plantation bloc: Jay Mandle's *The Roots of Black Poverty*, Dwight B. Billings Jr's *Planters and the Making of a "New South,"* and Jonathan Wiener's *Social Origins of the New South*. These works focused on the persistence of semifeudal planter domination in the post-Reconstruction South. Although I classify this period as capitalist, each of the works is of major importance to the reconsideration of New South development policies. Each author demonstrated that the industry-minded New South merchant and middle classes did not overthrow or dominate the plantation blocs, they allied with them. According to Wiener:

> With the rise of the Populist movement, planters realized that white tenants were not their allies in a struggle between agrarian and industrial society, but in fact were their worst enemies. Industrialists recognized that the repressive system presided over by the planters was necessary in the context of popular unrest. Once the industrialists had dropped their anti-planter agrarian program, once they had conceded that planters would remain a dominant class and that the south would develop along the Prussian road, a coalition between the two became possible. It was the threat from below that brought the planters and the industrialists together.[13]

This reinterpretation allows us to understand the internal workings of the present day multiregional Southern state. One form of development occurred in the predominantly White area, the New South, while planter bloc domination persisted in the predominantly African American regions collectively known as the Black Belt. Among other things, this agreement established the practice of industrial redlining which continues today (see page 202).

As the South descended into agricultural depression during the late 1970s, important scholars such as Numan Bartley, Pete Daniel, Gilbert Fite, Jack Temple Kirby, and Gavin Wright joined the debate over the impact of New Deal policies in preserving plantation power. Simultaneously, William Falk, Thomas Lyson, Daniel Lichter and others scholars focused on documenting the devastating impact of the current crisis on rural Black communities. A study prepared for the Southern Growth Policies Board found that corporations and state officials were directly contributing to the expansion of racial inequality:

> state development agencies openly admit that businesses did not like to move into counties where more than one-third of the population was black and that they did little to encourage the selection of those counties if this factor would jeopardize recruitment.[14]

A recent contribution to the revision of Southern development history in the period after World War Two was James Cobb's 1992 work on the Mississippi Delta, *The Most Southern Place on Earth*. Like Grubbs, Kirby, and Daniel, Cobb adopts the African American and populist tradition of plantation criticism. His focus is on the alliance between the Delta planters and the federal government during the civil rights movement of the 1960s. He illuminates an argument made by African Americans in the early 1960s that the final pushing of Blacks out of their plantation homes, and out of the region, was a direct response to the threat of African American political empowerment:

> Those who explained the failure of blacks in the Delta and elsewhere in the southern plantation belt to make more progress during the civil rights era often cited the enduring influence of paternalism, referring to the historic dependence of black tenants on their white landlords. In fact, however, it was a new form of paternalism, one introduced by the federal government, that played a major role in shaping events in the Mississippi Delta throughout the post-New Deal decades. Since the 1930s the Delta has increasingly moved into the federal orbit as Washington subsidized the reduction of cotton acreage and succeeded the planter as the primary source of support for the region's seasonally employed black laborers.[15]

Although I do not believe that the Delta order is anachronistic, I do agree with him and the many other scholars and observers on two critical points. First, the Delta regime of inequality is not the result of too little capitalism, too little development. Second, in many ways the entire United States is rapidly becoming the "Delta writ large":

> many of the human and material extremes that were the keys to the Delta's identity either as the "South's south," or "America's Ethiopia" were shaped not by its isolation but by pervasive global and national influences and consistent with interaction with a federal government whose policies often confirmed the Delta's inequities and reinforced its anachronistic social and political order as well ... the social polarization that is synonymous with the Mississippi Delta may be observed wherever and whenever the pursuit of wealth, pleasure, and power overwhelms the ideals of equality, justice and compassion and reduces the American dream to a self-indulgent fantasy. As socioeconomic disparity and indifference to human suffering become increasingly prominent features of American life, it seems reasonable to inquire whether the same economic, political, and emotional forces that helped to forge and sustain the Delta's image as the South writ small may one day transform an entire nation into the Delta writ large.[16]

Finally, none of the above studies on New Deal agricultural policy and the current rural crisis has examined the organization of planters known as the Delta Council, formed in 1933 by the wealthiest planters, bankers, merchants, and industrialists in the Mississippi Delta. Absent from many of the works cited is a discussion of how the Delta Council spawned the National Cotton Council, creating one of the Sunbelt's most powerful economic blocs. The Delta Council's *de facto* administration of state and federal agricultural agencies in the region has also received scant attention. Little mention is made of how the Citizens' Council movement emerged from the Delta Council's membership in 1954 to combat desegregation nationally and how it later evolved into the reordering of the national political party system. Also, the role of the Delta Council in the creation of a Mississippi intelligence agency designed to subvert the civil rights movement and community development organizations and projects must be included in the development history of the region. Far from being a federal parasite, the Delta Council is a regional predator. While the story of federal policy and multinational corporations is seductive, regions still matter. It is only through an examination of organized power in the region that regional institutions, relations, and movements can be understood and structures of inequality may be dismantled.

## The Blues Epistemology

Many of the valiant efforts of African Americans for an alternative path of development before, during, and after the civil rights movement of the 1960s were defeated in a consciously organized manner. Yet the meaning of this experience to future reform efforts is critical. In the Delta, the tradition of development theory and practice among working-class African Americans continues to be marginalized in debates over public policy. The elimination of state-sponsored segregation and reenfranchisement were the beginning, and not the end, of the historic African American agenda in the rural South. However, there is more involved here than just a political agenda: there is a distinct perspective on who they are and where they are, on their predicament, and on who is responsible. Like other blocs in the region, working-class African Americans in the Delta and in the Black Belt South have constructed a system of explanation that informs their daily life, organizational activity, culture, religion, and social movements. They have created their own ethno-regional epistemology. Like other traditions of interpretation, it is not a monolith; there are branches, roots, and a trunk. This central tradition is referred to in this work as the blues epistemology.

The blues perspective emerged among the two generations that witnessed the overthrow of slavery, ten years of freedom, the overthrow of Reconstruction and the beginning of ninety-five years of what has been called the "Second Slavery," namely disenfranchisement, debt peonage, Jim Crow, and legally sanctioned official and private terrorism. The Delta plantation bloc led the overthrow of Reconstruction and the defeat of Populism in the South. If the blues were based solely on suffering, this history would be reason enough to declare the Delta the cradle of the blues; approximately sixty of the eighty blues performers recorded between 1890 and 1920 were born in either the Mississippi Delta, Memphis, Tennessee, or Jackson, Mississippi. According to performer Shelby Brown, the relationship between the blues and Mississippi was not a coincidence:

Why do you think they blues in Mississippi? Because of the way they used to plow the folks here, chop cotton at daylight in the morning. They would get out there and work so hard, they be even looking at the sun, saying, "Hurry, hurry, sundown. Let tomorrow shine" ... They wanted the sun to go down so they could stop working. They learned the blues from that. Most anything like that [backbreaking work and lost love] will give you the blues. And Mississippi got more of it than anywhere 'cause all the blues people come up here singing the blues.[17]

The birth-to-death relentlessness of the Delta system was captured by blues-man Robert Shaw:

> Living ain't easy and times are tough.
> Money is scarce, we all can't git enough.
> Now my insurance is lapsed and my food is low.
> And the landlord is knocking at my door.
> Last night I dreamed I died.
> I couldn't afford a casket,
> And embalming was so high,
> I got up from my sick bed because I was too poor to die.
> Now ain't that blue?[18]

The vision of those trapped inside this system was expressed in song by the muleskinners who sang to the sun, "Hannah," as they built the Delta's levees:

> Go down, Ol Hannah, doncha rise no more,
> If you rise in the morning, bring judgement day.
> Go down, Ol Hannah, doncha rise no more,
> If you rise in the morning, set the world on fire—set the world on fire.[19]

Born in a new era of censorship, suppression, and persecution, the blues conveyed the sorrow of the individual and collective tragedy that had befallen African Americans. It also operated to instill pride in a people facing daily denigration, as well as channeling folk wisdom, descriptions of life and labor, travelogues, hoodoo, and critiques of individuals and institutions. It is often forgotten that the blues are also defined by those songs, music, stories, jokes, dances, and other visual and physical practices that raise the spirit of the audience to unimaginable heights. The men and women who performed the blues were sociologists, reporters, counselors, advocates, preservers of language and customs, and summoners of life, love, laughter, and much, much more. Daphne Duval Harrison's 1990 study of blues women, *Black Pearls: blues Queens of the 1920s*, demonstrates that through blues channels there also flowed images of African American women as independent symbols of authority. She cites Ralph Ellison on this last point:

Bessie Smith might have been a "Blues Queen" to the society at large, but within the tighter Negro community where the blues were a total way of life, and major expression of an attitude toward life, she was a priestess, a celebrant who affirmed the values of the group and man's ability to deal with chaos.[20]

After achieving mass distribution nationally and internationally through recordings, the blues as a system of explanation began to influence both popular, and academic, literature and criticism. According to literary critic Henry Louis Gates, this marked the end of one major African American cultural movement and the beginning of another. He observes that the transition from the literature of the Harlem Renaissance to a blues-based literature was signaled by Sterling Brown, a Harvard-educated African American professor of English at Howard University:

> By 1932, when Sterling Brown published *Southern Road*, his first book of poems, the use of black vernacular structures in Afro-American poetry was controversial indeed ... what was generally called dialect, the unique form of English that Afro-Americans spoke, was thought by whites to reinforce received assumption about the Negro's mental inferiority ... Middle class blacks ... thought that dialect was an embarrassment, the linguistic remnant of an enslavement that they longed to forget ... Brown's book of poetry, even more profoundly than the market crash of 1929, truly ended the Harlem Renaissance primarily because it contained a new distinctly black poetic diction ... the black common man whose roots were rural and Southern ... Brown renders in a style that emerged from several forms of folk discourse, a black vernacular matrix that includes the blues and ballads, the spirituals and worksongs. Indeed, Brown's ultimate referents are black music and mythology.[21]

In *Southern Roads* Brown wrote about one of his favorite performers who, like Bessie Smith, was so popular that sometimes she sparked hysteria when her traveling show came to town:

> O Ma Rainey
> Sing yo' song
> Now you's back
> Whah you belong
> Git way inside us,
> Keep us strong ...
>
> O Ma Rainey
> Li'l an' low;
> Sing us 'bout de hard luck
> Round' our do';
> Sing us 'bout de lonesome road
> We mus' go ...[22]

The Harlem Renaissance was replaced by the more consciously Blues Renaissance. Brown not only used the language of the folk, he addressed working-class themes in poems using blues lyrical construction. As a poet, critic, and the "Dean of Afro-American literature," Brown spent the next fifty years integrating the blues aesthetic into African American literature. Also in the early 1930s, in "Blueprint for Negro Literature," novelist and Mississippi native son Richard Wright launched a powerful critique of African American literature and social commentary. He argued forcefully that the blues form, subject, and folk vision must become the basis for African American social explanation and literature. Wright engaged in discussions with members of the Chicago School of Sociology and began sociological investigations of African American daily life so that he could better express the blues perspective in his novels and essays. In 1959, writing from exile in Paris, Wright argued that the blues was the music both of the wretched of the earth and of the beautiful ones not yet born:

> Not only did those Blacks, torn from their tribal moorings in Africa, transported across the Atlantic, survive under hostile conditions of life, but they left a vivid record of their suffering and longings in those astounding religious songs known as the spirituals, and their descendants, freed and cast upon their own in an alien culture, created the blues, a form of exuberantly melancholy folk song that circled the globe. In Buenos Aires, Stockholm, Copenhagen, London, Berlin, Paris, Rome, in fact, in every large city on earth where lonely, disinherited men congregate for pleasure or amusement, the orgiastic wail of the blues, and their strident offspring, jazz, can be heard.
>
> Yet the most astonishing aspect of the blues is that, though replete with a sense of defeat and down-heartedness, they are not intrinsically pessimistic; their burden of woe and melancholy is dialectically redeemed through sheer force of sensuality, into an almost exultant affirmation of life, of love, of sex, of movement, of hope.
>
> No matter how repressive was the American environment, the Negro never lost faith in or doubted his deeply endemic capacity to live. All blues are a lusty, lyrical realism charged with taut sensibility.[23]

While the blues continued to be developed as a theory of African American aesthetics by Langston Hughes in literature and by Romare Bearden in the visual arts, the social sciences remained unscathed. Wright's conception of the blues as social criticism deeply influenced succeeding generations. During the 1950s authors and blues critics such as Ralph Ellison and Albert Murray both deepened the understanding of folk vision and examined the blues foundations of other musical forms, particularly jazz. Brown's students at Howard University were also well grounded in the blues. One of the most notable was poet–critic–activist Amiri Baraka, formerly known as LeRoi Jones, who both wrote the landmark *Blues People* in 1961 and led the Black Arts Movement. Baraka's work opened up an endless number of avenues for research on the blues as the cornerstone of an African American national identity. Another key figure in this movement was Larry Neal, who in 1971 defined the "blues ethos" in African American culture in the following manner:

> The blues, with all of their contradictions, represent, for better or for worse, the essential vector of Afro-American sensibility and identity. Berthing themselves sometime between the end of formal slavery and the turn of the century, the blues represents the ex-slave's confrontation with a more secular evaluation of the world. They were shaped in the context of social and political oppression, but they do not, as Maulana Karenga said, collectively "teach resignation." To hear the blues in this manner is to totally misunderstand the essential function of the blues, because the blues are basically defiant in their attitude toward life. They are about survival on the meanest, most gut level of human existence. They are, therefore, lyrical responses

to the facts of life. The essential motive behind the best blues song is the acquisition of insight, wisdom.[24]

Working from this lineage of blues aesthetic criticism, the Black Arts Movement of the 1960s was founded on the premise that working-class African American culture was beautiful. This declaration was in direct opposition to the "deviant" and "pathological" labels placed on it by social scientists, politicians, and cultural critics. The Black Arts movement also influenced African American scholars who were engaged in fundamental critiques of institutions, disciplines, and methodologies. However, those laboring in the social sciences were unable easily to overcome the "scientific" prejudices against popular culture in general and the denial of the existence and longevity of ethno-regional epistemologies in particular.

This was not the problem encountered in the daily life of African Americans, since the blues tradition informed both thought and action, critique and celebration. A popular rebirth of the blues and blues-based music occurred in the early 1980s and continues to spread. In many ways the blues offers a multiethnic working-class vision of a flawed United States haunted by its own practices of ethnic oppression and enforced poverty. In the face of this reality, the blues and its extensions offer an unapologetic celebration of life, resistance, spiritual affirmation, community, social and humanity, and the highest levels, the "upper rooms," of African American culture and philosophy.[25]

In *Development Arrested* I attempt to bridge the gap between the blues as a widely recognized aesthetic tradition and the blues as a theory of social and economic development and change. This I do by returning the blues back to its roots as a critique of plantation social relations and their extensions. Several major theoretical barriers disempowered such an approach in recent times. First, the reification of urban street culture detached explanation from its blues–folk roots; the analysis of African American social life as urban became definitive and the rural South became derivative. Second, in many of the recent studies on the African American aesthetics, there is an overemphasis on what is termed "expressivity". Both the creator and the audience are systematically marginalized when questions of social power and social conflict are excluded from discussions of artistic expression. I will argue that what is being expressed in the blues and its extensions is a critique of plantation culture in all its manifestations. Also present in this form of expression is the desire to develop communities independent of plantation monopoly. A third theoretical barrier has been that a theory of orature and its uses was needed. Fourth, in order to recover African American development thought through orature, the structure of social explanation and action devised by enslaved African Americans must be explored as well.[26]

Understanding representational structures of African Americans created within the bowels of the plantation requires the theoretical integration of several approaches to political economy, cultural criticism, institutional analysis, regional transformation, and periodization. By reestablishing the original connection between regional political economy, culture, and consciousness, we now have the beginnings of a method of investigation capable of recovering forgotten conflicts between the plantation tradition of explanation and the blues tradition of explanation within the Delta. It becomes possible to reclassify seemingly unconnected events and to track the generational efforts of African Americans both to resist plantation monopoly and to reaffirm their identity in one place. When the seemingly invisible link between older African American development traditions, such as cooperatives, town building, and land reform, and more recent social movements is established, we are able to evaluate the twelfth regional crisis in the Delta since the eighteenth century and to open the window called the Lower Mississippi Delta Development Commission in order to view the contending power blocs in motion.[27]

## The Lower Mississippi Delta Development Commission

The LMDDC provides a perspective on the dreams realized and dreams arrested in the Mississippi Delta. All the elements required for a critical study of the region emerged during the eighteen-month life span of the commission. The simultaneous deterioration both of community life in the Delta, and of the Delta's political economy is daily producing divergent definitions of development and crisis. Created in 1988, the Lower Mississippi Delta Development Commission represented a plea to the federal government from a section of the region's leadership to support and expand the physical, institutional, and symbolic landmarks of the New South, New Deal, and Great Society mobilizations. Without federal support, the future held only more plant closures, a collapsing rural social and physical infrastructure, further outmigration, the resurgence of the dominant plantation bloc, and ever-deepening social conflict.

In many ways the federal tradition of regional planning in the United States began in the South as an attempt to resolve North–South schisms. For example, the Reconstruction program in the 1860s, the Tennessee Valley Authority (TVA) in the 1930s, and the Appalachian Regional Commission (ARC) in the 1960s were all created to address problems of economic collapse and integration in various regions of the South. The benefits of federal intervention were the following: the restoration of cotton profitability through the establishment of African American peonage in the case of Reconstruction; the generation of electric power for the Northeast, Midwest, and South through the construction of dams and power plants in the case of the TVA; and the accelerated exploitation of coal resources based on new highway construction in the case of the ARC. Yet, in each case, the working-class constituency was jettisoned while Northern corporate blocs and the dominant blocs of regional capital reaped the primary benefits. Additionally, the planter bloc's historic influence over numerous Congressional committees and sub-committees, particularly the cotton, rice, sugar, and tobacco subcommittees, meant that the US Department of Agriculture became a *de facto* regional planning body for the South. Often used to reinforce segregation, state and local *de facto* industrial policy and planning also emerged in the South earlier than in other regions. Consequently, based on the historical record, the LMDDC posed a fundamental danger to impoverished communities in general, and to African American communities, in particular.[28]

After the proposals for a commission emerged as a bill sponsored by US Senator Dale Bumpers of Arkansas, hearings were held in the summer of 1988. During the Congressional hearings, poverty, collapsing social programs, deteriorated infrastructure, and falling agricultural productivity were the issues most often addressed. Additionally, many of the participants testified that growth based upon the relocation of manufacturing plants was at a dead end and that communities that continued to engage in competitive industrial recruiting using local tax, infrastructure, and land incentives would only end up reducing local services and deepening their fiscal crisis. This rare examination by Congress of the depths of rural and regional exhaustion spurred political leaders from the Texas-Mexico border and the Western Plains also to propose federal commissions.[29]

The interim report, *Body of the Nation*, was presented to Congress on 15 October, 1989. The final report, *Realizing the Dream . . . Fulfilling the Potential*, was delivered to Congress and the White House on 14 May, 1990. In his letter of transmittal to President Bush, Governor Clinton placed the region's problems within a global context:

> If we do not implement a single recommendation made in this report, a lot of Americans who live in the Delta are going to do fine in the 1990s: those who are well educated, on the cutting edge of change, and able to take advantage of the emerging global economy. But millions of people will be left behind, and the region as a whole, including its successful residents, will not achieve its full potential . . . Being in the vanguard of change need not be a distinction limited to the freedom-hungry citizens of Eastern Europe or Poland or the aggressive business people of Singapore or Korea. The people of the Delta belong in that vanguard. They want to be there, and they can be if each of us will do our part.[30]

Although President Bush did not respond directly to the ten-year plan submitted, his Secretary of Housing and Urban Development did. In June of 1990, future vice presidential nominee Jack Kemp discussed the global illustrations used by Clinton:

> Bless them, they can't seem to get it in their mind that they are preaching democratic capitalism in Poland and Eastern Europe and they won't allow us to try it in the Delta . . . I equally reject the idea [that] massive federal infusion of funds to the Mississippi Delta or Downtown Buffalo or to Watts is the solution to poverty in America.[31]

Ironically, two years later, in the heat of a presidential race, both Kemp and Clinton were in south central Los Angeles promising federal aid in the wake of the largest urban rebellion in United States history. The LMDDC and its recommendations did not fare as well as Clinton's presidential bid. It was scheduled to become defunct as of 30 September, 1990. Although Clinton raised hopes in 1994 by designating much of the Mississippi, Arkansas, and Louisiana Deltas as Enterprise Communities, enterprise zones, he simultaneously dashed them by giving control over the Mississippi Delta Empowerment Zone to one of the most powerful planter organizations in the world, the Delta Council.

From its inception in 1988 to its demise in 1991, the LMDDC was continually attacked, both externally and internally, by regional leaders representing the plantation bloc who felt threatened by any discussion of their role in intensifying economic monopoly, ethnic conflict, and poverty. While these issues were never addressed squarely, the predominantly African American staff of the LMDDC inserted two paragraphs in the report that hinted at the true nature of inequality in the region:

> Strained race relations have historically compounded the problems associated with poverty in the Delta. The Delta's economic, social and cultural structure of life has often reinforced tensions between ethnic groups and worsened the economic subjugation of African Americans. This reality has stood in the way of economic development efforts. The changes brought on by the civil rights movement and recent reforms in education policies and spending have helped to make up for decades of low investments in human development. However, much work remains if the region is to overcome the legacy of its past.
>
> ... industrial redlining, a practice by which industries systematically avoid locating in certain areas, has been widely perceived as an impediment to recruitment efforts in the Delta. At the Commission's meeting Clarence Wright ... requested that the Commission address the impact of industrial redlining in those instances in which industries avoid locating in areas where the African American population is 30 percent or higher. The extent to which this policy has adversely affected the Delta is a concern which has subsequently been raised by other citizens. In preparation for its Final Report, the Commission plans to conduct research to assess the incidence and impact of industrial redlining on economic development efforts in the Delta.[32]

These two subjects were not what the commissioners wanted to address, and the idea of studying industrial redlining and other racist practices was quickly denounced and abandoned. For those viewing the region from the blues perspective these issues meant the difference between leaving and staying, living or dying. However, those operating from the dominant plantation bloc tradition objected to any serious discussion of how to address poverty and ethnic relations outside a discussion of what they saw as the region's principal problem, the crisis affecting agriculture. Preoccupied with industrial recruitment and new infrastructure, the New South bloc assisted the plantation powers in hundreds of ways, including objecting to any full explorations of the past as being too divisive.

To appease the plantation bloc, the LMDDC embarked upon a road that limited debate on what was and on what will be. Instead, it focused on a future, a federally subsidized future, in which the historic structures of regional inequality are neither talked about or addressed. By contrast, the present work will examine the historical origins and current manifestations of planter bloc hegemony, the appeasement of it, resistance to it, and the roads still open to regional development based on economic democracy, social justice, and cultural sanctity.[33]

# 2

# The Blues Tradition of Explanation

... had it not been for the blues, the black man wouldn't have been able to survive through all the humiliations and all the various things going on in America ... he had nothing to fight with but the blues ... the blues is the facts of life.

Willie Dixon[1]

Although they call it the blues today, the original name given to this kind of music was "reals." And it was real because it made the truth available to the people in songs ...

Henry Townsend[2]

The blues epistemology is a longstanding African American tradition of explaining reality and change. This form of explanation finds its origins in the processes of African American cultural construction within, and resistance to, the antebellum plantation regime. It crystallized during Reconstruction and its subsequent violent overthrow. After two hundred years of censorship and ten short years of open communication, the resurrected plantation bloc thoroughly demonized all autonomous forms of thought and action for another century. The blues became the channel through which the Reconstruction generation grasped reality in the midst of disbelief, critiqued the plantation regime, and organized against it. The Mississippi Delta is the home of the blues tradition in music, popular culture, and explanation. It is therefore fitting that this popular consciousness is used to interpret both the continuous crisis in the Delta and African American attempts to create a new regional reality based on cultural freedom and economic and social justice.

This chapter will attempt to demonstrate that the blues epistemology is embedded, necessary, and reflective. It is a self-referential explanatory tradition among working-class African Americans in which development debates occur. The blues epistemology was first fully explained by the Mississippi author Richard Wright in 1937. Wright developed this approach originally as part of his studies on African American daily life and as part of a music-based critique of African American literature. The discussion below extends his theory into the field of regional studies by integrating several related discourses.[3]

Edward Soja argues that physical, functional, and cultural definitions of regions fail to explore fully the processes that distinguish regions: construction, reproduction, crisis, and the conscious activities of institutions and social movements. The analysis of this "social-spatial dialectic" is a central feature of the emerging regional critique. According to Anne Gilbert, the relational concept of the region traces its origins to the intense debates over the relationship between ethnicity, gender, and consciousness and political economy that occurred during the 1960s and 1970s. Distinctive regional identities and relations are constructed, and reproduced, through mobilizations and countermobilizations:

> the existence of a particular region is assumed to depend on the actual domination of certain social groups in the regional structure. If a group within this structure is strong enough to impose standardization in a certain area at a certain time, the regional entity emerges, and its differentiation from other areas is sharpened. If the groups within a given regional structure are instead too weak to generate some sort of unity, they are integrated by groups dominant at other scales and the regional differentiation associated with the former disappears. The regional whole comes from the power of certain groups to impose their values and norms upon the majority and the cultural solidarity necessary to the specification of an area.[4]

To comprehend this process, a dynamic conception of how various regional blocs respond to, and anticipate, the general processes of uneven development must be utilised. Several conceptions are key to this undertaking. First, successful regional reproduction is not solely dependent upon preserving, at all costs, a comparative advantage in the production of a single commodity or group of commodities. Also, the ability of dominant regional blocs to maintain control over the regional structure cannot be assumed. Third, ethnic and gender divisions of labor are reproduced and reinforced within all aspects of the region's institutions, sectors, and spatial organization. What comes from the entire discussion is that a distinctive regional or subregional "state" emerges. Finally, the relational approach also enables us to see through the mask of normality that hides the permanent state of crisis in the Delta.[5]

The term "regional bloc" is used in the body of this work to understand the forces constructing and contesting regional power structures. The bloc can be conceived of as an alliance, a bargain, or a contract between disparate ethnic, gender, class, and other elements. The goal of the regional bloc is to gain control over resources and over the ideological and distributive institutions governing their allocation. The institutions and movements of the dominant group are typically explained in terms of moral, psychological, biological, and intellectual imperatives and superiority. According to Antonio Gramsci, after the dominant or hegemonic bloc "creates a new ideological terrain," it "determines a reform of consciousness and of methods of knowledge ... when one succeeds in introducing a new morality in conformity with a new conception of the world, one finishes by introducing the conception as well." Similarly, Barbara Fields argues that race relations must be understood in the context of the drive by dominant blocs to portray themselves as natural while identifying, classifying, disciplining, and institutionalizing difference, "deviance," and nonconformity. For Peter Jackson, the "real innovation in Gramsci's work was the realization that, in capitalist societies, hegemony is never fully achieved – it is always contested . . . Resistance may not always be active and open, often it will be latent and largely symbolic."[6]

Blocs, agendas, and movements that challenge the dominant regime are often eliminated from the historical record and from popular memory by the normal workings of the dominant institutions. In *Farmer Movements in the South, 1865–1933*, Theodore Saloutos provides the following insights into the importance of these movements:

> society is composed of ephemeral groups with whom many of us are in disagreement, and for whom many academicians in particular have nothing but contempt. But these people existed, agitated, and proselytized; they constitute a significant part of their times . . . The amazing thing about all this is that—despite the numerous errors and reversals—so much of what these people dreamed about and aspired for became an accepted part of our agricultural thinking long after the visible structure of their organizations had melted away.[7]

The above discussion of relational regions and regional blocs provides a theory of social change that can be incorporated into the blues epistemology. Attempts by working-class African Americans to establish social democracy within a plantation-dominated economy provided the material basis for an ethic of survival, subsistence, resistance, and affirmation from the antebellum period to the present. The kin, work, and community networks that arose from these efforts served as the foundations of thousands of conscious mobilizations designed to transform society. Through a historical examination of these little-documented, long-forgotten, and seemingly ephemeral organizations and agendas, African American traditions of explanation, development thought, and social action become visible once again.[8]

Edward Said's *Orientalism* is an invaluable study of the military, political, economic, and academic foundations of the worldview of a dominant bloc. To Said, the material dependency of the imperial power upon the colonized produces an internally consistent imagery that is increasingly detached from how the colonized actually live their lives. Therefore, for Europeans the Orient "can become a discourse, a career for poets, journalists, scholars, soldiers, priests, administrators, etc . . . However, in the final analysis, it is the hegemony of one region over the other which gives durability to this phenomenon."[9] Similarly, many scholars, etcetera, outside the African American community in the Delta have built careers interpreting and managing African American life and culture. One of Said's most important contributions is his assertion that orientalism is not dogmatic or a single-minded grid, but as complex as the individual authors who have produced thousands of works on the subject. The key to understanding this complexity is the positional superiority of one region, bloc, class, or ethnic group over the other. Also important are the desires, repressions, investments, and projections circulating within that culture which weigh upon the imagination and logic of the individual. This approach allows the combined evaluation of social science, humanities, and policy studies in terms of their relationship to regional power structures.

Briefly reviewed below are examples of the ways in which some regional blocs define themselves, the region, its history, and the "other." First, Benedict Anderson suggests that blocs make investments in creating "imagined communities" which command emotional legitimacy. These communities are not coterminous with humankind or even with all segments of a region. They are, however, bound by deep horizontal networks of kinship, fraternity, sorority, and obligation. These networks and material relations are often explained not in terms of class or political affiliation or by rational calculation, but in terms of being sovereign in relation to their "gods," national ethnic and regional destiny, golden pasts and golden futures. Raymond Williams suggests that all these golden periods are used both to spur memories and to provide intellectual discipline in preparation for future mobilizations.[10]

Born in the Delta city of Vicksburg, Mississippi, in 1915, the late bluesman Willie Dixon worked tirelessly to get the blues recognized as a social philosophy and to get its performers the respect they have been so systematically denied. In his 1990 autobiography *I Am the Blues*, he explains how the working-class African American representational structure, the blues, has maintained its grip on a constantly shifting reality despite the pressures of falsification, distortion, romanticism, cynicism, piracy, and commercialization:

> All the blues songs actually related back to Africa or some African heritage things ... By knowing about yesterday, how things came along and are still advancing, it can give you a greater idea of what the future could be. This is why the blues represents the past, the present and future ... It's necessary for people to know all the various parts of the blues and the various things that have happened in the blues so they won't make the mistakes in the future that have been made in the past.
>
> They've got blues books out there that tell a little about everybody—his name and what songs he sang—but they don't have none of the actual blues experience involved ... Ninety-nine percent of the people that wrote stories about the blues gave people phony ideas and this gave the blues a bad reputation. They had people believing the blues was a low-down type of music and underestimating the blues one hundred percent. The majority of people have been taught to stay away from the blues because the world didn't actually want you to understand what the blues want.
>
> The majority of the blues have been documented through time with various people involved with the blues. All of this is unwritten facts about the blues because these blues have been documented but not written—documented in the minds of various men with these various songs since the first black man set foot on the American shore ... My old man would explain it all so we accepted his philosophy more than we did anybody else's because it made sense.[11]

## The Blues as Epistemology

> Lacking the handicaps of false ambition and property, they have access to a
> wide social vision and a deep social consciousness. They display a greater
> freedom and initiative in pushing their claims upon civilization than even the
> petty bourgeoisie. Their organizations show greater strength, adaptability,
> and efficiency than any other group or class in society.
>
> Richard Wright[12]

The intellectual traditions and social organizations through which working-
class African Americans lived, understood, and changed their reality have
typically emerged in spite of, and in opposition to, plantation powers. This
conflict is one of the defining features of African American social thought.
From the unique experience and position of the enslaved Black Southern
working class there emerged a self-referential classificatory grid. This distinct
and evolving complex of social explanation and social action, this praxis,
provided support for the myriad traditions of resistance, affirmation and
confirmation that were to follow. This pillar of African American identity is
referred to in this work as the blues epistemology.

In the following chapters the historical evolution of two blocs will be traced.
Most familiar to the reader is the plantation bloc and its system of representation. This fragment of society can be generally viewed as a Southern ethno-
class grouping engaged in the monopolization of resources, power, historical
explanation, and social action. The plantation classificatory grid has at its
center the planter as the heroic master of a natural ethnic, class, gender, and
environmental hierarchy. African Americans in general, and African American women in particular, are at the bottom of this order. The growth in power
of the first bloc was directly linked with the growth in potential power of the
second bloc, the blues bloc. The blues bloc consists of working-class African
American communities in the rural South and their diaspora. The ontology,
or worldview, embedded in these communities has provided a sense of
collective self and a tectonic footing from which to oppose and dismantle the
American intellectual, cultural, and socioeconomic traditions constructed from
the raw material of African American exploitation and denigration.[13]

In the African American experience, the plantation bloc set the parameters
of this conflict for several centuries as it attempted to suppress independent
thought, cultural expression, and action. To ensure the autonomy of thought
and action in the midst of constant surveillance and violence, African Americans constructed a highly developed tradition of social interpretation. This
practice finds its origins in the secret societies prevalent during slavery. During
this period, African, Native American and European intellectual traditions
were forged in the crucible of the plantation South. What emerged was a
highly developed introspective and universalist system of social thought and
practice whose influence upon the modern world can never be underestimated.

The blues epistemology rests on two foundations. The first involves the constant reestablishment of collective sensibility in the face of constant attacks by the plantation bloc and its allies, and in the face also of a daily community life that is often chaotic and deadly. Therefore, the location, timing, and forms of communications necessary to reestablish the conditions for collective thought and action are of critical importance. Across a constantly changing and dangerous terrain, the first question faced by an African American musical, literary, religious, and political performer/investigator is how can an individual express the thoughts of the audience authentically when authentic thoughts and actions are routinely and violently condemned. Consequently, those able to link historic African American objectives and expressions with present realities and visions of the future are often viewed as having been the recipients of ancestral gifts.

This brings us to the second aspect of the blues epistemology, social relations in the plantation South as one of the foundational pillars of African American culture. The plantation was a site both of conflict and of cultural formation. Even many of the descendants of the 6 million African American migrants who left the South between 1910 and 1970 (3 million of them between 1950 and 1970 alone) still measure social progress and spirituality in relation to their physical and psychological distance from "down home." For many of the diaspora communities in the Northeast, Midwest, Southwest, and West, the 1980s represented a reversal of progress, the collapse of the Second Reconstruction, and the return to the older forms of oppression that they fled the South to escape. Segments within some of these communities had dismissed the blues many years ago. For example, the biographer of B. B. King, a native of Clarksville, Mississippi, described the reception King received in the early 1960s during national tours:

> His appearances on these tours gave him exposure to young, racially mixed, audiences, and they might have bridged the waters around his cultural island. But they didn't. On the contrary, they isolated him further because the audiences were cold, indifferent, at times even hostile to his music . . . They . . . were impatient with his slow tempos and mournful lyrics . . . Sometimes he was booed. The heckling came more from black teenagers than from whites, a fact he attributed to the blues being associated with black Americans' poor origins in this country.[14]

During the 1980s the blues were rediscovered by one generation of African Americans while another generation created rap which reaffirms the historic commitment to social and personal investigation, description, and criticism present in the blues. However, the question remains of how African Americans investigate and explain changing social relations when they still live in or adjacent to plantation-dominated counties and states; and where, in some instances, the same African American working-class families and the same White planter families have coexisted with, and combated, each other sometimes for over 300 years?

Some of these questions were addressed during a series of seminars held in 1988 and 1989 by the Margaret Walker Alexander Research Center for the

Study of Twentieth Century African American Culture at Jackson State University in Mississippi. According to the Duke University Professor of Religion, C. Eric Lincoln, those African Americans who stayed in the South were heroic:

> because they did, America has been changed ... True freedom cannot be imposed from the outside, it has to originate in the hearts and minds of the people who want to be free. There were such people in the South—people who stayed put, but people who were no less determined to see America be America. Their names were legion: Medgar Evers, Fannie Lou Hamer, Rosa Parks, Martin Luther King, Jr, Daisy Bates, Wiley Branton, Fred Shuttlesworth and ten thousand others whose names are known only to God, but whose faith, whose determination and whose sacrifice brought us to where we are ... many who had once quit the South in despair, came bringing unexpected succor, encouragement and reinforcement. But the brunt of the battle was borne by the black citizens of the South, the African Americans who stayed "down home" determined to make "down home" a true and viable home for themselves, for their posterity, and for every American of whatever race, or creed or color.[15]

Described as the "Mother of the Modern civil rights movement," Rosa Parks compared the past and the present:

> I felt that we were intelligent people and we must exercise our freedom. I felt that we should have our own self worth and think of ourselves as first class citizens in spite of the obstacles. I feel the same way today, that we should not feel that because we are in a certain location we must feel helpless, oppressed and accept the persecution, the pressure and intimidation that is placed on us.[16]

Novelist, essayist, Professor Emeritus of English and Director Emeritus of the institute Margaret Walker Alexander addressed the accomplishments of those who stayed to lead the so-called Southern Revolution:

> Black people who stayed built social institutions, families, churches, businesses, and other social organizations ... Those who stayed here therefore built a nation within a nation. We are a completely Black nation. Segregation forced us into every profession, business and vocational endeavor. We became self-sufficient despite the fact that billions of our dollars went regularly into the coffers of our oppressors.[17]

At the very end of Dr Martin Luther King Jr's life, he recognized that the movement would remain hollow so long as it failed to address the entirety of plantation relations so eloquently explored in depth by the blues. He came to realize that the plantation complex was central to both the construction and destruction of African American identity and aspirations. This is why the march King was organizing at the time of his death had as a goal a nationwide general strike directed at the Mississippi Delta plantation bloc. King along with many other African American leaders only discovered the power and continued relevancy of the blues epistemology after a long and circuitous route.

Cultural critic Richard Powell argues that the blues is an aesthetic found in

African American art and life throughout the USA, and that it has philosophical foundations that are essentially humanistic:

> The term "blues" is an appropriate designation for this idea because of its association
> with one of the most identifiable black American traditions that we know. Perhaps
> more than any other designation, the idea of a blues aesthetic situates the discourse
> squarely on: (1) art produced in our time; (2) creative expression that emanates from
> artists who are empathetic with Afro-American issues and ideals; (3) work that
> identifies with grassroots, popular, and /or mass black American culture; (4) art that
> has an affinity with Afro–US derived music and/or rhythms; and artists and /or
> statements [whose] raison d'etre is humanistic.
>
> Although one could argue that other twentieth century Afro–US musical terms
> such as ragtime, jazz, boogie-woogie, gospel, swing, bebop, cool, rhythm and blues,
> doo-wop, soul, funk, go-go, hip-hop, or rap are just as descriptive as "the blues,"
> what "the blues" has over and above them all is a breadth and mutability that allows
> it to persist and even thrive through this century. From the anonymous songsters of
> the late nineteenth century who sang about hard labor and unattainable love, to
> contemporary rappers blasting the airwaves with percussive and danceable testimo-
> nies, the blues is an affecting, evocative presence, which endures in every artistic
> overture made toward black American peoples.[18]

According to the African American folk critic Stephen Henderson "the blues
continues as its own reference point ... speaking the truth to the people in
the language of the people." Like other working-class and peasant knowledge
systems, it has been denigrated by hegemonic institutional structures and by
African American scholars, artists, professionals, entrepreneurs, and political
figures hoping to put some distance between themselves and their demonized
working class.[19]

The legendary Richard Wright commented on this last tendency in a historic
1937 article:

> Generally speaking, Negro writing in the past has been confined to humble novels,
> poems, and plays, [by] prim and decorous ambassadors who went a-begging to white
> America ... For the most part these artistic ambassadors were received as though
> they were French poodles who do clever tricks ... On the other hand, these often
> technically brilliant performances by Negro writers were looked upon by the majority
> of literate Negroes as something to be proud of ... That the productions of their
> writers should have been something of a guide in their daily living is a matter which
> seems to have never been seriously raised ... it became a sort of conspicuous
> ornamentation [and] it became the voice of the educated Negro pleading with white
> America for justice ... Rarely was the best of this writing addressed to the Negro
> himself, his needs, his sufferings, his aspirations.[20]

According to Wright, these yearnings were met, in different ways, by two
African American institutions: the Black church and the blues. Both the Black
church and the blues emerged in rural areas where Black political and
economic institutions were subjected to constant surveillance and often
destroyed. Both prospered in Southern cities and spread throughout the
Northern and Western diasporas. With its theology of liberation and common

metaphorical language, the church helped to move the social, cultural, economic, and human rights goals forward while giving institutional and physical form to the African American vision of the ideal community and utopia. Although the schism between the church and the blues is often emphasized, the two shared music, adherents, and leaders. According to Wright, it was difficult for individuals to divorce themselves from the blues given that its text was folkloric and its philosophy was based upon both materialism, realism, and spirituality:

> The blues could be called the spirituals of the city. They are the songs of a simple people whose life has been caught up in and brutalized by the inflexible logic of modern industrial existence ... Since the best-known blues have love as the main theme, people have a false idea, an incomplete one, of their true range and role in the life of Black people. There also exists blues which indict the social system and they have been judged not commercial enough because of this satirical bent ... Common, everyday life, the background of our national life, is to be seen through the blues: trains, ships, trade unions, planes, the Army, the Navy, the White House, plantations, elections, poll tax, the boll weevil, landlords, epidemics, bosses, Jim Crow, lynchings ... All such blues are as natural for the Black people as eating and sleeping, and they come as a rule out of their daily experience. Their very titles indicate the mood and state of mind in which they were written.[21]

However, Wright believed that because it was embedded in daily life, the knowledge which flows through the blues channels was typically "unwritten and unrecognized":

> It was, however, in a folklore molded out of rigorous and inhuman conditions of life that the Negro achieved his most indigenous and complete expression. Blues, spirituals and folk tales recounted from mouth to mouth; the whispered words of a black mother to her black daughter on the ways of men, the confidential wisdom of a black father to his black son; the swapping of sex experiences on street corners from boy to boy in the deepest vernacular; work songs sung under blazing suns—all these formed the channels through which racial wisdom flowed.[22]

In his works, Wright connected ethnic and class consciousness with daily life. He identified orature in general and music in particular as a point to begin the study of African American representational structures. Ruth Finnegan's exploration of the relationship between oral traditions and social theory in "Literacy versus Non-literacy: The Great Divide" represents an important contribution to this endeavor:

> When people wish to make a basic distinction between different societies or historical periods, one of the commonly invoked criteria is literacy ... those wishing to avoid the connotations of "primitive," " uncivilized," and "aboriginal" tend to turn to a description of "non-literate" or "pre-literate."[23]

It is assumed that non-literate translates into a lack of intelligence. It is assumed that societies which are without writing are without true culture. What is clear is that non-literate societies have their own lyrics, panegyric poetry, religious poetry, love songs, prose narratives, and drama, often referred to as folklore:

> individuals in societies without such formal institutions are not without an oppor-
> tunity for literary education in the broader sense. The Akan child in the West
> African forest areas grows up hearing spoken, sung and intoned poetry, as well as
> the special verbal poetry for horns and drums and the constantly recurring imagery
> of proverbs, while a little further east the Yoruba are exposed from birth to tonal,
> metaphor-saturated language which in its ordinary prose form is never far from
> music in the aural impression it gives and which has produced an extensive variety
> of spoken art characteristic of the people.[24]

Tradition in both form and content are also components of orature; however, the function of orature is social, moral, educational and pragmatic, and not simply entertainment or art for art's sake:

> The fact that oral literature is unwritten does not ipso facto absolve the poet from
> adhering to locally accepted canons of aesthetic form ... nor prevent him from
> delighting in the elaboration of beauty in words and music for its own sake. To be
> sure, there is often little interest among non-literate and semi-literate peoples in the
> individual personality of the author, particularly of the romantic and intense kind
> characteristic of a certain period of western literature or western capitalism. Nor is
> there often an idea of copyright.[25]

Using this approach, we can begin to understand the fullness of an oral tradition. The demands of performance significantly structure African American orature, particularly the traditions that have emerged through the interaction between language, music and movement. As explained by Harrison, language represents a layer of orature that possesses its own dilemmas:

> The blues ... are a means of articulating experience and demonstrating a toughness
> of spirit and re-creating that experience. Two qualities highly valued in the black
> community, articulateness and toughness, are thus brought together in this art form.
> Fluency in language is considered a powerful tool for establishing and maintaining
> status. Thus a man or woman who has mastered the art of signifying, rapping, or
> orature ... is held in high esteem (the present-day phenomenon of grand masters of
> rap music demonstrates the continuation of this value among blacks in cities).[26]

Music is similarly an important component of orature. Several recent studies have identified the continuation of numerous African vocal, instrumental, and composition traditions in the blues. They have also noted the continuity of the role of performers as educators. African string instruments range from the one-string bow to the twenty-one-string kora. Furthermore, in various parts of Africa, griots, musical families, and orchestras serve as historians, genealogists, counselors, reporters, diplomats, and social, cultural, and economic innovators. It was not a great leap from the stringed instruments of Africa to the diddly bo, the violin, the banjo, and, later, the guitar in the Americas. Despite intense efforts at suppression, the African musical sensibility and scale were preserved:

Aaron Copeland has also noted the technically specific nature of the blues scale and feels that this African element is a most unique contribution to American music. The blue or flattened note, sung just under the note as it should have been sung on the Western musical scale, has become almost the hallmark of the blues ... Blue notes are not notes played out of tune but notes played in a specific way. It was created when slaves tried to fit African scales to European scales.[27]

Language and music also intersect with performance styles. Lomax believes that these too are heavily informed by African practices:

It became clear that black Africa had distinctive performance styles, quite as formal as those of Western Europe ... Careful comparisons showed that black African nonverbal performance traditions had survived virtually intact in African America, and had shaped all its distinctive rhythmic arts, during both the colonial and postcolonial periods. It was this unwritten but rich African tradition that empowered the creativity we had encountered in the lower depths of the Mississippi Delta.[28]

This complex of language, music and performance must be understood as a whole. Albert Murray has taken to task those who associate blues music and lyrics with a state of emotional depression. Attempts to analyze the lyrics separately as literature ultimately fail because meaning and abstraction in the blues emerges from the simultaneous interaction between language, music, and movement.

Blues music is always an artful combination of incantation and percussion. It is not always the song in the conventional sense of the word ... The essential message is usually conveyed by the music, whether vocal or instrumental ... verbal statement can be contradicted and in effect canceled by any musical counter-statement. If the lyrics laments but the music mocks, that statement is not one of lamentation but mockery ... The words may bemoan the loss of a lover, but if the singer is also involved with such choreographic gestures as finger popping, shoulder rocking, and hip swinging all the while, the statement can hardly be considered a form of bereavement.[29]

Sidran attempted to link this "oral physicality" to the process of the construction of individual and community identities:

The essential nature of communication through rhythm is an unknown quantity due primarily to a lack of interest on the part of Western science. Rhythm ... is the cultural catharsis Fanon has suggested is necessary to black culture ... it simultaneously asserts and preserves the oral ontology ... it is on this basis that black music can be seen ... as a source for black social organization ... [According to Raymond Williams] "the process of communication is in fact the process of community."[30]

Finally, it is often assumed that societies reliant upon orature are isolated and ethnocentric. First ethnocentrism is part of the daily bread of "literate cultures." Second, written

literature, particularly the printed word, does indeed provide certain opportunities for wider communication. But so too can oral literature. We can instance the

traveling jellemen of the Great Western Savannah region of Africa who created a
vast cultural area throughout many different kingdoms and linguistic groups by their
arts of word and music; the wandering Azmaris of Ethiopia who helped to bring
about a striking uniformity of Ethiopian poetry among the many groups of the area;
the unifying effects of their reverence for Homer among the disparate Greeks; or the
early poets of Ireland who in the absence of towns or any centralized political system
... were the only national institution – all performing the same kind of functions as
the medieval jugglers and minstrels of Western Europe or their counterparts in the
Arab World.[31]

Similarly Black musicians have created a vast cultural region of global
proportions through the spread of the blues and blues-influenced genres such
as jazz, gospel, rhythm and blues, rock and roll, country and western, reggae,
soul, funk, and rap. Furthermore, the blues, its schools, and its various
extensions can be considered a national institution on a par with the Black
church. It has its own schools and masters. According to Gates, among the
African American art forms, in music given the "required mastery of technique
and a highly critical audience, there evolved a tradition of master not found in
literature." Poet Amiri Baraka also juxtaposes the traditions:

> American Negro music from its inception moved logically and powerfully out of a
> fusion between African musical tradition and the American experience ... It is,
> indeed, a chronicler of the Negro's movement from African slave to American slave,
> from freedman to citizen. And the literature of the blues is a much more profound
> contribution to Western culture than any other literary contribution made by
> American Negroes...[32]

There has always been a great deal of diversity in the blues, particularly in the
form of distinct local and regional schools. Constant movement and migration
ensured both continuity and further differentiation. The local traditions were
created and maintained by individual performers and audiences who shared,
and built upon, a set of foundational songs, sounds, techniques, instruments,
lyrics, language, dances, etcetera. The interaction between local schools and
the distinctiveness of regional power structures, daily life, and aesthetics
become the foundation of the regional blues traditions, those of the Delta,
Piedmont, Texas, Chicago, etcetera.

The blues emerge immediately after the overthrow of Reconstruction.
During this period, unmediated African American voices were routinely
silenced through the imposition of a new regime of censorship based on exile,
assassination and massacre. The blues became an alternative form of communication, analysis, moral intervention, observation, celebration for a new
generation that had witnessed slavery, freedom, and unfreedom in rapid
succession between 1860 and 1875. Perhaps no other generation of a single
ethnic group in the United States, except for Native Americans, witnessed
such a tremendous tragedy in such a short period of time. Performer Cash
McCall described the blues as the almost magical uncorking of the censored
histories of countless people, places and events:

Well, in the old days, you see, you weren't allowed to express your feelings all that much. A lot of stuff was bottled up inside. Coming up from the old days until now ... You can't explain it in a conversation so the best way to do it is to sing.[33]

On the other hand, guitarist Willie Foster described them as the irrepressible voice of daily anguish:

The black folks got the blues from working ... You work all day long, you come home sometimes you didn't have nothing to eat. You got the blues."Lord have mercy I ain't got nothing." You sit down and cry. You ain't got nothing to eat. And that's where the blues come from.[34]

The multiple perspectives and levels of expression inherent in the blues operating within a rigid racial hierarchy ensured that the study of the blues would proceed with great difficulty. One of the key problems identified by Stephen Henderson was that the community that created the blues was deemed incapable of analyzing them:

while one may admit to the existence of "folk poetry" or of a "folk" poet, the category of folk critic is unthinkable ... on the assumption that unlettered people lack sufficient capacity for judgement, even of the works which they create themselves ... Folk poetry is thus a lower form of expression which must be subjected to the informed discursive intelligence before it becomes a great literature or "real poetry."[35]

Beginning in the 1910s, scholars began examining the blues using the categories and standard of Anglo-American and European musical and poetic traditions. Still prevalent, this tradition of blues scholarship actively distorts the history of the blues while crippling its philosophical implications for African Americans and the world at large. Within the emerging African American literary tradition, the exploration of blues forms and themes was begun by Langston Hughes, Sterling Brown, Zora Neal Hurston, and other writers in the Harlem Renaissance and the New Negro movement. Blues as criticism arose during and after the Great Depression from authors such as Richard Wright, Ralph Ellison, and Albert Murray, and during the Black Arts Movement of the 1960s important contributions were made by Amiri Baraka, Larry Neal and others. In the present period, many African American scholars working in the disciplines and fields of music, history, folklore, drama, poetry, art, literary criticism, cultural studies, theology, anthropology, etcetera have acknowledged the blues as a hearth of African American consciousness. As stated earlier, the social sciences remain a barrier not breached.

The continual presence and growth of this tradition will exponentially expand the crisis that has continued to sweep through the social sciences and the humanities as a result of the domestic and international movements of the 1950s and 1960s. There is now an intensified struggle over interpretation in the midst of another national and international expansion in the popularity of the blues. For example, in years past White scholars have criticized African Americans for their lack of interest in the blues. Lomax recently made the following observation:

The error in African-American studies had been to look to print and to language for evidence of African survivals. For instance, musicologists discovered that American blacks performed many European-like melodies, but failed to notice that the whole performance context—voicing, rhythmic organization, orchestration—remained essentially African. Such scholarship turned university-trained black intellectuals and writers away from the heritage of their parents, who had a nonprint, nonverbal heritage that the educated falsely labeled "ignorant." Nonetheless, it was because of this culturally biased "ignorance" that African culture had been largely passed on in America—that is, through nonverbal and oral channels, out of the reach of censorship.[36]

Similar observations were offered by Samuel Charters:

> With the rise of the black middle class new musical forms and styles have emerged, but the root language for it all is still the blues and when black historians and black sociologists begin the assessment of what has been the cultural achievement of the years in America, it is to the blues that they will have to turn for many of their answers.[37]

These observations both celebrate and denigrate African American working-class intellectual traditions. Not only did the audiences and performers create, listen and shape the blues, they were also its first students and scholars. The epistemology, or perspective, of these folk intellectuals eventually began to influence numerous "educated" African American artists, writers, and professors who were more likely to be recognized by the dominant institutions. However, such an essential feature of American identity as Black music could not be left to the interpretation of Blacks themselves, whether working-class or middle-class.

The struggle over who will interpret Black music is an intellectual battle that has been raging throughout the nineteenth and twentieth centuries. The above authors seem to want to forget the existence of this conflict and their role in it. They also fail to understand that African American Studies was a movement led by the African American working class. This movement should be seen as a stage in the further institutionalization of both the African American development agenda and the blues epistemology. It can also be viewed as an intensification of the debates over, not just African survivals, but American survival. The authors must evaluate their own work in light of these realities. They must also examine the strong resistance to accepting African American intellectuals on the part of the guild-like fraternity of White Black music scholars.

Rosemont argues that slightly below the surface of traditional blues scholarship is a "dark truth" that is being consciously avoided because few American institutionalized scholars, African American or White, wish to confront the full implications of African American culture:

> It should be emphasized, since so many critics pretend not to notice it, that all authentic blues and jazz share a poetically subversive core, an explosive essence of irreconcilable revolt against the shameful limits of an unlivable destiny. Notwith-

standing the whimpering objections of a few timid skeptics, this revolt cannot be "assimilated" into the abject mainstream of American bourgeois/Christian culture except by way of diffusion and/or outright falsification. The *dark truth* of Afro-American music remains unquestionably oppositional. Its implacable Luciferian pride—that is, its aggressive and uncompromising assertion of the omnipotence of desire and imagination in the face of all resistances—forever provides a stumbling block for those who would like to exploit it as mere "entertainment," a mere ruse to keep the cash register ringing. Born in passionate revolt against the unlivable, the blues and jazz demand nothing less than a new life.[38]

Willie Dixon sung about this dilemma in "You Can't Judge a Book by Its Cover":

> You can't judge the sugar by looking at the cane
> You can't judge a woman by looking at her man
> You can't judge the sister by looking at her brother
> You can't judge a book by looking at the cover.
>
> You can't judge the fish by looking at the pond
> You can't judge the right by looking at the wrong
> You can't judge one by looking at another
> You can't judge a book by looking at the cover.[39]

The above discussion has attempted to establish the terrain upon which the blues epistemology emerged and now operates. During the last three hundred years, the African American working class has daily constructed their vision of a non-oppressive society through a variety of cultural practices, institution-building activities, and social movements. By doing so, they have created an intellectual and social space in which they could discuss, plan, and organize this new world. The blues are the cries of a new society being born.

# 3

# The Social-Spatial Construction of the Mississippi Delta

Plantation regimes create, institutionalize, and manage extreme levels of conflict. Therefore, the current crisis in the Delta is not one of failed policies, underclass behavior, illiteracy, rural poverty, labor market mismatch, or social "backwardness." Responsibility for the coexistence of great poverty besides great wealth rests squarely at the feet of a dominant regional bloc that has fought every effort to expand the parameters of social, economic, and cultural justice. In *Cotton Kingdom of the New South*, Robert Brandfon described the incendiary implications of this three-hundred-year engagement over the essential meaning of development:

> the largest of the planters of the Yazoo Delta were some of the wealthiest planters in the world. And they lived in Mississippi, the poorest state in the Union! ... The enclaves of wealth amidst overwhelming poverty produced the setting for new political configurations that jolted the South for decades thereafter.[1]

Between the Native American expulsion known as the Trail of Tears and the Great Depression of the 1930s, the Yazoo–Mississippi Delta was carved out of an impenetrable complex of swamps and hardwood forests. Prior to colonization, the Lower Mississippi Valley was imagined by Easterners as a future empire that would eventually rival the Nile Valley civilizations. Consequently, allusions to those ancient empires are still scattered throughout the Valley: Cairo, Illinois; Luxora, Arkansas; Memphis, Tennessee; Alexandria, Louisiana; etcetera ... For African Americans, the Delta came to represent a slavery within slavery and oppression of biblical proportions.

In African American, and Southern, historiography, the term Mississippi Plan usually refers to two planter-led movements which began in the Delta and spread rapidly throughout the South: the 1875 overthrow of Reconstruction, and the 1890 constitution "legalizing" African American disenfranchisement and segregation. In this work, the phrase "Mississippi Delta Plan" is used throughout to distinguish twelve major mobilizations launched to restructure the region's political economy. This chapter reviews the construction, reproduction, and demise of six of the Delta regimes prior to 1875.

## Mississippi Delta Plan 1: The Trail of Tears

Plantation systems are a method of colonization that imposes upon social landscapes a distinct regime of political, economic, and ethnic regulation. Central to these regimes is their monopolization ethic: the total elimination, marginalization, or exile of indigenous people and small landowners. Therefore, the expansion of the plantation regime southward and westward resulted in the destruction of one Native American nation after another.

In approximately 700 AD, native nations of the Lower Mississippi Valley began to become more fully integrated with the Aztec and Mayan cultural spheres. Known as the Mississippian transformation, this movement was defined by the adoption of several institutions: communal ownership, hierarchical religious structures, centralized government, large towns, formalized class structures, mound building, and a corn-centered agricultural economy. Standing at the center of trade routes extending from Guatemala to Wisconsin, and from Oklahoma to South Carolina, Mississippi Delta nations such as the Tunica, the Yazoo, and the Natchez were integral links in this new international complex.

The Mississippian period lasted more than eight hundred years, yet its demise was rapid. As a consequence of numerous European invasions, the native population in what would become known as the South, the southeastern region of North America, declined from more than one million people in 1492 to only two hundred thousand people by 1692. Three European nations were involved. First, after their destruction of native people in the Caribbean, the Spanish began to capture the indigenous people of the Southeast and enslave them on the islands of Cuba, Puerto Rico, and Santo Domingo. The rapid depopulation of the Southeast, the flight of native people to the interior forests, and a series of native revolts in Florida, Georgia, and South Carolina were all attributable both to this growing slave trade and to the introduction of influenza, measles, smallpox, and typhus.

The age of uninterrupted warfare in the Lower Mississippi Valley began soon after the military expedition of Cuban governor Hernando de Soto to Florida in 1539. After massacring fifteen hundred Choctaw warriors who refused to bring him treasure, de Soto took a less violent approach with the Tunica. Upon reaching their great walled capital of Quizquiz, his expedition was immediately surrounded by an army of four thousand. Attacked throughout the Lower Mississippi Valley, de Soto and his men stumbled upon the Mississippi River in 1541 shortly before his death.[2]

Second, beginning in 1586, English settlers proceeded southward from North Carolina and Virginia to engage in genocidal wars for the lands of the Algonquian, the Yamasee, the Appalachee, and other nations. In 1691, the British established trade relations with the eight thousand Chickasaw of northern Mississippi. Guns, ammunition, metal knives, axes, cooking equipment, beads, thread, alcohol, and livestock were exchanged for native goods such as honey, corn, furs, salt, herbs, livestock, cotton, and enslaved natives.

The British-encouraged slave trade resulted in the devastation of smaller Delta and Gulf Coast nations, many of whose members ended up on the auction blocks of Charleston.[3]

Third, the French destroyed the Natchez civilization under similar circumstances. They settled near present-day Natchez, Mississippi, in 1729. In the same year, the commander of Fort Rosalie demanded Natchez land for use as plantations. In response, the natives seized the fort and three hundred prisoners. In 1730, a combined army of French, Tunica, and Choctaw forces defeated the Natchez and sold most of the nation's members into Caribbean slavery. Those who escaped joined the Chickasaw in numerous battles against the French and their Choctaw allies between 1720 and 1763.

The Native American nations were often surrogates in the larger conflict between the British and the French, and the deadliness of their rivalries increased greatly during the eighteenth century. Although the two European nations were engaged in a global competition for raw materials and markets, French colonial policy originally emphasized the establishment of scattered fur trading outposts while the British focused on both trade and settlement. The British viewed plantation slavery as the most efficient institution for producing agricultural exports. Accelerated attacks upon Native American social structures came as a result of several events. The rising European demand for deerskin products led to an unprecedented slaughter of wildlife, which in turn created a Native American dependency upon the most commonly offered exchange goods, guns and alcohol. Additionally, the rapid expansion of the African slave trade increasingly made both native labor and native people superfluous in the eyes of the expanding plantation regime.[4]

Although several native nations had been able to use the British–French rivalry to preserve their lands and enhance their trade position, 1763 marked a turning point: the English won the Seven Years War, the French renounced their claims to Louisiana and Canada, and the Spanish ceded Florida. In order to prevent further British incursions, the Ottawa chief Pontiac organized a grand pan-native alliance that stretched from Canada to the Gulf of Mexico. Fearing war and the disruption of trade, King George III proclaimed that British colonists could not venture beyond the Appalachian Mountains. However, British control over the American settlers and merchants was disintegrating rapidly as the drive for plantation-generated wealth took on a life of its own.

By 1772, settlers, traders, and speculators had used debt and violence to force the Creeks to cede 2 million acres to the state of Georgia and the Cherokee to cede 17 million acres to the states of Tennessee and Kentucky. Furthermore, according to historian Eric Williams, the fight between Britain and New England merchants for control over the Southern and Caribbean plantation trade, particularly the sugar and rum trade, was the primary motive behind the Revolutionary War of 1776. Future President John Adams claimed that he was at a loss as to why Americans "should blush to confess that molasses was an essential ingredient in American independence."[5]

By 1790, in the South, the native population was less than 60,000, Whites totaled more than 1 million, and African Americans numbered more than 500,000. The British defeat and the French and Spanish withdrawal led to rapid changes in the brutal "frontier" lands of the Old Southwest. The Mississippi Delta was still impenetrable but the nearby Mississippi River city of Natchez rapidly gained prominence as a center for steamboat traffic, for westward-bound settlers, and for commerce related to the surrounding cotton and sugar plantations. It was also the southern terminus of the 450-mile Natchez Trace road which originated in Nashville and stretched along the eastern boundary of the Mississippi Delta. This road became known nationally as the center of banditry and excess.[6]

Also, in the 1790s, cotton madness gripped the South, the United States, and England. Southern cotton production, African enslavement, and the British industrial revolution proceeded hand in hand. Several major technological inventions fueled this boom, including the 1793 introduction of Eli Whitney's cotton gin. Between 1793 and 1801, cotton production in the United States grew from 3,000 bales to 100,000 bales per year.[7]

Organized in 1798 and dominated by the Natchez planters, the original Mississippi Territory extended from the Chatahoochie River in western Georgia to the Mississippi River. Among the growing number of White planters and settlers hungering for cotton land, Native Americans were depicted as murderous and thieving savages and as shiftless and lazy drunks. This representational system emerged despite the fact that settlers were selling the alcohol and they were the ones actively "stealing Indian land and property, killing any Indian who refused to move, and breaking every White law and treaty obligation."[8]

The Chickasaw, the Cherokee, and the Choctaw, the so-called "civilized tribes," soon found themselves surrounded by people who saw their sacred forests, their burial places, and their ceremonial and hunting grounds as vacant and unused commodities. There was little appreciation for the Native American land stewardship practices that had maintained both ecological abundance and social diversity. The settler worldview saw the ecosystem in all its biodiversity as isolable and exploitable parts: forests became timber, deer became fur, water became irrigation, and people became slaves.[9]

The rising demands of the speculators, planters, and settlers who dominated territorial and state governments turned federal treaties into mere ploys for obtaining more land. Native resistance, and continued French, British, and Spanish aspirations were adeptly broken by Virginia enslaver and planter Thomas Jefferson who devised a three-pronged strategy for the removal of indigenous peoples. First, as early as 1791, he suggested to President Madison that upon subduing hostile Native Americans the federal policy should change from "war to bribery." Second, in addition to being invited to commit fraud and intimidation to gain land, Indian agents were instructed to impose upon the native nations a narrower vision of land and agriculture that was devoid of religious significance. The final strategy centered around using federal trading posts as mechanisms for the rapid expansion of native consumption and debt. Between 1801 and 1805, President Jefferson's administration negotiated three treaties with the Choctaw in which 7.6 million acres of land were ceded in exchange for less than $100,000 in debt.[10]

Debt, forced assimilation, and military alliances with the new republic undermined attempts to create a new pan-native alliance. The leaders of the three "civilized tribes" believed that they could guarantee peace by adopting American constitutional, religious, educational, plantation, and slavery practices. Consequently, the Shawnee chief Tecumseh and his brother, the Prophet, were unsuccessful in their effort to convince the three nations to join a new continental federation. Instead, during the war of 1812, the Choctaw helped General Andrew Jackson to defeat the British at New Orleans and then helped the Mississippi Militia to defeat the Creek rebellion in Alabama. While the Choctaw were hailed as heroes, much of the Creek nation was extinguished after Jackson seized 22 million acres of their land in Georgia and Alabama. Seeking peace, the Chickasaw ceded all claims to land south of Tennessee in 1816. These events signaled the beginning of rapid colonization as farmers and planters from Georgia and South Carolina flooded into the Black Belt, the 320-mile-long crescent-shaped swath of extremely fertile black soil extending from western Georgia through Alabama to northeast Mississippi.[11]

Increasing demand for Native American land led state and federal authorities to target their allies, the "civilized" Choctaw, for the first removal program because they were considered less likely to resist. The chief US negotiator in 1820 was the war hero and Memphis land speculator, General Andrew Jackson. He presented the Choctaw with two options, removal or extinction. "If the Choctaw children of your father the president will adopt the measures here recommended, they will be happy; if they should not they may be lost forever."[12]

With an intimate knowledge of the destruction of their neighbors, the Choctaw signed the Treaty of Doak's Stand on 18 October, 1820. Approximately 5 million acres of rich Mississippi Delta land were exchanged for 13 million acres of poor, sandy, and sterile land in the Oklahoma Territory. For their efforts, Jackson and the Mississippi general Thomas Hinds were declared heroes. In 1821, the Mississippi legislature named the state capital Jackson and the surrounding county Hinds in their honor. Millions of acres of Delta land were now available to the cotton planters; few Choctaw showed any inclination of moving, however.[13]

Planters along with US senators and representatives from Alabama, Florida, Georgia, Mississippi, North Carolina, and Tennessee formed an alliance in 1827 for the rapid and total removal of the Choctaw and the Cherokee. In 1828, Georgia and Mississippi planters announced their intention to ignore all federal treaties and immediately to extinguish all Native American legal rights, privileges, and franchises. Yet their militias were not powerful enough to defeat the native nations without assistance from federal troops.[14]

When Jackson was elected President in 1828, there were 23,000 Native

Americans in Mississippi, more than the native population left in all the Northern states combined. Ignoring US Supreme Court decisions on native sovereignty, Jackson signed the Indian Removal Act of 1830. During the same year, bribes and threats were used to entice Choctaw chief and Jackson ally Greenwood LeFlore to sign the Treaty of Dancing Rabbit Creek. This event led to the rapid deportation of 18,000 Choctaw, Chickasaw, Cherokees, and Creeks to Oklahoma in forced marches plagued by cholera, malaria, blizzards, starvation, violence, and more than 7,000 deaths. Considered one of the most barbaric single events in US history, the seven-year horror appropriately known as the Trail of Tears signaled the ideological and territorial consolidation of the Deep South plantation regime. At the heart of this barbaric regime was Mississippi, already considered the most undemocratic state in the new nation. As a result of the influence of the Natchez planters, the 1817 constitution guaranteed the complete domination of planter power: voting was restricted to taxpaying and property-owning White males; candidates for governor had to own at least 600 acres of land; and many appointed positions had unlimited terms.[15]

The militaristic nature of plantation production was heightened by the anticipation of epic profits from the alluvial soil. Following the Trail of Tears, plantations and towns began to spring up along the Mississippi Delta's rivers. The interior swamps and forests remained undisturbed because of the lack of levees and roads and the presence of numerous bears and panthers. Since the Mississippi River is the catch basin for two hundred other rivers, the rich alluvial soil promised yields 100 percent above the Southern average. Yet the promise of swift destruction posed by annual flooding required an extremely high level of coordination, study, experimentation, and infrastructure development. Also, by 1830, 50 percent of Mississippi's 137,000 residents, and 60 percent of the Delta's 1,976 residents, were African Americans. The desire of planters to control both the African American majorities and the annual ravages of the region's rivers led to the creation of extremely high levels of class and ethnic solidarity between the planters and working-class Whites. The intersection of these trends marked the birth of the Delta as the super-plantation region of the South.[16]

The first major production and financial crisis encountered by this emerging bloc would lead to a decade-long capital and credit drought. Between 1833 and 1836, the federal government sold 8.3 million acres in Mississippi to syndicates of speculators. When President Jackson required all payments to be made in gold and silver rather than bank notes, the syndicates, their lenders, and the cotton merchants of New Orleans all failed during the Panic of 1837. As cotton prices collapsed on Wall Street in 1839, bank failures and an international depression ensued. As the value of a Delta acre plummeted from $1.25 to 25 cents, new settlement essentially ceased until the late 1840s.[17]

## Mississippi Delta Plan 2: The Rise of Capitalist Slavery, 1837–59

The consolidation of planter economic and ideological hegemony in Mississippi during the late 1830s spurred the movement for Southern independence. Future Confederates viewed the sparsely settled Delta as a potentially endless source of wealth that was capable of financing the entire new nation. There is a strong tendency within the historiography of Southern slavery which views the plantation regime as a decaying and dying system by the mid-nineteenth century. This theory rests upon several pillars. Planters are viewed as semi-feudal overlords who governed a non-capitalist complex. Extending the argument further, since capitalism was penetrating all regions of the world, it was just a matter of time before the anachronism of slavery and its fake aristocracy would be overthrown by capitalism, that is, Northern industrial, manufacturing, trade, and political forms.

This modernization paradigm is more prescriptive than descriptive. First, it exhibits an urban, trade, and manufacturing bias. Merchant capitalism and industrial capitalism are discussed without considering the possibility that capitalist development often, as in the case of England, is established in the countryside first. Second, since free labor is considered to be a prerequisite for capitalism, it is argued that enslaved laborers could not be part of the working class. This theory ignores the fact that enslaved Africans had been "freed" or alienated from their land, tools, communal rights, hereditary privileges, and subsidies of nature. They were subsistence wage workers, and the largest section of the US working class. The mere fact that major rural Southern planters did not talk or dress like urban Northern manufacturers does not change the fact that both were capitalists. Neither does it change the reality that capitalism in every period, including the present, can exist and thrive based on slavery and other forms of unfree labor. According to Marx, the chattel slavery plantation system was a central key pillar of industrial capitalism:

> Direct slavery is as much the pivot of our industry today as machinery, credit, etc . . . Without slavery no cotton, without cotton no modern industry. It is slavery which has made the colonies valuable; the colonies have created world trade; world trade is a necessary condition of large scale machine industry . . . Thus before the traffic in Negroes began, the colonies supplied the old world with only very few products and made no visible change in the face of the earth. Slavery therefore is an economic category of the highest importance. Without slavery, North America, the most progressive country, would be turned into a patriarchal land. If North America were wiped off the map of the world, the result would be anarchy, the total decay of trade and modern civilization. But to let slavery disappear is to wipe North America off the map of the world. Since slavery is an economic category, it has existed in every nation since the world began. Modern nations have merely known how to disguise slavery in their own country while they openly export it into the New World.[18]

In the sphere of consciousness, the Northern modernization model is also unable to explain the continued viability of planter forms of representation, especially in fiction, history, folklore, theater, and the social sciences. The mass production of both romanticized versions of plantation life and of negative African American stereotypes are defining features of the national popular culture. These traditions have been the foundations of various anti-African-American alliances across race, ethnicity, class, gender, regional, and national lines from the antebellum period to the present.[19]

A closer examination of the rise of capitalist slavery in the South reveals not a static, decaying system of production, but one that was constantly restructured to meet new demands generated by global competition and by ethnic and labor conflicts. For example, according to John Moore, after the Panic of 1837, planters with little capital relied upon the reorganization of the labor process and technological innovation to intensify production and restore profitability: "By means of mechanization, crop diversification, soil conservation, and refined methods of managing slaves (particularly the gang system), plantations evolved to a peak of effectiveness just prior to the Civil War."[20] After the introduction of the cotton gin, Mississippians were producing the largest crop in the nation. Production soared from 20,000 bales in 1821 to 387,000 bales in 1839. An ideal plantation in the 1850s consisted of sixteen hundred acres, costing $90 per acre, with 135 Black workers producing one to two bales an acre. High levels of capitalization and indebtedness meant that only the wealthiest, often absentee, planters in the South or North could meet such requirements. For example, Tunica County

> became the newest frontier of plantation capitalism and the hottest outpost of the empire of cotton. Because of the high cost of clearing undergrowth, building levees, and digging draining canals, only large-scale operators even attempted to make a go of planting in Tunica. They brought in thousands of slaves to clear and cultivate the land. Those Blacks not killed by cholera or weakened by swamp-bred disease, dug ditches, felled huge cypress trees, and made dazzling crops of cotton, a bale or more to the acre. Land prices rose ... making Tunica's land the second most expensive among all counties in Mississippi and among the costliest in the South.[21]

The official end of the African slave trade in 1808 did not choke off the availability of African American labor. First, the slave trade continued at lower levels until 1861. Second, farms and plantations in the Southeast were increasingly dedicated to the internal slave trade: that is, to the raising and selling of Black children and adults to planters in the Delta, Texas, and other more fertile lands. Mississippi's population rose significantly, from 136,000 and 48 percent African Americans in 1830 to 791,305 and 55 percent African Americans by 1860. The state had the highest percentage of Blacks in the nation. In the Delta, the population grew to 71,631 persons and 61 percent African Americans in 1840, and to 177,887 persons and 72 percent African Americans in 1860. Memphis emerged as the unofficial capital of the region with a population of more than 20,000 persons by 1860. Actually, many considered the city to be part of Mississippi until 1832 when surveyors proved it was in Tennessee.[22]

During this period the plantation was used as a settlement institution to secure the firm establishment of modern capitalist slavery on the Old Southwest frontier. The barbarism and cruelty accompanying the colonization of the Deep South quickly gained international attention. Marx attempted to distinguish previous forms of slavery from the capitalist form of slavery that was quickly emerging in the South:

> But as soon as people whose production still moves within the lower forms of slave-labor, corvee labor, etc. . . . are drawn into the whirlpool of an international market dominated by the capitalist mode of production, the sale of their products for export becoming their principal interest, the civilized horrors of overwork are grafted on the barbaric horrors of slavery, serfdom, etc. . . . Hence the Negro labourer in the Southern states of the American union preserved something of a patriarchal character so long as production was chiefly directed to immediate local consumption. But in proportion, as the export of cotton became of vital interest to the states, the overworking of the Negro and sometimes using up his life in 7 years of labour became a factor in a calculated and calculating system. It was no longer a question of obtaining from him a certain quantity of useful product, it was now a question of production of surplus-labor itself.[23]

While enslavement was *per se* barbaric, among African Americans being sold down the river to the Delta conveyed a sense of betrayal, the beginning of life that was both further removed from the possibility of escape and innately closer to some unknown, unflinchingly evil savagery. The Delta had become representative of the daily destruction of human life in the South. Work had come to mean the year-round non-stop toil of the gang labor system: land clearance and preparation in late winter; planting in the spring; clearing swamps and forest during the summer; and picking cotton from the fall to sometimes February—picking cotton on ice. Few allowances were made for pregnant women and, consequently, infant mortality was extremely high. Several travelers took note of this form of barbarism which also became known as the original "factories in the fields."[24]

Sam Chatmon, of the famed Chatmon family of musicians, offered a description of how children were fed on the plantation where his father lived:

> old colored ladies, they would always be the ones to take care of the young kids. And they had a trough to mix bread and stuff up in so the children could eat . . . Yeah, a trough! Just like pigs![25]

Those who resisted work were subjected to torture. For example, an elderly woman was chained to an ant-infested log for days for refusing to follow orders. African Americans lived in barrack-like cabins often seven to a room. While state law did not prohibit torture, murder was subject to a range of fines that rose as the price of Black life rose from $700 in 1845 to $1,800 in 1860. Not only was rape institutionalized, some African American women came to view conception and birth as part of a cycle in which they would eventually see their children consumed by this cannibalistic regime.[26]

Since all the region's wealth was concentrated in the purchase of land and

African Americans for the purposes of cotton production, town and city were severely inhibited. This was truly a mining enterprise in which all social and public considerations were secondary to production. As a total institution, the plantation was town, home, workplace, recreational area, religious grounds, prison, and cemetery.[27]

Settlement based on slavery, peonage and disenfranchisement created a situation where the planter was judge, jury, and executioner within the boundaries of his or her properties. On the other hand, the local state continuously intervened in cotton production and the most minor aspects of African American daily life. Yet, state

> government rarely interfered in the lives of its [white] citizens, concerning itself primarily with the problems and maintenance of the cotton economy. Keeping credit fluid, easing transportation difficulties, and regulating and protecting slavery were the accepted functions ... of the legislative and administrative branches of the state ... When the state became involved in the lives of [white] Mississippians, however, it did so to uphold law and the existing social order rather than to effect social change. In 1848, for example, the state treasury paid out more to reimburse slave holders for executed slaves than for a vaccination program, the school for the blind, and the Chickasaw Indian school combined.[28]

Although political life was dominated by the Natchez and Black Prairie planters, the rapidly growing numbers of White petty planters, small farmers, timber workers, and herders who settled the Piney Woods, the Hills, and the southern portions of the state were fast becoming influential. The planters and these refugees from the failed farms of Virginia, the Carolinas, and Georgia served as the pillars of a uniquely Southern state ideology that combined a commitment to both slavery and Jacksonian democracy. Among Southern scholars, this phenomenon is termed "Herrenvolk democracy." Among Whites, intra-ethnic and inter-class unity in the Southern states was preserved so long as Native American lands were provided, slavery was protected, and direct competition between Whites and African Americans was avoided. Internally, the fate of critics was typically banishment, torture, or death. Externally, planters continually created a series of regional, national, and international alliances to preserve their hegemony. The constant creation of repressive reproductive social structures turned the Southern Black Belt into the most highly regulated region in North America.[29]

In such a society, planters insisted on being the final interpreters of the physical, social, and biblical destiny of African Americans. The control of planters over representation was an essential feature of the ethnic alliance between White planters, small farmers, and laborers, as was a fear of the economic consequences of abolition:

> It therefore mattered a great deal who was in a position to interpret the behavior of slaves for a society as a whole, especially when the slaves acted in ways that appeared to contradict the racial assumptions of the planters ... Such latitude and the nature of the "daily contact with genuine slavery" that planters had as a result [of ownership]

allowed them to believe they had special insight into the behavior of Blacks and that it was their right and responsibility to take authority when the actions of slaves became a matter of public concern. It also encouraged non-slaveholders to believe that it was in their own best interests to have planters speak for white society when any slave refused to accept "that situation in life which it has pleased God to place him."[30]

Mississippi planters tried to define their regime as both a necessary and a fortunate occurrence. This perspective was supported by the construction of a grid of representations designed to reinforce the belief that the planters were the masters of a world of their own creation. In his study of planter ideology, Singal notes the bizarre ontological break that occurred in the Deep South: "Why after all, should early nineteenth century southern Americans, the ideological heirs of Jefferson and Madison, suddenly develop exotic visions of establishing themselves as feudal barons on the southwestern corner of the American frontier?"[31]

The origins of this intellectual turn of events are found at the conjuncture of three economic and social movements. First, the Native American genocide and expulsion, and the accompanying cotton boom in Alabama and Mississippi, made the 1830s a time of unprecedented opportunity and of unprecedented threats. In the Deep South, numerous fortunes were rapidly made and lost by the sons of Tidewater and Carolina planters, aspiring yeoman, small farmers, and landless soldiers. The invention of the myth that they were part of a Cavalier aristocracy was an attempt to drape an emerging class of previously marginal figures with a cloak of genetic supremacy. Second, the constant threat of African American rebellions, such as Nat Turner's 1831 revolt in Southampton, Virginia, threatened to cast this grasping element into the same permanent state of terror that defined African American life. As a result, the Anglo tradition of African and African American demonization was elevated to both an institutionalized civic religion and a career.[32]

Third, the growth of the abolition movement in the North sparked increased repression in the South. The planters of the Black Belt cotton kingdom began to refer to themselves in terms of nobility and omnipotence. While titles such as knights, dragons, cyclops, emperors, kings, patricians, aristocrats, and cavaliers began to litter the social landscape, as usual the extremism of the Delta's "pharaohs" was unrivaled. The planters' mythical ethno-regional system of explanation placed them at the center of the new cotton kingdom. Additionally, the planters attempted to convince others that they were the ideal leaders and that the South was the model of social stability and civilization that the other regions should follow. "Only the Cavalier possessed the heroic force of character which was required to hold back the restless flood of savagery that threatened to overflow the country."[33]

As the basis for much of American political thought the US Constitution's declaration of "self-evident" rights could have posed a problem if the nation was not engaged in building a continental empire. After 1820, the examples of the ancient slave empires of Greece and Rome were widely celebrated as proof that slavery was a universally beneficial force in civilization. As is evident in the use of Greek and Gothic revival architectural styles for their homes, planters extracted elements from several golden ages to make their social order seem natural, "classical," and timeless. Discussed below, the emerging plantation representational grid positioned the planter as the noble and heroic alternative to the selfish Yankee, the criminal immigrant, the savage Southern poor Whites, and to the childlike, yet demonic, enslaved African American. Out of this ontological shift emerged a new epistemology, a reorganization of cultural and academic categories and texts. African American scholar Addison Gayle Jr argued that, the plantation school of literature eventually came to dominate American cultural thought from the 1830s to the present:

> The Plantation Movement occurred almost simultaneously with the Transcendental Movement ... The rise of the Plantation Movement and the demise of the Transcendental can be attributed to the fact that the former went back ... to the Aegean "for confirmation of its faith," while the latter went back to Germany for the same reason. Between Immanuel Kant and Plato lay a world of difference, not only in the philosophical approaches, but in views of man and society. The voice of Kant calling upon men to be open-minded, to be inquisitive, to approach the complex problems of men in humanitarian terms fell on deaf ears in a nation where prejudice, dogmatism and simplistic approaches to problems, human and social, were and still are the norm. Given the choice between Platonic idealism and Kantian transcendentalism, the South chose to ally itself with the Greek mind, and thus became the embodiment of the American Myth.[34]

Planters, African Americans, plantations, and slavery were central themes of the mid-century literary wars. Borrowed in part from the works of Sir Walter Scott and other English romantic novelists, the imagined community of the nouveau riche planter, in the form of the plantation romance novel, gained widespread national popularity during this period. Harriet Beecher Stowe's *Uncle Tom's Cabin* and numerous other works that relied on a caricature and subversion of this form were key elements in the abolitionist attack.

According to Gaines, of all the popular culture traditions in the United States, the plantation tradition is the "most spacious, and the most gracious." There are three central components of its appeal. First, the "American love of feudalism" is realized in the romance of the Southern estate. "However we may vaunt our democracy, our imaginative interests are keenly appreciative of social gradations and our romantic hunger is satisfied by some allegory of aristocracy.... the plantation, alone among native institutions, satisfies this craving for a system of caste."

Second, the

> plantation, again, furnishes through the person of the genuine darkey, essentially the most conspicuous figure of the tradition, the closest native approximation to a type almost as old as history, proverbially dear to the masses as opposed to the literati:

the folk figure of a simple somewhat rustic character, instinctively humorous, irrationally credulous, gifted in song and dance, interesting in spontaneous frolic, endowed with artless philosophy ... the darkey is the assumed source of a large body of unwritten humor, or at least is credited with a collection of floating anecdotes, real and spurious, more so than any other of our makers of vulgar comedy."

Finally, in the relatively young United States, the plantation furnishes a native-born golden age for European refugees. "The plantation romance remains our chief social idyll of the past; of an Arcadian scheme of existence, less material, less hurried, less prosaically equalitarian, less futile, richer in picturesqueness, festivity, in realized pleasure that reeked not of hope or fear or unrejoicing labor." This golden age came complete with a menu of plantation food and with plantation cooks such as Aunt Jemima and Uncle Ben. The American pantheon found in the plantation romances that emerged in the 1830s came complete with a focus on luxury, gambling, the hunt, dueling, the heroic transported aristocracy, the manners of highly bred ladies and gentlemen, the cult of true womanhood, the faithful old manservant or uncle, the devoted mammy, the pitiful slave, the violent slave, the lusting slave, the minstrel, the tragic mulatto, etcetera.[35]

Abolitionist papers, poems, novels, essays, autobiographies, sermons, songs, orations, lectures, and articles were all geared around contrasting the noble and defenseless enslaved African American against the cruel, brutal, foolish, and unchaste planter and his minions. African American narratives such as the works of Frederick Douglass also stressed this contrast. Although limited by abolitionist representations and criminalized by planters, the eyewitness testimonies of the Black refugees represented an extension of one intellectual movement, African American Realism, into Northern thought and literature.

Planters relied heavily upon biblical explanations to rationalize slavery. As the "descendants of Ham," African Americans were considered

an inferior people who benefitted by enslavement [and this] could be shown by the most cursory examination of their history in Africa and in America. In Africa they were forced to endure a life of ignorance, war, murder, polygamy, and paganism. Slaves there were eaten, women were mere beasts of burden, and the worst forms of heathenism prevailed.[36]

Soon, the plantation social science tradition also began to emerge. In *Cannibals All*, George Fitzhugh, one of the earliest sociologists in the USA, combined biblical and ancient justifications of African slavery with an advocacy of the enslavement of Northern White workers as well. As a social reform, his proposal would guarantee both lifelong employment and subsistence, an alternative to the "madness" of Northern libertarians who are

in daily expectation of discovering a new Social Science, that will remedy all the ills that human flesh is heir to. They belong to the schools of Owen, Louis Blanc, Fourier, Comte, and German and French Socialists and Communists."[37]

In his 1854 work *Sociology of the South or the Failure of Free Society*, Fitzhugh presented key features of the planter epistemology that continue to influence public policy. African Americans were described as ignorant, wicked, and irresponsible, "grown up children." Therefore, they must be subjected to perpetual social management under some direct rule of which they were not a part, preferably "military despotism":

> Now, it is clear the Athenian democracy would not suit a negro nation nor will the government of mere law suffice for the individual negro. He is but a grown up child, and must be governed as a child, not as a lunatic or a criminal. The master occupies toward him the place of parent or guardian. We shall not dwell on this view, for no one will differ with us who thinks as we do of the negro's capacity, and we might argue till dooms-day, in vain, with those who have a high opinion of the negro's moral and intellectual capacity.
>
> Second, the negro is improvident; will not lay up in summer for the wants of winter; will not accumulate in youth for the exigencies of age. He would become an insufferable burden to society. Society has the right to prevent this, and can only do so by subjecting him to domestic slavery.

For Fitzhugh, there were other adult dependents in society that had to be managed:

> In truth, woman, like children, has but one right, and that is the right to protection. The right to protection involves the obligation to obey . . . If she be obedient, she is in little danger of maltreatment; if she stands upon her rights, is coarse and masculine, man loathes and despises her, and ends by abusing her. Law, however well intended, can do little on her behalf.[39]

He went on to argue that the fall of feudalism was a tragedy of immense proportions. And that the extension of political, social, economic, and human rights in England and France only produced uncontrolled crime and poverty. "How slavery could degrade men lower than universal liberty has done, it is hard to conceive." Unions of the poor were said to be unable to protect themselves from competition as long as liberty existed and, therefore, could only lead back to a form of slavery less humane than that of the planters:

> Slavery to an association is not always better than slavery to a single master. No association, no efficient combination of labor can be effected till men give up their liberty of action and subject themselves to a common despotic head or ruler. This is slavery, and toward this socialism is moving.[40]

Therefore, social reform movements dedicated to the extension of human rights and economic security were by definition unnatural and unhealthy:

> The knowledge of numerous theories of radical reform proposed in Europe, and the causes that have led to their promulgation, is of vital importance to us. Yet we turn away from them with disgust, as from something unclean and vicious. We occupy high vantage ground for observing, studying, and classifying the various phenomena of society; yet we do not profit by the advantage of our position. We should do so, and indignantly hurl back upon our assailants the charge, that there is something

wrong and rotten in our system. From their own mouths we can show free society to be a monstrous abortion, and slavery to be the healthy, beautiful, and natural being which they are trying, unconsciously, to adopt.[41]

Social chaos could only be prevented by the Southern gentlemen planter who was the restrained, honorable, and heroic paragon of virtue. Only the Cavalier had the moral authority and the biological superiority to discipline society using heavy doses of shame and violence. Thus, the planter was the ideal civilizing agent for Blacks, for the South, and for the world. The French observer Alexis de Toqueville had a differing opinion of the plantation intellectual tradition:

> They have, if I may put it this way, spiritualized despotism and violence. In antiquity men sought to prevent the slave from breaking his bonds; nowadays the attempt is made to stop him from wishing to do so ... my indignation is not directed to the men of our day who are the authors of these outrages; all my hatred is concentrated against those who after a thousand years of equality, introduced slavery into the world again.[42]

Finally, antebellum doctors were marshaled to complete the grid of plantation bloc explanation. For example, in his travels Frederick Law Olmsted encountered a professor at the University of Louisiana who was studying the African American desire to escape and rebel as a form of nervous disorder. The organic semifeudal order defined and described by the planters themselves is still accepted as fact by some historians and social scientists. However, this was the representational grid that the plantation bloc created to argue for the inevitability and permanence of their rule. In reality, planters lived in the midst of the competitive, revolutionizing, destructive, and chaotic swirl of frontier capitalism.[43]

Throughout the period of slavery and after, the plantation bloc attempted to limit Black initiative and imagination. For example, as late as 1864 Texas passed a law mandating a brand or ear mark for African Americans pretending ownership of land. In the midst of slavery, enforced paupery, and censorship, however, there arose the African American domestic economy. This cash-and-barter economy was driven by the individual initiative, social solidarity, spatial segregation, and subsistence needs of enslaved and free Blacks. It would be false to say that this was a wholly American-derived phenomenon. In much of Africa, the institution of individually owned and alienable private property was absent, as was the institution of plantation-based capitalist slavery. Generally, communal ownership and cooperative work responsibilities were based on highly ritualized family, gender, peer, village, and ethnic practices. These structures exhibited high degrees of social control and to some extent prevented the rise of strong centralized states. While the Arab and European slave trades brought to the continent an age of perpetual warfare, it is still inconceivable to imagine the individual shock of those involved in the process of being kidnapped and separated from their families, imprisoned, chained, transported across a vast ocean, sold, resold, and then forced to work in another's fields.[44]

Inevitably, this process gave rise to an African development ethic in the Western Hemisphere centered around mobilizing for the purposes of cooperation and the reestablishment of social autonomy. In the midst of heavily armed settlers on a constantly moving frontier of continental proportions, this ethic took different forms in North America from those it took in the Caribbean and South America. The nascent African American group economy had several related circuits connected by kin networks, cultural affinity, the plantation regime, resistance to it, and state regulation. This complex was centered around numerous interlocking components: plantation gardens; the owning and raising of livestock; the production and sale of clothes, furniture, wagons, and crafts; the provision of entertainment, medical, spiritual, and gaming services; wages from self-hire; compensation derived from being hired out; the covert ownership of businesses and property; and free Blacks who sold their labor and owned land and businesses. Secret Christian and non-Christian religious practices held the community together as did family, the arts, and experiences with escape, resistance and rebellion. The budding associational life of African Americans was placed under perpetual surveillance. Yet the combination of overt, and covert, market and non-market activities ensured the reproduction of this complex even under circumstances of constant assault.[45]

The group economy was reproduced through several processes. First, the desire to acquire and consume drove many people into these enterprises. Second, some planters supported its growth as a means of social control, as a means of supporting their Black children without manumission, and as a method of profiting from hiring-out workers. Third, and most important, African Americans were motivated by a desire for autonomy. One of the most analytically debilitating myths about plantation workers and peasants is that they passively accommodate themselves to the dominant institutions. In such discussions, the freedom ethic becomes the sole possession of the people destined to rule while some other theory must be found to explain why others cannot run their own affairs. This "hierarchy of freedom" thesis prevents an understanding of how all people attempt to guarantee subsistence and social independence in an unlimited number of ways:

> In the rural areas with the largest concentration of Blacks—eastern North Carolina, the Sea Islands of South Carolina and Georgia, the Black Belt of Alabama, the Mississippi Delta, and the sugar parishes of Louisiana—the dominant motive was probably the desire for autonomy. Indeed, by planting crops, raising farm animals, hunting and fishing, Blacks could distance themselves not only from the impersonal forces of the marketplace but from their overseers and masters as well. These goals— subsistence and independence ... were nothing more than the central priorities of peasants throughout the world.[46]

The African American representational structure emerged out of opposition to the totalizing practices of plantation institutions. The central organizing vision was one of a land where there were no plantations and no planters. As a result of the structure of the plantation regime, land reform was the only solution to the question of guaranteeing subsistence, formalizing the group economy, and gaining political, cultural, and personal dignity and freedom. From this powerful polarity emerged the blues Culture. It contained an apocalyptic form of Christianity populated by devils, heathens and pharaohs. Also present were cosmologies derived from African and Native American traditions, which were populated by known and unknown human, animal and plant spirits, and by the forces of nature. The blues culture possessed an explanatory grid based on observations of daily life. African American realism as institutionalized in the blues and its derivations would speak of a world simultaneously full of misery and resilience.

The acceptance of certain tenets of Christianity did not mark the death of African cultural retentions since many of the traditional religions in Africa, and European Christianity, were syncretic and filled with a pantheon of personages and combinations of practices. Selectively appropriated Native American and Anglo-American practices were incorporated into a complex of African-derived oral, religious, organizational and agricultural practices. Emerging out of the rich tradition of African song-centered orature, and under conditions of intense censorship, secular and sacred songs became the fountainheads of cultural transmission and social explanation. Furthermore, as a result of the extremely hierarchical class structure of Southern plantations, African American working-class thought would come to find its fullest expression in the blues: "a collective expression of the ideology and character of Black people situated at the bottom of the social order in America."[47]

The ability and right of African American organizations and individuals consciously to accept, reject, or contemplate various dogmas was considered as heresy by the plantation bloc. However, independent explanation flourished in the form of secular-sacred secret societies. After first being outlawed in Maryland and Virginia in the 1690s, the "secret meetings reached a climax under the militant leadership of Nat Turner ... [who] fomented a slave insurrection of such significance as to cause England and America to debate the greatest social problem of the century."[48] These societies relied heavily upon the secular-sacred song traditions to communicate. In *Black Culture and Black Consciousness*, Lawrence Levine discussed the role of the secular song tradition in community building:

> it gave a sense of power, of control. If it did not affect the material well being of its creators, it certainly did have an impact upon their psychic state and emotional health. It allowed them to assert themselves and their feelings and their values, to communicate continuously with themselves and their peers and their oppressors as well ... Black secular song, along with other forms of oral tradition, allowed them to express themselves communally and individually; to derive great aesthetic pleasure, to perpetuate traditions, to keep values from eroding, and to begin to create new expressive modes. Black secular song revealed a culture which kept large elements

of its own autonomous standards alive, which continues a rich internal life, which interacted with a larger society that deeply affected it.[49]

However, there is a danger that the dichotomy between secular and sacred may be overstated. The social-spiritual life and practices of Africans and African Americans are rich, varied, and still not fully understood often because the categories used to understand them were developed by academic, cultural, religious, and military missionaries pursuing their own exploits for which African Americans were merely raw materials. Therefore, oral and song traditions, community building activities, and social movements must be understood in terms of the distinctive transformation of African American Southern culture:

> The initial cultural heterogeneity of the enslaved doubtless had the effect of forcing them at the outset to shift their primary and social commitment from the Old World to the New, a process which often took their European masters centuries to accomplish.[50]

Rapid homogenization meant that numerous African practices and traditions would become the pillars of African American culture. Many African American oral forms emerged and coexisted in the antebellum South: spirituals, seculars, worksongs, arhoolies (hollers), ballads, and stories of folk heroes and tricksters, bandits, lovers, jokers, fools, leaders, and saints. The line dividing African American sacred and secular song was a plantation construct designed to institutionalize the censorship of the secret societies and other instances of collective autonomy. In *Negro Slave Songs in the United States*, Miles Mark Fisher examined the transformation of African American song after the 1830s:

> Negro cultists did not see their behavior as either good or bad, but they did know that they were prepared to accept death. It is not accidental that Negros who so consistently envisioned the good life, as do all human beings, suddenly turned and sang about death in North America, in the first half of the nineteenth century ... A postwar variant ... also likened the deaths of African cultists to the crucifixion of Jesus.[51]

According to Fisher, the turn to death themes in the spirituals was partly due to the execution of Nat Turner in 1831. Soon after, many songs included references to the coming "judgement day" for the plantation regime and, later, for the Confederacy – "Can't stand the fire." Turner's rebellion also sparked a movement that spread White Christian missionaries across the South in order to establish churches for African Americans that used only approved songs. The battle over lyrics and music censorship, sacred and secular, has been fully engaged ever since.

Yet the blues as a mobilization was still several decades away. This was the era of Nat Turner, Harriet Tubman, Frederick Douglass, John Brown, and the Black and White abolitionists. The violent overthrow of the plantation regime in the South was preached openly all over the North and covertly all over the South. Growing panic took hold of Mississippi in response to the four uprisings in the state between 1826 and 1860. Often referred to as "slave revolts", African American insurrections of the period can be understood more accurately as local social, agrarian, and human rights movements that had the potential of rapidly becoming a revolution of immense geographic proportions.

Southern legislatures continually attacked both the growing group economy and political activism. It was believed by many planters that free Blacks, such as Gabriel Prosser and Nat Turner, were the strands linking various immobile plantation populations for the purposes of independent accumulation, resistance, and rebellion. Four months after the Turner rebellion, the Mississippi legislature passed a law severely restricting the activities of free Blacks: 39 lashes for each violation of preaching the gospel, i.e. religious activism; and all those between age sixteen and fifty who were not awarded a pass to travel, a license, had to emigrate. The wave of fear resulting from the discovery of plans to launch a Vicksburg rebellion in 1841 further fueled legislative hysteria: manumissions now required a special act of the legislature; free Blacks were barred from immigrating; and those who remained were constantly attacked and illegally expelled.[52]

On their way North, refugees from the Delta and other parts of the state either had to wade through treacherous alligator-infested swamps, secretly board boats, or stay on the run for months while "slave catchers" followed them around the country. The socially totalizing aspects of plantation production enabled the planter bloc in Mississippi to build a modern police state on top of slavery using all-encompassing laws and a minutely detailed pass system that renders the concept "Orwellian" completely feeble.[53]

Finally, in many ways, the Civil War was occurring in the South long before 1860. Expansion of the plantation regime kept African Americans mobile, scattered, and disorganized; halting expansion would reduce planters to little more than prison guards facing perpetual revolts from Blacks, and from poor Whites as well. Consequently, the extension of plantation slavery to the West, to the Caribbean, and to Central and South America was considered to be an imperative:

> Thus, radical Mississippi Southern Rights leader and Cuba filibusterer C. Pinckney Smith remarked to the Adams County Southern Rights Association in May 1851 that the exclusion of the South from California would endanger the South because confinement of its Black population might incite race war.[54]

Therefore, for social, political, and production reasons, the leadership of this capitalist complex fought to expand. The plantation system was not dying a slow death due to land exhaustion, rather it was struggling to expand and conquer. By the 1850s, cotton demand, production, and profitability had reached unprecedented heights. So much wealth was generated that key elements within the colonization-minded Mississippi wing of the Southern plantation bloc felt they would be better served by organizing their own nation.

## Mississippi Delta Plan 3: Cotton Empire Autonomy, 1858–61

> When Israel was in Egypt's land, O let my people go!
> Oppressed so hard they could not stand, O let my people go!
> O go down Moses, Away down to Egypt's land,
> And tell King Pharaoh, To let my people go![55]

The late 1850s was a period marked by numerous planter bloc mobilizations. The Confederate independence movement was founded upon the premise that Lower Mississippi Valley cotton—white gold—would be used to finance the war and the new republic. It was also assumed that the British dependency upon cotton would assure immediate diplomatic recognition and the continuation of trade. Not surprisingly, the Lower Mississippi Valley was the first Southern region targeted for occupation by the Northern troops.

Although only 10 percent of the Delta's land had been cleared, the region was viewed as rich enough to finance an entire nation. Between 1850 and 1860, the value of Mississippi Delta farmland tripled as production and productivity rose dramatically. Several millionaires were among the eighty-one planters who had personal fortunes of more than $100,000; four Delta counties ranked among the thirty-six wealthiest in the nation. Expanded production led to a significant increase in population. From 1850 to 1860, the total population in Bolivar, Coahoma, Issaquena, Tunica and Washington counties rose from 20,621 to 36,972; 83 percent of the residents were African American. By 1860, Mississippi's African American population of 437,404 was significantly larger that its White population of 353,889 persons.[56]

Still, annual flooding operated to deter additional development and investment in the Delta. To rectify this situation, planters organized the General Levee Board in 1858. This body was dedicated to constructing 262 miles of levees from Memphis to Vicksburg at a cost of $6.25 million. Although only 142 miles were completed prior to the Civil War, the projected increase in property values by the year 1868 was put at $150 million. One of the world's largest public works projects, the levee system was, and is, one of the defining features of Delta capitalism.[57]

The sale of Delta land increased dramatically between 1846 and 1860. Assessed values tripled in five years; from $7.7 million in 1853 to $23.4 million in 1857. By 1858, anticipation of the wealth to be derived by the levee system emboldened many Mississippi planters and their allies throughout the Black Belt to launch what they thought would be a very profitable movement for independence. Along with being the leading manufacturer of cotton gins, Mississippi was producing one-fourth of the nation's cotton. The nation envisioned would be the center of the "Velvet Empire"—the Confederate South as the center of a colonial empire encompassing most of the Caribbean, Central America, parts of Mexico, and Bahia in Brazil.[58]

However, this vision of expansion and imperialism was not initially shared by all White factions in Mississippi. The flood of small White farmers into the northern portion of the state after the Chickasaw cession of 1832 resulted in the weakening of Natchez planters' domination of the legislature. The establishment of Jacksonian democracy based on manhood suffrage instead of property qualifications also threatened planter control. The national Jeffersonian Democratic Party split into the pro-slavery, pro-Union, and planter-dominated Whig party, on the one hand, and the pro-slavery, pro-secession, and small-farmer-dominated Jacksonian Democrat Party on the other. Although opposed to South Carolina's secessionist strategy in the 1820s and early 1830s, by 1840 Mississippi's political leadership was fully co-operating with this movement. Furthermore, an 1846 Congressional attempt to form a cordon of free states around the slave states reunited the pro-slavery factions.[59]

Passed in 1850, the Fugitive Slave Act required all public officials to return African Americans who escaped back to their "owners." However, the law was often ignored in the North and West due to rising abolitionist sentiment. Outraged about nonenforcement, John Quitman, the Governor of Mississippi and a leader of the Cuban and Mexican annexation movements, convinced the state legislature to call a secession convention of slave states in Nashville, Tennessee, in 1850. This, however, was unsuccessful. In a reaction to the planters' threat to homesteading, in 1854 the Republican Free Soil movement swept the national elections in New England and the Midwest, and formed a majority in both houses of Congress. Congress passed the Kansas–Nebraska Act in the same year in order to enable the territories of the Louisiana Purchase to decide individually whether they would allow slavery.

Despite the shift in Congress, the plantation bloc still had supporters in the executive branch. The Secretary of War in the Pierce cabinet, Delta planter Jefferson Davis, proposed a series of rail and road improvements under the guise of military necessity in order to move huge numbers of African Americans and planters across the desert into California and New Mexico prior to the latter states' votes on whether or not to join the Union as slave states. The election by the Democrats of President Buchanan in 1856, and the US Supreme Court's Dred Scott decision in 1857, temporarily appeased the contending forces. In the Scott case the court ruled that enslaved African Americans were the property of their enslaver and could not claim citizenship rights even if residing in a free state. However, Buchanan's attempt to get Kansas admitted as a slave state in 1858 failed.

Properly fearing the Republican Free Soil movement, abolitionists, and African American revolts, in December 1859 the Mississippi legislature voted to expel all free Blacks. Several days before the decisive presidential election of 1860, an editorial in the *Vicksburg Weekly Sun* expressed the belief that the federal system was now an unbearable fetter on the expansion of plantation-bloc capitalism and empire:

> in the Union the South cannot expand beyond her present limits; out of it she can extend her institutions over Mexico, Cuba, San Domingo, and other West Indies

islands and California, and thereby become the most powerful Republic that ever the sun shone upon.[60]

In December 1860, the secession of South Carolina was followed in January by the secession of Mississippi, Alabama, Georgia, Florida and Louisiana. In Mississippi, eighty-three of the one hundred secession convention delegates were slaveowners. Eventually joined by Arkansas, North Carolina, Tennessee, Texas, and Virginia, the Confederacy was formed in February 1861. Three months before the Confederate attack on Fort Sumpter in 1861, Mississippians seized Fort Massachusetts on Ship Island off the Gulf Coast. Delta planter Jefferson Davis was elected President of the Confederate States of America. In previous years, Davis had been a West Point graduate, a Warren County planter, leader of the Mississippi regiment in the Mexican War, son-in-law of US President Zachary Taylor, a Congressmen, a gubernatorial candidate, President Pierce's Secretary of War, and a US senator. He held the latter position before resigning to head the new republic. In many ways, Davis defined, and still defines, what has been called "Mississippi imperialism". In 1848, Alexis de Toqueville attempted to describe the origins of this regional imperialism:

> Those Americans who go out far away from the Atlantic Ocean, plunging into the West, are adventurers impatient of any sort of yoke, greedy for wealth, and often outcasts from the states in which they were born. They arrive in the depths of the wilderness without knowing one another. There is nothing of tradition, family feeling, or example to restrain them, laws have little sway over them, and mores still less. Therefore, the men who are continually pouring in to increase the population of the Mississippi Valley are in every respect inferior to the Americans living within the former limits of the Union. Nevertheless, they already have great influence over its counsels, and they are taking their place in the government of public affairs before they have learned to rule themselves . . . [When a state has a population of 2 million and is one quarter the size of France] it feels itself strong, and if it continues to want union as something useful to its well-being, it no longer regards it as necessary to its existence, it can do without it, and although consenting to remain united, it soon wants to be preponderant.[61]

The independence-minded planters in Mississippi were still heavily dependent upon outside factors for cotton financing, transport, and sales. A key element in the strategy of the Union Army was to split the Confederacy along the Mississippi River and blockade the Gulf of Mexico. When this was successfully completed, river traffic came to a halt and cotton production declined dramatically. However, major fortunes were made by those who were able to produce cotton in the Delta, run the blockades, and sell it in the markets of New Orleans and Memphis.[62]

## Mississippi Delta Plan 4: "Cotton Closed Their Eyes to Justice"

> Union military occupation transformed the Mississippi Valley from the heartland of
> slavery to a testing ground for free labor ... [To] a degree unmatched in other
> Union-occupied parts of the South, ongoing warfare affected the character of the
> new order, repeatedly upsetting the plans, and reshaping the expectations, of all
> participants.[63]

The capture of Memphis and New Orleans in 1862, and the continued
resistance of Confederate forces in Vicksburg, placed the Delta at the center
of the North's efforts to divide and bankrupt the Confederacy by exercising
control over Mississippi River and Gulf of Mexico commerce. Although
generals Ulysses S. Grant and William T. Sherman held the northern Delta,
southward to Baton Rouge could only be patrolled by gunboats. On 23
September, 1862, President Abraham Lincoln issued the Emancipation Proclamation with the twin aims of both freeing and arming enslaved and free
African Americans in order to disrupt the Confederacy from within and
without.

By December 1862, Union soldiers were seizing livestock and burning
plantation houses, gins, and crops in the region. African Americans who had
knowledge of the landscape and of Confederate troop movements helped
Sherman and Grant to seize and torch various cities. The conflict resulted in
more than 22,000 African Americans moving into Memphis area army camps
and refugee centers known as "contraband camps." The latter were organized
Black settlements where houses, hospitals, schools, and gardens were soon
built.[64]

The threat of re-enslavement resulted in African American regiments
guarding these villages and their families from attacks by planters, Confederate bands, and Union troops. Outside the regimental villages, women, children
and the elderly faced unemployment, hunger, disease, and death. Schemes to
move them North ran into immediate opposition. The Free Soil movement
increasingly lost interest in African American freedom after the passage of
the Homestead Act of 1862, while White urban workers viewed the potential
immigrants as unwanted competitors. Ignored as a policy option was recognition of, and support for, the self-governed camps and villages. Of the many
Black settlements that arose during the occupation, perhaps the most famous
was Davis Bend, a community of six plantations managed by Benjamin
Montgomery south of Vicksburg.[65]

In December 1863, Lincoln's Proclamation of Amnesty and Reconstruction
guaranteed the re-establishment of regional planter hegemony. It allowed
repentant planters and their newfound Northern partners, typically investors
and army officers, to reclaim confiscated land. In the Lower Mississippi Valley
this new alliance would later come to defeat every attempt by African
Americans to occupy or lease land, to regulate and raise wages, or to improve
living and working conditions.

In the Lower Mississippi Valley of 1864, there were around 124,000 free African Americans: 41,000 served as soldiers or army laborers; 72,500 worked either on plantations or in the wood yards, cities, and freedmen villages; and 10,000 were being directly assisted by the government. In the latter group, one third paid for this assistance from profits generated through growing crops on leased land. If these workers had been given the confiscated lands a new type of democracy could have emerged in the Delta. Instead, the federal government chose to take advantage of historically high cotton prices to revitalize planter power and plantation capitalism.

The new system was run by regional commissioners who would lease African Americans living in the Union camps to work for one year on plantations owned by the same, now loyal, planters they had recently escaped from. They were also forced to work on confiscated plantations leased to new planters such as Northern entrepreneurs, cotton speculators, civilian employees of the army, and Southern unionists.

The growing number of federally controlled estates returned to the former planters was quickly extinguishing the dream of fundamental land reform. In this new form of coercion, Blacks had no choice of employer. They were paid wages in name only and often had to get permission to leave. The numerous Black squatter settlements that emerged during the war years were destroyed and their crops and livestock were seized as Grant moved south. Those holding the leases were given the livestock and crops of the African American residents while Union troops forced them into the fields. Soon, Blacks began to strikes for better wages, hours, and conditions, and for the ability to grow food.[66]

The great movement of people during this period led to the rise of African American urban life in Memphis, Natchez, Vicksburg, and Helena, Arkansas. Many benevolent societies, churches, and schools were established, some with Northern philanthropic support. However, to solve the shortage of labor in the countryside, federal officers began to require Blacks to have passes to be in the city. This was followed by the mass expulsion of those not employed by a "responsible white person."[67]

General Hawkins, administrator of the Northeast Louisiana Delta, objected to the preservation of land monopolies and believed that the failure to break up plantations into small farms would have a devastating impact on the future Southern society. Additionally, he viewed the lessees as

> men who cared nothing how much flesh they worked off the Negro provided it was converted into good cotton at seventy five cents per pound . . . Cotton closed their eyes to justice just as it did in the case of the former slave master.[68]

## Mississippi Delta Plan 5: Presidential Reconstruction, 1865–66

During Presidential Reconstruction, the planter bloc did not wither away. As administered by Lincoln and his successor, Andrew Johnson, this first Reconstruction focused on immediately restoring production under planter hegemony. The federal government mobilized to further marginalize all manifestations of African American freedom: the growing group economy, the autonomous agrarian communities, labor unions, and other assertions of independence. As the federal administrators blended in with the planter bloc, the attempted return to civilian rule witnessed a movement by planters to reestablish slavery with federal assistance. By 1865, Union military officials in the Delta were fully engaged in forcing African Americans back under planter hegemony by forcing them to work on the plantations, by enforcing illegal contracts, by banning mobility, by sanctioning torture, and by withdrawing their troops.[69]

Many of the governors and state legislators in the Lincoln–Johnson Reconstruction governments were former Confederate leaders. These governments passed Black Codes similar to the one passed by the Mississippi legislature that set the punishment for interracial marriage as life imprisonment. Although planters had lost their property rights in individual African Americans, now "Blacks at large belonged to whites at large."[70]

Spanning the years 1865 to 1867, Presidential Reconstruction under former Tennessee governor Andrew Johnson allowed former Confederates who swore loyalty to the Union to participate in the conventions called to create new constitutions. Blacks were unable to participate because they were not eligible to vote under the previous constitution. Mississippi was the first Southern state that held a convention. As a condition of readmittance into the Union, the new constitution had to abolish slavery. Led by the new governor of Mississippi, Delta planter William Sharkey, the convention voted for abolition in August 1865, yet the question of African Americans' civil rights was ignored. After the election of 1865, the Delta planter and former Confederate brigadier-general Benjamin Humphreys became governor. In his inaugural address, Humphreys proclaimed "that ours is and shall be a government of white men."[71]

These conventions and the Black Codes they adopted in 1865 gave only a "passing nod to the Emancipation Proclamation and the Thirteenth Amendment."[72] One of the key similarities between this mobilization and previous, and future, movements was the conscious attempt to limit the social vision of African Americans. Or, in the words of the *Jackson Daily News*, "We must keep the ex-slave in a position of inferiority. We must pass such laws as will make him feel his inferiority." Among other things the Black Codes "provided for the 'binding out' of young black children as apprentices. Former owners of the children were given first choice. Blacks had to have a home or a job by January 1, 1866, or be fined as vagrants. If they could not pay the fine they were 'hired out,' with former owners given the first option . . . [and] they could not own guns."[73]

Due to the planter-defined labor shortage, there were numerous experiments with labor systems such as cash wages, sharecropping, gang labor, the use of northern supervisors, and re-enslavement in the interior. As a guide, the Freedman's Bureau suggested a pay level of fifteen dollars a month, housing, medical service, and some rations. The Freedman's Bureau set wages, supervised contracts, and established schools and hospitals. It also had the authority to distribute seized or abandoned lands to African Americans, yet it refused to do so.

The spread of the wage system did not ensure profitability and there was a great dissatisfaction over payment. One couple earned $39.30 in 1868 of which $38.25 was deducted by the planter. The lack of capital in the region made the payment of cash wages before or during the growing season difficult. The burden was shifted to the workers and their children.

Some planters attempted to combine a wage system with tight social controls. The Deer Creek Planters Association attempted to establish uniform wages, hours, and contracts. They set monthly wages at six dollars a man and four dollars a woman. Alternatively, they would feed and house laborers in exchange for three bales of cotton. According to Cobb:

> [the] proposed working hours were daylight to dark, six days per week with Sundays free ... Failure to perform as expected would bring immediate dismissal without compensation. ... Renting land to the freedpersons was deemed acceptable only in "exceptional cases." Members also agreed not to employ workers who had been discharged by fellow members.[74]

The gang system also reemerged on some plantations. Under the supervision of White overseers, sixty to seventy men and women would plow the fields simultaneously; other women and children would chop weeds; while still others other would clear fields. In another arrangement, instead of cash wages, food, clothing, tools, and seed were provided during the season. Upon harvest, these items were deducted from the sharecroppers' half of the crop. As under slavery, those protesting were sometimes tied by the thumbs and whipped. During the winter, it was not uncommon to see bands of homeless and starving families scrounging for food from wherever they could get it. As we will see, enforced homelessness and hunger as a labor control policy has remained a preferred strategy of Delta planters throughout the region's history.[75]

This search for a reproducible regime of capital accumulation and social regulation occurred amidst a rapidly deteriorating built environment. Railroads, levees and roads had collapsed, trade was at a standstill, and several towns remained in ashes. Broken levees and flooded fields were once again the domain of bears, alligators, mosquitoes, panthers, wildcats, and wolves.[76]

In the urban centers, social collapse was the order of the day. In 1866, the cotton-industry-dominated cities of Memphis and New Orleans erupted in a wave of violence that shocked the nation. African Americans were robbed, killed, raped, and burned. Also torched were their homes, churches, and schools. After a three-day police-led massacre in Memphis that left forty-six persons dead, a local newspaper proclaimed: "Thank heaven the white race are once more rulers of Memphis." Under the leadership of former Confederate general Nathan Bedford Forrest, the great-grandfather of the fictional character Forrest Gump, the city became the national headquarters of the Ku Klux Klan. Similarly, in New Orleans on 30 July, 1866, a convention of Black Republicans and White Unionists was attacked by a mob led by White policemen and firemen. Also investigated by Congress, this attack resulted in the deaths of thirty-four Blacks and the wounding of hundreds of others. The Union military commander called it "an absolute massacre, a murder which the mayor and police perpetrated without the shadow of necessity."[77]

## Mississippi Delta Plan 6: Radical Reconstruction, 1866–75

In no other period in our history have so many ordinary people become heroes overnight, until the Second Reconstruction of our own time.[78]

Oh My God! How long before my ass will be kicked by every Negro that meets me.[79]

In 1865, the Mississippi legislature passed a law prohibiting Blacks from renting land or housing outside town limits. Whites who sold or rented land to Blacks were subjected to physical attacks. The Fourteenth Amendment which protected both the rights of the individual and Black citizenship was unanimously rejected. Observing the massacres of New Orleans and Memphis, and the general legislative thrust, one planter boasted, "the nigger is going to be made a serf."[80]

Threatening to turn Mississippi into a frog pond rather than let the former Confederates back into Congress, Northern radicals launched what has been termed Radical, or Congressional, Reconstruction in 1865. The purpose of this movement was temporarily to break the back of the reemerging planter bloc, and of Herrenvolk unity, by empowering Black voters. Radical Republicans swept the congressional elections of 1866 and soon passed an extension of the Freedman's Bureau and the Civil Rights Act in 1866 over President Johnson's vetoes.

The Southern state governments organized by President Johnson were nullified by the Reconstruction Act of 1867. In their place were created five military districts; Mississippi and Arkansas fell into the fourth district. After swearing an oath to the national government, Blacks and Whites were allowed to vote for delegates to new constitutional conventions. Before rejoining the Union, each state had to adopt a constitution guaranteeing African American civil rights. Therefore, the Mississippi Constitution of 1868 removed all property qualifications for serving on juries, holding public office, and voting. It also guaranteed freedom of speech, freedom of assembly, freedom of the press, free public education, proportional apportionment, and unrestricted mobility.

Planters responded immediately by forming the Democratic White Men's Party of Mississippi. The central principle of this body was as follows:

> *Resolved:* That the nefarious design of the Republican party in Congress, to place the white men of the southern states under the governmental control of their late slaves, and degrade the Caucasian race as the inferiors of the African negro, is a crime against civilization of the age, which needs only be mentioned to be scorned by all intelligent minds.[81]

The new constitution was defeated by voters in 1868 and martial law continued. After Ulysses S. Grant became President in 1869, the document was finally accepted. The new state legislature had 107 members; 82 of whom were Republicans; of those, 30 were Black. James Alcorn, a Coahoma County planter, was elected provisional governor. In February 1870, Mississippi was voted back into the Union and the most prominent African American political leader in the Delta, Hiram Revels, took his seat as the first of two African American Mississippians to hold a US Senate seat during this period. Another Black leader, John Roy Lynch, became Speaker of the House in 1872. Other African American political leaders from the Delta included James Hill, Mississippi's Secretary of State, Thomas Cardoza, Superintendent of Public Instruction, Israel D. Shadd, Speaker of the Mississippi House of Representatives, and US Senator Blanche K. Bruce who became the nation's leading Black politician, and dispenser of Republican patronage, prior to the rise of Booker T. Washington. As the Delta was a national center of political thought and action for African Americans, conflicts there were bound to be monumental.

It will be argued throughout this work that the mass of intelligent and resolute leadership found within Delta led to a century-long campaign to portray these communities as passive, criminal, and ignorant. The depth of denigration heaped upon Black Mississippians was directly related to the depth of their resistance to planter hegemony. Mississippi's Reconstruction government overturned the Black Codes of 1865, approved the Fourteenth and Fifteenth Amendments, and passed the Civil Rights Act which prohibited discrimination in public places and on public vehicles. It also began the process of rebuilding railroads, bridges and levees, in addition to constructing schools, hospitals and asylums for the first time in the state's history.[82]

By 1870, there were 193,797 persons in the Delta, 130,117 of whom were African American. Although the African American population represented 67.1 percent of the total population, in counties such as Washington and Issaquena more than 85 percent of the residents were Black. The Delta was the center of power for the state's 60,000 Black voters; 90 percent of the White Republican voters also resided there. Numerous Black officials assumed office throughout the region, including such positions as sheriff and tax collector. The legitimacy of these officials rested upon mass organizations, known as Loyalty and Union Leagues, that promoted African American unity, land holding, and self-defense.

During the Civil War, many of the plantations had been confiscated by Black residents, and they were either run cooperatively or divided into smaller plots. At the end of the war, African American political leaders, soldiers, and several Radical Republicans supported a development program based upon plantation confiscation and land redistribution, that is, forty acres and a mule. This would have essentially defeated the plantation system and set the South upon a development path based on small farms and democratic rights.

In *Black Property Owners in the South*, Loren Schweninger summarized the material basis of the imagined community that underlay the African American development agenda of the period:

> It was natural for Blacks to have a passion for the land. For generations they had worked the soil, planting, cultivating, harvesting, tending gardens, and raising live-stock. Like most rural people who derived their sustenance from the soil, they respected the land and its bounty. Some of them felt a certain "proprietorship" over their garden plots, and, to some extent, over the provision grounds beyond. As freedmen they saw the possession of land as a symbol of a new beginning, a new independence. Some believed that ownership would release them from the control of their former masters. Others believed that they deserved a portion of the land that they had worked on all their lives—whites should be forced to relinquish their old plantations as punishment for holding a people in bondage. As was the case during the Antebellum period, some Blacks spoke of "getting ahead," taking advantages of new opportunities, and becoming "acquisitive." Whatever the mixture of motives, former slaves saw landownership as a symbol of freedom.[83]

Northern governmental support for limited land reform began with the passage by Congress of the Confiscation Act of 1861 over the objections of Lincoln. Authored by Senator Thaddeus Stevens of Pennsylvania, the act resulted in the army acquiring and distributing land to 40,000 freed persons in the Sea Islands of South Carolina and Georgia. Active between 1864 and 1872, the Freedmen's Bureau (the Bureau of Refugees, Freedmen, and Abandoned Lands) was authorized to do the following for African Americans in the South: lease them forty acres of land, negotiate their labor contracts; and settle them on abandoned or confiscated plantations. After the war, the Freedman's Bureau in Mississippi held more than 80,000 acres of abandoned and confiscated land. Yet, the decision to defeat the land reform movement had been made earlier by those seeking to reestablish the North–South alliance.[84]

In July 1865, the policy of land redistribution was revoked by Johnson immediately upon Lincoln's assassination. Johnson ordered that all confiscated lands be returned to those planters who had either received a presidential pardon or who had taken an oath of loyalty. This policy was implemented at the behest of planters who feared that the armed Black regiments would lead the mass seizure of land. However, plantations continued to be appropriated by African American rural workers. The situation became so tense that in

January 1866 Governor Sharkey of Mississippi insisted that the President remove the nine thousand Black troops and officers in the state because they inspired hopes, and fears, that land distribution was imminent. Known as the blues, many of these troops were removed and then mustered out of the army.[85]

Formal and informal restrictions were combined with violence to ensure that only a few Blacks were able to obtain land. The purchase of land was a political act and was thwarted at every turn; by 1870, there were only 2,009 rural landowners among the 85,788 rural African American families. Those who did acquire land often obtained small, marginal plots under the auspices of either military authorities or philanthropists.[86]

Yet land conflicts intensified. Those Union troops, those blues, who had defended African American life and labor during the war did not abandon their leadership role once they were mustered out of the army. Republican Governor Humphreys seemed to be aware of their commitment when, in 1867, he issued the following warning:

> if any such hopes or expectations [of land redistribution] are entertained, you have been grossly deceived, and if such combinations or conspiracies have been formed to carry into effect such purposes by lawless violence . . . you cannot succeed.[87]

In part, this threat was directed against the Union Leagues and Grant Clubs that were organized by Blacks and Whites in rural areas to hold political forums and escort voters to the polls. The Union Leagues movement was a mobilization designed to create a broadly based Republican Party in the South by encompassing Black Freedpersons and, to a smaller extent, White yeoman from the hills and mountain areas. The Union Leagues' National Council claimed three thousand chapters (local branches) in the South by 1867. Initially, it encouraged political activism and education among Blacks rather than land confiscation. However, as it tapped into the Black political insurgency in Mississippi its agenda was transformed and its ranks grew rapidly.[88]

In his keynote address before the Mississippi Constitutional Convention of 1868, Alston Mygatt, the president of the Mississippi Union League, clearly stated the league's vision of a golden future:

> large landed estates shall melt away into small divisions, thus densifying population; cities shall grow, towns spring up, mechanism flourish, agriculture becomes scientific, internal improvement pushed on, free schools flourish in every district and loyal men shall rule.[89]

The leadership of the Mississippi Union League came from, and organized in, the newly established Black churches. It also gained the support of numerous fraternal and social aid societies, educational groups, and other organizations, including the secret societies that were formed during slavery. The platform of the Mississippi Union League was clearly stated: "freedom, free schools, free ballot box, free jury box, free every thing." Its growth was initially slowed by conservative officials within the Union Army and the

Freedman's Bureau. In August of 1869, the Union Leagues' National Council sent a Black lawyer named William T. Combash to Sunflower County to organize Union League chapters in the Delta. During the same period, Grant replaced the hostile military commander, General Ord, with General Adelbert Ames. Although Republicans swept the Mississippi election of 1869, few Blacks were appointed to office even though they were the majority of Republican voters.

According to Fitzgerald, the democratic structure of the Union Leagues in Mississippi and Alabama allowed their Black leadership to turn them from purely electoral activity to agrarian reform. The organization began to create militias for self-defense which would eventually emerge as a major issue within the Republican Party. Martial drilling, parades, and mass action demonstrated an independent capacity both for activism and for defining self-interest. Temporary work stoppages lasting for days would be called to hold militia conferences. Their "enthusiasm for martial activities reflected hostility to the whole coercive regime derived from slavery, and, in practice, it proved one more force tearing apart the centralized plantation." Eventually, Ames sent troops to crush Combash's followers and Combash was hung by the Ku Klux Klan. These and other attacks tore apart the Mississippi Union League's 100 chapters, and they began to disband in the face of unceasing terror and treachery.[90]

Attempts to re-create the gang labor system and reintroduce the Black Codes failed as African Americans refused to follow the sunup-to-sundown regime: no work was performed on Saturdays; women withdrew their labor from planter control; workers either boycotted or fled brutal planters; strikes were called; the right to own and rent land was demanded; and new towns were established. Of all the Union Leagues in the South, the Mississippi Delta chapters were among the few able to force planters to lease land to African Americans. As late as 1874, one of the last units in the state began drilling near Vicksburg in order to protest high rents.[91]

The vision of a new society upheld by the Union Leagues rapidly turned into a nightmare by the early 1870s. The rise of planter-organized terror resulted in the destruction of the Union Leagues. Soon African American schools were burned, Northern teachers were driven from the state, the leaders of Black political organizations were assassinated, and the membership was massacred. Increasingly, voting became fraudulent as Blacks in the Delta were "voted." In the midst of this wave of reaction, the Ku Klux Klan still did not enter the Delta in force as a result of continued resistance by former Union League chapters.[92]

Without land reform, African Americans were faced with a housing and food crisis of immense proportions. While towns such as Vicksburg and Memphis were experiencing moderate growth, the rising demand for agricultural labor in the countryside meant that Blacks living in the cities were constantly being driven out. Although the freedmen villages offered a seemingly ideal form of town development, they were dismantled and the land they were built upon was returned. Families were placed in the position of being forced to appropriate livestock and crops or starve. This led to a massive expansion in punishment; neither starvation nor homelessness were crimes, but those attempting to feed their families were placed in peonage.

No reforms in housing or food distribution were forthcoming. In the case of the African American majorities in the Delta, their ability to mobilize quickly and in a united manner made their Union League activities particularly frightening to the planters and to the Ku Klux Klan. In part, living in the centralized plantation quarters and squatter camps enabled them rapidly to defend themselves. Therefore, from the planter's perspective, this settlement pattern had to be abolished. As cotton production and land prices rose after 1868, few African Americans were able to raise the cash necessary to meet the rising rents. Out of this situation the sharecropping system began to emerge which, along with the practice of furnishing goods for debt, created the foundations of the new economic order, debt peonage. Yet the establishment of sharecropping and the abandonment of the gang system did not necessarily mean the abandonment of the slave quarters that had been transformed into bases for African American social action. According to Fitzgerald, centralized housing was dismantled for the primary purpose of crushing the Union Leagues movement in the South:

> neither co-optation nor economic intimidation tamed the League insurgency; only massive violence destroyed it. Taking advantage of the dispersal of the freedmen, the nightriders adopted a practice that allowed them to take on adversaries one at a time, and neither the League nor the Republican governments devised any effective defense. The destruction of the Republican Party's mass base devastated its electoral strength ... [and] the large landlords were increasingly able to dictate terms to the labor force. The net effect was to help stabilize decentralized tenant farming, in its various forms, as the norm of postbellum agricultural production, an event of critical long-term importance in southern history.[93]

By the early 1870s, the *Economist* of London, the *New York Times*, the Boston Board of Trade, the plantation bloc, and the Ku Klux Klan were all in agreement as to the basic socio-spatial outlines of the next phase of restructuring, regimentation, and domination. Not only did African American labor have to be returned to the fields it had to be spatially fragmented for the purposes of social control. After the financial Panic of 1873, and during the six years of economic depression that followed, the plantation bloc mobilized in order to perfect further this new regime of social, economic, political, and intellectual destruction in order to achieve a complete restoration of power.

# 4

# The Shotgun Policy and the Birth
# of the Blues

Generated by what many historians call the Mississippi Plan, the 1875 conflict in the Mississippi Delta would play a significant role in shaping national politics for the next century. Regional transformation in the form of the overthrow of the Reconstruction governments, and the restoration of the planter wing of capital, doomed Black, Native American, and many White communities to renewed disenfranchisement and exploitation. This movement severely deformed national political life and its social and cultural vision. Once again the United States plunged forward along the path of "development" without concern for human rights.[1]

The planter development agenda during this period focused on warring with, and disciplining, an African American majority that rebelled in the most fundamental ways by taking up arms, rewriting the state constitution, governing, and seizing land. Threatened by the potential establishment of democratic production through democratic politics, planters and their allies attacked the electoral institutions. With the recapturing of the electoral process, the full power of the state and the monopolization of production could be rearticulated once again for the purpose of stable planter-dominated capital accumulation.

The emergence of the so-called Second Slavery in the South was one of the most disgraceful and bloody episodes in US history. What is more disturbing is how often the general formula of this mobilization has been repeated. As explored in later chapters, Black Belt history is replete with the same scenario: planter restoration through the abandonment of African American labor by Northern capital, Northern labor, and Southern labor.

Also during this period, the blues emerged as the sounds of daily life, work, imprisonment, and rejuvenation in the face of a sea of misery. While fulfilling the function of entertainment, and fueling social interaction, the blues held the feet of the community to the fire of African American realism. It disempowered the powerful and popular development arguments of planters and some African American leaders. These arguments were designed to limit African American social vision and social movements by asserting several related propositions: that less was more; that the future was the present; that the planters were really humanitarians; that the plantation was a home; that

Blacks were now free; that the working class was ignorant and uncivilized; that the upper and middle classes were civilized and superior; and that Blacks were incapable of running their own affairs without guidance from above.

## Mississippi Delta Plan 7: The Shotgun Plan of 1875

"Carry the election peaceably if we can, forcibly if we must."[2]

The mobilization that defined this period was signaled in 1870 by James Alcorn, a Delta planter and the state's first Republican governor. He advocated limited Black suffrage and active White participation in the electoral process in order to ensure that Reconstruction was a "harnessed revolution." In 1871, Republican US Senator and former Reconstruction military governor Adelbert Ames accused Alcorn of cooperating with the planter bloc and of allowing the Ku Klux Klan to operate in the state. In the 1873 governor's election, Ames defeated the Democrat-supported Alcorn. African Americans assumed key positions in the Ames administration and in the legislature: President of the Senate, Senators (nine), Speaker of the House, Representatives (fifty-five), Lieutenant Governor, Secretary of State, and Superintendent of Education.[3]

One of the most important lessons to be learned from Delta history is the relationship between representation, social control, and taxation. Democrat organizations such as the White Men's Clubs and the Taxpayer League grew rapidly. The latter was composed of planters who accused the Reconstruction governments of mismanagement when they were not complaining about the cost of governmental services, high taxes, and the state debt. They wanted social service monies redirected to levee construction and the retirement of their own back taxes. One traveler found that at

> every town and village, at every station on the railroads and rural neighborhood in the country, he heard Governor Ames and the Republican Party denounced for oppressions, robberies and dishonesty as proved by the fearful rate of taxation. White Leaguers knew . . . that they must appeal to the world as wretched downtrodden and impoverished people.[4]

Planter William Alexander Percy led a movement to regain control of the Washington County Board of Supervisors and thereby reduce the taxes on planter-owned land. After a minor gun battle, Percy entered the legislature and organized Washington County as a base from which to attack the Republican state government. In a book written in the late 1930s, Percy's grandson reveled with unbounded pride in the accomplishments of his ancestors:

> These were the men who . . . bore the brunt of the Delta's fight against scalawaggery and Negro domination during reconstruction, who stole the ballot boxes which,

honestly counted, would have made every county official a Negro, who had helped shape the Constitution of 1890, which legally disenfranchised the Negro.[5]

To regain control over the regional political economy, Delta planters turned the elections into armed affairs as they tried to oust "all bad and leading negroes." During the Vicksburg election of 1874, Democrat rifle clubs armed the White population and marched 500 strong to remove Republican office-holders. After Blacks tried to reinstate the Black sheriff a massacre ensued; twenty-nine blacks were killed immediately and up to three hundred were executed randomly throughout the countryside for several days before federal troops arrived to stop the assassination squads. In the same year, a two-county massacre occurred after a lightly armed Black militia occupied the Tunica County courthouse after local White officials refused to prosecute a White man who murdered a young black girl. Approaching the 1875 election, Black and White Republicans were beaten and killed, schools and churches were burned, and cannons were shot into rallies. Massacres also occurred in the Delta towns of Yazoo City, Friars Point, Rolling Fork, Vicksburg, and in the state capital, Jackson. In nearby Clinton, trainloads of White Democrats from throughout the state came to participate in a massacre of between twenty and fifty Black Republicans. The riots and assaults began to multiply, and every Black candidate in every county was "threatened, shot, or forced to resign."[6]

A key tactic in this movement was the highly developed art of provoking riots during African American political events. One such "riot" at a Black Republican rally in Coahoma County resulted in 250 unarmed delegates being chased and murdered over several weeks by 1,500 heavily armed White Democrats brought into the county from throughout Mississippi and Arkansas. Attacks occurred on other fronts as well. Several Black political leaders were used to defeat the African American masses. At the behest of Democrats who later reappointed him to his former post as President of Alcorn College, the Black politician Hiram B. Revels wrote a letter to President Grant stating that bloodshed would have been unknown if the Reconstruction government had not appointed, and Blacks had not voted for, Black and White Republicans who were "unprincipled adventurers."[7]

During the months before the governor's election of 1875, hundreds of citizens wrote to Governor Ames asking for protection. "WE COLORED CITIZENS" of Vicksburg wrote the following letter in September 1875:

The rebels turbulent; are aiming today to go to Satartia to murder more poor Negroes . . . This Confederate military all over the State are better prepared now for fighting than they was before the war. They intend to hang you, or get some secret scoundrel to kill you.[8]

In response to Ames's request for troops, Grant replied, ". . . the whole public is tired of these annual autumnal outbreaks in the South." According to the African American US Representative John Lynch, Grant refused assistance because Ohio Republican leaders believed that Mississippi was already lost to the Democrats and that if Black rights were made an issue Republicans would lose the Fall national elections. Ames formed a militia composed of five Black and two White regiments. He soon disarmed them as part of a peace agreement with the Democrats. While Ames believed that fair elections would ensue, the Democrats were scouring the South for cannons.

Election day in November 1875 began with cannon fire aimed at Black voters and ended with numerous massacres. With the assistance of White militias from Alabama, polling places were turned into armed encampments. The Republican vote in Yazoo County declined from twenty five hundred persons to just seven; Democrats carried sixty-two of Mississippi's seventy-four counties. Facing impeachment proceedings and death threats, Ames was forced to resign and flee the state; a former store clerk and former Confederate colonel replaced him as governor.

After the election, Grant concluded that "Mississippi is governed today by officials chosen through fraud and violence." In 1876, Grant also surrendered; Southern Democrats in the US House of Representatives were able to block the army appropriations bill until Grant agreed to remove most of the federal troops from the South.[9]

Alternatively known as the Mississippi Plan of 1875, Redemption, and the Shotgun Plan, this Delta strategy was used to overthrow Reconstruction governments throughout the South. This movement reestablished the plantation bloc's leadership of a militarized regional regime that exercised a complete dictatorship over politics, production, and class, ethnic, and gender relations. The key remaining question was how such a regional regime could reproduce itself in a national political economy increasingly dominated by a new bloc, Northern Robber Barons.[10]

The answer lies in the Delta plantation bloc's seemingly perpetual state of mobilization. Confronted by the Mississippi River on one side and competitive White farmers on the other, this bloc also had to maintain hegemony in the midst of a hostile African American majority. This social and spatial brew produced a leadership fanatical in its determination to violate all human rights and every law in order to maintain power. Its survival also depended on convincing potential allies of the rationality and success of its approach. Therefore, the Delta bloc was always attempting to mobilize internally and externally in the Lower Mississippi Valley, the Black Belt, the South, and the North, and also in other nations.

For example, as early as 1879, Delta planters were engaged in a new regionwide mobilization. Later known as the National Cotton Planters' Association, the Mississippi Valley Cotton Planter's Association was formed to preserve planter control, end the African American flight to Kansas, and promote scientific production and diversification. The objectives of this organization were focused on labor and sectoral coordination; it stressed the elimination of small producers through land concentration and through reducing tenants and sharecroppers to the position of voiceless dependants. The Robber Baron phenomenon was not simply the domination of national and international communities by a few firms and sectors emanating from the North. The other regional blocs did not disappear; instead regional alliances were restructured.[11]

## The New Regional Order

After regaining regional hegemony through armed revolt, the planter bloc made the first item on its agenda the reorientation of the entire political economy toward meeting two objectives: reestablishing the plantation as the dominant institution, and expanding cotton production. Consequently, even though town development lagged, levee and rail construction created new fortunes.

In many ways, the primacy of plantation-centered development limited urban growth. Although the Mississippi Delta's population grew significantly, from 193,797 in 1870 to 355,208 in 1890 (77 percent African American), the region was still as the Native Americans had left it. For example, in 1880, there were only two towns of over one thousand people in the Delta between Memphis and Vicksburg: Clarksdale and Greenville. Few roads existed in a landscape laced with bayous, while vast stands of cypress, gum, and cane provided habitat for numerous species including bears and panthers.

Although Memphis stood on the verge of becoming a major urban center, it was still a frontier town obsessed with commerce and not the conditions of its residents. War refugees and the rebirth of the cotton trade doubled the population of Memphis between 1860 and 1870, from 23,000 to 40,000. Yet poor sanitation practices sparked an outbreak of yellow fever that killed 5,800. The evacuation that followed was accompanied by numerous bankruptcies and the eventual loss of the city's charter.[12]

The intersection of war, plantations, and the frontier also produced a fragmented infrastructure. The haphazardly organized levee system was effectively destroyed by the combined cirumstances of war, lack of maintenance, uneven construction standards, and the bankruptcy of local governments. The massive levee construction project launched by the planters permanently tied their fate to the federal treasury.

After 1877, two levee districts were formed, each with the power to tax property owners for construction, maintenance, and repair. In 1879, the Delta bloc convinced the US Congress to create the Mississippi River Commission, a body that funded the levee and navigation projects of the Army Corps of Engineers. One of the first projects, river channelization, created a more rapid flow by deepening and straightening the river. This activity alone eventually shortened the route between Memphis and New Orleans by 170 miles. As yet uncalculated is the large number of Irish American and African American workers who lost their lives building and maintaining what was one of the world's largest public works eventually stretching from Cairo, Illinois, to New Orleans.[13]

Levee building on the Mississippi River did not alter the constant flooding and slow-moving streams characteristic of the interior. These factors severely hindered the movement of the steamboats that transported most of the crop to market. This situation was radically altered after railroad capitalist Colis Huntington purchased one of the small planter rail lines built in the 1870s. As part of the sale, he also gained ownership of 774,000 acres of Delta land. Run through virgin forest, the line stretched 445 miles, from Memphis to New Orleans. Combined, levee and rail construction created a triple boom in land values, cotton production, and timber.

The new cotton production regime stabilized around a number of interlocking events. First, the fertility of the soil made the Delta lands the most productive in the South. Second, levee and rail construction allowed lands covered by forests and bayous to be brought into production. Third, rising land prices changed financing practices. Now planters were able to finance production by mortgaging the land instead of providing cotton merchants with a crop lien.

Expanded production required additional labor. However, many of the African Americans already in the Delta wanted to leave after the overthrow of Reconstruction. "Kansas Fever" took hold of this community as thousands in Mississippi and Louisiana left for Kansas, Oklahoma, and Texas. Imagined communities were partially realized in the form of the small town and small farm democracies that they established. The Kansas exodus threatened the entire system of labor control constructed by the Delta bloc. They responded by creating the Mississippi Valley Cotton Planters' Association to coordinate their violent response and to solidify their control over the region.[14]

Simultaneous with their efforts to prevent labor from leaving, efforts were made to bring labor into the region. The erection of a pass system in the cities operated to push African Americans into the countryside. Known as "bulldozing," this practice continuously forced African Americans out of trades and occupations in favor of White workers. While this phenomenon clearly operated, and operates, during recessionary periods, breaches of any social restriction often resulted in the flight or banishment of individuals or entire communities. Delta planters also heavily recruited Blacks in the neighboring hill section to the east. Although this led the Mississippi legislature to pass two labor anti-enticement bills in 1884 and 1890, the Delta had effectively become a heavily traveled destination and departure point for African Americans from throughout the South.

Once in the production complex, Blacks were prevented from engaging in economic activities outside of sharecropping and wage labor. Without land, capital, or money, destitute African Americans were mined for their labor. The new labor system had several interrelated components: prison labor, gang labor, wage labor, sharecropping, and tenancy. Prison labor was a political and ethnic policy designed to recapture labor without compensation. The state used vagrancy laws and an array of other statutes to imprison Blacks who were then leased out to planters for $50 per year, or forced to produce cotton on state-owned prison plantations or leased to levee contractors. A Mississippi grand jury in 1887 found that "most have their backs cut in great wales scars and blisters with skin peeling off in pieces as the result of severe beatings." Many lost their lives when they were forced to protect levees during the numerous floods.[15]

Second, there were numerous attempts to reinstitute gang labor. Black labor contractors or squad leaders recruited, supervised, and often led work in the fields. Blacks were kept in semi-bondage through several mechanisms. Wages were received monthly or at the end of annual contracts. At times, workers were not allowed to leave the plantation until the end of the contract, and at other times they were forced to leave before settlement, extinguishing a family's claim on the crop. Even though wages were extremely low, workers were forced to incur grossly inflated debts for food, clothing, and rent. Debt opened the door to both imprisonment and disenfranchisement.

Another form of debt creation, impoverishment, and unfreedom was share-cropping. This practice was viewed by the planters as the solution to the problem of guaranteeing harvest labor during peak demand. Supplies of food, clothing, and livestock were advanced or "furnished" at the beginning of, and during, the season. Although these debts could, hypothetically, be resolved at settlement, sharecroppers often worked year round without income and under strict supervision. At settlement time they were typically defrauded. The planters' expanding monopolization of land, labor, and credit forced ever larger numbers of Blacks and Whites into sharecropping and debt peonage after the 1890s.

Those who could rent land often preferred to be on or near unimproved acreage which offered opportunities for hunting, fishing and greater autonomy. Renting land to African Americans met the needs of large landowners and railroads interested in expanding cotton production. However, these were highly politicized events. Any form of economic autonomy was considered a direct threat to the entire regime. Land ownership was resisted and there was a general agreement among planters not to rent.

Similar to the antebellum period, planter political and economic control over the majority-Black counties after 1875 allowed them to exert a heavy influence on state, Southern and national politics. The dominant group in the Delta was perhaps better organized and coordinated than its counterparts elsewhere in the South. Levee construction, land concentration, the immobility of agricultural investment, cyclical threats in the form of weather and pests, highly developed kin and educational networks, and overwhelming Black majorities in a majority-Black state all served as an impetus for the construction of a highly regimented state regime.

The creation of the Democratic one-party state in Mississippi enabled Delta planters and their allies effectively to control the levers of state power. For the entire period between 1876 and 1890, the governor's office was held by two former Confederate colonels, John Stone and Robert Lowry. During this era, they gave individuals what seemed to be life appointments to state and county offices. Behind the scenes, the political machinery of the state was controlled by another pair of planter bloc leaders who also reordered national political structures, J. Z. George and L. Q. C. Lamar.[16]

The plantation-dominated state was minimalist in terms of social service provision and interventionist in terms of guaranteeing stable accumulation. In the first year after the overthrow of the Reconstruction government, the state budget was cut by half. Most of the funds dedicated to education, health and the disabled were eliminated. Five key state institutions were then constructed: disenfranchisement, Black Codes, the one-party state, the malapportionment of legislative districts (gerrymandering), and labor peonage. By the 1890s, the political life of the state was completely debased: debates were suppressed, all issues were subordinated to appeals for racial solidarity, and political power was increasingly concentrated in the hands of major racists and major capitalists. Although six Blacks remained in the state legislature by 1890, most of the Black and White Republican officials had been bulldozed from office and their constituents had been eliminated from the voter rolls.[17]

According to Brandfon, the emergence of the Delta as a major production and political complex served further to deform and polarize Southern economic and political life. Although the region's potential was widely known, the lack of infrastructure prevented the full realization of profits. During the 1880s, the center of the cotton kingdom shifted from the Carolina and Georgia uplands, and the Alabama and Mississippi black prairies, to Texas and the Delta swamps. This intra-regional shift had a far-reaching effect upon the entire South:

> Indeed, the concentration of railroads, capital, and labor into the alluvial lands to the neglect of the South's poorer cotton lands, which were unable to compete, led to the latter's too rapid deterioration ... The sharpness of the divisions between the Delta and the hills made more turbulent the political reactions of the 1890s, and these in turn imprinted upon the South for generations the curious mixture of progressivism and clownishness that was the redneck political order.[18]

The federal government also put its imprimatur upon African American disenfranchisement. The United States Supreme Court declared the Civil Rights Act of 1875 unconstitutional because the Fourteenth Amendment could not prevent discrimination by individuals, only states. The Supreme Court further ruled that laws requiring racial separation did not imply inferiority; they were merely an exercise of state police power. In the National Compromise of 1877, the Republican presidential candidate, Rutherford B. Hayes, won a highly contested election over his Democratic opponent Samuel Tilden. In exchange for electoral college support, Hayes agreed to meet the demands of the White supremacist Southern Democrats: the further removal of federal troops; noninterference in state and local elections; federal appointments for key leaders; and massive financial support for infrastructure projects, including the Mississippi River Commission.

To accomplish the economic and political restructuring of the region described above, the Delta plantation bloc engaged in a sustained effort to transform social explanation. First, within the South, the Herrenvolk ideology was relied upon to reconstruct and reproduce intra-Southern White unity. Second, in the post-war period, Confederate images were redeployed. Patriotic societies and militias such as the United Daughters of the Confederacy and the United Confederate Veterans would eventually spread throughout the region as did the myth of the "Lost Cause". The myth that the Confederacy was a golden past lost to current and future generations of Whites was personalized, politicized, and preserved in numerous forms. As early as 1864, the editor of the *Southern Literary Messenger*, Frank Alfriend, proposed a blueprint for Southern literature that would unite and educate Southern Whites across class lines.[19]

The third pillar of plantation bloc social explanation was an attack on the so-called New South movement, its Northern capitalist allies, and its imagined consequences: industrialization, pollution, corrupt government, and labor mobility. However, Daniel Singal argues that there remained a great deal of ideological similarities between the plantation bloc and the merchant-led New South movement. Although more formally oriented to accomplishing the goals of manufacturing capital, the latter possessed its own definitions of capitalist behavior. Like the planter bloc, it relied heavily upon the codes of ethnic oppression, class domination, and British Victorianism.[20]

The fourth shift in social explanation involved an appeal to North–South White ethnic unity. The New South program was obviously predicated upon uniting white Northern capitalists with white Southern leaders and resources. Many Northerners saw a program of interregional ethnic unity as the only path to national unity, international expansion, and stable capital accumulation. Confederate leaders were now key elements within the national Democratic Party and they were allowed to do what they wanted with the Union's African American allies. Also stressed in both regions were the historic ties of kinship, Protestantism, and Anglo, Scotch, and Irish ancestry. Upon these foundations Anglo-Saxonism arose in the 1880s. Unlike the doctrine of Manifest Destiny which announced the intention of the United States to control the entire Western Hemisphere, this new movement was global in scope. The new national "humanitarian" mission was to "civilize" all the inferior races.[21]

The final pillar of plantation bloc representation relied on reproducing the myth of Black progress and a companion myth of Black degeneracy. Both were used to support policies preserving the planter's role as the final judge, jury, and executioner of African American life. For example, the 1879 Cotton Planters' Convention in Greenville issued a formal appeal to the "Business Men and Benevolent Societies of the North" not to assist Blacks in their exodus to Kansas. In this document both myths were used. First, the Delta was described as an African American utopia:

And hence we invoke the fair minded people of the North and West ... to prevent the destruction of the industrial interests of the white and black alike of the

Mississippi Valley. It is not true that the negro in the Valley of the Lower Mississippi is subjected to prejudice of race, any personal abuse, any extortion, any denial of political, legal, or social rights, any personal discomforts of want, to which he would in his condition be subjected in a greater degree at any other place on the American Continent.[22]

Therefore, the desire of Blacks to leave this utopia came not from the elimination of a whole generation of leadership, from massacres, rape, forced family separations, disenfranchisement, and debt peonage, but from the deficient inner workings of the African American personality:

With many, and we fear with most of the emigrants, they exhibit the delusion of religious mania, and either of their own conceit or under machinations of the emissary, believe that the Almighty has called them to a Land of Canaan. Added to this wonderful credulity of the negro, ever ready as he is to listen to the marvelous and hopeful to an absurd degree, it is not surprising that he should be demoralized, enticed from his contracts and crops, and crazed with the fever of emigration.[23]

## The Death of the Blues and the Birth of the Blues

Between 1863 and 1875, the plantation regime in the South was visually confronted with its own mortality. While Northern military occupation was considered a defeat of immense proportions, the greatest possible abomination to the planter's worldview was the sight of their "property" armed. Vincent Harding argues that these "bluesmen" haunted the Southern psyche:

those black men in blue are central to any proper understanding of the self-liberating movement of their community in the year of Jubilee [1865]. Only when we comprehend the meaning of their presence do we see the powerful potential for revolutionary transformation in the South which they represented. Only then can we sense the logic of the white Southerners who stood rigidly against the rushing black tide, and understand what was lost to the struggle when the black military vanguard was removed.[24]

Even in the late 1960s, the sight of an African American man in a military uniform provoked panic and violence in much of the Deep South. Known as the "Black and Blues," African American regiments of the 1860s both defended Black communities and led their movements. After they were mustered out of the Union Army, these former soldiers were the backbone of the Union Leagues and of the Mississippi militias that protected the Reconstruction governments. The attempt to suppress the blues completely, and any memory of them, led to their rebirth.

Just as the death of Nat Turner marked the restructuring of African American spirituals, the death of the Black and Blues marked another restructuring of African American social explanation and music. This new form of representation reflected the views of a defeated community that had only briefly tasted freedom. Also defeated was Reconstruction and the first regional planning institution in the United States, the Freedman's Bureau. The death of the Black and Blues, of the Freedman's Bureau, and of Reconstruction marked the birth of the blues.[25]

After 1875, every aspect of daily life was increasingly segregated along ethnic lines. Yet during the 1880s, the Black population in the Mississippi Delta grew by 60 percent and Whites were outnumbered seven to one. A White community gripped by fear forced separation in schools, churches, and railroad cars; even the courts used separate bibles. Mississippi led the nation in lynchings, tar-and-featherings, whippings, and human burnings. There is no way to estimate accurately the thousands upon thousands of African American community leaders and members who were murdered during this period. One can only speculate on the impact of this pogrom upon the younger generations.

Although thoughts, speech, and actions were increasingly censored, still there was greater mobility than under slavery. The medium of communication that united this censored, yet mobile, generation was the blues. William Barlow argues that this form of explanation was a tool used to share censored ideas and memories:

> The critical role the rural blues played in revitalizing the black oral tradition during the post Reconstruction era has yet to receive proper recognition. The black population in the South was still overwhelmingly agrarian and non-literate. The oral tradition was still a primary communication channel between individuals and the community and between one generation and the next ... Blues songs documented the temper of the times and thus preserved the historical legacy of a people still confined to the lowest echelon of the social order ... They dramatized the cultural vitality and rebelliousness of the participants, evoking race and class solidarity.[26]

The agonies of the 1870s and the blues are permanently intertwined. The turmoil generated by the overthrow of the Reconstruction governments created many homeless families and orphans. It also created a new occupation for the former "slave catchers"; they now traveled the roads of the South looking for men and boys that they could kidnap and imprison within the levee camps. In those camps, the prisoners became muleskinners and laborers. To the bosses, and their Black and White enforcers, Black life was so expendable that they would kill a man for injuring a mule. According to former muleskinner Walter Brown, levee workers were paid either weekly, monthly, semiannually, or not at all:

> All it was, was a privileged penitentiary. When you worked, you wasn't locked up. But other than that, it was just like a penitentiary. They paid you what they wanted you to have. If you didn't do it like they want, somebody's gon beat you up.[27]

Brown recalled that in the levee camps everyone sang at the same time. "Aw, everybody and everybody. You couldn't hear your ears. And some of 'em could sing so good till the mules would go hollerin. People don't believe that, but that's true." The levee hollers and those of the fields, prisons, docks, and streets became the central elements of blues lyrics and music. Even in the levee camps, the blues accompanied and united African Americans at work and at family, organizational, religious, and other social gatherings. Like many other writers, Lomax recognizes the unifying and expansionary aspects of the blues:

> it could be argued that the new song styles of the Delta symbolized the dynamic continuance of African social and creative process as a technique of adaption. Moreover, the birth of the blues and the struggle of its progenitors could be seen as a creative deployment of African style in an American setting, the operation of African temperament in new surroundings. In a sense African American singers and dancers made an aesthetic conquest of their environment in the New World.[28]

For Lomax, the blues were an aesthetic intervention produced as a by-product of African American oppression:

> The tales and songs return again and again to a few themes—to the grievous and laughable ironies in the lives of an outcast people who were unfairly denied the rewards of an economy they helped build. One black response to this ironic fact was to create the blues – the first satirical song form in the English language – mounted in cadences that have now seduced the world. It is heartening that both the style and inner content of this new genre are bold symbols of an independent and irrepressible culture.[29]

However, the blues and the spirituals are not simply mechanistic responses. They are the conscious codification of African American folk wisdom. The derivatives of these forms such as jazz, gospel, rock and roll, rhythm and blues, funk, and rap all refer back to these anchors and their insights. These new musical genres are documentary in nature. That is, they still must explicitly, or implicitly, address African American consciousness of this period and the intellectual/performance traditions that emerged during it. They are popular in the true sense of the word: generated by and for an evolved community of consciousness and memory.

The blues and spirituals traditions became the law for African Americans living in a lawless environment. Barlow suggests that they were

> a mix of personal sentiment and collective memory. They were focused on the present but they were framed in the folklore of the past. Many rural blues were "cautionary folktales" designed to uphold traditional values and foster group cohesion; they were commonsense lessons on how to survive in America as have-nots.

They were the secular/sacred visions of public/individual morality that were based on both idealism and realism. In essence they became foundational pillars of the African American civil religion. As such these forms are used by every generation to revitalize the African American development ethos. They became key rituals used to define and redefine the Black identity. Therefore, it is quite preposterous to argue, as some music scholars have, that the blues are either too commercialized or that they are dead in the African American community and are now the province of its White adherents and celebrants. The role that blues plays in revitalizing African American culture was captured by Amiri Baraka in his discussion of African Americans as "Blues people."[30]

Although African Americans were not simply "have-nots," they were systematically oppressed. Still, they were "haves" in terms of their determination. A standard plantation myth is that after the defeat of Reconstruction, African Americans were quiescent for the next century until they were disturbed again by Northern "outside agitators." However, the movement against the plantation bloc came immediately and in several forms. First, African repatriation efforts expanded, as did efforts to establish communities in the Caribbean, Mexico, and Central America. Second, although prior to Reconstruction there was a long history of efforts to emigrate to other regions, after the 1875 election "Kansas fever" took hold. One Black Vicksburg resident, J. C. Embry, wrote thus:

> Whether I stay there till after the campaign and election will depend upon the attitude of the administration toward us in that section. If those fellows are to be allowed to arm and persecute us at pleasure as they have done the past season, we must all of necessity soon abandon the state and the south entirely.[31]

In the Delta, emigration clubs, along with positive letters from friends and family members who had left, fueled the movement west. Although the planters tried to interrupt this flow, some White publishers in the state believed it had positive benefits:

> One thousand negroes will emigrate this season from Hinds and Madison counties, Miss., to Kansas. We hope they will better their condition, and send back so favorable a report from the "land of promise" that thousands will be induced to follow them; and the immigration will go on till the whites will have a numerical majority in every county in Mississippi.[32]

While exact figures are unavailable, by 1879 more than 30,000 African Americans had fled violence and landlessness in the Southern states to purchase land and construct towns in Kansas and Oklahoma. The origins of this movement lie in the much larger Black town movement which began on plantations during slavery and reemerged during the Civil War in the form of the freedmen villages. These town-building efforts continued in the South and represent a third form of mobilization against the 1875 revolt. Stretching from Maryland to Texas, incorporated and unincorporated African American towns still dot the Southern landscape.

Perhaps the most famous and the largest town was the Delta community of Mound Bayou. After the Civil War, the African American, Benjamin Montgomery, who had formerly been enslaved by the Confederate president Jefferson Davis, bought Davis's Warren County plantations after they had been confiscated by the Freedmen Bureau. From 1866 to 1878, the self-governing plantation community at Davis Bend was the third-largest cotton producer in the South. By 1878, relatives of Davis regained ownership and forced Montgomery to leave and the community of several hundred to disband. With a number of the Davis Bend settlers, Montgomery's son Isaiah purchased 1,500 acres of forested land from the Louisville, New Orleans and Texas (LNO&T) Railroad in 1887. The land was then cleared and the acreage was divided into numerous cotton farms. Founded in 1888, by 1907 Mound Bayou had grown to a town of eight hundred families, and it was surrounded by several hundred Black farm owners.[33]

Kenneth Hamilton argues that Mound Bayou and the other Black towns of the period were mainly developed by boosters (that is, land developers), who used racial pride as a marketing technique. First, he asserts that the town was actually planned by the LNO&T as part of its strategy to create additional rail traffic by selling its land to encourage expanded cotton production. He concludes that it was the most successful Black town because

> the town promoters helped to ensure the continual development of Mound Bayou ... by skillfully securing new settlers and outside financial assistance through the manipulation of boosting themes laced with black nationalism ... [in addition, it was successful because] Isaiah Montgomery, as Joe Davis's [brother of Jefferson Davis] teenage body servant and private secretary, had learned how to speculate and how to ingratiate himself with powerful whites for the purpose of making money.[34]

For Hamilton, the Black settlers were just another market tapped into by shrewd promoters. Therefore, the town movement was "neither insignificant nor of special importance." Unfortunately, Hamilton misses the historic implications of the search for utopias and promised lands by African Americans in the South and the continued viability of Mound Bayou as a symbol of pride in the Delta. Many of the post-Reconstruction leaders who lived in Mound Bayou suffered for their activism.[35]

The fourth form of countermobilization was civil rights protests. Segregated street cars and other aspects of Jim Crow were resisted. In 1889, Black leaders from forty counties met in Jackson to denounce the criminal suppression of the Black vote and to call for federal intervention.

The fifth response was the Colored Farmers' Alliance, considered by several scholars to be the largest African American organization in US history. As part of the national Populist movement, the Southern Farmers' Alliance organized thousands of small White producers throughout the South around a platform of farm debt reduction and higher agricultural prices. Barred from membership, Black small farmers, sharecroppers and field hands formed the Colored Farmers' Alliance (CFA) in Houston County, Texas, in 1886. Generally supportive of the Populist Party, the Colored Farmers' Alliance had a membership of 1,250,000 and a platform that promoted self-help, buyers' and sellers' cooperatives, school construction, farm loans, farm ownership, collective bargaining, and political action. Its major differences with the Southern Farmers' Alliance centered around the latter's opposition to the federal protection of African American voting rights and to a cotton pickers' strike called by Black farmers.[36]

When Oliver Cromwell began organizing for the Colored Farmers' Alliance in Leflore County, Mississippi, there were 14,276 Black and 2,597 White residents. First, in small meetings and then in larger rallies, Cromwell urged African American farmers to join the Colored Farmers' Alliance and to purchase their supplies at the Southern Farmers' Alliance cooperative store in Durant. This posed a direct threat to the intricate web of food and debt dependency created by the planter–merchant monopoly. After planters threatened Cromwell with death and demanded that he immediately leave the state, seventy CFA members marched peacefully through Shell Mound in military formation to protest intimidation and to demonstrate their resolve.

Reports that a Colored Farmers' Alliance meeting was occurring in Leflore County early in September 1889 were taken by some planters as evidence of an impending "race war." After turning many private White militias away, the Governor sent three regiments to Minter City to ensure that the CFA members were unarmed. Once this was done the regiments withdrew and allowed the massacre of CFA members to proceed. There were no reports of Blacks being armed or of Whites being shot, but estimates of the number of African Americans murdered range from twenty-five to one hundred. The numerical disparity of this estimate is a product of the cotton curtain of silence that repeatedly descends over the Delta.[37]

The consistent attack on Black leadership, and the random attacks on the young and the old, became part of daily life and consciousness. From the planters' perspective, there was no development without terror. From the African American perspective, there could be no development when every independent economic and political action was violently suppressed. Although short-lived, the Union Leagues of the 1870s and the Colored Farmers' Alliance of the 1880s represented the continuation of the blues tradition of African American explanation and action that has reemerged generation after generation. These landless and small-farmer movements were first and foremost directed against the plantation regime. Both were also intellectual movements operating outside and against the planter grid of representation. Both emerged out of the stream of African American daily life and from the tradition of organized attempts to reorder plantation relations.

Yet in Mississippi by the late 1880s, the unity between the planters and the small White producers of the hills and other sections was disintegrating in the face of the growing monopoly of the former and the increasing bankruptcy of the latter. A 75 percent fall in cotton prices was forcing the White yeoman and tenant down to the level of the Black sharecropper. The split in the Democrat Party, the formation of the Populist Party, renewed African American activism, and the potential for federal supervision of elections meant that, theoretically, the African American electorate would again hold the balance of power in state politics.

According to one of their own, Delta planters "saw the handwriting on the wall." The social–spatial fix that resolved this deep crisis resembled the coup of 1875. Planters moved rapidly to formally disenfranchise African Americans, to further restrict their mobility, and to launch another wave of violence. This time, however, they also moved against the rebellious white populist elements through a program of white disenfranchisement. Once again, a mobilization of the Delta plantation bloc would serve as the model for innovative forms of oppression for the entire South. In *Black Reconstruction*, Du Bois commented on the deepening tragedy of this period:

> God wept; but that mattered little to an unbelieving age; what mattered most was that the world wept and still is weeping and blind with tears and blood. For here began to rise in America in 1876 a new capitalism and a new enslavement of labor. Home labor in cultured lands, appeased and misled by a ballot whose power the dictatorship of vast capital strictly curtailed, was bribed by high wage and political office to unite in an exploitation of white, yellow, brown and black labor, in lesser lands, and "breeds without law." Especially workers of the New World, folks who were American and for whom America was, became ashamed of their destiny. Sons of ditch-diggers aspired to be spawn of bastard kings and thieving aristocrats rather than rough-handed children of dirt and toil.[38]

# 5

# Segregation, Peonage, and the Blues Ascension

The old men of the present generation can't afford to die and leave their children with shotguns in their hands, a lie in their mouths, and perjury on their souls, in order to defeat the negroes. The constitution can be made so that this will not be necessary.[1]

The danger posed to the Delta planters by their 1875 counterrevolution was that it recognized the principle of universal White male suffrage. The removal of class restrictions on voting made the growth of the White and Black populist alliance even more formidable. The resolution of this conflict between violently disenfranchised Black majorities and land-hungry White tenants on the one hand, and planters and railroads on the other, came in the form of Mississippi Delta Plan 8 in 1890. In the midst of this intense conflict the blues became a national and an international language.[2]

After the Republicans gained control of the presidency and both houses of Congress in 1888, US Senator Henry Cabot Lodge introduced a Fair Elections bill designed to guarantee federal supervision of Southern elections. To prevent federal intervention, Whites in the Hills and planters in the Delta entered into a new intra-state and intra-ethnic agreement to disenfranchise African Americans constitutionally. Actually, many Republicans outside the South opposed the Lodge bill. They wanted to reenter Southern politics with White allies and jettison African American party members. Faced with further marginalization, several Black leaders sought an accommodation with Mississippi Democrats. The price was their support for efforts to disenfranchise their own. Isaiah Montgomery of Mound Bayou set the national tone for the African American capitulation faction in the South by offering a "peace bush" or olive branch to the delegates to the 1890 constitutional convention. The only Black delegate, in a famed speech to the convention he expressed his willingness to sacrifice two-thirds of the Black vote in the name of peace. This event preceded Booker T. Washington's famous capitulation during the Atlanta Exposition by five years. Montgomery's surrender was celebrated nationally by opponents of civil rights, and it was printed verbatim in the *New York World*.[3]

Montgomery and several other African American leaders thought that the franchise would be taken from "illiterate" Blacks, not from the educated and property-owing elite. Governor James K. Vardaman was unambiguous as to the meaning of the new constitution:

> I am just as opposed to Booker T. Washington as a voter, with all his Anglo-Saxon reinforcements ... as I am to the coconut-headed, chocolate-colored typical little coon, Andy Dotson, who blacks my shoes every morning. Neither is fit to perform the supreme function of citizenship.[4]

The new constitution granted the franchise to all adults except "idiots," the insane, Native Americans, and women. It banned biracial education, interracial marriage, and voting by those with criminal convictions. The poll tax as a disenfranchisement tool was reinforced by literally dozens of overlapping practices: literacy tests, a constitutional understanding clause, property tests, secret ballots, character tests, complex registration procedures, long residency requirements, the grandfather clause, and the White primary. Many of these tactics had a disproportional impact upon African Americas because of their higher rates of imprisonment, impoverishment, and illiteracy. Additionally, the fear of physical and economic attacks created a permanent state of chaos which forced many families and individuals to make a series of moves in and out of the region. Also to the planters' political advantage, these requirements served to disenfranchise poor Whites.

After approving the constitution, the convention declared it in force without a vote because the delegates feared that the voters would reject it at the polls. This constitutional fraud was upheld by the Mississippi Supreme Court and the US Supreme Court in the 1898 case of *Williams v. Mississippi*. Under the apportionment rules drawn up by members of the Delta plantation bloc, each Mississippi House member from a majority-Black county represented 675 adult White males while members from majority-White counties represented 1,168 adult White males. For the Senate, the numbers were 1,891 and 3,681 adult White males respectively. After Black disenfranchisement, this formula prevented planters from being overwhelmed by poorer Whites in the legislature. Furthermore, in order to protect planters from populist-inspired taxes, new revenue measures could not be enacted unless they received a three-fifths majority. Therefore, the future battles for Black re-enfranchisement represented a direct attack on planter power.[5]

At the center of the 1890 mobilization was the call for White unity and further violence against Blacks. With their ranks composed of ruined and debt-ridden White farmers in southwest Mississippi, the White Cappers movement emerged between 1890 and 1910. Through intimidation, murder, and the burning of churches and schools, whitecapping forced Black workers out of the lumber industry and drove them off land they rented or owned. Blacks were forced into the Delta until the Governor intervened, while planters feared another mass exodus of Blacks. Those White populists who insisted on preserving their alliance with their Black counterparts were also threatened. The *Vicksburg Commercial Herald* warned, "Don't monkey with white supremacy: it is loaded with determination, gunpowder and dynamite."[6]

According to Neil McMillen, "Negrophobia" took hold of the state. Characteristic of this condition was "the ceaseless agitation, indiscriminate cursing of the whole Negro race often to cheering crowds." Based on racial fundamentalism, this new civil religion quickly spread throughout the South and then to the rest of the country. Several observers noted that not only had the North surrendered, but it had joined the Confederacy. By 1925, national Ku Klux Klan membership reached 8.9 million, with Northern states having the most members: Michigan 875,000; New Jersey 720,000; Texas 450,000; Kentucky 441,000; Ohio 400,000; Florida 391,000; Nebraska 352,000; California 350,000; Iowa 350,000; Illinois 300,000; New York 300,000; Pennsylvania 300,000; Arkansas 150,000; Mississippi 93,000; and Louisiana 50,000.[7]

## The Alluvial Empire

After the adoption of the Mississippi Plan of 1890, planter hegemony was reproduced through internal reorganization, major infrastructural projects, and the infusion of capital from outside the region. From 1890 to 1919, timber workers and sawmills cleared 4 million acres of forest, leaving a wasteland of stumps. Railroads began selling land to settlers at attractive terms: cut-over land purchased for $1,500 an acre could then be sold when cleared for $7,500 an acre. In 1892, the Illinois Central Railroad Company (ICRRC) purchased the LNO&T railroad, and earnings from its Delta line proved to be greater than all the other ICRRC operations combined. In order to expand production and settlement, the railroad began to finance land purchases. Beginning in 1910, the ICRRC marketed the region to potential farmers and investors through a series of pamphlets. Under the name the Southern Alluvial Land Association, the plantation bloc also began to promote the multi-state Delta region through a 1919 pamphlet entitled *The Call of the Alluvial Empire: Containing Authentic Information about the Alluvial Region of the Lower Mississippi Valley States of Arkansas, Tennessee, Mississippi and Louisiana.*[8]

Capital availability became less of an issue in consequence of rising land values and expanded production. With the guarantee of levee protection and with land values rising above those of the best Iowa farmland, banks rushed to provide loans for new Delta plantations. It was claimed that "banks lend more money on alluvial soil than upon any other land in the South." Unleashing this flood of new capital were Memphis banks such as the Union Planters Bank, Bank of Commerce and Trust Company, Guarantee Bank and Trust Company, several Mississippi and Arkansas banks, and the National City Bank of New York.[9]

The Northern-owned and -oriented rail network linked major Northern cities to the new inland cotton markets and manufacturing centers of the South: Atlanta, Birmingham, Memphis, and Nashville. With a population of

120,000 persons in 1900, 48 percent of whom were Black, Memphis grew to become the second largest city in the South behind New Orleans, which had 287,000 persons.[10]

Memphis also became a national trading center that supplied the thousands of plantations and rural towns in the so-called Alluvial Empire: the Mississippi Delta, the Arkansas Delta, the Louisiana Delta, the Missouri Bootheel, western Tennessee, and beyond. The headquarters of this regional commercial complex was the Memphis Chamber of Commerce. In the process of becoming an international center of cotton production and trade, Memphis became the home of the largest cotton warehouses in the world, the largest inland cotton market in the world, the largest producer of cottonseed products in the world, the largest hardwood market in the United States (exporting $100 million annually), the second-largest drug market in the nation, the nation's third-largest grocery market, and the largest mule and car market in the South. The city was now served by ten rail trunk lines, by two bridges across the Mississippi River, and by fourteen national and interstate highways.[11]

These events transformed Memphis, and its famed Beale Street, into a major African American cultural center. The city was christened by W. C. Handy's "Memphis Blues," an ode to the mayor, Edward H. "Boss" Crump:

> Mr Crump don't 'low no easy riders here
> Mr Crump don't 'low it—ain't goin' have it here
> We don't care, what Mr Crump don't 'low
> We gonna bar'l house anyhow
> Mr Crump can go and catch his-self some air.[12]

The Mississippi Delta's population grew from 355,208 in 1890 to 478,060 in 1910 to 548,290 by 1920. The African American portion of the population fluctuated: 76.8 percent in 1890, 90.8 percent in 1910, and 75.6 percent in 1920. In what has been referred to as the Great Migration, 148,000 African Americans and 111,900 Whites left Mississippi between 1910 and 1920. While the wartime demand for labor in the Northern manufacturing cities sparked much of this movement, McMillen suggests that the oppressive practices of the Democratic Party and the plantation bloc had a great deal to do with Black and White emigration.[13]

The Delta's production system yielded the highest cotton-bale-per-acre averages in the world. One observer predicted that the "Cotton Kingdom would become as efficient as any northern factory system, make profits as never before, and thus provide general prosperity for a new South." With just 30 percent of Delta lands under cultivation in 1900, planters boasted that they could outproduce the rest of the Cotton Belt states combined. In part because of the amazing fertility of the soil, between 1909 and 1915, as the boll weevil infestation devastated cotton producers throughout the South, cotton yields in the Delta actually increased.[14]

During the boom, in 1911, British investors purchased a bloc of thirty to forty thousand acres for $2–3 million. This marked the beginning of the Delta and Pine Land Company, arguably the largest plantation in the world. The purchase arose out of the desire of Manchester textile manufacturers to guarantee the most efficient forms of production and the highest-quality crop. The Delta Pine and Land Company and other large plantations utilized the latest scientific management techniques:

> A centralized office made all major management decisions determining hours of work, the amount and kind of fertilizer and such used, the maintenance and improvements required, the tools, equipment, and mules to be used, the boll weevil poisoning to be applied. Supervisors or overseers directed the work and saw to it that the workers followed the routine set by the manager.[15]

This brings us to the question of the organization of labor in the Delta. The principal labor institution, sharecropping, was defined in promotional materials in the following manner:

> Half and Half—tenant supplies labor and one-half of fertilizer if used—while the landlord supplies the house, land, garden, tools, work animals, feed, and fuel. Each receives half of the crop. The landlord exercises careful supervision over the share-croppers who are considered as laborers—hired to do the work in return for half the crop and use of the house, etc.[16]

This definition is significant. At least formally, the promoters did not consider sharecropping anything more than a system of hired labor designed to guarantee harvest. Although some historians have referred to sharecropping as a feudal retention, for the plantation bloc it was merely a capitalist innovation used to immobilize free labor for at least nine months out of the year. The second most common labor system was share-renting. Tenants used their own labor, stock, feed, and tools. The planter provided the buildings, land, and fuel in exchange for one-fourth to one-third of the crop. Another variation, cash-renting, required the tenant to pay the planter cash instead of crop shares.

In 1910, 92 percent of the Delta farms were operated by sharecroppers or renters of whom 95 percent were Black. Of all the arrangements, sharecrop-ping was the most profitable for the planter. A USDA study in 1911 found significantly different outcomes from the various labor arrangements. The cash renter averaged $478 per crop while the planter got a return on investment of 6.6 percent. Under the share-renting arrangement the returns were $398 and 11.8 percent respectively. However, under sharecropping, the farmer received only $333 while the landlord return was 13.6 percent.[17]

Sharecropping was wrapped in violence and fraud. The harvest and the settlement were governed by state crop lien laws which gave merchants and planters control over the crop division, distribution, and marketing along with debt collection. Even after bumper crops, planters would often claim that the sharecropper still owed money and would have to remain on his plantation for another season to pay off the debt. By mid-winter, not only were many sharecroppers in debt after nine months of work, but cash advances were typically reduced or suspended. Many sharecroppers secretly moved during this post-harvest period to escape these manufactured debts, the likelihood of imprisonment for refusal to pay or attempted escape, and the specter of starvation if they acquiesced. Beginning with field preparation in the spring, advances were made again, in the form either of poor-quality clothes and food, or of cash. These advances were credited to the tenant's account at interest rates typically above 25 percent. Those who challenged this year-in and year-out system of exploitation often found themselves or their family members imprisoned, beaten or murdered.[18]

A 1923 argument between Black sharecropper Don Pullen and White plantation manager W. T. Saunders over settlement resulted in the latter being killed. A posse of one thousand White men searched the swamps near Drew. Depending the source, Pullen killed 4, 17, or 19 Whites and wounded 8, 38 or 40 others before being machinegunned. He either died immediately or was dragged through the streets and then killed.[19]

According to Clarksdale blues performer Will Stark, no African American was safe during the cotton harvest:

> They had to work—or fight! When they come after a man to work, he had to *go*. For instance, Mister Hobson or Mister Clark or Mister King or Anderson or any of these people out of town wanted some hands to chop the cotton or plow, it make no difference who he was, he must *go*. They would go into colored people's houses and git the children out who had never been worked none—schoolgirls—and make *them* go out and pick cotton ... Of course the boss didn't do all this, the officers here in town would take um and when they got out on the plantation they had to work—or fight ... [What happened to those that fought?] They just *whipped um up*. Some of um I heard they whipped to death ... One bossman out here about Tutwiler ... made a man work and chained his wife in bed at night to make sure they wouldn't run away.[20]

After the overthrow of Reconstruction, numerous laws were passed by Southern legislatures allowing plantation owners to hold workers in lieu of the payment of private and public debts. Delta planters increasingly resorted to debt peonage. A 1900 law punished tenants who entered into new contracts without giving notice to their former employers. A 1904 law increased the prosecution of vagrancy while a 1906 law provided criminal punishment for those who left a contract after small advances. Repeated appeals by family members to the US Department of Justice concerning persons who were kidnapped and held on farms or in prison chain gangs for years at a time were simply ignored. This emerging system of unfree labor allowed planters once again to buy and sell people, this time through the purchase and sale of their debts.[21] As editor of the National Association for the Advancement of Colored Peoples' (NAACP) journal the *Crisis*, W. E. B. DuBois railed against debt peonage as a state-enforced system of involuntary servitude:

> let me point out that the practice of peonage in the rural South, where not less than a quarter of a million black laborers are held to service on the plantations by force

in direct defiance of laws and wise industrial policy, has been buttressed by a system of statutes and administration which applies to all rural black labor and white, and which makes a body of legislation positively astonishing in its reactionary and medieval aspect ... makes a body of law which carries force and fraud on its very face.... Where else in a modern industrial land could a girl [of] fourteen, accused by the landlord's bookkeeping of receiving an advance wage of $7 and of refusing to carry out further her contract to pick cotton, be fined $75 or twelve months in the chain gang?[22]

Finally, those men and women who drained the swamps, and who worked on the prison farms and in the levee and sawmill camps, faced death from working too hard and death for not working hard enough. African Americans continued to die building and shoring up the Lower Mississippi River levee system. The brutality used in levee construction was unsurpassed. According to one worker, after a man fell into a pit with his wheelbarrow "they just dump the next dirt on him and leave him there—cover him up and forget him." This phenomenon was captured by the following blues song:

> Looked at the sun and the sun was red
> I looked at my partner, he was falling dead,
> But we just kept on *moving*
> It was tough
> We just kept on moving
> We *had* to move
> Look out! Shot![23]

This regional complex was defended by politically and economically active planters and their family members who also served as sheriffs, judges, lawyers and merchants. Alliances within the plantation bloc were cemented through culture, schooling, and marriage. These families expanded into other businesses such as cotton gins, cottonseed oil mills, real estate, insurance, publishing, banking, and cotton factorage. They also formed land companies to purchase properties in the Delta areas of Arkansas, Louisiana, and Missouri, further cementing the alluvial valley alliance. In addition to educational, political, and military ties, interregional bonds were established through the vertical integration of local firms into powerful national bodies such as the Standard Oil Company which dominated the American Cotton Oil Trust.[24]

In terms of state expenditures, the agenda of the Delta planters revolved around infrastructural improvements designed to increase agricultural productivity. The state began funding the Delta Experiment Station which was established in 1904 in Stoneville with funding from the USDA. By 1929, 95 percent of the cotton acreage in the Delta was planted with strains developed at the station. In addition, increasing private and state support accelerated the construction of levees as did the massive infusion of federal funds provided in the Randsdall–Humphreys Act of 1917.[25]

The plantation bloc also continued its domination of state offices, from the legislature to local sheriffs. State officials acted as enforcers of plantation ethnic, social, and labor regulations. Increasingly, the intensity of oppression and censorship returned to levels found prior to abolition. The rise of curfew, vagrancy, and peonage laws signaled that a crisis was at hand. For example, a 1920 state law mandated a $500 fine or six months imprisonment for anyone found "guilty of printing . . . information, arguments or suggestions in favor of social equality." The rising crisis was due, in part, to renewed African American mobilizations. Another key element of this crisis was the "Revolt of the Rednecks"—an insurgency against planter domination emerging from the predominantly White counties of the Hills, Piney Woods and the Gulf Coast.[26]

## Planter Thought: From Fiction to the Social Sciences

As in previous periods, the Delta planter bloc developed forms of representation that both rationalized and preserved their regional domination. However, what is distinctive about this period is the expansion of the plantation tradition of explanation from its base in history and fiction into the newly emerging social sciences. Although increasingly integrated with Northern capital, the planter bloc still held on closely to its belief in empire. A 1919 promotional pamphlet clearly expressed the view that the Deltas were destined for greatness:

> When its 20,000,000 acres are in cultivation, it will be one of the world's greatest production centers. The alluvial empire has started to bloom. Its blossom bids fair to permeate the world with a rich fragrance.[27]

Belief in regional superiority extended to belief in the supremacy of the planters themselves. They still held to the view that the structures of inequality they created were a symbol of their generosity and paternalism. This mythical paternalism was in reality a production system organized around institutionalized starvation, discrimination, violence, fraud, debt and enforced dependency. For Walter Sillers, a Delta planter and Speaker of the Mississippi House of Representatives from 1944 to 1966, paternalism was similar to the relationship between a dog and his owner:

> no law abiding Negro is afraid of violence. He not only knows he is valuable to the white man, more so than his mules and fine horses, but he also relies upon the kindly feeling of justice of the white man.[28]

In the 1890s, the plantation bloc epistemology was bolstered by several cultural/intellectual movements. First, there was "The Lost Cause" movement, which during this period became a civil religion dedicated to memorializing plantation culture and the Confederacy. The mid-1880s marked the beginning of a South-wide, local elite-led, century-long movement to erect monuments to the Confederate dead and to the Confederacy. Found in almost every courthouse square, these statues were constructed by local memorial associa-

tions whose activities were celebrated in the publications of the Southern
Historical Society, the United Daughters of the Confederacy (founded in
1894), and the Confederated Memorial Associations of the South. For Campbell, sections of the Southern White clergy played a critical role in simultaneously silencing the opponents of the plantation regime while celebrating
its defenders:

> Confederate political and military figures became in sermons "the Christian heroes
> of the ages" and assumptions that the cause was lost were dispelled with assurances
> that with "the providence of God" and "steadfastness to principle" the South would
> in effect triumph. The South could well regard adversity as a sign of God's favor: "it
> is better to be chastened than to be let alone" was a favorite theme.[29]

Another key component in the formation of this civil religion was the
Southern Historical Society, which had been founded in New Orleans in 1869
by several former Confederate generals. Marching under the banner of "lest
we forget," efforts to memorialize the Confederate dead were soon transformed into a celebration of the South, slavery, the Confederacy, the war,
White supremacy, multi-class White unity, and the Democratic Party. They
were also a celebration of the domination of Blacks, the denial of their human
rights, and the destruction of their families, institutions, culture, and communities. Additionally, museums were created and magazines, newspaper articles,
biographies, multi-volume studies, and even playing cards began to issue forth
at a dizzying rate.

Soon articles on local color and plantation nostalgia began appearing in
Northern journals. Perhaps the greatest influence upon the urban masses of
the North was the traveling minstrel shows which were later integrated into
the budding film industry. It is therefore not surprising that among the pillars
of this new film industry were the 1915 film by D. W. Griffith, *Birth of a
Nation*, which celebrated the birth of the Ku Klux Klan; the 1935 film starring
Shirley Temple, *The Littlest Rebel*, which celebrated the Confederacy; and the
ever-popular 1939 film *Gone with the Wind* with its intimate celebration of
planters and plantation life. Hundreds of films, radio programs, books, and
advertisements fed into the movement to restore the luster of the planter, of
the plantation bloc epistemology and of the Confederacy.[30]

A second central feature of the reproduction of planter hegemony and
South/North reconciliation during the 1890s was the institutionalization of the
plantation bloc's view of economics, history, biology, psychology, and sociology. Academic discussions of African American life, deemed the "Negro
problem," were dominated by a diverse group of Southern planters, sons of
planters, Confederate soldiers, historians, and political economists who
believed in the inferiority of Blacks and the impossibility of assimilation. Many
received their advanced training at Northern universities and went on to
publish a body of works in the leading sociological journals. In essence, they
were the founders of academic racial discourse and the race relations industry
that was built upon it.

Using Herbert Spencer's social Darwinism, this group believed that disenfranchisement and the Black Codes were the most appropriate mechanisms to manage a Black population that had lapsed into the barbarism of their ancestors once the civilizing institution of slavery was removed. At the turn of the century, this was the dominant academic explanation of the "Negro problem." Columbia University's Franklin Giddings, the USA's first full professor of sociology, was a leading figure in the plantation social science movement. His 1896 observations sound strikingly similar to two current theories of African American inferiority, underclass ghetto isolation and the lack of appropriate role models:

> The negro is plastic. He yields easily to environing influences. Deprived of the support of stronger races, he still relapses into savagery, but kept in contact with whites, he readily takes the external impress of civilization, and there is a reason to hope that he will acquire a measure of reason.[31]

Empirical works in a similar vein began to emerge upon the national stage. Joseph A. Tillinghast's *The Negro in Africa and America*, published by the American Economics Association in 1902, and Jerome Dowd's 1907 study *The Negro Races* were widely influential comparative examinations. These authors argued that all people of African ancestry shared a similar set of debasements: criminality, lack of industrial efficiency, exceptionally strong reproductive powers, the lack of science and art, polygamy, heathen religions, unusual sexual proclivities, neglect of the young, and ignorance. According to Tillinghast, "the sensory motor activities of the West African brain produced both potent passions and a feeble ability to control them."[32]

Of all the Southern sociologists, Alfred Holt Stone and Howard Odum had the most lasting influence. In many ways Stone was the theorist of Delta plantation bloc mobilizations. The writings and practices of Stone are perhaps the clearest example of the influence of the Delta plantation bloc upon the national disciplines of history and sociology. The son of a classics professor who later became a Confederate captain and a Delta politician, Stone attended the University of Mississippi, practiced law in Greenville, owned a relatively large cotton plantation, and served in the Mississippi legislature. He attended the Mississippi constitutional convention of 1890 as a delegate and voted in favor of stealing the ballot from African Americans. Later in life, he served as a vice president of the Delta Council, the dominant planter organization. Treated as the authority on the "Negro problem" by the largest philanthropists in the nation, Stone lectured at universities throughout the USA.

"Is Race Friction Between Blacks and Whites in the United States Growing and Inevitable?" was a paper Stone delivered before the American Sociological Society in 1907. It was so controversial that it and responses to it found their way into several 1908 issues of the *American Journal of Sociology*. His concepts reached a wider audience in a book published by Doubleday in 1908, *Studies in the American Race Problem*.[33]

Stone's theory of racial antipathy rests on the premise that White racial

prejudice was the natural result of such racial differences as physical appear-
ance, intelligence, customs, and religious beliefs. Antipathy between the races
would be lessened by the abandonment of "the novel claim to equality made
by the negro after emancipation." For Stone, one of the "commonest mis-
takes" of those asserting equality is that they see slavery as the foundation of
race friction. He then harkens back to Fitzhugh's claim that slavery was a
superior social institution:

> The institution, *per se*, was not only not the cause of the problem, but, on the other
> hand, it actually furnished a basis of contact upon a plane of theoretical equality . . .
> The late Professor Shaler, of Harvard, summed up with absolute accuracy the
> function of slavery in making possible relations of mutual amity between the white
> and negro races in this country when he declared that, "the one condition in which
> very diverse races may be brought into close social relations without much danger of
> hatred, destructive of social order, is when an inferior race is enslaved by a superior
> . . . it remains to be seen whether the race hatred lost during the period of slavery
> will return in the condition of freedom."[34]

Stone argued the movement of significant numbers of Blacks into White areas
would also result in increased ethnic hatred and race war. This theory
introduced social physics into the social sciences through the proposition that
when the concentration of Blacks reaches some magic percentage, degradation, conflict, and destruction would ensue:

> Just as a heavy increase of negro population makes for an increase of friction, direct
> legislation, the protection of drastic social customs, and a general feeling of unrest or
> uneasiness on the part of the white population, so a decrease of such population, or
> a relatively small increase as compared with the whites, makes for less friction,
> greater racial tolerance, and a lessening of the feeling of necessity for severely
> discriminating laws or customs.[35]

For Stone, racial friction was absent during slavery "due to the general
acceptance by the negro of the status assigned him by the white race."
Conversely, Northern-encouraged Black assertiveness would cause greater
friction because the feelings of superiority were stronger among Anglo-Saxons
than any other race. The promotion of social equality and intermarriage, along
with attempts by educated Blacks to develop ethnic consciousness and solidarity, would not only threaten Anglo-American civilization but would lead to a
race war. Above all, the sanctity of the social order superseded Christian and
democratic principles.

After noting the demand for equality by W. E. B. DuBois and other
"Americans of African descent whose mental attainments and social equipment identify them much more closely with the Anglo-Saxon than with the
Negro masses," Stone quoted sociologist Edward A. Ross, author of the 1905
work *Foundations of Sociology*:

> The superiority of a race cannot be preserved without pride of blood and an
> uncompromising attitude toward the lower races . . . the net result is that North
> America from the Behring Sea to the Rio Grand is dedicated to the highest type of

civilization; while for centuries the rest of our hemisphere will drag the ball and chain of hybridism.[36]

Among the May 1908 respondents to Stone's paper was W. E. B. Du Bois, then a professor at Atlanta University. At the time, Du Bois was also a reluctant participant in a 1907 study Stone was conducting for philanthropist Andrew Carnegie on the history of African American economic cooperation. Yet his contempt for the plantation bloc epistemology, for Stone's ideas, and for Stone himself were barely masked. First, Du Bois argued that slavery was a failure "because it denied growth or exception on the part of the enslaved and kept up that denial by physical force." Those who expected Blacks not to aspire were "bound to disappointment":

There is today in the South growing protests from the masses of Negroes, protests to which whites are yielding today and must yield . . . protest is not confined to a few leaders, it is not confined to the North; it is not confined to mulattoes.[37]

Second, Du Bois believed that conflict was not inevitable if the White South moved away from the "absurd stand" that inferiority was absolute and unchangeable. The issue of incompatibility and repugnancy between Black and Whites had to be studied scientifically. It would then be proven to be

a most ludicrous and harmful conglomeration of myth, falsehood, and desire . . . we must realize that not only does the modern world spell increased and increasing contact of groups and nations and races, but that indeed race or group segregation is impossible.[38]

Third, in response to Stone's conclusion that the problems of Black–White relations had only two solutions, assimilation or separation, Du Bois argued that neither were possible:

Race segregation in the future is going to be impossible primarily because these races are needed more and more in the world's economy. Mr Stone has often expressed the cheerful hope that the Negro would be supplanted by the white man as the worker in the South. But the thing does not happen. On the contrary there are today more Negroes working steadily and efficiently than ever before in the world's history.[39]

Finally, Du Bois addressed the authors cited by Stone:

Finally, rhetoric like that quoted by Mr Stone is not in itself of particular importance, except when it encourages Philistines who really believe that Anglo-Saxons owe their pre-eminence in some lines to lynching, lying, and slavery, and the studied insult of their helpless neighbors. God save us from such social philosophy.[40]

The last sentence of Stone's reply to his respondents seemed directed at Du Bois:

Something has been suggested as to the rights and wrongs involved in the situation, and about what might be if only men would just be honest, and so forth. My only reply is that I did not come here to discuss ethical questions. I am just now concerned with the hard, stern, inexorable facts in the case.[41]

This last comment clearly demonstrates how the claim of objectivity arose and how it was used to mask the organization of the social science disciplines in the United States around basic tenets of the plantation bloc epistemology from their inception. Such claims are still used today to mask the continued centrality of these categories. Individuals and institutions that objected to and deviated from this foundational subversion of the social sciences were swiftly persecuted.[42]

Stone's theory that reforms designed to promote ethnic equality would lead to race wars was used to defend Southern and Northern resistance, inaction, and gradualism. Even though his theories were marginalized by the 1960s, they were constantly being remodeled and re-presented by scholars in the South and North, White and Black. His works have always been venerated at the center of plantation bloc thought: the planter-led organizations and research institutes located at the USDA's Delta Branch Experiment Station in Stoneville, Mississippi.

Another important intellectual figure to emerge partly out of Mississippi was Howard Odum, the "father of regionalism." At the turn of the century he received an MA in English from the University of Mississippi, a PhD in Psychology from Clark University, and a PhD in Sociology from Columbia University. In his 1910 study of African American communities in Oxford, Mississippi, and other Southern towns, Odum systematically presented the planter thesis of African barbarism and Black inferiority:

> First, the negro easily responds to stimuli, that is, he is controlled by present impulses. This results in almost complete lack of restraint, including both yielding to impulses and inertia. Second, this free response tends always to pleasure, sometimes the pleasure being more or less unconscious in the simple giving way to impulse and the breaking down of restraint or in negative feelings of non-exertion. The negro is therefore inactive. Third, the negro tends to carry all responses to an extreme. He loves plenty of stimuli. This exhausts and degenerates his vital powers. Fourth, the negro has little capacity for sustained control. This applies to sustained efforts, conduct in general, morality, convictions and thought. He is therefore weak in social and self-control and lacking in self-direction. Fifth, he does not, therefore, lend himself to the development of permanent qualities through the working out of essential processes. Sixth, he is, therefore, superficial and irresponsible ... He has no pride of ancestry and is not influenced by the lives of great men. The negro has few ideals and perhaps no lasting adherence to an aspiration of real worth. He has little conception of the meaning of virtue, truth, honor, manhood, integrity.[43]

Odum went on to describe the hundreds of African American blues songs he collected and, in the process, he became the founder of a school of blues criticism that, to this day, annually generates thousands of scholarly and journalist defamations of the blues, of blues-derived musical forms, and of African Americans. Initially, the blues were for Odum, "Openly descriptive of the grossest immorality and susceptible of unspeakable thought and actions rotten with filth ... the superlative of the repulsive ... Must he [the African American] continue as the embodiment of fiendish filth incarnated in the tabernacle of the soul?" During the 1920s, Odum attempted to maintain his position as a leading expert in the "Negro field" by capitalizing on the growing national popularity of the blues. Due to their growing popularity among Whites, he chose to mask his overtly racist characterization of African Americans and of their songs with the new scientific racism of anthropology. Blacks and the blues were now to be investigated as anthropologists investigate any other "primitive" people. He then proceeded to coauthor two works on African American songs and author three biographical works on bluesman John Wesley "Left Wing" Gordon, profiles of a "primitive man in the modern world."[44]

Folklore and songs were considered by Odum to be passageways into the "psychic, religious and social expressions of the race." They could be used to "advance the successful study of the common development of the human intellect and primitive thought." He suggested that the blues were principally concerned with three subjects or concepts: "loneliness and melancholy," "the love relationship between a man and a woman," and "self-pity." Stunting the categorical range of possibilities inherent in the blues was part of a larger project to confine African Americans, their culture, and their aspirations to a "natural" and "primitive" cell that could never be opened since this would mean the death of "civilization."[45]

Stone, Odum, and the other social theorists were speaking as supporters of the overthrow of the Reconstruction governments, of legalized disenfranchisement, of apartheid, and of lynching. The explanations and scenarios laid out by each attempted to convince audiences that not only was Black political leadership a farce but also any form of African American autonomy was doomed to failure without close White supervision. These formulations represented a direct extension of the plantation tradition of explanation. Serving as the foundation of many current sociological theories of Black degeneracy, the authors of these studies claimed that they found "scientific" evidence supporting the planter's command that African Americans had to be managed for their own good and for the good of the society at large. Consequently, the planter stood as hero, as superman, and as a bulwark of civilization defending it mightily against African barbarians and their heathen excesses.

Finally, the representation of African barbarism by Northern and Southern scholars also fed directly into the international policies of the period. Theories of tropical inferiority, "White" unity and supremacy, and mythic paternalism were combined to become the intellectual foundations of US imperial expansion and of the establishment of new plantation regimes in Haiti, Hawaii, Cuba, the Philippines, Puerto Rico, the rest of the Caribbean, Central America, Asia, Africa, and the rest of Latin America.

Yet there were splits within the national social science community between those operating from the plantation tradition and those reform-oriented academics who emphasized scientific objectivity and empiricism. A 1909 attack upon the Tillinghast–Dowd thesis by the Columbia University physical anthropologist Franz Boas would eventually serve as the basis for the emergence of a distinct liberal cultural-determinist school of social science in the North.

Although Boas originally believed that Blacks had smaller brains than Whites, he also believed that their debased state was not caused by their African heritage: slavery and peonage had both destroyed their rich African heritage and oppressed them for generations.

In a 1917 article, the University of Chicago sociologist, Robert E. Park, a former assistant to Booker T. Washington, argued that segregation was supportable on sociological rather than biological grounds. He was thus a transitional figure in sociology who stood between the instinctive and environmental schools. A mixture of biology and sociology, racism and sexism can be found in his theory that Blacks, like Africans, exhibit a particular temperament which may eventually be broken through immigration and miscegenation:

> Everywhere and always it [the African race] has been interested in expression rather than in action; interested in life itself than its reconstruction or reformation. The negro is, by natural disposition, neither an intellectual or idealist, like the jew; nor a brooding introspective like the East Indian; nor a pioneer and frontiersman, like the Anglo-Saxon. He is primarily an artist; loving life for its own sake. His metier is expression rather than action. He is, so to speak, the lady among races.[46]

Park also believed that the process of assimilation had been interrupted by the abolition of slavery. Segregation had brought with it a Black nationalist movement organized around a distinct moral authority and separate institutions such as towns, churches, schools, and hospitals. Park concluded that the "races seem to be tending in the direction of a bi-racial organization of society, in which the negro is gradually gaining a limited autonomy." As Park was one of the founders of the Chicago School of Urban Ecology, his revised theory that migration, class differentiation, education, assimilation, and intermarriage would eventually eliminate the inferior attitudes and behavior of lower-class Blacks found its way into the writings of his students, such as Black sociologists Charles Johnson and E. Franklin Frazier, and into current debates on the African American "underclass." During the 1920s, the theories of Boas and Park were ignored by many scholars still committed to proving Nordic supremacy. In the South, the responses to the new paradigms were exceedingly hostile. For example, an article on "The Pathology of Prejudice" by African American sociologist and Morehouse College professor E. Franklin Frazier yielded death threats that forced him to flee Atlanta.[47]

The emergence of theories of ethnic assimilation, convergence, and equality marginalized but did not eliminate the plantation bloc theories, institutions and practices. For example, one of the central categories of the plantation bloc was the house slave. This class was considered superior to field slaves because the planter's civilizing influence had removed their natural inclination to disorder. This theory of class structure held that if the "low class," uncivilized, field slaves were left to themselves they would adopt chaos as an occupation. Therefore in the absence of direct White contact, contact with the more assimilated Black elements would eliminate threats to White domination by the "primitives."

This role model theory remains firmly implanted in popular, academic, and state discourse as do theories of the natural domination of Whites over Blacks, and of capital over labor. In research on African American communities, this perspective translates into the assumption that members of the Black middle class are the natural leaders of the Black working class. Consequently, the social-spatial isolation of the latter from Whites and from Black middle-class role models is said to cause behaviors reflective of an imagined return to a state of nature and "jungle" life. Modern authors working in this "underclass"/plantation sociological tradition, such as William Julius Wilson, Nicolas Lemann, and Charles Murray, then proceed to search for the cultural, psychological, Southern, African, or genetic genesis of African American degradation to support this proposition. What they are really expressing is their fear; a fear of the social vision and leadership of a centuries-hardened people. In his 1930 work *The Rural Negro*, historian Carter G. Woodson addressed this phenomenon in the course of a critique of the interracial cooperation movement:

> Interracial cooperation about which we hear so much signifies mainly the keeping of the Negroes satisfied with getting less than their share of the loaf, while the whites are being persuaded to be a little more lenient ... Sometimes one inquires as to what the enlightened Negroes are doing to direct attention to these things. The inevitable answer is that they are doing absolutely nothing in the open ... the intelligent Negroes in the South are more timid than the riffraff ... When cornered the Negro rough element will sometimes fight it out down to death, but under such circumstances the Christianized Negroes hold indignation meetings or take their troubles to God in prayer.[48]

Bessie Smith, the "Empress of the Blues," described the toughness of the "riffraff" and "rough elements", and her admiration for them, in her 1930 song "Black Mountain Blues":

> Back in Black Mountain, a child will smack your face. (2x)
> Babies cryin' for liquor, and all the birds sing bass.
> Black Mountain people are as bad as they can be. (2x)
> They uses gunpowder just to sweeten their tea.[49]

## The National Expansion of the Blues

> Oh, the Blues has got me on the go.
> They roll around my house, in and out my front door.
>                                                  Bessie Smith[50]

It has not occurred to the members of the neo-plantation school of social science that working-class Blacks have their own epistemology, their own theory of social change, and their own theories of class and ethnic depravity. The next section will focus upon this blues epistemology as the embodiment of African American daily life, social explanation, and social action.

In 1890, one out of ten African Americans in the United States lived in

Mississippi. Blacks were attracted to the region because of the high concentration of African Americans there, because of expanding production opportunities, and the economic ruination of other Southern regions, and because of the ethnic cleansing activities of whitecappers in the other parts of the state. Approximately, 60 percent of Mississippi's population was African American, 743,000 of a total of 1.3 million residents. One quarter of the state's African Americans lived in the Delta where they outnumbered Whites by seven to one. By 1910, Issaquena County was 94.1 percent Black, Tunica County was 90.6 percent, and Quitman County, at 76.5 percent, was the only one of the eighteen Delta counties where the African American population was below 80 percent. The Delta became both a refuge and a prison for African Americans. The monopolization of land and capital was accompanied by increasingly restrictive state laws governing debt and mobility. As voting essentially ceased, African Americans were locked out of local county and state politics. At every turn, the remnants of autonomy were destroyed as planters tried to extract more labor for less and less compensation.[51]

Often unrepaired for years, plantation housing consisted of shotgun and dogtrot cabins. Families of as many as fifteen members would crowd into the one- and two-room shacks. Clothes were often made out of sewn-together flour and feed sacks. Whenever possible, vegetables and milk were used to supplement the daily diet. However, planter restrictions on the creation and use of small garden plots and the tiny patches of land not dedicated to cotton production meant that families had to rely on the overpriced, poor-quality food furnished by the plantation commissary: salt pork, canned beans and peas, corn, and lard. As a consequence, high rates of infant mortality, pellagra, and rickets were common features of this regime. Blues musician Willie Foster recalled his own troubled birth near Leland in 1922:

> there wasn't no hospital for no black people then. You had to be *sick*. But just having a baby, you'd just holler down the street, "Tell Miss so-and-so to come here," ... my mother was picking cotton about 500 feet from the house. And the pain struck her [and] that's where I was born, on that cotton sack.[52]

Enforced illiteracy and miseducation were also hallmarks of the era. In 1880, Black illiteracy in the region was 75 percent compared to 17 percent for Whites. By 1890, the White schools had 53 pupils per teacher while Black schools had 103; biracial education was constitutionally banned. Because of the widespread use of child labor, schools were kept closed during the harvest season, from October to December, and were often closed again as early as February so that preparations for planting could begin.[53]

As discussed previously, African Americans believed land to be the cornerstone of African American economic, political, and social autonomy and development. However, hopes of building upon this foundation were crumbling in the face of increasing land concentration. Land ownership rates among African Americans were significantly lower in the states of Arkansas, Louisiana and Mississippi than they were in the Upper South. Although the number of farms owned by Blacks in these three states increased from 3,910 to 50,290 between 1870 and 1910, they were marginalized by cotton price fluctuations, small holdings, marginal lands, taxation, the denial of loans for improvements and production, multiple heirs, illegal evictions, and terrorism. As a percentage of total farm owners, Black farmers in the Delta declined from 7.3 percent in 1900 to 2.9 percent by 1925. In Tunica County, Black landowners outnumbered Whites three to one, yet they only owned 10 percent of the total acreage. The number of Black tenants also declined as planters began to rely on timber companies to cut and clear land.[54]

African Americans were also being marginalized in the region's towns. A rigid ethnic division of labor restricted the vast majority of African American workers to a few occupations within the White-run sectors and households. Yet urban and rural workers were able to support the growth of Black business districts organized around service provision: barbershops, grocery stores, bars, coffee houses, tailors, laundries, millinery shops, funeral parlors, etctera. While Black-owned and White-owned firms operating in these districts were generally small, some did provide Black owners and employees with a modicum of personal autonomy. However, Black businesses were not autonomous. In addition to being faced with the economic instability generally associated with small firms, they were also the victims of segregation when it came to location, expansion, community leadership, political participation, and access to capital and White patrons. A few Black firms were able to negotiate this highly charged environment and evolve into major institutions. On the other hand, Black business people accused of economic competition by their White counterparts faced being exiled, beaten, tarred and feathered, buried alive, etcetera.[55]

In response, African American mutual aid societies expanded their activities in the Mississippi Delta. The Knights of Pythias, the Knights and Daughters of Tabor, the Church of God in Christ, and other organizations provided burial, health care, and educational services. Black churches, and various Northern charities and foundations, funded the construction of high schools and colleges: Mary Holmes in 1892, Okolona in 1902, Utica Junior College in 1903, Mississippi Industrial in 1905, and the Prentiss Institute in 1907.

Mutual aid societies performed many of the functions of a state determined not to provide any public services or relief. Disenfranchisement protected the state from the demands of a Black electorate. Though Black "post-office" Republicans continued to receive patronage from the national government, 93 percent of the appointments made by Republican presidents went to White Democrats. In one famous incident, the African American postmistress of Indianola, Minnie Cox, was forced to resign because a Black holding such a position was considered "a menace to white civilization."[56]

Out of 147,000 potential African American voters, only 8,600, 5.8 percent, were registered by 1892. In the Delta of 1904, working-class Blacks could not vote while working-class Whites could. However, the poll tax kept 50 percent of the 120,000 White voters from registering. According to Isaiah Montgomery of Mound Bayou, middle-class Blacks could vote but, if their votes proved "troublesome later on," they were retroactively discarded. A consistent defender of the new regime, Montgomery considered the constitution of 1890 a good law that was simply administered poorly.[57]

Jim Crow, the institutionalization of censorship, and violence through the restoration of the antebellum Black Codes were designed to reinforce plantation bloc hegemony by restricting mobility, speech, and thought. The day-to-day life of the plantation bloc was organized around the perpetual monitoring of the behavior of Blacks *and* Whites. After 1900, African American domestics, professionals, and politicians were forced out of residences in White neighborhoods and were attacked if they were out of the Black districts after curfew. No recreational facilities or libraries were built in Black areas, and those located in White areas were for Whites only. Theaters had Black sections as did public transportation. In the Delta, Black drivers were even forbidden from overtaking White motorists.[58]

Wealth, home improvements, and ambition often had to be hidden. Servicemen in uniform were assaulted, whilst post office workers scratched the title Mr and Mrs from mail sent to Black residents. Threatened and actual beatings, death, disfigurement, and exile were heaped upon African Americans who objected to verbal insults. According to Richard Wright, the wide range of forbidden conversational topics led many Blacks to minimize social contacts with Whites. At an early age, Blacks had to learn which word and subjects were forbidden:

> American white women; the Ku Klux Klan; France and how the Negro soldier fared there; the entire northern part of the United States; the Civil War; Abraham Lincoln; U. S. Grant; General Sherman; Catholics; the Pope; Jews; the Republican Party; slavery; social equality; communism; socialism; the 13th, 14th, and 15th Amendments to the Constitution; or any topic calling for positive knowledge or manly self-assertion on the part of the Negro.[59]

While interracial love affairs between Black men and White women often resulted in either exile or death for the man, White men constructed a system whereby numerous Black women were forced into sexual relations with them through rape, economic coercion, physical threats, and murder. Delta bluesman Big Bill Broonzy recounted the following incident:

> one white boy down there was liking the same girl that this colored boy was liking, and he told this colored boy not to marry this colored girl because he wanted her hisself . . . So the [Black] boy . . . and the girl run off . . . got married and they come back . . . they went and killed his daddy and they killed her. Then they killed his mother and then one of his brothers, . . . they killed him . . . they killed twelve in that one family. That was in 1913. The boy was named Belcher . . . at a place called Langdale, Arkansas.[60]

According to the annual reports emanating from Tuskegee, between 1882 and 1927 Mississippi led the nation with 517 reported instances of African American lynchings. Approximately thirty reported lynchings occurred in the

Delta between 1880 and 1901. Yet, a brief review of the Black press of the period will immediately convince the reader that the above figures represent a massive undercount of the deaths caused by shootings, beatings, and other forms of individual, planter, mob, and official violence. One well-publicized event occurred in the aftermath of the 1904 murder of Sunflower County planter James Eastland, uncle of the future, famous segregationist US Senator James Eastland. The lynching of Luther Holbert and his wife took on a gruesome carnival atmosphere:

> While the funeral pyres were being prepared, they were forced to suffer the most fiendish torture. The blacks were forced to hold out their hands while one finger at a time was chopped off. The fingers were distributed as souvenirs. The ears of the murderers were cut off. Holbert was beaten severely, his skull was fractured, and one of his eyes, knocked with a stick, hung by a shred from the socket . . . The most excruciating form of punishment consisted in the use of a large corkscrew in the hands of some of the mob. The instrument was bored into the flesh of the man and woman, in the arms, legs, and body, and then pulled out, the spirals tearing out big pieces of raw, quivering flesh every time it was withdrawn.[61]

Many were forced into exile. In 1890, Ida B. Wells Barnett, a Memphis teacher and publisher, printed the first statistical record of lynchings in the South. Soon afterwards, a group of young men opened a grocery store in a Black Memphis neighborhood. The White merchant nearby charged them with the crime of competition and tried to close their store with the assistance of a mob. The armed Black merchants defended themselves and were subsequently lynched. In 1892, after Wells Barnett printed the names of those accused of the lynching, she was forced to flee the city permanently.

After relocating to Chicago, she led the Anti-Lynching Bureau of the National African-American Rights League, and in 1909 she became one of the founders of the National Association for the Advancement of Colored People (NAACP). The same types of atrocities, censorship, and daily exploitation drove many others out of the region. For example, the same incident that resulted in Wells Barnett's exile convinced several hundred Blacks, including the congregations of two churches, to leave Memphis for Oklahoma.[62]

Others chose the path of conciliation. There arose a wide-ranging institutional network based on an alliance between one section of African American leadership, Democratic state officials in the South, Northern Republican Party leaders, and Northern philanthropists. One of the African American leaders of this alliance was Isaiah Montgomery of Mound Bayou, who counseled activists that this "is the white man's country . . . let them run it."[63]

Development debates in the African American community were exhibiting signs of other fundamental schisms. One of the most enduring debates revolves around the question of regional identity. Although this issue is rarely addressed explicitly, distinct regional histories and realities have required distinct development agendas. Northern agendas often emphasize political advancement, employment opportunities, and human rights, whilst Southern agendas emphasize these elements plus resource ownership and control, cultural recognition, and the formation of cooperative and autonomous institutions.

Although growing rapidly, the newer Northern Black communities were typically confined to spatially minute portions of states and regions. For African Americans outside the South, the isolated urban "ghetto" was both the dominant spatial form and the overriding subject of discourse. The predominantly White suburbs became the measure of development while the predominantly White rural areas were often considered dangerous spaces that had to be transversed in order to reach another urban community or the South.

On the other hand, Southern Blacks could still touch the living legacy of an era when their defenders helped to establish their citizenship, secure their political leadership, and implement their development agenda. Consequently, the regional golden age of Reconstruction, its crucifixion, and resurrection became their civic religion and the rod used to measure the meaning of development and progress in the South. The landscape of this imagined community was populated by millions of African Americans physically linked across more than five hundred thousand square miles. The blues grew in importance as the cultural medium that both united the Southern African American working-class communities and continually reeducated the burgeoning Northern, Midwestern, and Western diasporas.

## Blues All Around

At its most fundamental level, the blues expansion was the full expression of the rise of an African American culture that was self-conscious of its space and time and, therefore, fully indigenous. The South was the space of origin, the African American hearth. It was the only place where the blues could be celebrated daily through a whole range of interactions with people and nature. They accompanied those who worked on the levees and roads, and in the forest, fields, and prisons. They surrounded them at home, in their neighborhoods and juke joints, and at picnics, churches and the other uncensored spaces where African Americans explored the parameters of their daily life, spirituality, and vision.[64]

The first phonograph records were created in 1897. This event, combined with the publication of blues scores by W. C. Handy in 1912, ensured that the blues were now accessible to the vaudeville, minstrel, and medicine show performers who traveled around the USA. By 1914 the first blues craze hit in the form of the recording of the songs of Handy and other Black and White songwriters. Typically the performers on these records were White minstrels who used degraded forms of Black speech. An example of this genre was "Nigger Blues," which was copyrighted by a White Dallas minstrel in 1913 and recorded by a White Washington, DC, lawyer in 1916. The first recordings of jazz in 1917 followed a similar pattern.[65]

The new and rapidly expanding recording industry extended the geographical range of the blues. Blues and jazz piano rolls were popular throughout the nation by 1916. In 1920, Mamie Smith sold more than 100,000 copies of her "Crazy Blues" on Okeh Records. Within a year, her success was duplicated by Ethel Waters, Bessie Smith and Ma Rainey. This burgeoning record industry became one of the principal communication mechanisms linking African American communities across the USA. According to Daphne Harrison:

> the largest record companies were selling up to five million copies of blues records per year, most of them to blacks, from 1920 through the 1930s. The recording industry may indeed have commercialized a folk art by standardizing format, cleaning up lyrics, and featuring women singers ... It is idle to argue whether they were closer to vaudeville blues or jazz singing than to authentic blues; what counts is that the audience for the recordings accepted and endorsed them as blues ... The blues singers' products were validated by their audiences, no mean feat given the role and behavior of black audiences. The performer was aware that her audience knew the music as well as she and would actively participate with singing, clapping, dancing and shouts of approval.[66]

Levine also argued in support of the proposition that commerce does not automatically translate into inauthenticity and irrelevancy:

> The Negro market not only existed, it was able to impose its own taste upon businessmen who ran the record companies and who understood the music they were recording imperfectly enough so they extended a great deal of freedom to the singers they were recording. Though blues became part of the commercial world of the entertainer and the record industry, they remained communal property and were vehicles for individual and group expression.[67]

Scholars such as Sherley Anne Williams and Hazel Carby assert that the women known as the "classic" blues singers of the 1920s solidified community values, heightened community morale, and constructed a national social space where reflection and analysis could occur. Recorded singers such as Ma Rainey, Bessie Smith, Clara Smith, Ida Cox, Alberta Hunter, Victoria Spivey, and Ethel Waters addressed many aspects of the chaotic relationships and gender-specific issues created by constant social upheaval, oppression, poverty, rural displacement, and the ideology of male supremacy. For Carby, the "language of the blues ... is the cultural terrain in which these differences were fought over and re-defined." Michelle Russell suggests that the blues should be understood as a pillar of democracy, as "the expression of a particular social process by which poor Black women have commented on all the major theoretical, practical, and political questions facing us and have created a mass audience who listens to what we say, in that form."[68]

Harrison's classic study of the blues queens of the 1920s catalogues the uses of the blues to examine social and personal conflicts such as alcoholism, drug addiction, abandonment, suicide, homelessness, etcetera. Harrison cites Sippie

Wallace's "Caldonia" as one of many songs where family and spousal abuse are discussed:

> You drink muddy water and you sleep in a hollow log. (2x)
> And you treat all your family just like a dog.[69]

For many, it was shocking to hear African American voices that proceeded from a non-Calvinist, non-Victorian view of social relations. It was equally shocking to hear working-class African American women discuss authoritatively the issues of the day. An example of this practice is Bessie Smith's popular Great Depression era song, "Poor Man's Blues":

> While you're living in your mansion, you don't know what hard times mean (2x)
> Poor working man's wife is starving; your wife is living like a queen.[70]

The establishment of an African American community of consciousness based on recorded blues and jazz was one of the most fundamentally significant and enduring mobilizations of this period. By the late 1920s, record companies were sending their agents to scour the Delta for performers who eventually dominated the market for recorded blues. Practitioners of the rural blues traditions were first recorded in 1923; among the most notable were the Texan Blind Lemon Jefferson in 1925 and the Floridian Arthur "Blind Blake" Phelps in 1926. Also recorded in 1926 by Chicago-based Okeh Records was the first performer who played in the Delta blues tradition, Freddie "Papa Freddie" Spruell. Observing the success of the smaller labels, major record companies such as Columbia, Vocalion, and Victor joined the search for new talent. By 1927, Memphis resident Jim Jackson had sold a million copies of his "Kansas City Blues."

The early recorded blues varied greatly in form; some styles were closer to minstrelsy while others were closer to jazz. However, the songs of many of those working in the Delta tradition were distinguishable by the rhythmic harshness of the beat, by the wincing guitar sounds produced by the knives and the sawn-off bottlenecks, slipped onto a finger and slid over the strings, and by the haunting screams and hollers of the vocalist. When compared to the Texas and Piedmont styles, the following descriptions are often applied to the Delta blues: "fragmentary lyrics," "narrow melodic range," "rudimentary vocal expression," "only slightly removed from speech patterns," "heavily rhythmic," "clamorous," "heavy," "harsh," "rough," "stark," "haunting," "eerie," "foreboding," and "frightening."[71]

The continual development of numerous blues families, teachers, schools, events and venues in the Delta meant that the blues was more of a community endeavor than just an individual occupation. For example, referred to by critics variously as the "Father of the Delta Blues," the "Voice of the Delta," and the "King of the Delta Blues," Charley Patton was actually a congregant, a member of a network of communities, artists, and apprentices.

Patton was born between 1881 and 1887 in the town of Bolton, near Jackson, and later lived on a plantation near Drew, Mississippi. He was at the center of an important group of musicians in and around Drew during the 1910s: Dick Bankston, Willie Brown, Josie Bush, Lucille Davis, Mattie Delaney, Jim Holloway, Lousie Johnson, Bertha Lee, Ben Maree, Jake Martin, Henry Sloan, and Mott Willis. While only a few members of this group went on to record, the younger members of this network went on to achieve much wider fame: Eddie "Son" House, Robert Johnson, Bukka White, Chester Burnett ("Howlin' Wolf"), Roebuck "Pop" Staples, etcetera.[72]

Patton's influence on the regional style is considered monumental for several reasons. First, he was a consummate entertainer who combined powerful lyrics, music, and performances. It would not be unusual to witness Patton throwing his guitar in the air, playing it behind his back, between his legs, and on his knees. Additionally, according to Palmer:

> Most of the rhythmic devices Patton uses have counterparts in West African drumming, and he uses them in an African manner, stacking rhythms on top of each other in order to build up a dense layered rhythmic complexity . . . Patton's command of vocal nuance is equally noteworthy . . . He stretches certain syllables and inserts split-second pauses between words in order to achieve a desired rhythmic effect . . . These vocal techniques, along with the ability to hear and execute microtonal pitch shadings, are basic attributes of superior Delta blues singing.[73]

Patton recorded fifty titles in four sessions between 1929 and 1934. Most examined the various aspects of daily life: incarceration, female–male relationships, traveling, floods, drought, sheriffs, a strike in Chicago, boll weevil infestation, and lovers' revenge. In his "Down the Dirt Road Blues," Patton captured the often-felt need of African Americans to escape the Delta:

> Everyday seems like murder here (my God I'm gonna sing 'em),
> Everyday seems like murder here,
> I'm gonna leave tomorrow, I know you don't bit more care.[74]

Clearly, Patton, Son House, and their many contemporaries in the Deltas of Mississippi, Arkansas, Louisiana, Missouri, and Tennessee were engaged in constructing a regional, and later national, African American community through a particular constellation of lyrical, musical and performance styles. Through blues realism they were also carving out a role for Delta blues performers as a collective which seriously contemplated the problems and inequities of the world around them. Their focus on humor, love, good times, religion, and nature allowed them to present a complete worldview to an audience whose boundaries were continually being widened through the wandering of the musicians, through mass migration, and through recordings.[75]

The insistent voices and music of these folk intellectuals could not be ignored by either Blacks or Whites. Therefore, this period also marked the beginning of a permanent national cultural crisis. The voices of the oppressed African Americans and their blues epistemology were now permanently linked to the new communication technologies. As this relationship broadened and deepened, it continually scraped the raw nerves of a nation forever worried about its identity, ethnicity, and morality, and about the true meaning of democracy.

Another social mobilization occurred within the sphere of religion. The line between blues and religion was never clear. Many performers, like Patton and his contemporary Eddie "Son" House, were preachers either before, during or after they were actively performing the blues. According to Booker Miller, a protégé of Patton, "The blues is kinda like workin' in church, I guess. Whatever the spirit say do, you do it." In Son House's 1930 recording "Preachin' the Blues," he speaks of the blues as a religion, a sermon, a spirit, a man, and a visitor:

> Oh, I'm gon' get me religion, I'm gon' join the Baptist Church (2x)
> I'm gon' be a Baptist preacher and I sure won't have to work.
> Oh, I'm gon' preach these blues now, and I want everybody to shout (2x)
> I'm gon' do like a prisoner, I'm gon' roll my time on out . . .
> Now I met the blues this morning' walkin just like a man (2x)
> I said good mornin' blues, now give me your right hand . . .
> Oh, I got to stay on the job, I ain't got no time to lose (2x)
> I swear to God I've got to preach these gospel blues.[76]

The blues-centered development ethic began to penetrate Christianity during this period. The African American Holiness, Pentecostal, or Sanctified movement erupted in Alabama, the Mississippi Delta and the Arkansas Delta in the 1890s: Reverend C. P. Jones founded the Church of Christ, Holiness USA in Selma, Alabama, in 1894; Reverend C. H. Mason founded the Church of God in Christ in the Mississippi Delta town of Lexington in 1895; and Reverend William Christian founded the Church of the Living God Christian Workers for Fellowship in 1899. Another feature of the proliferation of small independent Holiness churches was the reemergence of women as formal religious leaders. Washington suggests that although the Black Pentecostal movement was influenced by the White movement, they were qualitatively different:

> Remembering the spirituals, hearing blues and jazz on the streets, and being of the streets, . . . [the] sects brought into their religious services everything that was denied blacks in slavery or was denied by black independents [churches]: dancing, tambourine playing, hand clapping, and screaming, as well as the usual speaking in tongues, and prophesying adapted from whites. As blacks became more mobile they increased in number and variety the instruments used in these services, in keeping with the new ones used by blues and jazz men.[77]

Anthropologist and folklorist Zora Neal Hurston argued that the African American sanctified movement was a cultural movement designed to reassert the primacy of older African and African American working-class forms of expression:

> The sanctified church is a protest against the high-brow tendency in Negro Protestant congregations as the Negroes gain more education and wealth. It is understandable that they take on the religious attitudes of the white man which are as a rule so staid

and restrained that it seems unbearably dull to the more primitive Negro who associates the rhythm of sound and motion with religion. In fact, the Negro has not been Christianized as extensively as is generally believed. The great masses are still standing before their pagan altars and calling old gods by a new name.[78]

For Hurston, this cultural rebirth fundamentally transformed African American consciousness as it spread institutionally and geographically:

> So the congregation is restored to its primitive altars under the new name of Christ ... The whole movement of the sanctified church is a rebirth of song-making! ... These songs by their very beauty cross over from the little storefronts and the like occupied by the "Saints" to the larger and more fashionable congregations and from there to the great world ... The Saints, or the Sanctified Church is a revitalizing element in Negro music and religion. It is putting back into Negro religion those elements which were brought over from Africa and grafted onto christianity.[79]

After William Joseph Seymour left his Holiness church in Jackson, Mississippi, in 1905, he went on to lead the Azusa Street Revival in Los Angeles. This blues movement quickly spread to fifty nations and now influences an estimated 360 million Pentecostals worldwide.[80]

### "Maybe I've done sumthin a little bit wrong, Stayed in Miss'ippi just a day too long."[81]

The vast array of hardships present in the Delta led to many tormented decisions to leave. These sentiments were expressed in Bumble Bee Slim's song "If I Make It Over":

> Well, I'm blue and evil, so many things to learn,
> So many days to worry, so many ways to turn.
> I had so much trouble, swear my nerves is weakenin' down
> I would swing on a freight train, but I'm afraid to leave the ground.
> Whistle keeps on blowin' an I got my debts to pay,
> I've got a mind to leave my baby, Lord I've got a mind to stay.[82]

The Delta was a center of numerous types of migrations, both international and domestic. Delta residents were among the several thousand African Americans who settled in Liberia between 1890 and 1910 under the leadership of Bishop Henry McNeil Turner of the African Methodist Episcopal Church. The Universal Negro Improvement Association (UNIA) also advocated emigration to Africa. Led by Marcus Garvey, the organization had more than one million members in the United States by 1923. Garvey concluded that deteriorating economic conditions would lead to a movement among Whites to

> get rid of the Negro problem ... just as the North American Indian was exterminated. African Americans should respond by resettling in Africa while the world is reorganizing itself, while political boundaries are being adjusted ... and establish some political stronghold of your own ... Fellows like Du Bois will not think of the

future, because they can get all they want ... But you, the common people, who
have nowhere to go, who have to struggle for your daily existence ... you should see
this danger that confronts us.[83]

UNIA membership grew in proportion to the increase in Ku Klux Klan
attacks. By the early 1920s it had established several chapters in the Deltas of
Arkansas and Mississippi. Although the UNIA had many external critics, its
refusal officially to challenge the Ku Klux Klan sparked internal disputes. At
the 1923 convention, some delegates took the position that Blacks should do
nothing to "antagonize" the Ku Klux Klan while others objected, saying it was
"cowardly to acquiesce in the intolerance the Klan exhibited."[84]

Another stream of migrants headed north. The migrants brought many
things with them to the North including their own form of criticism. They
immediately challenged Northern social theories and social practices in often
unexpected ways. For example, in 1893 a partially blues-influenced musical
form, ragtime, battled plantation architectural traditions on the streets of
Chicago. The plantation's representative was "White City", built specifically
for the World's Columbian Exposition in Chicago:

> Officially American city planning places its date of birth from 1893, for if once it had
> been claimed that all roads led to Rome, now it would be said that all city plans
> stemmed from the dreams of that Great White City in Chicago ... it would stand as
> a promise and pledge that the fullness of the human spirit could come to fruition in
> this new art of city making ... [It] was the expression of this spirit; symbolizing
> purity and light, it stood as the climatic expression of a more trustful unity and a
> forecaster of the beginnings of a planned civilization of cities, of the hope of a more
> noble existence.[85]

A plaza surrounded by monumental government buildings, the "Great White
City" was designed to symbolize the creation of the new American empire
based on the architectural, class, and ethnic principles of the Roman and
Greek empires. These ancient hierarchies were also the intellectual role
models for the Southern plantation regime. The architects commissioned to
design this series of pillared civic buildings were to provide classical models to
their profession that would subordinate the "national tendency to experiments
in design." Instead of marbled White unity and purity, the nation's elite
received Black "Rags." Visitors shunned White City in order to patronize the
saloons where famed Black ragtime pianists held forth.[86] In *Ragtime: A
Musical and Cultural History*, Edward Berlin argues that the great cultural
phenomenon unveiled at the 1893 Chicago World's Fair was not White City,
but ragtime which subverted the classical aspirations of the American elite, an
event that has been repeated generationally:

> Many of the nation's cultural leaders looked on with horror as Ragtime, the first
> recipient of the new musical technology, engulfed the nation. They had envisioned
> the country's musical life "maturing" along the supposedly well-ordered lines of
> European musical academicism. Instead they witnessed the intrusion of a music that
> stemmed not from Europe but from Africa, a music that represented to them not the

civilization and spiritual nobility of European art but its very anti-thesis—the sensual depravity of African savagery, embodied in the despised American Negro.[87]

As a result of the wartime labor shortages between 1915 and 1920, more than 100,000 Blacks left Mississippi for factory and domestic work in Memphis, St Louis, Detroit, and Chicago. As a service to manufacturers along their line, free passage was often provided by the Illinois Central Railroad. Approximately, 560 miles to the north, Chicago rapidly emerged as a Delta blues center. Barlow identified several reasons for this:

> First, the city was a key refuge for black migrants, especially from the densely populated Mississippi Delta ... Second, the city was also an underworld stronghold with well-entrenched mobster operations organized along ethnic lines, and a sizable red-light district ... And third, the city was surpassed only by New York as a center for show business during the first decades of the twentieth century.[88]

There were other reasons why Chicago was attractive. Voting, employment, educational, and health opportunities were available here that were non-existent in the South. Additionally, distributed throughout the South, the *Chicago Defender*, the largest African American newspaper in the country, systematically encouraged migration by showcasing the city's advantages. While the Black population rose from 15,000 in 1890 to 50,000 by 1915, job opportunities during World War One helped to expand the population to 109,000 by 1920. Chicago was also the second-largest recording center in the country. Okeh, Paramount, and Brunswick/Vocalion were successful in selling a variety of blues and jazz styles during the 1920s and 1930s. African Americans nationwide had quickly purchased phonographs and they were being regularly supplied with new records sold by the Pullman porters. Soon musicians from throughout the South were visiting and settling in Chicago.[89]

By the late 1920s, Chicago blues were dominated by pianists from Chicago and a variety of Southern states, such as Thomas Dorsey, Clarence Lofton, Charles Davenport, Jimmy Yancey and boogie woogie pianists Clarence "Pinetop" Smith, Albert Ammons, and Meade Lux Lewis. The pianists found plenty of work in the thousands of bars, clubs, and juke joints in the city. Additionally, record companies favored piano and guitar duets and Hokum bands. Chicago was the center of Hokum music, in Barlow's phrase a "happy-go-lucky" musical style closer to the Black minstrel and vaudeville tradition than it was to the raw Delta blues. Among the guitarists favored for duets were Tampa Red and Big Bill Broonzy.[90]

One of twenty-one children, William Lee Conley (Big Bill Broonzy) was born near Mound Bayou in 1893. He started working in the fields with his family in the Arkansas Delta at seven, and by ten his uncle had begun to teach him how to play a one-string fiddle made out of a cigar box. Broonzy sang in several bands, preached the gospel, worked as a coal miner, and served in the army during World War One before returning to Arkansas. As soon as he got off the train, a White town resident told him to "get you some overalls because there's no nigger gonna walk around here with no Uncle Sam's uniform." His refusal to readjust caused him to both leave for Chicago in 1920 and to write the following song:

> I ain gon raise no mo cotton
> I declare I ain gon raise no mo corn.
> Gal, if a mule started runnin away with the world,
> Oh, lawd, I' gon let him go ahead on.[91]

During the day, Broonzy worked at the Pullman company and at night he played at rent parties where he encountered and learned from legendary blues veterans such as Sleepy John Estes, Blind Lemon Jefferson, and Papa Charlie Jackson. Barlow describes Broonzy as the archetypical Chicago bluesman from the late 1920s until the rise of Howlin' Wolf and Muddy Waters after World War Two. He was also considered extremely influential because he overtly criticized the plantation epistemology in his lyrics. A good example of his approach was the 1928 song "When Will I Get to be Called a Man":

> When I was born in this world, this was what happened to me,
> I was never called a man and now I'm fifty-three.
> I wonder when will I be called a man,
> Or do I have to wait until I get ninety-three?[92]

Jazz can also be considered a blues-based movement if we examine the people who gave it birth, its blues elements, and the role it has played for successive generations. According to several scholars, jazz developed around the turn of the century, after the blues had already reached a mature stage. Many of the musicians credited with founding the jazz movement were already thoroughly grounded in the various blues traditions that surrounded New Orleans. Buddy Bolden is generally considered to be the founder of this new integration of blues and rags. He often could be found entertaining the young and old at parks and, by 1906, at a dance hall renamed after his theme song, a blues called "Funky Butt." Other key New Orleans-based founders of jazz included King Oliver, Sidney Bechet, Johnny Dodds, Jelly Roll Morton and Louis Armstrong. As they moved upriver to Chicago and other points north during the 1920s this group backed many of the classic blues singers: Ma Rainey, Bessie Smith, Mamie Smith, Alberta Hunter, and Clara Smith. Additionally, performers such as Fletcher Henderson (a former member of the W. P. Handy Band), James P. Johnson, and Coleman Hawkins ensured that the blues would remain a central touchstone in jazz composition and performance.[93]

During the 1920s, the blues epistemology increasingly became a key component of African American literary and performing arts. It flowed through the poetry of Sterling Brown and Langston Hughes, and through Jean Toomer's landmark novel *Cane*. Blues-related music and dance emerged in numerous musical comedies, films, and cartoons, in symphonic and classical music, and in the "new" phenomenon known as "social dancing." A constant flow of new, often African inspired, dance "crazes" gripped Whites across the nation, particularly in the North. Some of these dances involved "scandalously" close contact between female and male partners, others demanded a great deal of physical exertion, and yet others required improvised, free-style movements that expressed the emotions of the performer. Also known as the Jazz Age, this period was marked by the emergence among Whites of a new physically unbound female icon, the blues- and jazz-addicted "flapper." The blues reached Broadway in all-Black cast productions such as *Shuffle Along* in 1921, *Blackbirds* in 1928, and *Hot Chocolate* in 1929. Blues-based musicals written by Whites soon followed: Jerome Kern's *Showboat* in 1928, George and Ira Gershwin's *Porgy and Bess* in 1934; and the influence of the blues was evident in the works of Irving Berlin, Oscar Hammerstein, Lorenz Hart, Cole Porter, and Richard Rogers. This process was duly noted by Langston Hughes in *Notes on Commercial Theater*:

> You've taken my blues and gone / You sing 'em on Broadway
> And you sing 'em in Hollywood Bowl, / And you mixed 'em up with symphonies
> And you fixed 'em / So they don't sound like me.
> Yep, you done taken my blues and gone.[94]

The growing popularity of blues, jazz, and minstrelsy among Northern Whites during the 1920s represented both the acceptance and the degradation of African American culture. At one level, this movement represented a broad expansion of the use of Black music to protest rigid social conventions, to heal the emotional and psychological traumas associated with the machine age, and to create a new cultural sphere by redefining the national identity. This acceptance did not imply the coming of social equality; in fact it was a period of the national expansion of the Ku Klux Klan and mob-led attacks on Black communities. Conversely, within the African American community, the blues stood as a philosophical arsenal, always ready, willing, and able to provide strategies for overcoming the tragedy of daily life, a form of resolve without which the more obvious social movements would have become impossible.[95]

## High Water Everywhere

The plantation powers faced numerous crises by the mid-1920s. First, beginning in 1907 the boll weevil infestation resulted in large crop losses even though the Delta's fertility meant that the degree of devastation was less than that felt by other regions. Second, although the timber boom of 1900 had catapulted state lumber production to third in the nation and for a time, the industry employed thousands, it had rapidly declined after the virgin forests were cut over. Third, after the World War One high price of 85 cents per pound, the price of cotton crashed three times before bottoming out at 10 cents per pound in 1931. As banks foreclosed on planters and tenants, sharecropping became the last resort for the unemployed of all ethnic groups.

Two other events dramatically deepened the conflict between the plantation bloc and the blues bloc: the Elaine Massacre of 1919 and the Mississippi River flood of 1927. The historic development agenda of working-class African Americans emerged again in 1919 in the Arkansas Delta town of Elaine. African American tenants in Phillips County had recently formed the Progressive Farmers and Household Union (PFHU). This secret fraternal order had among its many goals raising funds to hire a lawyer to represent members in rent, share, and wage disputes. According to PFHU members, the sheriff, several deputies, and several other Whites raided their meeting at a church and opened fire. After the smoke had cleared, one White person was dead and another was wounded. What occurred next is known as the Elaine Massacre:

> The white bush telegraph delivered the news throughout the region within hours. Armed whites gathered from other parts of Arkansas as well as from the neighboring states of Tennessee and Mississippi. Many blacks were simply hunted down in the canebrakes, but there was apparently some resistance. The official figures cited 5 white dead and 25 black. Walter F. White, of the National Association for the Advancement of Colored People, who made an on-site investigation, estimated that as many as 100 blacks had been killed. The courts held speedy trials shortly thereafter and sentenced 12 blacks to die and 80 to prison terms.[96]

The Elaine Massacre was a watershed event. It confirmed the belief of many Blacks that the Alluvial Empire and the entire plantation system had to be immediately dismantled. This attack, along with those that occurred after World War One during the Red Summer of 1919, radicalized an entire generation. Yet reports of outrages continued to pour out of the Delta.

The biblical Mississippi River flood of 1927 is generally considered to be the greatest of all floods in the United States. It rained almost continuously in the Delta from the summer of 1926 to April 1927. On 21 April, a wall of water 20 feet high demolished the new levees built near Greenville. The rushing waters created a lake 75 miles long and 100 miles wide. Then, during the first week of May, tornadoes and earthquakes pounded the region. Water completely covered the land until August. Several African Americans died immediately and more than 400,000 were placed in the 154 Red Cross camps established in Arkansas, Louisiana, and Mississippi, 18 of them in the Mississippi Delta. Whites were escorted to camps in the hills while 142,000 Blacks were held in squalid Delta encampments at gunpoint by the Mississippi National Guard. White mobs attacked Blacks trying either to reach safe ground in the Hills or to leave the region. The mass imprisonment and drownings associated with the flood were immortalized by Charley Patton in his nationally popular 1929 songs "High Water Everywhere" and "High Water Everywhere, Part Two":

> The whole round country, Lord, river has overflowed
> Lord, the whole round country, man, is overflowed
> I would go to the hill country, but they got be barred.
> . . . So high the water risin', I been sinkin' down
> Then the water was risin', at places all around
> It were fifty men an chillun, come sink and drown.[97]

In the Red Cross camps, Blacks were not allowed to leave or to talk to outsiders without the permission of the soldiers. Refugees were taken at gunpoint out of the camps to shore up the remaining levees. Richard Wright described such a scene in "Down by the Riverside":

> As they neared the levee Mann could see long, black lines of men weaving snake-fashion ... The levee was a ridge of dry land between two stretches of black water ... At the water's edge men unloaded boats; behind them stood soldiers with rifles ... Suddenly a wild commotion broke out. A siren screamed. On the levee-top the long lines of men merged into one whirling black mass. Shouts rose in a mighty roar ... Lawd! thought Mann. The levee's gone![98]

When Walter White, the president of the NAACP, came to the region to investigate, he discovered that free Red Cross supplies such as food, clothing, seeds, and other supplies were going directly to displaced Whites and planters. They were then sold to penniless Blacks to create new debts. Denied cots and dressed in rags, many African Americans lived in muddy camps in full sight of boxcars filled with clothes. The *Chicago Defender* accused the flood relief director, leading Delta planter Leroy Percy, of denying aid to families headed by women. It also claimed that "waste was dumped in the Negro section of Greenville and that the dead bodies of Negroes were slit, loaded with sand, and sunk in the river."[99]

Percy explained the logic behind the mass imprisonment in the midst of disasters. "If we depopulate the Delta of its labor we should be doing it a grave disservice." In other words, the planters were primarily concerned with preventing other planters and Northern labor agents from recruiting their tenants. These practices shocked the entire nation and went a long way in delegitimizing the carefully constructed image of the plantation regime. According to Daniel:

> Though complaints of peonage had spurred the investigation, the conditions in the flood area suggested a way of life not very different from slavery days. The flood emergency had simply washed the system into the open ... The tragedy of the policed concentration camps was not so much the willingness of the National Guard to prevent movement or even of the planters to demand closed camps, but that almost all white Mississippians had become so accustomed to controlling black labor by force that such prescriptions seemed appropriate and necessary.[100]

An intense sense of outrage swelled up within the national African American community. Based on genuine concern and on a fear of mass outmigration and the rise of radical leaders, in May, the president of Tuskegee Institute, Robert R. Moton, sent an investigator who confirmed the worst. Moton then contacted his fellow Republican Herbert Hoover. Soon to be the President of the United States, Hoover was then serving as the Secretary of Commerce and was in charge of national relief efforts. At Moton's behest, Hoover ordered the creation of the federal Colored Advisory Commission in order to inquire into the "proper treatment of the colored folks in the concentration camps." One of the commission members, the poet Langston Hughes, was shocked at what he saw in the camps: "Some were surrounded by National Guardsmen. Negroes were not allowed outside the gates without the permission of their landlords who were waiting for the water to subside so they could force these refugees back into semi-slavery."[101]

After the commission's initial investigation, the US Attorney General, the National Guard, the Red Cross, and the Federal Bureau of Investigation all denied that the widely reported conditions existed. In August, Moton and the Urban League's journal *Opportunity* praised the work of the Red Cross. Yet, reports of great suffering and of planters obtaining free Red Cross supplies and selling them to sharecroppers continued to filter out. Moton suggested that maybe the residents of the Mississippi Delta should be colonized in Alabama to prevent them from leaving the South. Even as economic and human rights conditions in the Delta deteriorated, the plight of the flood victims disappeared from public view as the Tuskegee machine turned its attention to gaining African American support for the Republican Party's presidential candidate, Herbert Hoover. By 1931, Langston Hughes captured in verse the persecution and abandonment of impoverished African Americans:

> That justice is a blind goddess
> Is a thing to which we poor are wise:
> her bandage hides two festering sores
> That once, perhaps, were eyes.[102]

# 6

# The Enclosure Movement

Devastated by the historic flood of 1927 and by a deep agricultural crisis, the Mississippi Delta fell into chaos. The planter bloc responded to this crisis by organizing two bodies for regional and sectoral domination: the Delta Council in 1935, and the National Cotton Council in 1938. The federal government's response was to intervene massively to restore plantation profitability. African American communities were also mobilizing to challenge once again the plantation regime.

## Revolution and Enclosure

The Delta enclosure movement decimated the region's democratic constituency just as the African American return to electoral activity was on the horizon. It also guaranteed the derailment of movements for land and resource redistribution while preserving the White supremacy alliance. As with the Choctaw removal, efforts were made to limit the historical vision of African Americans; the rights obtained earlier were now deemed revolutionary, while the violence of mass eviction and the total monopolization of resources were depicted as the inevitable march of progress.

First, after the Mississippi flood of 1927, Congress appropriated the unprecedented amount of $325 million for flood control in the Lower Mississippi Valley. Planters benefited immensely from the rapid rise in land values, from the opening of new lands, and from activities associated with levee building and river channelization. The second federal intervention also operated to preserve and reproduce planter power in the face of a severe cotton overproduction crisis. Although cotton acreage grew to meet increased demand during World War One, it continued to grow as foreign and domestic demand fell after the war: it was 28.6 million acres in 1921, 44.6 million acres in 1926, and 40.8 million acres in 1933. Both the cotton price and farm values declined by 50 percent between 1919 and 1933—the per pound price of cotton fell below five cents. The result was a national financial and manufacturing crisis: Northern financial and manufacturing sectors were so heavily dependent upon cotton profitability that the basic outlines of their response to the crisis, the

Agricultural Adjustment Act (AAA), was submitted to and accepted by
Franklin Roosevelt prior to his election as president in 1932.[1]

Termed by Pete Daniel and other scholars the Southern Enclosure, the plan
was designed to rescue Northern financiers heavily invested in plantation and
farm ownership:

> the pattern of land ownership had changed dramatically by the turn of the century,
> and concentration continued thereafter. Many farmers who expanded acreage and
> secured loans during World War I could not pay off their loans; their creditors
> foreclosed ... [It was estimated] that life insurance companies and banks owned 30
> percent of all southern cotton land in 1934.[2]

The first AAA was enacted early in 1933 based on the following rationale:

> That the present acute economic emergency being in part the consequence of a
> severe and increasing disparity between the prices of agricultural and other commod-
> ities, which disparity has largely destroyed the purchasing power of farmers for
> industrial products, has broken down the orderly exchange of commodities, and has
> seriously impaired the agricultural assets supporting the national credit structure.[3]

On 19 June 1933, the Roosevelt administration announced a program that
would pay landowners cash to plow up 30 percent of the cotton acres already
planted: approximately 10 million acres or 3 million bales. Planters received
enormous subsidies for reducing acreage, and payments were structured to
allow maximum flexibility.[4]

Extension agents often gave the few payments addressed to sharecroppers
directly to the planters as profiteering and usury were encouraged by official
action and inaction. Those who were forced to buy their necessities from the
plantation commissary saw already inflated prices rise to new heights, as much
as 50 percent above normal area retail prices. In some cases, the interest on
cash advances to sharecroppers was calculated at 25 percent per day. Finally,
the rapid increase in federal relief payments and commodity distribution
programs allowed planters gradually to dismantle the furnishing system and
end their responsibility for the survival and reproduction of African American
labor. Yet, planter control over these programs allowed them to decide who
ate and who starved, who was poorly housed and who was homeless, and who
lived and who died.

The scion of one of the oldest and most powerful planter families William
Alexander Percy, future Delta Council president, complained about federal
relief practices to Roosevelt's AAA finance director and Delta planter
Oscar Johnston: "such dishonesty is widespread and disruptive of interracial relations, disintegrating to the planters, and conducive to making
the tenants distrust and even hate the white man." Johnston responded that
even though "such practices were the rule rather than exception," he would
reject any effort to legislate against it "as long as man is made in his present
image."[5]

Operating within and outside the New Deal regime, liberal rural reformers often joined the propertyless in their condemnation of existing conditions and in calls for land reform. A 1934 report issued by the federal Mississippi Valley Committee described the typical Delta sharecropper as "an object of pity, and too often contempt. He is the victim of a system no less bad in many ways than slavery." Yet, for all their good intentions, the liberal reformers within the Resettlement Administration and the Farm Security Administration (FSA) had the luxury of underestimating the power and dedication of the Southern plantation bloc and its ally Roosevelt.[6] Planters and their political allies were able successfully to attack and deform rural programs initiated by the liberal faction. Roosevelt signed the Agricultural Adjustment Act on the same day he signed the Emergency Relief Act of 1933. By 1934, director Harry Hopkins reorganized all rural relief programs within his Federal Emergency Relief Agency (FERA) into a single bureau, the Division of Rural Rehabilitation and Stranded Populations. In 1935, this division was moved to the Resettlement Administration headed by Rexford Tugwell, only to be moved to the Farm Security Administration (FSA) in 1937. The FSA provided loans and technical information to help tenants and sharecroppers purchase farms. Many of the projects in the Delta, such as the 106-unit 9,300-acre Mileston Farms project in Holmes County, had a lasting influence upon the supporters of land reform and participatory democracy. Yet the federal government, instead of developing a systematic program for land reform, created a confusing array of loan programs, cooperatives, collectives, and colonies, paraded them around, and removed them like so many musical chairs.[7] According to Daniel, by the mid 1930s it had become painfully obvious even to the federal rural reformers that the AAA movement was plowing under the experimental resettlement programs in the process of creating the foundations for the neo-plantation complex:

> The significance of increasing land concentration lay as much in the changing organization as in size. As the report noted, "if these changes mean that the typical plantation is eventually going to be highly commercialized with all the workers reduced to the lowest possible economic position of wage laborers, the continuance, let alone the increase in the number and size of plantations, is in direct conflict with the stated policy of the department [US Department of Agriculture] in achieving for all those engaged in agriculture a reasonable level of living" ... The report predicted ... local economies would be disrupted, small towns would disappear, and social stratification and unrest would increase.[8]

From beginning to end, the AAA was a planter-dominated affair. A central figure in the entire episode, and one of the principal architects of New Deal cotton policies, was Delta attorney and banker Oscar Johnston, also known as "Mr US Cotton." His prominence in the Delta and in international cotton circles derived from his management of the world's largest cotton plantation. Owned by British textile manufacturers and centered in Scott, Mississippi, the 40,000-acre Delta and Pine Land Company (D&PL) stretched across Bolivar and Washington counties. Early in 1933, Johnston joined the AAA to handle the sale of 2.4 million bales of surplus cotton. He then served as vice president of the federal Commodity Credit Corporation (CCC) and as the AAA director of finance for five years. He went on to become the manager of the Cotton Producers Pool, CCC envoy to Latin America and Europe, director and vice president of the Delta Council, and the founder, and long-time president, of the National Cotton Council. Throughout the entire period of his federal employment, Johnston continued to serve as the principal manager of the D&PL even though the plantation received over $100,000 in federal production control payments in 1935 alone. Johnston stood at the center of political and policy debates over cotton, the Delta, the South, the national economy, and African Americans. Rather than being a great individual achievement, his career defines the neo-plantation core that was the heart of the New Deal, Fordism, and the welfare state.[9]

The third planter mobilization involved the creation of the Delta Council in 1935. Through a multitude of highly coordinated policy and planning activities, this organization has effectively dominated the region for the last sixty years. Prior to the Depression, planters in the Delta were highly organized, but labor shortages and conflicts, flood control, infrastructure development, and the political, economic, and cultural suppression of the African American majority necessitated numerous agreements between the planters and between them and their allies, White and Black. The first inklings of what in 1935 would become the Delta Chamber of Commerce emerged soon after the flood of 1927. The name was changed to Delta Council in 1938 because it was felt that President Roosevelt viewed chambers of commerce as "a stiff collar organization for the rich man" and he being "a friend of the common man" preferred the more democratic sound of the word "council." The change in name did not change the fact that the organization was created and dominated by planters, cottonseed mill owners, and bankers.[10]

Originally, the council's two dozen directors were elected by the body's eighteen county units. Several committees were established to ensure effective regional planning and coordination: agricultural development, finance, executive affairs, flood control, livestock, health, forestry, research, education, transportation, taxation, farm policy, industry, labor, and race relations. Through its economic, political, and policy monopoly, the Delta Council was able effectively to dominate local and county governments. The federal government was also targeted. Immediately after the Delta Council's formation, it attempted to lobby Congress and the Roosevelt Administration on issues of concern such as lower tariffs, increasing cotton research funds, and flood control. In fact, municipal councils, county supervisorial boards, levee boards, and the regional branches of state and federal agencies, such as the United States Department of Agriculture (USDA), and the Army Corp of Engineers were all considered adjuncts of the council. Representations of each received honorary memberships and were expected to contribute funds. Additional contributions came from local utilities, while newspapers and radio stations donated space and time. The headquarters of the organization was, and still is, located in the Stoneville, Mississippi, administration building of the USDA's Delta Branch Experiment Station.[11]

The fourth mobilization of Delta planters during this period was designed to attain sectoral unity through the formation of the National Cotton Council, "the voice of the farflung cotton empire." This powerful Memphis-based industrial coordinating council rapidly extended its influence throughout the South, the Southwest, nationally, and then worldwide. It also formed the backbone of the modern Sunbelt economic and political alliance. Additionally, the National Cotton Council proved a powerful and unrelenting foe to all civil rights, labor, and social reforms in addition to becoming one of the most powerful post-World War Two economic organizations in the world. In a speech to the Delta Council, Oscar Johnston, then president of the National Cotton Council, heralded the birth of this new bloc in the following manner:

> one year ago this month . . . the Delta Council sponsored a movement, the outcome of which resounded around the entire world . . . Following an address by Assistant Secretary of State Francis B. Sayre, a meeting was held at which it was decided there should be a National Cotton Council, [and] *that the activities of the Delta Council should be spread throughout the belt, from Virginia on the Atlantic to California on the Pacific.*[12]

Two Delta planters and Delta Council leaders, Oscar Johnston and W. T. Wynn, formed the NCC in the Fall of 1938 in Wynn's living room. At the behest of Wynn, Johnston served as its president from 1938 to 1947, as chairman of the board from 1938 to 1952, and as honorary chairman of the board from 1953 to 1955. Wynn served as treasurer from 1938 to 1954, president during 1955, and as chairman of the board in 1956. The NCC formally began its operations in the offices of the Delta Council and initially relied completely upon its staff. For example, the Delta Council's executive vice president, Rhea Blake, went on to serve as the NCC's secretary and executive vice president from 1938 to 1969.[13]

The entire Delta complex was involved in the NCC movement, from the planters in Mississippi to the Cotton Exchange and warehouses in Memphis to the cotton shippers in New Orleans. The organization was first introduced during the Delta Council's annual meeting in June 1938. In the same year, the NCC Committee on Organization met at the Peabody Hotel in Memphis. The five segments of the industry were formally represented: producers, ginners, warehousemen, merchants, and cottonseed crushers; textile mill owners joined later. Fourteen state units were also in attendance: Alabama–Florida, Arizona, Arkansas, California–Nevada, Georgia, Louisiana, Mississippi, Missouri–Illinois, New Mexico, North Carolina–Virginia, Oklahoma, South Carolina, Tennessee–Kentucky and Texas.[14]

Johnston's strategy was to unite the often hostile state and sectoral fragments through an organization which served as both a regional and an industry advocate. The NCC would work to increase demand, to expand and coordinate promotional and advertising activities, and to secure foundation and government funds for research on crops, products, markets, and new technologies. In addition to preserving and reinforcing draconian ethnic and labor regulations, the NCC is credited with speeding mechanization, improving ginning standards, reducing fire losses, increasing cottonseed margarine consumption, lowering tariffs on the manufactured goods of major cotton importers, and encouraging cotton's use in high fashion. Also developed was a national cleanliness campaign designed to encourage more laundering, more changes of attire, the purchase of more clothes, and, therefore, the purchase of more cotton. Although it claimed to be apolitical, officers of the NCC stated that the organization would attempt to "set Southern opinion in motion in support of those [cotton industry] principles."[15]

This enormous movement was able to exert substantial power over the cotton sector and over social reform policies in the South. For example, the FSA established 10,000 cooperatives nationwide, 3,500 in the South, for the joint purchase and use of agricultural machinery by small farmers. In 1943, after the NCC and the Farm Bureau requested members to report rumors of mismanagement by this "un-American collectivist agency," the planters and large farmers represented by these two bodies successfully proposed legislation for the break-up of the FSA's farmworker housing, loan, and cooperative programs.[16]

The general thrust of the flood control, the AAA, the Delta Council, and the NCC mobilizations was to restore profitability to cotton production while preserving plantation bloc dominance. This was accomplished through the formation of six new alliances or blocs: a new interregional alliance (North–South) between the planters, Northern finance capital, and the federal state under the blanket of the AAA; an intra-regional (Mississippi Delta) bloc centered around the Delta Council; a multi-state bloc composed of the Delta Council and allied organizations in the Delta areas of Arkansas, Louisiana, Missouri, and Tennessee; a Southern cotton bloc centered around the NCC; an interregional bloc, South and Southwest, coordinated by the NCC; and an intra-sectoral alliance of cotton textile manufactures, cotton producers, financiers, importers and exporters under the tent of the NCC that stretched around the world.[17]

The Delta planters were not simply victims of the new global division of labor emerging from the Depression-era crisis. Through several mobilizations planters were able to impose large sections of their agenda upon the Mississippi Delta, surrounding states, the South, the nation, and the world. Their opponents within federal and state governments, and within the African American and labor movements, were simply unprepared for a resurgent planter intervention.

## Daily Destruction

The enclosure movement in the Delta was not, as some have argued, based on the transition of feudalism into capitalism; rather, it marked the movement from capital-scarce, labor-intensive plantation production to capital-intensive, labor-surplus neo-plantation production. In the process, millions fled the South in horror, and thousands of African American communities were destroyed seemingly overnight.

The Southern Enclosure marked the end of African American population growth and the beginnings of a new mass migration out of the region. By 1930, there were 1.5 million African Americans in twelve Northeastern states, 1.1 million in eight Midwestern states, and 1,010,000 in Mississippi alone. By 1950, the African American percentage of Mississippi's population fell below 50 percent for the first time since the mid-1800s: 986,000 persons of a total state population of 2,178,000 persons. Between 1930 and 1950, the Delta's population fell from 619,000 to 609,000 persons and the African American population declined from 440,000 to 409,000. However, these raw numbers mask the eviction of one-third of the sharecropping families and their sub-sequent movement from plantation communities into the hamlets, towns and cities of the Delta. For example, between 1940 and 1950 the Delta's rural farm population declined dramatically, from 316,000 to 257,000 persons.[18]

How did this social destruction occur? First, the federally funded enclosure led to the removal of less fertile and marginal lands from production. It also led to the eviction of sharecroppers and tenants from the most fertile lands which were then cultivated using machines and chemicals. Once the relationship between eviction (enclosure) and yields was established, additional evictions generated more funds for equipment purchases and then even higher yields, and even more evictions. This process has been referred to as being "tractored" off the land. The problem of obtaining high yield *and* high-quality cotton awaited the genetic engineering of varieties specifically adaptable to a new generation of yet undeveloped mechanical cotton pickers, defoliants, and ginning equipment.[19]

Economic activities in the South were diversified based on the introduction of new crops and on new sectors such as dairying and manufacturing. In the Delta, the last premier cotton region in the South, diversification occurred much more slowly. The Delta plantation bloc was generally hostile to manu-facturing because it feared competition: labor shortages, rising wages, and the political and social challenges generated by unionization. The establishment of value-added industries such as textiles and food processing was resisted until near the end of World War Two. The Delta Council's view of manufac-turing shifted after the organization's leaders became worried that without stable jobs providing an income capable of supporting a family, returning White veterans would leave the region and the African American majority would increase again.[20]

Labor relations were marked by the institutionalization of new forms of economic and physical terror that were specifically designed to drive African Americans either materially downward or physically out of the region: share-croppers and tenants were evicted; cabins were burned and plowed under; and entire plantation-based communities were leveled. Those evicted expanded the pool of available wage labor and increased the downward pressure on wages in the region. Between 1930 and 1940, the number of tenants in the region declined by 62 percent. The day laborers who worked for wages were part of the growing number of homeless families created by the AAA. As their plantation houses were destroyed, many moved to the small towns and cities. Large sections of the region's residents became dependent upon the Works Progress Administration (WPA) for employment, relief payments, and food. This agency also served the needs of the planters who required that federal relief payments and public work projects be suspended during the harvest in order to force Blacks back into the fields.[21]

Under the WPA, Blacks received a maximum wage of $30 a month while Whites received $42. Skilled Blacks were classified as unskilled and unskilled Whites were classified as skilled. Of the 10,000 white-collar WPA positions in the state, only six were occupied by Blacks. In September 1936, thousands of African American WPA workers in Mississippi were dismissed in a matter of several days only to be replaced by White workers. The purpose of this action by federal authorities was to force Blacks into the fields to work as cotton pickers for 50 cents per hundred pounds of cotton picked and on other jobs paying the same wage rate. This action sparked mass meetings throughout the African American community. One participant asked the question most pressing on minds of those attempting to stay in the region:

> Where is the law and the constitution? Are we living under the alleged government where all men are said to be equal under the law or are we not living under an administration under which discrimination and a belittling system of caste reign supreme?[22]

Dependency and exploitation continued to be reproduced through pay struc-tures. One family of African American sharecroppers reported clearing a profit only six times in thirty-six years. Hired pickers were paid 60 cents per day in 1932 and $1 a day by 1935. Women cotton pickers made $3 to $6 a week while domestics earned only between $1.50 to $2.50 a week. As wages rose during World War Two, African Americans tried to avoid field and kitchen work that paid starvation wages. Women who received money from their husbands in the armed forces ceased working, especially on Saturdays and Sundays, even though planters enlisted Black preachers to convince them that it was their patriotic duty to return to the kitchens of their White employers.[23]

African Americans who refused to work in the fields found their food allotment cut by the WPA and Mississippi welfare agencies. They were then jailed as vagrants and forced into the fields under armed guard. The prison plantation, Parchman Farm, awaited those committed to resistance. Much of the Delta production complex was physically constructed, sustained, and subsidized by thousands of imprisoned African American men and women. The Delta ethnic and labor control institutions such as the convict lease system, chain gangs, and the 21,000-acre prison plantation at Parchman were all nationally infamous for their brutality. After a visit to Parchman, music historian Alan Lomax reported on the lengths that the prisoners went to avoid the torture of daily life:

> the state prisons of the South in many ways resembled concentration camps, both in the way they treated blacks and in their intimidating effect on the black community ... The horrid shadow of this remorseless system, in which so many men disappeared, lay over the whole South, carrying a threat that has not entirely vanished ... The prisoners rose in the black hours of the morning and ran, at gun point, all the way to the fields, sometimes a mile or more, their guards galloping behind on horse back. At work they were divided into squads, with the swiftest worker in the lead. The others were required to keep pace with him, and anyone who did not keep up, no matter what the reason, was sure of severe punishment. I met one old-timer, respectfully nicknamed "the River-Ruler" because he'd been the leader of the number-one gang on the number-one farm in the penitentiary for twenty years. The River-Ruler's feet had turned into bags of pulpy bones from the long years of pounding the earth of the penitentiary fields. In the words of the song, he had run and walked "till his feet got to rollin, just like a wheel" ... Everywhere we heard of men working till they dropped dead or burnt out with sunstroke. "Knocking a Joe," or self-mutilation, was one way out. The sight of a one-legged or one-armed man who had chopped off his own foot or hand with an ax or a hoe was a common one.[24]

Lomax recorded the following song near Tunica:

> In the South, when you do anything that's wrong, (2x)
> They'll sho put you down on the county farm.
> They'll put you under a man called Captain Jack, (2x)
> Who'll write his name up and down your back.[25]

This system of ethnic and labor exploitation was coordinated by the Delta Council and the Mississippi State Employment Service. The latter agency would also identify men and women for cotton picking and, if necessary, arrange transportation. In addition to using Mexican nationals and German prisoners of war, the council also insisted that Selective Service Boards should defer military service of employees considered critical to production. When the federal government ruled that migratory laborers were to be paid 30 cents an hour minimum wage in 1942, Walter Sillers, the president of the Delta Council and the Speaker of the Mississippi House of Representatives, obtained a federal exemption for the entire region.[26]

In the middle of the Depression, the threat of eviction was devastating. In his 1938 work *Uncle Tom's Children*, Richard Wright described a Delta community's fight against enforced hunger and a preacher's personal struggle to overcome his doubts about leading this movement:

Sistahs n brothers, they tell me the Deacon Boards done voted me outta the church. Ef thas awright wid yuh, its awright wid me. The white folks say Ahma bad nigger n they don wanna have nothin else t do wid me ... Sistahs n Brothers, las night the white folks took me out t the woods. They took me out cause Ah tol em yuh was hongry. They ast me t tell yuh not t march, n Ah tol em Ah wouldnt. Then they beat me. They tied me to a tree n beat me till Ah couldn't feel no mo. They beat me cause Ah wouldnt tell you not t ast fer bread.[27]

Controlled by Delta planters from top to bottom, the state and county AAA committees completely ignored profiteering, usury, and all manners of fraud while successfully blocking calls for investigations. Consequently, evictions and beatings occurred when tenant complaints to federal officials in Washington worked their way back to the planter-dominated county committees.

The alternatives to agricultural labor were few. Throughout the South, many Blacks had already been bulldozed out of trade and service occupations after 1890, and after every economic downturn more were forced out of their occupations by unemployed Whites. For some, there was still "work" on the levees. However, the following conversation between bluesmen Big Bill Broonzy and Memphis Slim reveals that levee building was an extremely deadly occupation:

[Big Bill Broonzy:] "Looky here Memphis. Did you ever work for the Loran brothers?"
[Memphis Slim:] "You mean ... Sho man, I've worked for the bigges part of the Loran family ... They always been and they still is ... some of them big business-mens in towns, some of them running extry gangs and levee camps and road camps. They were peoples wouldn't allow a man to quit unless they got tired of him and drove him away ... And remember how the boys used to sing:

I axed Mister Charley
What time of day.
He looked at me
Threw his watch away.

Big Bill: He the man originated the old-time eight-hour shift down here. Know what I mean? Eight hours in the morning and eight more in the afternoon ... You couldn't *tell* um you was tired ... They'd crack you cross the head with a stick or maybe kill you. One of those things. You just had to keep on workin ... From what they call "can to can't" ... You start to work early in the mornin, and work right on till you can't see no more at night.[28]

During the 1940s, ten percent of the South's Black population left. Testifying before the 1940 hearings of a Congressional Subcommittee Investigating the Interstate Migration of Destitute Citizens, Delta Council representatives argued contradictorily that mechanization had not caused displacement and that further migration was unlikely because mechanization has "advanced as far as feasible." This double-consciousness or twoness in planter thought can more simply be called two-facedness. The AAA and mechanization were just the beginning of an ethnic cleansing project openly advocated by leading politicians and social scientists.[29]

## Planters Explain Enclosure

Although they initially supported the stabilization and eviction aspects of the AAA, the plantation blocs throughout the South became increasingly hostile to federal social intervention. In much of the Black Belt, the planters were the state. Like ranches and mines, plantations evolved as total social institutions with distinct regional, state, electoral, administrative, and judicial practices. While reform impulses emerging in Mississippi could be easily blocked, the possibility of new national regulations, standards, and rights was perceived as a fundamental threat to "states' rights," that is, regional autonomy. Therefore, the plantation blocs throughout the South engaged in a prolonged attack upon the "centralizing" influences of the New Deal.[30]

In the Mississippi Delta, the planter bloc asserted that its knowledge of what African Americans wanted and needed was not only superior to the knowledge of any outsider, it was superior to the knowledge and desires of African Americans themselves. To get this message out, the Delta Council considered new forms of regional promotion. Tourists were encouraged to attend annual plantation balls in costume or to visit dude plantations. The first National Cotton Picking Contest was scheduled for the Fall of 1939 as a way of killing two birds with one stone. It would "turn the spotlight of the nation upon this section of Mississippi, and turn the attention of the darkies to the necessity of picking a better grade of cotton." Union organizers and social reformers were to receive a much more violent welcome. In 1944, the Delta Council adopted a resolution that essentially summarized its approach to organized labor from the 1930s to the present:

> opposing any organization of farm labor as a dangerous movement which would serve to cause disunity and a breach of faith. The plantation system as a partnership is successful only when there is mutual understanding and mutual effort.[31]

Throughout the history of the region, the Delta bloc has complained about labor shortages. The perception of shortages can only be understood in terms of a regional economy that was constructed upon ever-expanding monopolies and the fundamental denial of social and economic justice. In the 1930s, acceptance of the planter-constructed term "labor shortage" required the closing of one's eyes to the AAA-induced evictions and hunger, to tractor-induced reductions in the availability of work, to debt peonage and starvation wages, and to migrations propelled by systematic human rights violations. In the midst of this general attack, discussions of the "shortage" of African American labor were replaced by discussions of their expendability. In 1940, according to former Mississippi governor and then US senator Theodore "The Man" Bilbo, the growing redundancy of African American labor required a return to the policies advocated by Thomas Jefferson and Abraham Lincoln: the forced removal of all 12.5 million African Americans and their resettlement in Africa. Similar to present-day urban and intelligence theorists, Bilbo argued that African Americans were the source of the South's industrial backwardness, crime, poverty, and disease. Since "all the education in the world ... cannot erase the physical and mental differences that divide the races," public education for this "prolific race" was considered an unfair burden upon White taxpayers. He also believed that 20,000 Blacks per year were crossing the color line by passing as Whites and that they would soon mongrelize and destroy the White race in America as it had done in Egypt.[32]

The dominant social science agendas also doomed African Americans to a subservient position by failing to address the historic claims of African Americans for the redistribution of political and economic power. Social scientists masked these demands by using abstract theories of poverty and behavior. This discourse protected planters by essentially relieving them of any responsibility for the conditions they created and reproduced. Roosevelt's Secretary of Agriculture, Henry Wallace, identified the central tenet of the new social science paradigm, one that was designed to make the new neo-plantation complex disappear from academic and policy discourse: "It must be recognized that the problem of sustaining indigent populations is not the problem of agriculture ... The problem itself is a sociological one and must be treated as such."[33]

Slowly, the planter bloc began to view the social sciences as a useful method of officially denying their oppressive practices without resorting to the increasingly unpopular biological and religious explanations of African American inferiority. Renamed "deviance" and "dysfunctionality", African American destitution could now be blamed on the inability of certain Blacks to assimilate White standards due to "scientifically" proven social, cultural, and psychological differences. Another pillar of this social science movement was the redefinition of monopolization and mass eviction as progress and modernization.

Although the Southern Enclosure process heightened the fears, and bolstered the confidence, of the plantation bloc, it also exacerbated existing schisms within Southern White explanation, within the Herrenvolk democracy. In the academic realm, the Agrarians of Vanderbilt University in Nashville viewed industrialization as a fundamental threat to agriculturally based social order. Conversely, Howard Odum and the regional sociologists based at the University of North Carolina believed that with proper planning, industrialization could raise the region's living standards while preserving its folk cultures. There were also popular traditions operating in the region such as the Appalachian critique of resource monopoly, the remnants of small farmer populism, and the growing labor movement. The new White populist critique of monopoly revolved around questions related to mass unemployment and poverty, around the exploitation of mill and other factory workers, and around the elimination of small farmers, tenants, and sharecroppers. During the 1930s and 1940s, works such as *Southern Exposure* spoke to the combined plight of Black and White Southern "farm folks" and their resistance to the destruction of community.[34]

In 1930, on the eve of the New Deal, a collective of twelve Southern novelists, poets, philosophers, historians and economists launched an attack on the influence of Northern capital, labor, and social theory. In *I'll Take My Stand: The South and the Agrarian Tradition*, the Vanderbilt Agrarians warned both Northerners and Southerners about the impending dangers of the urban and industrial order and about the need to preserve a society based on plantations, small farms, segregation, the Democratic Party, and White supremacy. This highly influential book was written for young Southerners who were abandoning their culture and agrarian heritage for "the industrial gospel." According to economist Herman Nixon, the origins of this New South gospel were to be found in the process of "industry gaining on agriculture and the up-country gaining on the plantation country in economic power." John Crowe Ransom outlined two potential responses. The "foreign Yankee invader" could be attacked until the region achieved some form of limited autonomy similar to Scotland, or the North could decide to restore part of the plantation bloc in order to maintain stability. Poet Robert Penn Warren prophetically counseled that Northern industry must enter the South as good citizens and must not pit Black workers against White workers for this would lead to riots. Instead, he advocated the continuation of industrial segregation (redlining) by locating manufacturing firms in the predominantly White areas only and by maintaining a single wage rate to prevent African Americans from undercutting White employment. Although the Agrarians are often classified as the irrational remnants of a dying order, many of the strategies outlined by Ransom and Warren were implicitly adopted by the federal government.[35]

The Agrarians were trying to limit the rising influence of a competing intellectual tradition, the New South school. The 1920s in the South were marked by the professionalization of public service, the rapid growth of public education, the consolidation of the social science movement on university campuses, and the beginnings of New South scholarship. The central goals of this movement were the orderly transformation of the cotton economy and national social and economic integration. Funds for the study of Southern social and economic problems increased dramatically after the Social Science Research Council, the General Education Board, and the Julius Rosenwald Fund decided to fund university-based research centers and the Commission on Interracial Cooperation. One journalist noted that the flow of federal and foundation research funds into the South turned the Depression into the "Golden Age of the Gadflies ... the sociological-research gadfly and the literary gadfly." Others referred to these highly trained racial gradualists as "Jim Crow, PhD" According to Dewey Grantham, this was a highly coordinated movement:

An informal but powerful directorate emerged during this period to establish lines of communication and understanding between the academic community in the South and the organizations interested in regional reform. The key figures were the triumvirate of Will W. Alexander, whose Commission Interracial Cooperation became a clearinghouse for Southern information and cooperation in race relations; Edwin R. Embree, president of the Rosenwald Fund, and Charles Johnson of Fisk University.[36]

The Institute for Research in the Social Sciences at the University of North Carolina, Chapel Hill, became "the single most important academic agency for the promotion of Southern regionalism in the social sciences." Now based at Chapel Hill, Howard Odum became an important figure in the New South research movement. By the late 1930s, Odum no longer publicly supported theories of the inherent inferiority of African Americans. He now believed that the social sciences should identify the causes of racial, social, and economic differences and then propose governmental interventions to elimi-nate them. His colleague at the University of North Carolina, T. J. Woofter, advocated interracial cooperation rather than governmental intervention. Eventually adopted throughout the South in the late 1960s, interracial coop-eration or biracialism essentially called upon White business, religious, aca-demic, and political leaders to meet regularly with "reasonable" African American community leaders in order to diffuse conflict and promote cooperation.

During this period Odum attempted to redefine the use of the term "regionalism" by limiting its association with questions of Southern White identity and rebellion. The old regionalism was renamed "sectionalism" while the new regionalism became a tool both for analysis and for multi-state planning. This methodology was a key component of the effort to build a constituency for massive federal economic intervention in the South. Among other things, Odum argued that federal action was required to reorient the development visions, theories and agendas of African Americans. In 1936, he observed that

> the tension among Negro leaders and spokesmen over the matter of political and civil rights is increasing . . . the danger in conflicts over Negro rights is increasing . . . [and] Negroes are less and less disposed to be content with what white people do about the race problem . . . The subordinate race has become acutely race conscious and is on the way to developing a nationalistic sentiment.

In order to protect the social order from the full implications of the rising tide of African American expectations, Odum recommended a psychological reorientation:

> a hardboiled, realistic, evolutionary hope for the future, rather than closed doors of opportunity and change. What is needed is . . . to magnify the episode and the treatment of the Negro both North and South, as a supreme example of race tragedy under conditions which need not exist any more in civilized society. There can be no doubt about the enormity of the tragedies and injustices. But it is too big a burden

to place on one or two generations the task of changing powerful folk ways of the centuries at one stroke. The races can go the whole way of political and civic equality without endangering their [biological] integrity.[37]

Odum was advising the region's leadership that their preservation depended not on a defense of tradition but on the tactical adoption of a modernist official language and the codes of behavior that signaled the acceptance of evolutionary racial gradualism. Similar to rhetoric in the 1990s, the violent past was now to be viewed as an unfortunate anachronism that was now at an end. Therefore, the new discourse would promote a psychological reorientation and a new set of aspirations to be shared by Black and White Southerners: national unity with regional integrity; regional economic growth without threatening the plantation bloc; and formal ethnic and civic equality combined with the acceptance of continued economic, social, spatial, and biological segregation. When combined, the Agrarian/New South epistemology served as a model for preserving the traditional structures of domination in the post-apartheid South.

In 1935, these many strands of Southern opinion met at an academic summit sponsored by the Southern Regional Committee of the Social Science Research Council. *Problems of the Cotton Economy*, the proceedings of this conference, contains papers presented by Will Alexander, Calvin Hoover, Charles Johnson, H. C. Nixon, Howard Odum, Rupert Vance, and the Delta planter-sociologist Alfred Holt Stone. The purpose of the conference was to set the federal intervention agenda and the social science research agenda in the South for the next twenty-five years. The conference call read as follows:

> Whatever condition adversely affects cotton directly threatens the economic life-stream of nearly one-fourth of the people of the nation, who constitute the population of the ten cotton states. Cotton and a high percentage of farm tenancy; cotton and a high ratio of Negro to white population; cotton and low family income; cotton and changing world conditions; cotton as king in the far flung area of the south and the appearance of new textiles; cotton and the one crop system; cotton and soil wastage; cotton and a debtor economy—all of these combinations, and more, are the problems of the cotton economy.
>
> The cotton economy is now confronted with troubling difficulties in making adjustments to changes in conditions of demand and supply in the world markets for cotton. If the advancement of chemistry and plant science should cause a material increase in cotton substitutes, and if a practical mechanical cotton picker should be developed, these problems of adjustment will become acute indeed.[38]

The Southern social science community was being organized for the transformation both of the cotton economy and of African American reality. Odum presented a research agenda for planned diversification and "regional reconstruction" which focused on new crops, dairying, forestry and wood products, farm chemical production, the balanced location of manufacturing plants, the development of consumer markets, job training, and the establishment of cultural institutions. As this planned diversification proceeded, surplus people, particularly African Americans, would be "redistributed":

> The Southeast, if it thus develops its people, can provide also a surplus of workers adequate to meet any shortage which may arise from limited migration to other regions. In this way, too, the region can help reduce its marginal and submarginal folk, plan wisely the redistribution of its rural population, and direct its public-welfare programs in the expectation of balanced rates of increase. In such a program may be found also new approaches to the better adjustment of its Negro and white population problem.[39]

A supporter of the eugenics movement, W. F. Ogburn of the University of Chicago, was even more emphatic about seeking a solution to the presence of African Americans. He wanted a special conference called on Southern population:

> Some of the issues which such a conference might profitably consider would be the extent to which submarginal populations can be shifted by economic forces, the possibilities of experimentation in population control on a local or semi-local scale, the desirability of decreasing the Southern population, and the probable effect on the cotton South of the approaching static national population.[40]

These comments occurred during a time when African American men in Tuskeegee, Alabama, were allowed to waste away with treatable syphilis and federally funded sterilization experiments were being proposed throughout the South. Increasingly, discussions within the Southern and Northern White leadership centered on limiting and eliminating the African American presence.

Finally, in 1933, the same year the AAA was launched, the federally funded Tennessee Valley Authority (TVA) was created. Although the TVA has had numerous incarnations during its sixty years in existence, its original mandate was infrastructure, energy, small farm, and rural community development. It also subsidized new academic and agricultural research programs, public administration programs, and state and local planning commissions throughout the South. This growing academic, governmental, and foundation-funded research and planning complex stressed the New South goals of regional integration and industrial development. Out of this movement came two works that defined ethnic and political discourse for two generations.

To produce Gunnar Myrdal's 1944 work on race relations, *American Dilemma*, numerous Southern social scientists were mobilized using a $250,000 grant from the Carnegie Foundation. Another huge contingent was assembled for *Southern Politics*, a comprehensive 1949 study of the Southern one-party state funded by the Rockefeller Foundation and authored by V. O. Key of the Political Science Department of the University of Alabama. Referred to as "the study to end all studies," Myrdal's program for the socially engineered integration and assimilation of African Americans came to define liberal orthodoxy until the 1970s. Myrdal's circular argument that White racism is caused by the differential treatment of non-Whites (White racism) makes

African Americans extraneous to policy debates. Racism is considered to be a product of lower-class Whites frustrated by competition with other ethnic groups; therefore, peaceful integration can occur only once their fears are addressed. Consequently, the decline of racism is viewed as being dependent upon economic expansion and not upon fundamental structural reforms.[41]

After the completion of *American Dilemma*, foundation support for the study of African American conditions and culture disappeared. W. E. B. Du Bois and numerous other African American scholars were forced to abandon works in progress. According to Du Bois, the structure of funded intellectual production had shifted radically:

> Up to this time the Negro himself had led in the study and interpretation of the condition of his race in the United States. Beginning with 1944, with accelerated speed the study of the Negro passed into the hands of whites and increasingly southern whites.[42]

Northern social science was also being transformed during this period due in part to Southern transformation, the massive African American migration northward, and the rise of a radicalized inter-ethnic labor movement. During the early 1930s, Robert Park of the University of Chicago moved from methodologies designed to prove inherent racial difference to those emphasizing cultural differences. He now believed that African Americans were assimilable although he still held onto Alfred Stone's position that "pure blacks" were more "docile, tractable, and unambitious." By 1937, he had accepted part of the theory that African Americans were a distinct caste, yet he argued that this relationship would not be transformed by legislation, but rather through economic and social progress and through interracial cooperation.

Park considered the migration, eviction, and dispersion of Blacks as progressive developments because they eliminated caste status and social distance. As African Americans moved from caste to minority, class would become the most significant distinction and there would be a declining significance of race; this proposition was to be echoed by the University of Chicago and now Harvard University sociologist William Wilson some forty years later. Conversely Harvard University and then University of Chicago professor W. Lloyd Warner cited sanctions against intermarriage, social mobility, and citizenship to argue that the Southern caste system channeled class relations and mobility along racial lines in a manner similar to the caste structure in India. Although the caste line was horizontal during slavery, African American progress was pushing it into a vertical position. However, Blacks were not similar to the European ethnic minorities because there was no opportunity for assimilation. Therefore, he concluded that as African Americans moved out of the South, the Northern social structure would increasingly come to resemble its Southern counterpart, that is, plantation relations writ large.[43]

Warner's caste theories inspired several important empirical works on the Mississippi Delta and neighboring counties: John Dollard's 1937 work on

Sunflower County, *Caste and Class in a Southern Town*; Hortense Powder-maker's 1939 work on Sunflower County, *After Freedom*; and the Allison Davis, Burleigh B. Gardner, Mary R. Gardner 1941 work on Adams County, *Deep South*. Dollard viewed White racial chauvinism as a sickness, while the authors of *Deep South* argued that African American mobilizations would push the caste line to a vertical position, creating separate but equal societies. The caste theory was attacked from various positions. African American sociologist Oliver Cox thought that the theory focused too much on attitudes and not enough on institutions and institutionalized violence. According to Vernon J. Williams, Charles Johnson believed that the forces of modernization were not properly recognized and that urbanization, industrialization, and class differentiation would eventually lead to the breaking down of caste barriers between Whites and Blacks.[44]

A student of Park, African American sociologist E. Franklin Frazier also believed that urbanization and industrialization would lead to the breakup of plantation relations. However, assimilation would occur at different rates depending upon which region African Americans migrated from. Although stable patriarchal families were encouraged on plantations in the older regions, "on the frontier of advancing slave power, beyond the reach of a humanizing public opinion, the slave was subject to arbitrary power of crude adventurers." House servants, town dwellers, "mulatto families," and those Blacks enslaved along the Atlantic Coast were more likely to exhibit the "normal patriarchal family structure" than those in the Delta and other parts of the Deep South. According to Frazier, the pattern of "matriarchy" was harmless on the plantation, but in the urban areas it led to chaos as familial ties became disorganized. Therefore, African American ghettos would be structured around concentric zones of disorganization: single-parent families followed by zones of successful two-parent families.[45]

Frazier was attempting to provide an evolutionary model of African American development from rural plantation debasement, matriarchy, and disorganization to urban rationality, industrial discipline, patriarchy, acculturation, assimilation, and "normality." "The very fact that the Negro has succeeded in adopting habits of living that enabled him to survive in a civilization based on laissez faire and competition, itself bespeaks a degree of success in taking on the folkways and mores of the white race."[46] In addition to perpetuating regional, gender, class, ethnic, color, and cultural biases, Frazier's earlier works have provided arguments like those developed by Nicholas Lemann with the veneer of rationality. In his influential 1992 work the *Promised Land*, Lemann, a prominent White journalist originally from New Orleans, argues that the source of Black "underclass deviancy" in Chicago is not William Julius Wilson's isolated ghetto, but the rural Delta where African American culture, humanity and morality were all destroyed. Frazier's works have also been used to support numerous attacks on the Black family and upon Black women. In fact at the 1965 White House Conference on the Family, presidential assistant Daniel Patrick Moynihan tried to reshape the entire national poverty agenda by arguing that matriarchy, not poverty, was the most urgent problem facing African Americans. The plantation bloc's social theory of African American moral bankruptcy remains deeply ingrained in the social "sciences."[47]

Du Bois began to advocate a program for a planned African American group economy in the South. In his 1940 work, *Dusk of Dawn*, Du Bois explained his program fully. African American workers and working-class culture were characterized as being both "retrograded," and as a raw material that must be refined, trained and governed by educated and cultured Blacks:

> No matter what the true reasons are, or where the blame lies, the fact remains that among twelve million American Negroes, there are today poverty, ignorance, bad manners, disease and crime ... Any poor, ignorant people herded by themselves, filled with more or less articulate resentment, are bound to be bad-mannered, for manners are a matter of social environment; and the mass of American Negroes have retrograded in this respect ... This means that Negroes live in districts of low cultural level; that their contacts with their fellow men involve contacts with people largely untrained and ignorant, frequently diseased, dirty, and noisy, and sometimes anti-social ... Allison Davis likens the group to a steeple with a wide base tapering to a high pinnacle. This means that while the poor, ignorant, sick and anti-social form a vast foundation, upward from that base stretch classes whose highest members, although few in numbers, reach above the average not only of the Negroes but of the whites, and may justly be compared to the better-class white culture.[48]

He concluded that his earlier program for creating a elite corp of liberally educated professionals, the Talented Tenth, required further refinement because they were becoming corrupted by their inability to regulate African American economic, social, and cultural life:

> [The Talented Tenth] fear desperately a vulgarization of emerging culture among them, by contact with the ignorant anti-social mass. This fear has been accentuated by recent radical agitation; unwashed and unshaven black demagogues have scared and brow-beaten cultured Negroes; have convinced them that their leadership can only be secured through demagoguery.[49]

Consequently, he proposed a form of limited regional economic autonomy in the South to be built upon the existing "partially segregated Negro economy" and to be led by the "aristocracy of talent." Turned inward it could raise incomes, health and education levels, lower crime, and better coordinate and finance political, social, and civil agitation. Consumer societies could be created, efficiently managed, and integrated into wholesale and factory operations:

> With its eyes open to the necessity of agitation and possible migration, this plan would start with the racial grouping that today is inevitable and proceed to use it as a method of progress ... instead of letting this segregation remain largely a matter of chance and unplanned development, and allowing its objects and results to rest in the hands of the white majority or in the accidents of the situation, it would make the segregation a matter of careful thought and intelligent planning on the part of

the Negroes. The object of that plan would be two-fold: first to make it possible for the Negro group to await its ultimate emancipation with reasoned patience, with equitable temper and with every possible effort to raise the social status and efficiency of the group. And secondly and just as important, the ultimate object of the plan is to obtain admission of the colored group to cooperation and incorporation into the white group on the best possible terms.[50]

This approach was attacked by his civil rights allies Francis Grimke, E. Franklin Frazier, Ralph Bunche, James Weldon Johnson, and Walter White. According to Danforth Stuart Green, Du Bois was forced to resign from the NAACP in 1934 because the "organization and its staunch integrationist orientation could not share the same billing with the aging intellectual and his voluntary segregation." Du Bois's concern with the long-term economic future of Southern African American communities was well placed, yet it was crippled by his views on working-class leadership, culture, and consciousness. Like Frazier, his preoccupation with high culture and elite guidance left little conceptual room for the blues: the dialectical ability of working-class communities to revitalize themselves using their own cultural reservoirs to push their own historic development agenda forward, ever forward.[51]

African American intellectuals were not immune to the deep psychic fear of the Black working class that plagued the plantation bloc. In the brave new modern world of the New Deal and World War Two, planters continued to resist the rising movement for social equality by using historical studies, autobiography, and fiction to represent African Americans as pre-modern beings. The more the forces of transformation swept the Delta, the more fiercely the planter bloc asserted that African Americans were unchanging, unchangeable, and unknown. For example, William Percy, a major planter, Delta Council member, Harvard Law School graduate, poet, and author, wrote one of the best-selling books of 1941, *Lanterns on the Levee*. A descendant of one of the original planter families to settle the Delta, Percy wrote of the burdens and dangers involved in relations with African Americans:

> Just about the time our proximity appears most harmonious something happens—a crime of violence, perhaps a case of voodooism—and to our astonishment we sense a barrier between. To make it more bewildering the barrier is of glass; you can't see it, you only strike it.[52]

Another acclaimed autobiography of the period was David Cohn's 1938 work *Where I Was Born and Raised*. Cohn believed that despite all the decades of unparalleled violence, howled supremacy, medical experimentation, religious instruction, cultural analysis, social science research, and eternal vigilance, members of the planter bloc knew that they suffered from a false sense of confidence. Their recurring nightmare in the nightmarish world they created was of the inevitable deepening and expansion of African American working-class social vision and social action. Cohn refers to this real American dilemma which confounded the planter, that is, how the African American was able to construct

> a world of his own from which the white is jealously excluded; of which he knows nothing and cannot ever know. His questing mind is impotent to break through its shut windows and barred doors. His penetrating eye is powerless to perceive what is hidden from untutored vision.[53]

## Shadows of Sharecroppers

During this period, African Americans entered into the ranks of the labor movement; into the calculations of the Democratic Party, into federal policy; and into the production decisions of capitalists in all parts of the USA. Many Blacks viewed this period as the beginning of the Second Reconstruction where the forces of modernization and state intervention would finally eliminate planter bloc power and all remnants of discrimination. Others saw only further monopolization, destitution, and violence.

During the social upheaval that characterized the enclosure, planter hegemony was maintained first and foremost by a system of legal and private terror. Laws, juries, and courts were not allowed to impede the authority of planters in particular, and Whites in general, to dispense immediate violence for real and imagined infractions of ethnic and class regulations. As described by White informants in *Deep South*, violence was considered the solution to seemingly every conflict:

> This is so well accepted as a practice that a white justice of the peace reported that "most of the planters when they catch one of their hands stealing ... will take them out and give them a beating ... It never gets to court." Not only is this practice generally recognized but many of the judges and lawyers thoroughly approve of it, one justice of the peace stating that he believed "in the whipping post for these petty crimes."[54]

Sharecroppers who objected to planter exploitation were treated similarly:

> they can't afford to take them to jail because they need them on the farm ... The boys [the whipping group] were at it again last night ... A lot of men from here went down to help them ... That is the way they do, help each other that way.[55]

An affair between a Black man and a White woman elicited the following response:

> A couple of years ago, some of the fellows around here took out six or eight Negroes, beat them, and made them leave town. They had a broad leather strap with holes in it and every time they hit one it would bring blood ... There hasn't been any trouble since, but some are getting pretty sassy now.[56]

For rape or claims of rape the punishment was certain death:

The Negro had been working for a white woman. After an argument, she claimed that he had attacked her. So they arrested him and brought him to jail here ... I never did believe that he attacked her ... But they had to hang him, there was nothing else they could do under the circumstances ... When they got to the jail the sheriff told them they might as well go back ... Of course they hung him legally after the trial.[57]

During the Depression, the African American community was trapped between the regular operation of institutionalized violence on the one hand and the collapse of Black land ownership, commercial activity, and occupational structures on the other. Between 1865 and 1900, Black merchants had been able to establish restaurants, groceries, banks, funeral homes, drugstores and several hospitals that mainly catered to their community, although some served Whites exclusively. Also, Black artisans and contractors had dominated the building and other skilled trades in many areas. According to several observers, manual labor was looked down upon by many Whites in the Delta.

African Americans had been preferred as workers in some sectors because they could be paid less than Whites and because the White community didn't sanction the brutal treatment of White labor. One White warehouse foreman described his approach to labor management in the following manner: "I take a club and beat the hell out of a couple of Negroes and conditions return back to normal." But in the 1930s the practice of denying credit to Black firms and the violent competition of White merchants for existing trade joined with shrinking regional incomes to destroy the service-based group economy. African American farmers were subjected to illegal seizures by banks, the poisoning of livestock, arson, etcetera.

Furthermore, manufacturing employment was held to be off limits. Begun in 1936 by business leader and future governor Hugh White, Mississippi's Balance Agriculture with Industry (BAWI) program promised to bring the expansion of manufacturing employment. Counties and municipalities were authorized to use tax-supported general revenues to back municipal bonds that were then used to "erect, build, purchase, rent or otherwise acquire industries, factories, manufacturing enterprises and buildings and building projects, and to conduct and manage these on behalf of the citizens." For firms promising to relocate, municipal bonds were used to construct facilities that were free of both rent and property tax. The BAWI was fundamentally a state-subsidized affirmative action program for unemployed White male workers, local White officials, local White business leaders, and Northern White manufacturers.

Governor White clearly believed that the program was designed to take advantage of, and foster, regional and ethnic competition. In the midst of the massive multiethnic mobilizations of the Congress of Industrial Organizations in the Midwest, Northeast, and West, he tried to impress prospective employers with his state's abundance of "native Anglo Saxons" who were peaceful when compared to the "disturbing elements so common in larger industrial centers."[58] Before the Delta plantation bloc would support the BAWI program, it extracted assurances from the BAWI board, on which several major planters sat, that all work would go to "native Anglo Saxons":

> in 1937 when Armstrong tire and rubber prepared to open its new plant in Natchez, company officials allayed local fears by announcing that the industry would employ "only a few coloreds for porters and mixing carbon black"—work thought to be too unrenumerative and distasteful for whites.[59]

In the midst of unprecedented economic hardships for African Americans, the state economy was restored almost entirely through federal funds. The New Deal stabilized planters, merchants, banks, and the state government. As a result of the AAA and other related programs, bank deposits, farm values, and farm incomes all doubled. Between 1933 and 1939, the federal government's direct expenditure in Mississippi totaled $450 million, while an additional $260 million entered state banks through ensured loans. As state tax receipts quadrupled, federal programs became the primary source of income, cementing a new form of regional dependency.

In the midst of this boom, African Americans communities still had to fund and build their own public schools while federal funds were being used to construct new facilities for White students. Overcrowding was also a major problem; one elementary classroom had 170 students in daily attendance. Monthly teacher salaries ranged from $75 to $200 for Whites and from $25 to $75 for Blacks. Typically, planters did not allow the children of sharecroppers and tenants to start the school year until November or December, after the cotton was picked.[60]

Medical attention was often nonexistent, and at times the sick traveled 150 miles to a hospital only to be turned away. In various public pronouncements, the Delta Council expressed its concern for African American health yet it did little to change the situation. Most programs emerged from the Black community or from national and state public health efforts. Although impoverished rural agricultural regions generally exhibit higher fertility rates, a 1940 study found that Blacks in the Deltas of Mississippi, Arkansas, and Louisiana had fertility rates significantly lower than both Blacks and Whites in the South and in the USA as a whole. Poor individual and family health, and high rates of infant mortality and childless families were the result of poor diets, a nonexistent health care system, and the failure to treat curable communicable and venereal diseases.[61]

The rapidly growing militancy of both the African American and the White working class began to fracture the power of the accommodationists. Many workers believed in the power of Roosevelt's New Deal to transform their lives. In his gripping 1992 recollection *Growing Up Black in Rural Mississippi*, Chalmer Archer Jr examined the social and psychological implications of Roosevelt's twin strategy of affirmative action for Black professionals and eviction for the masses. To those leaving the South, the WPA, the Northern Democratic Party, and Roosevelt's Black Cabinet were seen as signs of progress:

But despite the hopeful talk, people were being stripped of many traditions ... The choices really did not seem to be choices ... In the outlying country areas, the past times of vast inequality haunted a poor everyday life and mocked the dreams of a productive future. An inheritance of dying rural communities matched the urban gloom ... I still remember Mrs Lula Washington sitting on her front porch in Balance Due, yelling at the top of her voice "Maybe what some people are saying is true that nothing will ever change, but it is time for all of us to start living a real life! We must have faith. We must believe strongly in the future!" Her faith was not enough to save her community. Her exhortations were addressed to the shadows, to the silent shapes of the Mississippi landscapes.[62]

## Blues Revolutions

each Monday and Wednesdays in our little neighborhood—there was nothin' else to do but sing—we would go from house to house singin'. Monday night maybe we would go to my house and Wednesday night we'd go to yours. And probably even Friday night because there wasn't much to do. And it seemed, like it kept us kind of close together. That was another part of the blues that's sorta like the church social workers. In other words, they kind of keep you up with everything that's happening.

Riley "B.B." King[63]

blues is a kind of revenge ... He couldn't speak up to the cap'n and the boss, but he still had to work, so it give him the blues, so he sang it—he was signifying and getting his revenge through songs.

Peter "Memphis Slim" Chatmon[64]

During this period, the Delta blues continued its march through regions, traditions, and institutions. A central figure in this movement was Robert Johnson. Born in 1911 south of Jackson, Johnson was raised by his mother in labor camps, on plantations, and in Memphis before she settled down with her new husband in the Delta town of Robinsonville from 1918 to 1929. As a teenager interested in both the harmonica and the guitar Robert would follow Charley Patton, Willie Brown, and Son House when they played at picnics, jook joints, houses, and country stores. He married in 1929, but his wife Virginia died in childbirth a year later.

An intense student of numerous musical styles, Johnson could make his guitar sound like an entire band. According to Honeyboy Edwards, Johnson would ramble from New Orleans to Ontario, from New York to Texas. He would play in front of stores and hotels, in levee camps, lumber camps, coalyards, bars, honkytonks, gambling joints, and movie theaters, at rail depots, picnics, dinners or fish frys, and in gambling joints, carnivals, and medicine shows. Almost all Johnson's songs were recorded between 1936 and 1937 in Dallas and San Antonio. When Johnson died in the Delta in 1938, he had just been booked to play Carnegie Hall in New York.[65]

Johnson's lyrics, Ellison observed, contained "an imagery that could be stark and horrific and was made more menacing by his use of the walking bass figure that was to become a common feature of Chicago blues" and Jamaican reggae. Johnson's influence resonates in the work of several generations of performers: Muddy Waters, Elmore James, Chester Burnett (Howlin' Wolf), Robert Lee McCoy (Robert Nighthawk), Ike Turner, Jimi Hendrix, Robert Lowery, Taj Mahal, Eric Clapton, Johhny Winter, Keith Richards, and Bonnie Raitt. A reissue of his works in 1990 broke blues sales records and became one of the top-selling records of the year.[66]

In addition to the Delta, Memphis and Jackson, another important blues center emerged in the river port city of Helena in the Arkansas Delta. By the early 1940s, Helena had over 10,000 residents and nearly 100 clubs, taverns, and "jook joints." It was a major destination, and sometimes home, for traveling blues performers such as Johnson, Howlin' Wolf, Elmore James, and Peter Chatmon (Memphis Slim), along with Helena-born artists such as Robert Nighthawk and Roosevelt Sykes. When the radio station KFFA opened its doors in 1941, the powerful harmonica player Aleck "Rice" Miller (Sonny Boy Williamson II) and guitarist Robert Lockwood became the hosts. Their *King Biscuit Time* program was heard throughout the Upper Delta and, as a result, Helena became a center for experimentation. Increasingly, the bass, piano, trombone, trumpet, and saxophone became part of the regional bands. By 1943, guitarist Robert Nighthawk had a competing show on KFFA which featured traditional blues, jazz, and the jump blues of Arkansas Delta native Louis Jordan. Many young musicians such as Jimmie Rogers and Little Walter came to Helena to learn and perform:

A number of young musicians who were still in their teens, many of them children of broken homes and already living on the road, were in and out of town during the early and mid-forties. They would congregate at the radio station, and sometimes they were allowed in to watch broadcasts. At night they would follow Sonny Boy and his band to their gigs, waiting for a chance to sit in ... [at age 14] Walter would wait for Sonny Boy to leave the bandstand ... and then, if nobody objected too violently, he would sit in ... Walter usually slept on a pool table in whatever joint he happened to be in, and he seems to have depended on the generosity of various gamblers and musicians for cigarettes and meals.[67]

Outside the region, Chicago continued to develop as a central place in blues culture. By 1930 there were over 25,000 nightclubs and bars. The blues found a comfortable home in the clubs, house parties, and other social events held in the predominantly Black South Side. As the enclosure proceeded, between 1940 and 1950, the Black population in Chicago nearly doubled, from 277,000 to 492,000, as a result of the continuous mass migration from the Deltas of Mississippi, Arkansas, and Tennessee. Thousands paid the $11.10 fare charged by the Illinois Central for the trip from Memphis.[68]

During the early 1930s, the recorded blues market in the city was dominated by Chicago-based performers who recorded for Columbia and Victor: Tampa

Red from Georgia, John Lee "Sonny Boy" Williamson from Tennessee, Washboard Sam from Arkansas, and Mississippians Big Bill Broonzy and Memphis Minnie. Lizzie Douglass, "Memphis Minnie," was born in 1897 near New Orleans and raised in the Delta town of Walls, just south of Memphis. Beginning in 1916 she was a partner of Willie Brown, the former partner of Charley Patton, and during the mid-1920s she played with the Chatmon family near Jackson. Settling in Chicago in the early 1930s, she was known as a powerful electric guitarist and vocal innovator. Langston Hughes described one of her performances as the intersection between the rural South and industrial Chicago:

> Then through the smoke and racket of the noisy bar float Louisiana bayous, muddy old swamps, Mississippi dust and sun, cotton fields, lonesome roads, train whistles in the night, mosquitos at dawn, and the Rural Free Delivery that never brings the right letter. All these things cry through the strings of Memphis Minnie's electric guitar—amplified to machine proportions – a musical version of electric welders plus a rolling mill.[69]

From the onset of the Depression, the blues as the voice of the African American community captured every intimate detail of the challenges faced by their audience and of the mechanism to resolve them. The songs were indicative of the times: "Broke Man Blues," "Cold Wave Blues," "Collector Man Blues," "Depression Blues," "Hard Road Blues," "Hobo Jungle Blues," "Insurance Man Blues," "Mean Old Master Blues," "No Dough Blues," "Poor Boy Blues," "Starvation Blues," "Tin Cup Blues," "WPA Blues," "Welfare Store," and Floyd Council's "Don't Want No Hungry Woman" which included the lines

> Hey the welfare didn't answer, the government paid me no mind
> Hey the government didn't answer, welfare paid me no mind
> Hey boy, if you think we goin' help you, swear you better change your mind.[70]

According to Barlow, two signal events occurred during the Depression to change the nature of blues in the city. First, the decline in record issues led many musicians toward experimentation and away from the formulaic blues preferred by the record companies. Simultaneously, the audience for the raw Delta blues and the performers of it were expanding daily. Innovation and tradition merged to create a powerful blues revival, a new "urban-industrial blues" sound:

> As the job opportunities in Chicago diminished in the aftermath of the depression, so did commercial pressures to make the blues conform to conventional pop standards. Left more and more to their own devices, Southside blues artists gravitated toward the traditional sources of musical inspiration in their own culture, and the Delta blues tradition became more deeply rooted in Chicago soil ... Blues artists in the city increasingly relied on the local black community for support and sustenance. They played for their friends and neighbors at rent parties, at never-ending jam sessions on the sidewalks of State Street, or in their own homes. In these settings, the blues were not a commodified form of commercial entertainment but a living

cultural tradition nourishing an ethnic group hard pressed by poverty and discrimination. As the collective voice of the black masses, the blues reaffirmed their historic
quest for equality, prosperity and freedom in the United States.[71]

One of the innovators of this new movement was Peter "Memphis Slim"
Chatmon who arrived in Chicago in 1937 and soon formed an experimental
band called the the Houserockers which included three saxophones—an alto
and two tenors. In the Delta and Chicago more and more instruments were
brought into the bands, there was more specialization, an increase in volume
and density, a wider range of tempos and structures, and a greater interplay
between voice and instrument through amplification. As introduced by Charlie
Christian and Aaron "T-Bone" Walker in the 1940s, the wailing amplified
electric guitar would become the instrument and sound that defined post-
World-War-Two culture.[72]

Jazz musicians were also engaged in radical experimentations in instrumen-
tation and composition. The heavily blues-grounded jazz bands of Kansas City
drew musicians from throughout the Southwest "territory": Texas, Oklahoma,
Missouri, Arkansas, and Louisiana. The bands and orchestras of Walter Page,
Bennie Moten, and Count Basie included musicians and singers who taught
the entire nation to swing or "stomp the blues": Coleman Hawkins, Oran
"Hot Lips" Page, Jimmie Rushing, Buster Smith, Big Joe Turner, Mary Lou
Williams, and Lester Young. Other seminal jazz figures—pianists Art Tatum
and Thelonious Monk, orchestra leader Duke Ellington, saxophonist Charlie
Parker, trumpeter Dizzy Gillespie, and vocalist Billie Holiday—deconstructed
or "riffed" the blues to create new styles. According to Albert Murray, this
blues movement in jazz consistently revitalized the foundations of social
identity and unity for a new generation:

> In no time at all, riffing traditional blues choruses in medium- or up-tempo in a
> steady pulsing Kansas City four/four beat was picked up by musicians elsewhere ...
> and was soon to become and remain the fail-safe tactic used by blues musicians
> across the nation on all occasions for calling Buddy Bolden's Children home to the
> good-time downhome ambiance of the Saturday Night Function.[73]

This was also a time when two Jackson, Mississippi, natives residing in
Chicago extended the blues epistemology into literature, specifically fiction
and poetry. Richard Wright came to this mission through his years of growing
up in and around Jackson. Wright had also been shaped by the murder of his
uncle during the Elaine Massacre of 1919. Most of his numerous works
revolved around a central theme; an in-depth and systematic exploration of
African American working-class consciousness—the blues epistemology. In
the June 1940 edition of *Atlantic*, Wright explained his method: "I wrote
*Native Son* to show what manner of men and women our 'society of the
majority' breeds, and my aim was to depict a character in terms of the living
tissue and texture of daily consciousness." Increasingly his writings were
developed along the principles of sociological investigation. While in Chicago,
Wright held numerous discussions with members of the Chicago School of

Sociology based at the University of Chicago and conducted numerous interviews with recent Mississippi immigrants in order to understand the political implications of daily life. He relied heavily upon the blues. He believed that they embodied the African American working-class perspective on daily life, work, and exploitation. For Wright, the blues were also a method to investigate these relations, an epistemology, and the foundation for social action.[74]

In order to preserve the organic connection between intellectual production and daily life, Wright relied upon the blues epistemology to undermine the increasingly rigid boundaries being erected around forms of social action, social inquiry, artistic production, and moral discourse. According to McCall, Wright upset the literary community:

> [Ralph] Ellison would later proclaim that "people who want to write sociology should not write a novel." But to say that is to deny the novel's traditional role with a bland assurance that "sociology" and "the novel" have nothing to do with each other. For Wright they do, very much. And his insistence in his fiction upon social commentary is usually accompanied by moral imperatives.[75]

Wright shocked the sociological establishment as well:

> In a speech given in November of 1960 Wright quoted what Robert Park, the sociologist had asked him twenty years previously: "How in hell did you happen?"[76]

By 1945, the works of Richard Wright, Chester Himes, and Ralph Ellison had been dubbed the Blues School of Literature by one of the fiction critics with the *Chicago Defender*. Zora Neal Hurston, Ann Petry, Margaret Walker Alexander and many other writers could have been placed in a similar category. Not only did these novelists embed blues music in the daily life of their characters, the daily life of their characters seem to be long extended blues songs. The literary blues first and foremost assumed the existence of a vital cultural womb. Only then were social realism, historical breadth, and the implicit call to action constructed.[77] The clearest statement of this epistemology can be found in Wright's "Blueprint for Negro Literature." This statement on the central role of the Southern rural African American working-class tradition of explanation has provided the theoretical underpinnings of African American literature and literary criticism for the last half-century.[78]

In Chicago at the same time as Wright, Jackson native Margaret Walker Alexander was also instrumental in developing the "Blueprint." She states that it evolved out of the Federal Writers Project of the WPA. The Chicago Writers Project included Wright, Walker, Ralph Ellison, Arna Bontemps, Frank Yerby, Saul Bellow, Nelson Algren and many other writers who went on to transform American literature. Wright also formed the South Side Writers group for the National Negro Congress. The members read widely in political economy and philosophy, and in Southern Gothic, American, English, Irish, and Russian literature. They specifically focused on African American dialect, spirituals, work songs, and folklore in order to develop a theory and practice of blues-based literature that placed the traditions of social action at its center.[79] Walker's poem "For My People" expressed the attitudes of a new generation and it became a standard of the freedom movement from the 1930s onward. It ended with a morally and spiritually driven call to action:

> Let a new earth rise.
> Let another world be born.
> Let a bloody peace be written in the sky.
> Let a second generation full of courage issue forth.
> Let a people loving freedom come to growth.
> Let a beauty full of healing and strength of final clenching
> be the pulsing in our spirits and our blood.
> Let the martial songs be written, let the dirges disappear.
> Let a race of men now rise and take control.[80]

In addition to the writers mentioned above, another wave of cultural workers entered Chicago from the Lower Mississippi Valley. Mass migration was accompanied by the establishment of numerous Black Sanctified and Holiness churches in Chicago. The participatory, expressive, and musical practices of these rural Southern working-class congregations were, in many ways, a blues movement or mobilization. It pushed a whole series of regional, class, and aesthetic conflicts to the fore, both outside and inside the four walls of the old-line Baptist and African Methodist Episcopal (AME) churches. The resistance objected to the integration of shouting, moaning, blues-based songs, new instruments, dancing, hand-clapping, and possession into the service. Some congregations split, with members leaving to found Presbyterian and Episcopal churches. In 1932, the senior choir director of Pilgrim Baptist Church in Chicago expressed his objections to Thomas Dorsey's attempt to standardize blues-based gospel songs for the services of the most prominent churches:

> I felt it was degrading. How can something that's jazzy give a religious feeling ...
> The only people who think it isn't a desecration are the people who haven't had any
> musical training—people who haven't heard fine religious anthems, cantatas,
> oratorios.[81]

Dorsey had come to Chicago in 1917 at the age of eighteen. As a blues pianist and composer known as "Georgia Tom," he played in Ma Rainey's Georgia Band and organized her Wild Cats Jazz Band in 1924. By 1932, he dedicated himself to capture in his writing the spirituality inherent in the blues:

> blues were really born shortly after slaves were free and they were sung the way
> singers felt inside. They were just let out of slavery or put out, or went out, but they
> hadn't gotten used to freedom. The spirituals you had a kind of feeling, you know a
> depressed feeling. They poured out their souls in their songs. They still had the
> feeling for a number of years, but not the persecution and all that. But blues is a
> digging, picking, pricking at the very depth of your mental environment and the
> feeling of your heart. Blues is more than just *blues*. It's got to be that old low-down
> moan and the low down feeling; you got to have feeling ... This moan gets into a

person where there is some secret down there that they didn't bring out. See this stuff to come out is in you ... Whether it's blues or gospel, there is a vehicle that comes along maybe to take it away or push it away. A man or woman singing the blues in the church will cry out, Holy, holy, holy.

Dorsey believed that as the blues became more closely associated with "unsavory places," certain religious segments of the community felt increasingly alienated from the music and the musicians. "Now people look down with derision, discontent, vulgarity on the blues ... Many blacks ... disavowed this heritage by seeking a religious ethos that excluded blues and the emotion that accompanied it." In *The Rise of the Gospel Blues*, Harris describes Dorsey's role in translating the blues aesthetic of the migrants for the "main line" congregations:

> commercialization nearly obscured the function of the blues as an element of black religion. Indeed, the more popular blues became, the more reason black churches, especially those that emulated white liturgies, had to consider it inappropriate. Dorsey sensed that the blues had to be recontextualized.[82]

Dorsey was able to systematically introduce his "gospel blues" songs, orchestration, and performance styles by training organists, other musicians, preachers, and choirs. His collaborations with the Reverend Theodore Frye and Sallie Martin were important first steps. However, his collaborations with a twenty-year-old, New Orleans-born gospel singer marked a turning point. Heavily influenced by Bessie Smith, Mahalia Jackson's rendition of Dorsey's "Take My Hand, Precious Lord," led to the acceptance of Jackson, Dorsey, and the gospel blues by the National Baptist Convention and the institutionalization of each as a pillar of African American culture and religion.[83]

The widespread destruction of rural communities and their rebirth outside the South nationalized the conflict between African Americans and the plantation bloc. The Chicago blues, the gospel blues, blues-based jazz, and blues-influenced literature signaled the national expansion of the blues epistemology. These new institutions revitalized the entire African American population on the eve of an era of unprecedented nationwide mobilizations. They confirmed and reaffirmed African American working-class social vision and cultural traditions in new cities and regions.

Within the Delta, the blues and spirituals worked to develop the vision, spirit, philosophy, and will necessary for African Americans to confront the plantation regime collectively and individually. Music accompanied almost every aspect of daily life and everyone was a performer in her or his own way. As an organizer, songwriter, and poet, John Handcox contributed to the efforts of the Southern Tenant Farmers' Union (STFU) to mobilize sharecroppers. "I had to leave Arkansas. I heard them talking about me. They said, 'We got a rope and we got a limb and all we need is John Handcox.'" In one of his most powerful songs, Handcox cursed the annual May Cotton Carnival of the Delta Council:

The planters celebrated King Cotton in Memphis, May fifteen / It was the largest gathering you most ever seen. / People come from far and near—to celebrate King Cotton / Whom the planters love so dear. / Thousands of flags were hung in the street, / But they left thousands of sharecroppers on their farms with nothing to eat. / Why do they celebrate cotton? Here, I'll make it clear: / Because they cheat, beat, and take it away from labor every year. / Cotton is King, and will always be, / Until labor in the South is set free.

The money spent for decorations and flags / Would sure have helped poor sharecroppers who are hungry and in rags. / Oh! King Cotton, today you have millions of slaves / And have caused many poor workers to be in lonesome graves. / When Cotton is King of any nation, / It means wealth to the planter—to the laborer starvation.[84]

## The Return of Elaine

> When a Mississippi sharecropper stuck his head up, he got it shot off.
> H. L. Mitchell, co-founder, Southern Tenant Farmers' Union[85]

The Mississippi Delta plantation bloc had actively participated in the massacre of between forty and one hundred members of the African American Progressive Farmers and Household Union of America in Elaine, Arkansas, in 1919 (see page 118). Among the seven Blacks and eleven Whites that formed the STFU in Tyronza, Arkansas, in 1934 was Ike Shaw, leader of the African American delegation and a former member of the PFHU. H. L. Mitchell, the future national secretary of the STFU, referred to Elaine at the founding meeting. "This time it is going to be different. We white men are going to be in the front, and when the shooting starts, we will be the first to go down."[86]

One year after its founding, the STFU had 25,000 members, headquarters in Memphis, and chapters in the Missouri Bootheel, eastern and south-central Texas, eastern Oklahoma, and western Tennessee. As soon as it began organizing chapters in the Mississippi Delta in 1935, a local organizer was murdered. Other locals were formed on the D & PL plantation in Washington County and at the Delta Cooperative Farm in Hilllhouse, Bolivar County. Established by the STFU and Sherwood Eddy with national foundation support, Hillhouse was an experiment in communal living, cooperative production, and interracial organizing. Although idealistic, the farm still maintained segregated facilities so as not to enrage neighboring planters. Among the trustees were the famed theologian Reinhold Niebuhr and John Rust, inventor of the mechanical cotton picker.[87]

The STFU's intellectual direction emerged from a combination of the African American blues and White populist development traditions. The STFU was also integrated into the larger national agenda of the rapidly growing Socialist Party of Norman Thomas. The origins of the Alabama-based Sharecroppers Union (SCU) are also found in the African American development tradition which was then integrated into the larger national agenda of the rapidly growing Communist Party. The latter's platform in the 1930s defined the Black Belt South as a separate nation possessing the right of self-determination. So certain of their success were these and other mass-based organizations that many of the conflicts between them revolved around what was to occur *after* the planters were dispossessed. The immediate agenda focused on the establishment of small-farmer and tenant cooperatives and rural unions, on preventing evictions, on racial/ethnic cooperation, and on securing federal funds for land reform.[88]

Noting the distinctions between the predominantly White though significantly integrated STFU and the predominantly African American SCU in Alabama, author Harold McDougall suggests that the STFU avoided fundamental issues related to African Americans and land reform. "The STFU was organized essentially to protect tenants from oppression by large farm landlords; [unlike the NSU] it did not specifically address the political future of the Black 'nation' in the South. The goal of land redistribution was never central to the STFU." However, at least initially, the organization did have a larger vision. In a 1936 letter, Clyde Johnson, secretary-treasurer of the Alabama Sharecroppers Union, expressed his reservations to Mitchell about the foundation support being received by the cooperative at Hillhouse. "Eddy is dangerous if he gets people to believe that this is the solution to union struggles and the sharecropping system." In response, Mitchell suggested that the debate between the STFU and the NSU was not over whether or not the planter lands should be socialized but over how the labor force would be reassembled:

> The Eddy adventure isn't very dangerous, it cannot wreck an organization of 25,000 people ... It is paternalistic and all that, but what about your soviet collectives, weren't they the same too. The state took the place of the philanthropist. He may get some liberals to think that the establishment of a few such farms is the solution but we who know what we are doing are going ahead with the struggle. We aren't thinking in terms of buying up all the land that we have paid for a thousand times over. But we are looking forward to the future when the whole south can come under the Collectivist Farm system. If the outfit in Miss. is a success we have demonstrated something: that the American "Peasant" does not have to be forced into collectivization.[89]

While both organizations advocated the creation of a federal agency to redistribute idle lands, several of the African American sharecroppers at Hillhouse had other ideas. Lee Hays and others used cooperative stationary to invite liberal STFU contributors from around the country to "send them firearms and weapons and [we] promise to send back a mess of Peachers." Paul Peachers was an Arkansas Delta plantation owner and deputy sheriff who was convicted of peonage for holding thirteen union members for an extended period in a stockade. In the same letter they spoke of arrangements they had made for the protection of sharecroppers, "a strong escort of about a hundred armed union men" and for protection of the farm: we are "preparing to construct a shooting plan for this place." The discovery of these plans shocked the White liberal managers of the farm who feared the reaction of local planters and the *Memphis Commercial Appeal*.[90]

By 1939, the STFU had eighteen locals and five hundred members in Mississippi, mostly in the Delta. The organization engaged in strikes for better wages and tried to press the federal government to force planters to return to sharecroppers their share of the AAA subsidies. By 1946, as part of the National Farm Labor Union, the STFU was demanding a wage for cotton pickers of $5.00 a day for ten hours' work. Planters had actually lowered wages in the previous year, from $3.00 per 100 pounds of cotton to $2.10. This meant the workers' eight-week seasonal total income declined from $180 to $126. STFU-organized cotton pickers struck, leaving 40 percent of the crop in the field. However, the planters were planning to lower wages even further. Mitchell filed a complaint with Chester Bowles, director of the USDA Wage Stabilization Board, to protest his agency's participation in "a secret meeting held by large plantation owners in Mississippi, February 12th, for the purpose of planning to cut wages paid to cotton choppers this season."[91] In a statement to the USDA State Wage Stabilization Board in Greenville on 6 March, Mitchell was reduced to pleading to the federal government and the planters to stop the implementation of a plan they had set in motion over a decade earlier:

> The Negro who said he had rather be on relief in California than on the best job in Mississippi, expressed the views of 90 percent of the Negroes in the Delta. If the larger Delta plantation owners continue their present policy of using agencies of the federal, state, and local government to keep wages down, the labor will continue to leave the state. If they are driven out in increasing numbers, plantation owners cannot cultivate and harvest crops until they get new machinery.[92]

The Wage Stabilization Board refused to endorse the proposed wage reductions because of fears of further strikes and legal challenges to planters who used the threat of violence and eviction to force sharecroppers to vote for reducing their own wages. While the plantation bloc had temporarily to accept the current rate of African American expulsion, they would soon devise other mechanisms to accelerate it. The STFU increasingly became marginal to the conflict between the African American working class and the plantation bloc. It did organize a seasonal migration of one to two thousand Mississippi workers to Maryland and New Jersey to work in canneries. It also launched a campaign to organize and increase the wages of five thousand Memphis cotton pickers who were trucked daily to the Arkansas and Mississippi fields. The STFU was less successful in its efforts to organize the thousands of Mexican workers "brought into Arkansas, Mississippi, and Missouri ... under the auspices of the State Agricultural Extension Service." Intensely exploited Mexican workers were being used by planters to accelerate the replacement and removal of sharecroppers. Using a combination of racial and moral appeals, Mitchell accused federal immigration authorities of "winking at the illegal entry of thousands [20,000] of 'Wet Backs', or Mexican citizens who . . . are being held in a state of peonage. They are promised 25 cents an hour but are forced to pay."[93]

Just as the Elaine movement was linked to earlier African American rural development movements, the STFU informed future movements. The organization, in affiliation with the AFL-CIO, continued working in other parts of the South and in California until the 1960s. At its height the STFU had 27,000 members in 204 locals in six states. Former members would later become involved in the United Farmworkers' Union (UFW) in California and the Student Non-Violent Coordinating Committee (SNCC) in the South. Thus the century-old African American agenda for rural transformation and development had again been both defeated and transmitted generationally. According to Neil McMillen, the planter bloc's response to the STFU land reform agenda was in keeping with previous and future tragedies:

> In the end, the union's message of hope and solidarity was no match for white terror. Nearly everywhere in the South, tenant organizations met determined and even violent white objection. But nowhere was the climate less favorable than in Mississippi . . . try as they did to remain undetected by the landlords until they found strength in numbers, the black locals were all too quickly crushed. Many members were threatened; some were driven away and others beaten and arrested; one was castrated . . . By the mid-1940s, white pressure had broken the back of the movement in Mississippi and everywhere else. There would be no further attempt to organize tenants until Fannie Lou Hamer formed the Mississippi Freedom Labor Union in 1965.[94]

The Delta planters have always known that their victories were only temporary. They viewed the growing number of strikes by cotton pickers, the growth of African American civil rights organizations, and the rising expectations of returning Black and White veterans as the beginnings of another threat to their regional hegemony. In 1947, a Coahoma County planter who was actively testing a new mechanical cotton picker in his fields wrote to several other planters that rapid mechanization would eliminate another significant portion of the population and that this would be the new final solution to their African American problem:

> I am confident that you are aware of the acute shortage of labor which now exists in the Delta and the difficult problem which we expect to have in attempting to harvest a crop this fall and for several years to come. I am confident you are aware of the serious racial problem which confronts us at this time and which may become more serious as time passes . . . I strongly advocate the farmers of the Mississippi Delta changing as rapidly as possible from the old tenant or sharecropping system of farming to complete mechanized farming . . . mechanized farming will require only a fraction of the amount of labor which is required by the sharecrop system thereby tending to equalize the white and Negro population which would make our racial problem easier to handle.[95]

# 7

# The Green Revolution

In the Delta of the 1940s, author Lilian Smith found "reaction rising like a great wave." The Delta Council, the National Cotton Council (NCC), and other institutions created during the previous period were reinforced by several new movements: a Green Revolution, the Dixiecrat Revolt, the Citizens' Council, and the Sovereignty Commission. The plantation bloc described each as an aggressive attack on godlessness in the form of organized labor, national and international governmental bureaucracies, and communism. In reality, once again—Mississippi Delta Plan 10—these hegemonic movements were designed to destroy the latest manifestations of the African American freedom movement.[1]

First, the national and international power of the NCC continued to grow rapidly. With the addition of more presidents of the Farm Bureau (an organization of elite farmers closely tied to agribusiness) and textile executives to its membership roster, its attacks on the "professional false gods" of organized labor began to be noticed. The president of the International Teamsters Union called for a national boycott of cotton products in 1946 and the NCC responded by mobilizing its congressional supporters to pass the Taft-Hartley Act over President Truman's veto. This action permanently crippled the union movement in the United States and the world. Another NCC victory came in the form of the European Economic Recovery Program of 1948, the Marshall Plan. Designed by an NCC founder, this massive undertaking was both an attack on European labor movements and a cotton export strategy. The NCC was also deeply involved in organizing and launching the Delta's Green Revolution through the initiation of annual Cotton Belt-wide conferences in cooperation with the Delta Council. Started in the late 1940s, these events brought together cotton producers, textile mill executives, machinery manufacturers, government officials, academics, and scientists for the purpose of assembling the components of a new economic, technological, and social order in the South.[2]

Another movement emerged as the conflict between Whites in the Hills and the Delta (see page 89) began to disappear. Fearful of a renewed era of federal social intervention, Mississippi Whites reunited under the banner of White supremacy and sent two of the nation's most radical segregationists to the United States Senate: the Delta planter James Eastland in 1942 and former governor Theodore Bilbo in 1946. A reinvigorated Delta plantation bloc occupied a central role in the Dixiecrat Revolt against the Democratic Party during the 1948 convention in Philadelphia. This movement originated in the Mississippi legislature's attack upon President Truman's support for the reforms suggested by the Commission on Civil Rights in 1947. When Minnesota's US Senator Hubert Humphrey called for a strong civil rights plank, the Southern delegates walked out of the national convention and traveled to Birmingham, Alabama, to join six thousand other participants in the States' Rights Party convention. The States' Rights Party—which viewed almost every federal intervention, except those that directly benefited the dominant regime, as unconstitutional—elected South Carolina plantation bloc leader US Senator Strom Thurmond as its presidential candidate and Delta Plantation bloc leader Governor Fielding Wright of Mississippi as its vice presidential candidate. Although the party carried only four states in the general election, the Dixiecrat Revolt set the stage for the eventual mass movement of Southern segregationists into the Republican Party.[3]

Although Wright and his successor as governor, Hugh White, supported the Democrats' presidential ticket in 1952, the Speaker of the Mississippi House, who was also a lifelong Democrat, announced his support for the Eisenhower–Nixon presidential ticket of 1952. A planter, a lawyer, and a former president of the Delta Council, Walter Sillers explained his reasons for defecting thus:

> We walked out of the 1948 convention because of the vicious, anti-Southern, socialistic, civil rights, FEPC [Fair Employment Practices Commission] platform; ... [Democratic presidential candidate Senator Adlai Stevenson of Illinois] advocates repeal of the Taft Hartley Law, ... [and of] the "filibuster" in the United States Senate, the only weapon left to the South to protect itself from ... [the] South hating majority; ... [He reportedly made a] statement to New Englanders recently that ... he will use his influence to keep any more industries from moving from that section to the South—a slap at our balance agriculture with industry program in Mississippi.[4]

Led by Chief Justice Earl Warren, on 17 May 1954 the US Supreme Court overturned the "separate but equal" precedent the court itself had established in the *Plessy v. Ferguson* case of 1896. In *Brown v. Board of Education of Topeka Kansas*, it ruled that the "separate but equal" doctrine had no place in public education because segregation itself generated in Black schoolchildren "a feeling of inferiority ... that may affect their hearts and minds in a way unlikely to ever be undone." But the Delta plantation bloc resisted implementation of the *Brown* decision. In anticipation of *Brown*, between 1952 and 1954 the state legislature took several steps: it created a program of teacher and school facility equalization as an alternative to ending segregation; it created the Legal Educational Advisory Committee (LEAC) to assemble the state's best public and private legal talent to plan defiance of the anticipated ruling; and it seriously considered proposals to abolish public education altogether. Soon after the 1954 ruling, the White Citizens' Council was formed in Indianola, the Sunflower County hometown of US Senator James Eastland. The original organizers were the manager of a large Leflore County plantation, a Yale-educated judge, a Harvard-educated lawyer, the manager of a local cotton compress, a banker, the town mayor, the city attorney, and seventy-five other members drawn from the local agricultural, commercial, banking, and governmental elite. The leadership of the Citizens' Council essentially over-lapped that of the Delta Council. In a letter to the editors of *Time* magazine written soon after the *Brown* decision, Citizens' Council leader and plantation manager Robert Patterson claimed that school integration was tantamount to economic, religious, and biological surrender:

> To impress the Asiatics, nine misguided political appointees have decided to change the way of life of 50 million Americans in 21 states of our great nation. If we red-blooded Southern Americans submit to this unconstitutional "judge made law" and surrender our Caucasian heritage of 60 centuries, the malignant powers of Commu-nism, atheism, and mongrelization will surely follow.[5]

Soon after *Brown*, a movement was launched by the NAACP throughout the South to assist its branches in petitioning local school boards to desegre-gate. In response, Sunflower County Citizens' Council initiated a program in July 1954 to organize a boycott of all African Americans who signed the petition. In Yazoo City, the fifty-three professionals who signed had their names printed in the local paper. Each of the Yazoo 53 was either fired, economically boycotted, forced to withdraw their names, or forced into exile.[6]

In the majority-Black areas of Mississippi, northern Louisiana, and Arkan-sas, the Citizens' Council's membership rapidly grew to over 300,000. Senator Eastland played a pivotal role in expanding the council's activities. In 1955, he called upon the state government to fund the movement. By 1957, he was regularly using the television studios of the US Congress to produce a fifteen-minute television program, *Citizens' Council Forum*, that was broadcast weekly on twelve television stations in Alabama, Georgia, Louisiana, Missis-sippi, Texas, and Virginia. The Citizens' Councils of America (CCA) was launched as a national organization in New Orleans in April 1956. Yet, "not until early in the 1960s when the indigenous segregation groups were either dead or dying did the Citizens' Councils of America begin to effectively coordinate racism in the South." The organization's reach eventually extended from Virginia to California before ebbing in the late 1960s.[7]

After the passage of the Civil Rights Act of 1960, the CCA called for the establishment of a separate African American state, for the passage of the African repatriation bill of US Senator Russell Long (D. Louisiana), and for the implementation of the "Negro relocation plan" of US Senator Richard Russell (D. Georgia), whose aim was to distribute the South's surplus Black population evenly among the states. To speed the expulsion of Blacks from the South, several CCA chapters forced evicted Black families onto buses headed out of the region. One of the Northern cities that they were sent to in 1962 was Hyannnisport, Massachusetts, the home of President John Kennedy.

The Reverse Freedom Ride program was a publicity stunt designed to get federal and Northern assistance for the "voluntary migration" and resettlement of Blacks. The plantation bloc seemed to be laughing at the entire nation as it made a joke out of its mass destruction of the African American rural community.[8]

Ten years after *Brown*, Mississippi was the only state that had avoided even token compliance. The CCA founded private White academies in 1964 and, by 1970, it controlled three small school systems with three thousand students. In the South as a whole, by the early 1970s there were three to four hundred segregated White academies, one hundred of them in Mississippi, educating 300,000 children.[9]

The CCA began to shock White Americans. Delta publisher Hodding Carter Jr opposed the council's growing "Gestapo" activities: blacklists, boycotts, night visits, and violence. In a speech before the 1955 national convention of the AFL-CIO, one of its vice presidents issued the following warning:

> The recent wave of terror and denial of constitutional rights in Mississippi and other Southern States must enlist our grave concern ... We must realize that a more terrible, a new and more powerful type of Klan is attempting to rise in the South today ... This time it is more dangerous, because it is ultra-respectable ... it counts among its members and supporters bankers, lawyers, powerful industrialists, and plantation owners ... state governors, United States Senators, and Congressman ... Remember its birth![10]

The CCA became an official Mississippi state institution when one of its organizers, Ross Barnett, was elected governor in 1960. In the late 1950s, several Southern state legislatures established sovereignty commissions that were designed both to publicize the benefits of segregation and to use McCarthyite tactics to destroy the human rights leadership. After Barnett's election, Mississippi became the first state to use its sovereignty commission publicly to fund Citizens' Council activities. The director of the commission, Erle Johnston, described the goal of the agency as the establishment of a form of interracial cooperation acceptable to the plantation bloc: a "policy of cooperation with Negroes in an effort to maintain segregation in Mississippi as being in the best interest and welfare of both races." The commission built a network of investigators and informants that could both systematically compromise an influential segment of the African American leadership and isolate and eliminate leaders who refused to submit. The commission often worked hand in hand with the CCA. For example, a CCA member was eventually convicted of the 1963 assassination of Jackson civil rights leader Medgar Evers. During the first trial, the Sovereignty Commission participated in tampering with the jury, suppressing evidence, and intimidating witnesses.[11]

Finally, during this period the push continued for multistate regional economic integration of the so-called Mid-South, that is, the Deltas of Arkansas, Louisiana, and Mississippi along with western Kentucky, eastern Tennessee, and southeastern Missouri. The Delta Council influenced development policy for the entire Lower Mississippi Valley based on its working relationships with the Louisiana Delta Council, the Arkansas Agricultural Council, and the Memphis Chamber of Commerce. Comprising forty-five counties in the Arkansas, Louisiana, and Mississippi Deltas, the core area of the Mid-South had a population of 1.3 million; it produced 20 percent of the nation's cotton crop, worth $500 million, and derived 43 percent of its regional income from cotton production. According to its official history, the "Delta Council is truly democracy at work." Yet in 1950 political scientist Stephen K. Bailey expressed the views of many in the region when he characterized the leadership as a dictatorship of the highest order:

> one of the wealthiest cotton areas in the world, the Delta is dominated politically and economically by an aristocratic junta called the Delta Council, which is made up of the leading cotton growers, bankers, lawyers and businessmen in the area ... In the last Congressional election ... less than one percent of the population took pains to or were allowed to vote.[12]

## The Neo-Plantation and the Green Revolution

The violent enclosure process that marked the birth of the Delta neo-plantation regime was fortified during this period by a Green Revolution. While Green Revolutions are usually conceived of as methods of achieving food self-sufficiency, Harry Cleaver argues that they are actually programs for "nation building." This program for rural and national transformation has its origins in the fifty-year battle after the Civil War between African Americans and Southern Populists, on the one hand, and Southern and Northern capitalists, on the other. The populist farmer organizations were weakened, hemmed in, and then defeated by the creation of a state and federal agricultural extension network, the Farm Bureau, and by new educational, health, and other institutions established by, or allied with, major banks, implement and chemical manufacturers, and commodity associations. As a pillar of post-war US foreign policy, Green Revolutions were launched in Mexico, India, China, and many other countries along the same strategic lines developed in the South. Internationally, a more dependent agricultural and rural leadership was created through the reorganization of production and credit structures. Not only did US foreign aid support the growth and power of those farmers most reliant upon US-produced machinery and chemicals, but new educational and health initiatives lent these extremely conservative and brutal rural elites the air of legitimacy they needed in order to defeat the social movements of dispossessed peasants and workers.[13]

Prior to the New Deal, a plantation was generally defined as "a tract with five or more resident families, including the landlord." The neo-plantation is defined as "a fully mechanized unit of at least 260 acres with at least four resident hired workers." According to Jack Kirby, the neo-plantation was constructed in four stages: the capitalization of planters through the AAA crop reduction program and other subsidies during the early 1930s; the mass eviction of sharecroppers; the dominance of the tractor and wage labor regime by the early 1940s; and, by the mid-1950s, by the introduction of the mechanical cotton picker, the elimination of hired labor, and the diversification of the regional economy. In the Delta, this last stage was followed by a Green Revolution.[14]

During the late 1940s, the general tendency in Delta cotton production was to rely more heavily on day labor and mechanical harvesting, and less on sharecroppers. Between 1953 and 1957, the acreage dedicated to cotton fell from 59 to 32 percent, the percentage of land farmed by sharecroppers fell from 56 to 39 percent, the cotton acreage worked by wage laborers increased from 44 to 52 percent; the number of mechanical cotton pickers increased by 46 percent; and the use of herbicides doubled.[15]

Although this period is often classified by the term "mechanization," this category inadequately describes one of the major social revolutions in the history of the United Sates. While wheat production was mechanized gradually over a fifty-year period, the Cotton Belt transformation swept through the Delta and the Black Belt in fifteen short years. Masked by the term "mechanization" is the astoundingly brutal attack upon rural African American communities and labor the transformation involved. Furthermore, the term fails to encompass the biological, chemical, hydraulic, geological, and organizational revolutions that were also occurring. Although International Harvester had introduced a commercially available mechanical cotton picker as early as 1941, hired labor was still required to remove weeds and leaves. Beginning in 1946, increased federal funding of cotton experiment stations, combined with research directed by the National Cotton Council, led to the development of a new technological package. The United States Department of Agriculture (USDA) research center at Stoneville established individual laboratories and plots devoted to every aspect of revolutionized cotton production: genetics, plant breeding, insect and disease control, mechanization, handling, ginning, packaging, fiber analysis, seed analysis, soil nutrients, and fertilizers.

To accelerate the transformation of cotton production, the Delta Council, the NCC, and the USDA held the first annual cotton mechanization conference at Stoneville in August 1947. In attendance were the presidents of farm equipment companies, land grant colleges, farm bureaus, and producer organizations, in addition to the directors of extension programs and experimental stations from throughout the South and Southwest. The conference also served as the stage on which International Harvester publicly introduced the first mass-produced cotton picker. The firm was planning to manufacture a thousand machines for the next season at its plant under construction in Memphis. The cost, size, and design of this cotton picker restricted its use to large, highly capitalized operations producing on flat lands characteristic of the Delta and the Southwest. As a key element of the movement to mechanization, General Motor's diesel engine division sponsored a conference at Stoneville in May

1949 to demonstrate and sell its new drying, cleaning, bailing, ginning, and seed handling equipment. Although small farmers were promised a cotton picker capable of meeting their varied soil and financial capabilities, the thrust of the conferences was to organize the forces of monopolization and to number the days of the small cotton farmer.[16]

While the new cotton picker eliminated harvest labor, workers were still needed to remove weeds and apply insecticide. At the 1947 mechanization conference the assistant to the secretary of the USDA, E. D. White, pledged that his agency would actively push to speed the process by initiating several programs, a sort of affirmative action for planters: reestablishing European export markets; establishing a working relationship between machinery manufacturers and USDA engineers, economists, agronomists, chemists, and plant pathologists; coordinating the breeding of compatible plants; working with textile mills to minimize machine damage to fibers; providing economic studies; providing credit for machinery purchases through the Farmers Home Administration (FmHA) and the Farm Credit Administration; and retraining and relocating displaced workers to "the extent possible":

> To summarize the thinking of those of us in the Department of Agriculture who work with cotton, I would say that we want to push cotton mechanization all we can and as fast as it is economically feasible ... I wish the picker, mechanical chopper, and other improved machines could come faster than we have good reason to expect.[17]

Federally funded herbicide research began in 1946. Ten years later, Memphis business leaders were calling on fertilizer, herbicide, and pesticide firms to relocate to the "Chemical Capital of the Mississippi Valley." Among the numerous firms operating in the region was Mid South Chemical, the oldest and largest ammonia-distributing company east of the Rockies. Co-owned by planter and former Delta Council president Ellis Woolfolk and Memphis business leader J. D. Wooten, the firm expanded to the point where it was annually covering 1.7 million acres of Lower Mississippi Valley farmland with Big N anhydrous ammonia fertilizer. The firm quickly acquired several new partners, including the New York oil firms Cities Services and Continental Oil. By 1965, the entire cotton crop was being sprayed repeatedly with chemical defoliants, insecticides, fungicides, and anhydrous fertilizers, and with pre-emergent, lay-by, and post-emergent herbicides, Use of these products tripled between 1964 and 1965 alone. Yields of two 500-pound bales per acre made the Delta complex the only Southern region competitive with the newly irrigated cotton kingdoms of Arizona, California, and Texas.[18]

The second major component of the Green Revolution in Delta production focused upon crop diversification: corn and small-grain breeding, soybean research, pastures and feed crops, horticulture, and timber. Based on varieties developed at Stoneville, a 500 percent increase in planting between 1949 and 1959 pushed soybean acreage ahead of the more valuable cotton crop. Wheat, catfish, livestock, nuts, vegetables, fruit, and oil seeds also became more common within the Delta, while timber production grew in several waves. In

1948 the Delta Council and the USDA Experiment Station established an experimental forest. In 1960, Mississippi established a program to assist landowners with timberland management in exchange for signing a ten-year lease with timber companies. By 1962, Mississippi was leading the nation in the harvesting of hardwood pulp, and by 1965 the growing number of timber plantations led the International Paper Company to locate a massive paper mill on the Yazoo River.[19]

Additionally, the Delta Council played an important role in establishing the regional rice industry. In 1950, Delta planters in Arkansas, Louisiana and Mississippi received federal allotments and acreage exemptions that aided the construction of a rapidly expanding rice complex. Modeled upon the NCC, the powerful Rice Council worked to cement an array of regional, sectoral, and political alliances. Although rice consumption in the United States rose rapidly, domestic overproduction forced producers to focus upon stimulating demand in Europe, South Africa, and Asia. Finally, diversification created a new set of problems for the region. Although the average annual rainfall is 52 inches per year, the growing irrigation demands of the rice sector, and the increasingly irrigated cotton and soybean sectors, led to the rapid depletion of streams, lakes, and aquifers.[20]

This period also marked the formation of a significant manufacturing presence. Under Fordism, continuous-flow manufacturing operations and thousands of workers were concentrated in massive plants throughout the Midwest and the Northeast. However, by the late 1940s, unionized labor was successfully organized across occupations, ethnicity, and sectors. Simultaneously, African Americans and organized labor were using their growing influence in the Democratic Party to stop the unchecked trampling of human and worker rights by corporations, landlords, and local governments. Therefore, in many ways, the movement of branch plants to the rural South represented an effort by corporations to continue their unregulated exploitation of ethnic differences, labor, and the environment.

The violent nature of the domination of African American labor in the Black Belt did not deter firms from locating in the Delta. Although only thirty-six manufacturing plants existed there in 1957, by 1965 the region was home to an additional eighty plants having a workforce of 15,000 and an annual payroll of $30 million. Previously indifferent to industrial development, the Delta Council used Balance Agriculture with Industry (BAWI) municipal bonds to subsidize plant relocations and construction expenses. The change in the Delta Council's position reflected its desire to provide stable employment for a declining White population. With the restoration of African American citizenship rights on the horizon, industrial development was deemed necessary for the political preservation both of the plantation bloc and of the White supremacist regime.[21]

Critics of President Roosevelt charge that the African American displacement policies at the core of the AAA ensured that the South would be a pro-segregation and anti-union bastion throughout the Fordist period. The Green

Whiteness on the vine, blood on the fields. A cotton plantation near Midnight, Mississippi, 1985.
(Courtesy of Robert T. Jones, Jr)

In many ways the Delta remains a sea of white gold. A cottonfield near Midnight, Mississippi, 1985.
(Courtesy of Robert T. Jones, Jr)

Hoeing cotton near Cleveland, Mississippi, in 1959. These workers were on the verge of witnessing the Green Revolution, the third planned dismantling of Black community life since 1933. It was accompanied by wave after wave of racist violence. (Courtesy of George Walker/the Library of Congress)

Picking cotton for $1 a day in a field near Cleveland, Mississippi, 1949. After World War II, and before African Americans regained their voting rights, planters began to use starvation and the mechanical cotton picker to drive them out of the Delta. (Courtesy of George Walker/the Library of Congress)

"Fixin' to Die" / The past as future? The nation recoiled in horror at the human disaster planters created in the Black neighborhood of Sugar Ditch, Tunica, Mississippi, 1979.
(Courtesy of Robert T. Jones, Jr)

*(next page)*
"Got My Mojo Working" / "Blow, Wind, Blow." McKinley Morganfield, "Muddy Waters" (1915– 83). The "muralist of the spirit" at work calling lost souls and rebuilding a sense of comunity, *c*.1980.
(Courtesy of Robert T. Jones, Jr)

"I'm a Man" / "I Can't Be Satisfied." Muddy Waters and Governor William Winter at the Muddy Waters Homecoming Day, State Capitol, Jackson, Mississippi, 1980.
(Courtesy of Robert T. Jones, Jr)

"The Hunter" / "Born Under a Bad Sign"/ "I Get Evil." Albert King (1924–92)
at the Delta Blues Festival, Greenville, Mississippi, 1982.
(Courtesy of Robert T. Jones, Jr)

"The Heartbroken Man" / "The King of Nelson Street" / "Going Back Home." Roosevelt "Bo Bo/Booba" Barnes (1936–96) performing at the Delta Blues Cruise, Greenville, Mississippi, 1989. (Courtesy of Robert T. Jones, Jr)

Folk artist and Bluesman James "Son" Thomas (1926–93) and band performing in a Leland, Mississippi, jook joint, 1989. (Courtesy of Robert T. Jones, Jr)

"We gonna pitch a wang dang doodle all night long, all night long." Jook joint in Greenville, Mississippi, 1985. (Courtesy of Robert T. Jones, Jr)

"Take My Hand, Precious Lord." Reaching for higher ground in a Yazoo, Mississippi, church, 1983. (Courtesy of Robert T. Jones, Jr)

The Otha Turner Fife and Drum Band is just one of two bands in the USA to maintain an African American musical tradition that is more than a century old. Turner (aged 89) and his band released their first album in 1980. Fife and drum music combines hymns and Black folk songs with polyrhythmic drumming. Pictured are Otha Turner, Blueswoman Jessie Mae Hemphill, and Charles Woods at the Delta Blues Festival, Greenville, Mississippi, 1986. (Courtesy of Robert T. Jones, Jr)

"Mellow Down Easy." A resident of Como, Mississippi, on his porch, 1989.
(Courtesy of Robert T. Jones, Jr)

Prodigal sons and daughters. A baseball game in Winstonville, Mississippi, 1976.
(Courtesy of Robert T. Jones, Jr)

Linking sacred nature with sacred communities. Baptizing members of Mount Nuel Church,
Red Bank, Mississippi, 1989.
(Courtesy of Robert T. Jones, Jr)

*(next page)*
"The Sun is Shinin'." The blazing Delta sun illuminates a church doorway in Clarksdale, Mississippi, 1980.
(Courtesy of Robert T. Jones, Jr)

"Well, the big bell is tollin', trouble here and gone." Are Black farmers destined for total elimination?
A Black farmer sells his vegetables on the side of a Rosedale, Mississippi, road, 1989.
(Courtesy of Robert T. Jones, Jr)

"The Train Kept Rollin'" / "I Would Hate to See You Go." Lady selling watermelons, Greenville, Mississippi, 1982. (Courtesy of Robert T. Jones, Jr)

"When things go wrong with you, it hurts me too." Teacher and students, Mound Bayou, Mississippi, 1976. (Courtesy of Robert T. Jones, Jr)

"Evil is goin' on home." The offices of the *Jackson Advocate* were firebombed on Monday, January 26, 1998. Official hostility toward this crusading newspaper has shielded the perpetrators of what has been called "a hate crime of the highest order." (Courtesy of Charles Tisdale, *Jackson Advocate*)

Revolution went further in ensuring that the plantation bloc minorities would be able to continue to monopolize political and economic power after the passage of the Voting Rights Act of 1965. During the first Beltwide Mechanization Conference at Stoneville in 1947, Oscar Johnston responded to critics who argued that mechanization would displace millions and lead to starvation:

> the word "displacements" is a misnomer. Rather the word "replacements" should be used ... It is impossible to charge mechanization with this population shift ... an actual shortage of labor made it impossible for the cotton-producing industry to meet acreage quotas ... The lessons of the past should provide adequate proof that mechanization of any industry or commodity has never resulted in anything other than progress.[22]

Johnston recommended that those in attendance pay close attention to the thoughts of a Birmingham columnist and conference participant Jack Temple Graves:

> The picker is going to put people out of work. Nothing gets around that. Some people say 2,000,000 in 20 years, others say 5,000,000 in five years. What will happen to them? God only knows, but if we are characterful and scientific about it, they will find better jobs eventually in something else. Some will move away from the South, perhaps, and if it lessens our Southern percentage of colored population and increases it in other places, the race problem will be easier for us to handle and for other places to understand.[23]

At the same meeting, the president of International Harvester, McCaffrey, argued that African American displacement had occurred, was now occurring, and would continue to occur without any significant impacts. Both Johnston and McCaffrey stated that the mechanical cotton picker was demanded because there was a labor shortage. This conclusion ignores the institutionalization of starvation based upon AAA-financed tractor purchases and evictions, the end of furnishings, the demolition of housing and communities, and the payment of below-subsistence wages. Invisible to Johnston and McCaffrey in 1947, the conflicts generated by African American displacement would soon grip the entire nation in the form of a historically unprecedented wave of urban and rural rebellions.[24]

There were other efforts to drive African Americans out of the regional economy and into new forms of destitution. In 1948, at the behest of the Delta Council, the Mississippi Unemployment Compensation Commission worked with Texas officials to bring two thousand Mexican workers in for the cotton chopping season. Simultaneously, the Delta Council established a program that sent African Americans to work for planters in North Carolina and Florida. Mexican laborers were brought into the region again to harvest the 1951 crop over the objections of labor unions and the Truman administration as "official eyes were blinked." Furthermore, the council ensured that those who remained would face a lifetime of destitution. It successfully lobbied the federal government to classify sharecroppers as self-employed persons, thereby eliminating their Social Security coverage.[25]

Several authors have suggested that the displacement of more than 3 million Black Southerners during this period was the foundation of the modern civil rights movement. The rural farm population in the Delta fell by 54 percent between 1950 and 1960. In 1965, more than 20,000 seasonal laborers were displaced from their 25 to 30 cents an hour "jobs" as machine-picked acreage increased from 69 percent to 95 percent of the regional total and as another one-third of the Delta's 925,000 cotton acres were taken out of production. Scenes of destitution covered the land. One visitor was "taken to a home where a woman lived with fourteen children, all of whom were naked from the waist down. They were burning cotton stalks in a barrel to keep warm. They had no bed and no food."[26]

## The New Crusaders

> Never, Never, Never, Never, Never, No-o-o Never, Never, Never
> Never shall our emblem go from Colonel Reb to Old Black Joe
> University of Mississippi (Ole Miss) fight song

As in previous periods, the plantation bloc revised its representational grid to explain the movements it both initiated and confronted. Embedded in Delta Council literature of the time was a worshipful reverence of the council's origins, a triumphalism in its historical accounts, and a warlike aggressiveness in its vision of the future. At the height of the civil rights movement, a *Delta Council News* editorial, "A Mighty Voice in the Land," used mythical and militaristic imagery to describe its regime:

> Personified, the Delta Council becomes the living, vibrating voice of motivation, and the sinew of the fabulously rich Mississippi Delta; ever alert to and aware of the needs of its own, but unhampered by envy or avarice towards others—the watchful sentinel and guardian of all Delta interests.[27]

Chemicals, machinery, resource monopolization, and African American evictions were celebrated as the foundations of this the world's greatest civilization. While the plantation bloc felt the sting of national and international criticism, most members believed that they were leading a holy crusade. Consequently, as the victories of the civil rights movement began to accelerate, a wave of physical and cultural terror was unleashed.[28]

The battle over segregation was essentially a war fought over which development path would dominate the region. One author considered the core of the Citizens' Councils ideology to be "Negrophobic ... the black man's presence could be tolerated only so long as the range of his economic, political, and social interactions with the white man's world could be defined." The first issue of the Citizens' Council's paper focused on denouncing the "tribal instincts of NAACP Witch Doctors who sought to replace the American concept of justice with the African Congo of centuries past." In a primer on race prepared for fifth-graders, the CCA described African Americans as a mixture of half child and half beast. As part of this movement, Carlton Putnam, the Princeton University and Columbia University educated former chairman of the board of Delta Airlines, published *Race and Reason* in 1961. In this work he attacked anthropologist Franz Boas's theory of the nonexistence of racial purity as "a pseudo-scientific hoax" which substituted "the demi-Goddess of Equalitarianism" for "the Goddess of Truth." In response to his efforts, the governor of Mississippi declared that a special day would be set aside throughout the state for the celebration and study of this book, the legislature urged that it be taught in school, and the CCA distributed it along with other tracts written by highly prominent Northern and Southern scientists that "proved" Black inferiority.[29]

Once again religion was introduced into the development debate. Though several Southern denominations tacitly supported the *Brown* decision, the Citizens' Councils deployed a contingent of clergymen who railed against this "blasphemy." After all, they argued, God and Jesus were segregationists and Christendom had to be defended from attacks by "multiracial collectivists and Social Gospelers." Theories of genetic destruction were used to oppose integration, as were the writings of political figures such as Bilbo, Thomas Jefferson, and Abraham Lincoln. Desegregation was portrayed as a direct attack on White women, who had to be protected from "mixed love," orgies, rape, and "sex atrocities." A prominent Delta jurist and Citizens' Council founder claimed that like "the modern lizard" Blacks had not evolved. The civilizations of Egypt, Babylon, Greece, Rome, India, Spain, and Portugal were all said to have fallen after drinking from "the cup of black hemlock," that is, after accepting Blacks as sexual and marriage partners. In the battle for the minds of the youth, books, films, music, organizations, and individuals were banned in favor of sanctioned texts, contests, and television shows. When James Meredith attempted to integrate the University of Mississippi in 1962, a publication linked to the CCA called for the execution of the "Marxist Monster" John F. Kennedy.[30]

Cognizant that its growing ranks contained union members, the CCA played the race card. It attacked the Congress of Industrial Organizations (CIO) when it adopted a platform plank that called for African American equality. Attacks on the welfare state were framed in the language of States' Rights, tax resistance, and anti-communism. Accordingly, it was claimed that the NAACP and the Supreme Court were implementing the program of world communism. This last line of reasoning allowed the CCA to build a national alliance with the arch-conservative John Birch Society based in the North and the West. The steady stream of hysteria notwithstanding, the regime still believed that the civil rights movement and its supporters would eventually be defeated. In his 1964 address before the Delta Council's annual meeting, US Senator John Stennis of Mississippi prophetically declared that even if the Civil Rights Act desired by "the imported racial zealots and agitators" and their allies in Congress was passed and signed into law, the tide would eventually turn because "those in other sections of the country are now feeling the pinch of the civil rights problem." Similarly, the ultimate victory of the plantation bloc was predicted by Congressman Jamie Whitten during a speech before the Thirtieth Annual Meeting of the Delta Council in 1965:

> voting rights is merely a front for a massive takeover by militant agitators. Once seized, this power will be used to control industry, agriculture, and even labor . . . we must continue to show restraint and respect for the law in the hope that as it becomes clear to the rest of the country that the South is only a beachhead to these radical leaders for a take-over of the nation, the laws will be changed.[31]

During this period, several leading White intellectuals in Mississippi questioned the rising levels of extremism and their own loyalties. In 1954, a Black teacher was shot after she objected to a White sheriff driving through her yard. When publisher Hazel Brannon Smith of the *Lexington Advertiser* both published the story and refused to denounce the *Brown* decision, she was sued, boycotted, threatened with death, and then bankrupted by a newly created segregationist newspaper. University of Mississippi history professor James Silver wrote an influential exposé on the growth of the Citizens' Council in 1963, *Mississippi: the Closed Society*. But while Pulitzer prize-winning publisher Hodding Carter of the *Delta-Democrat Times* fought to keep the Ku Klux Klan out of the Delta from the 1920s onward, he did so because "this lower class, noisome white-garbed snake" had no right to interfere with the operation of "noblesse oblige" exercised by the "cosmopolite" planters. As late as 1960, Carter was still certain that "segregation will remain a fact for a long, long time." Personal contradictions only intensified as the horror of expulsion and the promise of freedom touched every household and forced every individual to decide who they were and who they wanted to become.[32]

### "Freezin Ground Was My Foldin Bed Last Night"
(Robert Johnson)

In many ways the Southern system of peonage was similar to a levee built to hold back the rising river of African American desires and visions. The energy building up behind it could be heard in mythically powerful music swirling around the region and its diaspora. The collapse of the Delta's levee unleashed a sixteen-year cultural flood. In the 1950s and 1960s, important blues movements emerged in Chicago, in Memphis, in Memphis again, and in Britain. As the legitimacy of planter-based forms of explanation declined, Delta performers and their multiple musical movements played a central role in spreading blues thought to every corner of the earth. These movements served to preserve, reconstruct, and revitalize African American and other communities and individuals throughout the world. The blues provided them with a compendium of folk wisdom that was relied upon in the heat of battles against ancient and ever-changing forms of exploitation. The blues was capable of undergoing constant metamorphosis without losing its central messages of global social justice and the sanctity of African American culture. Therefore, as the process of global alienation intensified, the blues always held out a hand to the lost, the dispossessed and the disavowed. Its position as the counternarrative of the American Dream enabled the blues to expand simultaneously with the power of the United States in the period after World War Two.

In the first of the new blues movements, a powerful social and cultural vision was hewn from the mangled lives of Delta refugees driven to Chicago by debt peonage, unemployment, homelessness, daily violence, enclosure, mechanization, and the Green Revolution. The chroniclers of their lives, their griots, emerged directly out of the schools and networks that had created the mythic figures Charley Patton, Son House, and Robert Johnson. Performers trained in the Delta blues tradition began recording in Chicago during the late 1940s and early 1950s. On their way to dominating the national Black record market and setting an international standard for blues performance, the Chicago blues school of the 1950s and early 1960s was also presenting a powerful celebration of the pantheon of Black culture and consciousness. Considered by many to be uncompromising and revolutionary, the music expressed the intense levels of dissatisfaction and resistance to domination present in the daily lives of African Americans in the aftermath of World War Two. Although often characterized as urban blues, as opposed to country blues, the Chicago school struck a deep resonating chord among Blacks north and south, east and west, urban and rural. The works and lives of the core members are constantly studied throughout the world and have entered the realm of global folklore: from Mississippi came McKinley Morganfield (Muddy Waters) and Albert Landrew (Sunny Land Slim) (1947), J. B. Lenoir (1952), Charles Burnett (Howlin' Wolf) and Elmore James (1953), Walter Horton (1954), and Aleck "Rice" Miller (Sonny Boy Williamson II) (1955); from Arkansas came Robert Nighthawk (1948), Junior Wells (1953), and Otis Rush (1956); from Memphis came Johnnie Shines (1950) and Willie Nix (1953); and from Louisiana there was Little Walter (1947).

Born in Rolling Fork, Mississippi, in 1915, Muddy Waters was raised on the Sherrod plantation in Coahoma County. He learned directly from Patton, Son House, Johnson and from the accumulated wisdom of numerous individuals, schools, and regions, and explained the process of intellectual exchange in the following manner: "It just came down from nation to nation, you know, from the top of the blues thing that all black people were into." By the early 1940s, Muddy Waters, his wife, uncle, and grandmother worked the same plot of land as sharecroppers and cleared as little as $100 a year after commissary debts were deducted. He recalled that the fields were full of the blues:

> Every man would be hollerin' but you didn't pay that no mind. Yeah, course I'd holler too. You might call them blues but they was just made-up things. Like a feller

be workin' or most likely some gal be workin' near and you want to say something to 'em. So you holler it. Sing it. Or maybe to your mule or something, or it's gettin' late and you wanna go home. I can't remember much of what I was singin' now 'ceptin I do remember that I was always singin' I cain't be satisfied, I be all troubled in my mind.[33]

In 1943, Muddy Waters caught an Illinois Central train headed to Chicago where, several years later he would begin recording. Unlike the pre-1939 period when large commercial labels dictated what music was recorded, Aristocrat/Chess/Checker, Savoy, King, Aladdin, Modern/RPM and other independent Chicago labels built their sales upon artists and material that captured the lives and determination of the refugees from the Delta and other Southern regions. Muddy Waters was able simultaneously to call lost and alienated souls back home and to contribute to the construction of new Black communities. "I had it in my mind I wanted to play close round Son House — between Son and Robert. I did Chicago a lot of good. A lot of people here didn't hear Son House or Robert Johnson because they didn't get a chance to ... you see, the blues is tone, deep tone with a beat ... By itself the sound would have never made it in Chicago." According to Little Walter, several innovations were adopted. "We went to putting time to the low-down Mississippi blues ... we learned the beat, learned what the people moving off of. Even if it's the blues, we still had to drive behind it." The Chicago blues of the early 1950s was defined by a combo composed of Muddy Waters and Jimmy Rogers on guitar, Little Walter on harmonica, and Baby Face Leroy, later Elgin Evans, on drums. A piano and a bass were eventually added. Numerous songs reached the top ten on the R&B charts: "I Can't Be Satisfied," "I Feel Like Going Home," "Louisiana Blues," "Rollin Stone," "She Moves Me," "I Got My Mojo Working," "I'm Your Hoochie Coochie Man," and "I'm a Man."[34]

Delta native Willie Dixon also played a key role in the construction of the Chicago blues during this period. Dixon was introduced to the blues at age twelve after he was imprisoned on a county plantation for taking plumbing from an abandoned house:

I really began to find out what the blues meant to black people, how it gave them consolation to be able to think these things over and sing them to themselves or let other people know what they had in mind and how they resented various things in life. I guess it kinda rubbed off on me because after you see guys die ...[35]

In Clarksdale, Dixon was arrested again and sentenced to thirty days for trying to catch a train to Chicago. While serving time on a plantation prison, he froze after seeing the overseer, Captain Crush, "tear flesh from a man with a two foot long strap named 'Black Annie'." He then called Dixon. "Hey come here ... Me? ... Yeah, you ... I go down there and this guy took that damn strap and hit me upside the head and I stayed deaf for almost four years." When he began to wonder why he wasn't released after thirty days, another inmate informed the thirteen-year-old Dixon, "You'll be here until the day you die." Escaping on a stolen mule, Dixon headed for Chicago.[36]

During the 1940s he sang and played bass with the Five Breezes, the Four Jumps of Jive, and the Big Three Trio. At Chess Records, and later at Cobra Records, he wrote hit songs for Chuck Berry, Bo Diddley, Lowell Fulson, Buddy Guy, Shakey Horton, Willie Mabon, Otis Rush, Magic Sam, Koko Taylor, Muddy Waters, Jimmy Witherspoon, and Howlin' Wolf. One day in 1956 he had five songs in the national R&B charts. Yet Leonard Chess "would always find one way or the other to take my money."[37]

Several of Dixon's most popular songs were organized around the conscious, fearless, and unashamed celebration of African American folk religion and its heroes. "The Seventh Son" was one who could "heal the sick and raise the dead." In "I'm Your Hoochie Coochie Man" the role of hoodoo in shaping human destiny was discussed. Predecessor of both the militant and the "gangsta," the unblinking bad man was the voice heard in "I'm Ready":

> I gotta axe handle pistol
> on a graveyard frame
> that shoots tombstone bullets
> wearing balls and chains . . .
> I'm drinkin' TNT
> Smokin' dynamite
> I hope some screwball
> start a fight
> *Chorus:* Because I'm ready
> Ready as anybody can be
> I'm ready for you
> I hope you're ready for me.[38]

Another key figure was Chester Arthur Burnett (Howlin' Wolf), who was born near West Point, Mississippi, in 1910 and moved in 1923 with his family to a plantation near the Delta town of Ruleville. Taught by Patton, Johnson, and his brother-in-law Aleck "Rice" Miller, Burnett left farming at age thirty-eight to become a performer and disc jockey in West Memphis, Arkansas. Moving to Chicago in 1952, he was renowned for several talents: for his ability to merge older Delta styles with the jump blues; for his epic harmonica performances; and for his field shouts and hollers in a voice so loud and intense that many felt it could stir the dead. Another critical member of the Chicago group was Elmore James. Born in 1918 on a plantation near Richland, Mississippi, as a teenager James performed with Johnson and "Rice" Miller. His electrified version of Robert Johnson's "Dust My Broom" reached the top ten on the national R&B charts in 1952. James was a radically innovative genius who, according to one critic, laid the foundations of both rap and heavy metal music. Also recorded during this period was Andrew Tibbs's heavily censored song about the nation's leading segregationist, Mississippi's US Senator Theodore "The Man" Bilbo, entitled "Bilbo is Dead." The blossoming of the blues epistemology in Chicago during the 1950s would soon reverberate around the world.[39]

## "... Playing the Blues, ... It's Like Being Black Twice" (Riley "B. B." King)[40]

The second blues movement of the 1950s and 1960s was led by the Beale Streeters of Memphis who represented the refugee-led cultural revitalization of growing Black communities in the urban South. In Memphis, new recording studios and radio programs began to capture the powerful voices, rhythms, and visions produced by the churning of social relations in the Delta. Instead of in Chicago, many of the young blues intellectuals began their recording careers closer to home; including Riley "B. B." King (1949), Bobby Blue Bland (1950), Rufus Thomas (1951), Ike Turner and the Kings of Rhythm (1951), Junior Parker (1952), Albert King (1953), and Little Milton (1953). As a group they were influenced by the Delta tradition, by the Texas blues, and by jazz.

King was born in 1925 on a plantation located between Itta Bena and Indianola and at age four he moved with his mother to live on a farm in Kilmichael. Although his mother died when he was nine, King continued to live in their cabin alone. In addition to milking cows and picking cotton, he attended a one-room schoolhouse with one teacher, thirteen grades, and ninety-two children. At age fourteen, his father brought him to Lexington, Several years later, King was married and living on the 1,000-acre Barrett plantation near Indianola with fifty other sharecropping families. He began singing with his mother in their Holiness church at age five and as a teenager he formed at least two gospel groups. On the weekends and during down times, he would travel throughout the Delta playing the blues in clubs and on the streets, singing "like a blind man." After crashing a plantation tractor, King grabbed his guitar and walked the 120 miles to Memphis. Performer Rufus Thomas first spotted him during one of the Beale Street talents shows where all contestants were given a dollar. "And B. B. was happy to come up and get that dollar ... One dollar. No soles on his shoes and a raggedy guitar."[41]

King stayed in Memphis with his cousin, blues performer Bukka White, and visited West Memphis in order to take lessons from Lockwood who was still broadcasting from there. He was also influenced by the recordings of Blind Lemon Jefferson, Robert Johnson, Lonnie Johnson, Louis Jordan, Lester Young, Charlie Christian, Django Reinhardt, and T-Bone Walker. By 1948, King had his own jump blues program on WDIA, a 50,000-watt country station that had just switched to an all-Black format. WDIA became known as the "Mother of Black Southern Radio," and King, Nat D. Williams, and Rufus Thomas and other WDIA disc jockeys reached an audience of nearly 1.3 million African Americans.[42]

While recording with the powerful Club Handy House Band of Willie Mitchell, Hank Crawford, and Phineas Newborn, on WDIA King would promote his own trio comprising himself and Johnny Ace on piano, and Earl Forrest on drums. This trio along with vocalists Bobby "Blue" Bland, Herman "Junior" Parker, and Arnold "Gatemouth" Moore was collectively known as the Beale Streeters:

> The blues lineages of Texas, Oklahoma, and Kansas City to the west, and Mississippi, New Orleans, and Georgia in the east fused there like a laser beam and a disparate group of teenagers banded together in its intensity. B. B. King was the oldest, though they were all born between 1925–30 ... when they all worked together, they called themselves the Beale Streeters, Chicago had become the center for the urbanization of the rural blues, but the Beale Streeters were out to modernize that urbanization.[43]

Scoring his first hit with Lowell Fulson's "Three O'Clock Blues," King began a forty-year trek back and forth across the world with his fifteen-piece band. The legacy of the Beale Streeters is similar to that of the Chicago blues performers: they expanded the geographic, musical, and generational range of the blues; they helped to reenergize and refocus communities that were both dying and being born. While they sang from a hunger without end, they also exhibited a sophistication, worldliness and world-weariness rarely associated with dispossessed rural youth. Considered an ambassador from the blues to the world, King has repeatedly argued for the sanctity and centrality of the blues worldview:

> For us (black Americans), the blues is almost sacred, like Gospel music, because it is a part of our culture, and a part of us ... As long as you've got black people, there'll always be the blues ... I don't class myself other than just a blues singer.[44]

In this period Memphis was also the site of a third blues movement, one that would catch an entire generation of White Southerners in its wake before sweeping other parts of the world:

> One March afternoon in 1951, a Delta highway patrolman spotted a flagrantly overloaded sedan wallowing up Highway 61 toward Memphis. Seven black teenagers were crammed inside, and a string bass, three saxophones, a guitar and amplifier, and a set of drums were crammed in with them and partly lashed to the vehicle's roof ... Eighteen-year-old Ike Turner, the ringleader of the group, was a Clarksdale native and something of a personality around town ... His band, the Kings of Rhythm, was a popular local attraction. The group played jumping dance music, including versions of the latest R&B hits, and were popular with some white teenagers as well as with younger blacks.[45]

Turner and his band were headed for Sam Phillips's Memphis Recording Service Studios, later renamed Sun Records. Born in Clarskdale in 1932, Turner was influenced by the *King Biscuit Time* radio program, and its hosts "Rice" Miller and Pinetop Perkins. The latter gave Turner lessons in boogie woogie piano styles. By age sixteen, Turner was working as a disc jockey and leading an eighteen-piece band; many of the band members had been taught by legends such as Earl Lee Hooker and Houston Stackhouse. The Rhythm Kings came to Memphis to record "Rocket 88," a song that reached number one in the R&B charts and one that Phillips called the first rock and roll song.[46]

Robert Palmer asserts that "Delta bluesmen had been rocking for years — the term was understood there musically as well as sexually at least as early as the thirties." He goes on to suggest that in the late 1940s, urban Southern Whites with a history of hiring African American entertainers, and listening to their latest recordings, were the first generation of White enthusiasts of rock and roll. Conversely, Judd Phillips, also of Sun Records, claimed that it "was the poor white seeking the soul expression. Not the uptown white, but the poor white." For Conway Twitty, a White Mississippi Delta native who gained popularity as both an early rock and roll and a country performer, the acceptance of the blues among younger rural Whites was "really inevitable. Every country musician today has been subjected to the blues." According to Michael Bane, the subjected found their way to Memphis:

> But in Memphis—*Memphis* of all places!—. . . A bunch of rednecks caught black music the way some people get the gospel . . . When Elvis walked down Beale Street . . . When Carl Perkins first went to an all black Baptist Church in Jackson, Tennessee . . . when Jerry Lee Lewis peeked in the window of a black church in Ferriday, Louisiana; when Conway Twitty listened to his first field hand singing the blues — they found missing pieces of themselves, and they went to Memphis to try and make other people understand their vision.[47]

Yet, as Judd Phillips once bluntly stated, "the Negro could not be accepted as an idol; it was a sin." Consequently, there were unimaginable fortunes to be made in preserving the racial barriers in cultural production and consumption. By the early 1950s, major record executives recategorized the rockin blues as "rockabilly," "country-blues," and "rock and roll." Simultaneously, Sam Phillips signed and developed White acts to sing and perform songs created by Black performers. He "kept saying that if he could find a white man who could sing with the black man's individuality and conviction he could make a billion dollars." In 1953, Phillips found his solution in the form of a young Memphis housing project resident named Elvis Presley. Born in Tupelo, Mississippi, in 1935, Presley had moved with his parents to Memphis at age thirteen. Every night he listened to African American performers such as Louis Jordan, Wynonie Harrris, Rosetta Tharpe, Roy Brown, and Big Boy Crudup on the *Red Hot and Blue* program of White disc jockey Dewey Phillips. In between attending high school, driving a truck, serving as a movie usher, and selling his blood, Presley spent countless hours learning African American song, dance, performance, hair, and clothing styles on Beale Street.[48]

Presley's first record for Sun was a cover of Arthur "Big Boy" Crudup's 1946 Delta blues hit, "That's All Right Mama." According to the White Georgian journalist Stanley Booth, the rise of White rock performers was not a new Memphis-based minstrel movement:

It was 1956, and for the past couple of years we had been hearing on the radio performers such as Fats Domino, Little Richard, the Platters, Jackie J. Brenston, Hank Ballard and the Midnighters, Ray Charles, Chuck Berry and Bo Diddley. Soon there were so many white performers doing the same kind of music as the black rhythm and blues artists—Elvis, Carl Perkins, Jerry Lee Lewis, Charlie Rich, Gene Vincent, Roy Orbison, Johnny Cash, Bobby Charles—that even if we didn't remember that Al Jolson and Jimmie Rodgers has appeared in blackface, we knew that race was irrelevant.[49]

Refusing to accept the notion that race doesn't matter, Gary Giddins and others argue that Presley and his contemporaries were still in touch with the tradition of minstrelsy. Giddins examines the use of African American bluesman Otis Blackwell by RCA and Presley. Blackwell wrote several major songs for which Presley was given undeserved co-authorship; Blackwell also provided demo tapes with arrangements for the band and vocal cues for Presley. The talent and persona of Blackwell, and the tradition he represented, were ruthlessly mined and mimicked in an effort ultimately designed to block a blues movement that could have demolished the most cherished ideals of White supremacist culture.[50]

The most pressing question was how to preserve the barricades of intellectual and physical segregation in the midst of the grand cultural and social revolution developing in the South. Songs, styles, arrangements, dances, clothes, voices, and even personalities were "covered" or masked. Soon after its release in 1951, "Rocket 88" was covered by a White country band from Pennsylvania, Bill Haley and the Saddlemen. The success of WDIA and other stations with rhythm and blues programming encouraged radio owners throughout the country to switch formats. Although White minstrels had carved out a significant niche in radio from the 1920s into the 1950s, the success of WDIA and other stations with rhythm and blues programming led owners and managers to seek out White announcers familiar with Black slang. One of the first practitioners of what Nelson George has called "blackface radio" was Allan Freed, a Cleveland disc jockey whose nighttime R&B show's signal reached a huge White teenage audience in a dozen states. He has been credited with coining the term "Rock and Roll"; a banner of the successful intellectual resegregation of the Black and White working classes, the term that distinguished the audience more than it did the music.[51]

The fourth blues movement partially emerged from the deep impact of the Chicago blues school upon the consciousness of European youth. Among the New York Left of the mid-1930s, a folk music movement had developed which had spread to London by the early 1950s. Blues performers with a strong political bent such as Leadbelly, Josh White, Sonny Terry, Brownie McGhee, and Big Bill Broonzy constantly traveled within this transatlantic circuit. When Big Bill Broonzy's health failed in 1958, he recommended that Muddy Waters go to England in his place. Waters quickly became popular and upon returning to England in 1962, he was followed around by a young group of admirers who had named their band after one of his 1954 songs, "Rollin' Stone."

Soon many blues performers, including the women from the classic era of the 1920s, were being booked at colleges and festivals, and on tours and television. Al Young remembered this period:

> By 1961 I was playing folk music in coffee houses and cabarets, and keeping company with so-called folkies, who relished being hip about the legends surrounding black country blues singers . . . The early sixties was the folk blues revival era. Enthusiastic and enterprising young Yankees were systematically journeying South, sojourning, and returning with valuable cargo.[52]

By the early 1960s the blues incubating in England recrossed the Atlantic in the form of the "British Invasion." This assault was led by a budding group of English guitarists such as Mick Green, Jeff Beck, Eric Clapton, Jimmy Page, Peter Townsend, and the Rolling Stones. All were heavily influenced by the recordings of Bo Didley, Little Richard, Ike Turner's Kings of Rhythm, Muddy Waters, and Howlin' Wolf:

> When the Stones first toured America, they were asked to appear on a nationally syndicated television pop show called "Shindig." Only, they said, if they could bring Howlin' Wolf in to do a guest spot. Howlin' Who? Few American teenagers had heard of the man, but there he was one night in prime time, moving his great bulk around the "Shindig" stage with unbelievable agility and screaming the blues for the millions.[53]

During a Beatles first press conference

> a reporter asked them what they most wanted to see. They immediately replied, "Muddy Waters and Bo Diddley." "Where's that?" asked the culturally ignorant reporter. The Beatles snickered. "You Americans don't seem to know your most famous citizens."[54]

The literary blues tradition was also significantly deepened and widened during this period. The social realism of William Faulkner had gained him many admirers including the African American novelist James Baldwin. Raised in Lafayette County on the western border of the Mississippi Delta, Faulkner was the great-grandson of a plantation owner who was also a Confederate colonel and a novelist. Beginning in 1929, he produced a series of novels that revolved around the transformation of a plantation society debilitated by its own mythology. Some critics charged that his realism was a form of studied ambivalence that allowed him to critique the Cavalier tradition without repudiating it. After winning the Nobel Prize for Literature in 1950, Faulkner ended his ambivalence over desegregation, vowing to join his fellow White Mississippians in "going out into the street and shooting Negroes." Baldwin attacked him and all others who advised African Americans to be patient and accept gradual change. Baldwin offered another view of Mississippi society in his 1964 play *Blues for Mister Charlie*. Set in Plaguetown, the acclaimed work was based on the murder of Emmett Till and was inspired by the assassination of Medgar Evers (see pages 176–7). In a 1974 novel, *If Beale Street Could Talk*, Baldwin presents "angry determined, hard talking blues people who recognize the motherfucker for what he is and, through the power of their love for each other, are able to overcome his power to oppress." Firmly embedded in the blues literary tradition, Baldwin saw the blues epistemology as a form of social realism that was essentially liberating:

> Now I am claiming a great deal for the blues. I'm using them as a metaphor ... I want to talk about the blues, not only because they speak of this particular experience of life and this state of being, but because they contain the toughness that manages to make this experience articulate ... And I want to suggest that the acceptance of this anguish one finds in the blues, and expressions of it, creates also, however odd this may sound, a kind of joy.[55]

Not all the recorded blues schools retained their position at the top of the commercial charts. The rhythm and blues and rock and roll performers such as Chuck Berry, Bo Didley, Little Richard, and Fats Domino eclipsed the national popularity of the Chicago and Memphis blues sounds by the mid-1950s. Yet according to Muddy Waters, all these traditions were treasured and preserved by the Southern Black audience, the collective griot and the archivist of African American culture:

> People there, they *feel* the blues ... They come from miles around to hear us, and if we get less than six-seven-eight hundred people, believe me that's a bad house! ... They pay two, three dollars a time to come in; maybe they don't eat the next day, but man, the place is really jumpin'![56]

## "Hellhound on My Trail"

> I got to keep moving, I got to keep moving,
> blues falling down like hail, blues falling down like hail
> Ummmm blues falling down like hail
> blues falling down like hail.
> And the day keeps reminding me there's a hellhound on my trail
> Hellhound on my trail, hellhound on my trail.
> > "Hellhound on My Trail," Robert Johnson[57]

> The real trouble is that you have given us schools too long in which we could study the earth through the floor and the stars through the roof.
> > Rev. H. H. Humes[58]

African Americans in Mississippi did not immediately benefit from the rising rates of Black voter registration in the South which occurred after the Supreme Court outlawed the White primary in 1944. The state legislature passed a constitutional amendment further restricting registration in 1954. Those few registered Blacks were paid personal visits by Citizens' Council members who threatened them and their families. In Belzoni, 52-year-old Rev. George Washington Lee was fatally shot in the head in May 1955 for refusing to remove his name from the voting rolls. After being visited by a bank president who was also a CCA member, 62-year-old Belzoni grocer Gus Courts was seriously wounded for his refusal to remove his name from the rolls. In Brookhaven, 63-year-old World War Two veteran and activist Lamar Smith was murdered in front of a crowd on the courthouse lawn. Although the state NAACP charged the CCA with direct involvement in the shooting of these key leaders, no one was ever convicted for committing these atrocities. As Black voter registration in the Delta fell, US Senator Eastland praised the work of the Citizens' Council. The federal government was finally forced to investigate electoral violations in 65 of Mississippi's 82 counties.[59]

In August 1955 the body of a fifteen-year-old African American youth visiting the Delta from Chicago was found floating in the Tallahatchie River. The brutal murder of Emmett Till for speaking to a White woman became an international incident. The NAACP blamed the CCA in a pamphlet entitled *M is for Murder and Mississippi*. Those charged with the murder were defended by the law partner of US Representative Jamie Whitten, Princeton graduate J. J. Breland, who believed that the accused were the glue that held the Delta together: "we've got to have our Miams and Bryants to fight our wars and to keep the niggahs in line." He also warned that if the North persisted with pushing integration, the "Tallahatchie River won't hold all the niggers that'll be thrown in it." None of the accused were convicted and Till's grandfather had to flee the state because he dared to testify against them.[60]

Despite international condemnation, the attack on the new Black leadership intensified. Born in Decatur, Mississippi, after graduating from the historically Black Alcorn State College in 1952, Medgar Evers came to the Delta town of Mound Bayou. His initial job was working as an insurance agent for the newly formed Black company Magnolia Mutual Insurance Company, owned by Dr. T. R. M. Howard. According to his wife Myrlie, he immediately underwent a deep, personal, transformation, a blues moment. He committed the remainder of his life to resurrecting the historical African American rural reform agenda:

> Here on the edge of the cotton fields, life was being lived on a level that Medgar, for all his acquaintance with the poor of both Mississippi and of Chicago's teeming black ghetto, found hard to believe. In a way, a horrified fascination with it drew him back again and again even as the sight of that of that long-ago pile of bloody clothing had drawn him to the place in the woods near Decatur where a Negro had been lynched ... It was a long time before Medgar was able to piece together all of the elements of this vicious system ... All during that long, unbelievably hot summer of 1952, Medgar sold insurance and gathered information. He was like a student driven by horror to learn more ... Sometime during that summer his anger reached a peak, and he began organizing chapters of the National Association for the Advancement of Colored People ... And for a time Medgar himself flirted intellectually with the idea of fighting back in the Delta. For a time he envisioned a secret black army of Delta Negroes who fought by night to meet oppression and brutality with violence ... a Mississippi Mau Mau.[61]

Evers organized these new chapters with Amzie Moore. Moore and Howard helped to create the Regional Council of Negro Leadership (RCNL) in 1951.

Mirroring the structure of the Delta Council, this body organized mass meetings so that Delta residents could hear such national leaders as Congressmen William Dawson of Chicago, Congressman Charles Diggs of Detroit, and NAACP lawyer Thurgood Marshall. Built by Howard, Moore, Aaron Henry, Richard West, Fannie Lou Hamer, and many others, the huge RCNL network included numerous local religious, fraternal, business, and community organizations. The RCNL addressed issues such as police brutality, voting rights, and making segregation expensive to local White businesses and "Uncle Toms" through economic boycotts. During the 1950s, the RCNL could hold mass meetings with thirteen thousand persons, and Moore claimed a membership of 100,000 in forty counties. This rarely discussed organization represented a continuation of the local organizing tradition upon which the national civil rights organizations would later build.[62]

After detailing the rising number of atrocities in the state, as field secretary of the state NAACP, Evers challenged the activities of the Federal Bureau of Investigation in 1959. "We are concerned that the lynchers of Mack Charles Parker are known to the FBI and state officials. However, despite this knowledge, not a single person has been arrested." The NAACP launched several campaigns during this period to investigate violence, register voters, and desegregate public facilities throughout the state. In 1963, Evers and the organization were heavily involved in a campaign to desegregate Jackson public facilities that involved a boycott of merchants, mass meetings, mass demonstrations, and the mass arrest of hundreds of children and college-age students. On 12 June 1963, after attending an evening mass meeting, Evers was assassinated by Byron De La Beckwith, a member of the Greenwood Citizens' Council. On the day of Evers's burial, a funeral procession of twenty-five thousand persons accompanied him to his final resting place. Truly a man of the people, Evers explained his motivations in the following manner:

> Ladies and gentlemen, I think it appropriate at this time that I make a confession to you before we go any further, and that is: I LOVE THE LAND OF MY BIRTH. I do not mean just America as a country, but Mississippi, the state in which I was born. The things that I say here tonight will be said to you in hopes of the future when it will not be the case in Mississippi and America, when we will not have to hang our heads in shame or hold our breath when the name Mississippi is mentioned, fearing the worst. But instead, we will be anticipating the best.[63]

## "I can't see a leader leading me nowhere if he's in New York and I'm down here catching hell."[64]

Out of the growing conflict in the Delta hundreds of new leaders emerged, including Fannie Lou Hamer. Her life experiences and determination came to symbolize for a new generation the historic African American rural reform agenda. Hammer was the youngest of twenty children, whose sharecropper parents were able to rent land and accumulate livestock and equipment in

Sunflower County until they were pushed back into destitution after a White neighbor poisoned their livestock. She and her husband Perry worked on various plantations for twenty years. In 1962, at age forty-five, she agreed to participate in the voter registration campaigns of the Southern Christian Leadership Conference (SCLC) and the Student Nonviolent Coordinating Committee (SNCC).

These campaigns had emerged from the rapid growth of the student wing of the freedom Movement. After four students from the historically Black North Carolina A&T College decided that they were going to be served at a segregated lunch counter on 1 February 1960, student sit-ins and boycotts were immediately launched in fifteen cities and five states. With the guidance of veteran activist Ella Baker, the student movement created SNCC, a regionwide organization, in April 1960. Now the vice president of the Mississippi NAACP, Moore requested SNCC to launch a voter registration project. According to SCLC leader Andrew Young: "We tried to warn SNCC. We were all Southerners and we knew the depth of the depravity of Southern racism. We knew better than to try to take on Mississippi."[65] In another mobilization, after the US Supreme Court declared segregation on interstate transport to be illegal, the Congress of Racial Equality (CORE) sent integrated teams of freedom riders to the South in 1961. After one of their buses was burned near Birmingham, SNCC joined the trek. With the backing of the Kennedy administration, and with a National Guard escort, the freedom riders rode west only to land in jail in the Delta's notorious prison, Parchman Penitentiary. The refusal of Governor Ross Barnett, a CCA member, to release the activists led the state branches of NAACP, SCLC, SNCC, and CORE to band together under the banner of the Council of Federated Organizations (COFO).[66]

The imprisonment of the freedom riders occurred near the time of the annual meeting of the Delta Council. The keynote speaker, President Kennedy's Secretary of Agriculture, Orville Freemen, canceled in response to to pressure emanating from the NAACP and the RCNL. Undaunted, the Speaker of the Mississippi House of Representatives and Delta Council leader Walter Sillers proposed a resolution,

> commending our officials and law enforcement officers for the orderly manner which they handled an invasion of our state by disorderly groups bent on producing an explosion of mob violence and lawlessness as occurred in our sister state of Alabama ... [These conspirators included] some unworthy newspapers, commentators, cheap politicians, irresponsible negro preachers, and minority groups.[67]

A majority of the council members on the committee considering the resolution voted against it. Sillers denounced their "timidity and complacency" as the first steps on the road to communism. In a letter to Sillers, fellow legislator and planter Edwin Hooker warned that "unless these race matters are handled properly ... these Delta plantations of ours won't be worth three cents on the dollar."[68]

Opposed to the confrontational methods of sit-ins and freedom rides, the Kennedy administration promised SNCC leaders federal protection and philanthropic support if the movement would shift its energies toward voter education. In 1961, C. C. Bryant of the McComb NAACP and Bob Moses, field secretary for the SNCC, tried to push a voter education registration drive by holding a mock election for African Americans, a freedom vote. Before the mock elections could be held, two Black Mississippians chose to run for the US Congress in two separate districts. Although they were defeated, this event

> captured the imagination not only of the state's Negroes but of the nation, [and] they were partly responsible for the influx of civil rights workers the following summer for Moses' voter registration drive.[69]

In June 1962, the COFO established seven voter registration training schools throughout the state by using local staff members and two hundred college students from around the USA who volunteered for the summer. In another mock election held in 1963, more than 88,000 disenfranchised African Americans selected the president of the state NAACP, Dr Aaron Henry, for Governor, and the Reverend Edwin King, the White chaplain of the historically Black Tougaloo College, for lieutenant governor over the White candidates. Despite these efforts, African American registration increased by only 6 percent.[70]

This failure was a product of the intensification of official persecution. Fannie Lou Hamer and eighteen others attempted to register to vote in Indianaola in August 1962. Instead of being allowed to register she was given a test on the state constitution. After the entire group was rejected, the bus carrying them was stopped and the driver was arrested for driving a bus the same color as a school bus. By the time Hamer returned to her plantation home, the owner already knew of her attempt to register and began threatening her family with eviction. Hamer went to stay with a friend in Ruleville and later that night shots were fired into the house. She fled Ruleville and later went to Nashville for a SNCC meeting. Her testimony riveted the audience while her voice joined those of the Freedom Singers, a group that infused the entire movement with powerful songs. Before finally being allowed to register in January 1963, she was evicted and her family's property was seized. After she became a SNCC field secretary, her activities were continually monitored by county and state officials, the Ku Klux Klan, the Citizens' Council, and the Federal Bureau of Investigation. A month after registering, Hamer and a group of activists were jailed in Winona, Mississippi, on their way back from a SNCC conference, for complaining after she and another Black woman were pushed away from the bus door so a young White girl could get on first. Jailed for three days, Hamer, June Johnson, and Annelle Ponder were all beaten. The women were held incommunicado without treatment and threatened with death before finally being found by US Justice Department attorneys. On 26 April 1964, COFO delegates formed the Mississippi Freedom Democratic

Party (MFDP) and decided to hold another Freedom Election in all the congressional districts of the state; in the Delta's Second congressional district, Hamer defeated the Democrat Whitten by 33,000 votes to 49.[71]

Upon the assassination of President Kennedy in November 1963, his Vice President, Lyndon Baines Johnson, was immediately sworn in as President. For many years a powerful congressman representing the Texas Cotton Belt, Johnson attempted to keep the Southern White electorate within the Democratic Party by censoring and compromising the freedom movement. Initially, however, the movement continued to gain momentum. During Freedom Summer in 1964, more than one thousand White students from the North were invited to the state for three purposes, according to Haynes Walton:

> First, COFO's voter registration forces obviously needed to be strengthened ... Second, in order to prod the federal government into taking action, direct action techniques were needed for dramatizing nationwide the plight of Mississippi Negroes. Third, Moses and the others acknowledged the need for some means of protecting those Negroes who had recently obtained the vote to ensure that they were not frightened off.[72]

In August, one Black student and two White students were killed in Neshoba County in August: James Chaney, Andrew Goodman, and Mickey Schwerner. A few days later, the MFDP delegates went to the Democratic Party's national convention in Atlantic City to challenge the credentials of the "lily white" Mississippi delegation. President Johnson and the liberal wing of the party campaigned on the basis of their civil rights "successes" even though Southern state party structures completely excluded African Americans. The exposure of the liberals' acceptance of segregation in their own party ranks threatened their legitimacy with African Americans, labor, and White liberals. When Hamer delivered an account of her beating in the Winona jail before a national television audience, the liberal wing of the Party was officially on trial.[73]

The fight over the seating of the MFDP delegation of mostly sharecroppers at the Democratic Party's national convention again placed the Delta at the center of a national debate over the meaning of American democracy, class, culture, and human rights. The Democratic Party feared disaster as the MFDP insurgents successfully lobbied other delegations for support. Although anticipating winning his own election, President Johnson feared an immediate White backlash and the permanent loss of Southern White electoral votes. US Senator Hubert Humphrey was ordered by Johnson either to crush the MFDP rebellion or be removed from the presidential ticket. Humphrey told his protégé, fellow Minnesotan and future Vice President Walter Mondale, to suppress the MFDP by any means necessary. He accomplished his assignment through secret meetings, and false statements, and by using information on the MFDP's strategy gathered from FBI informants in the Freedom Movement. Instead of unseating the entire Mississippi delegation, Johnson, Humphrey and Mondale offered the MFDP two at-large seats to be selected by

Johnson (this was to ensure Hamer would not be selected). Humphrey pleaded with Hamer to accept the compromise so that he could become vice president and push the civil rights agenda. According to Edwin King, prophetically Hamer expressed no sympathy for Humphrey's position:

> Senator Humphrey. I know lots of people in Mississippi who have lost their jobs for trying to register to vote. I had to leave the plantation where I worked in Sunflower County. Now if you lose this job of vice president because you do what is right, because you help the MFDP, everything will be all right. God will take care of you. But if you take it this way, why, you will never be able to do any good for civil rights, for poor people, for peace, or any of those thing you talk about.[74]

The United Auto Workers' president, Walter Reuther, was brought in to convince Martin Luther King Jr and the SCLC to support a compromise; his tactic was to pledge badly needed funds for voter registration. Finally, Rev. Edwin King, Aaron Henry, and Bob Moses of the MFDP were invited to a secret meeting with Mondale, Reuther, Humphrey, Bayard Rustin, Rev. Martin Luther King, and Andrew Young. Fannie Lou Hamer was purposely excluded and a deal was done. Chana Kai Lee, among others, has argued that this event marked the opening of a new era of conflict between the blues Bloc and the old and new Black elite. This disastrous compromise pushed the historic African American rural reform agenda out of sight for the next thirty-five years, isolated its adherents, and forced these perpetually plundered communities once again to to defend themselves by themselves.

## The End of Legitimacy

The failure of the Democratic Party to break with the plantation bloc spurred African Americans to search for autonomous forms of development. SNCC leader James Forman recognized the growing schism between working-class Blacks and the national liberal agenda:

> Atlantic City was a powerful lesson, not only for black people from Mississippi . . . No longer was there any hope, among those who still had it, that the federal government would change the situation in the Deep South. The fine line between state governments and the federal government, which we had used to build a movement, was played out.[75]

Similarly, after Congress refused to remove White Mississippi legislators and congresspersons who gained their seats in racially rigged elections, Hamer identified the Northern liberal as the plantation bloc's last line of defense:

> Racial progress? Almost a hundred years ago John R. Lynch placed this same kind of challenge before the House of Representatives. He was a black man from Mississippi and he succeeded with white Yankee help. But we failed a hundred years later with native white Mississippi help and Yankee opposition. So you see this is not Mississippi's problem, it is America's problem.[76]

The Delta's plantation bloc faced another challenge; federal cotton policies were contradictory. Subsidies didn't compensate for declining crop prices and the increasing costs of equipment, fertilizers, pesticides, defoliants, etcetera. The decline in crop prices was due, in part, to a federal program designed to assist textile mills and machinery manufacturers by expanding lower-cost foreign production. The government was providing technical assistance and financing for cotton Green Revolutions in Argentina, Brazil, Egypt, El Salvador, Greece, Guatemala, India, Iran, Mexico, Nicaragua, Pakistan, Spain, and Sudan. When Orville Freeman raised support prices for cotton in the early 1960s, the demand for domestic cotton from domestic mills declined even further. Additionally, domestic profitability was further undercut by national acreage reductions, price reductions in rayon, and increased imports from foreign textile mills.[77]

Stability and uniformity in federal policy, the limiting of funding for foreign producers, and the resurgence of the power of domestic producers were not achieved until 1965. Overall, Johnson was engaged in promoting disunity within the Freedom movement and unity among domestic cotton producers in an effort to establish the conditions necessary for the resurgence of plantation bloc power.

# 8

# Poor People and the Freedom Blues

The Black Power slogan did not spring full grown from the head of some philosophical Zeus. It was born from the wounds of despair and disappointment. It is a cry of daily hurt and persistent pain ... It is no accident that the birth of this slogan in the civil rights movement took place in Mississippi — the state symbolizing the most blatant abuse of white power. In Mississippi the murder of civil rights workers is still a popular pastime. In that state more than forty Negroes and whites have been murdered over the past three years, and not a single man has been punished for these crimes. More than fifty Negro churches have been burned or bombed in Mississippi in the last two years, yet the bombers still walk the streets surrounded by a halo of adoration. This is white power in its most brutal, cold-blooded, and vicious form.

Rev. Martin Luther King Jr, 1967[1]

Before the Poor People's March on Washington set off from the Mississippi Delta town of Marks in the summer of 1968, its principal organizer had already been assassinated in Memphis, the capital of the Delta. On a previous visit to Marks, the Reverend Martin Luther King Jr had been profoundly shocked when he found himself in the midst of starving children. After so many monumental achievements and awards, King and millions of others were forced to ask themselves how had defeat been snatched from the jaws of victory? After years of fighting for human rights throughout the world, King realized, as had many before him, that this question could only be answered by directly confronting the Delta plantation bloc.

## The Poor People's March on Washington

Slowly, observers outside the Delta's African American community began to realize that the plantation bloc was in the final stages of implementing the plan advocated by Bilbo, by the regional sociologists at Chapel Hill, and by the Citizens' Councils: to hold back "this black tide which threatens to engulf us" by distributing "the Negroes more evenly throughout the country." By 1964, members of the Mississippi legislature were openly advocating the expulsion of African Americans, and the legislature passed a bill authorizing the felony prosecution and sterilization of Black women on welfare who had a second child out of wedlock. Punishment for this "crime" was later reduced to a misdemeanor that could result in a jail term of 30 to 90 days or a $250 fine. Called the "genocide bill" by its critics, this law was still part of the state criminal code in the early 1990s.[2]

The movement to secure the right to vote was met with mass evictions. The number of cotton choppers fell by 75 percent between 1964 and 1967. Those attempting to remain in the Delta witnessed the end of freely distributed federal commodities in 1962 and their replacement by food stamps sold by planters. Now the unemployed, homeless, and starving residents had to beg planters for loans with extortionate rates of interest in order to buy food stamps so that they could then purchase poor-quality food. By 1966, the year-round labor force on the plantations was down to 20,000 tractor drivers and mechanical cotton picker operators. The use of the cotton picker shifted the critical day-labor demand period from fall cotton picking to spring cotton chopping, hoeing, and weeding. The introduction of aerially sprayed herbicides further reduced the day-labor workforce from 21,000 persons in 1962 to 14,500 in 1965. Homeless, without food or income, 12,000 African Americans fled the Delta in 1967 alone, leaving behind what the Delta Council called a "grand labor force made up of grandparents and grandchildren."[3]

Movements to improve the economic position of African Americans such as the Council of Federated Organization's effort to secure wages of $1 an hour for agricultural labor were also met with mass evictions. Organizing on the Andrews plantation in Washington County in May 1965 led to evictions, picketing, violence, and then to the construction of Tent City by the newly homeless families on the land of a neighboring Black farmer. As the newly formed Freedom Labor Union rallied support around the evicted families, the county welfare agency moved to deny them food.

The burning of fifty crosses throughout the state by the Ku Klux Klan on 4 January 1966 signaled the end of the "moratorium on violence" called for by the state's "responsible" White leadership in the fall and winter of 1965. On 24 January 1966, the MFDP, the Freedom Labor Union, and the Delta Ministry held a 700-participant Poor People's Conference for two days at the Mount Beulah Center. On the last day, the leadership sent a telegram to President Johnson requesting federal assistance with slowing the evictions, housing the growing number of homeless, feeding the starving adults and children, and preventing the outbreak of a new wave of racist terror. After the White House failed to respond, fifty members of the group staged a "live-in" at the abandoned Greenville air force base. Evicted again, some of the homeless moved to form a new community, Freedom City, on 400 acres near Greenville while the rest of the group moved into the Mount Beulah Center.[4]

On 5 June 1966, the first Black student to enroll at the University of Mississippi, James Meredith, began a pilgrimage for voting rights through the Delta, from Memphis to Jackson. On 6 June, he was shot, although not fatally, by a White sniper as he crossed into Mississippi. The march was restarted by

Delta residents and joined by Fannie Lou Hamer of the MFDP, Stokely Carmichael of the SNCC, Floyd McKissick of CORE, Martin Luther King Jr of the Southern Christian Leadership Conference (SCLC), and many other national leaders. The threats, attacks, and police whippings that accompanied this march radicalized African Americans throughout the country. Not only did the slogan "Black Power" emerge for the first time from this Delta pilgrimage, so did a new Martin Luther King Jr.

Dr King soon underwent a profound transformation, a phenomenon described in this work as a "Blues transformation." In his autobiography, SCLC vice president Ralph Abernathy describes how a new King was created during the march when they briefly visited a small school house in the Delta town of Marks, in Quitman County:

> We looked around the primitive school house and saw them watching us, wide-eyed and silent . . . Then I realized what it was: virtually all of them were under weight . . . As if reading my mind the teacher glanced at the clock. "Can you excuse me," she said. "It's lunchtime. I need to feed them. It won't take a minute. Please don't leave." We watched as she brought out a box of crackers and a brown paper bag filled with apples. The children sat quietly as she took out a paring knife and cut each apple into four parts. Then she went around to each desk and gave each child a stack of four or five crackers and a quarter of an apple. I watched with a growing awareness of what we were seeing. This was not just a snack. This was all these children would be eating for lunch. I nudged Martin. "That's all they get," I whispered. Turning to me he nodded his head and I saw that his eyes were full of tears which he wiped away with the back of his hands.
>
> [Later that evening, King spoke to Abernathy:] "We've got to do something for them . . . We can't let that kind of poverty exist . . . I don't think people really know that little school children are slowly starving in the United States of America. I didn't know it." . . . It was true. He had grown up in a middle-class household, as had I. Neither of us had ever gone hungry, nor had any of our family. Oh, we had seen some poor homes in our ministries but we had never lived in a poverty pocket like northern Mississippi. So that day we were confronted with something we knew existed but had never seen first hand. "We'll go to Washington and camp out if necessary" he said . . . "Then something would be done." . . . "When do you want to do this?" I asked him. "As soon as possible . . . We'll go for broke. We'll move the whole operation to Washington and stay there until we get a hearing."

However, according to Abernathy, all of the staff of the SCLC were not as enthusiastic as King:

> The most vocal adversaries to the idea were James Bevel and Jesse Jackson . . . "How do we bail out?" they asked. "If we don't succeed, if we don't get any concrete results, then how do we bail out of the situation?" . . . Martin listened with barely constrained anger. He had seen a vision in Marks, Mississippi, that would haunt him for the rest of his short life.[5]

Several months later nine US senators on the Subcommittee on Employment, Manpower and Poverty of the Senate Committee on Labor and Public Welfare visited the Delta. The delegation included senators Jennings Randolph, Clai-

186186

DEVELOPMENTDEVELOPMENT ARRESTED

borne Pell, Edward Kennedy, Robert Kennedy, and Jacob Javitz. They visited a family of thirteen whose daily diet consisted of grits and molasses for breakfast, no lunch, and beans for supper. Some of the children did not attend school because of distended stomachs, chronic sores, and a lack of shoes. While mechanization-generated unemployment was generally blamed, the subcommittee observed:

> It [mechanization] has accelerated sharply, due to factors associated with the agricultural minimum wage. In the Delta alone, it is estimated that some 40 to 60 thousand people will either be without or almost without cash income by this summer. It is our strong belief that this economic upheaval has reached a level of emergency, as grave as any natural disaster.[6]

Two weeks after their return they wrote President Johnson that the "shocking" and "widespread" malnutrition and hunger in the Delta constituted an "emergency situation." The subcommittee recommended that the Secretary of Agriculture provide free food stamps for families without income, provide reduced-price food stamps for low-income families, investigate overcharging, and distribute free surplus federal commodities. The Executive Branch, the OEO, and the Department of Health, Education and Welfare were all requested to go upon an emergency footing. The Johnson administration refused. However, food and other donations began to flow into the Delta from around the United States and from church congregations in Australia, Botswana, Britain, Cameroon, Canada, Denmark, East Asia, Finland, France, Germany, Holland, India, New Zealand, South Africa, and Switzerland.[7]

Rooted in the historic African American development tradition, in 1967 the Poor People's Committee decided that a national movement was necessary to halt the Delta plantation bloc mobilization. Their agenda was adopted by King, the SCLC, and by organizations in the Delta, Mississippi, and the nation as a whole. It was agreed that Mississippians would lead the nation in a march on the Capitol against expulsion, starvation, and other forms of oppression. After the Poor People's March on Washington was announced, Black and White middle-class leaders essentially sided with the plantation bloc when they launched a campaign to isolate the movement. King's long-time aide Bayard Rustin refused to participate, the NAACP and the Urban League refused to comment, and the White liberal Southern historian C. Vann Woodward asked in a prominent article, "What more do they want?"[8]

Many key individuals and organizations in Mississippi and the USA decided that they could not turn back. President Johnson had failed to implement and fund much of the civil rights and anti-poverty legislation he authored and Congress was content, in King's words, to play "Russian Roulette with riots." King believed the civil rights movement as a whole had become bogged down for two years by the "paralysis of analysis" and that this period of indecision had to come to an end:

> America is at a crossroads of history and it is critically important for us, as a nation and a society, to choose a new path and move upon it with resolution and courage

... Unrest among the poor of America, and particularly Negroes, is growing rapidly
... And so we decided to go to Washington to use any means of legitimate nonviolent
protest necessary to move our nation and our government on a new course of social,
economic and political reform ... In this way we can work creatively against the
despair and indifference that have so often caused our nation to be immobilized
during the cold winter and shaken profoundly in the hot summer.[9]

King was undergoing a revitalization, a resurrection, a "Blues transformation."
He was moving away from being the model of African American pragmatic
uplift and into a folk immersion, a baptism in an older tradition. After years
of being a leading light in the Second Reconstruction, he already understood
the necessity of raising the banner of the Third Reconstruction:

"For years I labored with the idea of reforming the existing institutions of the
society, a little change here, a little change there," Martin said in the Summer after
Chicago. "Now I feel quite differently. I think you've got to have a reconstruction of
the entire society, a revolution of values."[10]

The conditions and consciousness of the rural African American working class
shocked and radicalized both King and Malcolm X in the last years of their
lives. In December 1967, King presented his plan for the Poor People's March
to the SCLC board. Beginning in April 1968, three thousand Blacks, Native
Americans, Chicanos, Puerto Ricans, and Whites would leave from their
respective communities to converge on the capital and force the immediate
implementation of a $12 billion economic bill of rights that guaranteed work
or livable incomes. As envisioned, the Poor People's Campaign (PPC) was the
first stage in a movement that would grow stage by stage into a national strike
against hunger, injustice, and the plantation bloc:

The demands were left intentionally vague, not restricted to specific legislation, in
order to guard against the seduction of empty promises and legislative feints. The
intensity and size of the campaign would be determined by congressional response.
An unfavorable response would result in thousands more converging on Washington
with the original contingent acting as non-violent marshals. The plan also envisaged
simultaneous demonstrations on the west coast.[11]

As part of this campaign, King wanted to organize Black tenants, domestics,
sanitation workers, and seasonal laborers into national unions. Therefore,
after two garbage workers were crushed to death by an automatic compressor
forty miles from Marks, Mississippi, in Memphis on 1 February, he felt
compelled to support the sanitation workers' organizing efforts. In the midst
of organizing the Poor People's Campaign, however, on 4 February King felt
it necessary to give his own eulogy at Ebenezer Baptist Church in Atlanta.
The congregation was told not to mention his degrees or his Nobel Prize after
he died. "I want you to be able to say that day that I did try to feed the
hungry, I want you to say that day that I did try in my life to clothe the
naked."[12]

In coordination with Delta leaders, King and the SCLC intensified their

Poor People's Campaign organizing efforts. In a letter to the SCLC staff on 8 March, 1968, field director Hosea Williams gave instructions to local staff around the country on the types of promotional activities they should arrange when Dr King visited. Ministerial, business, professional, civil rights, community, and youth leaders were to be organized, along with mass meetings that would include mock trials. "You must organize the mock trial as well . . . America must be tried for stealing 4 million mules and 80 million acres of land [from] her supposedly newly freed blacks over a hundred years ago." On 17 March, Dr King met with a co-founder of the United Farm Workers, Caesar Chavez, in Delano, California, before beginning a national tour to drum up support for the PPC. He interrupted his schedule to return to Memphis on 28 March to lead a march of eight thousand persons in support of the sanitation workers. During the Memphis protest, battles between the police and youths led to 120 arrests. Within a few hours, three thousand National Guardsmen entered the city to impose a dusk-to-dawn curfew. King left Memphis only to return on 3 April to lead another demonstration in order to prove the feasibility of nonviolence. The city attorney informed King that White supremacists in and around Memphis were intent on killing him. At a church rally that night, King spoke of the vision he had had at Marx:

> Longevity has its place, but I'm not concerned about that now. I just want to do God's will. And He's allowed me to go up to the mountain. And I've looked over, and I've seen the promised land . . . I'm not worried about anything. I'm not fearing any man. Mine eyes have seen the glory of the coming of the Lord.[13]

The next morning, King was assassinated while standing on the balcony of the Lorraine Motel in the Delta's capital city, Memphis. That night, more than 100 African American communities in over 100 cities erupted in rage and flames. Undeterred, the SCLC sent out thousands of telegrams to remind those who were wavering why the march had to go on:

> The late Dr Martin Luther King Jr's last dream was to turn the poorest county in America—Quitman County, Mississippi—from a "dungeon of shame to a haven of beauty." On Dr King's last visit to Marks, Mississippi . . . multitudes of men women and children ran to him, crying to him as though he was Jesus, telling him of their suffering and despair, their joblessness, their hunger, and their need for clothing to him. Some were even without shelter to live. Many presented their starving children who were dying of malnutrition.[14]

On 29 April several PPC leaders arrived in Washington, presented agency heads with a list of demands, and promised to return to get their answers in ten days. On 2 May, after a memorial service at the Lorraine Motel, the campaign began with a two-day march from Memphis to Marks. Approximately two to three hundred people from Marks and surrounding towns and plantations moved to a second Tent City, to prepare for the journey—some would never return. Caravans of busses and cars called Freedom Trains departed from Milwaukee, Maine, and Marks on 7 and 8 May. In each of the seven cities that each caravan passed through, rallies were held and busloads of activists joined the pilgrimage. Abernathy led the caravan out of Marks in a wagon pulled by two mules named Stennis and Eastland. On 9 May, the Southern caravan was entertained by the Temptations, the Supremes, and Harry Belafonte in Atlanta. Although the Western caravan stalled temporarily, activists promise to continue by any means necessary. The national coordinators received the following telegram from the West: "Tijerina says he can't raise enough money for buses from New Mexico, some of the poor people there plan to sell their own blood so they can make the trip." By 19 May, the Resurrection City encampment, located on the National Mall between the Lincoln Memorial and the Capitol building, had two thousand residents and was growing at a rate of five hundred persons per day.[15]

According to Abernathy, "Five years ago [during the 1963 March on Washington] we pleaded for the Black man. Today we plead for the Indians, the Mexican Americans, the white Appalachians, the Puerto Rican, and the Black man." Indeed, as evidenced by the list of participant organizations, this was perhaps the most historic multiethnic event in the nation's history. Presented was the agenda of the Third Reconstruction.[16]

Resurrection City was in many ways a utopian/imagined community come to life. It was a new democracy with its own city hall, a city council (sixteen officers, two selected from each ethnic and geographical group), a city manager, marshals, and a daily newspaper, *Truth and Unity News*. New institutions emerged during the two-month life of the settlement, including the Poor People's University, a library, the Coretta Scott King Day Care Center, and the Many Races Soul Center. A two-hundred-person construction crew installed sewer and electric lines, toilets, fences, kitchens, telephones, and washing machines, and erected a tent city. Major grocery stores supplemented the 500 tons of donated food and hot meals were trucked in daily from Howard University.

This grand coalition had a number of far-reaching demands. At the Department of the Interior, Native Americans sought "an end to paternalism; the right to control their destiny; complete control over the Native educational system; greater assistance for those Indians relocating to the cities; and a study of legal ownership of the disputed lands under the treaty of Guadalupe-Hildalgo." Native Americans also went to the Smithsonian Institute to press for the return of the remains of their ancestors. The delegation that met with Secretary of Labor Willard Wirtz demanded that the federal government immediately become the employer of first resort for the unemployed and underemployed; that it fund public works jobs immediately, include unemployed and underemployed workers in unemployment statistics; cancel contracts with firms that discriminated; extend equal employment requirements to subcontractors; hire more persons to investigate discrimination; include the voices of the poor in program planning, policy decisions, and administration; and give local residents control over programs that served them. Wirtz promised 100,000 new jobs by January, but, according to Abernathy, "he still refuses to push for a new strong bill . . . to create new jobs in the public and private sector ... And we're going to keep the pressure on until he changes his mind."[17]

Delegations delivered key demands to Secretary of State Dean Rusk: guarantee the land rights of the Spanish-speaking people of the Southwest; withdraw support from South Africa and from Portugal's occupation of Guinea-Bissau, Mozambique, and Angola; end the Bracero Program with Mexico; and stop the employment of Green Card holders as strike breakers until the poor in the USA are employed. The answers received from Rusk were characterized as reiterations of "time worn policies." Similar encounters occurred at the OEO, and at the departments of Health Education and Welfare, Housing and Urban Development, and Justice.

Yet the central dynamic of the march was between the African American participants and the USDA over what was to be done in the Mississippi Delta. The demolition and liquidation of African American community life in the Delta were denounced at every turn. A nonofficial Resurrection City newspaper, *Soul Force*, reprinted the following statistical analysis compiled by the influential journalist I. F. Stone:

> Eastland Plantation Inc. received government handouts of $157,930 or $13,161 a month. Poor children on ADC welfare in Mississippi receive $9 a month and thousands of them are starving. In other words, the United States of America pays one racist Senator's plantation in one month about the same amount that is provided for 1,462 children in Mississippi.[18]

After receiving a visit from Abernathy in April outlining the campaign's demands, Orville Freeman, the Secretary of Agriculture, delivered a terse communiqué. "I would like to emphasize my belief that it would be tragic for those who share our hope for a better life for the poor to use farm programs as a scapegoat." In a May meeting with Freeman, the Poor People's Campaign demanded that the USDA expand the school lunch program; expand the food stamp program and make food stamps free; support poor-farmer cooperatives; support the right of farm workers to bargain with employers; raise the agricultural minimum wage; end employment discrimination in USDA agencies and offices, and increase the nutritional value of freely distributed food. The PPC also demanded should that Freeman cease his attempt to return to the Treasury $227 million in supplemental food program funds; and that the USDA should respond immediately to hunger-plagued counties like those in the Delta.[19]

It had taken African American mobilizations in the Delta and a national march on the Capitol to restore political importance to the relationship between agricultural policy and rural and urban poverty and oppression. The agricultural blocs now faced an alliance consisting of numerous organizations that advocated various forms of land and labor reform in the South, in the Southwest, on Native American lands, and in Appalachia. These historic regional movements were being linked on the steps of the Capitol with newer urban movements, often composed of rural refugees. Furthermore, institu-

tional indifference only served to alienate and radicalize the march participants. The head of direct action, Hosea Williams, made the following
declaration during one of the daily 500-person mini-marches on the USDA:

> We are coming out of those shacks. We are ready to bleed ... This is our building
> and our labor paid for it ... we'll go when we want to and not before ... We have
> our job and the police have theirs.[20]

There was a great deal of underlying tension in Resurrection City about the
future, especially among the youth who were more influenced by the Black
Panthers and other leaders more radical than those present. Many felt the
march to be the end of one era and the beginning of another. Yet the citizens
of Resurrection City were bolstered by numerous expressions of support. A
Solidarity Day march on 19 June drew a crowd of one hundred thousand
people from around the United States. During his remarks, Abernathy concluded that the federal institutions would only be responsive to intense
vigilance and struggle:

> We went to Mr Freeman at the Department of Agriculture and demanded that the
> hungry of this nation be fed. At first he told us he was doing everything he could.
> But we kept after him. . . . So by August 1 there will be a food program in every one
> of the thousand poorest counties in this country—that includes over 200 counties
> that did not have food programs on June 1. We're going to keep after Mr Freeman,
> too, until he . . . makes food stamps free to people who can't afford them.[21]

The growing official condemnation of the march was accompanied by a
growing police presence, an increasing number of conflicts between police and
youth, and by a rise in the numbers of attacks on official Washington such as
the stoning of the Supreme Court. When the police came to evict the
occupants of Resurrection City on 19 June, a rebellion erupted in the city and
the National Guard was mobilized. Abernathy was subsequently arrested for
refusing to dismantle Resurrection City. US Senator and planter Strom
Thurmond (R. SC) led the official chorus denouncing the march and the
inability of its leaders to be satisfied: "the public has paid an astronomical cost
for two months of disorder and violence in Washington, and the Poor People's
Campaign representatives have been received at levels of government no
other group could ever reach." Before he died, King had predicted that the
failure of the Poor People's March would lead to deep and rapid national
polarization. Abernathy expressed the same despair in a statement issued
from his jail cell on 27 June, now realizing that the nation's leaders had
accepted the plantation bloc's doctrine that the destruction of community life,
particularly the destruction of African American community life, was little
more than a standard business practice and that the persons affected were
meaningless and inconsequential:

> In spite of all of our efforts to make America provide an adequate diet for all her
> citizens, the House Agriculture Committee voted against money for free food stamps
> and the Federal District Court denied our petition to enjoin Secretary Freeman from

returning to Treasury some $227 million dollars which is urgently needed to provide food for almost 3 million Americans who exist on sub-standard diets. *This is indeed a sick country.*[22]

## The Movement to Break the Movement

In the quotation that begins this chapter, Dr King concluded that Black Mississippians were dominated by "white power in its most brutal, cold-blooded and vicious form." What must be added to this formulation, and what has been demonstrated throughout this work, is that plantation power in the Delta survives through the creation of multiple forms and identities: old alliances are continuously being recast; new alliances are constantly being constructed; and new movements are perpetually being launched.

By the mid-1960s, the plantation bloc was amassing power at many different levels. The Delta Council was engaged in the direct management of the region. The National Cotton Council was securing new federal subsidies and cementing new national and international alliances. The electoral activities of the Citizens' Councils solidified a swing constituency that has become the obsession of both the Democrat and Republican parties. The Sovereignty Commission effectively subverted the African American community development agenda, while new manufacturing firms adopted existing plantation relations. Overnight, the War on Poverty turned into a war on the poor.

First and foremost the power of the Delta plantation bloc rested upon the ability of the all-White, 3,500-member, Delta Council to control key intersections of the regional complex. Representing the allied interests of the region's White planters, bankers, politicians, engineers, teachers, lawyers, judges, bureaucrats, and journalists, the Delta Council managed the pace and intensity of African American expulsion, hunger, unemployment, homelessness, and disease. Its control over county and local government proved critical in thwarting the numerous counter-movements designed to halt its community destruction agenda.

Since all members of the boards of supervisors in each of the Delta's eighteen counties were considered Delta Council members upon election, the organization was able to influence and control public policies and programs directly. Those African Americans who engaged in strikes, protests, and voter registration efforts were typically threatened with the termination of food assistance and with the state taking custody of their children. In *Our Land Too*, Tony Dunbar describes how this public-private partnership operated during the 1960s to enforce dependency:

> The boards of supervisors in Mississippi, which in the Delta is to say the planters, have no legal authority over the county welfare departments, but do have considerable influence to wield against them. Those tenants on the supervisors' plantations in Humphrey's County having any claim to eligibility receive welfare benefits that seem guaranteed for the elected term of their boss. This guarantee, which acts as an

incentive for good work, also serves the planter as an assurance that none of his tenants will cause any trouble.[23]

The Delta Council also played a central role in destroying and coopting the War on Poverty while it simultaneously fought to maintain control over the employment practices of new industries. Its representatives traveled to various states and nations to recruit firms by offering them county-financed tax, plant, and infrastructure subsidies. These recruiters tried to dispel "false" images of racial tension while simultaneously demanding that no unions were to be brought into the region; plants were to remain non-union; wages were to remain low; and hiring was to occur along specific racial lines.[24]

Manufacturers could take advantage of a labor market where, in 1965, wages for cotton pickers were as low as 30 cents an hour, $3 for a ten- to twelve-hour day. The federal government mandated wages of $1 an hour for agricultural workers in 1967. Even though this agricultural wage was lower than the national wage, sub-minimum, a heavily used loophole removed the agricultural minimum wage coverage for piecework, such as cotton picking, thereby creating a sub-sub-minimum wage rate. Additionally, national laws preventing children younger than sixteen years of age from working during school hours were ignored. Despite the elimination of the agricultural wage differential in 1976, the cotton piecework exemption was retained. Black workers and their families were trapped in a tangled web of tragedy and failure. This web was spun from the mutually supporting practices of the Delta Council, regional manufacturers, the Mississippi Employment Security Commission, local police, the state prison system, and the Mississippi departments of Agriculture and Commerce, Economic Development, and Public Welfare.[25]

During this period the National Cotton Council (NCC) attempted to preserve regional and industry unity while blocking the advance of foreign cotton producers and the manufacturers of manmade fibers. At the height of the starvation and eviction of African Americans in the Delta, the NCC was able to secure massive federal subsidies for cotton producers. In 1962 the Kennedy administration imposed restrictions on the rising flow of imported textiles and agreed to subsidize the cost of domestic cotton purchased by domestic mills. Inserted in the Food and Fiber Act of 1965 was a cotton subsidy program designed by NCC leader and former Delta Council president G. C. Cortwright and President Lyndon Johnson. This program was still considered a national scandal in the 1990s. The example of Delta Council leader Roy Flowers is instructive:

As a long time beneficiary of governmental generosity, planter Roy Flowers of Coahoma County personified the manner in which, over three decades, federal agriculture and welfare policy had reinforced rather than undermined the wealth and power of the reactionary Delta planters. Flowers, whose income was approximately one million dollars in 1966, received over $210,000 in federal payments in 1967. He had come to the Delta in 1908 as a store clerk earning twenty-five dollars per month. By the early 1960s, he claimed to own everything within forty-nine square miles,

including seven thousand acres in cotton, four gins, a bank, the entire town of
Mattson, and, in his own words, "more niggers than anybody in Mississippi."[26]

A 1969 study by the Committee on Farm Policy of the National Council of
Churches found that Mississippi Delta planters were being subsidized more
than any agricultural group in the country. "In 1966, there were more
payments over $50,000 in each of eight Mississippi counties than in the states
of Iowa and Illinois combined ... In the seven states of Iowa, Illinois,
Nebraska, Minnesota, Wisconsin, Indiana, and Ohio, 165 producers received
checks of $25,000 or more, as compared with the 194 in Mississippi alone who
received payments of $50,000 or more." In 1967, under the Agricultural
Stabilization and Soil Conservation's subsidy program, the Delta and Pine
Land (D&PL) Company, "the world's largest plantation," received a subsidy
totaling $653,253 while the 5,000-acre Eastland Plantation Inc., owned by arch
segregationist US Senator James Eastland, received $157,000.[27]

Another NCC intervention was the creation of the International Cotton
Institute (ICI) in 1966. The governments of India, Mexico, Spain, Sudan, the
United Arab Republic and the United States formed the organization for the
purpose of expanding the world's consumption of raw cotton. The body's first
executive director was a former manager of the Delta Council. One of the
ICI's major activities was the annual cotton orientation tour co-sponsored by
the NCC and the Foreign Agricultural Service of the US State Department.
The twenty-two Asian textile mill owners who would visit the Delta on the
1975 tour represented nine Asian and Pacific Island nations which at the time
consumed 45 percent of US cotton production: Bangladesh, Hong Kong, India,
Indonesia, Japan, Malaysia, the Philippines, Thailand and Taiwan.

Several events and innovations signaled the birth of a new world cotton
kingdom in 1975: high oil prices significantly increased the production costs of
synthetic fibers; a new generation of textile mill machinery became available;
flame-retardant fabrics and durable press finishes were introduced; consumer
demand in Asia rose rapidly; and there was an explosion in the worldwide
consumer demand for 100 percent cotton denim jeans. The NCC's logo
became inescapable; the white cotton boll on a dark background trademark is
seen daily in clothing stores, supermarkets, television commercials, etcetera.
Similarly, the NCC theme song which heralded the triumph of the plantation
bloc over the reborn African American freedom movement is so ubiquitous
that it can be sung unflinchingly by prominent African American performers
such as Richie Havens and Aaron Neville. Fundamentally, the NCC's theme
song, "The Touch, the Feel of Cotton, the Fabric of Our Lives," is the funeral
dirge of the civil rights movement and of the Second Reconstruction.[28]

During the late 1960s, the Citizens' Council of America (CCA) was still
actively engaged in trying to preserve segregation and limit the impact of
newly won voting rights in the South. According to one interpretation, the
aggressively violent nature of the CCA subsided after 1965 because the
Mississippi Economic Council and the Mississippi Manufacturing Association

felt that continued noncompliance with the *Brown v. Board of Education* decision, the Civil Rights Act of 1964, and the Voting Rights Act of 1965 would hamper efforts to recruit manufacturers. Yet, by the mid-1970s, Citizens' Council founder Robert Patterson could still claim that the "change is almost indiscernible . . . we're integrating because we're forced to integrate . . . We're not submitting to it." For example, in the city of Greenwood, CCA members resisted integration by turning bars and restaurants into private clubs, by boycotting hospitals and stores, by driving a pro-integration White editor into exile, and by using a roving gang of enforcers, which included the man who assassinated Medgar Evers, to beat African Americans who patronized theaters and other integrated facilities. Throughout the Delta, school boards continued to resist integration and the CCA's private White academies continued to expand.[29]

Many CCA members found their way into the reborn and resegregated Republican Party of the South. According to J. Earl Williams, "Racial Republicanism" arose after the Dixiecrat Revolt of 1948 and was marked by the "substituting [of] the expressions 'civil rights' and 'states' rights' for race" in political discourse. Between 1948 and 1964, the percentage of the presidential vote received by Republican candidates in the Deep South (Alabama, Georgia, Louisiana, Mississippi and South Carolina) increased from 18 percent to 63 percent. The Southern Strategy of the Republican Party was first formulated during the Kennedy–Nixon race of 1960 and was founded upon attracting White voters who wanted to resist desegregation and re-enfranchisement. By the 1964 Johnson–Goldwater race, five of the six states carried by Goldwater were the Deep South states. In a 1962 article the *Louisville Courier Journal* heralded the birth of "Racial Republicanism":

> The truth is that this Republican upsurge, if that is the word, owes much of its momentum to the very thing that has kept the South in one-party bondage for nearly a century—an unreasoning passion to maintain "white supremacy" which the Supreme Court sometime ago made an outlawed relic of the past.[30]

The lack of a clear attack on civil rights by Nixon and the Northern Republicans prevented the immediate integration of the CCA into the party. Instead, leaders in Mississippi, Georgia, Louisiana, and Alabama began to advocate election of a "true" Southern conservative. In 1968 and 1972, they provided the foundations of George Wallace's third party candidacy. With the election of Georgia peanut planter and former Democratic governor Jimmy Carter to the presidency in 1976, "Racial Republicanism" was split for a time before reassembling in the form of a national Christian fundamentalist movement. Forming a regional alliance with Southern "Racial Republicanism" in the late 1960s, former California governor Ronald Reagan rode this movement to the Oval Office by splitting the South in his defeat of Carter.[31]

The Republican hold on the South in presidential elections would be broken again in 1992, when President George Bush, an adopted Texan, was defeated by two White New South conservatives operating under the banner of the

Democratic Leadership Caucus (DLC). The DLC was the leading force behind
the creation of the "Super Tuesday" alliance between Southern legislatures.
Beginning with the 1988 election, most Southern states scheduled their primaries on the same day in order to ensure the election of a Southerner to the
presidency. Four years later, two DLC leaders from Delta states were elected
President and Vice President: Bill Clinton of Arkansas and US Senator Al
Gore. Calls for Southern bloc voting had simultaneously emerged from the
New South Democrats, Racial Republicans, and the heirs of the CCA in the
growing Southern nationalist movement. The emergence of the latter and its
associated militias were to mark the full restoration of plantation ideology in
the nation's political and cultural life. In a 1982 tract directed against the
"New York oligarchy," "the race traitor Jimmy Carter," "the mongrelatto
nation," and "the Washington/Wall Street slave masters," the "Yankee
Regime" was said to have

> reduced the average White from freeman to serf and the average Black from servant
> to scavenger . . . 40 sq. feet and a rat more accurately describes the reality of Yankee
> racial justice . . . They simply have no values which [correspond] to our own ideals of
> truth, loyalty to kindred, spouse, parents, ancestors, and God. They are restless
> seeking out one loathsome thing after another: socialism, atheism, miscegenation,
> pornography, sexual perversion, mannish women in fox holes, womanish men in the
> kitchen, drugs, abortion, etc.[32]

During the 1960s and 1970s the Mississippi Sovereignty Commission continued
to play an instrumental role in derailing anti-poverty efforts, in destroying
independent African American mobilizations, and in constructing alliances
between Black leaders and the plantation bloc. For example, the War on
Poverty in the Mississippi Delta was lost in less than two months. On 18 May
1965, the principal federal anti-poverty agency, the Office of Economic
Opportunity (OEO), awarded a grant of $1.4 million to the summer Head
Start Program of the Child Development Group of Mississippi (CDGM).
Rapidly, 83 centers serving 6,400 children were established, often in the
freedom houses and freedom centers started by the Delta Ministry, the
Council of Federated Organizations (COFO), the Student Non-violent Coordinating Committee (SNCC), and the Mississippi Freedom Democratic Party
(MFDP). Most of the 1,100 staff members were local women who were both
mothers and civil rights activists. The employment opportunities created by
the program meant that some of these women would be free of plantation-
related dependency for the first time in their lives.

Just one month and eleven days after the Head Start program began, the
plantation bloc began implementing a plan that would lead to the destruction
of the CDGM and the defeat of the War on Poverty in the Delta. In a letter
of 29 June, Governor Paul Johnson informed national OEO director Sargent
Shriver that the CDGM was "an effort on the part of extremists and agitators
to subvert the lawful authority in Mississippi and create division and dissention
between the races." On the same day, the US Senate Appropriations Com-

mittee, at the behest of US Senator John Stennis (D. MS), sent an accountant and a counsel to Mississippi to gather damaging information on the CDGM. The Sovereignty Commission provided these investigators and the OEO with information obtained from two informants placed in the central Head Start office.

To block the direct federal funding of organizations in the future, the state accepted the OEO's plans to establish Community Action Program (CAP) agencies in the various counties. The boards were appointed by county supervisors: a cabal composed of plantation owners, Delta Council members, and arch White supremacists. Fannie Lou Hamer doubted that the "landowners on the CAP board, who got us into poverty in the first place, are about to get us out." The CAP agencies immediately began to close CDGM projects and replace them with ones managed by the county boards or their allies. Hamer denounced the use of federal funds to intensify political and class divisions in the African American community:

> Now, the ministers, to get a little money, are selling their church to the white folks so the CAP program can run Headstart ... They're these middle-class Negroes, the ones that never had it as hard as the grassroots people in Mississippi. They'll sell their parents for a few dollars. Sometimes I get so disgusted I feel like getting my gun after some of these school teachers and chicken-eatin' preachers.

After two year of investigations, illegal surveillance, suspensions, audits, press attacks, closures, firings, layoffs, threats, and treachery of every description, the CDGM died in December 1967.

Shriver gave Mississippi Action for Progress (MAP) control over the bulk of the CDGM's funding and project areas. MAP was a state anti-poverty organization with a twelve-member board appointed by the governor of Mississippi. Among the board members of MAP were the NAACP's state president Aaron Henry, journalist and publisher Hodding Carter III of the *Delta-Democrat Times*, and two former Delta Council presidents whose families have dominated the region for much of the twentieth century, Leroy Percy and Oscar Carr Jr. Another Delta resident, Owen Cooper of Yazoo City, was appointed chair of the board. Cooper was also president of the Mississippi Economic Council and of the Mississippi Chemical Corporation, one of the largest agricultural chemical firms in the world.

As early as October 1965, a report to the Executive Committee of the Delta Ministry concluded that the War on Poverty in the Delta was shaping up as an attack on the leadership, movements, and dignity of impoverished African Americans:

> It is now kosher to have poor people represented on poverty agencies but not in a majority ... In areas such as the Delta where a remnant of paternalism and white beneficence remains, there is a desire to maintain that system in which the white man acts in behalf of the poor Negro ... These complications, coupled with the political sagacity of the political structure, have created a context in Mississippi in which the poverty program is contributing to the further rape and emasculation of

the Negro community, enabling the white political structure to intensify even more strongly its hold on community life, and to demonstrate that the War on Poverty is either as its critics maintain "war against the poor" or is administered by bureaucrats too insensitive to the human needs, morality, and the politics of the South, as to be hopelessly an assault on the integrity of the poor.[33]

According to the former director of the Sovereignty Commission, "the NAACP—once the ugliest letters in the language of Mississippi whites— seemed to be the best agency for communication at the national level." Regardless of this budding alliance, the commission continued its wide-ranging spy network and its use of blackmail and terror to fracture African American organizations. Informants were used to help officials defeat boycotts, strikes, and suits. Individual activists and organizations were discredited in the local and national press through the use of doctored photographs and false reports. The Sovereignty Commission also launched investigations of requests for state agency reports that were made by individuals and organizations beyond the Mississippi border while food and clothing donations from out-of-state agencies, churches, and organizations were redirected to groups approved by the plantation bloc. Additionally, cooperatives and land development projects that sought out-of-state funding were subverted either before their proposals were completed or after funding had been received. The Sovereignty Commission finally disbanded in 1973 after many Whites began to object to the extension of its surveillance activities to their communities.[34]

Finally, the great social torture of African American communities in the Delta was protected by a veritable arsenal of national political power. Representing a portion of the Delta, representative Jamie Whitten essentially controlled agricultural programs as the chairman of the House Appropriation Committee and its Subcommittee on Agriculture. By the time he retired in 1994 after fifty-two years in the House, Whitten had broken all congressional service records. In the late 1960s, representative Thomas G. Abernathy (D. MS) was chairman of the Cotton Subcommittee of the House Committee on Agriculture. As chairman of the Senate Finance Committee and later as chair of the Senate Armed Service Committee, Mississippian John Stennis blocked interventions by regularly threatening congresspersons, agencies, and programs until he retired in 1989, after forty-two years in office. As chairman of the Senate Judiciary Committee after 1956, Eastland pocketed or defeated almost all the civil rights bills reaching his committee for an entire decade. In his role as chair of the Internal Security Subcommittee he continued where Joseph McCarthy left off by persecuting civil rights, antiwar, campus, and labor groups until his retirement in 1978. Eastland was proud of his accomplishments:

After 1950 they [civil rights measures] were blocked ... Do you know why? Because of seniority, I was maneuvered into chairmanship of the Civil Rights Subcommittee. Yes ... Eastland of Mississippi [tapping his chest] ... became boss of the committee that had all of the civil rights bills! And they said I broke the law and so I did! You know the law says the committee has got to meet once a week. Why, for the three years I was chairman, that committee didn't hold a meeting. I didn't permit them to meet. I had to protect the interest of the people of Mississippi. I had special pockets in my pants and for three years I carried those bills around in my pockets everywhere I went and every one of them was defeated.[35]

Congresspersons representing the planter blocs of surrounding states were just as powerful during the 1960s: Senator John McClellan of Arkansas chaired the Senate Government Operations Committee and the Senate Permanent Investigations Subcommittee; Representative Wilbur Mills of Arkansas chaired the House Ways and Means Committee; Senator William Fulbright of Arkansas chaired the Senate Foreign Relation Committee; Senator Allen Ellender of Louisiana chaired the Senate Agriculture and Forestry Committee; Senator Russell Long of Louisiana chaired the Senate Finance Committee; and Senator John Sparkman of Alabama chaired the Senate Banking and Currency Committee. Far from being a parasite on the federal government, in much of the region the plantation bloc *was* the federal government.

Although considered by some to be the patron saint of the civil rights movement and the War on Poverty, President Johnson actively assisted the demise of the movement. Immediately after the 1964 Democratic convention in Atlantic City, Douglass Wynn, chair of the Johnson–Humphrey campaign in the state and one of the members of Mississippi's regular "lily white" delegation, went directly to President Johnson's LBJ Ranch. Wynn was the son of Billy "High Water Bill" Wynn, one of the first Delta Council presidents and co-founder of the National Cotton Council, and he was the son-in-law of Johnson's personal attorney, the powerful Texan Edward A. Clark. When he returned from his visit with Johnson, Wynn declared civil rights was a "dead issue" and the MFDP was "an extra-legal lawless bunch of hooligans." As suggested by the following quote from *Newsweek*, Northern institutions also seemed poised to dismantle the MFDP:

Fannie Lou Hamer, the Freedom Democrats' leading mouthpiece, is showing disturbing demagogic tendencies—attacking middle class Negroes and whites, American policy in Vietnam, and Martin Luther King.[36]

With White House assistance, Wynn formed the Loyal Democrats of Mississippi (also known as the Loyalists) with the same MAP leaders that had just defeated the CDGM: Aaron Henry, Charles Evers, Hodding Carter III, along with planter and Delta Council leader Oscar Carr. Along with the Prince Hall Masons, the Black teachers' organization, and the AFL-CIO leadership, MFDP representatives joined with the Loyalists to successfully challenge the seating of the Regular Democrats at the 1968 convention in Chicago—the Loyalist delegation was approximately 50 percent Black and 50 percent White. For Carter, "it showed that there are victories that can be won by people working together." Conversely, although she participated in the coalition, Hamer believed that the Loyalists were formed to prevent a 90 percent Black delegation from being seated; that would be "too much recognition for a

bunch of niggers. So why not step on the bandwagon and take it over." SNCC
leader Unita Blackwell stated that Hamer felt the Loyalist movement "lost
the truth. It lost the real and basic feeling of the grassroots because all the
guys was in again—the big wheels from Mississippi and all these guys that you
see now jumped up on the back of this and became big and famous people."
SNCC leader Hollis Watkins remembered that many in the MFDP felt the
same way. "They felt that it truly did not represent the constituency and the
masses of poor black people. And when you look at what happened over the
long run, you can say now in retrospect that was the correct position."[37]

## The Green Revolution Economy

Writing in 1967, economist Michael Piore concluded that the enclosure process
and the civil rights movement in the Delta were fundamentally linked:

> Suddenly, in the space of two years, the Negro part of the economy has been totally
> eliminated. In the spring of 1960, seasonal employment in the Mississippi Delta
> totaled 30,510; in the spring of 1965, it was 32,328. Last spring seasonal employment
> was cut almost in half, from 32,328 to 16,571 . . . This spring it fell by over half again
> to 7,225 . . . Incomes of Negroes in the Delta have always been among the lowest in
> the nation, but today, numbers of families have no income at all. What was once
> malnutrition and accumulated diseases has become virtual starvation. Even in the
> summer months, many families were begging from door to door . . . The beginning
> of agricultural displacement follows upon the Civil Rights Summer of 1964 and
> coincides with the Voting Rights Act [1965] and the shift in tactics of the white
> community from outright violence to reliance upon economic retaliation.[38]

By 1970, approximately 700,000 Blacks who had been born in Mississippi lived
elsewhere. Especially hard hit were African American women farm workers,
75 percent of whom were no longer in the labor force. The principal desti-
nations of those leaving the region were Chicago, Memphis, Louisiana, Alabama, Missouri, and California. Partly as a result of the expulsions, the African
American population in Memphis grew by 123,000, 67 percent, between 1960
and 1980. Through its huge agricultural chemical, paper, and furniture industries, the city remained directly tied to neo-plantation crop and timber
production. It maintained its position as the second-largest inland freight port
on the Mississippi, as the largest spot cotton market in the world, and as the
second-largest processor of soybeans, and the third-largest center of food
processing in the USA. Yet Memphis was also being transformed. Beginning
in the late 1950s, city officials launched numerous efforts to turn the famed
Beale Street into the "Disneyland of the blues." According to Michael Bane,
many of these efforts were unsuccessful because Beale Street was "black,
without shuffling, without apologies . . . It was still a different world, a black
world that refused to pay even lip service to the idea of integration . . . The
first step was [to] declare Beale Street dead, which was absolutely not the
case." Additionally, the city seemed to punish the Beale Street community for

being the site where the Reverend Martin Luther King was assassinated; hundreds of buildings were bulldozed within a year of his death:

> The policy that failed so spectacularly in Southeast Asia worked spectacularly in Memphis ... bluesmen who had spent forty years of their lives along Beale Street were resettled in different areas of town away from the clubs, the honky-tonks, the other musicians. [It] was razed except for a four block segment listed with the National Register of Historic Places ... "This city spent 26 million dollars over the past twenty years to create the look of Hiroshima in 1946," said Memphis State University historian Dr F. Jack Hurley. "Only in Hiroshima, we did it a lot quicker."[39]

While one of the centers of Black life in the region was being dismantled, Stoneville, the center of the plantation bloc, and of the Delta Council, was rapidly becoming one of the largest agricultural research centers in the world. Between 1967 and 1982, the number of federal research scientists there grew to 125, the number of federal research laboratories grew to 7, and the number of national and international chemical companies on site grew to 14, including several major British, French, German, and Swiss firms. Third only to California and Florida in the concentration of chemical research firms, Stoneville's pro-chemical attitude was attractive to companies interested in the minimally regulated testing of experimental herbicides, fungicides, insecticides, and genetically engineered organisms.[40]

Inflation and rising energy prices pushed the cotton industry into crisis again in 1976. Although cotton was still king in the Delta in 1981, generating a crop worth $450 million, federal polices reducing crop acreage resulted in successful diversification: a soybean crop valued at $300 million, a wheat crop worth $50 million, and a rice crop valued at $154 million. The two largest rice mills in the USA were built in the Delta in 1977 by Pacific International of California and Uncle Ben's of Houston. Catfish farming expanded to 80,000 acres and was generating an annual income of $200 million. Another growth area was timber. In the 1930s the Delta Council established a 2,500 acre tract near Stoneville, which became the US Forest Service's Southern Hardwoods Laboratory in 1962. Scientists at the laboratory developed a fast-growing hardwood that was thirteen inches in diameter and eighty feet tall after only seven years. The neo-plantation timber industry grew with similar rapidity and led to massive paper and lumber mills being constructed in the region.[41]

The development of the irrigation infrastructure in the 1950s enabled the growth of rice and pond-grown catfish production to expand rapidly during the 1970s and 1980s; between 1980 and 1984, irrigated acreage increased from 467,000 to 700,000 acres. As a result, even though the region received between 50 and 60 inches of rain annually, groundwater was being extracted faster than the aquifer could be recharged. One Arkansas Delta farmer described the situation in the following manner:

> Streams often dry up or are at such a low flow that the water cannot be used for irrigation. During the times of most need, streams have their lowest levels ...

Farmers have had to go deeper and deeper to get enough water to irrigate their crops. In some areas the shallow aquifer has been exhausted of its waters.[42]

As the demand for irrigated water continues to rise so do the losses attributed to evaporation and chemical damage. The expanding catfish and rice industries maintain hundreds of thousands of acres of water-filled ponds under the unrelenting summer sun. In the case of cotton and soybeans, the poisoning of what was once the richest soil in the world has led to an increasing reliance on irrigation. According to R. Neil Sampson of the American Forestry Association:

> the most damaging misconception was the notion of the soil as a mechanical part of the system . . . If soil-as-machine were damaged, it could simply be repaired . . . a soil deficient in nitrogen was easy to fix: nitrogen was added in the form of commercial fertilizer. Low on water? Irrigate. Too much water? Drain . . . But the soil is not a machine, it is a bio-geological ecosystem.[43]

This mechanistic approach to ecosystems increases yields for a few years before completely altering the patterns of microbial activity and of carbon and nutrient cycling. As yields fell, more irrigation and more powerful fertilizers and pesticides were required to maintain existing production levels. Alternative approaches were discouraged by banks which will only lend money for high-yield production practices that require larger and larger amounts of fertilizers, pesticides, herbicides, and fungicides. Fordist mass-production manufacturing and Green Revolution mass-production agriculture meet in the waterways of the Delta. Untreated agricultural and manufacturing wastewater pours into the Mississippi from producers in the twenty-five state watershed; 42 percent of the 552 million pounds of toxins poured into all US waters were dumped into the Mississippi. Additionally, Memphis has more than 112 hazardous waste sites scattered throughout the city which in the 1990s were partly responsible for fishing being banned within a thirty-mile radius and for fish kills that stretched from Memphis to the Gulf of Mexico. South of the Delta is "Cancer Alley," an 80-mile corridor between Baton Rouge and New Orleans that is the home of 25 percent of the nation's chemical industry, including 136 major petrochemical plants and seven major oil refineries. The dozens of previously unknown organic compounds born on the bottoms of Lower Mississippi Valley waterways have caused widespread deformities among the region's fish and wildlife. Along the river are found the highest mortality rates in the USA and, in Cancer Alley, the highest rates of lung cancer in the entire world. One recent study concluded that the "river has been transformed into a chemical soup beyond human understanding." Another observer described the region's environment as one "massive human experiment."[44]

The tripling of the numbers of industrial plants and of employment in the Delta during this period is often attributed to the success of various regional and state local development incentives, principally the use of long-term, low-interest, tax-exempt bonds under the Mississippi Agricultural and Industrial

Board. Although the growth of cities and manufacturing employment in the state limited the influence of the plantation bloc in the legislature, industrialization was another "harnessed revolution." The increasing outbreaks of violence after 1964, combined with the campaigns of CORE and the NAACP to boycott firms that continued to locate in states that maintained segregation, led various industrial promoters and business leaders to moderate official extremism. According to one industrial recruiter, one "lynching and we've wasted two hundred thousand dollars in magazine advertising." To improve the image of the state, on 3 February 1965 US Senator John Stennis read into the *Congressional Record* a resolution of the Mississippi Economic Council that supported voting rights. According to Cobb, this declaration did not mean that economic segregation was at an end:

> Developers generally assumed that incoming plants would hire no blacks unless all or parts of their operations required labor so arduous, distasteful, and low-paying as to be unappealing to most whites ... A Yazoo City development leader admitted in 1966 that he and his colleagues were not seeking employment opportunities for blacks ... white leaders feared a black political takeover if a chance for industrial employment should stem the tide of black outmigration.[45]

Consequently, the growth of manufacturing in the Delta did not significantly upset traditional relations because the Delta Council continued to exercise control over the types of firms that moved into the region. Through this form of industrial redlining, it was able to preserve old ethnic and class divisions while creating new ones. The following statement was included in the Delta Council's 1986 semi-official history: "Delta Council members have never envisioned an industrial strip. They have observed that industry and agriculture are compatible, and their objective is to continue to seek those industries which will improve the economic quality of life for Deltans."[46] Undergirding this seemingly innocuous language was the determined belief that the region and its people were the possession of the council's members and that only they could understand, and devise solutions for, its problems.

Those who deny the existence of industrial redlining typically refuse to examine its roots in segregationist theory and practice, the specific evolution of regional power, or the internal and external communications of the dominant regional bloc. Many public officials and scholars would rather use Delta planter Alfred Stone's turn-of-the-century tipping thesis to explain why so few firms locate in counties that are more than 30 percent African American. This thesis holds that because Whites fear being in the minority, they flee or avoid an area with a large or growing presences of non-Whites. Statistically "proving" this simplistic formulation is considered more acceptable and desirable than examining the conscious creation of segregated places. Another example of the tipping thesis is the argument that firms do not locate in areas with large African American concentrations because there are too few skilled or educated workers. First, not only are investments in skills training for African Americans limited, graduates are often denied employment. This argument is further undermined by the case of Tuskegee, Alabama, which has a highly educated workforce with many professionals, a generous industrial development program, and no firms in its industrial park. Asked why he wouldn't locate in this 90 percent black city, a White manufacturer responded simply "Who would I eat lunch with?"[47]

Industrial redlining and industrial screening policies in the Delta led to employment stagnation; between 1969 and 1986, manufacturing employment grew slightly from 28,000 to 34,000. Firms offering improved wages, working conditions, and training were discouraged in favor of low-wage, low-skill, and non-union enterprises. Firms offering more than this were (and still are) considered threats to the painstakingly crafted regional system of social control. These plantation bloc reproductive practices fueled continual outmigration. Many young Blacks with aspirations felt they had to flee the region, while those with skills were discouraged from entering it. By the early 1980s, the manufacturing boom in the rural South was unraveling. In the Delta, Boeing, General Motors, and Schwinn closed their plants, eliminating more than one thousand workers. The only readily identifiable growth industries are catfish processing in the Delta and chicken processing in adjacent regions.[48]

In summary, the success of the Green Revolution created the conditions necessary to undermine the freedom movement, labor movements, stable communities, and stable families. The technologies and social regulations adopted by planters created a form and a scale of production that is deadly to the region's people and its environment. The belief that manufacturing would lift the regional standard of living has been replaced by a realization that new technologies are not by themselves progressive. Plantation relations can be reproduced under a variety of conditions so long as there is no systematic challenge to the dominant bloc.

## The Modernist Planter

The language of modernity and evolutionary progress undergirded the new alliance between the plantation bloc, Northern industrialists, and a segment of the African American leadership. Within the South, the interracial cooperation approach to creating intra-regional alliances reached the Delta last. This movement emphasized the gradual changing of ethnic relations through interpersonal communication, electoral politics, judicial decisions, and economic growth. The planters gave up little when they supported these biracial programs and adopted the modernist forms of social explanation.

Several corporate leaders encouraged planters to adopt the language, if not the spirit, of progress. They suggested that it was now necessary to conceal plantation bloc ideology with the mask of social science discourse. Explicitly hostile race-centered and region-centered explanations were replaced with discussions of farm efficiency, industrial development, labor markets, competitiveness, regional convergence, and sociologically acceptable definitions of poverty. The deep desire of Blacks for manufacturing employment meant that they were particularly susceptible to descriptions of a coming industrial utopia framed in the objectivist language of Northern social science.

At the 1965 annual meeting of the Delta Council, the editor of the *Memphis Commercial Appeal*, Frank Ahlgren, advocated the abandonment of open combat. Not only did he view racial conflict as "the number one problem confronting the region," he believed that expanded industrial recruitment programs would help to reduce the race issue to an issue of employment. "If we could mechanize the farms, why can't we mechanize the race problem? . . . Machinery stands for industry, and industry means jobs." In an address to the Delta Council in 1968, the chairman of the General Electric Company, Gerald Phillipe, offered a similarly utopian vision of regional peace based on manufacturing growth:

> With the long heritage in agriculture and with growing industrial abilities, the Delta has a rare opportunity to attain a truly balanced economy . . . an economy in which men can work, prosper, and raise their families in a beautiful environment.[49]

Among the powerful New South alliances built upon the false belief that industrial growth would eliminate racial inequality was the L. Q. C. Lamar Society formed in North Carolina in 1969. Lamar was a Delta planter, lawyer, congressman, professor, and diplomat who drafted the Mississippi secession legislation, the plan for the 1875 overthrow of Reconstruction, and the program for North–South reconciliation that expelled African Americans from the national body politic. Members of the L. Q. C. Lamar Society included several of the South's leading writers, educators, politicians, and businessmen. The title of the society's 1972 book *They Can't Eat Magnolias* used the Mississippi state flower to issue a warning that the segregationists, particularly those based in Mississippi, would kill industrial growth and lead the region to a monumental disaster. In addition to containing a supportive letter from liberal US Senator Edward Kennedy, the work contained an essay criticizing the racialized "Southernization of the United States" policy advocated by President Nixon and presidential candidate Governor George Wallace of Alabama:

> Richard Nixon's "Southern Strategy" is more than an attempt to carry the states of the old Confederacy. It is instead an acknowledgment of the fact that recent upheavals have reduced the political preoccupation of all Americans to a common denominator. And the success of George Wallace's march northward in the past two presidential campaigns bears grotesque witness to Lincoln's prediction over a century before that the nation "will become all one thing or all the other."[50]

Conversely, in the same work, the New South Democrats and Republicans in the Lamar Society proposed interracial cooperation strategies to address problems such as community development, hunger, housing, multiethnic coalition politics, school integration, education, and increasing Southerner control over "their own" economy. Celebrated throughout this volume was the emergence of pragmatic and "populist" Southern governors such as Jimmy Carter of Georgia, Dale Bumpers of Arkansas, etcetera. However, for New South Democrats to reintroduce Lamar's name into the battle of the Second Reconstruction signaled a certain level of capitulation to the plantation bloc and acceptance of their continued domination of certain industries and certain rural regions.

Through the deployment of non-controversial language, the plantation bloc could make its expulsion and Green Revolution projects appear to be beneficial to the larger society. For example, a 1967 *Delta Council News* editorial reminded planters that one of the consequences of the mass expulsion of African Americans was "dilapidated and unsightly buildings that mar and detract from the beauty of the countryside." Visible from highways, these former homes and communities were considered a threat to tourism. Therefore, as a regional housekeeping measure, they should immediately be dismantled, plowed under, or burned. After the 1962 publication of Rachel Carson's exposé of the dangers of agricultural pesticides, *Silent Spring*, Congressman Whitten wrote *That We May Live*, in which he argued that the proponents of the unregulated and massive use of pesticides were protecting American consumers from "science fiction" accounts that would destroy not only agriculture, but also low-cost food and clothing, and, ultimately, American civilization.[51]

Carson was attacked for challenging the prevailing scientific wisdom of various federal agencies and manufacturers. This crisis of explanation and legitimacy also extended to the social sciences and the humanities as a new generation of African American, Asian, Caribbean, Latino, Native American, feminist, environmental, and working-class oriented White scholars devastated the dominant intellectual paradigms and institutions with withering attacks. Fueled by social movements throwing off the shackles of racism, colonialism, and class exploitation, new disciplinary critiques and the search for new intellectual paradigms fueled a remarkable period of investigation and experimentation throughout the world. However, by the mid-1980s, intellectual retrenchment returned the official dialogue back to discussions of moral and genetic depravity as African Americans were once again being identified as the cause of their own exploitation. As in previous periods, White Southerners defined the African American problem for Northern social science by reaching into the bowels of planter explanation. In 1991, New Orleans-born journalist Nicholas Lemann wrote the following in his best-seller *Promised Land*:

> All through the nineteenth century, white Southerners claimed that poor blacks were fundamentally inassimilable as full-fledged Americans, and they used this idea to justify slavery, and then the ending of Reconstruction, and then the institution of Jim Crow laws. In order to prove that claim wrong, Booker T. Washington, more than a century ago, embarked on his life's work as an educator. In the black slums of the big cities, firsthand observers from W. E. B. Du Bois to E. Franklin Frazier to Richard Wright to Kenneth Clark voiced concern about the condition of the social fabric there. In other words, this is really an old problem that has become more

isolated and concentrated and, as a result, gotten worse and more obvious. For most of this century, racial reformers put off its solution so that the goal of black freedom from discrimination could receive full attention. Now it is the most significant remaining piece of unfinished business in our country's long struggle to overcome the original sin of slavery.[52]

Lemann argues that the planter's knowledge of the African American character was not only superior to that of Northerners, it was superior to the knowledge African Americans had of themselves. Since African Americans are incapable of moral regeneration on their own, Lemann called upon the nation, that is, Whites, to do it for them. The celebration of this classic plantation bloc vision of African Americans as violent children led by charlatans fuels the thousands upon thousands of new social theories and policies designed to discipline, punish, and control the inherently amoral. It marks the return to national respectability of the plantation tradition of African American micro-management. Yet what Lemann has not considered is the ability of the despised and "fundamentally inassimilable" African American working class to continue their challenge of the plantation bloc and its ideology. He truly fails to understand the extent to which the moral, intellectual and social action traditions forged by previous generations of working-class African Americans remain both prophetic and decisive.

In June 1983, at the behest of, and accompanied by, the Reverend Jesse Jackson, President Reagan's Assistant US Attorney-General William Bradford Reynolds conducted a six-county tour of Mississippi to investigate voting irregularities. At hearings in the Delta towns of Belzoni, Greenwood, Indianola, and Marks, Jackson and Reynolds were given eyewitness accounts of numerous and systematic attempts to prevent Blacks from voting: plantation owners and factory managers made their black employees work overtime on election day; absentee ballots were mailed late; those with no cars had to travel long distances to register; those attempting to register had to produce birth certificates, social security cards and driver's licenses; registration offices were arbitrarily closed by officials; polling places were moved out of Black communities and into White ones; and there were racially motivated municipal annexations and gerrymandering. In response, the Justice Department sent ten federal examiners to five Delta towns to register voters for the August election. However, the *Memphis Commercial Appeal* denounced this quest for full voting rights as cheap theatrics:

> Poor Mississippi, every four years at about this time, the state attracts national attention for its lack of progress in race relations. There is a reason for that of course: Presidential politics, like old-time vaudeville, likes nothing so much as it does an emotionally liquored up audience that knows the punch lines in advance ... When it comes to providing a stage for that type of show, Mississippi, with its long tortured history of racial injustice, is a political huckster's dream. Everyone knows blacks have gotten a bum deal in Mississippi—and everyone knows when to shout "Amen!" when reminded of those past injustices.[53]

What is most interesting about this argument is how existing and well-documented examples of continued oppression are both denounced and rendered invisible. In "What is the South," an essay in his 1992 book *Entirely Personal*, the Arkansan editor Paul Greenberg suggests that facts, particularly those related to the lives of African Americans, are inconsequential in a region where the Confederate Golden Age is still lovingly cherished in many quarters:

> "The past is never dead," said Faulkner. "It is not even past." ... We are the only part of the country to have been defeated explicitly, and defeat lasts longer than victory and is in some ways sweeter. Whether we learned anything from the defeat is problematic; we were not so much instructed as fascinated by the experience. Its effect has not been cautionary but romantic. The politicians we honor are not the most effective or successful, but the dreamiest. How else explain the worship of Jefferson Davis? ... Southernism itself is a curious, alien patriotism, the product of both America and of the separate nation we were for four long, arduous years, perhaps longer. We are still a different country in the important, informal, ways that are most enduring.[54]

Increasingly in the region and its institutions, accounts of continued and growing oppression are treated as fiction. As the plantation tradition of social explanation once again rises to the fore, dialogue is being replaced by violence. Yet the necessity of the blues as ontology, as epistemology and as a development agenda is also reemerging, just as it did after 1965.

## Blues Power, Soul Power

The central and defining role of the blues and its derivations for the African American working class has been understood, denied, celebrated, and manipulated by a variety of political, social, and cultural movements. What many of these individuals and organizations have failed to understand is the transcendent social agenda inherent in the blues tradition.

Since the 1930s, Northern, Southern, and European Whites have scoured the Delta hoping to "discover" something "lost" during the evolution of Western European civilization. Anthropologists, artists, film-makers, folklorists, historians, journalists, missionaries, musicians, musicologists, novelists, and working-class blues lovers have made pilgrimages into the "wilds" of the Delta hoping to find the last real bluesman and blueswoman: someone knowledgeable about modern capitalist society yet not bowed by its cynicism. This is a search both for the last "uncivilized primitive" and for the keepers of the flame of humanity.

The image of the "primitive" was preserved through several mechanisms. In the form of music criticism, plantation bloc ideology operated to prevent a realistic understanding of the blues as a critical and inseparable part of working-class African American identity. One intellectual barrier was constructed around the practice of equating the blues with pain. When not being conceived of as the expression of pain the blues are examined as the products of poverty and oppression. One critic went so far as to use positivistic social science to predict the exact time when the social progress of African Americans would destroy their relationship to the blues. In his 1974 work *Soul Music*, Michael Haralambos relies on social physics to develop several charts and graphs which scientifically "prove" that as Blacks advance economically (ethnic convergence), and as Jim Crow declines (Black Belt convergence), the blues will die out:

> the decline of the blues is primarily a function of the decline of Jim Crow to which the music, and the attitudes and strategies it presented, was adapted. Economic hardship alone fails to explain the blues. Rather, it is economic hardship in concert with Jim Crow that produced the situation to which the blues was adapted. With the removal of Jim Crow, black Americans have the opportunity to improve their situation, they have cause for hope and optimism. With Jim Crow and its ultimate sanction gone, the barrier so long considered impenetrable has broken down . . . now for the first time, black Americans have hopes for sustained improvement. . . . [As] the black struggle gained momentum there was a corresponding decline in the demand for the blues. Blues is embedded in and adapted to a situation that no longer exists.[55]

Similarly, the blues are often equated with family hardship. In attempting to explain why one veteran bluesman was seemingly unemotional when he played, Alan Lomax made the following observation about blues legend Sam Chatmon:

> To Sam, the blues were first of all another kind of dance music. He sang about the bitterness of Delta love in a rather matter of fact voice, without either the keening of a Robert Johnson, the ironic merriment of Eugene Powell or Papa Charlie Jackson, or the rage of Son House. Perhaps he was too old to care, but I suspect that he came from this stable family background, the anguish of the blues did not touch him as it did others.[56]

Fatherlessness is a related theme emphasized by interpreters, translators, and critics. The implicit adoption of two fatherless White orphans by a legendary Chicago bluesmen was one of the central storylines in the extremely popular minstrel film *The Blues Brothers*. Many other critics have managed to immerse themselves in streams of African American culture without fundamentally altering their belief in White supremacy. In his 1982 book *White Boy Singin the Blues*, Bane writes, "I can't recall the exact moment I figured out that I could grow up to be a nigger." The so-called "White nigger" is a derogatory term used to refer to those Whites who demonstrate an affinity for Black culture. Sometimes there is also an acceptance of the African American social vision. At other times the social agenda is rejected in favor simply of putting on the mask of the "primitive" in order to engage in "primitive" behavior. Writing in 1975, Paul Garon criticized sections of "white bluesdom" that have used the blues as a vehicle for preserving and extending social oppression:

The male chauvinism that is so manifest in the blues is not without a historical base which makes it more easily understandable. Yet the "white blues" world while sharing this historical base ... could, with its connections with the counter-culture, be expected to be in touch with other currents as well, not the least of which would be the women's liberation movement. Still, this has not prevented the "white bluesman" and rock singers, in a pathetic attempt to reinforce their own self-esteem and masculinity, from borrowing from their black "fathers" precisely those lyrics and songs containing the most derogatory estimations of women's potential. Removed from their historical base and their socio-economic settings, these songs as purveyed by white adolescents are sickly, pale and offensive ... Thus "art for art's sake" becomes "do your own thing."[57]

He goes on to observe that many White women have come to appreciate the liberatory aspects found in the blues:

there seems to be an ever-growing number of white female blues enthusiasts, many of whom voice a strong preference for women blues singers. Undeniably, there is a strong element of identification in the refusal to accept further degradation ... there is implicit in the blues a "feminist" critique of society, linked to this is a broader critique of repressive civilization ... [and of] the general level of degradation of human life throughout the world at the present time.[58]

Two fallacies are committed by scholars who declare that the Black blues tradition is dead and that White "bluesdom" is the inheritor of the estate. The first fallacy rests upon the assumption that the blues were transmitted to White guardians by a process that is both mechanistic and linear—mechanistic in that it assumes that the essence of the blues can be obtained through interacting with individual musicians and by consuming records, films, books, and other memorabilia. Also, the supposed linear evolution of the blues from one ethnic group to another, from Black fathers to White sons, rests upon several somewhat disconnected responses: that the blues are dead within the African American community; that younger African American performers are now marginal and are incapable of dictating trends; and that the blues cannot now belong to any one group. These rationales for blatant cultural imperialism rests upon an assumed power to define African American music and then repackage and market it to the world atomistically, that is, unconnected to African American life and thought. It would be a grave mistake to examine the blues as a lifeless commodity devoid of powerful internal dynamics. Always implicit is the potential to expand, deepen, and transform African American, American and world culture for a purpose. If we examine what was occurring within the African American community after 1965, we find a grand revitalization of blues culture.

    In the era after World War Two, the federal government quickly recognized the international popularity and power of the blues and jazz. At the height of the civil rights movement, the Cold War and the Vietnam War, blues and jazz musicians were continually flown to Africa, Asia, Europe, Latin America, and the Middle East in order to promote American cultural hegemony. However,

State Department officials soon realized that they were potentially assisting in spreading criticism of the country's ethnic, class, and cultural regime. For example, after a 1966 performance in East Berlin, Junior Wells was forced by the FBI to sign a statement promising that he would never perform his anti-war "Vietcong Blues" again.[59]

Although the civil rights movement is primarily identified with freedom songs derived from the spirituals, blues and blues-based gospel, jazz, rhythm and blues, and soul music were still the daily bread of the Southern Black working class. Cognizant of this fact, Dr King attempted to recruit several prominent blues musicians to join his 1967 Chicago marches. Junior Wells declined because they, like many African Americans, refused to accept racist abuse passively:

> I would have marched with him once but he was talkin' that non-violence thing. He asked was I non-violent. Because me, him, and Willie Dixon and them was talkin'. I said, "Yeah, I'm non-violent. But I *am* violent if somebody hits me." And he said, "Well I'm glad you explained yourself but you have to be non-violent to walk with us." So I didn't walk with 'em. Willie didn't walk. But I had a whole lot of respect for him and the people who walk with him and do that thing.[60]

In 1968, Muddy Waters, Little Walter, Otis Spann, and Willie Dixon drove all night from Chicago to perform at the Poor People's March on Washington. Waters told the entertainment coordinator, Alan Lomax, that they went "by the headquarters this morning, but those preachers didn't seem to know who we were." To a wildly enthusiastic crowd Waters sang

> Well if I feel tomorrow like I feel today,
> I'm gonna pack my suitcase and make my getaway.
> I be's troubled, I'm all worried in my mind,
> And I never be satisfied, And I just can't keep from crying.

The contradictory nature of the blues is often found by examining the relationship between lyrics and instrumentation. As described by Lomax, behind the heartbreaking introspective lyrics of the above song was a gargantuan rhythm of mythological proportions:

> Back of the poetry that expressed their discontent rose the big sound that Muddy and his friends had been cooking up, the sound of their new wind, string, and percussion combo. It had many voices: a closer-miked harmonica, wailing and howling in anguish and anger like the wind off Lake Michigan; Muddy's lead guitar, with the bottle neck crying out the blues all up and down the six strings, a rhythm guitar behind, both amplified by big speakers so every crying note, every beat, could be heard a quarter mile away; a drum set, heavy on the back beat, traps, blocks, and cymbals sizzling and cracking in counterrhythms; a big bass fiddle, transformed by Willie Dixon into a tuned zither, slapped and plucked to emit a bass countermelody like a bull about to charge; and swanking it on a grand piano, Otis Spann, filing in all the cracks with a surging boogie . . . This was America's newest orchestra.[61]

The mythic power of this new Chicago/Delta blues sound was matched by the equally liberating and powerful sound of soul. Beginning in the late 1950s, a new blues- and gospel-based cultural revival emerged in the South. Several labels played a prominent role in this movement: in particular Stax, Sun, and Hi based in Memphis; Capricorn Records in Macon, Georgia; and Fame Music in Muscle Shoals, Alabama. Several labels in Los Angeles too were prominently involved. The music that was recorded was variously categorized as rhythm and blues, soul, Southern soul, country blues, country, Southern rock, rock and roll, and funk.

Soul marked the beginning of a celebration of African American folk dance, folklore, humor, language, cuisine, theater, poetry, and visual arts. Earlier, the traditional denunciation of Southern Black culture by Whites in the North and South had been joined by elements within the Black communities of the North and by assimilation theorists from a variety of ethnic and class origins. However, the convergence of the soul, freedom, Black history, and Black arts cultural movements countered the growth of this tendency. Slavery, sharecropping, and the Southern heritage were no longer badges of shame. The heroic struggles of African Americans in the South were now recounted, treasured, and celebrated just at the point when a vastly expanded diaspora could have fragmented into a thousand contending pieces.

By the 1960s, Memphis had become the center of soul music and Memphis-based Stax Records had become known as "Soulville, USA." As Stax evolved, it supported directly many of the local and national protests and projects that arose in the Black community. The legendary core group of Stax performers, writers, and managers infused energy, emotion, and realism back into Black popular music of the 1960s and 1970s: the Bar-Kays, William Bell, Booker T. and the MGs, Isaac Hayes, Albert King, Wilson Pickett, David Porter, Otis Redding, Sam and Dave, the Soul Children, the Staple Singers, Johnny Taylor, Carla Thomas, and Rufus Thomas. Stax was also the first label to record the contemporary and profoundly intellectual folk humor of Richard Pryor and the sermons of the Reverend Jesse Jackson. Another Memphis-based label, Hi Records, was the home of monumental blues–soul–gospel artist, Al Green.[62]

Although influential internationally, the Memphis-based studios began to decline by the mid-1970s. By the early 1980s another blues revival was under way within the African American community. Z. Z. Hill's second album for Jackson-based Malaco Records, *Down Home Blues*, expressed for many African Americans the intellectual need to escape a seemingly meaningless existence by returning to a place and a state of mind where they could "take off their shoes." The song stayed on the R&B charts for 100 weeks and greatly expanded the audience for other performers who were either Jackson-based or on the same label: Denise LaSalle, Latimore, Little Milton, Mckinley Mitchell, and Bobby Rush. Malaco and LaJam records have been successful in reaching Black consumers across economic and age categories. Among the influential blues artists residing in the Mississippi Delta in the mid-1980s were Roosevelt "Booba" Barnes, Jackson Ranie Burnette, R. L. Burnside, Frank Frost, Monroe Guy, Jessie Mae Hemphill, Raymond Hill, Jimmy Holmes, Big

Jack Jonson, Junior Kimbrough, Jack Owens, Lonnie Pitchford, Eugene Powell, Wilbert Lee Reliford, James "Son" Thomas, Wade Walton, Elmore Williams, Johnny Woods, and Hezekiah and the House Rockers.[63]

Throughout this period, through dozens of albums and thousands of performances, B. B. King expanded the audience for the blues on all continents. Also, several of the 1920s blues queens, such as Alberta Hunter and Sippie Wallace, resurrected their careers in the mid-1970s. In the 1980s, Robert Cray, Bonnie Raitt, and Stevie Ray Vaughn achieved wide popularity among predominantly White audiences. However, the blues continued to be locked out of the vast majority of R&B, rock, and jazz venues and mainstream media. Famed bluesmen such as King and John Lee Hooker eventually gained wider exposure and airplay as a result of collaborations with rock bands such as U2. Blues influences could also be found in the works of reggae artists such as Bob Marley; the poetry of Amiri Baraka, Larry Neal, Gil Scott Heron and the Last Poets; the novels of James Baldwin; the plays of August Wilson; and the collages of Romare Bearden. Blues were also an integral part of the Southern rock which emerged in the 1970s based on the music of the Allman Brothers, the Marshall Tucker Band, Charlie Daniels, Lynyrd Skynrd, and ZZ Top.

In the Delta, the blues are finding institutional expression in several forms. The Delta Blues Festival founded and run by MACE (Mississippi Action for Community Education) regularly attracts audiences of forty thousand for the summer event. Also held yearly are the Medgar Evers Homecoming Festival in Jackson, the B. B. King Blues Festival in Indianola, and blues seminars at Jackson State University. More than 120 other festivals are held annually in thirty-three states and four foreign countries. Also important in the institutionalization of the blues has been the Center for the Study of Southern Culture at the University of Mississippi, its magazine *Living Blues*, and its blues archives built around the B. B. King Collection. Also, in 1979, the Delta Blues Museum was established in Clarksdale.

Not surprisingly this institutionalization process is enough to give the blues the blues. In many instances, African American history, daily life, consciousness, and cultural artifacts are used with little systematic input from African Americans and with little concern for their historic and current development agendas. In many ways they have been relegated to the role of raw material for debates over class, gender and ethnicity within White working-class communities in the South, other regions of the United States, Britain, and other nations in Europe. What are we to make of this phenomenon?

Presented earlier in this work was the thesis that rock may be an extension of the nineteenth-century minstrelsy tradition in which blackened-face performers simultaneously degraded African Americans while attempting to escape Victorian censorship. Another perspective is offered by Pattison who traces the origins of and attitudes found in blues-inspired rock to a much earlier European intellectual tradition which was preserved through the South's isolation:

Rock begins in the imposition of white Romantic myth on black Southern music . . . A school of Romanticism now proclaimed that man in his native state is indeed a willful animal and that in his naked desire lies his highest nobility . . . The ideal breeding ground for rock should be somewhere steeped in the ideas of nineteenth century Romanticism, especially Romantic notions of the primitive. It should be an area that has a history of translating Romantic ideas into action . . . It should be a locale remote from the mainstream of Western culture . . . All these conditions were met in the American South of 1954 . . . The South has scored as great a victory in rock as it did at Manassas and now is the purveyor to the globe of a vulgar, democratic music that could have emerged where slavery and the myths of the black primitive collided.[64]

The question of whether the blues extension known as rock and roll has become the basis for a revival of the institutions of primitivism, minstrelsy, and Southern cultural nationalism is complicated. These Western cultural traditions have maintained a dangerous and parasitical relationship with African and African American culture for over five centuries. However, to focus solely on the representational devices of these institutions denies the power of the blues to transform human consciousness by introducing the uninitiated to alternative conceptions of spirituality, time, place, change, individual expression, and social responsibility. The blues remains a revitalizing element that continues to preserve, discuss, and reinterpret the hard-learned lessons of the past while maintaining an unblinking gaze upon the present and the future. Although the blues has been appropriated for many purposes, there is an underlying foundation of truth which cannot be denied or masked; there are still forgotten agendas demanding fulfillment. The continuity of the taut relationship between the blues and the truth of the African American experience was captured in the 1970s by the Last Poets in their work "True Blues I" excerpted below:

True Blues/ ain't no new news/ 'bout who's been abused/ I sang the Blues when the missionaries came passing out bibles in Jesus' name./ I sang the Blues in the hull of a ship beneath the sting of the slavemaster's whip./ I sang the Blues when the ship anchored at the dock, my family being sold on the slave block./ I sang the Blues being torn from my first born and hung my head and cried when my wife took his life and then committed suicide./ I sang the Blues on the slavemaster's plantation helping him to build his free nation./ I sang the Blues when he forced my wife to bed, Lord knows I wish he was dead./ I sang the Blues on land, sea and air about who, when, why and where./ I sang the Blues in the summer, fall, winter and spring, I know sho'nuff blues is my thing./ I sang the Blues black. I sang the Blues blacker. I sang the blues blackest. I sang about my sho' nuff Blue Blackness.[65]

## No Bailing Out

There were to be no easy victories, or "bailing out," for the majority of African Americans who remained in the Delta after 1965. Consequently, many national leaders chose to distance themselves from the ongoing rural crisis. First, the educational system began to desegregate and resegregate simultaneously. In the late 1960s, the US Department of Justice sued the state to carry out the *Brown* decision of 1954. In response, several regional banks lent the Citizens' Council $600,000 to start a tax-exempt, private White school system while the state paid the students' tuition. Second, basic services were still denied African American residents. A former SNCC and MFDP leader, Mayor Unita Blackwell of Mayersville, described what she found when she assumed office:

> Well, wasn't any decent housing ... We had roads that was not paved; we didn't have a water system—decent water. We started getting water because I started a utility district.... [Fire, police, and water services were absent] "because the whites who controlled the area didn't think people needed them ... I was the president of the National Conference of Black Mayors ... and that climate of "certain services in certain areas" was everywhere ... You will find that it's a climate of keeping other people down, or keeping all the money in one area. It's the same with education. The thread runs all the way through."[66]

Third, Blacks were still dependent upon the plantation bloc for credit, loans, and jobs. According to one African American leader, "Blacks won't get over $2,000 in loans unless they sell their mother and grandfather, while Whites get $50,000." In a 1970 speech, at the University of Illinois, the sole African American legislator in the Mississippi at the time, Robert Clarke, charged that the state had prevented industry from entering because it feared it would help both Blacks and Whites escape dependency:

> We need unionism ... but the state government has always been against this one hundred percent ... [Black communities have] no doctors, dentists, or health centers; they [have] the highest illiteracy and infant mortality rates in the United States. Some [have] no garbage or sewage disposal systems, safe water supplies, adequate electricity, banks, or public libraries ... We need outside help.[67]

Fourth, the rise of the Black elected officials in rural Mississippi has been severely overstated. According to Frank Parker, there were significant electoral gains by African Americans during this period. Increases in Black voter registration were responsible for disproving the myth of incompetency, and there was also "a decline in the systematic use of terrorism," a curtailment in "the use of racial demagoguery in political campaigns," and the creation of coalitions that "elected Cliff Finch governor in 1975, William Winter in 1979, Bill Allain in 1983, and Ray Mabus in 1987." Yet these historic electoral victories were both limited and systematically undermined by White bloc voting and gerrymandering. For twelve years after his election in 1967, Delta native Robert Clarke remained the only African American sitting in the Mississippi House of Representatives; he was then joined by Aaron Henry, president of the Mississippi State Conference of the NAACP. While the number of Black officials holding city and county elected positions increased from 57 in 1970 to 254 in 1980, they still represented a small percentage of the total. In the twelve Delta counties where African Americans were over half the voting-age population in 1980, the percentage of county officials who were African American was typically far below 50 percent: Bolivar 7 percent; Coahoma 16 percent; Holmes 44 percent; Humphreys 25 percent; Issaquena 5 percent; Leflore 13 percent; Quitman 11 percent; Sharkey 8.3 percent; Sun-flower 0.0 percent; Tallahatchie 4 percent; Tunica 12.5 percent; and Washington 3.6 percent. Despite proclamations of a New South, by the late 1980s there was only one African American sitting on the five-member county boards of county supervisors in each of the Delta's eighteen counties.[68]

Additionally, the new Black political leadership in Mississippi was rife with fundamental schisms. A 1978 letter from Shirley M. Watson of the Mississippi State Conference of the NAACP to the associate director of Branch and Field Services of the national NAACP contained a serious indictment of NAACP leaders. According to Watson, president of the Mississippi State Conference Aaron Henry, Mayor Charles Evers, and field director Emmett Burns had aligned themselves politically with Republican candidates, and Henry was implicitly supporting the plantation bloc leader US Senator James Eastland, the ultimate enemy of civil rights:

> Dr Henry's recent speeches and letters with regard to Eastland are bringing undue hardships to the Miss. State Conference ... Dr Henry doesn't have to use the word "Endorse" for him to get support from the Black community for Eastland. I want to know where does it stop ... My feelings are not as Mr Evers that Dr Henry should be removed ... I have been hurt to even hear Aaron talk about Eastland as he has ... we will lose members and workers. I am still upset that the NAACP's program would be jeopardized in times like these, when segregation has taken on a new growth, and discrimination is present on every sphere. Peace and God Bless.[69]

In response to sustained defeats on the education, health, economic, service provision, and electoral fronts, community groups relied heavily on the donations of private foundations to tackle the problems of the region. Missis-sippi Action for Community Education (MACE) was successful in obtaining major grants for many of its Delta programs: adult literacy, cattle raising, consumer and cooperative buying leagues, credit unions, emergency food and food stamp distribution, health services, job counseling, welfare registration, supermarket construction, etc. Founded in 1969, the Delta Foundation focused on the development of Black-owned businesses, job training, public service improvement, and regional development planning. Another group that com-bined local self-help with external support was the Federation of Southern Cooperatives (FSC). By the late 1980s, the FSC had helped to develop more than one hundred Black cooperatives throughout the South, five of which were in the Delta. The FSC had been started in Atlanta in 1967 after the coming together of twenty-two cooperatives and credit unions launched by the freedom movement.

Other reform movements also had an impact on the region. By the mid-

1960s, the Nation of Islam had purchased farmland in Mississippi and five Southern states for the stated purpose of building a foundation for African American economic self-sufficiency. In 1971, the Republic of New Africa (RNA) also bought land in Mississippi:

> as the first step toward a Black republic in the South, [it] had its purchases nullified outright by the state of Mississippi. The RNA residence in Jackson was raided by state police and FBI agents allegedly seeking a fugitive. The ensuing gun battle left one FBI agent dead and led to the imprisonment of eleven RNA members, five for life.[70]

Many of these comprehensive community development efforts addressed problems related to the daily operation of the Green Revolution neo-plantation political economy. Black land loss continued as a result of out-migration, title and tax disputes, illegal seizures, conflicts between multiple heirs, and the denial of loans for production, land and equipment. Generally, loans were available for young and propertyless Whites entering farming for the first time, while African Americans were being pushed out and kept out. Federal agencies, particularly the USDA, have played a central role in the systematic legal, illegal, and violent efforts to eliminate the remaining Black farmers. In the massive 1971 study of Black land loss by the Black Economic Research Center, *Only Six Million Acres*, the investigator assigned to the Mississippi Delta found a wide and ongoing conspiracy.

> There is serious evidence that white bankers, federal loan agencies (the Farmers Home Administration and the Federal Land Bank) and local merchants conspire to force blacks into foreclosure. There have been examples of reprisals against blacks who helped fellow blacks save their land.

In 1986, the house of a Black USDA employee in Arkansas was burned to the ground after he filed a discrimination claim against his agency and against administrators in his office who he accused of being members of the Ku Klux Klan. When Southern agriculture descended into crisis in the 1980s, for every White farmer that had to quit agriculture, five Black farmers were forced to leave the land.[71]

Finally, the new institutions, communities and leaders that emerged out of the Delta freedom movement were not the creation of the SNCC, SCLC, CORE, NAACP, or Delta Ministry. They were not the creation of innovative public officials in Washington, DC, or important social theorists in New York. They emerged from the daily lives and the collective history of the people of the Delta, just like the blues. For example, long after Delta conflicts had faded from the national headlines, Fannie Lou Hamer was still driven by her mission to give flesh and bone to the historic dream of an ideal community. In 1970, she formed the Freedom Farm Cooperative for the purpose of helping displaced farm workers become self-reliant. At one point, the cooperative had 680 acres of land devoted to cotton production, 200 units of low-income housing, a day care center, and a garment-manufacturing plant.

In many respects, the Freedom Farm mirrored the historic African American rural reform agenda. Yet new economic, educational, and political opportunities buttressed belief in evolutionary and inevitable social progress. In the minds of many it was not necessary to remain focused on transforming plantation structures: poverty, racism and the structures of plantation bloc domination would wither away naturally. Nevertheless, although job training replaced land and labor reform as the immediate development objective for part of the leadership, the much older tradition of social explanation and social action continued to operate. Fannie Lou Hamer so clearly expressed this older tradition, the blues development ethic, that she was and still is considered to be a prophet for a new social order. According to a recent biographer:

> Mrs Hamer also spoke to the platform committee the Saturday before the convention began. Along with Lawrence Guyot, she presented the Freedom Democrats' ideas for dealing with rural poverty; theirs were not words to make Delta planters sleep easy. The Freedom Democrats wanted outright grants of free land—take it from the land "now being subsidized to lie unused"—along with government advice and long-term, low-interest loans, for farm cooperatives. The MFDP also wanted a guaranteed annual income, fair representation for the black and the poor on all state agencies receiving federal funds, expanded day care, free and complete medical care for every person from birth to death, expanded federal food programs, and free higher education. The Freedom Democrats knew few of these programs could be achieved without an end to the war in Vietnam, and they also sought an end to compulsory military service. They wanted to halt arms shipments to the Middle East, the resumption of diplomatic relations between the United States and Cuba as well as the United States and China, and an arms embargo against South Africa.[72]

Rather than constituting dreams, most of this agenda came directly out of the blues development tradition and its emphasis upon participatory democracy and global social justice. On 27 September 1971, Hamer made a speech in Ruleville, Mississippi entitled "If the Name of the Game is Survive, Survive." In it she described her vision of what was necessary to bring this new society into being:

> Of course I will agree with the late Doctor Martin Luther King's "non-violent approach" in some cases, but in other cases, one has to take a more militant approach and I am not referring to turning the other cheek ... The new militancy on the part of Blacks and many young Whites has caused not only the Deep South but the North as well to realize that racism is an unnecessary evil which must be dealt with by "men and governments" or by "men and guns." If survival is to be the name of the game, then men and governments must not move just to postpone violent confrontations, but seek ways and means of channeling legitimate discontent into creative and progressive action for change.[73]

She viewed the impending political victories in the South as the first step toward constructing representative and responsive governments dedicated to meeting basic needs. The breakup of the plantation regime through land reform was considered a central component of the "ultimate goal of total freedom":

> The concept of *total individual ownership* of huge acreage of land by individuals is at the base of our struggle for survival ... individual ownership of land should not exceed the amount necessary to make a living ... Cooperative ownership of land opens the door to many opportunities for group development of economic enterprises which develop the total community rather than create monopolies that monopolize the resources of a community.[74]

Therefore, African American politicians, economists, and planners should be dedicated to restoring the principle of self-government in their communities based on a long-range vision of social and economic development.

> As we move forward in our quest for progress and success ... we must not allow our eagerness to participate to lead us to accept second class citizenship and inferior positions in the name of integration. Too many have given their lives to end this evil. So stand up black men, this nation needs you, mothers need you. In your hands may lie the salvation of the nation.[75]

Fannie Lou Hamer died in 1977. According to SCLC president Ralph David Abernathy, the death of Hamer "marks the beginning of the end of the era of aggressive militant nonviolence." To Georgia state legislator and SNCC worker Julian Bond, she was "the articulator for the Southern movement who continued to fight long after SNCC's summer soldiers abandoned Ruleville and the rural south, shell shocked by too much of what was daily life for her." While others basked in the glow of temporary victories, she marched on. The impact of Hamer upon the African American, labor, and women's movements cannot be overestimated. She and her co-workers taught a powerful lesson to those now facing the rapid dismantling of the formal structures of African American progress, the rise of widespread racist terrorism, and the intensification of economic exploitation. It is impossible to escape plantation bloc relations, ideology, and practices by denying the vision of the blues.[76]

# 9

# The Crises of Tchula, Tunica, and Delta Pride

The mid-1980s was a time of crisis and renewal for the African American community in the Mississippi Delta. State and federal fiscal policies intensified the struggle for basic survival. The renewal of activism may best be understood as a community response to the collapse of the Second Reconstruction. Four examples are presented below in order to provide a better understanding of the beginnings of a multidimensional crisis which still affects the region.

## Eddie Carthan and the Tchula Crisis

The removal and imprisonment of the African American mayor of Tchula, in Holmes County, shocked the Black community in Mississippi and in the US. This incident hinted at the unthinkable: that after a quarter-century of legal reforms, federally monitored elections, and Black electoral gains, African Americans were still unable to defend themselves against open political coups launched by the plantation bloc. The Tchula incident was a watershed event that intensified divisions within the biracial Loyalist coalition that had come to dominate the Democratic Party of Mississippi.

In 1977, Eddie Carthan was elected as the first African American mayor of Tchula. Historically, many White-dominated local and county governments in impoverished predominantly African American areas have refused to apply for federal programs that would benefit the African American working class. Additionally, when they did apply for and receive funds, they were typically used to improve White communities only. In his first term, Carthan was able to bring more than thirty federal housing, health, and community development programs, many for the first time, to his town of three thousand residents. According to several observers, Carthan's success in lessening Black dependency resulted in him being attacked by the White and Black members of the plantation bloc.

After Carthan refused to take a reported $10,000 bribe from planters, the town aldermen cut his salary by 90 percent, changed the locks on City Hall, and appointed their own sheriff. When Carthan, an alderman, and five deputies tried to retake city hall they were arrested and sentenced to three years in prison by a judge who was also the sister-in-law of the newly appointed sheriff. After an alderman loyal to the plantation bloc aldermen was killed during a robbery in 1982, Carthan and his brother were charged with the murder. The prosecutor's call for his execution led activists to picket the governor's mansion and launch an international campaign for his release. Although it took a jury only one hour to find the two innocent, Carthan and his supporters within the United League of Holmes County continued to face reprisals.[1]

The Carthan incident raised new fears that the use of political office, fabricated charges, biased prosecution, and judicial collusion in the Delta would become the pillars of a new era of attacks launched against African American leaders nationwide. For example, the county board of supervisors system in Mississippi has been repeatedly described as institutionalized corruption. Not only was it designed by the plantation bloc, the Mississippi constitution still requires that each county supervisor must be a landowner. Each of the five supervisors per county has traditionally had complete personal control over county funds, workers and equipment in their districts; therefore attempts by state leaders to centralize county management have been strongly resisted. Kickbacks, patronage, and favoritism in service delivery led to a Federal Bureau of Investigation probe—Operation Pretense—which resulted in the arrest of 57 supervisors in twenty-six targeted counties. Several boards have been denounced for their discriminatory electoral practices. Although Tallahatchie County is almost 60 percent African American, its first Black county supervisor was not elected until 1986, and then only after 80 percent of his opponent's ballots were disqualified for being fraudulent.[2]

The state legislature is another level of government that has been able to resist reforms. Representing the Delta counties of Issaquena, Sharkey and Warren, Mississippi House Speaker C. B. "Buddy" Newman continued the tradition of plantation bloc control of the Speaker's chair. In March 1985, eleven Black legislators charged him with making committee assignments on the basis of race and not seniority or merit. Questions were also raised in the African American community concerning the participation of African American legislators in eroding gains of the civil rights movement. *Jackson Advocate* editor Charles Tisdale's 1991 postmortem on the civil rights movement charged that some Black political leaders were assisting with the dismantling of the Second Reconstruction. He cited the support that a majority of African American legislators gave to a bill giving the Mississippi Attorney General $364,000 to fight the Voting Rights Act extension and a bill revoking the charters of local governments. Framed as a cost-saving measure, the latter proposal would also eliminate half of all the African American elected officials in the state:

> the revolution [Rosa] Parks inspired has long ago been short-circuited and its African American beneficiaries sent down what Stuart Chase calls "the Road to serfdom." The destabilization of "The Movement" was not accomplished solely through the

efforts of intransigent white racists. A more telling blow to African American self-determination was delivered by the recently empowered African Americans themselves. They, unfortunately, selected a breed of selfish and grasping leaders to represent them in the councils of this nation. This group is the color, but not the kind, of the recently enfranchised African American masses in this state. And, in the main, these elected officials have grown fat and corrupt feeding at the public trough while urging the Black masses to "register and vote" in order to further empower themselves.[3]

The state judicial system was particularly resistant to the civil rights gains. A 1985 class action suit filed by African American attorney Ellis Turnage charged that the at-large judicial election system, in which candidates are elected on a state-wide or city-wide basis, was designed to ensure the perpetual defeat of Black candidates, in consequence of racial bloc-voting. Although Reuben Anderson was appointed and then elected to the state Supreme Court in 1986, at the time only one of the state's forty Circuit Court judges and none of its 39 Chancery judges were Black. Several suits have been filed attempting to force the creation of majority-African-American single-member judicial districts.[4]

The election of Ronald Reagan to the presidency in 1980 sparked numerous movements in the African American community, including the short-lived National Black Independent Political Party. In 1981, two African American women in their seventies, Maggie Bozemen and Mary Wilder, were arrested in Pickens County, Alabama, and given jail sentences for alleged voting registration fraud. Many civil and human rights activists viewed the prosecution of Bozeman, Wilder and several other Deep South activists by the US Department of Justice as accomplishing two key goals of the Republican Southern strategy: limiting Black voter registration and preventing the election of African Americans in rural counties. The alliance formed to resist this attack, the Rainbow Coalition, rapidly expanded out of the South to incorporate hundreds of voting, human, and labor rights organizations nationwide. As part of its strategy to stop Reagan's wide-ranging attack on social programs, the Rainbow Coalition served as the foundation for a 2-million-person increase in Black registered voters and for two presidential bids by the Reverend Jesse Jackson, in 1984 and 1988. The famed African American poet, novelist, Jackson State University English professor, and political activist Margaret Walker Alexander called the candidacy of Jesse Jackson "the most important thing for Black people all over the world. Get rid of Reagan! It is imperative! It is absolutely a question of life and death!"[5]

Record Black participation in the 1984 Democratic presidential caucus in Mississippi resulted in African Americans capturing several key state and county party offices and in Jackson winning the popular vote, although Mondale won the most delegates. *Jackson Advocate* political analyst Mike Alexander, the coordinator of the state Jackson campaign, noted that there were those who believed that the campaign to democratize the Democratic Party in the South signaled its demise. "Jackson has called for an end to dual

registration, at-large elections, gerrymandering, and second primaries as violations of the 1965 Voting Rights Act which deny Blacks the full impact of
their voting strength ... Predictably, the 'new pact' between Blacks and the
Democratic Party is being blamed for 'dividing the party.'" For the Rainbow
Coalition, the abolition of the second primary became the litmus test for party
unity. Black members of the Loyalist coalition formed in the 1960s were
pushed from party leadership positions by a coalition formed between a new
generation of insurgents and older activists such as Walker Alexander, state
Senator Henry Kirksey, and SNCC veterans Johnny Walls and Hollis
Watkins.[6]

One of the main beneficiaries of the Rainbow Coalition was Mike Espy.
The boundaries of the Delta's second congressional district had been redrawn
in 1982 to make the voting-age population 50 percent Black, yet the Democratic candidate, African American state Representative Robert Clarke from
Holmes County, still lost to Webb Franklin, a White Republican lawyer and
former judge. During the 1984 election, Vice President George Bush traveled
to the Delta to help Franklin in his successful bid to defeat Clarke once again.
For Tisdale, Clarke's defeat was the product of specific plantation bloc actions:
"an estimated 2,000 Blacks have fled the district because of legal and economic
terrorism launched specifically to ensure Clarke's defeat." He also blamed the
defeat upon the failure of Black political leaders to mobilize the community:

> Black Mississippians, politically speaking, are asleep—their dreams of empowerment,
> generated by the insurgencies, blood, sweat, and deaths of over 100 years of struggle
> are being smashed against the rocky crags of betrayal by those they elected to lead
> them.[7]

In 1985, former Assistant Attorney General Mike Espy, contested the seat.
Espy was the 31-year-old grandson of the founder of the state's first African
American hospital, a member of a prominent family that owned a chain of
nine funeral homes in the Delta. Espy believed he could win the seat by
advocating jobs, economic development, nutrition, and education for Blacks
while simultaneously supporting the agenda of White planters and farmers
ravaged by the agricultural crisis. These farmers and planters objected to
Franklin's alliance with Reagan to block farmer bailout legislation. Furthermore, Espy argued that the election of a Black congressperson could prove
profitable to the plantation bloc. "From a business standpoint a Black candidate would be entertained more warmly in some areas of the world than some
others. From all sides except the reactionary side, it makes sense to have a
black Congressman from Mississippi." Espy received the support of both the
*Jackson Advocate* and the *Jackson Clarion Ledger*, respectively the most
freedom-oriented and the most conservative newspapers in the state. Jesse
Jackson campaigned for him vigorously and the Rainbow Coalition generated
a huge turnout. Espy became the first Black congressperson elected in
Mississippi and in the rural South since the 1880s. He easily won reelection in
1988 and 1990 before being appointed Secretary of Agriculture by Clinton in

1993. In 1995, however, he was forced to resign after being accused of accepting gifts from several powerful agricultural blocs, including long-time Clinton benefactor and Arkansas poultry empire Tyson Foods. A character flaw of both Espy and Clinton is their deep-seated need to be accepted by the agricultural aristocracy.[8]

Throughout the early 1980s, the human rights situation in Mississippi continued to worsen. The legislature disbanded Mississippi's covert intelligence agency, the Sovereignty Commission, in 1974, and by 1979 several plaintiffs filed a suit to open the records of the commission. Federal Judge Harold Cox allowed limited access in 1984. One of the immediate outcomes was the reopening of the investigation of the assassination of Medgar Evers and the retrial and conviction of his assassin. The files documented the involvement of the governor and the Sovereignty Commission in attempts to influence the jury. In general, the opening of the files, and the continued restriction on their availability, have opened both old and new wounds surrounding the subversive activities of a generation of White and Black politicians who are still part of the state's leadership. Equally disturbing were the more than twenty African American males found hung under suspicious circumstances in state jail cells since 1990. Approximately 38 percent of Mississippi's population was African American in 1991, yet Blacks represented 71 percent of the state's prison population and 60 percent of the prisoners on death row. As in the legendary days of old, prisoners reported that they had been beaten to unconsciousness for refusing to work in the prison's shops and on the cotton plantations of the world-infamous Mississippi state penitentiary at Parchman. Similarly, when African American historian Manning Marable looked at the South in 1984, he found that "almost one million of the region's 14.5 million blacks are arrested every year ... The root cause of racial discrimination, poverty, and unemployment, remain permanently in place while the illusion of black equality is perpetuated within public discourse."[9]

Finally, between 1980 and 1985, Charles Tisdale, editor of Mississippi's largest African American newspaper, the *Jackson Advocate*, had his office burglarized and fired into, his daughter shot at and run off the road, and his home burned. In an article citing several cases of the selective prosecution of Black officials and the non-prosecution of Whites who beat, harassed, or murdered Black residents, he concluded that the end of the Second Reconstruction was at hand:

> Quasi-official legal terrorism together with its economic counterpart have been the traditional harbingers of Black political disempowerment from the time of the First Reconstruction when Black office holders were swept from office and hundreds of would-be Black voters killed. Today they are not less so.[10]

## Tunica and the Crisis of African American Community Life

It is ironic that Tunica should play a defining role in the debate over the destiny of the Mississippi Delta. As one of the most heavily African American counties in the nation, Tunica was also a center of regional conflict during the First Reconstruction. After being reported first by the *Jackson Advocate* in the fall of 1984, the plight of African American families living in Tunica gained national attention. This revelation of abhorrent conditions had two effects. First, it created a national intellectual crisis of the advocates and theorists of eventual regional, ethnic, social, and economic convergence who were unable to explain how Tunica could happen. Second, it created a crisis of legitimacy for the welfare state and its supposed social safety net. African American communities began to view Tunica not as a remnant of the past but as an omen of the future.[11]

Considered the poorest county in the nation, Tunica had a population of 7,050 African Americans and 2,594 Whites in 1980. In the three preceding decades, enclosure and the Green Revolution had gutted the county: the number of employed African Americans fell by 85 percent and the total population declined by 10,000 persons. In 1984, 67 percent of African Americans families lived in poverty; their median family income was $6,000 and the mean annual income of those relying on public assistance was only $2,365. At $31 per month per child, Tunica county had the lowest Aid to Families with Dependent Children (AFDC) benefits in the nation. The official unemployment rate was 26 percent and the Black high school graduation rate was only 14.3 percent. Managing and reproducing this devastation were several plantation bloc millionaires who thoroughly dominated the economic and political life of the community. With an average farm size of 1,514 acres, 81 percent of the land in Tunica County was dedicated to agriculture and livestock production.[12]

In the city of Tunica, the Black community of Kestevan Alley, also referred to as "Sugar Ditch," became nationally known as the epicenter of parasitic and bacteriological infections, malnutrition, and hunger. Running behind a group of dilapidated houses, the ditch had been part of the city since 1927. It had no water or sewer connections even though the three White subdivisions annexed after it did. Yet Black residents still had to pay city water fees. The roach- and rat-infested shacks of Sugar Ditch were rented to tenants for between $35 and $65 a month. If the rent was paid on time the merchants owning the properties would provide loans to purchase food and clothing at exorbitant rates of interest. According to one resident, the rats ate more of her food than her family did.[13]

In December 1984, the predominantly African American National Association of Health Services Executives (NAHSE) filed charges against the city with the federal Office of Revenue Sharing. The complaint stated that the town delivered water and sewer services based on race. After an investigation, the charges were upheld and a letter of noncompliance was sent to Governor

Bill Allain in March 1985. In July, Reverend Jesse Jackson, Mississippi senator Henry Kirksey, and congresspersons Charlie Hayes of Chicago and Augustus Hawkins of Los Angeles convened a hearing in the city. Calling the residents "hostages . . . [and] victims of terrorism," Jackson announced that his organization, People United to Save Humanity (PUSH), was going to adopt the residents. In the face of this pressure, the city ordered property owners to connect water and sewer lines or face condemnation. The landlords immediately began to evict their tenants, stopping only when they were blocked by a suit filed by North Mississippi Rural Legal Services. In August, the tenants were subjected to a series of attacks: the beating of a ten-year-old by three White adult men; bricks being thrown at their homes; the nightly firing of guns around the neighborhood; and the attempted arson of one of the houses. In response to these attacks, one mother stated: "[If] I catch somebody out there, that's where I'm going to leave him."[14]

After reports on CBS's *Sixty Minutes*, NBC's *Nightly News*, and in hundreds of newspapers, Mississippi officials brought in trailers to house the residents. By December, NAACP leaders announced that they had worked out an arrangement with the Farmers Home Administration (FmHA) to finance a new forty-unit apartment complex outside the city limits; critics charged that this plan was an attempt to dilute Black voting strength in the town. Tunica was emblematic of the numerous Southern communities that the civil rights era passed by. Additionally, the abandonment of federal regulatory oversight in counties such as Tunica has allowed the plantation bloc system of regulation to flourish. For example, NAHSE discovered that the city spent or planned to spend more than $1 million in federal neighborhood redevelopment funds on downtown beautification and for a barrier to block off Sugar Ditch from sightseers rather than on provision of basic services. It also found that Black patients had been denied treatment at Tunica County Hospital; it mattered little whether or not they were in the middle of labor or whether they were bleeding from gunshot wounds. According to syndicated columnist Alfreda Madison, Tunica "is a prime example that President Reagan's New Federalism won't work. It is only a revival of the old states' rights policy."[15]

In many ways, Tunica was simply a surface manifestation of the crisis of African American community life in the Delta. Although the Delta is widely recognized as having one of the highest infant mortality rates in the USA, the relationship between infant mortality and agriculture is rarely mentioned. Deadly pesticides such as DDT were used to carpet the Delta during the 1950s and 1960s. Banned pesticides are still secretly used, and approved pesticides are improperly applied. These chemical time bombs continue to work their way through the reproductive systems of area residents, particularly mothers, decades after exposure has ended. National, state, and local public health officials have yet to act upon a growing body of evidence that suggests that pesticide poisoning in the South from the 1920s onward has created a massive health crisis that affects African Americans of every age in every region of the United States.

Dr George Furr of Clarksdale suggests that the connection between pesticides and infant mortality lies in the heavy use of eight chemicals now banned. "Authorities say DDT we used then will be in our systems for ten to fifteen years stored up in our body fat." In his opinion, chemicals directly ingested and those that entered the food chain are responsible for the high rates of adult, infant and fetal mortality. Pesticide-contaminated mothers' milk is also suspected as the cause of many infant deaths. Because of his views, planters refused to send Furr patients and he eventually stopped practicing obstetrics. The author of a *Jackson Advocate* investigative report on infant mortality concluded that in "the final analysis, Mississippi state health authorities' failure to pinpoint the cause of high Black infant and fetal death rates and make an effort at reversing or at least slowing down the trend, may be viewed by many as genocidal." In addition to facing threats from the plantation bloc, Delta doctors are few, isolated from other doctors and medical schools, and declining in number. Consequently, HIV, syphilis and other diseases are spreading at nationally unprecedented rates. The economic development impact of the collapsing health infrastructure was described by Harold Armstrong of the Office of Rural Health in the Mississippi Health Department: "If you lose your physicians you lose your hospital, and then you can't recruit business and industry."[16]

Major studies of hunger in the Mississippi Delta were performed in 1967, 1968, and 1977. Two studies were undertaken in 1984: one by the Harvard University School of Public Health and one by a presidential taskforce. The latter studies found that after a decline in chronic malnutrition between 1968 and 1977, by 1984 conditions were again similar to those found at the height of evictions of the mid-1960s. The elderly and the young were particularly at risk. Reductions in federal food assistance programs, and expanding unemployment, were creating chronic malnutrition in children, making them much more susceptible to death from dysentery, measles, meningitis, and other afflictions.

In such an environment, the common practice of fishing, hunting, and picking of fruits, nuts and vegetables to supplement diets becomes a double-edged sword. On the one hand, many attempts to secure food are defined as trespassing and, on the other hand, there are numerous contaminants in the environment which have led to numerous bans on commercial fishing and on drinking river water, from Memphis to New Orleans. In 1990, *Newsweek* found a litany of environmental problems in the Mississippi Delta:

Cotton is a compilation of bad horticultural traits. It has a raving nitrogen dependency and is prone to rot. The boll weevil is just one of the half dozen pests it attracts. Cotton uses just about every pesticide known to man ... that is especially true here, amid the vibrant insect and microbial life of the Delta ... There are plenty of old farmers who remember washing the walls of their homes with a solution of DDT ... there are no standards for pesticide residue in the crop ... Frank Mitchener, one of the largest cotton farmers in Mississippi, facing a bollworm invasion, sprayed his fields with the banned pesticide toxaphane last summer. Nobody might have known, but for a four-inch rainfall that washed most of the pesticide into Cassidy Bayou, [and] killed fish up to six miles down stream ... A coalition of black farmers around Clarksdale has set out to grow organic vegetables, but found that in order to escape the countryside's pervasive pesticides they actually had to locate their plots in town. W. C. Spencer tried to switch his land from cotton to soybeans ... but his beans withered and died from herbicides in the soil.[17]

African Americans, Native Americans, Latinos, Asian Americans, Pacific Islanders, and working-class Whites have increasingly become aware that their communities have been the targets of unregulated chemical use and of chemical, nuclear, and hazardous-waste dumping. This awareness has sparked a growing multiethnic environmental alliance composed of community, labor, religious, and civil rights organizations throughout the South. Yet the historic and ongoing pesticide poisoning of African Americans has not been frontally attacked.[18]

The crisis in community life exemplified by Tunica also extends to education. The creation of kindergartens was finally approved by the Mississippi Senate in 1982; however, implementation was delayed until 1986 so that new classrooms could be built in order to avoid integration. In 1990, nationally, in terms of teacher salaries and per pupil spending, Mississippi ranked 43rd and 49th respectively, while Arkansas ranked 48th and 50th. Institutionalized underfunding was compounded by institutionalized racism and corruption. For example, African American parents in Indianola initiated a successful 6-week boycott of schools and merchants in 1985. The purpose was to force the predominantly White school board to hire a local Black educator as superintendent for the 93 percent African American school district where the administration was almost completely White. At the time, allegations were made that the school board was continuing the 1960s and 1970s practice of funneling funds from predominantly Black public schools into the coffers of the all-White private academies attended by their children.[19]

African Americans continued their efforts to resist the merger and closing of the severely underfunded historically Black colleges and universities. In the heart of the Delta, Mississippi Valley State University (MVSU) in Itta Bena was threatened with closure in 1985. Alcorn State in Lorman faces a similar fate, while Jackson State in Jackson is attempting to ward off the dismantling of programs and a potential merger. The Mississippi College Board voted on Martin Luther King's birthday in 1986 to close down Valley and to reduce Alcorn from a university to a college. It was suggested by some that MVSU be turned into a prison. During the course of the battle to "keep Valley open," students marched on the state capital. As the only college available to many African Americans in the Delta, the severely underfunded MVSU has numerous supporters throughout the Black community and even among some White conservatives who did not relish the idea of increased Black enrollment at the overwhelmingly White and better-funded Delta State University.[20]

A suit filed in 1975, by Jake Ayers and three other African American plaintiffs, charged that Mississippi was operating a segregated college system in defiance of the Civil Rights Act of 1964. The plaintiffs expected that the decision would lead to an equalization of funding and an upgrading of Historically Black Colleges and Universities (HBCUs). The Fifth Circuit found that the state was guilty of operating a dual higher education system. Conversely, in September 1990, the Fifth Circuit Court of Appeals found that Mississippi's policy was race-neutral. These were the opening salvos in what would become a full-scale attack both upon HBCU's and upon the resegregation of predominantly White universities and colleges. As in the past, the plantation bloc's path to power was paved with the broken dreams of African Americans.

## The Delta Pride Strike of 1990

In 1986, the eleven-hundred-member, predominantly young, female, and African American workforce at Delta Pride won a significant victory by voting to join local 1529 of the United Food and Commercial Workers Union (UFCW), the largest local in Memphis. The organization of the Indianola facility was accomplished despite the firing of a dozen union organizers; physical threats; intimidation; and a pre-election party where workers were entertained by prominent blues performers and cautioned by Fayette mayor Charles Evers. Several catfish-processing plants in Belzoni and Tunica had been closed just prior to the strike in order to break the effort to unionize the industry.

The largest catfish-processing concern in the world, Delta Pride is owned by 180 plantation owners who have turned part of their farms and plantations over to growing catfish in huge excavated ponds. The firm's 1989 sales totaled $144 million. While Delta Pride was planter-owned, the second- and third-largest processors in the region were major agribusiness firms: ConAgra and Hormel. Approximately 85 percent of the catfish consumed in the United States is produced and processed in Mississippi.[21]

By 1986, the $650 million a year industry processed fish from seventy-five thousand Delta acres, employed four thousand workers, and generated an annual payroll of $40 million. By 1990, annual sales reached $875 million and the industry's total economic impact upon the state economy was estimated to be $2 billion. Yet production workers were paid only $4.05 an hour and they received no holidays and no benefits. In one plant, a male foreman followed the women into the doorless bathroom to ensure their quick return to the assembly line. Cuts and the loss of fingers are common for the women who work all day in ankle-deep water filleting 300 pounds of catfish each. These workers are overseen by a manager who strolls the catwalk above the assembly line timing each with a stopwatch. The combination of the pace, the conditions, and the demands of the machinery has resulted in many workers being permanently crippled by carpal tunnel syndrome. Regional economic depression and widespread unemployment ensure that workers will stay on the job despite their injuries until they are no longer physically able to work.[22]

On 13 September 1990, the two thousand members of local 1529 authorized a strike of Delta Pride after overwhelmingly rejecting the firm's final contract offer. This action began the largest strike of African American employees in Mississippi history. The company immediately hired 218 permanent replacements. Strikers were threatened with criminal prosecution for picketing and, after a scuffle with police, ten were arrested. One woman picketer was beaten by Indianola police officers. Soon after this incident, shots were fired at a building while the union met inside. In the midst of the conflict, the mayor of Indianola chose to resign as Delta Pride's lawyer; he had been the firm's lawyer since 1981, six years before he became mayor.[23]

After securing support from the NAACP, SCLC, PUSH, and the AFL-CIO, the workers arranged a hearing before the Congressional Black Caucus in Washington, DC. At an 11 October hearing, workers complained of being forced to process moldy green fish and of machines caked with fecal matter. The chair of the hearing, Rep. William Clay (D. MO), accused Rep. Mike Espy of being a "gigolo" for not standing up for his constituents and for trying to prevent the hearing from occurring. Considered the strongest congressional promoter of the catfish industry, and an ally of the Delta Council and other agribusiness groups, Espy argued that intervention by the Congressional Black Caucus was not necessary because it would give the "impression that it is a racial situation when it is largely economic." This race-is-not-a-factor argument was repeated almost verbatim by the company's president. "This is not a racial issue, it is an economic issue."[24]

The Congressional Black Caucus sent a letter to the president of Delta Pride on 19 October advising him that "compromise, not confrontation, is the course Delta Pride should be pursing at the moment." Meanwhile, the workers rapidly organized a nationwide supermarket boycott of Delta Pride's catfish fillets. The organizing effort attracted national attention and many believed it to be the birth of a new movement. Among those who came to support the strike was the national UCFW vice president Willie Baker. She argued that the strike could turn around the entire labor movement. "The toughest state to organize is Mississippi. The toughest part of Mississippi is the Delta. And this is the heart of the Delta." As part of the strike settlement reached in December 1990, most of the workers were rehired yet the replacements were not fired. This was done, in part, because the grueling pace, and the foul and dangerous conditions, "naturally" caused a high rate of labor turnover.[25]

The farm crisis of the 1980s severely eroded agricultural profitability and led to a restructuring of the entire agricultural political economy. Unable to gain entry into the European markets and priced too high for consumers in poorer countries, domestic crops such as soybeans, wheat, and corn all faced a crisis of overproduction. In addition, the movement of US capital into the production of Brazilian soybeans for importation into the United States helped to devastate domestic soybean producers. Two of the top four farm machine manufactures failed—Allis Chalmer and Massey Ferguson—and International Harvester was dismembered. A June 1990 General Accounting Office report on the lending practices of the Farmers Home Administration (FmHA) found that there were 7,415 farm delinquencies in Mississippi, 5,071 in Arkansas, and 4,361 in Tennessee. With the second-highest debt load in the nation, Mississippi planters, ranchers, and farmers owed more than $1.5 billion in loan repayments to the FmHA. For many, federal subsidies had become the sole source of profit.[26]

Additionally, agricultural subsidies faced a growing attack in Congress by officials from predominantly urban and suburban districts. As part of international trade negotiations, President Bush sought to reduce government participation in the commodity programs in order to allow market forces to regulate production. However, among the numerous agriculturally dependent regional blocs in the United States, the Delta plantation bloc is more protected than most. The eventual rise to national power of politicians from the Delta states has not been its only advantage: the federal government has never wavered from its commitment to rice and cotton export promotion. One major effort is designed to introduce Arkansas and Mississippi rice, more than 60 percent of US production, into Japan. Another major program subsidizes China's Mississippi and Arkansas cotton purchases. With total sales of $1 billion in 1990, Dunnavant Enterprises of Memphis, the world's largest cotton broker, completed the world's largest cotton sale ever to China in October 1990: 500,000 bales worth $200 million. China became the world's largest producer and consumer of cotton in 1986 while the United States remains the world's largest exporter.[27]

The African American communities in the Delta are in the grips of a highly capitalized and subsidized internationally oriented agricultural complex that is in the throes of a massive transformation having global implications. Public officials charged with the responsibility of halting the further degradation of rural communities are both products of this complex and have a very limited voice in its affairs. Therefore, there has been little inclination among the regional leadership to rethink the whole complex, little inclination to address neo-plantation monopoly, and little desire to revisit the African American development agenda. In many ways, this narrow vision ensured that the Lower Mississippi Delta Development Commission would tail behind the plantation bloc. Also, it guaranteed that the impoverished African American communities of the Delta would once again have to challenge the seemingly unchallengeable and win a battle that initially appeared unwinnable.

## The Current Crisis of Development Planning

Crafted from the New South ideology and Mississippi's Balance Agriculture with Industry program, the practice of Southern economic development proceeded in the decades following World War Two from the parasitic expectation that Northern firms would eventually locate branch plants in the rural South to take advantage of relatively lowcost labor and resources. Towns, cities, and states competed with one another by constantly lowering corporate taxes and by providing free facilities and infrastructure. The Southern states were able to guarantee their comparative advantage so long as the plantation bloc of each state was able to ensure that the rural African American counties were the sites of the most depressed wages, the worst living conditions, permanent disorganization, and widespread human rights violations. This ensured that there would always be a pool of unemployed workers willing to work for less; a section of predominantly White counties dependent upon local officials to attract plants and to protect them from ethnic economic competition with the predominantly Black districts; a large segment of untaxed agricultural producers and manufacturers; a state tax base dependent on placing new sales taxes on the poor; minimal infrastructure in the predominantly Black counties; and minimal services throughout a state. This complex of dependencies enabled the Southern states to defeat wave after wave of union organizing efforts.

This regime has been eclipsed, and rural manufacturing is now declining in the rural South. Between 1977 and 1984, non-metropolitan manufacturing employment in Arkansas, Louisiana, and Mississippi declined significantly as a result of widespread layoffs and plant closures. Historically, ethnic and class instability in the South destabilizes the entire United States. The collapsing low-wage economy in the South spawned a new industry, crisis studies: *After the Factories* and *After the Factories Revisited* by the Southern Growth Policies Board; the edited volume *Rural South in Crisis*; the study *Halfway Home* published by the Southern Governors Conference; and *Shadows in the Sunbelt*, a report written by MDC for the Ford Foundation and R. J. Reynolds in 1986. The one finding consistent between studies was that though the historic Southern "Buffalo Hunt" for new plants was over forever, public officials could think of nothing else to do:

> For a majority of counties in the rural South ... the economic forecast is dark and growing darker ... For the past several years the trends in manufacturing have become increasingly stacked against rural communities ... Even in the traditional manufacturing industries which have historically favored the rural South, the trends now favor urban areas ... The combined effects of these negative trends is producing a revolution in the economy of the rural South ... The counties in the South which have shown the fastest growth in recent years are those whose workers are the best educated. Yet the rural South has traditionally been among the least educated regions in the nation. The decline in the rural economy promises to be especially difficult for special segments of the population—particularly blacks ... The stampede of plants to the South is definitely over—especially for the rural areas that lack a skilled workforce, transportation, infrastructure, and cultural amenities. Yet the hunters continue in their pursuit ... Literally thousands of local groups have been formed to recruit new industries ... making recruitment one of the few remaining growth industries in the rural South.[28]

In response to this deepening crisis in agriculture and manufacturing, combined with the withering of the federal state, regional blocs throughout the USA began to reassert their direct control over the local political economy and over social relations, including ethnic relations. The Delta's plantation bloc mobilized to devise and implement Mississippi Delta Plan 12. Since the mid-1980s, the Democratic Leadership Caucus, the Memphis Area Chamber of Commerce, the Mississippi legislature, the Mid-South Foundation, Mississippi Power and Light, the Delta Council, the political leadership of Arkansas and Louisiana, and other bodies have been formulating strategies to transform the region without any participation by the African American community.[29]

The Delta Council began its mobilization in the spring of 1987 with the decision to prepare a comprehensive study to be "used as a tool for planning the region's future." A research team of more than thirty professors was assembled by Professor Arthur Cosby of the Social Science Research Center at Mississippi State University and the project was funded by the Cooperative State Research Service of the USDA. The advisory committee was composed of major planters, university officials, and several African American politicians. In addition to an inventory of the regional economy, education, health, infrastructure, leadership, poverty, and race relations, the chair of the advisory committee, Hugh Smith, believed that the study should also address other issues.

> Attitudes are also something we need to assess. We need to create optimism. This business of negative thinking destroys initiative. Good wholesome and optimistic publicity catches the eyes of those who are looking ... we need to establish pride in our communities, clean them up, run them efficiently, and develop our primary resources—people, land, and water. We need to set a course and get after it.

The authors of the final report believed that "this undertaking was one of the cornerstones to the next fifty years of the social and economic development of the Mississippi Delta."[30]

The effort by the Delta Council to devise a fifty-year plan for regional transformation was temporarily bogged down before full funding was secured. Its high-profile image was eclipsed by the April 1988 announcement of the creation of the Lower Mississippi Delta Development Commission (LMDDC). Whether the LMDDC was a preemptive strike by New South Democrats fearful of plantation bloc Republicans or a platform for Governor Clinton's presidential aspirations, what is certain is that it died a slow and tortuous death due to unrelenting attacks by the plantation bloc. Yet there were numerous attempts at reconciliation. One such attempt was on the day when three Delta state governors made a pilgrimage to the Delta Council.

## The Commission Movement

On 13 May 1988, governors Ray Mabus of Mississippi, Bill Clinton of Arkansas, and Charles E. "Buddy" Roemer of Louisiana traveled to the Delta town of Rosedale, Mississippi. Each took a boat out to a barge anchored in middle of the Mississippi River. On the barge they would sign two regional cooperation agreements. The first, the Governors' Agreement, created working relationships designed to address infant mortality, adult illiteracy, worker training, rural infrastructure, and the improvement of the tri-state region's business climate and national image. The second document, the International Cooperation Agreement, established tri-state regional ties with specific foreign governments in the areas of technology, tourism, trade, industry, education and culture. This document was signed by the governors and was then presented to the Japanese ambassador to the United States, who was also on the barge. According to ambassador Matsunaga, there is "a very strong interest on the part of Japanese industry to develop investments and industrial interests in this area." He specifically mentioned the falling dollar and the cheapness of US imports, an implicit reference to cotton.[31]

Each of the relatively young, Ivy League-educated, reform-oriented, New South governors spoke of the region as a center of unemployment and poverty. They also stressed that competition between their states had become suicidal. Since their economies were already highly integrated, particularly those of the Deltas of each state, tri-state cooperation was a seemingly natural foundation upon which to build future growth. As the governors continued their press conference, the ambassador boarded a speedboat for Cleveland, Mississippi, so that he could deliver the keynote address of the fifty-third annual meeting of the Delta Council. The governors were not far behind. One journalist described the three as "bright young politicians who can ill afford to jeopardize their political careers by upsetting the white business and social structure in the Delta."[32]

Of all of the governors, Clinton best articulated the position and the dilemma of the New South Democrats, whose electoral success depends on continued industrial development in the growing, predominantly White counties and upon Black votes in declining, high-unemployment rural and urban areas. During a June 1988 interview with the *Arkansas Democrat*, Clinton discussed the crisis facing the region, shifts in plantation bloc thinking, and his intent to shield himself from any serious conflict:

> eastern Arkansas [the Arkansas Delta] has always been my political base . . . there is no question in my mind that those counties have been held back by the dominance of what I call old plantation attitudes over there about what the proper place of blacks is and what the proper place of whites is. Thirty years ago when America dominated the international market place in manufacturing and agriculture, east Arkansas was the most prosperous place in the state. Even though there was always a lot of poor people there, at least all those poor people had jobs . . . The white leadership . . . now understand that their counties are never going to be prosperous

in the way they were in the 1950s, when agriculture was booming, when manufacturing was booming, and white people take the cream, and at least they give everybody a job, and everybody's happy and keeps their mouth shut.

Yet, according to Clinton, attitudes in the Arkansas Delta have recently changed:

> Is it because there's sweetness and light coming from over there? No, it's because I think more and more white people understand the economic realities . . . The blacks are going to have to rise with the whites . . . I can't do it for them. They're going to have to do it for themselves, and they're going to have to do it together. And if they don't, they're not going to make it.[33]

In this overview, Clinton attributes to the plantation bloc the discretion to write history as it sees fit. No mention is made of the existence of an independent African American development vision. By also ignoring the historical conflict over monopolization, he can only offer superficial and deceptive remedies based on an organic conception of regional development, that is, African Americans and poor whites "rising together" to "build a bridge to the twenty-first century" under the direction of the plantation bloc.

As originally proposed, the Lower Mississippi Delta Development Commission would require eighteen months to produce a ten-year economic development plan for the region of 214 counties and parishes consisting of the alluvial valley sections of seven states: Mississippi, Arkansas, Louisiana, Illinois, Kentucky, Missouri, and Tennessee. The boundaries exactly matched those established by the Mississippi Valley Project during the New Deal and those used by the Army Corps of Engineers to plan river control projects in the Lower Mississippi Valley. As the earliest major proponents of the LMDDC, Bumpers and Clinton described their vision of the best-case scenario. According to Bumpers, it included "such projects as a Delta parkway system, river crossings, harbor facilities and roads that would help link the area to the rest of the nation's economy." Furthermore, he added, "with adequate port facilities, the Delta shoreline should be able to attract heavy industry that could benefit from transportation opportunities."[34] Clinton wanted to resurrect the 1930s entente between the New South industrial promoters and the plantation bloc, namely, Mississippi's Balance Agriculture with Industry program:

> we want to develop the Mississippi River from Memphis to New Orleans along the same lines as the Rhine River in Germany has been developed. That is, we want to have industry and agriculture side by side . . . we want to diversify agriculture and take advantage of the fact that out west, in California, there will be more and more pressure on water, more and more pressure on land, which will open vast new markets for vegetable and fruit production in this part of the country.[35]

During the initial Congressional hearings on the LMDDC bill, members of the New South bloc invoked African American poverty in order to forward the agenda of racially segregated industrial development and plantation reproduction. Although the New South leaders had never lifted a finger to assist the people of Tunica or the people living in the dozens of Tunicas in all seven states, they shamelessly exploited it as a symbol of depression. Tunica was repeatedly used as an example of the dreaded past, as the epicenter of poverty, as "America's Ethiopia," and, even worst, as a disease. For example, without addressing the issue of causality, Bumpers noted the fact that thirty-one of the poorest counties in the USA were in the Lower Mississippi Valley, describing the situation as "a cancerous condition that should not have been allowed to grow."[36]

Just as Tunica was used during the hearings to create sympathy and a sense of urgency, the Appalachian Regional Commission (ARC) was used as an example of the positive benefits of federally funded multistate regional planning. Michael Wenger, the Washington representative of the ARC, spoke of the success of the agency in halving poverty, illiteracy, and infant mortality while building roads, sewers, and housing in the 397-county, 13-state, region since 1964. In the regional press, Professor Ron Eller of the University of Kentucky presented the other side of the ARC: most of the federal money spent went for highway construction (65 percent of $5.5 billion); the counties that were impoverished twenty-five years ago are still impoverished today (two-thirds of the counties are in greater poverty than they were in 1964); and boom-and-bust industries and absentee owners still dominate the region.[37]

Most observers expected that the bill authorizing the LMDDC would be passed quickly because the regional leaders still dominated several key congressional committees: long-time Delta Council guardian Representative Jamie Whitten (D. MS) was chair of the House Appropriations Committee; Senator John Stennis (D. MS) was chair of the Senate Appropriations Committee; Senator Thad Cochran (R. MS) was the ranking Republican on the Senate Appropriations Committee; and Senator Jim Sasser (D. TN) was the chair of the Senate Budget Committee. The effort to pass the enabling legislation in the Senate was led by Arkansas Democrat Senator Dale Bumpers and in the House it was led by Representative Michael Espy.[38]

After the bill had been approved by the Senate Appropriations Committee on 9 June 1988, to speed passage Bumpers, Espy and Cochran asked Whitten to insert the first year's funding, $2 million, into the $44 billion national agricultural appropriations bill. Whitten stunned his Mid-South colleagues by refusing. He wanted the passage of separate legislation and a $780,000 limit on first-year funding. Although he had previously testified in support of the LMDDC, he now argued that too much money would be used for hearings and press releases. Whitten also invoked the myth of planter omnipotence: "We already know what the problems are." Bumpers responded, "[You're] not going to be able to go down there and throw money off the I-40 bridge, you have to have a plan." After sustained pleading from numerous colleagues, friends, and relatives, Whitten inserted the act in the appropriations bill, Public Law 100–460. The Lower Mississippi Delta Development Act was signed by President Reagan on 27 September 1988.[39]

When the seven governors announced their appointments to the LMDDC on 1 November 1988, African Americans and women were noticeably absent. Clinton, Mabus, and Roemer appointed themselves. The governors of the four other states made the following appointments: Jay Hedges, director, Illinois Department of Commerce and Community Affairs—later replaced by Rhonda Vinson, a professor at Southern Illinois University; Lee Troutwine, commissioner, Kentucky Department of Local Government; Charlie Kruse, a farmer and director of Missouri's Department of Agriculture; and Ed Jones, a plantation bloc supporter and recently retired congressman from Tennessee. Clinton was named chair of the LMDDC at the first meeting in Memphis on 14 November 1988. On his last day in office, Reagan appointed John Shepperd, a St Louis attorney, who was also a fellow at the conservative Hoover Institute and former president of the American Bar Association. Reagan also appointed Webb Franklin, a Greenville, Mississippi, lawyer and former congressman who had been defeated by Espy in 1986. In the absence of an African American appointee, the appointment of Franklin was viewed as a direct affront, and a calculated insult, to African Americans.[40]

The lack of inclusion of African Americans sparked intense debate within the region. One of the first participants was Governor Clinton who said that although it was "terrible," he was not going to resign. "If we all got off tomorrow and appointed blacks . . . would the commission be more effective, or would it be less effective but more credible with the black community? I mean it's a dilemma." The editor of the Pine Bluff (Arkansas) *Commercial Appeal*, Paul Greenberg, referred to the dilemma of Bumpers and Clinton as "Rationalizing Jim Crow":

> It is hard to believe but even now, 25 years after the civil rights movement was sweeping the country, the senior senator from Arkansas is asking blacks to submit to the most obvious of slights: the appointment of a lily white commission to tackle the economic problems of the Mississippi Delta, one of the great expanses of black poverty in the nation . . . Bumpers said "Their voices are going to be heard . . . just as though the commission was all black" . . . Will they be just as eager to testify, to share their ideas and fears and hopes . . . Obviously not. One black ministerial group has already called for a boycott . . . Bumpers invites us to concentrate our attention on the hired hand [the executive director's position], not on the commissioners. That's a smooth move but not very original. Clinton took the same tack. What both have done is to rationalize, not justify, the make-up of the commission, which comes entirely close to resembling an all-white club.[41]

Less than a week later, Arkansan Clarence Wright, the African American field director for Save the Children Foundation, denounced complaints about the absence of Black commissioners. He proposed a series of reforms that were generally adopted by the LMDDC: the hiring of a Black executive director; the inclusion of urban counties with large African American populations in the commission boundaries, namely, Jackson, Little Rock, Memphis, Baton Rouge, and New Orleans; the appointment of African American alternates; involving Black newspapers and small businesses; and mandating affirmative action in hiring. For Wright, the LMDDC was

> a much-needed initiative that is rapidly going sour. The hue and cry over the racial makeup of the commission and the executive directorship needs to stop. Poverty not race is the primary issue before the commission. This opportunity to define poverty within a regional context should not be lost.[42]

On 11 February 1989, Wilbur Hawkins Jr was chosen as executive director. At the time, Hawkins was a Tennessee Valley Authority (TVA) resource development project manager in West Tennessee and Northeast Mississippi. Almost immediately, Senator Bumpers took Hawkins to Forrest City, Arkansas, in order to halt a boycott of the LMDDC launched by the Phillips County, Arkansas, chapter of the NAACP. Chapter president Jimmie Wilson denounced the support given to the LMDDC by state NAACP president the Reverend Ellihue Gaylord:

> by participating in a discredited process, you lend it credibility or some hint of credibility. These people are going to fall on their face because you can't have credibility with nine white people on a commission. They have no blacks, no women, and one token hanging from nine strings.[43]

Due to the slow work habits of the commissioners, five months of the LMDDC's eighteen-month life had elapsed before its office was open. The office was located on Shelby Farms on the eastern outskirts of Memphis. Here, the state had taken over a 1,000-acre cotton plantation and created Agricenter International, a combination office park, exhibition center, recreational center, and functioning cotton plantation. Agricenter was the administrative center of the region's plantation bloc, and on its board sat the president of Union Planters National Bank of Memphis, a retired executive vice president of the National Cotton Council, and the executive vice president of the Delta Council, Chip Morgan. The location of the LMDDC on an isolated former cotton plantation ensured invisibility, secrecy, inaccessibility, and fueled suspicions that the LMDDC was a new threat to the historic African American development agenda. Another early criticism was that regional elites had complete access to the LMDDC while the impoverished masses had none. At the first meeting, a reporter observed that "the only ones with out-stretched hands … [were] planners, consultants, and university types passing out business cards." The three governors and the four other commissioners mainly came together for bimonthly hearings, and Mabus and Roemer often missed those. Another reporter remarked that "the body largely had remained invisible—except for when it took the occasional flak for being too white, too lazy, or both."[44]

Pressured to become more active, between March 1989 and 14 May 1990, the commission held 17 work sessions, 14 public hearings in the seven states, and 10 conferences or round tables. In every session the commissioners had to confront several related problems. First, they had to explain the origins of regional poverty in a way that exonerated the plantation bloc from blame. Additionally, as a federal body they tried to avoid discussions of Northern colonialism even though this is a central theme in White popular and political culture in the South. For example, during the LMDDC's Agriculture Conference, Arkansas congressman Bill Alexander relied upon colonial discourse tradition to construct an explanation of Southern poverty that left the plantation bloc completely blameless:

> From a historical perspective, the Delta—like much of the rural South—never really recovered from a bloody war partially fought in its fields and fought by and about its sons and daughters. We came out of the Civil War behind the rest of the country and despite a century and a quarter of moderate progress, the Delta has stayed behind the rest of the country ... I do not believe that remaining an economic colony is the status we want for our region.[45]

Despite the willingness of the African American community to reopen the historic debate over racial and class domination, and Alexander's willingness to reopen the historic debate over regional domination, the New South partisans chose strategies designed to censor, silence, and lower expectations. At the beginning of the LMDDC's life, Louisiana governor Buddy Roemer used all three approaches simultaneously. "The commission's work is not about handouts. The commission's work is not to criticize the past." The *Economist* picked up on this official preoccupation with avoiding detailed and open discussions of the past and present. "Mr (Kevin) Smith likes to say that the Delta is not so much an area of destruction as one of untapped potential. If the commission paints too bleak a picture . . ." The writer left this sentence incomplete in order to convey the fear some leaders felt. Painting a too-realistic picture of exploitation could both scare away potential investors while fueling anger within African American and White working-class communities.

Once the responsibility for African American poverty was removed from the shoulders of the plantation bloc, the cornerstones of the plantation bloc's system of representation of African Americans could then be used. The myth of Black failure was quickly deployed and poverty, criminality, and promiscuity were described as inherent character flaws. During the Itta Bena, Mississippi, hearing, Commissioner Webb Franklin said, "We went to Tunica County this morning, Sugar Ditch Alley ... there are people who live in those same houses because they won't leave ... they want to stay there." According to Commissioner Shepherd, the region's drug problem had less to do with crushing poverty than it had to do with the uninhibited behavior of young Blacks who "sell their own people into the slavery of drugs ... it's as true today as it was when they got on these ships ... that the white people are getting the bulk of the money." The theme of African Americans being a timeless people, capable of little and satisfied with anything, was also resurrected by Clinton's director of the Arkansas Industrial Development Commission, Pat Harrington: "The work force is not as culturally adapted to industrial work. They don't have the history, a background to work in factories . . . They do what they have always done well."[46]

One suggestion of what could be done with idle, seemingly untrainable, African American labor came from Louisiana planter Carl Bater:

> Think about using these people that are idle to develop an . . . efficient . . . energy system . . . that would be a great accomplishment of your whole program . . . I'm tired of these prisoners sitting on their behinds and doing nothing; they should be creating their own power by either pumping an air tank with pressure or elevating water to turn a wheel . . . Now that'll give them something to do and it'll be fruitful.[47]

Once the plantation bloc was absolved and African Americans were denigrated, the LMDDC's deliberations could focus clearly upon wealth instead of poverty, upon opportunity instead of ongoing destruction. Once the regional vision was narrowed into acceptable parameters, the crisis of community was recast in terms of the problems affecting the plantation bloc and agribusiness alone. This process was outlined by Representative Bill Emerson of Missouri (D. MO):

> The fact of the matter is that our tremendous agricultural resource is our strongest asset . . . our agricultural economy is in a period of transformation, and we must be at the leading edge of what is being molded and shaped today . . . part of this process must be a mental metamorphosis—refocusing our direction as agriculture becomes a more and more market oriented field.[48]

Representing the largest owner of timber lands and lumber mills, the vice president of Anderson-Tully, Tony Parks, reminded participants in the LMDDC's Agricultural Conference that poverty should not make people lose sight of how fortunate they were. Like Emerson, Parks views the region as a resource, as an object detached from social relations. The entire region, and nature in general, is conceptualized as a single plantation or mine to be exploited carefully, by its owners, but exploited nevertheless.

> While having some of the lowest per capita income in the country, the majority of people do not realize how blessed we are with the productivity of the natural resources located in the Delta region. During the last seven years we have seen the bald eagle . . . and the black bear. Through wise conservation and timber and wildlife management practices, we can continue to manage this resource to the benefit of the economy and the environment.[49]

Consistent with the opinions expressed by many at the agricultural conference, Louisiana sugar planter and Farm Bureau vice president Martin Canciene wanted to make sure that the commissioners never forgot that all social programs must remain subsumed under the hegemony of agribusiness:

> When you're talking about . . . rural development and budget outlays, you have to remember one thing . . . we have to maintain a certain unique atmosphere in the rural areas of this country otherwise we're going to lose something that we'll never be able to get back . . . in pushing for rural development let us . . . not take away from our agricultural programs.[50]

## The Blues and Public Policy

The blues tradition of social explanation emerged repeatedly from African Americans who believed that the LMDDC and the rest of the regional elite lacked the moral authority, the legitimacy, to determine their future. The 5 September hearing in Helena, Arkansas, was boycotted. The co-leader of the boycott, Jimmie Wilson, the president of the Phillips County, Arkansas, NAACP, believed that the commission had become dangerous to African American interests. "It doesn't reflect the faces of the people who need help. It reflects the faces of the people who created the problem":

> I underestimated how damaging a circus of this nature could be. As long as there is a Delta Commission, and as long as it is the focus of the news media, no one is going to be forthcoming—from the congressional delegation, the Southern Governors Conference or elsewhere—to deal with the real problems. Everyone is standing behind a blockade called the Delta Commission that is a three ring circus allowing people to come out and basically have a religious exercise, talk and cry and purge themselves of the great ills that befall society. Then everybody goes home, and the Delta Commission compiles statistics that have already been compiled, and the governors go back to their mansions and talk benevolently about the problems, but they won't dare ask for new taxes to solve those problems.[51]

Those African Americans who did choose to testify did not speak of the region as a bountiful resource; rather they viewed regional relations as a structure that was both crippling and deadly. According to farmworker counselor Earl Moore, progress and the rhetoric of progress and opportunity had come to a dead end:

> We said back in the 1960s when we started OEO [the Office of Economic Opportunity, the lead agency in the Federal War on Poverty] that we wanted to teach people how to fish and that if we gave them fish they'd be back everyday. So we came up with JTPA or CETA [federal job training programs]. Ladies and gentlemen, folks, the pond is dry ... We are teaching people to fish in a pond that does not have fish.[52]

Dr Jerry Campbell of the Helena, Arkansas, Regional Medical Center expressed similar sentiments with regard to the collapse of health care:

> Today, all the hospitals in the Delta are suffering financially because of the federal government and the way they discriminate against rural providers. Choosing to live in a rural area should not be a death wish.[53]

In the same vein Avery Alexander, a legislator from Louisiana, spoke of how the entire environment had been turned against the African American community:

> Should we celebrate or mourn the fact that among African American women, near Saint James ... vaginal cancers are 36 times the national average ... here in Louisiana ... we have found the job promises empty and the risk of poisoning inevitable.[54]

Another central and historically consistent theme in blues explanation is that the planter bloc and its monopolization of power and resources are still the region's principal problems. According to Arkansas attorney Ollie Neal, the planter bloc is perfectly satisfied with silencing African Americans and excluding them from development policy debates. "Half of the population in the deep Delta is African American and almost none of the leadership. That cuts out half of the ideas, half of the enthusiasm ... half the team is sitting down not by choice but by acquiescence, in part, and by insistence of the white population." Dr Ronald Meyers, a physician in both Belzoni and Tchula, Mississippi, explained the mechanics of exclusion:

> I mean here you've got an industrial development foundation who has applied, applies, for grants, federal grants, state money to improve the community and they won't meet. They will not meet ... with what they call political and religious groups [black political, community, and church leaders] ... and these are the same people that the money is being channeled through for community development, but the black community is not even allowed to talk to them.[55]

The Reverend Carl Brown of Marks, Mississippi, asserted that the local knowledge of African American residents was both superior to and more meaningful than, a million studies:

> And so you're about to approach Congress ... and I'm wondering how effective will that report be ... it needs to be understood the blacks are still not part of this process. [Executive Director Hawkins: How are you not a part of this process?] We're part of it in your book, we're part of it in your report but I live the process ... we walk up here and make it look so good ... you've got people out there suffering and that's the real world ... let me show you what it's like ... I'm afraid tonight that in the final analysis, when this report is in, the same agenda will proceed and I hope not because ... we've been the victims of studies for a long time. You've done studied us to death![56]

Several African Americans informed the commissioners that their community was aware of the extent to which the plantation bloc was aligned against it and that they were determined to survive, to struggle, and eventually to win. For example, Mr Hewitt of Lake Providence, Louisiana, came to the witness table after the leading civic officials from his town had just presented a glowing description of their town as a model for the creation of retirement communities in the region. He railed against this approach and the hundreds of other models offered to, and developed by, local groups without any significant African American participation:

> Lake Providence is not a role model for no place ... It's a place of evilness where they work down on each other. They don't want to help each other to success. They want to put it all in their pocket.[57]

The African American president of the Greenwood, Mississippi, city council and former SNCC leader David Jordan explained:

A segment of the people ... have been completely excluded. We have a generation of individuals, from ... twenty through fifty, that are out there that nobody cares what happens to ... If for some reason we could go away and disappear then maybe that would work, but we'll be around.[58]

To the Reverend Gwynn, the plantation bloc's grip on regional power had to be broken:

In terms of dismantling the good ole boy network ... If your grandfather didn't have contacts with Mister Charlie then you're in trouble ... So we're looking at trying to dismantle that in order to let the best people use their own skills and opportunities to go forward and not be held back.[59]

Finally, the Reverend Rufus McCain of Quitman County predicted dire consequences if the dominant regime was not dismantled:

Thomas Jefferson once said, "Any nation that expects to be ignorant and free expects that which never was and will never be" ... If we don't see drastic changes ... in Mississippi and the LMDDC, we will meet our doom just as other empires who rode into oblivion.[60]

In July 1989, the reauthorization of the LMDDC came up before Congress. Rep. Whitten again refused to include $1 million for it in the $42 billion agriculture appropriations bill. He objected to any focus on poverty when the real problem, in his view, was the declining federal support for agriculture and flood control projects. "They don't need a study about how bad it is. We know it is." Before Whitten agreed to the continuation funds, he extracted an agreement that the LMDDC would turn its attention to agriculture and the problems of the plantation bloc.[61]

LMDDC's first report, *Body of the Nation*, was distributed on 16 October 1989. According to the authors, federal funding formulas needed to be changed to reflect differing regional realities. Certain federal policies were identified as producers of regional inequality: uneven defense expenditures, the lack of job training programs for the long-term unemployed; a bias in community development funding patterns toward urban areas with an older housing stock; and policies requiring local and state governments to match federal education and welfare grants which, it was claimed, discriminated against poorer jurisdictions. Regional political leaders continually expressed their lack of confidence in federal and state governments and their belief in the supremacy of private-sector leadership and public–private partnerships. "Partnership" still meant the public subsidy of privately owned firms. Many town leaders felt there were only two choices: compete with other towns or wither away through layoffs, plant closures, and the annual exodus of the young. Yet even successful towns saw the firms they recruited pack up and move again in less than five years. The suggested reliance on the private sector in a situation of high capital mobility and corporate downsizing meant that the LMDDC had fallen victim to the Southern and American tradition of economic myth-making and its use of unflinching optimism to mask the most brutal realities. This point was made by columnist Paul Greenberg after *Body of the Nation* was issued.

> The report uses the phrase "private sector" not in any realistic sense but as a magical incantation. Repeat it often enough and maybe something will happen. Or maybe not. This isn't a blueprint for economic development, it's a manual for a cargo cult.[62]

Before the LMDDC's final report was sent to Washington, the debate over the commission's future intensified. Clinton advocated a ten-year continuation of the LMDDC as a state and federally funded organization which would lobby for regional development while it monitored the implementation of the recommendations. According to Bumpers, however, two years earlier the report might have shocked Congress into action but now "the federal government, the states, and the cities are in a terrible fiscal crisis." Declaring that "we've got plenty of structure, the problem we have is delivery," plantation bloc representative Franklin visited the Bush White House three times before the release of the final report in order to coordinate the defeat of any effort to create another ARC.[63]

The final report of the LMDDC was entitled *The Delta Initiatives: Realizing the Dream . . . Fulfilling the Potential*. The report was delivered to Congress by Clinton and Hawkins on May 7 1990. It was delivered to the White House by Clinton on 14 May, exactly two years to the day after the Mississippi River governors' summit and one day before the annual Delta Council meeting. In a letter of transmittal to Bush, Clinton wrote that we "agreed that the Delta was an enormous, untapped resource for America, that it can and should be saved. We agreed that our goal should be nothing less than full partnership for the Delta." The report was designed as a handbook primarily for use by state and federal legislative bodies and agencies. It contained more than 400 recommendations divided into four major issue areas: human capital development, natural and physical assets, private enterprise, and the environment.[64]

Several new initiatives were launched immediately before and after the final report was submitted: the construction of a massive new prison near Espy's home town, Yazoo City, and the creation of the Delta Higher Education Association, a consortium for joint programs, and for faculty and student exchanges, between 105 colleges and universities in the seven states. By the summer of 1990 politicians from the LMDDC states had formed the Delta Caucus in Congress. Rep. Espy was the chair of the twenty-seven-member caucus and Rep. Bill Emerson (D. AR) was its vice chair. The caucus opted for changing funding formulas in a variety of programs rather than advocating the creation of a new regional commission. According to Emerson, the caucus was looking for "trains that are leaving the station to which we may attach some targeted opportunities that are in line with the report." Still raising the "plantations first" banner, Rep. Whitten argued that "appropriations alone won't solve the Delta's problems. Congress will have to address the underlying problems of the farm economy."[65]

Clinton and other leaders considered establishing the Delta Development

Center to provide technical assistance for various development projects and to track implementation of the recommendation of the LMDDC's final report. The proposed center was to be funded by contributions of $50,000 from each of the seven states, by $100,000 saved from the original $3 million federal budget, and by $250,000 from Congress. By September 1990, the LMDDC movement began to unravel. The governors of Mississippi and Louisiana declined to contribute. Whitten refused Espy's request that he write in $250,000 for the center in the $50 billion agricultural appropriations bill. Bumpers also balked, stating that he wanted the $100,000 to go back to the Treasury. The LMDDC officially expired on 30 September 1990. According to Greenberg, attempts to perpetuate the commission were just as useless as the commission itself:

> Waste has a way of generating more waste—indeed of demanding it in the most elevated and inflated prose. If only it could be harnessed, the cubic footage of gaseous verbiage in this report would have been enough to gin all the cotton produced between Cairo, Ill. and Pte. a la Hache, La., in any one fiscal year—with enough left over to fuel two and half gubernatorial campaigns in Arkansas.[66]

Greenberg's weekly attacks on the LMDDC led many to believe that his was a genuinely populist critique of social inequality and waste. In October 1990, Greenberg revealed himself as a plantation bloc supporter after all:

> If Bill Clinton is interested in doing something productive with that $50,000 a year, he might consider a new down-to earth home-grown outfit called the Arkansas Delta Council. It's just been formed on the successful model of the 55 year old Mississippi Delta Council.[67]

But the planter bloc was satisfied with the LMDDC to the extent that it was one of the few times that the national spotlight had been focused on the region without its practices being roundly denounced. For Chip Morgan, executive vice president of the Delta Council, this was the LMDDC's "greatest contribution." Franklin believed that President Bush should not be blamed for his refusal to assist the region: "I'm not so sure there's anything within his power to directly alleviate problems." In general there was a strong bias against any solutions that "smack of more bureaucracy or industrial planning." According to Cochran, "I'm not for creating a permanent commission to try to be nursemaid to the region." The plantation bloc clearly feared any new federal comprehensive development program that would reduce African American dependency.[68]

# 10

# Writing the Regional Future

The conflict between working-class African American communities and the dominant plantation bloc has been so intense for such an extended period that the region and its people are constantly being misunderstood. The sociological categories developed to explain conditions in other regions falter in the Delta. Similarly, the reforms, plans, and policies that appear feasible elsewhere are irrational when applied in the region. While no single community in the Delta possesses more knowledge about the region's hidden boundaries, the unspoken categories, and the invisible utopias than its African American community, the Lower Mississippi Delta Development Commission (LMMDC) proceeded from the premise that no such wisdom existed.

In order to accomplish its goal of preparing a ten-year development strategy for the Lower Mississippi Valley, the LMDDC held hearings, conferences, and tours, it funded studies, it deliberated, and then it offered more than four hundred recommendations. However, nothing in any of the written statements and interviews of LMDDC officials indicated that they were engaged in a significant challenge to the dominant plantation bloc production and policy regime. There were no signals that significant participation by the African American community was wanted or missed. It was from these narrow boundaries that the reports and recommendations were generated. Consequently, social science and development planning theories and methods served only to marginalize further African Americans and their social development traditions.

The central conflict in much of the region is between a dispossessed and impoverished bloc of African American communities and a monopoly-oriented plantation bloc that dominates the region's political economy and social relations. Although the LMDDC identified several hundred ways to restructure and reform regional development patterns, they all proceeded from the same basic assumption: that the plantation bloc monopoly was the foundation upon which new regional order was to be built. Consequently, in reading the various texts associated with the LMDDC, it is possible to excavate from the statements, documents, and actions of various authors their position on, and relationships to, the structures of regional inequality. This archaeological approach will be used below to recover from the LMDDC's hearings, conferences, and studies a discourse on the future of African

American communities. The primary goal of this interrogation is to open a window onto this central debate and upon proposed strategies for resolving the crisis. This approach was designed to discover the key elements of the plantation bloc's development agenda for the coming period, that is, Mississippi Delta Plan 12.

Four sets of LMDDC documents generated between 1988 and 1990 will be relied upon: conference reports; transcribed conference and hearing testimony; twenty of the thirty studies authorized and financed by the LMMDC; and the detailed recommendations found in the final report, *The Delta Initiatives: Realizing the Dream . . . Fulfilling the Potential*. While many of the discussions address problems in each of the seven states, the primary focus here is upon the eighteen-county Mississippi Delta. Published in 1992, the 300-page Delta Council study *A Social and Economic Portrait of the Mississippi Delta* will be used to highlight further the debates in the Mississippi Delta. The evaluation of these debates and agendas relies on categories of investigation developed out of the foundations of the blues epistemology: the working-class African American community-centered tradition of development thought and practice and its critique of the plantation bloc, its political economy, and its tradition of social explanation.

## Social Policy: The New Dependency

In the course of the LMDDC debates over future social policy, it was readily admitted that the existing education, health, and housing policies were a failure and that these failed systems were now collapsing. One of the persistent criticisms of the commission's recommendations was that outside of requesting new federal funds, no strategy was developed for assisting state and local governments deeply mired in fiscal crisis. Without a fundamental intellectual and social transformation, more residents will become dependent upon constantly shrinking programs. This leveling and winnowing process will translate into new forms of dependency, new forms of devastation, and a new exodus.

### The educational crisis

After existing in a state of crisis for decades, the regional educational system sank to a new bottom in the 1980s and 1990s. The LMDDC held only one conference on the subject and commissioned only one study: *The Role of Higher Education in Improving the Economic Climate of the Lower Mississippi Delta Region*. The seeming lack of interest in primary and secondary education was a consequence of the recent completion of major educational reform campaigns in most of the states and of a desire to avoid any discussion of the taxation of large agricultural landowners.

Several educational goals were identified in the final report of the LMDDC (*The Delta Initiatives*): development of public and private programs to ensure that "all parents will be competent to serve as their children's first and continuing teacher"; use of federal subsidies, state regulatory improvements, tax credits, and revolving loan programs to provide every family with access to safe and affordable child care; improvement of science, math and English competency by rewriting federal education regulations to allow the targeting of comprehensive services to rural low-income students; solution of the teachers' shortage by state actions to devise new certification programs and encourage businesses to donate staff; and rewriting of federal job training and adult literacy program guidelines to allow more funds to be spent on basic skill and literacy training. The fifth subject addressed was high school dropouts: only 54 percent of all adults had a high school diploma but only 38 percent of African American adults; on average, 25 percent of all students drop out every year. One problem identified was the existence of educational tracts for the majority of Black students that were so inadequate and inferior that they effectively pushed students out of school. In the study funded by the Delta Council, the view of African American education as a burden finds complete expression:

> most of the population of the Delta neither needed nor wanted education for all children. In fact, compulsory education has only become statutory within the last decade ... the emergence of early federal programs to support education was a mixed blessing ... higher educational attainment might actually disqualify a person from getting the low-level jobs that are available. Third, federal efforts to integrate schools have resulted in the 'flight' of many prosperous white families to private schools within the Delta. This has weakened community and financial support for the public schools.[1]

In addition to integration, another reason offered by White parents to explain the creation of White private schools was the "teaching of evolution and sex education." The authors went on to note that industrial redlining, lack of business diversity, and the state of the schools would prevent most firms from locating in the Delta.[2]

In 1992, twelve of the seventeen Mississippi school districts on academic probation were in the Delta. Many of the thirty-six school districts in the Delta have less than three thousand students each. Most of the schools suffer from advanced deterioration of buildings, heat and ventilation problems, and a severe lack of supplies. In 1988, in the eleven most heavily African American counties in the Delta, the graduation rate was only 25.9 percent. These disparities are better understood when governmental contributions are compared. The US average per pupil expenditure in 1982 was $2,701: 9.3 percent federal, 47.4 percent state, and 43.3 percent local. In Mississippi, the average per pupil expenditure was $1,784: 24.3 percent federal, 56.7 percent state, and 19 percent local. Local governments in the Delta contribute less to education than other localities in the state. This is partially a result of the deep poverty in which most families find themselves; approximately 86 percent of the students in the public schools receive free school lunches. The inability of parents to pay significant property taxes to support the schools is a consequence of plantation domination.[3]

Additionally, the very low rates of taxation on agricultural land serve to subsidize the planter while ensuring that badly needed social programs and infrastructure such as public schools and residential water systems are not funded. Agricultural and uncultivated land represents approximately 40 percent of the total assessed value of real property in the Mississippi Delta. In eight of the eighteen counties the percentages are much higher: Coahoma, 54 percent; Holmes, 50 percent; Humphreys, 53 percent; Issaquena, 87 percent; Quitman, 53 percent; Sharkey, 59 percent; Tallahatchie, 60 percent; and Tunica, 64 percent. Yet assessment rates, assessed value, and therefore, taxes are kept at very low levels at the behest of planters. As the process of land consolidation continues, the tax base of local and county governments will become even more dependent upon a smaller number of planters. The LMDDC refused to examine the central role the plantation bloc has played in gutting public education and destroying the lives of African American youths.[4]

### The health crisis

On the issue of health care access, the LMDDC called upon the national government to establish national health insurance in addition to providing Medicaid access for workers transitioning off welfare. One of the LMDDC recommendations was for the states to ensure that those in need received the Medicare, Medicaid, food stamps, and Women, Infants, and Children Nutrition Program (WIC) benefits they are entitled to. This suggestion was made because the state agencies and county offices administering these programs would arbitrarily ignore or deny applications from qualified African Americans. Even some Whites reported receiving similar treatment. Some persons who apply for food stamps are contacted two years later or not at all. Sometimes the distribution of benefits is done only on the approval of a planter, while state social service agencies work to discourage applicants and purge the rolls as often as possible. The results of these practices are staggering and serve as a partial explanation of why the Delta is the epicenter of infant mortality in the United States.[5]

The LMDDC study performed by Professor Frank Farmer of the University of Arkansas at Fayetteville found that, when compared to the rest of the USA, death rates in the Delta were higher across all age, ethnic, and gender groups, and for all causes of mortality. Death rates for Blacks in the rural areas of the region are higher than those of rural non-Whites in other parts of the USA from age one to age forty-four. While the neonatal (less than one month) mortality rates of African Americans in the Delta are similar to those of non-Whites in other parts of the United States, the post-natal (age one month to one year) rates are significantly higher: 7.42 per thousand to 5.47 per thousand. In a paper presented at the LMDDC Rural Poverty Seminar, Dr Jocelyn Elders observed that since 1960, adolescents have been the only age group with rising rates of mortality. The causes of this "new morbidity" were rising rates of car accidents, suicides, drug abuse, AIDS, homicides, chronic illness, and physical impairment:

> When the 60 percent of the adolescents living in poverty and not covered by Medicaid are combined with their uninsured parents and siblings in an environment of rural health facility closures and doctor flight, the outcome is that many youths choose to leave rural communities.[6]

Elders's recommendation that comprehensive, school-based clinics be established partially addressed one of the key aspects of health problems in rural areas: people often have to travel long distances to visit doctors and clinics. No viable rural transportation system exists in areas where many residents don't have access to cars. In the United States as a whole, there are 213 physicians per hundred thousand persons while in the Lower Mississippi Valley there are only 87 per hundred thousand. The existence of fewer facilities and fewer personnel is creating a situation where treatable diseases can rapidly turn into epidemics. For example, 246 cases of syphilis were reported in Washington County in 1989 compared to 21 reported in 1988.

The LMDDC made twenty-four specific recommendations for improving health care access, including encouraging state departments of corrections to "institute programs which train minimum security prisoners for ambulance and fire protection in small communities." In a place where high and rising rates of mortality, facility closures, personnel shortages, and transportation failures collide with a state and local fiscal crisis, major reforms funded by existing local resources are highly improbable. With the failure of national health care reform, the only alternative remaining for local government is either extraction of increased contributions from the plantation monopoly sector or passive acceptance of the growing deadliness of regional life.[7]

*The housing crisis*

The LMDDC study *Housing Problems and Solutions in the Lower Mississippi Delta Region* was prepared by researchers from the University of Arkansas at Pine Bluff under the direction of Dr Jaquelyn McCray. Unlike many of the other studies, this report identified the origins of the housing crisis in the region as lying firmly within the conflict between working-class African American communities and the plantation bloc:

> the housing problems of the region are the result of the historical presence of the black population and the fact that the social, political, and economic agenda of the region was created, sanctioned, and nurtured on the economic exploitation and social isolation of this population.[8]

In 1980, there were approximately 2.2 million housing units in the 214 counties in the LMDDC's boundaries, of which 1.4 million were owner-occupied. The median value of the owner-occupied units was $9,282 and the median rent was $41 per month. In the Mississippi Delta, the median rent in Holmes, Humphreys, Issaquena, Quitman, Tallahatchie, and Tunica Counties ranged from $17 to $27 a month. In the seven-state region, nearly 105,000 units lacked complete plumbing and 171,000 were overcrowded. The median value of African American owner-occupied units was $5,113 with minor variations between the states: $3,170 in southern Illinois, $4,157 in the Arkansas Delta, $7,069 in Louisiana, and $6,030 in Mississippi. Approximately 43.6 percent of all Black-owned homes were valued at under $5,000.The authors of this study concluded that the 492,000 units of owner-occupied housing valued at below $5,000 and most of the 396,000 rental units rented for less than $40 a month have "little or no potential for rehabilitation." The housing crisis was intensified not only by unregulated building construction and land, but also by hostile state agencies:

Such characteristics include the absence of community services in poor and black communities. Across the region, open ditches, dirt roads, and poor or no drainage systems are standard environmental conditions. Although many communities do have public sewage systems, some are ineffective and most are not available beyond short distances of the town boundaries ... In one community, the air was filled with the aroma of open sewerage. Water stood in almost every yard, and moisture problems associated with poor drainage were so severe that trees as well as wood framing on houses suffered from advanced stages of decay.[9]

During the LMDDC forum on "Rural Housing Needs in the Lower Mississippi Delta Region," a panelist discussed the refusal of the Delta states to enact building codes and landlord–tenant laws. First, none of the LMDDC states has a statewide housing code. Second, local governments in urban areas that have building codes cannot or will not enforce them. Third, although the requirement that landlords maintain their rental units in a habitable condition—known as the warranty of habitability—has been recognized in forty-eight states since 1970, it has not been recognized in either Arkansas or Mississippi. In Tennessee and Kentucky warranties don't apply to rural areas, while in Louisiana a landlord's failure to carry out repairs cannot be used as a defense against eviction. For ten years in a row, between 1979 and 1989, the Mississippi legislature defeated an exemption-packed bill requiring landlords to make basic repairs. Little relief is expected from a judiciary that has decided neither to protect tenants from retaliatory evictions nor to protect workers from retaliatory firings.[10]

The authors of the housing study recommended a comprehensive housing program similar to the federal Model Cities program of the 1960s. Local nonprofit management would play a central role in a program of massive construction and rehabilitation while nonprofit bodies with larger social agendas, of which housing was just a part, would be favored as either the primary developer or as partners with for-profit-firms. The LMDDC's report recommended the following: using the Community Reinvestment Act to get financial institutions involved in low-income housing rehabilitation and construction;

using federal tax breaks, grants and loans by utilities, state-assisted sweat-equity programs, and state revolving housing trust funds to encourage first-time home ownership; revising the federal tax code to encourage rental construction; continuing federally subsidized low-income and elderly housing programs; providing loans and grants for owners to meet the code require-ments; enacting landlord–tenant laws in each state; and encouraging federal and state governments to fund homeless shelters with comprehensive services.[11]

If implemented, many of these recommendations would improve dramati-cally the quality and quantity of housing and housing services in the region. Yet without the active participation of community-based organizations in the housing policy design and implementation process, these suggestions will never see the light of day. For example, an LMDDC conference paper on landlord–tenant law suggests that the forces capable of pushing such reforms through the legislatures are not yet present. "One of the likely reasons that the Delta states have not kept up with trends in housing law is the lack of any real organization around housing issues. In Mississippi, for example, passage of the landlord tenant bill has been urged by a small group of five to ten people who work on the bill each year. There has been no tenants' group or housing coalition to back passage." The consequences of the dismantling of the Mississippi freedom movement continue to reverberate in the region. Reforms to improve the conditions of the impoverished can be suggested by even the most conservative because there is little likelihood that fundamental change will occur. Several participants in the LMDDC debates reasoned that what was needed most was a new freedom movement.[12]

### Institutionalized rural poverty

The LMDDC's seminar on "Rural Poverty and the Family" was indicative of the exclusionary and silencing strategies that impoverished African Americans face daily in the Mississippi Delta. Funded by the LMDDC and the Tennessee Valley Authority, the event was convened by the John Stennis Institute of Government, the Sociology Department of Mississippi State University, and the Nelson Rockefeller Institute of Albany, New York. The seminar was held in February 1990 at the Delta branch of the Mississippi Agricultural and Forestry Experiment Station at Stoneville, the headquarters of the Delta Council. Without the effective participation of the rural poor, thirty to forty policy makers, foundation executives, and academics discussed rural poverty in the halls of an organization dedicated to its preservation and expansion.

The stated objective of the conference was to "to provide information ... to the private sector and to providers of public services that will enhance their ability to support rural families." In one of the first papers, Dr Farmer concluded that simply raising incomes of African American female-headed households will not necessarily change mortality patterns. Community-wide solutions were needed in those places where deep poverty is compounded by sexism, racism, and rural isolation. Other seminar participants concurred; poverty could not be overcome without addressing the deadly legacy of institutional intransigence. For example, Dr Frances Henderson, director of the Division of Nursing at Alcorn State University, reported that many rural service providers use their authority not to empower people but to control them by withholding information and benefits. According to Dr Alma Page, Professor of Sociology at Southern University, "counties in the Mississippi Delta have the lowest participation in AFDC (Aid to Families with Dependent Children) and Head Start Programs." For Doris Barnette of the Alabama Department of Public Health, the Mississippi Delta had become a living corpse, a museum of medical and social horrors that attracts both missionaries and poverty professionals as tourists:

> It is the only place that I have ever been where there is a relatively large group of fairly wealthy people and a large, large number of very poor people. The world we live in most often has the middle income people making the rules ... Here in the Delta ... the wealthy people can attend to their own needs; the poor do not have the power or political clout to get their needs met, and a few middle income folks wander about, most of them being human service professionals who spend time in the Delta, and then go on to something else.[13]

One of the most insightful criticisms of the structure of social policy decision-making was made by Professor Bonnie Thornton-Dill of the Center for Research on Women at the University of Memphis:

> we have to look at the political and economic structure of communities. We have to look at the resources that exist there and how those resources are divided—who controls them and what needs to be done to change that distribution and control. If we accept the notion that poverty is a characteristic of communities, we cannot assume that we can bring about change by giving the same groups who have run the community all the time the resources to develop new programs.[14]

This approach stands in direct contrast to strategies based on the premise that providing funds to the dominant leadership is the only course that should be followed. The latter position was supported by R. J. Felix, a program officer with the Henry J. Kaiser Family Foundation, who argued that the War on Poverty's Office of Economic Opportunity (OEO) failed because too much autonomy was given to groups representing the poor:

> one of the things that they did that historians now say might have been a political mistake is that they bypassed the state infrastructure and dealt directly with community level organizations, especially in the South. And sometimes, when the federal government pulled out, there was no local money that came back into local communities. Basically, the community level organizations were left to fend for themselves because of the political damage that was done as a result of by-passing state and local infrastructures.[15]

This naïve and revisionist account of the period has become a widely accepted explanation. The Delta planter bloc violently resisted the freedom movement and the War on Poverty while attempting to coopt programs that it could not immediately dismantle. In the early 1960s, African American, Native American, Chicano, and Asian American communities, and other working-class communities, were both abused by and shut out of the "state and local infrastructure." They were the ones being continually damaged and had little reason to expect, then or now, that there would ever be a sudden outpouring of "local money" to confront poverty.

Rural poverty is a direct product of rural relations of power. It cannot be confronted in the absence of fundamental social, economic, cultural and political democracy. Democracy can't be guaranteed in an environment defined by extreme resource inequality. Farmer argued that "policies that are intended to ameliorate poverty in the Delta areas should focus on enhancing community development and local action." For example, in the area of health care this would require a series of actions designed to build a comprehensive system dependent on local resources and people: expanding the number of residents trained in health care delivery; establishing working relationships between health care providers and economic development officials; encouraging regionalism or institutional cooperation across state boundaries; encouraging scientists and educators to study the problems of local development; using the Cooperative Extension Service to educate residents on local development issues; and using federal "funding which supports local action that focuses on addressing the social sources of poverty."[16]

This approach centers on the expansion of community participation and the extension of democracy based upon the collaborative efforts of residents, community organizations and institutions. Still, it is a service delivery model that offers no explanation of how impoverished communities will marshal the power needed to implement it. Autonomous organizations capable of challenging dominant institutions cannot be wished into existence. In past periods, an alliance of autonomous Delta organizations created and pushed an anti-exploitation and pro-democracy comprehensive agenda. Present and future efforts will require both an in-depth knowledge of these past strategies, a familiarity with other national and international reform movements, and a working knowledge of the offensive currently being mounted by the neo-plantation regime.

## Economic Development: The Past as Future

The central goal of the LMDDC was to assemble a ten-year economic development plan. Although the commission was able to generate four hundred recommendations, the conflict between the main development traditions defeated attempts to create a unified vision of the region's future. The New South branch of the region's leadership emphasized expanded manufacturing, infrastructure construction, small-business development, and new technologies. The continued growth of manufacturing was considered necessary to raise the standard of living for some of their African American constituents while preserving the stability of White working-class communities. Creating a multistate regional development commission along the lines of the Tennessee Valley Authority or the Appalachian Regional Commission was viewed as the most effective way to coordinate the political power, funds, and resources necessary to implement this agenda. This form of regional planning was resisted by the plantation bloc. Its producers' councils are committed to allowing only those federal and state interventions that they can directly manage. This alternative form of regional planning is designed to preserve neoplantation-bloc hegemony at the expense of increasingly impoverished African American and White communities.

One of the implicit goals of the LMDDC and its chairman, Bill Clinton, was to rebuild the alliance between the New South and the plantation bloc while continuing the long tradition of incorporating a small segment of the African American community. This formula for the construction of regional unity required avoidance of a thorough debate on the value of existing regional power structures. The challenge of planning the reproduction of power without a discussion of power was left to the social scientists. These scholars avoided the risk of open debate over power and resource distribution by attempting to prove objectively that the wisest course of action was to always invest limited revenues in existing sectors, institutions, and structures of inequality.

The LMDDC-commissioned study *Socioeconomic Change in the Labor Markets of the Lower Mississippi Delta, 1975–86* clearly demonstrates the effective limits of a social science based on positivism for the critical study of regional relations. Produced by two professors with the Louisiana Agricultural Experiment Station, the report used Local Labor Market Areas (LLMAs) as a category to analyze work patterns. As defined, LLMAs are a group of counties with a combined population of at least 100,000. LLMAs are distinguished by economic interactions such as commuting patterns.[17]

Between 1980 and 1986, of the twenty-seven LLMAs within the LMDDC boundaries, the two Mississippi Delta LLMAs, Leflore and Washington, showed every indication of being mired in a crisis of profound proportions. In 1980, the percent of families in poverty in them was 33.7 percent and 41.6 percent respectively, while the LMDDC and national rates were 21.2 percent and 13.3 percent. They also had the highest unemployment rates, the lowest per capita incomes, and the highest rates of population loss in the region. In 1980, the Leflore and Washington LLMAs were 48.7 and 59.8 percent African American respectively. Additionally, the percentage of African Americans in poverty was four times that of Whites. Yet despite these glaring inequalities, the two social scientist authors of the LMDDC study torturously tried to avoid any discussion of the relationship between race and poverty:

> Racial composition is another factor often associated with the prosperity of local areas ... We have included this factor to examine if the distribution of the black population in the Delta region is associated with economic performance. Although

the findings reported ... cannot be used to draw conclusions about causal relationships between racial composition and economic performance, we found a high
coincidence of the percent of a LLMA's Black population and rank based upon per
capita income. Those LLMAs ranked in the bottom third had substantially higher
concentrations of black residents.[18]

During the recession of the early 1980s, the region deteriorated faster, and
then recovered slower, than the USA as a whole. The authors constructed a
model to determine why the region fared so poorly. After running several
regressions, they concluded that the presence of a growing finance, insurance
and real estate sector was a good indicator of growth while Southernness and
Deltaness were indicators of decline. These last two categories are based on
comparison of the South to other national regions and of the Delta to other
Southern regions. Of no significance for growth was the percent of population
between 20 and 34 years, high school completion, federal investment, urbanity,
or the percentage of African Americans.[19]

Thus positivism in one fell swoop eliminated the meaning of over a century
and a half of ethnic regulation and social conflict. The entire documentary
record of the region demonstrates that public and private investment decisions
were, and are, based on race. Only the use of a methodology that defines
social reality in terms of the scientific analysis of randomly selected and
narrowly defined categories could come to a conclusion that both masks and
rationalizes continued economic monopolization and ethnic exclusion. The
major recommendation of this report sounds as if it could have been written
at the birth of the New South movement in the 1870s:

> While agricultural policies are likely to affect the socioeconomic conditions in the
> rural LLMAs, it is important to realize that long-term success ... depends on
> attracting new manufacturing and service industries.[20]

Although the general thrust of Southern economic development practice is, at
least rhetorically, moving away from complete dependency upon industrial
recruitment strategies, this bankrupting strategy is here again advocated
uncritically. This is one of the characteristic features of positivism as a
methodology. Policy can be advocated solely on the basis of statistical corre-
lations without a nod to history or present reality. Issues such as social,
economic, and cultural justice are categorically excluded, and policy recommendations become just as random and subjective as the variables selected.
Positivism allows the hegemonic bloc to prove scientifically that it is a superior
formation because it is impossible to test alternatives that do not exist. It is
used as a cloaking device, as a silencing strategy, and as an attempt to make
struggling and conscious humans scientifically invisible and voiceless numbers.

Another approach to explaining the relationship between race and economic
development was taken by Mississippi State University professor T. David
Mason in a study prepared for the Delta Council. He attempted to answer the
question: why are 85 percent of the poor in eight Mississippi Delta counties
African Americans?

[It] can not be denied that poverty in the Delta is rather uniformly a black phenomenon ... it would be difficult, to say the least, to deny that discrimination in labor markets exists in the Delta ... Poverty and race are inextricably connected in the Delta, and it will be difficult to alleviate the economic problem of poverty without addressing the social problems of racial conflict and overt discrimination. Racial hostility is also intimately connected to the general economic underdevelopment of the region because, ultimately, racial discrimination is economically inefficient ... Economic growth and development in the Delta will always be suboptimal so long as racial discrimination is allowed to distort the markets for human capital, credit, housing, and other goods and services.[21]

The human capital category proceeds from an ideological assumption of how social and economic change occurs, and it evaluates statistics accordingly. Relying on Gary Becker's 1957 work *The Economics of Racism*, racism is then defined ahistorically as an irrational activity that negatively affects capitalist development. Like the slavery-as-feudalism analogy, the human capital approach in economics and the other social sciences asks the observer to focus on a romanticized vision of "real" capitalism and not upon existing capitalism and the very gritty, chaotic, and "creatively" destructive features common in its day-to-day reproduction of inequality.

Finally, the LMDDC-funded study *Expanding Export Industry Employment in the Lower Mississippi Delta* had as its goal the formulation of a sectoral investment strategy for public officials. A portfolio approach was used to identify those sectors most likely to have the greatest long-term and short-term employment benefits to particular subsections of the seven-state region. As its name implies, the portfolio theory of economic development practice is derived from "modern financial management strategies ... used to select assets from a group and to determine in what proportion these assets should be combined in order to achieve the highest growth rate for a given level of volatility." Community assets (people, facilities, programs, resources, firms, etcetera) generate funds (taxes, loans, and grants) that can be used to invest in new or existing firms, sectors, and projects.[22]

What is claimed by this supposedly rational method is not superior knowledge but superior technique, namely flexibility. It would enable officials to respond quickly to increasingly contradictory shifts in firm, sectoral, and local government performance. In the absence of the global ordering characteristic of Fordism, "casino capitalism" has taken hold. Not only do local jurisdictions gamble their resources on the job- and revenue-generating potential of plants, technologies, trade, tourism and other activities, but localities themselves have become commodities or objects to be gambled with by firms seeking short-term, above-average profitability. Consequently, the stock-market approach to community development is proposed as a solution both to the inability of local government to implement long-term economic development strategies and to the seductiveness of panaceas:

One group proclaims "The future lies in high tech" while another exhorts "Go after real industry—plants with assembly lines and smokestacks." Another group urges

"Forget industry. Tourism is the answer." The next group argues "Roads, bridges, slackwater ports—that's what will bring industry to the Delta." The banner waving and hyperbole results, in part, because little objective analysis exists to show what has and hasn't worked, creating the opportunity for quick-fix salesman to pitch their solution to the region's woes.[23]

The study's authors focus on those sectors most likely to export their production and, therefore, to generate income for the region, namely agriculture and forestry, mining, construction and manufacturing industries. The issues of local ownership and control, sustainability, and justice are not considered. When the authors examined industrial employment in the export sectors of the forty-three heavily, and historically, African American counties and parishes of the "Central Delta Counties" of Arkansas, Louisiana, Mississippi, and Missouri, a pattern of unrelenting economic decline and rapid decay were found:

> Export industry employment peaked in 1978 in the central counties ... Export industry employment in the central counties contracted an average of −1.1% each year from 1969 to 1986. Since 1978, the average loss has been an astounding −2.8% per year ... Farming and industry had 24,477 fewer jobs in 1986 than 1969, and 27,000 fewer jobs [in 1986] than in 1978. Some 29,000 farm workers were displaced from 1969 to 1986 largely by mechanization and concentration of landholding. At the same time, textile, apparel and leather industries that moved south in the 1960s and early 1970s to take advantage of the Delta's low-cost labor began moving to southeast Asia and Latin America in search of even lower cost labor.[24]

The LMDDC recommended that the number of minority businesses in the region be increased by 25 percent in ten years. Small market shares, shortages of capital and expertise, and discrimination were cited as barriers to the growth of these firms. The favored solution came from an LMDCC-funded study completed by the Booker T. Washington Foundation, *A Market Study to Define the Prospective Business and Economic Development Benefits Generated by Section 1207, Public Law 99–661*. This report focused on the use of a US Department of Defense procurement program which had as its goal directing 5 percent of all DOD authorizations to minority contractors. Based on this study the LMDDC recommended the following:

> Representatives from state government, the private sector, and the minority businesses in the Delta should establish a regional partnership program to develop and implement a five-year plan to mobilize resources to enable minority business to obtain capital, management, technology, and technical assistance required to compete for the Department of Defense and other governmental contracts.[25]

This approach to expanding the African-American business community in the Delta begged the question. The recommended reliance upon the rapidly downsizing defense sector and upon increasingly embattled affirmative action programs ignores the role of regional elites in actively marginalizing Black firms. No state or local programs were suggested to rectify this situation. Clearly, the implication is that without the availability of non-intrusive federal funding, that is, federal interventions and programs that would leave the regional structures of domination and exploitation untouched, the states would refuse to act; the past would remain the future.

## Ethnic Supremacy Tourism

Authors of the LMDDC conference report on tourism concluded that "the Delta doesn't give itself enough credit for serving both as the cradle of jazz, blues, gospel, country and western, rock n' roll, and rhythm and blues . . . and as the inspiration for some of the most renowned writers in the history of American literature." One of the major recommendations in the LMDDC's final report was that a regional tourism entity be created. This agency would assist local communities with inventory, research, financing, infrastructure, and training. The reason for the previous failure of leaders to recognize the birth of major international cultural movements in the region can be found in the plantation bloc tradition of denying the genius inherent in African Americans, Native American, Asian American, Latino, and working-class White communities. It is also a result of the intense censorship visited upon musicians, authors, artists, and others critical of the regime.

For many years, the principal tourist activity in the Mississippi Delta consisted of tours and celebrations focused upon monuments to White supremacy: plantation homes, Civil War battlefields, romanticized reenactment of plantation life, the tragedy of cotton production, and racist collectibles. Part of the current growth in tourism is now being sparked by a growing interest in African American history, cultural practices, and social movements. Large numbers of national and international tourists are drawn to the Delta blues Festival in Greenville, the King Biscuit blues Festival across the river in Helena, the blues Museum in Clarksdale, and the entertainment districts found along Beale Street in Memphis and in the French Quarter in New Orleans. Civil rights tourism is also a growing activity. In 1992, the Civil Rights Museum in Memphis was opened on the former site of the Lorraine Motel, the place where Dr Martin Luther King Jr was assassinated. Annually, tours, conferences, anniversary celebrations, memorials, and other events throughout the region are held to mark the highlights of the African American movement to transform the South. Civil rights pilgrimages are particularly popular among young people of all ethnic groups from all over the world.[26]

Therefore there was an intense debate between the plantation bloc and African Americans over how the region's histories and cultures should be represented and promoted. In this conflict over whose image of the Delta would be inscribed on the landscape, the primary question was, will the censoring of the African American experience continue? Frances Smiley, director of the Alabama Department of Tourism's Black Heritage Program took the following position:

A continued collective embarrassment/timidity on the part of the current power structure regarding the relationship between Black history and Southern US history hinders a positive approach toward marketing Black heritage tourism. No organized, multi-state approach for inventory/research and marketing of Black heritage sites exists. A prevailing mindset connotes and celebrates Civil War history/tourism with plantation pilgrimages, and battlefield reenactment, yet fails to endorse the presentation of the ways Black Deltans participated in this pivotal era of struggle. In short, Delta tourism misses an enormous opportunity by not seizing its own history, by not accepting and realizing that it is all of our history.[27]

Susan Eddington, president of the Black United Fund of Louisiana, argued for the need to include African American voices when depicting the region's history:

> it is not enough to celebrate the plantations throughout the South without heralding the slaves who worked the land, the slaves who often built and certainly maintained the monuments that today are so dearly cherished. We must also celebrate the sons and daughters of these slaves for their contributions . . . When you go to a plantation . . . [or] in New Orleans, where you might find slave quarters . . . the experience of the slaves is not the one that's given; it's usually from the perspective of the family of the slave holder.[28]

To include these voices, the voices of the enslaved and their descendants, is often seen as a threat to the legitimacy of the plantation bloc. It would make suspect the entire plantation bloc tradition and its continued claims of cultural, economic, social and ethnic privilege. Furthermore, the disassembly of this tradition and the elevation of African American, and populist, traditions of resistance and culture could provide White Southerners with alternative and sustainable conceptions of tradition, morality, democracy, and justice to identify with. While the blues is increasingly being approached by Whites as a shared heritage, African American history remains censored and plastered over by numerous Civil War novels, movies, and miniseries.

Proposals for a Delta African American Heritage Trail were included among the initiatives presented in the LMDDC final report. The region was referred to as "a microcosm of the African American experience in this country by representing all forms of expressive culture (music, folklore, literature), a wealth of historical sites from all ways of life (urban and rural, river and inland), and all significant eras from slavery to freedom." The proposed tourism agency would be responsible for establishing the trail along one or two north–south routes paralleling the river and for coordinating research through African American studies, Southern studies, anthropology, and history academic programs and departments. Another proposal advocated the creation of Native American-based tourism linking archaeological sites, the Trail of Tears, and existing communities.[29]

Tourism as a development strategy presents numerous problems. When it is conceived of as just another form of economic competition between communities, questions of appropriation, commercial exploitation, ownership, resource distribution, and employment are left unanswered. For example, not discussed during the tourism proceedings were the thousands of impoverished African American and other women who work as minimum-wage hotel maids under extremely exploitative conditions. In the absence of a tourism agenda that has emerged from community-based decision making, a community's heritage can be turned against it and used to reproduce and expand the existing structures of exploitation.[30]

## Agricultural Policy: The New Green Revolution

The early 1980s crisis of the Delta Green Revolution was characterized by falling land prices, falling exports, rising rates of farm foreclosures, numerous bank failures, rising production costs, soil erosion, wetland degradation, groundwater depletion, and ever-widening pesticide, herbicide and fungicide contamination. The accelerating global mobility of capital and the attendant declines in new plants relocating to the rural South has resulted in a renewed emphasis by cash-strapped states upon assisting the relatively immobile export-oriented agricultural sectors.[31]

Since the mid-1980s, the combination of wetland protection regulations, mandated acreage reductions, and the introduction of higher-yielding varieties and new equipment has changed the production and marketing cost structure for the entire cotton complex. Additionally, yield-oriented federal and private lenders require farmers to adopt the most capital-, technology-, and chemical-dependent forms of production. All these forces are operating both to drive smaller farmers out of business and to encourage land consolidations.[32]

According to W.A. Percy II, vice chairman of the Farm Policy Committee of the Delta Council, the 1985 US Farm bill reduced federal outlays to the region's principal crops, cotton and rice, by more than 50 percent. Yet both regional crops gained a greater share of world markets. During the period of the LMDDC, Cecil Williams, executive vice president of the Agricultural Council, the Delta Council's sister organization in the Arkansas Delta, outlined the plantation bloc's strategy for increasing cotton profitability based on less federal subsidy, acreage expansion, and a new round of Green Revolution technologies:

> With the present varieties and chemicals, cotton is probably the most profitable crop grown in the area. It definitely is if you take government payments out of the picture, heaven forbid. With the new cotton pickers that will pick 30 inch rows, cotton could likely be profitably expanded to a lot of acres ... Most of this land would come out of soybeans which are not very profitable ... With proper incentives, farmers could level more land, install irrigation systems and make other investments which would reduce risks and increase profitability ... Perhaps we need to work toward a farm program that would induce farmers to plant more cotton and rice and less soybeans.[33]

One of the leaders of the new Delta Green Revolution is the California bio-technology firm Calgene. In the words of one of its vice presidents, the firm is focusing on revolutionizing the cotton economy in preparation for an era of declining government subsidies, rising fuel costs, and restricted chemical use:

> Calgene also owns Stoneville Pedigreed Seed Company, the nation's second largest cottonseed company based in Greenville, Mississippi ... Calgene is pursuing the development of genetically engineered cotton varieties that improve the profitability of the crop, either by increasing yields or decreasing input costs. We are developing varieties that are resistant to herbicides, thereby improving the economics of weed control. We are also developing insect-resistant cotton.... [G]enetically engineered cotton varieties will improve the environment, and the quality of life for the entire Delta by reducing the use of agricultural chemicals and/or causing a shift to less environmentally damaging ones.[34]

As a package, this new environmentally correct Green Revolution is the subversion of the original intention behind low-input and sustainable agriculture. In the LMDDC study prepared by the Rainbow Whole Foods Co-op of Jackson, *Alternative Foods and Sustainable Agriculture: Health and Wealth from Delta Soils*, the American Society of Agronomy's definition of sustainable agriculture and the Institute of Alternative Agriculture's definition of low-input production were cited:

> [Sustainability] over the long term: (1) enhances environmental quality and the resource base on which agriculture depends; (2) provides for basic food and fiber needs; (3) is economically viable; and (4) enhances the quality of life for farmers and society as a whole.
>
> [Low input production seeks to] optimize management and the use of internal production units in ways that provide acceptable production levels of sustained crop yields ... which result in economically profitable returns. The approach emphasizes such cultural and management practices as crop rotations, recycling of animal manures, and conservation tillage to control soil erosion and nutrient losses to maintain or enhance social productivity.[35]

At some point, these techniques were detached from the demand for economic democracy and were turned on their head to become sustainable, genetically engineered, cotton neo-plantation agriculture. While the export-oriented planters demonstrated their flexibility by coopting sustainable techniques and discourse, the advocates of alternative crops wanted to replicate the multi-institutional structures characteristic of the populist cooperatives. For example, the LMDDC study *Alternative Crop Production and Marketing Strategies for Farmers in the Lower Mississippi Delta Region* begins from the premise that the revitalization of rapidly declining rural communities depends on the "diversification of traditional agricultural production and marketing." The recommendations generated by the Rainbow Whole Foods Co-op also focused on the need to create a new regional institutional infrastructure. Bargaining associations would be formed to organize the sale, marketing, financing, processing, warehousing, distribution and research activities associated with regional associations dedicated to the selling of locally grown products. These associations would also negotiate with governmental institutions, banks, and labor. Legislation and state support would be needed for several initiatives: creating incentives for organic farming; experimental development of a community-based food supply system; formulation of a regional diet based on locally grown foods; and introduction of naturally processed foods from local businesses using locally grown ingredients.[36]

This last study clearly imagines a regional future fundamentally different from the agribusiness models. Yet the idealistic notion that states are willing to lessen their support of cotton and rice in favor of small-farm food production seems to miss the point that cotton and rice are not just crops; they are also highly mobilized political factions. The visionary and activist approach to production policy is also present in the labor and welfare policies advocated to complete the twelfth Delta mobilization. For example, while some state agricultural officials believe that expanded vegetable production could provide year-round employment in the region's fields and greenhouses, the lack of available and exploitable labor remains a major barrier:

> The cheap migrant labor that had sustained similar enterprises in the past is no longer available. In addition, the minimum wage rate is not considered affordable to some farmers. Many potential farm workers are reluctant to accept the minimum wage.[37]

According to one agricultural hearing participant, what was needed to resolve the shortage of readily exploitable labor was a "reorganization of the welfare system to encourage, not destroy the work ethic, family life and morality." On welfare reform, fellow plantation bloc allies and Southerners President Bill Clinton of Arkansas and US House Speaker Newt Gingrich of Georgia were all in agreement. The transfer of welfare policy formulation and implementation to states in 1996 created a new national system of unfree Black labor overnight. Plantation bloc beneficiaries include manufacturers who already depend upon high rates of unemployment, turnover, and injury. Large numbers of African Americans now face being forced into the fields, factories, and offices of the Delta as a new era of bondage is being born.[38]

## Resource and Environmental Policy: The Sustainable Plantation

The LMDDC also examined the restructuring of timber, water and environmental policies. Much in evidence during the LMDDC's existence was the conflict between major row crop producers and major timber/paper corporations. Many hardwood forests were "converted" to row crops as a result of the high agricultural commodity prices of the late 1960s and 1970s. Conversely, falling commodity prices in the mid-1980s provided an opportunity for "afforestation" on the now-fallow fields. By 1970, seven major pulp–paper corporations owned or controlled over 30 million acres of forest land in ten Southern states. By 1980, 150,000 families were engaged in hauling and harvesting timber for these firms. By the late 1980s, 34.6 million of the 76.7 million acres in the Lower Mississippi Valley were covered by forests. Timber harvesting has become highly mechanized and the flat Delta lands are perfect terrain for the use of mechanical scissors, each of which can cut dozens of trees a day.[39]

The section of the plantation bloc that is fully dedicated to row crop production has generally resisted incursions by the timber industry into the core Delta counties. They have also expressed suspicion of federal wetland regulations as an attempt to preserve fallow land for forestry. In its final report, the LMDDC saw the issue differently; federal wetland policies were viewed as preventing forest creation and exploitation:

> Current definitions do not adequately differentiate the quality and quantity of wetlands. For example, a pristine cypress swamp and a commercial loblolly pine plantation may be placed in the same wetland classification.[40]

While sawmill employment is likely to be minimal, 35 employees per plant, and the pay for mill workers and harvesters is low, the ecological costs from mill pollution are extremely high. Yet the LMDDC recommended that federal, state, and local governments should finance timber industry expansion:

> Financing must be made available for state-of-the-art plants. Congress, state, and local government should consider creating limited tax incentives to forest product industries . . . State and local government should increase infrastructure development to support expansion of the forest products industries.[41]

When there are many communities without sewers, homes without plumbing, when colleges face the threat of closures, and school systems face bankruptcy, the LMDDC arrogantly recommended subsidies for international timber monopolies. Monopoly timber production, much like catfish and chicken processing, holds out the potential of reinforcing plantation relations in some areas, reintroducing these relations in others, and introducing these relations for the first time in still other areas.

Many farms have better water delivery systems than rural homes and towns. This fact was highlighted in a workshop on agribusiness and water during the conference on "Economics, Energy, and the Environment in the Lower Mississippi Delta." The lack of water systems has led to depletion of ground-water and to contamination of shallow wells by leaking septic tanks. This public health hazard is compounded by seepage of agricultural chemicals into the aquifer recharge areas located to the north of the Delta. In the region itself, layers of clay prevent aquifer recharge by ground and river water. This feature holds pesticides and herbicides closer to the soil surface and hastens their entry into new crops and into wells, streams, and rivers that people depend upon for drinking water. Now being pumped at rates 40 percent faster than recharge, groundwater supplies will not be able to sustain the current production levels of rice, catfish, and cotton.[42]

The workshop participants recommended an immediate, and long-overdue, US Environmental Protection Agency study of air emissions in the region:

> Acidity levels of precipitation in the Lower Mississippi Valley have often reached pH's of 3.0–4.0, or the acidity of vinegar. This is a result of air emissions from heavy industry both within and west of the seven state region . . . populations along certain reaches of the river have some of the highest cancer-incidence rates in the nation and breathing problems are common.[43]

Nevertheless, the LMDDC's recommendations on the environment were generally based on the philosophy that reform means allowing major resource users to set policy. "Sustainable agriculture is one that is productive, competitive and profitable." The obvious question here is, profitable for whom and competitive with what? Instead of creating public water management districts, the LMDDC's solution to the problem of groundwater depletion was to let the plantation-bloc-dominated USDA regulate farm and plantation water use. In the areas of air, water, and waste management, the LMDDC advocated more stringent federal and state regulation. Yet again there appeared to be a bias toward the self-defeating process of rule writing by the major users and regulation by agencies locally dominated by pollution producers. Masked under the banner of environmental protection, this is a recipe for theft and murder committed on a grand scale.[44]

The environmental debate within the LMDDC did not address substantively the question of social inequality and the monopolization of resources. The fact that African American, Native American, and impoverished White communities are often the targets of air, water and waste polluters was not mentioned. Racially discriminatory local government practices in water system funding, administration, and delivery were also ignored. Since the monopolization of resources in the region distorts every policy decision, sustainability has been redefined to mean preserving the Green Revolution plantation structure at huge human and environmental costs.

## Leadership Policy: The New Paternalism or the Manufacture of Dissent

Several of the LMDDC-funded studies were specifically written to provide strategies for the reproduction of the dominant leadership and its institutions. The emphasis of these studies was upon establishing working relationships between major owners and managers on the one hand, and a section of the African American and organized labor leadership on the other. The models offered advocated what Noam Chomsky has called the manufacturing of consent:

> [Walter] Lippman ... argued that in a properly-functioning democracy there are classes of citizens ... the specialized class, the responsible men, carry out the executive function, which means they do the thinking and planning and understand

the common interests. Then there is the bewildered herd, and they have a function in democracy too. Their function in democracy, he said, is to be spectators, not participants in action ... They'll just cause trouble. So we need something to tame the bewildered herd, and that something is this new revolution in the art of democracy: the manufacture of consent.[45]

In several studies prepared for the LMDDC, the authors consciously set out to create models of cooperation for the purpose of manufacturing consent without expanding democracy. The LMDDC study *The Labor–Management Cooperation Model and Its Impact on Economic Development and Other Socioeconomic Issues* identified several reasons why labor relations must be reorganized:

> The 1990s will require a new kind of workforce. A workforce ... able to adapt quickly to global competition and new technological advancements ... Because the life expectancy of current jobs is only about seven years, continuous retraining of workers must be a high national priority ... The efforts to improve workplace literacy, skills and training; the spirit required to improve worker attitudes, improve work ethics and instill pride; the overall energy required to improve quality and increase productivity; will require a total commitment by business from top to bottom. It will require a high level of on-going cooperation between labor and management.[46]

Another LMDDC study, *Interstate Cooperation, Regionalism, and Economic Development in the Delta*, identified the manufacture of a new regional identity as a key concern:

> The first step toward the development of any meaningful cooperative venture among the Delta states must be the psychological unification of its residents into a recognizable, cohesive region with their own identity. Rather than focusing upon the competitive aspects of development in the various states, both the public and private sectors must understand and focus upon the benefits they accrue via the success of their neighbors. This will require that both governments and citizens identify themselves with the Delta as their cultural and economic home. Attitudes toward regional participation must be reshaped so that the Delta region takes on a psychological aspect of importance nearly equal to attitudes about state loyalty, giving the people a sense of "connectedness" with other Delta residents.[47]

Increasingly dependent on external investors, leadership groups or blocs are aggressively leading the charge to package (bind) and commodify their localities. This necessitates the assassination of participatory democracy and the regimentation of social thought:

> It necessitates labor and management to focus on common goals rather than divisive issues ... Churches of different denominations must present themselves collectively; public and private entities have to come together on what is best for a community. It is also required that where circumstances warrant, race relations must be improved and negative perceptions overcome.[48]

The strategy outlined above seems designed explicitly to play on the fears of African Americans, organized labor, and unorganized workers concerning employment and instability by recategorizing these fears as common goals: "the group would then develop a strategic plan for the accomplishment of non-threatening goals and objectives such as media relations, substance abuse, education, and many other timely and appropriate topics." The central features of this model are derived from industrial psychology and the race relations industry. The image and feel of meaningful action are manufactured while images and organizations considered to be "divisive" are to be dismantled. Under this model, discussions of work conditions, wages, unequal provision of services, institutional discrimination, housing and occupational segregation, community investment decisions, resource monopolization, and human rights violations would be severely censored. The manufacture of consent is accompanied by the destruction of dissent:

> A group involved with working on race relations issues can go a long way in showing prospective businesses that a community cares and is progressive ... Race relations issues become explosive at times where there is no vent to allow frustrations to be siphoned off before an eruption occurs. The labor management cooperation model furnishes an organized approach to such a release of tension and frustration.[49]

As part of the effort to manufacture consent, the LMDDC held an "Ecumenical Conference on Economic Issues" in Little Rock, Arkansas. Conference organizer Paul Purdy placed ecumenicism within an economic development context. "A community with a good moral climate, excellent schools, a workable and efficient government, a trained labor force and excellent transportation facilities will likely attract industries." In his speech before the conference, Governor Clinton stressed his belief that a new morality must be enforced upon the people of the region:

> this morning when I got up ... Hillary asked me what I was going to do today. And, I said, "Well, I'm going to start off the day with 200 preachers and a half dozen Rabbis." And she said, "Well, if anybody ever needed it, you do." Government has had to learn that there is not necessarily a program for every problem, and that all the good intentions of the world can come crashing down if there is not good motivation in the inside of the people we are trying to help. So government has tried to find new ways to impose personal responsibility on the people who would be the beneficiaries of tax dollars, whether they are business people, having to comply with stricter compliances, in order to get loans and grants, or welfare recipients, who in return for a check, have to sign a contract, promising to pursue a path of independence, through education, training, and job placement.[50]

Clinton's call for help was not based on asking churches to help design new welfare and other social policies. The churches' role was to ameliorate the negative impacts of governmental and corporate policies:

> A church cannot exist outside the world, beyond the doors of sanctuary. And so what we're trying to do today is to find some common ground ... Which churches have been most successful in working with local social service agencies, to pick up all the people falling between the cracks in society, and help them get started again?

And if it works in a place in Mississippi why aren't we doing it everywhere? The government cannot do this alone.[51]

Speaking for the more impoverished churches, the African American chair of the conference, and executive director of the Louisiana Interchurch Group, Reverend James Stovall warned that it "would be a mistake to assume that the churches have the resources or the skills to solve the basic problems of the area." While some churches viewed cooperation with governmental agencies and the economic elite on economic development matters as a high priority, others saw their primary mission as mobilizing their congregations and communities to achieve social and economic justice by fighting these same institutions.[52]

The final report on the restructuring of regional leadership was prepared by Clarence Wright: *Race Relations: A Strategy for the Lower Mississippi Delta Region*. It also focused on the use of a particular model of leadership to turn negative race relations into an economic development opportunity. Wright argued that Delta race relations must be reinterpreted "in a strategic, positive, forward thinking, and problem solving manner" in order to exploit this resource and capture economic benefits from a painful past:

> the Lower Mississippi Delta region has confronted each and every dimension of the race relations issue to varying degrees over the past four decades. Our history over the last two decades in the area of race relations is rich, progressive, and valuable. This region can "teach" this country and other nations volumes about the issue of race relations. This capacity, this resource should not be hidden, but aggressively marketed nationally and internationally.[53]

As a public relations strategy, Wright's approach contains touches of brilliance. As a strategy for regional social justice it suffers from a common flaw that has been found throughout many of the LMDDC works. The plantation bloc is not mentioned and its monopolization of power is left unaddressed. Surprisingly, the LMDDC accepted several of Wright's proposals. However, in the final report, most of Wright's recommendations were seriously watered down. The call for heightened federal civil rights enforcement became a demonstration program on race relations and cooperation. His call for state civil rights laws and regulatory bodies became a request that the US Civil Rights Commission (CRC) fund the mobilization of "state advisory committees to convene a coordinated series of race relations hearings and regional race relations conferences to report on regional progress in interracial cooperation." The LMDDC remained silent on several of Wright's recommendations: for enactment and enforcement of fair employment and affirmative action laws by the states; and for a Civil Rights Commission investigation of industrial redlining. These ideas did not spring forth from Wright's mind alone. Many of the points in this agenda are over a century old and are firmly based in the historic African American development agenda. The distance Wright placed between himself and the organizations that fought for these goals on a daily basis represented a fundamental diminution of the power and potential of the blues tradition.[54]

In its own study, representatives of the plantation bloc concluded that the civil rights revolution will only recede in the coming years. The principal editor of the Delta Council's 1992 study, Professor Arthur Cosby of Mississippi State University, provided the council with several economic and policy projections. Among them was his belief that the significance of race is declining, not in daily life, but in public policy:

> The national transition to a multi-ethnic society may also set limits for the future of the Delta. When there are many ethnic groups who may qualify for "minority status," the significance and importance of minority status as a legal and political identifier diminishes. Consequently, we should not expect significant new governmental or judicial targeting of a specific minority group for affirmative action treatment. Nor should we expect substantial new federal initiatives to eradicate poverty or health care problems in the Delta simply because the region has a majority black population. For example, there will likely be a diminished support for government set-aside programs for blacks or for strengthening of affirmative action guidelines. The emergence of a multi-ethnic society, at least at the national level, will diminish race as a category.[55]

If the Delta Council proceeds from the assumption that African Americans will be increasingly disempowered for the foreseeable future, then the manufacturing of consent takes on a new meaning. Except for minor efforts to incorporate small leadership factions, for the majority of Blacks social relations will become increasingly dangerous. An example of this deep schism is found in the chapter on leadership and economic development written by Judith Porter, chair of the Department of Sociology at Bryn Mawr College:

> Black and white leaders have differing perceptions of the cause of poverty. All black leaders, in contrast to white leaders, see the black population as having a good work ethic; for instance, "People want to work. They're getting up at 5:00 a.m. to catch a bus for a minimum wage job in the catfish factory. That tells you something." Blacks stress lack of jobs and racial discrimination rather than values and attitudes as the major causes of current poverty, though low skill levels are seen as a perpetuating factor.
>
> Black community organizers are the ones who blame lack of welfare rather than welfare itself for the continuation of poverty "People who don't have jobs often don't apply for food stamps. The atmosphere in the food stamp office is one of denial. People go there who have no food, no place to stay and the office tells them they have to wait a month. That's cruel, and discourages people from getting help they need." Thus, lack of economic development is seen as a cause of poverty for blacks. For white leaders, on the other hand, poverty is seen as an impediment to economic development.[56]

With these thoughts in mind, the "New Paternalism" might more appropriately be termed the "New Cruelty." This is exactly what Porter found when she asked a plantation bloc leader his vision of the region's future:

Ten years down the pike, I see beautiful fields of cotton and soybeans, the growth of industry, and a program to encourage out-migration, which will solve a lot of problems.[57]

# 11

# The Blues Reconstruction

If there is no struggle there is no progress. Those who profess to favor freedom and yet deprecate agitation are men who want the crop without plowing the ground; they want the rain without thunder and lightening. They want the ocean without the awful roar of its many waters . . . power concedes nothing without a demand. It never did and never will. Find out just what any people will quietly submit to and you have found out the exact measure of injustice and wrong which will be imposed upon them. The limits of tyrants are prescribed by the endurance of those whom they oppress.
                    Frederick Douglass, speech in New York, 3 August 1857

It has been an underlying theme of this book that plantation production is one of the most monumental burdens ever placed upon any community. It disfigures every nation, region, and ethnicity it touches. African American communities in the Delta have borne this burden with the help of the blues for over 170 years. It is finally time that this burden be lifted. African Americans in the Delta are more than ready to shift their attention away from surviving the dangers of daily life to the building of stable families and communities in a region where plantations are no more.

As many African American rural communities move from a permanent state of crisis toward social and fiscal collapse, the plantation bloc is attempting to establish a new regime of orderly accumulation and social regulation. The foundations of this new regime of oppression are the intensification of social inequality through an ever more irrational and absurd monopolization of regional resources that is secured, in part, by ethnic warfare. Yet there is no guarantee that the present mobilization of the Delta plantation bloc and its national and international allies will be successfully institutionalized. The critical unknown is the determination of African Americans to implement the historic development agenda of the Union Leagues, the Colored Farmers' Alliance, the Progressive Farmers and Household Union, the Southern Tenant Farmers' Union, the Mississippi Freedom Democratic Party, Fannie Lou Hamer, and the millions of souls whose lives and consciousness have been shaped by Southern trials and travails. Even though the plantation bloc has successfully disfigured even minor reforms and has buried numerous visionary movements, these defeats do not diminish the ultimate wisdom of these goals, the efforts to attain them, or the monumental victories they have birthed. This rich blues tradition remains as relevant today as it was two centuries ago. It is the only basis upon which to construct democratic, sustainable, and cooperative communities. These blues movements have not only defined African American identity in the region, they remain the fountain from which flows the ideas necessary to enable African Americans to confront once again those who loudly and arrogantly proclaim their right to determine the region's destiny by dominating all who live within its borders.

The Lower Mississippi Delta Development Commission (LMDDC) chose to ignore the African American tradition of expanding political, economic, and cultural democracy in the region in favor of a development path designed to solve the crisis of the plantation bloc. Many of the recommendations adopted by the commission would increase economic monopolization and dependency on the one hand, and ethnic domination and suppression on the other. During this critical period, the future imagined by the twelfth Delta plantation bloc mobilization is being confronted by African American efforts to resurrect the blues tradition and call into being the Third Reconstruction.

## The Twelfth Mobilization

The Delta's political schisms have once again occupied center stage in the life of the USA. Immediately after the LMDDC closed its doors, social relations in the Delta states became further polarized by deep schisms over race and development. One of the best ways to view this process is to examine the fate of the three governors who served as LMDDC commissioners.

After switching to the Republican Party, Louisiana governor Buddy Roemer placed third in the 1991 primary. The general election was an intense battle between Democrat Edwin Edwards and his Republican opponent David Duke. The eventual winner, Edwards, was a former governor and congressman who was also a former president of the International Rice Association. Duke was the leader of the National Association for the Advancement of White People and former leader of the Louisiana Ku Klux Klan. In the 1995 race, African American congressman Cleo Fields was defeated in the general election by Republican Mike Foster, a large sugar planter who reportedly is the great-grandson of a former governor who was also the founder of the Knights of the White Kamellias—a Louisiana variant of the Ku Klux Klan. After reviewing recent events in the state, Bernard Broussard of the Lafayette NAACP concluded, ". . . you'd swear the Civil War was never even fought."[1]

Mississippi governor Ray Mabus lost his reelection campaign in 1991 to millionnaire Republican Kirk Fordice, a Delta construction company owner from Vicksburg. Fordice immediately sent shock waves through the African American community when he expressed his desire to bring the "Reagan Revolution" to Mississippi, cut educational spending, repeal the Voting Rights

Act of 1965, veto legislation designed to increase the penalties for crimes motivated by racial, ethnic, or religious hatred, and to call out the National Guard rather than implement a federal court order to equalize funding between Black and White state universities. After the election of Fordice, the fight for fair political representation intensified greatly. According to his Democratic opponent in the 1995 governor's race, Dick Molpus, "Fordice leads more by venom than vision."[2]

The federally mandated electoral redistricting in Mississippi in 1993 resulted in the election of a record number of Black legislators being elected in the state. During the swearing-in of the new legislature in 1994, Fordice announced his plan to downsize the body from 174 to 90 members in the House and from 60 to 30 members in the Senate. Viewing this proposal as an attempt to eliminate African Americans, women, and rural representatives, the Legislative Black Caucus promptly walked out. Eventually tabled, the Fordice proposal would have reduced the number of Black legislators from 42 to 7. According to African American representative Ed Blackmon of Canton, this "sounds like 1894 instead of 1994."[3]

The third Delta governor initially did a great deal better than his fellow commission members. The 1992 election of Bill Clinton to the US presidency represented the realization of the principal goal of the Democratic Leadership Caucus (DLC). One of the founders of the initially all-White DLC in 1985, Clinton became its chair in 1991. In a 1990 interview, a DLC leader, Senator John Breaux of Louisiana, argued that a presidential candidate had to be found among the "more conservative Democrats in the South and West where the future of the Democratic Party lies." Even though Arkansas had not enacted significant civil rights laws during his tenure as governor, Clinton's influential cadre of African American supporters and his working knowledge of African American culture made him a more viable candidate than Senator Albert Gore of Tennessee or Sam Nunn of Georgia.[4]

The election of Clinton as President and Gore as Vice President and the subsequent appointment of Espy as Secretary of Agriculture meant that politicians from the Delta states had risen to the pinnacle of national power. However, fellow Southerners in the Republican Party launched an attack on the Clinton that has yielded a never-ending series of disclosures, exposés, investigations, resignations, and prosecutions. Despite numerous attempts at appeasement through retracted nominations, forced resignations, firings, budget cuts, new corporate subsidies, etcetera, the Democratic Party continued to suffer from an unprecedented number of local, state, and national defeats and defections.[5]

Many of the attacks on the DLC New South Democrats were orchestrated by Mississippi Delta plantation bloc lawyer Haley Barbour who became chair of the Republican National Committee after the 1992 election. The Barbour family's law firm has been a key fixture in the region since the late nineteenth century. Claiming to have "spent enough money to to burn a wet mule," Barbour was one of the principal architects of the 1994 and 1996 Republican elections strategy that resulted in radically conservative Republicans capturing both the US House of Representatives and the US Senate. After the 1994 congressional elections, members and allies of various Southern plantation blocs assumed strategic leadership positions: Representative Newt Gingrich of Georgia, Speaker of the House; Senator Thad Cochran of Mississippi, chair of the Senate Republican Conference; Senator Trent Lott of Mississippi, Senate majority whip; Senator Strom Thurmond of South Carolina, chair of the Senate Armed Services Committee; Senator Jesse Helms of North Carolina, chair of the Senate Foreign Relations Committee; Representative Dick Armey of Texas, House majority leader; Representative Bob Livingston of Louisiana, chair of the House Appropriations; and Representative Bill Archer of Texas, chair of the House Ways and Means Committee. When Senator Robert Dole resigned from the US Senate in May 1996 to run for president, both the two main contenders for the position of Senate majority leader were from Mississippi: Senators Thad Cochran and Trent Lott. A few years earlier the man who was to win the contest, Trent Lott, engaged in the following exchange on the relationship between the Southern past and national policy with a writer from the increasingly influential *Southern Partisan*:

> *Partisan*: At the Convention of the Sons of the Confederate Veterans in Biloxi, Mississippi you made the statement that "the spirit of Jefferson Davis lives in the 1984 Republican Platform."
> Lott: . . . all the ideas we supported there—from tax policy to foreign policy, from individual rights to neighborhood security—are things that Jefferson Davis and his people believed in.[6]

According to a Democratic Party official, "Southern Republicans have perfected the art of polarization. There are a lot of other things going on, but race is never far from the surface." House leader Gingrich has been no less definitive in resurrecting plantation bloc ideology. In response to a particularly brutal crime, Gingrich used this ancient strategy of intertwining discussions of crime, drunkenness, drug addiction, laziness, lack of intelligence, and otherness to implicitly argue that African Americans present a threat to "civilization":

> Now a country which has this kind of thing going on—and this is not an isolated incident; there's barbarity after barbarity. And we shake our heads and say, "Well, what's going wrong?" What's going wrong is a welfare system which subsidized people for doing nothing; a criminal system which tolerated drug dealers; an educational system which allows kids to not learn and which rewards tenured teachers who can't teach, while destroying poor children who it traps in a process with no hope. And then we end up with the final culmination of a drug-addicted underclass with no sense of humanity, no sense of civilization, and no sense of the rules of life in which human beings respect each other.[7]

According to Fordice, no one should be mistaken about the origins of this Republican movement and where its true leadership comes from:

> Much has been said and written about the new revolution in our nation's capital and the Contract with America. But when I examined the composition of this new

revolution, I noticed something very striking. Virtually every reform measure being discussed has either already been done in Mississippi or is in the process of being done in Mississippi.[8]

Clinton's role in the debates over the twelfth plantation bloc mobilization and African American destiny in the Delta can best be unserstood by examining several recent federal policies.

## Empowerment Zones and Enterprise Communities, December 1995

The Los Angeles Rebellion of 1992 emphasized the fundamental relationship between human rights and development. After the revolt, President Bush immediately proposed the creation of several federal enterprise zones. Although this agenda had been advocated previously by the Reagan administration, it was successfully resisted by African American, Latino, and labor organizations who feared both the neo-plantation corporate domination of neighborhoods and heightened labor exploitation. Although new enterprise legislation was passed by Congress, Bush vetoed the program after his defeat by Clinton. Upon assuming office, President Clinton reintroduced the legislation and it was passed with heavy bipartisan support.

The site selection process for the new Empowerment Zone and Enterprise Community (EZ/EC) Program began in September 1993. Proposals from around the USA were considered for designation as one of the three rural and six urban Empowerment Zones or one of the thirty rural and sixty-five urban Enterprise Communities. The urban programs were to be managed by the Department of Housing and Urban Development while the rural programs were assigned to the Department of Agriculture. The Enterprise Communities would receive $3 million in funds and a wide array of federal incentives and exemptions in addition to being granted the authority to issue tax-exempt facility bonds. Rural and urban Empowerment Zones were scheduled to receive a federal commitment of $40 million and $100 million respectively. Each were guaranteed all benefits provided the Enterprise Communities plus tax credits for employers, federal property tax reductions, and additional tax incentives for smaller firms.[9]

In December 1995, Clinton announced that seven rural Enterprise Communities would be established within the LMDDC boundaries: one in the southern portion of the Mississippi Delta, two in the Arkansas Delta, two in the Louisiana Delta, one in the Missouri Bootheel, and one in Tennessee. Three urban Enterprise Communities were also designated in the region: Monroe and New Orleans in Louisiana, and Jackson in Mississippi. Additionally, a portion of the Mississippi Delta was designated as an Empowerment Zone. Two organizations were selected to co-manage what is now known as the Mid-Delta Empowerment Zone. The first is a very small predominantly African American nonprofit development corporation, the Delta Foundation, while the other, the Delta Council, coordinates a multi-billion dollar international agro-industrial complex. By this one act, Clinton finally proclaimed himself and his administration to be defenders of the agenda of the Delta Council and of the plantation bloc that it represents.[10]


## Welfare reform, August 1996

> The bill closes its eyes to all the facts and complexities of the real world ...
> Peter Edelman, former Assistant Secretary for Planning and Evaluation, US
> Department of Health and Human Services[11]


Throughout his 1992 campaign for the presidency, Governor Clinton promised to "end welfare as we know it." His other campaign slogan, "two years and you're off," signaled his intention to ensure that there would be no relief from the new forms of dependency he was contemplating. In this attack on the economically weakest segments of society, Clinton overthrew a system of social guarantees developed during the Great Depression for the purpose of limiting mass starvation and other brutal forms of exploitation.

Clinton's signing of the Personal Responsibility and Work Opportunity Act of 1996 signaled the end of several federal entitlements. States now have the right to determine who receives Aid to Families with Dependent Children (AFDC) benefits and for how long. By the year 2000, some 50 percent of all families now receiving aid will be required to contribute from twenty to thirty-five hours of free labor to the state per week while 90 percent of all two-parent families now receiving aid will have to meet the same requirement. All assistance to teen parents and those convicted of drug possession, distribution, or use will be eliminated, and in addition no family or individual will be able to receive aid for more than five years. Newly unemployed adults are only allowed to receive food stamps for three months out of every thirty-six. The new law neither protects families from being wrongly terminated from the remaining entitlement-programs nor does it protect families and communities caught in cyclical or prolonged economic recessions. It also mandates the denial of food stamps and Supplemental Security Income to current and future legal immigrants, the elderly, the disabled, and children. While Clinton acknowledged that the bill would negatively impact 2.6 million people, he tried to suppress damning data from a study he commissioned: even under its most optimistic scenario, 11 million families would suffer a permanent loss of income.[12]

Even prior to Clinton's signing of the Republican-authored bill, states had been requesting and receiving numerous exemptions to the requirements of the AFDC program. One out of every three children in Mississippi lives in poverty. Additionally, the state pays the lowest benefits in the USA: $120 a month for a mother and two children. Subsidized or free school lunches are received by six out of ten children in Mississippi; for some of these children this lunch is their only meal of the day. None of these harsh realities prevented Clinton from approving Fordice's "experiments" with the lives of 50,000 destitute families on welfare, 82 percent of whom are African American. One exemption allowed the state of Mississippi to deny an extra $24 a month to a mother having another child while on welfare. Another exemption sanctioned Fordice's "Work First" program in Mississippi. Under this arrangement, food stamp and AFDC checks are turned over directly to private employers who disburse them as wages only after they are satisfied with an individual's work, attitude, subservience, etcetera. According to columnist Robert Scheer, the

> President has also approved a Mississippi program that seizes food stamp and welfare money from recipients and uses it to subsidize a mandatory work program. A welfare mother must accept a minimum wage job in the private sector mostly paid for with federal funds. In what may herald a return to the plantation economy, this time around subsidized with federal funds, the private employers put up only a dollar an hour of their own money ... Perhaps Clinton was drawing on his own experience as chairman of the Mississippi Delta Commission, which managed to do nothing to improve the lot of the poor in the most impoverished region of the country. Illiteracy and unemployment rates remain just where they were.[13]

These exceptions and the provisions of the welfare reform act have essentially given state governments the right to design their own enforced hunger and enforced poverty policies. State governments have also been given the authority to further delegate the policy and management functions, including the determination of eligibility and benefits, to county governments, charities, religious organizations, nonprofit corporations, and private firms. This has spawned a new growth industry—the design of "innovative" approaches to creating new forms of unfreedom: state, private, and family bondage; deadly competition between the poor and the working poor; poverty-enforced migrations; heightened levels of social surveillance; and an unquantifiable array of ethnic and racial oppressions.

Peter Edelman, Assistant Secretary for Planning and Evaluation at the US Department of Health and Human Services, and husband of Children's Defense Fund founder Marian Wright Edelman, resigned his post after Clinton signed the welfare reform bill in 1996. Attacking Clinton's decision to sign the bill, Edelman did not mention the fact that the entire leadership of the Democratic Party boycotted the signing of the bill. Neither did he mention Clinton's cynical and pathetic use of an African American single mother from Arkansas during the signing ceremony. But Edelman does provide an insightful analysis of welfare reform as being little more that a disguised package of massive budget cuts. Scheer charged Clinton with "giving opportunism a bad name." He suggests that the attack on public assistance for the poor launched by Clinton and US Senate majority leader Lott of Mississippi was an election-year ploy recommended by a political consultant who simultaneously worked on both their reelection campaigns, Dick Morris. With a somewhat different take on why the bill was signed, Edelman believes that Clinton unnecessarily capitulated to the conservative Republicans in Congress and then cynically used the threat of a Dole victory to silence and prostrate potential opponents:

The same defacto conspiracy of silence has enveloped the issue of whether the bill
can be easily fixed. The President got a free ride through the elections on that point
because no one on his side, myself included, wanted to call him on it. He even made
a campaign issue of it, saying that one reason he should be re-elected was that only
he could be trusted to fix the flaws in the legislation. David Broder wrote in the
*Washington Post* in late August that re-electing the President in response to this plea
would be like giving Jack the Ripper a scholarship to medical school.[14]

Again, with the stroke of a pen, Clinton had implemented one of the core
agenda items of the plantation bloc: the destruction of the six-decades-old
national social compact and the creation of a new generation of economically
defenseless African American.

*Proclaiming the new cotton kingdom, 15 May 1995*

The plantation bloc has been able to thrive even though numerous scholars
and activists declared it dead. The concept of institutional rents is useful for
understanding how the plantation bloc was able to use its economic, political,
ethnic, and cultural power to extract a wide variety of subsidies from a variety
of institutions and alliances. Regional blocs such as the Delta Council and
sectoral organizations such as the National Cotton Council mobilize to extract
institutional rents and then use these subsidies for several purposes. In
addition to building institutions and alliances that they control, they also use
subsidies to crush the growth of independent movements advocating alternative development agendas.[15]

How are these rents extracted? First, the federal pillars of the neo-plantation
regimes are found in the United States Department of Agriculture (USDA)
and its numerous agencies. Not only does the USDA support the production
and social goals of agribusiness, it also acts to accelerate the demise of rural
African American communities, institutions, farms, and farmers. Congressional committees, particularly the rice, cotton, and sugar subcommittees,
effectively operate as permanent sectoral and regional lobbyists. Equally
important are the billions of dollars' worth of water projects constructed and
managed by the US Army Corps of Engineers. Agencies such as the federal
Department of Health and Human Services, the Department of Education,
the Environmental Protection Agency and the Department of Justice contribute in many ways, including refusing to investigate the daily perversion of
laws, policies, and programs in the region.

At the state and local levels, selective and biased prosecutions, a racially
unbalanced judiciary, and the use and nonprosecution of random and systematic acts of violence by law enforcement officials and employers can also be
classified as institutional rents. The deeply embedded traditions of industrial
redlining, occupational segregation, and union busting also fall within this
category. State research and infrastructure funds are used to fund planter bloc
projects while local school systems, hospitals, and governments collapse. State-
regulated utilities, water and health systems either directly support the plan-

tation bloc's development agenda or implicitly support it through their failure to regulate. Additionally, local water and sewer services, health care, and education are either underfunded, selectively funded, or unfunded. Finally, the exemption of plantation lands from taxation severely limits local fiscal capacity and necessitates an increased dependence upon declining federal and state funds.

Looked at from the standpoint of institutional rents, the LMDDC was an extended search designed to identify the institutions capable of providing new rents for continued regional domination. Both the plantation bloc and the New South bloc were engaged in planning for the preservation and extension of their power in the face of a receding federal government. Yet in many ways the New South bloc is once again capitulating to the plantation bloc and its plan to create a new institutional regime based upon not only expanded cotton production with genetically engineered plants, but also a new round of mechanization, a new Green Revolution, new sustainable technologies, minimal local government, the pauperization of the working class as a whole, and a new campaign to demonize African Americans. In other words, currently being implemented is the twelfth Mississippi Delta plan, a new enclosure, and a new Trail of Tears.[16]

This new era was triumphantly proclaimed on 15 May 1995 by Clinton's Secretary of Agriculture, Dan Glickman. On this day the Delta Council traditionally holds its annual meeting and the Cotton King and Cotton Queen are crowned in Memphis. Before an assembly of Latin American textile manufactures attending the Cotton USA seminar, Glickman outlined the boundaries of the new cotton kingdom:

> We're your neighbor and we want to be your grower. We have a huge, huge area that is suitable for growing cotton. It includes 17 states. It stretches from California in the West to Virginia in the East, 2,500 miles; it reaches from Brownsville, Texas north some 800 miles into Kansas. Our number 1 and 2 cotton producing states, Texas and California, are half a continent apart. Throw in the Mississippi Delta and you have a diverse production area that falls across different climate zones, sees different weather patterns, faces different pest problems. This diversity is a strength. No flood, no drought, no ravage of insect or disease is going to cripple our total cotton-growing potential in a given season . . . we have tamed rivers, brought water into deserts, and put the forces of science at work against crop pests. Today South Carolina produces more cotton on 223,000 acres than it did on 2.8 million acres in 1918 . . . In Georgia . . . 1.25 million acres of cotton may be planted this year. Cotton will likely top peanuts as Georgia's number one cash crop . . . Cotton is king once again, and not just in the South.[17]

The Clinton administration's support for the new continental cotton empire, and for the neo-plantation blocs that govern it, seems to know no bounds. The plantation blocs were partially bound and chained by moral vision and federal laws only after centuries of struggle by African Americans for social, economic and cultural justice. Clinton and Congress have unleashed this brutal international regime once again upon African American communities and workers in the rural South.

## Burning all illusions, Christmas 1995

"The devil is still around," concluded the Reverend W. D. Lewis, the 92-year-old pastor of the Little Zion Baptist church of Boligee Alabama. His church and another a few miles away were burned on the night of 11 January 1996. Another nearby church was destroyed by an arsonist just days before Christmas 1995. On the night of 8 January 1996, the multiethnic Inner City church in Knoxville, Tennessee, was torched. The fame of the associate pastor, Reggie White of the Green Bay Packers, finally forced the national media to recognize that a pattern of assaults had been emerging over several years.

Almost a year earlier four Black churches in the western Tennessee portion of the LMDDC region were burned. On 4 April 1993, the twenty-fifth anniversary of the assassination of the Reverend Dr Martin Luther King Jr, three white youths used hymnals to set fire to Springhill Freewill Baptist church and Rocky Point Missionary Baptist church in the southwestern Mississippi portion of the LMDDC region. As the flames rose, the perpetrators yelled, "Burn, nigger, burn!" The rampage continued during the first week of February 1996 when three Black churches within the LMDDC boundaries were attacked in Zachary, Louisiana, ten miles from the state capital of Baton Rouge. Since Christmas of 1995, attacks on Black churches have grown in number and spread geographically to every region of the United States.[18]

Approximately thirty-six African American churches were burned during the first six months of 1996. The list of states where Black churches were attacked continued to grow throughout 1996 and 1997: Alabama, Florida, Georgia, Kansas, Kentucky, Louisiana, Maryland, Mississippi, New Jersey, New York, North Carolina, Oklahoma, Oregon, South Carolina, Tennessee, Texas, and Virginia. According to a US Justice Department study, between 1990 and 1996 over 216 churches, mosques, synagogues and temples were burned or vandalized. Over half these attacks occurred since January 1995 and the most common targets were African American houses of worship.

Strange theories of why Black churches were being targeted by arsonists began to emerge. Morris Dees, the White director of the Southern Poverty Law Center, suggested that the Alabama attacks were related to the deer hunting season: "you have a lot of hunting clubs up there, and a lot of drunk white boys who might be angry not getting a deer ... It's still bigoted, insensitive and intimidating, but it's not organized." Buddy Lavender, the White mayor of Boligee, speculated that the perpetrators might be Black drug dealers angered by anti-drug sermons or Black community activists trying to spur an apathetic community by manufacturing racial violence.[19]

According to the Reverend Mac Charles Jones of the National Council of Churches, "the investigation should be turned squarely in the direction of White supremacist groups." Yet Clinton and members of his administration steadfastly refused to draw any connection between the attacks even though a wave of racist bombings, murders, shootouts, standoffs, takeovers, and quasi-military formations were springing up throughout the South and throughout the USA. African American ministers and others denounced the administration both for its inaction and for its initial attempts to blame the ministers and congregations of the destroyed churches for the attacks. This practice continued until the Center for Democratic Renewal threatened to file harassment and intimidation complaints against the Federal Bureau of Investigation and the Bureau of Alcohol, Tobacco, and Firearms.

Clinton's response to the growing national outrage against the attacks and to the criticism of his administration was to convene a meeting of Southern governors on the wave of terror to discuss prevention, enforcement, and prosecution; noticeably absent were the governors of Alabama, Louisiana, and Mississippi. He was also forced to acknowledge that race was a determining factor, saying, "[we] do not now have evidence of a national conspiracy. But it is clear that racial hostility is the driving force behind a number of these incidents. This must stop."[20]

Yet Black churches continue to be attacked. What is behind the church arsons? Some would argue that the new wave of federal, state and local policies designed to isolate, oppress, and impoverish African Americans has no organic relationship with the arsonists attempting to destroy the social and spiritual centers of Black rural society. Nevertheless, although many social scientists, planners, and politicians resist any linkage between human rights and economic development, the two are inseparable. The rural Black communities of the Delta and the South who must confront all these disasters simultaneously have never had the luxury of distinguishing whips from chains.

## The Road Backward

There are already indicators of what the Delta will become if the twelfth mobilization of the plantation bloc is successful. First, Mississippi's economic development strategy can still be discussed in terms of imperialism while its community development policies can still be discussed in terms of colonialism. In a 1991 article on the Governor's Commission on Workforce Excellence, *Jackson Clarion Ledger* business columnist Dan Davis wrote that the state "doesn't need to move into a competitive position to compete with Louisiana, Arkansas or Alabama. Those have long since quit being Mississippi's economic rivals. Now we're competing with Japan, Germany, and Korea." In the same edition, another columnist attacked a candidate for governor that was not sufficiently in tune with this worldview:

Wayne Dowdy has been critical of Mac Holladay, head of the state Department of Economic and Community Development, for his recruitment of high tech industry. Dowdy has strongly suggested that those efforts are misplaced—that Mississippi

can't compete with Silicon Valley, New Jersey and Massachusetts. Like hell we can't
... don't tell me Mississippi can't compete with anybody for anything.... Where we
are is the best possible of all states ... I subscribe to the redneckism: "I'm proud to
be here."[21]

The colonial aspect of community development policy is also evident. First,
the tax revenues generated by the one million visitors per month who
patronize the booming casino industry in Tunica, along with the tens of
thousands who patronize the casinos on the Gulf Coast, have led many to
believe that the state's fiscal crisis has been permanently resolved. In what
Fordice has termed the "Mississippi Miracle," a state debt of $75 million in
the early 1990s had been replaced by a rainy-day fund of $200 million by 1995.
A recent estimate calculated the annual contribution of gambling to the state
treasury at $150 million. Welfare rolls have declined by 16 percent, from
60,000 to 50,000, and 30,000 gambling-related jobs have been created in
consequence of a growth in casino, construction, hotel, and restaurant employment. According to one economist, when "you're at the bottom, it's easy to
grow fast." Not only is the state per capita income still the lowest in the
nation, another economist suggests that, despite the growth of the casino
sector in Tunica, the "Mississipi Miracle" will miss the Mississippi Delta.[22]

Similar to the history of manufacturing in the Delta, the gaming industry is
reproducing racial and class inequality. The highly unstable gaming sector
survives by draining the income and savings of the already impoverished
residents of the Mid-South. Several planters actually own casinos, and the
planter-dominated Tunica County government unsuccessfully attempted to
block the use of new tax revenues to improve the 98 percent Black school
district. A coalition of Black parents and teachers finally forced the county
board of supervisors to dedicate 12 percent of casino-generated tax revenues
to the schools. Other conflicts have erupted around the refusal of the casinos
to hire Blacks for nonmenial jobs and around their refusal to do business with
firms owned by Blacks and women. In this 75 percent African American
county, 75 percent of casino jobs are held by nonresidents. Additionally, high
rates of job turnover have meant that, after an initial drop, there has been
significant growth in Black unemployment in Tunica.[23]

Second, the colonial aspect of community development policy is also evident
in Quitman County, which is 65 percent African American, where plantation
bloc powers continue to treat monies dedicated for county, state, and federal
programs as their personal accounts. According to Robert Jamison, president
of the Quitman County Youth Center, federal funds are systematically
diverted from meeting the needs of impoverished Black families, some of
whom live four families to a house:

> The white elected officials here do not see a problem with housing or jobs ... When
> officials send off for Community Development Block Grants (CDBGs) and the
> money returns to the community it is used on roads and bridges instead of housing
> and other necessities ... one [county] supervisor, who lives on a road six miles long,

spent an entire Block Grant on paving the road leading to his home. And his house is the only one on that road.[24]

After major floods hit Quitman County in April and May 1991, residents were forced to suffer through both the destruction of their homes and official indifference to their homelessness, hunger, and nakedness. White communities received the lion's share of the $750,000 flood assistance granted by the Federal Emergency Management Agency, while African American flood victims were moved to a community hall located in a White subdivision where they were provided with little food and no showers. When Jamieson inquired about the provision of showers he was told by local administrators that "we're talking about getting a concrete slab and a water hose to wash them off."[25]

Another key indicator of conditions in the Mississippi Delta, public education, was also feeling the brunt of the plantation bloc assault. Its decline continued, and in the early 1990s, Black parents in Yazoo County launched a boycott of local schools and businesses after they discovered that the White-dominated school board was diverting funds. According to boycott leader Linda Shaeffer, a "child receives $19.30 for textbooks every year and no textbooks have been purchased in 12 years." Another leader, Gladys Beasely, noted that there "aren't any college preparatory classes in the school, no foreign language classes or classes with lab. If one of our students is lucky enough to get to college, they would have to take remedial classes."[26] When a young person is fortunate enough to run this gauntlet and graduate from high school, he or she finds rapidly diminishing opportunities for a college education. In 1975, Jake Ayers Sr and twenty-one Black students filed a suit to end Mississippi's practice of starving the state's historically Black Colleges and Universities (HBCUs) of funds while building new facilities and programs at predominantly White colleges and universities. Although the suit was dismissed by US District Judge Neal Biggers Jr on 11 December 1987, the Fifth US Circuit Court of Appeals overturned Biggers's ruling two months later. On appeal, by a margin of 8 to 1, in 1993 the US Supreme Court supported the plaintiffs' contention that Mississippi was operating a segregated higher education system which severely and intentionally crippled the state's HBCUs. Yet the Court offered no remedy, preferring instead to allow the state to craft a solution. The Mississippi Board of Trustees of the Institutions of Higher Learning interpreted this ruling as a green light for dismantling the African American institutions. The board attempted to close the Mississippi Valley State University (MVSU) and merge its programs under the predominantly White Delta State University. It considered proposals to reopen MVSU as a prison facility and discussed the closure of the 124-year-old historically Black Alcorn State University.[27]

The ruling in the *Ayers* case immediately spurred other state educational boards in the South to push harder for the merger, consolidation, and/or closure of the remaining HBCUs. In December 1993, the Black Mississippians'

Council for Higher Education (BMCHE) held a major protest on the state-house steps under the banner "No Closure, No Merger." Alvin Chambliss, the lawyer who represented the plaintiffs, predicted that if "Black and poor people are not educated then Black and poor citizens of the state would have been summarily executed without any hope of success in life." The former president of Clark-Atlanta University, Elias Blake, also decried the state's plans:

> How can you close Mississippi Valley and still maintain that you are not promulgat-ing educationally destructive policies toward Black people? Educational death means the end of Black civilization as we know it in America. Black colleges are the engine that moves the Black masses, and if the engine dies the train stops.[28]

Instead of accepting the closure and merger plan, in 1995 Biggers awarded Jackson State University $30 million for endowments and programs while simultaneously raising admission standards at the three historically Black public universities to the same level as those of the historically privileged White universities. The plaintiffs appealed to the Fifth Circuit to block the implementation of the new standards, charging that this practice would devastate the three HBCU's which, together educate 60 percent of the state's Black college students. A study by the plaintiffs found that Biggers's 1995 ruling had resulted in a 32 percent decline in the number of Black students eligible to be admitted to the fall 1996 class of eight public universities. Additionally, Black freshman enrollment fell by 14 percent at the three historically Black institutions and by 9 percent at the five historically White institutions. Ruling on the appeal in April 1997, the Fifth Circuit acknowl-edged that the new admission standards could be viewed as a new form of discrimination. "We agree with the plaintiffs that it would be inappropriate to remedy the traceable segregative effects of an admission policy in a system originally designed to limit educational opportunity for black citizens by adopting a policy that itself caused a reduction in meaningful educational opportunity for black citizens." However, the judges of the Fifth Circuit still ruled that the district court's plan to exclude a significant portion of the Black students who survive the horrors of public education in the Delta and the rest of Mississippi was "a proper exercise of discretion."[29]

Other changes in the administration of justice bode ill for the future. There have been simultaneous increases both in the numbers of judicial decisions eliminating laws designed to protect African American human rights and in the seriousness of human rights abuses including law enforcement officials. The Fifth Circuit has led all federal courts in the attack on affirmative action programs. In June 1996, it delivered a stunning, if not fatal, blow to state efforts to end racial segregation in higher education. In the *Hopwood v. Texas* case, the court ruled that race cannot be used as a criterion in admission decisions at the University of Texas Law School or at any of the predominantly White public educational institutions of higher learning in its jurisdiction: Mississippi, Louisiana, and Texas. When Norma Cantu, assistant secretary for the Office of Civil Rights in the US Department of Education, tried to limit the impact of the ruling to the University of Texas, a political uproar erupted in Texas. US Senator Phil Gramm (R. Texas) successfully demanded that Clinton's Secretary of Education, former South Carolina governor Richard Riley, rescind Cantu's directive. According to Blake, the *Hopwood* and *Ayers* rulings represented "the closing of the doors to the elite universities and graduate and professional schools at the top . . . [and] closing the door for the mass of blacks at the bottom."[30]

The judicial attack on rural African American communities in the South was also carried out by the US Supreme Court which, between 1993 and 1996, eliminated predominantly African American congressional districts in Georgia, Louisiana, North Carolina, and Texas. In the North Carolina case it declared that irregularly shaped districts constituted "racial gerrymandering." Later, it ruled that shape was inconsequential; now any racially cognizant redistricting was a violation of the Equal Protection Clause of the US Constitution. After the dismantling of her district, Rep. Cynthia McKinney (D. GA) observed that it "is sad that almost 100 years after *Plessy v. Ferguson*, this country and the Supreme Court have not been able to move beyond the question of fundamental rights for this country's African American population." In May 1997, the Supreme Court used a case emerging from a dispute over Black representation on a Bossier Parish, Louisiana, school board to limit severely the ability of federal officials to use provisions of the Voting Rights Act of 1965 that were designed to "block proposed changes in state and local election systems that might hurt the political clout of Blacks and other minority voters." The Supreme court thus essentially endorsed a new wave of policies designed to exclude Blacks and Latinos from representation on state and local elected boards and legislative bodies in the South. It has provided the veneer of legitimacy to discriminatory practices such as the dilution of voting strength, the elimination of existing districts, and the blocking of new attempts to ensure proportional representation. Essentially, the Supreme Court's rulings represent an abandonment of the movement for full democracy through the silencing and isolation of the historic African American development agenda.[31]

With the abandonment of federal oversight, the justice system in Mississippi is urgently exploring new and unknown depths. After passing legislation requiring prisoners to wear striped uniforms, the state legislature began to discuss denial of their access to television, telephones, and showers. Still unsatisfied, several legislators began to consider the "burning and frying" of those convicted of serious crimes and "returning executions to the county seat." According to Fordice, his goal is to make Mississippi "the capital of capital punishment."[32]

Additionally, local officials have been charged with extralegal execution of prisoners. Between 1987 and 1993, there were 47 "suicides" within local jails, 24 by Black inmates and 23 by White inmates. Accompanying many of these deaths have been charges of official involvement. African American leaders from around the USA gathered in Atlanta in February 1993 to announce their intention to launch an investigation. The newly formed Commission on Human Rights Abuses held hearings in Mississippi in March of the same year. After hearing testimony from relatives of the deceased, and evidence on other events in the state, commission member Rev. Joseph Lowery, president of the Southern Christian Leadership Conference, stated, "we are outraged with what Mississippi is doing to its Black and poor citizens, thus we must call for sanctions against Mississippi and all its goods and services." He also charged Fordice with launching "an ethnic cleansing of state government."

By May 1993, the Civil Rights Division of the US Department of Justice had been forced to investigate the deaths. Previously, President Clinton had stated that evidence of official wrongdoing was absent. However, reports in the *Jackson Advocate*, the hearings, and a segment on NBC's *Dateline* news program all brought to national attention the inconsistencies present in official accounts and the circumstances surrounding the deaths of several of the men. For example, Scott Campbell died on 9 October 1990 in a jail in Philadelphia Mississippi. Philadelphia is the town where three SNCC workers were murdered in 1964 and where Ronald Reagan launched his presidential campaign in 1979. At the time of his death, Campbell, who was Black, was dating the daughter of a local White police officer. Soon after his "suicide," five hundred hooded Ku Klux Klan members paraded through the streets of town in what one observer described as a "celebration."[33] Another disputed suicide involved Andre Jones, the son of the president of the Jackson NAACP, Esther Jones Quinn, and the stepson of Charles X Quinn, a leading Nation of Islam minister. Contradicting the Simpson County coroner, a privately hired pathologist initially concluded that Jones had been murdered. Support for the charges of an official coverup was provided by the former Medical Examiner of Mississippi, Dr Lloyd White. In a letter to the publisher of the *Jackson Advocate*, White claimed that he was forced to resign because he insisted on unpoliticized autopsies:

> Only a thorough impartial, objective, investigation carried out by competent authorities immune from the influence of state or national politics, will provide you, Mr Tisdale, with any really substantial basis for long term change ... It probably isn't going to be possible for this to be done because of the deep rooted moral sickness which permeates every pore and fiber of contemporary Mississippi government ... No, Kirk Fordice and his cronies don't want a competent, independent medical examiner, who can impartially investigate jail deaths ... [Until] a proper medicolegal death investigation system can be established, the slaughter of Black citizens by the ignorance, incompetence, and malfeasance of white Mississippi law enforcement officials, with encouragement and full approval of white Mississippi politicians, will continue unabated, and your families, homes and communities will remain defiled forever by stain of innocent blood.[34]

The influence of both the White Citizens' Council and the Sovereignty Commission continues to deform the historic African American development agenda. The opposition of the Citizens' Council to school integration served as the foundation for the establishment of private White academies and

Christian schools throughout the South. According to one account, this multistate network formed the backbone of two conservative movements: the Moral Majority and the Christian Coalition. Often referred to as the "radical right," during the 1990s the Christian Coalition has waged several battles to become the dominant faction in the Republican Party.

The numerous attempts to open the files of another 1950s organization, the Sovereignty Commission, ran into surprising opposition from several Whites and Blacks who had participated in the civil rights movement. The Sovereignty Commission had established a network of African American and White informants, some of whom are said to be still active in public life. In 1993, the Reverend L. D. Bass of the Jackson Ministerial Alliance and the Jackson Human Rights Coalition demanded that the Sovereignty Commission's intelligence files be opened despite the objections of public officials and private individuals:

> the commission has committed acts of evil against us, to maintain white supremacy through every institution in Mississippi . . . The state Sovereignty Commission should be brought out of hiding . . . They are the drug child of sick minds. They look back with warped minds and take pride in human slave auctions.[35]

The Reverend Bass's wish may have come true, although not in the manner that he expected. Attitudes, policies, and practices contained since the 1960s have come out of hiding. Like dominoes, one institution after the other has succumbed to the romance of the plantation bloc's restoration. Economic crisis alone does not explain the psychological satisfaction that many of the current movements take in punishing African American communities for the transgression of demanding democracy. However, the success of the Mississippi Delta plan twelve is not assured. Among other things, its success or failure is contingent upon how the African American community will respond. What is the wall, bulwark, or antidote that can halt the spread of this sickness? The Third Reconstruction, a blues reconstruction.

## The Sun Never Set upon the Blues

> In a way, the message, in one form or another, or even the text itself, has always been liberation, not only the liberation of Black people but of the entire nation; not merely of man in society but of the human psyche in the world. Liberation not only from oppression but from the deadly corrosives of prejudice and spiritual meanness.
>
> Stephen Henderson[36]

> You can't hurt the blues. Everything else can come along, die right out but them blues will always stand, you cannot hurt them because it's a spirit there . . .
>
> Bob Myers[37]

The development path of the Mississippi Delta plantation bloc must be abandoned. At its best it reproduces permanent social crisis that daily plows under communities, families, and aspirations. At its worst, it permanently holds open the gates to new forms of segregation and slavery. As argued throughout this work, a new development path does not have to be invented. For over a century and a half, working-class African American communities and their allies have continuously experimented with creating sustainable, equitable, and just social, economic, political, and cultural structures. Just as it was inevitable that a new plantation bloc mobilization would occur, it was also inevitable that the long-suppressed alternative would be resurrected.

The plantation bloc and its various allies are fanatically committed to denying the spiritual significance of folk culture, rural communities, land, and agriculture; to limiting visions of what is possible; limiting the range of acceptable issues for discussion; to limiting participation in decision making; and defining both leadership and potential solutions narrowly. These ethno-regional class practices reflect a profound fear of the realization of the blues development tradition. The translation of working-class African American aesthetic and ethical movements into the reorganization of regional life in the Delta is, by definition, a transformation that will reconstruct the United States and the world.[38]

The blues courageously explores the origins, varieties, and consequences of life lived in a brutal and loveless society. It is also the voice of those who are dedicated to the preservation of their humanity. The blues is a vision of a society that is dialectically polyrhythmic, a democracy where both cooperation and individual expression thrive. This philosophy is expressed in, through, and beyond the music.

For Barlow, the blues can be conceived of as a form of African American cultural resistance organized around four elements. First, there is the blues soundscape composed of a wide variety of calls, shouts, hollers, grunts, screams, and the sounds of pain, ecstasy, violence, movement, animals, machines, weather, etcetera:

> The use of blue notes was at the heart of the blues sound; they gave it a subversive character, a dissonance instantly recognizable in both vocal and instrumental render-ings. In addition, the blues sound relied heavily on the use of tonic chords, which provided immediate release form musical tensions. Polyrthyms, which exploded tensions by stacking different rhythms on top of each other, thereby adding a dense repetitive, and fluid locomotion to the overall blues sound. Finally, there were a wide variety of vocal techniques, and suggestive pitch tones that masked the blues voice in order to invoke tonal memories.[39]

For Barlow, the lyrical text and the performance were two key elements of African American resistance and affirmation:

> The blues texts were also bulwarks of cultural resistance, providing a composite view of American society from the bottom. They were not linear narratives, but were circular and indirect in their discourse, in keeping with African custom. They focused

on the everyday life of the black masses—their working conditions, their living conditions, prison experiences, travels, sexual relationships ... Blues performers meshed orature and music by engaging in instrumental, voice and visual styling. They affected certain mannerisms and sang their songs in ways calculated to enhance their ability to communicate with their audience intimately and profoundly ... performance was the true test of the blues artists; it was the medium through which they honed their skills and perfected their calling as communicators of black cultural resistance and renewal.[40]

Lastly, blues performers represented the pantheon of African American personalities and practitioners who were condemned as rebels by the larger society while simultaneously being worshiped, celebrated, envied, and feared by the Black community: wanderers and natural forces, "ladies' men" and "wild women," hell raisers and earthshakers, hoodoo doctors and voodoo queens, tricksters and prophets, warriors and saints.[41]

The interaction between the blues soundscape, text, performance, and pantheon is fundamentally the expression of a distinct theory of social organization: participatory democracy at work. Democracy is evident in the author's claim of ownership of, and responsibility for, the ideas expressed. These individual expressions are participatory to the extent that the author's ideas resonates with an audience possessing a wealth of knowledge. Through the exchange of intellectual, emotional, and physical ideas, the author and the audience jointly determine their collective destiny.

Centuries of censorship and persecution have been visited upon African Americans who chose to explore, preserve, and build upon their folk culture. Even in the present period, African American leaders continue to denounce or marginalize working-class African American folk culture. They often claim that Black culture was lost, stolen, or broken. This assertion is generally followed by a program for accelerated cultural integration or for the creation of a new man and woman. The civilizing, even imperial, thrust of certain, middle-class segments toward Black working-class thoughts and practices is a problem that is perhaps more pressing than any other. Not only is working-class African American culture not broken or deviant, it is a powerful world culture held together, and expanded, by repeated blues movements.

This brings us to the question of the role of indigenous knowlege in social construction. The creation of sustainable communities requires a reconciliation between African Americans and their own folk culture. Often neglected, the conscious and strategic defense of this culture must become a guiding principle of daily living. So too must its development. Otherwise, past practices and events will continue to be treated as one-dimensional, abstract, and irrelevant by future generations. If the cross-generational experience of African American history and culture teaches any lesson, it teaches that democracy can only be secured through reliance on the experience and thoughts of the masses and through strict adherence to participatory forms of governance. The privileging of indigenous knowledge, of blues epistemology, and of millions of organic intellectuals denies power to another elite-led regime of stagnation. What is left? A society where every member is both a teacher and a student.

If we are to build a society where working-class knowledge and participatory democracy are truly treasured, we must understand that the South is the center of African American culture, not its periphery. The Delta then becomes understood as a Mecca. Future political and economic movements must view African American folk culture as a central, and necessary, element in the construction of new institutions and new regional realities. The "civilizing" activity of providing "nondeviant" role models for the creation of new men and women must come to an end. Instead, an all-out effort must be undertaken to celebrate and valorize the millions upon millions, living and dead, who met the regimes of daily destruction with unshakeable dignity. In the same vein, the lands, rivers, streams, air, plants, and animals of the region must be restored to their sacred status. Until then, "every hill and molehill," every blade of grass, every flutter of the flag, and every note that is played must be contested.

Land, labor, sectoral, and other reforms must be accompanied by an intellectual transformation. Using the blues to reconceptualize African American life and history is a very old practice indeed. Unfortunately, the agenda for a new democracy, for the Third Reconstruction, has been written, played, recited, and sung thousands and thousands of times without being recognized. The goal of this work has been solely to open a window in order to see the blues all 'round.

We were on top again. As always, again. We survived. The depths had been icy and dark, but now a bright sun spoke to our souls. I was no longer simply a member of the proud graduating class of 1940; I was a proud member of the wonderful, beautiful Negro race.

Oh, Black known and unknown poets, how often have your auctioned pains sustained us? Who will compute the lonely nights made less lonely by your songs, or by the empty pots made less tragic by your tales?

If we were a people much given to revealing secrets, we might raise monuments and sacrifice to the memories of our poets, but slavery cured us of that weakness. It may be enough, however, to have it said that we survive in exact relationship to the dedication of our poets (include preachers, musicians and blues singers).

Maya Angelou, *I Know Why The Caged Bird Sings* [42]

# Postscript

In April of 1997, more than two years after Clinton awarded the Delta Council control of the Mid-Delta Empowerment Zone (MDEZA), not a dime of the $40 million in direct federal grants available had been spent. Led by the Delta Council, the plantation bloc and Governor Fordice's Mississippi Department of Human Services, the state organization charged with monitoring the expenditure of funds had blocked the release of any monies that might remotely contribute to development of the African American community.[1]

In July of 1997, before she could complete her daily three-hour round trip, Carrie Ann Bridges of the town of Glendora in Tallahatchie County fell asleep at the wheel. (After the termination of her own and her family's welfare benefits she had found work on the second shift at a poultry plant seventy miles away.) The after-midnight crash killed Carrie Ann Bridges and her aunt, leaving her four children, aged one to eleven, motherless. The question remains, will Clinton and Congress take personal responsibility for the consequences of cynically titled welfare reform law, the Personal Responsibility and Work Opportunity Act of 1996? Who *will* take responsibility for the death of Carrie Ann Bridges or is she just an inconsequential footnote to a new epic tragedy that is being written with the blood and tears of African Americans in the Delta?[2]

On Tuesday, March 18, 1998, the United States Circuit Court of Appeals ordered the release of 124,000 pages from the files of the Mississippi Sovereignty Commission. The documents contained the names of more than 87,000 activists who had been spied upon, harassed, smeared, falsely jailed, beaten, or murdered between 1956 and 1977 as part of the campaign to destroy the Mississippi Freedom Movement. Despite major media commentary on the "sinister" past and on the "progress bought by martyrs' blood," there were no discussions of the relationship between the Movement's decapitation and the current horrors afflicting African American communities in Mississippi.[3]

On Monday, January 26, 1998, the offices of the *Jackson Advocate* were firebombed. Relied upon numerous times in the writing of this book, the crusading newspaper sustained more than $100,000 in building and equipment damages. A spokeswoman for the Southern Christian Leadership Conference, Stephanie Parker-Weaver, described the attack as a hate crime of the highest order. In calling for a hate crime investigation by the Federal Bureau of Investigation, the Bureau of Alcohol, Tobacco, and Firearms, and the US Attorney for the Southern District of Mississippi, African American Congressman Bennie G. Thompson (D. MS) stated that the "*Jackson Advocate* has been a backbone of the community for nearly sixty years." Although the newspaper has been attacked more than twenty times since the late 1970s, publisher Charles Tisdale declared: "I'm not going to be intimidated ... We are going to fight, fight, fight."[4] Contributions can be sent to the *Jackson Advocate*, P.O. Box 3708, Jackson, MS 39207 (601-948-4122).

Dedicated to introducing young people to the blues and to assisting elderly and sick performers, the late Willie Dixon's Blues Heaven Foundation can be reached at 2120 S. Michigan Ave., Chicago, IL 60616 (312-808-1286).

# Notes

## 1 What Happens to a Dream Arrested?

1. See the testimony of Dr Jocelyn Elders, US Congress, Senate, Committees on Environment and Public Works and Small Business, *Joint Hearing on S. 2246: A Bill to Establish the Lower Mississippi Delta Development Commission*, 100th Cong., 2nd sess. (Washington, DC: US Government Printing Office, 1988), 48.

2. Lower Mississippi Delta Development Commission, *Body of the Nation* (Memphis: LMDDC, 1989), n.p.

3. Edgar Thompson, "The Plantation: The Physical Basis of Traditional Race Relations," in Edgar Thompson (ed.), *Race Relations and the Race Problem* (Durham: Duke University Press, 1968), 192–4.

4. George Beckford, *Persistent Poverty: Underdevelopment in Plantation Economies of the Third World* (London: Zed Books, 1983, orig. 1972); John Hebron Moore, *The Emergence of the Cotton Kingdom in the Old Southwest: Mississippi, 1770–1860* (Baton Rouge: Louisiana State University Press, 1988); Thompson, 1968.

5. C. Vann Woodward, *Origins of the New South, 1877–1913* (Baton Rouge: Louisiana State University Press 1980, orig. 1951), 336. See also Neil R. McMillen, *Dark Journey: Black Mississippians in the Age of Jim Crow*, (Urbana: University of Illinois Press, 1990), 48–54.

6. Robert L. Brandfon, *Cotton Kingdom of the New South: A History of the Yazoo Mississippi Delta from Reconstruction to the Twentieth Century* (Cambridge: Harvard University Press, 1967).

7. National Archives, Files of the Mississippi Valley Committee, "The Lower Mississippi Valley Region: Partial and Preliminary Report", Box 41, July 31, 1934.

8. Harry Cleaver, "The Origins of the Green Revolution," PhD thesis, Stanford University, 1975, 243–356.

9. Aldon D. Morris, *The Origins of the Civil Rights Movement: Black Communities Organizing for Change* (New York: Free Press, 1984), 235.

10. Ibid., 234–5.

11. Donald H. Grubbs, *Cry from the Cotton: The Southern Tenant Farmers' Union and the New Deal* (Chapel Hill: University of North Carolina Press, 1971), xii.

12. Donald Grubbs, "The New Deal and the Roots of Agribusiness," statement to the First National Conference on Land Reform, 1973, 2–3 (in possession of author). For a detailed discussion of the historiography of the enclosure movement see Numan V. Bartley, "The Southern Enclosure Movement," *Georgia Historical Quarterly*, 71/3 (Fall 1987), 438–50 and Jack Temple Kirby, *Rural Worlds Lost: The American South 1920–1960* (Baton Rouge: Louisiana State University Press, 1987).

13. Dwight B. Billings Jr, *Planters and the Making of a "New South": Class, Politics and Development in North Carolina, 1865–1900* (Chapel Hill: University of North

Carolina Press, 1979); Jay R. Mandle, *The Roots of Black Poverty: The Southern Plantation Economy After the Civil War* (Durham: Duke University Press, 1978); Jonathan Wiener, *Social Origins of the New South: Alabama 1860–1885* (Baton Rouge: Louisiana State University Press, 1978), 227.

14. Stuart A. Rosenfeld and Edward Bergman, *Making Connections: After the Factories Revisited* (Research Triangle Park, NC: Southern Growth Policies Board, 1989), 33. For the scholarly debates see: Bartley, 1987, 444–50; Pete Daniel, *Breaking the Land: The Transformation of Cotton, Tobacco and Rice Cultures since 1880* (Urbana: University of Illinois Press, 1985); Gilbert Fite, *Cotton Fields No More: Southern Agriculture 1865–1980* (Lexington: University of Kentucky Press, 1984); Kirby, 1987; Gavin Wright, *Old South, New South: Revolution in the Southern Economy Since the Civil War* (New York: Basic Books, 1986); William Falk and Thomas A. Lyson, *High Tech, Low Tech, No Tech: Recent Industrial and Occupational Change in the South* (Albany: State University of New York Press, 1988); and Daniel T. Lichter, "Race and Underemployment: Black Employment Hardship in the Rural South," in Lionel J. Beaulieu (ed.), *Rural South in Crisis: Challenges for the Future* (Boulder: Westview Press, 1988).

15. James C. Cobb, *The Most Southern Place on Earth: The Mississippi Delta and the Roots of Regional Identity* (New York: Oxford University Press, 1992), 253.

16. Ibid., 333.

17. See interview with Shelby Brown, Leland, Mississippi, 1974, in William Ferris, *Blues From the Delta* (New York: Da Capo Press, 1978), 42.

18. Ibid., 43.

19. Alan Lomax, *The Land Where the Blues Began* (New York: Pantheon Books, 1993), 284–5.

20. Daphne Duval Harrison, *Black Pearls: Blues Queens of the 1920* (New Brunswick: Rutgers University Press, 1988), 7; Ralph Ellison, *Shadow and Act* (New York: Random House, 1964), 78.

21. Henry Louis Gates, Jr, *Figures in Black: Words, Signs, and the "Racial Self"* (New York: Oxford University Press, 1987), 225–7.

22. Sterling Brown, *Southern Road* (New York: Harcourt Brace and Company, 1932), 63.

23. Richard Wright, Foreword in Paul Oliver, *Blues Fell This Morning: Meaning in the Blues* (Cambridge: Cambridge University Press, 1990, orig. 1960), xiii, xv.

24. Larry Neal, "The Ethos of the Blues," in *Visions of a Liberated Future: Black Arts Movement Writings* (New York: Thunder's Mouth Press, 1989), 107–8. See also: Ellison, 1964; LeRoi Jones, *Blues People: Negro Music in White America* (New York: William Morrow and Company, 1963); Albert Murray, *Stomping the Blues* (New York: Da Capo Press, 1976).

25. Houston Baker, *Blues, Ideology, and Afro-American Literature: A Vernacular Theory* (Chicago: University of Chicago Press, 1984); William Barlow, *Looking up at Down: The Emergence of Blues Culture* (Philadelphia: Temple University Press, 1989); Mary Ellison, *Extensions of the Blues* (New York: Riverrun Press, 1989); Julio Flynn, *The Bluesman: The Musical Heritage of Black Men and Women in the Americas* (London: Quartet Books, 1986).

26. Michael T. Taussig, *The Devil and Commodity Fetishism* (Chapel Hill: University of North Carolina Press, 1980).

27. Costis Hadjimichalis, *Uneven Development and Regionalism: State, Class, and Territory in Southern Europe* (London: Croom Helm, 1987); Ann Gilbert, "The New Regional Geography in English and French Speaking Countries," *Progress in Human Geography*, 12/2 (1987), 209–28; David Harvey, *Limits to Capital* (Oxford: Basil Blackwell, 1982); Margaret FitzSimmons, "The New Industrial Agriculture: The Regional Integration of Specialty Crop Production," *Economic Geography*, 63/4 (October 1987), 334–53; Edward Soja, *Postmodern Geographies: The Reassertion of Space in Critical Social Theory* (London: Verso, 1989).

28. Clyde Weaver, *Regional Development and the Local Community: Planning, Politics and Social Context* (Chichester, England: John Wiley and Sons, 1984) 95–9; Frank So, Irving Hand, and Bruce D. McDowell (eds.), *The Practice of State and Regional Planning* (Chicago: American Planning Association, 1986).

29. "New Dawn for the Delta: Commission battles deadline to forge goals, credibility," *Memphis Commercial Appeal*, 21 May 1989, B7.

30. LMDDC, *The Delta Initiatives: Realizing the Dream ... Fulfilling the Potential: A Report by the Lower Mississippi Delta Development Commission* (Memphis: LMDDC, 1990), n.p.

31. *Arkansas Democrat*, Little Rock, 14 June 1990.

32. LMDDC, 1990, Appendix A II 26.

33. For a discussion of the reproduction of power through masking the existence of alternative development traditions see Christine Boyer, *Dreaming the Rational City: The Myth of American City Planning* (Cambridge: MIT Press, 1986); Richard E. Foglesong, *Planning the Capitalist City: The Colonial Era to the 1920s* (Princeton: Princeton University Press, 1986); Michel Foucault, *The Order of Things: The Archaeology of the Human Sciences* (New York: Vintage Books, 1970); Edward Said, *Orientalism* (New York: Vintage Books, 1979); Marc Weiss, *The Rise of the Community Builders: The American Real Estate Industry and Urban Land Planning* (New York: Columbia University Press, 1987).

# 2 The Blues Tradition of Explanation

1. Willie Dixon, "A Tribute," *Living Blues*, 103, May–June 1992, 47.

2. Cited in Barlow, 1989, 326.

3. It is argued throughout this work that the blues are a necessary feature of African American identity. For Gramsci, to "the extent that ideologies are historically necessary they have a validity which is 'psychological'; they organize human masses, they form the terrain on which men move, acquire consciousness of their position, struggle, etc. To the extent they are 'arbitrary' they only create individual movements, polemics, and so on." See David Forgacs, *The Antonio Gramsci Reader: Selected Writings, 1916–1935* (New York: Schocken Books, 1988), 199.

4. Anne Gilbert, "The New Regional Geography in English and French Speaking Countries," *Progress in Human Geography*, 12/2 (June 1987), 209–28, 217. See also Soja, 1989, 118–137, 92–93; Roman Szporluk, *Communism and Nationalism: Karl Marx versus Frederick List* (New York: Oxford University Press, 1988), 8–9. For Szporluk, the placement of narrow class-based analysis at the center of social investigation is a recipe for misinterpreting most of the last two centuries. "Leaving aside the crude reductionism involved in its assignment of ideologies to particular economic classes, this approach overlooks the fact that the nineteenth and twentieth centuries were periods when new national communities were being formed, when various groups, regional identities, and religious communities were being transformed into nations. While liberals, conservatives and socialists indeed responded to the industrial revolution within already existing societies and polities, there were also nationalists [and regionalists] who were engaged in establishing new communities and who, in the process, asked how the Industrial Revolution affected the position of their respective nations—often nations in the making —versus other nations."

5. Hadjimichalis, *Uneven Development and Regionalism*, 1987; Phillip McMichael, *Settlers and the Agrarian Question: Foundations of Capitalism in Colonial Australia* (Cambridge: Cambridge University Press, 1984), xi–xii; Margaret FitzSimmons, "Agricultural Regions as Social Contracts: Family and Industrial Farming in the United States," September 1989, 10 (paper in possession of author); G. L. Clark, "The Crisis

of the Midwest Auto industry," in Allen J. Scott and Michael Storper (eds.), *Production, Work and Territory: The Geographical Anatomy of Industrial Capitalism* (London: Allen & Unwin, 1986), 127–47; Howard Odum, *Southern Regions of the United States* (Chapel Hill: University of North Carolina Press, 1936), 11; Phyllis A. Gray, "Economic Development and African Americans in the Mississippi Delta," *Rural Sociology*, 56/20 (1991), 238–9.

6. Peter Jackson, *Maps Of Meaning: An Introduction to Cultural Geography* (London: Unwin Hyman, 1989), 53. See also: Forgacs, 1988, 190, 192; Barbara Fields, "Ideology and Race in American History," in J. Morgan Kousser and James McPherson (eds.), *Region, Race and Reconstruction: Essays in Honor of C. Vann Woodward* (Oxford: Oxford University Press, 1982); For key critiques of the use of transhistorical conceptions of ethnicity, race, and gender see the following works: Bonnie Thornton Dill, *Our Mothers' Grief: Racial and Ethnic Women and the Maintenance of Families* (Memphis: Memphis State University Center for Research on Women, 1986); Paula Giddings, *When and Where I Enter: The Impact of Black Women on Race and Sex in America* (New York: William Morrow, 1984); bell hooks, *Ain't I a Woman: Black Women and Feminism* (Boston: South End Press, 1981); Michael Omni and Howard Winant, *Racial Formation in the United States: From the 1960s to the 1980s* (New York: Routledge and Kegan Paul, 1986).

7. Theodore Saloutos, *Farmer Movements in the South, 1865–1933* (Berkeley: University of California Press, 1960), vi.

8. On the recovery of African American consciousness through the study of social movements see Robert A. Hill (ed.), *Marcus Garvey and Universal Negro Improvement Association Papers* (Berkeley: University of California Press, 1986); Gerald Horne, *Communist Front?: The Civil Rights Congress, 1946–1956* (Rutherford, NJ: Fairleigh Dickinson University Press, 1988); Robin Kelley, "Hammer n' Hoe: Black Radicalism and the Communist Party in Alabama, 1929–1941," Ph.D. thesis, University of California, Los Angeles, 1987; Neil McMillen, *Dark Journey: Black Mississippians in the Age of Jim Crow* (Urbana: University of Illinois Press, 1989); Nell Irvin Painter, *Exodusters: Black Migration to Kansas after Reconstruction* (Lawrence: University of Kansas Press, 1986). On kinship see Kay Young Day, "Kinship in a Changing Economy: A View from the Sea Islands," Robert L. Hall and Carol B. Stack (eds.), *Holding on to the Land and the Lord: Kinship, Ritual, Land Tenure and Social Policy in the Rural South* (Athens: University of Georgia Press, 1982), 11–24.

9. Said, 1979, 5. See also Boyer, 1986; Foucault, 1970; V. Y. Mudimbe, *The Invention of Africa: Gnosis, Philosophy, and the Order of Knowledge* (Bloomington: Indiana University Press, 1988).

10. Raymond Williams, *The Country and the City* (New York: Oxford University Press, 1973; Benedict Anderson, *Imagined Communities: Reflections on the Origins and Spread of Nationalism* (London, Verso, 1983), 14–16; Taussig, 1980, 4. For Taussig, the categories used to classify present regional relations are also rife with phantom objectivity: "to their participants, all cultures tend to present these categories [time, space, matter, cause, relation, human nature, and society] as if they were not social products but elemental and immutable things. As soon as such categories are defined as natural rather than as social products, epistemology itself acts to conceal understanding of the social order. Our experience, our understanding, our explanations—all serve merely to ratify the conventions that sustain our sense of reality unless we appreciate the extent to which the basic building blocks of our experience and our sensed reality are not natural but social constructions."

11. Willie Dixon, *I Am the Blues: The Willie Dixon Story* (New York: Da Capo Press, 1990), 3–4.

12. Richard Wright, "Blueprint for Negro Literature" (orig. 1937) in Addison Gayle, Jr, *The Black Aesthetic* (Garden City, NY: Doubleday, 1971), 333–47, 333–4.

13. Christopher G. A. Bryant, *Positivism in Social Theory and Research*, (New York: St Martins Press, 1985), 1.

14. Charles Sawyer, *B. B. King: The Authorized Biography* (London: Quartet Books, 1982), 86.

15. C. Eric Lincoln, "Those Who Stayed," in Doris Smith (ed.), *Those who Stayed* (Jackson, MS: Margaret Walker Alexander Research Center for the Study of Twentieth Century African American Culture, Jackson State University, 1990), 8.

16. Rosa Parks, "One Who Stayed, Remarks," in Smith, 1990, 12.

17. Margaret Walker Alexander, "From Field to Factory," in Smith, 1990, 27; William Ferris, "Folklore and Black Migration from Mississippi," in Smith, 1990, 18. During one of the forums William Ferris, Professor of Anthropology, Director of the Center for the Study of Southern Culture, and one of the founders of the Blues Archives at the University of Mississippi at Oxford, suggested that in "approaching the Mississippi Delta it is interesting to view the region as a black cultural nation. The Delta's rich traditions have shaped its political leaders as well as its musical performers. In approaching black migration from the Mississippi Delta, we should also consider parallels of migration from Caribbean nations such as Jamaica, Trinidad, and Haiti."African American societies in the South and the Caribbean are similar to the extent that they are part of the African diaspora; they are recently indigenous Western Hemisphere cultures forged within plantation, dominated societies; each relies heavily upon the tight intertwining of musical and intellectual traditions; and they each have developed powerful and influential diasporas.

18. Richard Powell, "The Blues Aesthetic: Black Culture and Modernism," in Richard Powell (ed.), *The Blues Aesthetic: Black Culture and Modernism* (Washington, DC: Washington Project for the Arts, 1989), 21–3.

19. Stephen Henderson, "Blues Poetry and Poetry of the Blues Aesthetic," *Sagala*, 3 (1983), 11.

20. Wright, 1971, 333–4.

21. See Richard Wright's introduction to the three-album set "Southern Exposure: The Blues of Josh White," 2 October 1940, cited in Michel Fabre, *The Unfinished Quest of Richard Wright* (New York: William Morrow and Company, 1973), 238. See also Flynn, 1986; Joseph Holloway (ed.), *Africanisms in American Culture* (Bloomington: Indiana University Press, 1991).

22. See Wright in Gayle, 1971, 336.

23. Ruth Finnegan, "Literacy versus Non-Literacy: the Great Divide," in Robin Horton and Ruth Finnegan (eds.), *Modes of Thought: Essays on Thinking in Western and Non-Western Societies* (London: Faber, 1973).

24. Ibid., 123.

25. Ibid., 128.

26. Harrison, 1988, 65.

27. Paul Oliver, *Savannah Syncopators: African Retention in the Blues* (New York: Stein and Day, 1970), 28–53; Ellison, 1989, 4.

28. Lomax, 1993, xiii.

29. Murray, 1976, 75–83; Jaques D. Lacava, "The Theatricality of the Blues," *Black Music Research Journal* 12(10) (Spring 1992), 127–39.

30. Ben Sidran, *Black Talk: How the Music of Black America Created a Radical Alternative to the Values of Western Literary Tradition* (New York: Holt, Rinehart and Winston, 1971), 11; Raymond Williams, *The Long Revolution* (London: Cox and Wyman, 1961), 55; Lomax, 1993, 331.

31. Finnegan, 1973, 141.

32. Gates, 1987, 31; LeRoi Jones, *Home: Social Essays* (New York: William Morrow & Co., 1966), 107. For a discussion of the relationship between local blues schools and regional traditions see David Evans, *Big Road Blues: Tradition and Creativity in the Folk Blues* (Berkeley: University of California Press, 1982), 252.

33. See interview with Cash McCall, "Cash McCall: A Refugee from the Cotton Fields," *Living Blues*, 103 (May–June 1992), 22.

34. Peter Lee and David Nelson, "Willie Foster: Right Out of the Cotton Field," *Living Blues*, 107 (November/December 1992), 33–8, 34.

35. Stephen Henderson, "The Blues as Black Poetry," *Callaloo*, 4/1–3 (February–October, 1981), 22–9.

36. Lomax, 1993, xiii.

37. Samuel Charters, *Legacy of the Blues* (London: Calder and Boyars 1975), 18.

38. Franklin Rosemont, "Preface," in Paul Garon, *Blues and the Poetic Spirit* ( New York: Da Capo, 1975), 7–8.

39. Dixon, 1990, 168–9.


# 3  The Social-Spatial Construction of the Mississippi Delta

1. Brandfon, *Cotton Kingdom of the New South*, 1967, ix.

2. See Southern Exposure, "When Old Worlds Meet: Southern Indians Since Columbus," *Southern Exposure*, 20/1 (Spring 1992), 14–45.

3. Faye Truex and Patricia Q. Foster (eds.), *The Tunica-Biloxi Tribe: Its Culture and People* (Marksville, LA: Tunica Biloxi Indians of Louisiana, 1987), 1–32. Still located in Point Coupee Parish in Louisiana, the Tunica are one of the very few Native American nations to have survived the colonization of the Lower Mississippi Valley.

4. Philip S. Robinson, *The Plantation of Ulster: British Settlement in an Irish Landscape, 1600–1670* (New York: St Martin's Press, 1984), 1–6, 1. "Plantation" is a sixteenth-century term used to describe the change in English colonial expansion policies within Ireland. As opposed to the "conquest and civilization" policy, the plantation "was an adventure officially sponsored by the nation-state and involved the transfer of an entire package of personnel, laws and materials into a new territory." During the Elizabethan period in the 1570s, state-sponsored plantations were increasingly considered too costly and they were reorganized upon the basis of private enterprise or entrepreneurship. In the early seventeenth century, English and Scottish Protestants were the principal personnel for the plantations in Irish Catholic Ulster and along the east coast of North America. Therefore, the plantation can be viewed as a military intervention, an entrepreneurial activity, and a colonizing institution.

5. Eric Williams, *Capitalism and Slavery* (London: Andre Deutsch, 1964, orig. 1944), 109, 120, 115. Under British rule, the prosperity of New England and the Mid-Atlantic states rested upon the slave trade and the sale of foodstuffs, wood products, and livestock to the South and to the plantation-dominated island colonies of the Bahamas, Barbados, Jamaica, and Trinidad.

6. See Bernard Bailyn, *The Peopling of British North America* (New York: Vintage Books, 1986). The brutality of the frontier is often lost due to a tendency within United States historiography to stress the eventual extension of political democracy. For Bailyn, this evolutionist preoccupation has led to classification of daily life as archaic, irrational, and anomalous in relation to the overall progression of the American ideal. On banditry see Harnett T. Kane, *Natchez on the Mississippi* (New York: William Morrow, 1947), 70–2 and Paul Wellman, *Spawn of Evil: The Invisible Empire of Soulless Men which for a Generation Held the Nation in a Spell of Terror* (Garden City, NY: Doubleday 1964). According to Wellman, in several Mississippi frontier schemes, African Americans were continually sold, kidnapped, and resold within a district until planters and authorities caught on. The captives were then murdered and buried in the swamps. Some Natchez Trace bandits marked their territory with raised poles topped by human heads.

7. Anthony Burton, *The Rise and Fall of King Cotton* (London: Andre Deutsch/British Broadcasting Corp., 1984).

8. Arthur DeRossier, *The Removal of the Choctaw Indians* (Knoxville: University of Tennessee Press, 1970), 23.

9. William Cronin, *Changes in the Land: Indians, Colonist, and the Ecology of New England* (New York: Hill and Wang, 1983), 19–33.

10. DeRossier, 27. Jefferson was one of the earliest theorists of the national fine art of limiting the social vision of Native Americans and African Americans. Jefferson hoped to direct Native American thinking away from communal conceptions of land and onto the competitive, hierarchical, agricultural ladder: "Toward effecting this object, we consider leading Indians to agriculture ... When they shall cultivate small plots of the earth and see how useless their extensive forests are, they will sell"[26]. Jefferson was an innovator in the creation of debt to further social dependency. "We shall push our trading houses, and be glad to see the good and influential individuals among them run in debt, because we observe that when these debts get beyond what the individual can pay they become willing to lop them off by a cession."[28] To Jefferson, national settlement would occur according to a plan of parallel colonization. "When we shall be full on this side, we may lay off a range of states on the western bank [of the Mississippi River] from the head to the mouth, and so, range after range, advancing compactly as we multiply." Also see Richard Van Alstyne, "The Significance of the Mississippi Valley in American Diplomatic History, 1686–1890," *Mississippi Valley Historical Review* 36 (June 1949 to March 1950), 215–38. The creation of parallel empires as a policy was also advocated by Alexander Hamilton and George Washington. Historian Frederick Jackson Turner also viewed the United States as "an empire, a collection of potential nations, rather than a single nation." He saw the Mississippi Valley both as "potentially the basis for an independent empire" and as the center of international and domestic conflict from 1686 until 1865 [215]. According to van Alstyne, US control of the Mississippi Valley enabled colonization of the Pacific Northwest, Mexico, and the Caribbean. However, he remained perplexed about what he called "Mississippi imperialism." "It is easier to recite the names of men from the Mississippi Valley who were prominent in the militant movements of the mid-century... . Andrew Jackson and Polk of Tennessee ... And the names of Robert Walker, John Quitman, Henry Foote, and Jefferson Davis give to the state of Mississippi an unusual notoriety as a hotbed of mid-century imperialism ... How are we to account for the imperialism of the leadership in the state of Mississippi? Was it ambition for territory for its own sake, or for territory that would buttress the political strength of the South alone?" [235, 237]. As we shall see in future chapters, Mississippi imperialism still remains a potent analytical category.

11. James W. Lowen and Charles Sallis (eds.), *Mississippi: Conflict and Change* (New York: Random House, 1974), 43. Tecumseh delivered a speech before the Choctaw outlining the threat posed if unity failed. "Before the whites came among us we enjoyed the happiness of unlimited freedom, and we knew neither riches, nor poverty, nor oppression. How is it now? Want and oppression are our lot. Are we not controlled in everything, and dare we move without asking permission? Are we not stripped day by day of the little that remains of our ancient liberty? Do they even now kick and strike us as they do their Black-faces? How long will it be before they will tie us to a post and whip us, and make us work for them in their corn fields as they do the Blacks? Shall we wait for that moment, or shall we die fighting before we submit to such shame?"

12. DeRossier, 1970; Thomas Perkins Abernathy, *From Frontier to Plantation in Tennessee: A Study of Frontier Democracy* (Chapel Hill: University of North Carolina Press, 1932), 262–76. Given partial credit for the founding of Memphis, Jackson illegally speculated in titles to land still in the possession of the Chickasaw. He was engaged in similar transactions for lands still in the possession of Native Americans in Florida, the Tennessee Valley, and Alabama.

13. DeRossier, 1970, 53–69.

14. Ibid., 93.

15. *Southern Exposure*, 20/1 (Spring 1992); and Cecil Sumners, *The Governors of Mississippi* (Gretna, Louisiana: Pelican Publishing, 1980), 4.

16. Moore, 1988, 118; and Cobb, 1992, 17. Also see Frank J. Welch, "The Plantation Land Tenure System in Mississippi," *Mississippi Experiment Station Bulletin* No.

385, June 1943, cited in Delta Council, *A Prospectus of the Yazoo Mississippi Delta* (Stoneville, MS: Delta Council, 1944), 38.

17. Robert W. Harrison, *Levee Districts and Levee Building in Mississippi* (Stoneville: Mississippi Agriculture Experiment Station, 1951), 8; Moore, 1988, 20. According to Moore, "the panic of 1837 ... performed a socially beneficial service by ridding the region of the plague of speculators. On the debit side of the ledger, many newcomers ... were wiped out ... and subsequently emigrated farther west to recoup their fortunes."

18. Karl Marx and Frederick Engels, *Marx and Engels on the United States* (Moscow: Progress Publishers, 1979), 68–9; Clyde Woods, "Slaves, Peasants and Capitalist Development in the United States South" (unpublished paper in possession of the author); Arthur Raper and Ira Reid, *Sharecroppers All* (Chapel Hill: University of North Carolina Press, 1941); Immanuel Wallerstein, "American Slavery and the Capitalist World Economy," in *The Capitalist World Economy* (Cambridge: Cambridge University Press, 1979), 202–21.

19. Alexander Saxton, *The Rise and Fall of the American Republic: Class Politics and Mass Culture in Nineteenth Century America* (London: Verso, 1990).

20. Moore, 1988, 18–36; Beckford, 1972, 3–5; David Harvey, *Limits to Capital* (Oxford: Basil Blackwell, 1982), 335–86. In his path-breaking study of world plantation systems, George Beckford argued that far from being an anachronism, plantation agriculture was, and is, an instrument of capitalist modernization. "It was an instrument of political colonization; it brought capital, enterprise and management to create economic structures which have basically remained the same; it brought together different races of people from various parts of the world to labor in its service and thus determined the population and social structure now existing in these places."

21. Cobb, 1992, 10; *Jackson Advocate*, 14 March 1985.

22. Moore, 1988, 118; James Phelan, *History of Tennessee: The Making of a State* (Boston: Houghton Mifflin, 1888), 317–18. As early as the 1820s, the Mississippi River was considered to be the "American Nile." On the name Memphis, according to Phelan the "origin of the name is not remote when we consider that the ancient city of the Pharaohs also stood upon the banks of a great river that in many respects resembles the Mississippi." United States, Bureau of the Census, *Ninth Census of the United States, 1870* (Washington, DC: 1872).

23. Karl Marx, "The Working Day," *Capital: A Critique of Political Economy* vol.1 (New York: International Publishers, 1979, orig. 1867), 236. While neo-classical historians characterized planters as capitalist because they were engaged in exchange relations, only recently have historians and economists who define capitalism in terms of production, such as Genovese, come to conclude that capitalism and slavery are not antithetical. See Eugene Genovese and Elizabeth Fox-Genovese, *Fruits of Merchant Capital* (New York: Oxford University Press, 1983). The reemergence of unfree labor in the late twentieth century has caused a fundamental revision of the meaning of capitalist free labor and a new understanding of contingency. See Robin Cohen, *The New Helots: Migrants in the New International division of Labor* (Hants, UK: Avebury, 1987); Robert Miles, *Capitalism and Unfree Labour: Anomaly or Necessity?* (London; Tavistock Publications, 1987); Roger Plant, *Sugar and Modern Slavery: A Tale of Two Countries* (London: Zed Press, 1987); Roger Sawyer, *Slavery in the Twentieth Century* (London: Routledge and Kegan Paul, 1986); Tom Brass, "Review Essay: Slavery Now: Unfree Labour and Modern Capitalism," *Slavery and Abolition* 19/1 (1988).

24. Lomax, 1993, 149; Cobb, 1992, 13–27. Several observers described these plantations as little more than death camps: "from the moment they are able to go afield in the picking season till they drop worn out in the grave, they are engaged in incessant labor, in all sorts of weather, at all seasons of the year without any other change or relaxation that is not furnished by sickness, without the smallest hope of any improvement in either their condition, their food or in their clothing"[22]. "It is calculated that in the county of Yazoo lying between the Yazoo and the Big Black Rivers, the Negroes die off every few

years, though it is said that in time each hand also makes enough to buy two more in his place." Although generally considered more privileged, the work of the house servant was also without end. "Mary's first chore was milking fourteen cows. She then cooked breakfast, swept the house, made the beds, dusted, washed the dishes, prepared meals for some of the other servants, nursed her own infant, and at last ate breakfast. Immediately thereafter, she cleaned the kitchen, prepared a huge mid-day meal, washed dishes, cleaned the dining room, washed a large batch of clothes and hung them out, and began preparing supper. After supper she milked for the second time that day, nursed her child, cleaned the kitchen and retired."[27]

25. Lomax, 1993, 382.

26. Cobb, 1992, 27.

27. Gavin Wright, *The Political Economy of the Cotton South: Household, Markets and Wealth in the Nineteenth Century* (New York: W. W. Norton, 1978), 125; Lloyd Best, "Outlines of a Model of Pure Plantation Economy," *Social and Economic Studies*, 17/3 (1968), 287.

28. See Christopher S. Johnson, "Poor Relief in Antebellum Mississippi," *Journal of Mississippi History* 49 (1987) 2–3; Stephen Shaffer and Dale Krane, "The Origins and Evolution of a Traditionalistic Society," in Dale Krane and Stephen Shaffer (eds.), *Mississippi Government and Politics: Modernizers versus Traditionalist* (Lincoln: University of Nebraska Press, 1992), p. 25.

29. See Charles Reagan Wilson and William Ferris (eds.), *Encyclopedia of Southern Culture* (Chapel Hill: University of North Carolina Press, 1989), 1,151; W. J. Cash, *The Mind of the South* (New York: Vintage Books, 1941); Edmund S. Morgan, *American Slavery, American Freedom: The Ordeal of Colonial Virginia* (New York: Norton, 1975).

30. Michael Wayne, "An Old South Morality Play: Reconsidering the Social Underpinnings of the Proslavery Ideology," *Journal of American History*, 77(3) (December 1990), 863.

31. Daniel Joseph Singal, *The War Within: From Victorian to Modernist Thought in the South, 1919–1945* (Chapel Hill: University of North Carolina Press, 1982), 13.

32. Peter Fryer, *Staying Power: The History of Black People in Britain* (London: Pluto Press, 1984), 136–7. As early as the second century, Africans were being equated with the devil in English folklore and literature. Early seventeenth-century expeditions to Africa spoke of encountering "satyrs, devils, monsters, amozins, and canniballs."

33. Carole M. Ornelas-Struve, *Memphis 1800–1900* (vol.1) (New York: N. Powers, 1982). Between 1835 and 1860, Delta and Memphis area planters so identified with the royalty and social order of ancient Egypt that some chose to be buried in iron "fisk mummy cases" designed to imitate the sarcophagi of the Egyptian pharaohs. Singal, 1982, 13, 17–18.

34. Addison Gayle Jr, "Cultural Hegemony: The Southern White Writer and American Letters," in John A. Williams and Charles F. Harris (eds.), *Amistad 1: Writings on Black History and Culture* (New York: Vintage Books, 1970), 5.

35. Francis Pendelton Gaines, *The Southern Plantation: A Study in the Development and Accuracy of a Tradition* (New York: Columbia University Press, 1925), 2–11.

36. Claude H. Nolen, *The Negro's Image in the South: The Anatomy of White Supremacy* (Lexington: University of Kentucky Press, 1967), 42.

37. Ibid., xiv.

38. George Fitzhugh, *Sociology of the South or the Failure of Free Society* (Richmond: A. Morris Publishers, 1854), 83.

39. Ibid., 214–15.

40. Ibid., 37, 44, 61.

41. Ibid., 81.

42. Alexis de Toqueville, *Democracy in America* (Garden City, NY: Anchor Books, 1969), 360–1.

43. Frederick Law Olmsted, *The Cotton Kingdom* (New York; Knopf, 1953), 95.

According to Olmsted, Dr Cartwight discovered two diseases of the nerves; drapetomania resulted in a irrepressible desire to flee, while the symptoms of dysaesthesia aethipoica were the breaking of tools, the abuse of livestock, the damaging of crops, and the challenging of overseers.

44. Walter Rodney, *A History of the Upper Guinea Coast, 1545 to 1800* (New York, Monthly Review Press, 1970). Rodney argues that it is not the great kingdoms that need to be studied but the absence of prisons. This absence was considered evidence of the presence of forms of governance that could inform current attempts to develop alternative state and non-state structures. Other recent authors have focused on Native American practices of environmental stewardship and governance as potential models.

45. Loren Schweninger, *Black Property Owners in the South: 1790–1915* (Urbana: University of Illinois Press, 1990), 30–59.

46. Ibid., 1990, 59–60.

47. Barlow, 1989, xii.

48. Miles Mark Fisher, *Negro Slave Songs in the United States* (New York: Carol Publishing Group, 1990, orig. 1953), 87.

49. Lawrence Levine, *Black Culture and Black Consciousness: Afro-American Folk Thought From Slavery to Freedom* (Oxford: Oxford University Press, 1977), 297.

50. Sidney Mintz and Richard Price, *The Birth of African American Culture: An Anthropological Perspectives* (Boston: Beacon Press, 1992), 46–7.

51. Fisher, 1990, 82. See also Barlow, 1989, 7–24.

52. Moore, 1988, 264–6. After Gabriel Prosser's rebellion in 1822, the ability of free Blacks to peddle goods between plantations was restricted; they could not attend meetings after dark where slaves were present, or be present when Whites were being taught to read or write. For verbally abusing a White person they would receive not more than 39 lashes on the bare back. The number of free African Americans in Mississippi declined significantly, from 1366 in 1840 to 773 by 1860 [118]. *Data News Weekly* New Orleans, 21 January 1995. Also on the minds of planters in the region was the large revolt that occurred in the parishes adjacent to New Orleans in 1811.

53. Charles L. Blockson, *The Underground Railroad: Dramatic First-hand Accounts of Daring Escapes to Freedom* (New York: Berkeley Books, 1989), 27–31.

54. Robert E. May, "Epilogue to the Missouri Compromise: The South, The Balance of Power, and the Tropics in the 1850s," *Plantation Society* June 1979, 201–25, 210.

55. Dena J. Epstein, *Sinful Tunes and Spirituals: Black Folk Music to the Civil War* (Urbana: University of Illinois Press, 1977), 246. "Let My People Go" was sung secretly in the South by African Americans for over fifteen years before being transcribed in September 1861. The first African American spiritual published with music and lyrics, it was used by abolitionists as evidence of the African American hatred of slavery.

56. Cobb, 1992, 30; Du Bois, 1983, 431.

57. Cobb, 1992, 29–31; Harrison, 1951, 1–23.

58. Harrison, 1951, 22; Percy Lee Rainwater, *Mississippi Storm Center of Secession, 1856–1861* (New York: Da Capo Press, 1969), 71–3; May, 1979, 201–25.

59. Rainwater, 1969, 16. The US Senator from Mississippi, Henry S. Foote, invited a US Senate supporter of the Wilmot Proviso—designed to form a cordon around the slave states—to come to Mississippi, where he "could not go ten miles into the interior before he would grace one of the tallest trees in the state ... I should assist myself in the operation."

60. Rainwater, 1969, 75.

61. De Toqueville, 1969, 377; see also Rainwater, 1969; Lomax 1993, 163. The importance of music was not lost on anyone in the Delta. According to one musician, "Jefferson Davis organized a band for his Negroes, and he hired a man in Vicksburg ... to teach them boys music. After they got so they could play, he bought um a uniform, and he name that band the Davis Bend Band. Escort him every where he went. Fourteen men in that band ... I played myself. Yeah, I played Dixie."

62. Howard Rabinowitz, "Southern Urban Development 1860–1900," in Blaine Brownwell and David Goldfield (eds.), *The City in Southern History* (Port Washington: Kennikat Press, 1977), 92–122.

63. Ira Berlin, Thavolia Glymph, Steven Miller, Joseph P. Reidy, Leslie S. Rowland, and Julie Saville, *Freedom: A Documentary History of Emancipation, 1861–1867* Series I, Vol. III (Cambridge: Cambridge University Press, 1990), 621–2.

64. Cobb, 1992, 35. In a several-month period, African American soldiers and spies helped Sherman seize the capital Jackson; Grant seize fortified Vicksburg; Sherman recapture and torch Jackson; and Sherman torch the largest Delta city, Greenville. Having perfected this formula for victory in the Delta, in May 1864 Sherman embarked on his March to the Sea, designed to spilt the South from middle Tennessee to northern Georgia. Sherman sacked and torched many cities including Atlanta.

65. Berlin, *et al.*, 1990, 748–9. In 1863, Union administrators confiscated these plantations which were owned by the Confederate President Jefferson Davis, his brother, and several neighboring planters. Seventy African American families were granted thirty acres apiece and, in 1865, an additional 5,000 acres were divided among 1,800 families who were organized into 181 companies and associations. Part of the community's success was attributable to the protection provided by several African American regiments. Stores, schools, medical care, a legal system, and local government were all found within this complex which cleared $160,000 in profits. Two of the plantations were returned to their owners during Lincoln's administration, and President Johnson returned Jefferson Davis's property in 1866. The African American who managed Davis Bend, Benjamin Montgomery, went on to found the town of Mound Bayou in the northern portion of the Delta.

66. Ibid., 632. Adult men were paid $7 a month, women $5, teenagers (12–15 years) half the adult wage, and younger children were paid no wages at all. From these wages, monopoly-priced clothing and food were deducted.

67. Matthew Josephson, *The Robber Barons: The Great American Capitalists, 1861–1901* (New York: Harcourt Brace and World, 1962).

68. Berlin *et al.,* 1990, 635.

69. Cobb, 1992, 48–9.

70. Arnold H. Taylor, *Travail and Triumph: Black Life and Culture in the South since the Civil War* (Westport, CT: Greenwood Press, 1976), 6–7; Kenneth Stampp, *Era of Reconstruction, 1865–1877* (New York: Vintage Books, 1965), 80.

71. Stampp, 1965, 78.

72. Taylor, 1976, 6–7. The first codification of the Black Codes by the Mississippi convention was the most repressive set of regulations in the South and served as a model for the other states: "by severely circumscribing the degree of liberty the former slaves were to enjoy, the codes attempted to transform the freedmen into a socially proscribed caste and an economically subservient proletariat. Several of the codes contained the following provisions: imprisonment for life for interracial marriage; serving on juries and testifying in court in cases involving Whites was prohibited; the buying or renting of farm land was prohibited; the ownership of real estate in towns or cities was prohibited; engaging in any form of employment other than agricultural labor without a special license was prohibited; those refusing to enter into contracts for their labor not fulfilling contracts were arrested and convicted of vagrancy and then forced to work for free; and "minors without parents, or with parents unable to properly care for them, were to be apprenticed to White guardians, preferably their former masters, who were to have essentially the same authority over them as masters over their slaves."

73. Lowen and Sallis, 1974, 146, 147.

74. Cobb, 1992, 58.

75. Ibid., 45.

76. Harrison, 1951, 25–9.

77. Dorothy Sterling, *The Trouble They Seen: Black People Tell the Story of*

*Reconstruction* (Garden City, NY: Doubleday, 1976), 92, 91. One of the incidents finding its way into the Congressional record was the story of an African American soldier's wife. "'The house had been set on fire and was burning ... When I went back, I walked upon the body of Rachel. She was dead and the blood was running out of her mouth. Her clothes were all burned off from her.' Question: 'How old was your daughter?' Answer: 'About fourteen years old.'"[92–3].

78. Ibid., xi.

79. Cobb, 1992, 42.

80. Vernon Wharton, *The Negro in Mississippi, 1865–1890* (New York: Harper and Row, 1965), 87.

81. Lowen and Sallis, 1974, 151.

82. Harrison, 1951, 31. The Levee Districts resisted efforts at reorganization by military officials. They requested the authorities to turn over to them "idle and unemployed" freedmen and later requested "vagrant and convict" labor for levee construction.

83. Schweninger, 1990, 145.

84. Gerald D. Jaynes, *Branches Without Roots: Genesis of the Black Working Class in the American South, 1862–1882* (New York: Oxford University Press, 1986). Jaynes outlines a course of events that doomed land reform. The Radical Republican program of "universal education, universal male suffrage, and universal small proprietorship" posed as much a threat to the growing power of Northern capitalists as it did to the prone Southern plantation capitalists. The stated policy of the Boston Board of Trade was that the federal debt, inflation, and the European trade deficit could only be eliminated by returning to the pre-war gold standard as soon as possible. Since "Cotton is gold anywhere in Europe ... the balance of trade must be paid in specie, unless paid in cotton which is to Europe the same as specie." The London *Economist* entered the debate in 1865 with a demand for an immediate return to both production and normal Atlantic trading relations since a large flow of gold was going to Egypt and Asia for cotton, never to return. "How the negroes will be regimented, ... into industrial gangs or squadrons again, does not seem clear. That in some way or the other they will be so 'regimented' – and either induced to work, or 'persuaded' to work, we entertain little doubt." In February 1865 the *New York Times* baldy concluded that "White ingenuity and enterprise ought to direct Black labor."[3–15].

85. W. E. B. Du Bois, *Black Reconstruction: An Essay Towards a History of the Part Which Black Folk Played in the Attempt to Reconstruct Democracy in America, 1860–1880* (New York: Atheneum, 1983), 433. Hodding Carter, *Lower Mississippi* (New York: Farrar and Rinehart, 1942), 289.

86. Schweninger, 1990, 146–7.

87. Cobb, 1992, 56.

88. Michael W. Fitzgerald, *The Union League Movement in the Deep South: Politics and Agricultural Change during Reconstruction* (Baton Rogue: Louisiana State University Press, 1989). The Freedman's Bureau had promised that land distribution would begin immediately after the war, and land confiscation was still being debated in Congress in 1867. According to a federal official, "the freedmen were ineradicably filled with the idea that the government is to divide the land among them about Christmas, and so will not make engagements to work beyond that time. Agents of the Freedman's bureau address them to disabuse them, but they will listen and then say 'This ain't no Yankee. He is a Southern man in disguise.'"[28]

89. Ibid, 170; Jaynes, 1986, 295. According to Jaynes, the Union Leagues were "hatcheries of radical economic experiments."

90. Fitzgerald, 1989, 66–70; Carter, 1942, 293.

91. Fitzgerald, 1989, 174–6. Planters who joined the League to foster good relations with Black labor were roundly denounced as scalawags and the home of former governor Alcorn was burned to the ground when he chose to rent.

92. Cobb, 1992, 62; Sterling, 1976, 361. Fitzgerald, 1989, 216–23. "One klansman

testified that 'in the lower counties along the river and in Yazoo country, you seldom hear of them [regulators]; the Negroes are so largely in excess of population that they never have anything of that kind down there."[225] Leagues continued to meet after the collapse of the state organization in 1870 and were still alive in various forms until the Vicksburg massacre of 1874 after which they all went underground only to reemerge again in the late 1880s.

93. Fitzgerald, 1989, 233; James Oakes, *Slavery and Freedom: An Interpretation of the Old South* (NY: Knopf, 1990), 199–200.

## 4 The Shotgun Policy and the Birth of the Blues

1. Kenneth Stampp, *The Era of Reconstruction, 1865–1877* (New York: Vintage Books 1965), 201.

2. Dorothy Sterling, *The Trouble They Seen: Black People Tell the Story of Reconstruction* (Garden City, NY: Doubleday, 1976), 438–9.

3. Cobb, 1992, 61.

4. W. E. B. Du Bois, *Black Reconstruction: An Essay Toward a History of the Part Which Black Folk Played in the Attempt to Reconstruct Democracy in America, 1860–1880* (New York: Atheneum, 1983), 449.

5. William Alexander Percy, *Lanterns on the Levee: Recollections of a Planter's Son* (New York: A. A. Knopf, 1941), 68–9. See also Cobb, 1992, 64–5.

6. Sterling, 1976, 458–9, 433–7; Cobb, 1992, 65. See the *Jackson Advocate* 25 July 1985, for a discussion of the Tunica massacre and the investigation of it by the US Senate in 1877.

7. Sterling, 1976, 454. Sterling describes the orchestrated creation of the new political regime in Mississippi in the following manner: "Provoking a riot became a fine art in Mississippi in 1875 when the conservatives adopted the 'Shotgun Plan' with the slogan 'carry the election peacefully if we can, forcibly if we must.' With a team of ex-Confederate generals at the helm, thousands of young white men were organized into cavalry and artillery companies. Equipped with the latest in repeating rifles, they drilled in the town squares and rode through the countryside threatening blacks and their white allies. Democratic clubs kept 'dead books' in which they ostentatiously wrote the name of Republican leaders. They shot off cannons at Republican rallies, demanding time for their own speakers and heckling their opponents. And they deliberately provoked riots which escalated into shooting wars"[438–40].

8. Sterling, 1976, 444.

9. Sterling, 1976, 453; James W. Lowen and Charles Sallis (eds.), *Mississippi Conflict and Change* (New York: Random House, 1974), 165; Stampp, 1965, 209.

10. Josephson, 1962.

11. Theodore Saloutos, *Farmer Movements in the South, 1865–1933* (Berkeley: University of California Press, 1960); William Hair, *Bourbons and Agrarian Protest: Louisiana 1877–1900* (Baton Rouge: Louisiana State University Press, 1969), 163. Saloutous argues that in the eyes of small farmers and sharecroppers, the large planters of the Cotton Planters' Association were the regional equivalents of the Robber Barons. "More basic to the survival of the association were the far-flung economic interests of the leaders who had invested in lumber, sugar, railroads, textile manufacturing, and brokerage firms, and who were anxious to exploit the natural and human riches of their region. They wanted to make efficient use of their resources, stress the staging of exhibits, field trials of labor-saving machinery, and expositions to instruct the planting community. Their labor, credit, managerial and production problems were those of the large-scale employer. Urban in outlook, dynamic, closely bound by social and economic interests, the large planters ... were the rural equivalent of big business and

monopoly, the very forces which in a competitive struggle threatened to drive them to the wall."[57]

12. Howard Rabinowitz, "Southern Urban Development, 1860 to 1900," in Blaine Brownell and David Goldfield (eds.), *The City in Southern History: The Growth of Urban Civilization in the South* (Port Washington, NY: Kennikat Press, 1977), 92–122, 103; United States, Bureau of the Census, *Eleventh Census, 1890* part 1 (Washington, DC: Government Printing Office, 1895).

13. William M. Cash and R. Daryl Lewis, *The Delta Council: Fifty Years of Service to the Mississippi Delta* (Stoneville, MS: Delta Council, 1986), 64.

14. Saloutos, 1960, 58.

15. Lowen and Sallis, 1974, 173.

16. Ibid., 169–70, 184–5. L. Q. C. Lamar and James Z. George were representative of the type of official that emerged in the Southern one-party state after 1875. Lamar was author of both the secession legislation and the plan for the 1875 counterrevolution. Intermittently, he was a planter, a lawyer, and a professor at the University of Mississippi. He resigned his congressional seat at the start of the Civil War and served the Confederacy as an envoy to England, France, and Russia. After 1872, he promoted regional reconciliation which he embodied while serving as a US Senator in 1876, as US Secretary of the Interior in 1885, and as a US Supreme Court Justice between 1888 and 1893. James Z. George helped Lamar draft the Ordinance of Secessions in 1861. As state Democratic Party chairman, he played a central role in coordinating the counterrevolution of 1875. After being appointed Chief Justice of the Mississippi Supreme Court in 1879, he left this position for the US Senate where he served from 1881 until 1897. While in the Senate he co-authored the Sherman Anti-Trust Act and became known as the "Father of the Department of Agriculture."

17. See the essay on "Jimmy Carter and the Americanization of Southern Politics," in Dewey Grantham, *The Regional Imagination* (Nashville: Vanderbilt University Press, 1979), 223–4.

18. Brandfon, 1967, 20.

19. Frank H. Alfriend, "A Southern National Literature", *Southern Messenger* May 1864. See Encyclopedia Britannica, *The Annals of America* (Chicago: Encyclopedia Britannica, 1976), v. 9, 490–3.

20. Cash and Lewis, 1986, 16; Brandfon, 1967, 3; Singal, 1982, 23–4. Singal explains the origins of planter representation in the following manner: "Its central tenets represent little more than the essentials of Victorian belief wrapped in southern garb ... the same worship of material success, the same diligence and practicality, the same outlook of steadfast optimism ... joined with and subsumed under the moral code of gentility, in the South as in England. For southerners, of course, things spiritual took the form of the Cavalier heritage, which was to ensure that the emerging society would be cultured, guided by gentlemanly standards of honor and run according to principles of paternalistic benevolence." In general the emerging New South movement was more concerned with social reform than the production-oriented Delta planters. For example, a long-term strategy for ethnic education was outlined by a reformist New South Alabama minister. Moral and industrial education would be provided for Whites; however, the irrational and barbaric needed a civilization program to condition them to accept permanent subservience. The principal tool in this effort would be primary schools designed to develop a Black middle class as a conduit of civilization. The pupils would primarily be taught punctuality and order: "even standing and sitting ... are to be performed under the control and direction of another."[31]

21. Frederick Merk, *Manifest Destiny and Mission in American History* (New York: Vintage Books, 1966), 238–47. Pastor of the US Congress, Josiah Strong was a key advocate of race-based imperialism as a humanitarian mission. According to Merk, Strong's social Darwinist views, found in his 1885 work *Our Country* set the tone for an era of interregional unity based upon the exploitation of other nations. "No war to exterminate the inferior races would be necessary. The feeblest of them would be wiped

out mercifully, merely by the diseases of and contacts with, a higher civilization, for which they were unprepared... . Races, somewhat stronger will simply be submerged. Decay already is far along in their superstitions and creeds. The dead crust of fossil faiths – Catholic, Mohammedan, Jew, Buddhist, and Brahmin – is being shattered. The pieces left in this process will be assimilated or simply neutralized by the stronger Anglo-Saxons. The plan of God is to weaken weaklings and supplant them with better and finer materials ... Prepare ye the way of the Lord!"[240].

22. Louisville Board of Trade, *Memorial of the Cotton Planters' Convention at Greenville Mississippi and the Response Thereto of the Louisville Board of Trade* (Louisville, KY: Louisville Board of Trade, 1879, Mississippi Department of Archives), 4; Nell Irvin Painter, *Exodusters: Black Migration to Kansas after Reconstruction* (Lawrence: University of Kansas Press, 1986), 216; Cobb, 1992, 70.

23. Louisville Board of Trade, 1879, 6.

24. Vincent Harding, *There is a River: The Black Struggle for Freedom in America* (New York: Vintage Books, 1983), 301.

25. Claude F. Oubre, *Forty Acres and a Mule: The Freedmen's Bureau and Black Land Ownership* (Baton Rouge: Louisiana State University Press, 1978). The Bureau of Refugees, Freedmen, and Abandoned Lands was the first, the largest, and the most powerful federal regional planning entity ever created in the United States. The Bureau operated a bank, schools, orphanages, labor–employer dispute courts, and model land reform projects. The bank had more than $31 million in deposits in 1872 before corrupt federal officials and the financial panic of 1873 wiped it, and the savings of hundreds of thousands of African Americans, out of existence. [161]. The bureau is generally referred to as an agency designed to help aimless African Americans adjust to freedom. In fact, it was responding to a crisis generated in the majority-Black rural counties where committees of African Americans were independently deciding which lands to occupy, and when and where to work, how to govern, and how to prevent planter restoration. Consequently the bureau can be examined as a planned federal intervention designed to redirect and defeat the realization of long-held visions of autonomy.

26. Barlow, 1989, 4–5.

27. Lomax, 1993, 241, 251.

28. Ibid., 232, xii.

29. Ibid., xiii.

30. Ibid., 4–5.

31. Painter, 1986, 154.

32. Ibid., 156.

33. Janet Sharp Hermann, *The Pursuit of a Dream* (New York: Oxford University Press, 1981); Schweninger, 1990, 165; Kenneth Marvin Hamilton, *Black Towns and Profit: Promotion and Development, 1877–1915* (Urbana: University of Illinois Press, 1991), 43–98. For more on Davis Bend, see Chapter 3, n. 65.

34. Hamilton, 1991, 84, 1.

35. City of Mound Bayou, *A Pictorial History of Mound Bayou: 95th Founder's Day Celebration, 1982* (Mound Bayou, MS: City of Mound Bayou, 1982). Mound Bayou is still a symbol of autonomous development.

36. Arnold Taylor, *Travail and Triumph: Black Life and Culture in the South since the Civil War* (Westport: Greenwood Press, 1976), 7.

37. William F. Holmes, "The Leflore County Massacre and the Demise of the Colored Farmers' Alliance," *Phylon* (September 1973), 267–9. According to one investigator, neither the National Guard, the governor, nor Black residents of Leflore County were forthcoming with accounts of the incident. However, there are several first-hand accounts by travelers who happened to be in the region. "J. C. Engle, an agent for a New York textile company, was 'in and about Greenwood' during the trouble. When he arrived at New Orleans several days later, he told reporters that Negroes 'were shot down like dogs.' Members of the posse not only killed people in the swamps, he said, but they

even invaded homes and murdered 'men women and children.' Engle recalled one act in which a sixteen year old white boy 'beat out the brains of a little colored girl while a bigger brother with a gun kept the little one's parents off.'" Several sources reported that the posse singled out four well-known leaders of the Colored Farmers' Alliance whom they shot to death: Adolph Horton, Scott Morris, Jack Dial and J. M. Dial. "A black undercover reporter sent to the region stated that the truth may never be known because terrified blacks dare not speak of the matter, even to each other." The lack of coverage of this event by the Mississippi press and the failure of federal and state officials to investigate led Holmes to wonder "how many other instances of violence greater and lesser magnitude occurred in that era and of which nothing is known." [272–73]

38. Du Bois, 1983, *Black Reconstruction* 634.

## 5 Segregation, Peonage, and the Blues Ascension

1. Lowen and Sallis, 1974, 183.

2. C. Vann Woodward, *Origins of the New South* (Baton Rouge: Louisiana State University Press, 1951), 336. For Woodward, the poll tax was a central feature of the Mississippi Plan of 1890. "In the Mississippi convention, the Delta counties had insisted upon the poll tax ... as their sine qua non, knowing that as a means of Negro disenfranchisement, it is worth all the rest ... It reduces the electorate and places political control of the state in the hands not of a minority of the voters alone, but of the minority of whites. [According to one observer,] poll tax gets rid of most of the Negro votes there, but it gets rid of a great many whites at the same time—in fact a majority of them."

3. McMillen, 1989, 50. Montgomery claimed that he was engaged in a noble effort to "purify the ballot [to] restrict the franchise to a stable, thoughtful and prudent element of our citizens. [This was] a fearful sacrifice laid down upon the burning alter of liberty ... an olive branch of peace ... the suffrage of 123,000 of my fellow-men at the feet of this convention."

4. Paul Lewinson, *Race, Class and Party: A History of Negro Suffrage and White Politics in the South* (New York: Oxford, 1932), 84–5; McMillen, 1989, 43. A spokesman for the Hills, Governor James Vardaman insisted that "Mississippi's constitutional convention was held for no other purpose than to eliminate the nigger from politics: not the ignorant or vicious but the nigger ... let the world know it just as it is."

5. Cobb, 1992, 88; Hanes Walton Jr, *Black Political Parties: An Historical and Political Analysis* (New York; Free Press, 1972), 84.

6. Taylor, 1976, 74; According to Lowen and Sallis (1974, 191) The *Bolivar County Democrat* issued the following warning: "We cannot believe that many of them will turn their backs on the white Democrats of the country and join the black brigade in the struggle for negro supremacy in our country ... the white people have determined to run Bolivar County and no combination of republicans, populists, and soreheads can defeat them."

7. McMillen, 1990, 6; Percy, 1941, 680; Molefi K. Asante and Mark T. Mattson, *Historical Atlas of African Americans* (New York: Macmillan, 1991), 95.

8. Brandfon, 1967, 86–91; see Illinois Central Railroad Company, *The Yazoo-Mississippi Valley* (Chicago: Illinois Central Railroad Company, 1910); Southern Alluvial Land Association, *The Call of the Alluvial Empire* (Memphis: Southern Alluvial Land Association, 1919); Ibid., *The West Side Delta* (Memphis: Southern Alluvial Land Association, 1920), n.p. *The Yazoo Mississippi Delta; The Garden Spot of America* (Greenwood, MS: Lawrence Printing Co, n.d). *The Call of the Alluvial Empire* stated that the Southern Alluvial Land Association was comprised of "lumberman who are clearing vast tracts of timber, [and] planters, banks, business houses, livestock breeders and other interest [such as publishers] having at heart the development of the Alluvial Empire ...

Twenty million acres of super soil, nestling in the Lower Mississippi Valley ... comprise the Alluvial Empire, the last and richest great area of America's undeveloped corn land available for agriculture." The Memphis Chamber of Commerce stood at the center of the Association. In the same pamphlet, the editor of the *Memphis Commercial Appeal*, one of the leading forces in the Chamber, assured Northerners that they would not be culturally isolated. "Southern people are not clannish neither are they provincial ... For the last forty years there has been a drift ... into the South. The population of Memphis is largely made up of people from Indiana, Wisconsin, and Illinois. Large plantations in the Delta are owned and operated by men, who when they were boys, plowed corn and cradled wheat on the Illinois prairies"[3, 29].

9. Southern Alluvial Land Association, 1919, 53.

10. Blaine A. Brownell, "The Urban South Comes of Age, 1900 to 1940," in Blaine Brownell and David Goldfield (eds.), *The City in Southern History* (Port Washington: Kennikat Press, 1977), 123–58; Rabinowitz, 1977, 127.

11. Southern Alluvial Land Association, 1920, 53.

12. W. C. Handy, *Father of the Blues: An Autobiography* (New York: Da Capo Press, 1969), 93.

13. McMillen, 1989, 259. See also: United States, Bureau of the Census, *Thirteenth Census, 1910* (Washington, DC: Government Printing Office, 1913). United States, Bureau of the Census, *Fourteenth Census, 1920* (Washington, DC: Government Printing Office, 1922).

14. Brandfon, 1967, 20; Cobb 1992, 99.

15. Cobb, 1992, 101.

16. Ibid.; *The Yazoo-Mississippi Delta* n.d., 18.

17. Cobb, 1992, 99.

18. Lowen and Sallis, 1974, 204.

19. David Evans, *Big Road Blues: Tradition and Creativity in the Folk Blues* (Berkeley: University of California Press, 1982), 191–2.

20. Lomax, 1993, 206–7, 468. Blues performer Big Bill Broonzy described the fate of African Americans who attempted to control who in their household would work. "I remember one time my auntie had a baby boy; about two or three years old. The white man came up there one day and he told him ... 'Say, Gerry ... I want you to get that woman out there and put her to work. There's no woman here sits up and don't work, set up in the shade, but Miz Anne.' 'Well, I'm sorry mister, but my wife is named Anne, too, and she sit up in the shade.' And he jumps off his horse ... my uncle whipped him, and run his horse on away and then beat him and run him away from there ... the white man went to town and got a gang ... he [my uncle] shot all four, five of them ... Fifty or sixty of them come out there and got him and killed [hung] him ... because he didn't want his wife to work out on the plantation when she had a baby there at the house to take care of and she was expecting another one pretty soon."

21. Lowen and Sallis, 1974, 207; McMillen, 1990, 154; Cobb, 1992, 104.

22. Danforth Stuart Green, "The Truth Shall Make Ye Free: The Sociology of W. E. B. DuBois," PhD thesis, University of Massachusetts, 1973, 175; Pete Daniel, *The Shadow of Slavery: Peonage in the South, 1901–1969* (London: Oxford University Press, 1973); Carter G. Woodson, *The Rural Negro* (New York: Russell and Russell, orig. 1930, 1969), 68. According to famed African American historian Carter G. Woodson, although involuntary servitude (except for those convicted of a felony) was declared unconstitutional by the Thirteenth Amendment to the US Constitution in 1867, "Alabama, Florida, Georgia, Mississippi, North Carolina, and South Carolina enacted, a generation later, evasive laws which provided for involuntary servitude for debt, and the courts of these states upheld such legislation ... From Mexico the planters had learned how to hedge around the letter of the constitution."

23. Lomax, 1993, 212, 214, 67–8. In 1904, a young White New England engineer named William Hemphill wrote a letter home describing conditions in his levee camp.

"If one white foreman shoots a couple of niggers on the works, and it by no means is an unheard of or infrequent thing, the work is not stopped ... Think of a white foreman, miles away from anywhere, working a hundred and fifty of the most reckless niggers in the world. It's a plain case of which you'd rather do, shoot or get shot."[217]

24. Donald Spivey, *Schooling for the New Slavery: Black Industrial Education, 1868–1915* (Westport, CT: Greenwood Press), 74.

25. Lewis and Cash, 1986, 63; *The Yazoo Mississippi Delta* n.d., 17–18.

26. McMillen, 1990, 9.

27. Southern Alluvial Land Association, 1919, 7.

28. Cobb, 1992, 117.

29. Edward D. C. Campbell, Jr., "Creation of a Past: Toward a Popular View of Southern History," *Journal of Regional Cultures*, Fall/Winter 1982, 31–9, 32.

30. Ibid., 35–7. Also see Donald Bogle, *Toms, Coons, Mulattoes and Bucks: An Interpretive History of Blacks in American Film* (New York: Continuum, 1989); Edward D. C. Campbell, *The Celluloid South: Hollywood and the Southern Myth* (Knoxville: University of Tennessee Press, 1981); Thomas J. Cripps, *Slow Fade to Black: The Negro in American Film, 1900–1942* (New York: Oxford University Press, 1977); Jack T. Kirby, *Media Made Dixie: The South in the American Imagination* (Baton Rouge: Louisiana State University Press, 1978); Peter A. Soderbergh, "Hollywood and the South, 1930–1960," *Mississippi Quarterly* Winter 1965–66.

31. Franklin H. Giddings, *The Principles of Sociology* (New York: Macmillan, 1896), 329.

32. Vernon J. Williams, *From Caste to a Minority: Changing Attitudes of American Sociologists Towards Afro-Americans, 1896–1945* (New York: Greenwood Press, 1989), 33–8, 59–69. Williams provides one of the most brilliant critiques of the evolving theory of race in social thought.

33. Alfred Holt Stone, "Is Race Friction Between Blacks and Whites in the United States Growing and Inevitable?" *American Journal of Sociology* 13 (March 1908), 676–697; Alfred Holt Stone, *Studies in the American Race Problem* (New York: Doubleday, 1908). See also the comments of five respondents including W. E. B. Du Bois, in "Discussion of Race Friction," *American Journal of Sociology* 13 (March 1908); Williams, 1989, 43; James Silver, *Mississippi: The Closed Society* (New York: Harvest Books, 1966), 17.

34. Stone, March 1908, 682–3.

35. Ibid., 680–1. Stone's "tipping thesis" remains a key component of current development policy debates in the areas of housing segregation, educational tracking, and industrial redlining.

36. Ibid., 684, 696–7.

37. Du Bois, 1908, 834; See W. E. B. Du Bois, *Dusk to Dawn: An Essay Toward an Autobiography of a Race Concept* (New Brunswick: Transaction Books, orig. 1940, 1984), 93. In *Dusk to Dawn* Du Bois expresses his amazement at how influential Stone was among Northern philanthropists.[84]

38. Du Bois, 1908, 835, 836, 837.

39. Ibid., 836–7.

40. Ibid., 838.

41. Alfred H. Stone, "Discussion of the Paper by Alfred H. Stone, 'Is Race Friction Between Blacks and Whites in the United States Growing and Inevitable?'" *American Journal of Sociology* XIII(6), May 1908, 840.

42. For example, Du Bois was increasingly unpopular in the South after 1905 when he sent out a call for the formation of the Niagara Movement which, after fracturing, evolved into the National Association for the Advancement of Colored People (NAACP) in 1909. Stone's attack on Du Bois and Du Bois's attack on Stone partially explains the funding blockade thrown up around Atlanta University by politically powerful planters, Washington's Tuskegee machine, President Theodore Roosevelt, the Rockefeller's

General Education Board, and other funders. By 1909, Du Bois understood that he had no choice but to resign if the university was to prosper.

43. Howard W. Odum, *Social and Mental Traits of the Negro* (New York: Columbia University Press, 1910), 13–14.

44. See ibid., 19; Singal, 1982, 135–47, 134.

45. Howard W. Odum and Guy B. Johnson, *The Negro and His Songs: A Study of Typical Negro Songs in the South* (Westport: Negro Universities Press, orig. 1925, 1972), 19–22. In 1925, Odum argued that an objective presentation of the "Negro," such as his, that emphasizes culture would create some empathy and goodwill among Whites for these "primitive" people. "If the musical nature and potential of the race can be emphasized again and again; if the good nature, the resourcefulness and adaptability of the Negro may be studied from varying viewpoints; if the Negro's skill and art may be presented in this way; if his hypocrisy and two-faced survival mechanisms may be suggested along with his good manners, his diplomacy, his artistic expression and rare harmony, then added values may be found in this volume."

46. Robert E. Park, "Education and Its Relation to the Conflict and Fusion of Cultures; With Special Reference to the Problems of the Immigrant, Negro and Missions," *Publications of the American Sociological Society* (December 1918), 59.

47. Williams, 1989; Kelly Miller, "Is Race Prejudice Innate or Acquired?" *Journal of Applied Sociology*, 11 (July–August, 1927), 520–4; Ellsworth Faris, "Racial Attitudes and Sentiments," in his Ellsworth Faris, *The Nature of Human Nature* (New York: McGraw-Hill Book Co., 1937), 317–19; Robert Park, "Our Racial Frontier on the Pacific," *Survey Graphic* 9 (May 1926), 196.

48. Carter G. Woodson, *The Rural Negro* (New York: Russell and Russell, orig. 1930, 1969), 236, 238.

49. Chris Albertson, *Bessie* (New York: Stein and Day, 1972), 175.

50. Bessie Smith, "In House Blues," *Bessie Smith: The World's Greatest Blues Singer*, Columbia Records CG33.

51. Taylor, 1976, 74.

52. Lee and Nelson, 1992, 33–8, 34. Dogtrot cabins consisted of two rooms separated by an open walkway. The shotgun cabin is a very narrow structure of African origin. See the architectural historian John Michael Vlach's note on African influences in C. R. Wilson and W. Ferris, *Encyclopedia of Southern Culture* (Chapel Hill: University of North Carolina Press, 1989), 139. According to Vlach, given "its history, the design of the shotgun house should be understood as somewhat determined by African architectural concepts as well as Caribbean, Indian and French colonial influences. Contemporary southern shotgun houses represent the last phrase of an architectural evolution initiated in Africa."

53. Taylor, 1976, 123; Hair, 1969, 122.

54. Schweninger, 1990, 166–71; Cobb, 1992, 91.

55. Schweninger, 1990, 228.

56. McMillen, 1989, 61–2.

57. Ibid., 57–71.

58. Handy, 81; McMillen, 1990, 11. While residing in Clarksdale, W. C. Handy engaged in the life-threatening business of smuggling Black newspapers such as the *Chicago Defender*, the *Indianapolis Freeman*, and the *Voice of the Negro*.

59. McMillen, 1989, 25; Taylor, 1976, 42. During this period, the African American doctor and dentist who organized the first NAACP branch in Vicksburg were tarred, feathered, forced to sell their property and then banished from the city. One historian argues that the national NAACP generally refused to mount a legal challenge to the constitutionality of Southern voting laws because it feared for the life of its lawyers. Richard Wright, *Black Boy: A Record of Childhood and Youth* (New York: Perennial Paperbacks, 1966), 253.

60. McMillen, 1989, 15; Handy, 1969, 79; Lomax, 1993, 468, 224. According to McMillen, the number of children produced by forced, coerced, and voluntary unions

spurred whites in Vicksburg to form an Anti-Miscegenation League at the turn of the century. Handy relates an incident which occurred in the New World red-light district in the Black section of Clarksdale, an area where prominent White politicians and planters gathered nightly. "One evening a vivid octoroon, who had been winking at our violinist, shared a drink with him. Her ofay company turned and put a pistol to the musician's temple. He promised to pull the trigger if he opened his mouth ... I recalled a saying that is almost an axiom among Negroes of the South ... more black men are killed by whites for merely conversing with colored girls of this type than for violating, as orators like to put it, the sanctity of white womanhood." [79]

61. Cobb, 1992, 114.

62. Alfreda M. Duster (ed.), *Crusade for Justice: The Autobiography of Ida B. Wells* (Chicago: University of Chicago Press, 1970), 53–8.

63. William H. Baldwin, "The Present Problem of Negro Education," *Journal of Social Sciences*, 37 (1899), 58; George Alexander Sewell and Margaret L. Dwight, *Mississippi Black History Makers* (Jackson: University Press of Mississippi, 1984), 160; Donald P. Stone, *Fallen Prince: William James Edwards, Black Education, and the Quest for African American Nationality* (Snow Hill, Al: Snow Hill Press, 1990), 158–61, 160.

64. Katrina Hazzard-Gordon, *Jookin: The Rise of Social Dance Formations in African American Culture* (Philadelphia: Temple University Press, 1990); Stephen Calt and Gayle Wardlow, *King of the Delta Blues: The Life and Music Of Charlie Patton* (Newton, NJ: Rock Chapel Press, 1988), 19.

65. Robert Palmer, *Deep Blues: A Musical and Cultural History of the Mississippi Delta* (New York: Penguin Books, 1981), 105–6.

66. Harrison, 1988, 56–7.

67. Levine, 1977, 225–7.

68. Hazel V. Carby, "It Jus Be's Dat Way Sometime: The Sexual Politics of Women's Blues," *Radical America* 20/4 (1986), 9–22, 16; Michelle Russell, "Slave Codes and Liner Notes," in Gloria T. Hull, Patricia Bell Scott and Barbara Smith (eds.), *But Some of Us Are Brave* (Old Westbury: Feminist Press, 1982), 130; Sherley Anne Williams, "The Blues Roots of Contemporary Afro-American Poetry," in Michael S. Harper and Robert Stepto (eds.), *Chants of Saints* (Chicago: University of Illinois Press, 1979), 123–35.

69. Harrison, 1988, 118

70. Albertson, 1985, 148–9; "Poor Man's Blues" by Bessie Smith c. 1930, 1958, Empress Music Inc. (Columbia G 30450).

71. Palmer, 1981, 105–11; Charles Keil, *Urban Blues* (Chicago: University of Chicago Press, 1966), 60.

72. Barlow, 1989, 40; Sheldon Harris, *Blues Who's Who* (New York: Da Capo, 1979), 410–11. Patton is also credited with influencing Honeyboy Edwards, Tommy Johnson, Johnny Shines, Muddy Waters, and many others.

73. Palmer, 1981, 64–6.

74. Charley Patton, "Down the Dirt Road Blues," on *Charley Patton: King of the Delta Blues*, Yazoo L-1020.

75. By the mid-1920s, Jackson was becoming a blues center, in part due to the presence of the Chatmon brothers band (the Mississippi Sheiks), Tommy Johnson, Skip James, Memphis Minnie Douglass, and one of the only record company talent scouts based in the Deep South, H. C. Spiers.

76. Calt and Wardlow, 1988, 94; Eddie "Son" House, "Preachin' the Blues," *The Legendary Son House: Father of the Folk Blues*, Columbia CS 9217; Palmer, 1981, 80–81.

77. Joseph R. Washington Jr, *Black Sects and Cults* (Lanham, MD: University Press of America, 1984), 108.

78. Zora Neal Hurston, *The Sanctified Church* (Berkeley: Turtle Island, 1981), 103.

79. Ibid., 104–5.

80. Iain MacRobert, *The Black Roots and White Racism of Early Pentecostalism in the USA* (Basingstoke: Macmillan Press, 1988).

81. Lomax, 1993, 152.

82. Oliver, 1990, orig. 1960, 60.

83. McMillen, 1989, 285; Robert Hill (ed.), *Marcus Garvey and the Universal Negro Improvement Association Papers* vol.V (Berkeley: University of California Press, 1986), 282.

84. Hill, 1986, 282, 652, 745, 672.

85. Boyer, 1983, 46.

86. Ibid., 48.

87. Edward A. Berlin, *Ragtime: A Musical and Cultural History* (Berkeley: University of California Press, 1980), 33, 22, 154. A cultural critic, songwriter and one-time president of the NAACP, James Weldon Johnson described how the rapid commercial appropriation of Ragtime served as the model for the future appropriation of African American cultural productions. "The first of the so-called Ragtime songs to be published were actually Negro secular folk songs that were set down by white men, who affixed their own names as composers. In fact, before the Negro succeeded in establishing his title as creator of his secular music, the form was taken away from him and made national instead of racial."[6].

88. Barlow, 1989, 42, 287.

89. Ellison, 1989, 7.

90. Barlow, 1989, 294–9, 32–3, 300–1; Peter Silverster, *A Left Hand Like God: The Story of Boogie-Woogie* (London: Omnibus Press, 1988); Palmer 149–51. An offshoot of the blues, boogie-woogie emerged in the late nineteenth century. Originally replicating the relationship between guitar and singer, it evolved into a distinctive style of piano solo. Many of the pianist followed the Santa Fe railroad lines to barrelhouses in isolated lumber and turpentine camps in Arkansas, Mississippi, Louisiana, Texas, and Alabama. Later moving to Chicago, Kansas City, St Louis, and New York, by the early 1940s, the practitioners and the sound were popular nationally. Boogie-woogie declined in the late 1940s only to be reincarnated in the "rockin" styles of the 1950s. The signature rolling bass was incorporated into gospel music by the time it reached Chicago in the 1920s, if not earlier.

91. Lomax, 1993, 423–35, 437.

92. Barlow, 1989, 301–3; Big Bill Broonzy, "When Will I Get To Be Called a Man," *Big Bill Sings the Country Blues*, Folkways Records FA 2326.

93. Grace Lichtenstein and Laura Danker, *Musical Gumbo: The Music of New Orleans* (New York: W. W. Norton, 1993), 28; Murray, 1976; Ellison, 1989; Gary Giddins, *Riding on a Blue Note: Jazz and American Pop* (Oxford: Oxford University Press, 1981); Frank Kofsky, *Black Nationalism and the Revolution in Music* (New York: Pathfinder, 1970); Sidran, 1971; and Ellison, 1989, 24–5.

94. Ibid., 1989, 218–68.

95. Sidran, 1971, 53–6. Sidran argues that the historic purposes the blues and jazz served in the Black community were fundamentally distinct from the purpose they served in particular White communities of the era. "The 1920s, first called the Jazz Age by F. Scott Fitzgerald, was a period of affluence, escapism, and extensive cross-cultural activity … for the first time, the music of the black culture—and 'vulgar' culture in general—became part of mainstream American expression … Heightened materialism … seemed to stimulate a need for its opposite—spirituality … In times of heightened materialism, emotional honesty takes on a revolutionary aura, and appears as an overt alternative to mainstream values. Black music can, and did, exist as a non-ideological spiritual outlet."

96. Lowell K. Dyson, *Farmers' Organizations* (New York: Greenwood Press: 1986), 289–90; Taylor, 1976, 92.

97. Charley Patton, "High Water Everywhere," on *Charley Patton: King of the Delta Blues*, Yazoo L-1020; Palmer, 1981, 75; Charley Patton, "High Water Everywhere, Part Two," in Calt and Wardlow, 1988, 205.

98. Richard Wright, "Down by the Riverside," *Uncle Tom's Children* (New York: Harper and Row, 1938), 81–2.

99. Daniel, 1972, 157.

100. Lowen and Sallis, 1974, 215; Daniel, 1972, 163.
101. Daniel, 1972, 155; Lowen and Sallis, 1974, 216.
102. Daniel, 1972, 166–7, 18; Langston Hughes, "Justice," *New Masses*, 7 (August 1931), 15.


# 6  The Enclosure Movement

1. Cash and Lewis, 1986, 21–27; Thomas Ferguson, "Industrial Conflict and the Coming of the New Deal," in Steve Fraser and Gary Gerstle (eds.), *The Rise and Fall of the New Deal Social Order, 1930–1980* (Princeton: Princeton University Press, 1989), 3–31, 15. According to Ferguson, the outline of the AAA was promoted by Rockefeller advisor Beardsley Ruml and accepted by Roosevelt forces on the eve of the Democratic National Convention of 1932.
2. Daniel, 1985, 168–9.
3. See Wayne D. Rasmussen (ed.), "The Agricultural Adjustment Act of 1933," *Agriculture in the United States: A Documentary History*, vol. 111. (New York: Random House 1975), 2,245. *Memphis Press Scimitar*, 17 April 1937. Between 1927 and 1937, the United States produced 69 percent of the world's cotton crop. Yet, its market share had declined to 51 percent by 1937. Market share declined due to the US demand for payment in dollars, and the high tariffs it placed on imported goods. These practices led Britain, continental Europe, and Japan (the latter consuming one-fourth of the world's cotton crop) to establish plantations in, or buy from, countries that had to purchase their manufactured products. Thus Black sharecroppers in the US were increasingly in direct competition with the colonized, semi-colonized, or extremely exploited cotton workers of India, Egypt, Brazil, Peru, and Argentina.
4. "Annual Report of the Secretary of Agriculture," US Department of Agriculture, 1934, in Rasmussen, 1975, vol. 3, 2,256–71. Siding with states' rights arguments, the United States Supreme Court ruled the first AAA's mandatory participation requirements unconstitutional in 1936. Released from these restrictions, cotton planters and farmers produced a bumper crop in 1937, thereby refueling the overproduction crisis. Roosevelt called Congress into special session to pass the AAA of 1938 which replaced mandatory participation with cash inducements. See Cobb, 1992, 192; Daniel, 1985, 171. Daniel argues that the payments to planters in 1933 are evident in agency records while those made to the insurers of Southern plantations were masked. "Only one insurance company appeared on the schedule of owners receiving $10,000 or more, yet these companies dominated the list of multiple owners that reported 150 or more farms under AAA contracts. Connecticut General Life Insurance Company did not appear on the 1933 Washington County [Mississippi] list, but in 1934 it received $31,679. The firm had 179 farms under AAA contract in 1934 or 1935, yet it was not the largest holder of cotton farms. John Hancock Mutual Life Insurance Company for example listed 1,580 farms under cotton contracts; Metropolitan Life had 1,141, Prudential 999, Aetna 705, Travelers 736, Union Central 609, General American 602 ... In all, fifty-five multiple landowners who reported 150 or more AAA contracts owned 10,858 cotton farms. Either these companies spread their holdings evenly over many counties or the payments were reported under other names, for only one appeared on the $10,000 list."
5. Cobb, 1992, 191.
6. Sherman Woodward, Harlan Barrows, and Gilbert White, "The Lower Mississippi Valley Region: Partial and Preliminary Report," the Mississippi Valley Committee, 31 July 1934, 9–10, Box 41, National Archives. The report went on to conclude that Delta labor and social practices required immediate reform. "Stabilization of the old social order in most of the region will accomplish little toward human betterment. The pernicious tenant system should be abolished as soon as practicable through readjustment

in land utilization and ownership, meanwhile the degrading mode of life which it tends to powerfully breed and perpetuate should not be permitted to spread."

7. Donald Holley, *Uncle Sam's Farmers: The New Deal Communities in the Lower Mississippi Valley*, (Urbana: University of Illinois Press, 1975), 13, 113, 125–7, 246, 284–5.

8. Daniel, 1985, 169–70.

9. Kirby, 1987, 63.

10. Cash and Lewis, 1986, 22; Albert R. Russell, *The First 40 Years: The National Cotton Council, 1939–1979* (Memphis: National Cotton Council, 1980), 4. A participant in the activities of both the Delta Council and its spawn the National Cotton Council for over forty years, Albert Russell gives a more succinct statement as to why the organization was formed. "The Delta country like the remainder of the Cotton Belt was looking for an answer to the cotton problem. The Delta veritably lived off cotton. Also, there was concern over moves within the USDA's Farm Security Administration to agitate the labor situation in the area. Delta leaders were sitting on top of a powder keg and knew it."

11. Cash and Lewis, 1986, 18–27, 30–31. The Delta Council has always maintained a lobbying office in Washington, DC, in order to accomplish more effectively the task of imposing a unified and regional cotton policy on the federal government.

12. See *Delta Council News*, December 1938; Delta Council, *Proceedings of the Annual Meeting, 1939* (Stoneville: Delta Council, 1939), 68, my emphasis. The birth of this new bloc was heralded in a 1938 article subtitled "Delta Council Project Given Approval throughout the Nation." The Delta Council enjoys the pride of parenthood, as its brainchild, the National Cotton Council … draws the attention of the world to its program to increase the consumption of American cotton." See Cash and Lewis, 1986, 46. In a 1986 history, the Delta Council is given sole credit for creating the NCC in order to blunt market erosion caused by the introduction of synthetic fiber. "Thus, the leadership of the fledgling Delta organization began the almost impossible task of creating a national organization to represent effectively all segments of the cotton industry in its competition for markets both at home and abroad."

13. Russell, 1980, 180, 182, 5; and *Memphis Press Scimitar*, 23 May 1955, 23 February 1959. As with Johnston, the career of W. T. "High Water Bill" Wynn was a sterling example of the political, sectoral, and social integration of the hegemonic planter bloc. Born in 1890, this planter and lawyer stood at the axis of regional power: partner in the Refuge Plantation; Delta Council president; National Cotton Council president and treasurer; Mississippi state representative; president of the University of Mississippi alumni board; president of the Delta Cotton Compress, the Delta Cooperative Compress, the Southern Credit Corporation, and the Bank of Lake Village, Arkansas; vice president of the Greenville Bank and Trust Company; and a director of the Columbus and Greenville Railroad, the Greenville Chamber of Commerce, Middle South Utilities, Mississippi Power and Light, and the United Gas Company. Helping to run his operations were his wife, sister of a local compress and warehouse firm president; his son, a Yale graduate and lawyer educated at the University of Mississippi and his daughter, a Smith graduate.

14. Russell, 1980, 1–9.

15. *Memphis Press Scimitar*, 16 October 1955; Russell, 1980, 19, 10.

16. Kirby, 1987, 58. Kirby argues that "Congress was stingy with small farm programs. Many of the homestead communities were capital starved or incompetently managed or both, but their inhabitants were blamed for their failures. Between 1937 and 1947, the FSA and the FHA made farm purchase loans to only 47,104 tenants (nationally), leaving, in 1945, about 1.8 million non-owners who were never assisted. The FSA made loans (averaging $4,500) to a grand total of 46 tenants in the entire commonwealth of Virginia. At this miserly rate of support, the elimination of tenancy and the achievement of the Jeffersonian dream of an America of stable freeholders would have required about four hundred years."

17. Delta Council, *Proceedings of the Annual Meeting of the Delta Council, 1942–1943* (Stoneville, MS: Delta Council, 1943), 28. The Delta Council also extended its policy and production coordination activities by helping to form similar bodies in the Deltas of Arkansas, Louisiana, Missouri, and Tennessee. Under this new global cotton regime, the favored production complexes in the United States were the plantations of the Delta and the irrigated cotton "ranches" of California, west Texas, New Mexico, and Arizona. To reestablish and maintain US market dominance, at the behest of the NCC, the US Export-Import Bank established a $100 million line of credit to finance the purchase of 800,000 bales of US cotton by European countries after World War Two.

18. Kirby, 1987, 51–79. See Odum, 936, 482; United States, Bureau of the Census, *Fifteenth Census of the United States: 1930*, vol. III, Part 1 (Washington, DC: United States Government Printing Office, 1932); United States, Bureau of the Census, *Seventeenth Census of Population*, vol. II, Part 24 (Washington, DC: United States Government Printing Office, 1952); Sandra Vaughn, "Memphis: Heart of the Mid-South," in Robert Bullard (ed.), *In Search of the New South: The Blacks Urban Experience in the 1970s and 1980s*, (Tuscaloosa, AL: University of Alabama Press, 1989), 99–120, 101. For a detailed discussion of population loss in the Delta see Richard H. Day, "The Economics of Technological Change and the Demise of the Sharecropper," *American Economic Review*, vol. 57 no. 3 (June 1967), 442.

19. Delta Council, *A Prospectus of the Yazzo Mississippi Delta* (Stoneville, MS: Delta Council, 1944), 42–3. By the early 1940s, the South was still the cotton kingdom: there were 13 million people involved in production, 2.5 million working cotton farms and plantations, 12,000 gins, and dozens of textile mills. Cotton products permeated the national economy and daily life: lint for clothing and bedding; linters for paper and film; and seed for salad oil, shortening, margarine, paint, varnish, cattle feed, fertilizer, washing powder, cosmetics, records, oilcloth, linoleum, and flour. Francis L. Gerdes, "Mechanization of Cotton Production in the Mississippi Delta: Its Relation to Cotton Quality and Marketing Practices," 35–51, 37; J. E. Adams, "Mechanization of Cotton in the Mississippi Valley with Emphasis on Agronomic and Engineering Aspects," 52–9, 54; both in *Proceedings of the Sixth Cotton Research Congress* (Dallas: State-wide Cotton Committee of Texas, 1945). Delta cotton acreage under plow fell from 1.7 million acres in 1930 to 1.06 million by 1946. The Delta counties had 1.2 million acres in cotton that produced 1,500,000 bales per year worth over $60 million in 1939. This yield represented 65 percent of Mississippi's total crop and more than half of the nation's high-quality long staple cotton. By the late 1940s, the yields per acre tripled due to the introduction of high-yield varieties of seeds, tractors, and crop rotation, improved insect control, and the use of mineral nitrogen as fertilizer.

20. Delta Council, 1944, 27–8, 21. Cash and Lewis, 1986, 73. Its shift in industrial policy was announced by the Delta Council in 1944. "Since considerable mechanization had taken place, it became increasingly obvious that new employment would be necessary for some of the servicemen." The treatment accorded Black servicemen was quite different. Many were attacked while stationed in the state and many residents were attacked in uniform when they returned.

21. See Cobb, 1992, 190, 194. See Joseph S. Vandiver, "The Rate of Reproduction of the Rural Negro in the Yazoo Mississippi Delta," unpublished master's thesis, Louisiana State University, 1946, 94, 190. According to Vandiver, by the 1940s the extremely low fertility rates in the region began to rise because smaller and childless families were capable of leaving and were the first to be evicted. Large families provided more labor, were less able to move, and, therefore, more subject to abuse. See *California Eagle*, 9 October 1936. The partisanship of Black Republicans allowed them to deromanticize the New Deal and the AAA, and to register fully their shock at the wholesale destruction of communities. The *California Eagle* reprinted an article in 1936 entitled "Negro Share-croppers of South Suffer under New Deal: Thousands are evicted from cabins formerly

occupied as tenants." The article cited a study by Dr A. B. Cox of the Bureau of Business Research of the University of Texas: "That from 1930 to 1935, the land in farms of all colored operators in the South decreased by 2,219,482 acres which represented a decrease of 945,216 acres for colored owners; 86,362 acres for managers; 492,415 for croppers, and 659,489 acres for other tenants."

22. *California Eagle*, 4 September 1936.

23. Cobb, 1992, 154; Cash and Lewis, 1986, 44, 199. Also see Welding, 1991, 176–203, 182.

24. Lomax, 1993, 258.

25. Ibid., 21.

26. *Delta Council News*, 11 October 1940, 9 September 1940; Cash and Lewis, 1986, 48; Delta Council, *Proceedings of the Annual Meeting, 1942–43*, 6.

27. Richard Wright, "Fire and Cloud," *Uncle Tom's Children*, 1938, 177.

28. Lomax, 1993, 462–4.

29. *Delta Council News*, September 1940. Reed Dunn of the Delta Council testified that "mechanization has caused no appreciable labor displacement." During the same hearings, H. L. Mitchell of the Southern Tenant Farmers' Union observed that in the Mississippi and Arkansas Delta's mechanization was displacing thousands: two to four families per tractor. The University of North Carolina sociologist Rupert Vance expressed an opinion widely held by those advocating African American expulsion. He argued that displacement was beneficial in that migration was necessary to raise the standard of living of the overpopulated South.

30. See Twelve Southerners, *I'll Take My Stand: The South and the Agrarian Tradition* (Baton Rouge: Louisiana State University Press, 1977, orig. 1930); Donald Davidson, *Attack on Leviathan: Regionalism and Nationalism in the United States* (Chapel Hill: University of North Carolina Press, 1938). Leviathan was the biblical sea beast used as a metaphor by Thomas Hobbes to describe an ever-expanding state. Vanderbilt professor Donald Davidson used the concept of Leviathan to denounce the New Deal intellectual climate which he believed rested upon centralization, industrialism, urbanism, Marxism, Freudianism, Easternism, futurism, Darwinism, etcetera. The 1980s revival of the attack on the federal government by Reagan conservatives was accompanied by a revival of the writings of Davidson and the other Southern Agrarians. See Russel Kirk, "The Attack On Leviathan: Donald Davidson and Southern Conservatism," *The Heritage Lectures* (Washington: Heritage Foundation, 1989), 6. Kirk describes the early attacks on the Twelve Southern Agrarians and what he considers their ultimate triumph in the battle over the direction of American literature.

31. Delta Council, *Proceedings of the Annual Meeting, 1943–44*, 1944, 35. In 1944, in the form of a resolution, the council delivered an edict on social reforms and African American participation in them. "The Delta Council knows these problems [education, health and housing] to be existent and, realizing the long experience of the people of this section in dealing with the development of the Negro race, believes that a continued effort by the leadership of the South will do more for the promotion of the Negro's interest than can be accomplished through union organization or social reforms originating in other sections of the country." During the same meeting, the violently enforced spatial segregation of African Americans was described as a positive social good. "With a view to promoting and preserving peaceful and satisfactory race relation and adjustments, the laws of Mississippi ... provide for the segregation of whites and Negroes in intra-state transportation of persons both on railroad trains, on buses, and street cars in towns and cities and on the highways." See also Delta Council, *Proceedings of the Annual Meeting of the Delta Council, 1939*, 29. Delta Council, *The Yazoo-Mississippi Delta: Organized Unified Coordinated: A Story of Great Men Doing A Great Work* (Stoneville: Delta Council, 1949), 16.

32. Theodore G. Bilbo, "African Home for the Negroes," *Living Age*, June 1940, 327–35.

33. *Delta Council News*, September 1940. Far ahead of his time in terms of masking fundamental social relations and economic crisis, prophetically Secretary Wallace recommended that those displaced from agriculture look to the service sector.

34. Stetson Kennedy, *Southern Exposure*, 1946, 276. In his 1946 work Kennedy offers an accurate prophecy of what small farming would become: "many financial groups have conspired to deny long term credit to the small farmer and at the same time have gone all-out financing big business farms and processing plants. By coupling this with a political campaign against adequate government programs for small farmers, these financial interests hope to establish a monopoly over farming whereby the surviving small farmers will be denied loans by the banker unless they agree in advance to sell their crops at the combine's processing plant at whatever prices are offered."

35. Twelve Southerners, 1977, "Statement of Principles" xxxviii–xlviii; Andrew Nelson Lytle, "The Hind Tit," 295; Herman Nixon, "Whither the Southern Economy," 193; John Crowe Ransom, "Reconstructed but Unregenerate," 22–4; Robert Penn Warren, "Briar Patch," 254–64, all in Twelve Southerners, 1977).

36. Grantham, 1979, 153–84, 153–62; Kennedy, 1946, 334.

37. Odum, 1936, 483–7.

38. Southern Regional Committee of the Social Science Research Council, *Problems of the Cotton Economy: Proceedings of the Southern Social Science Research Conference* (Dallas: Arnold Foundation, 1936), v.

39. Ibid., 51–71, 63–4.

40. Ibid., 86.

41. Saxton, 1990, 4–5.

42. Walter A. Jackson, *Gunnar Myrdal and America's Conscience: Social Engineering and Racial Liberalism, 1938–1987* (Chapel Hill: University of North Carolina Press, 1990), 263–71, 269. See also Grantham, 1979, 165–80.

43. For Parks's views see Williams, 1989, 152, 161, 162. W. Lloyd Warner, "American Caste and Class," *American Journal of Sociology*, 41 (September 1936). See also Wilson, 1979; Allison Davis, "A Comparative Study of American Caste," in Edgar Thompson (ed.), *Race Relations and the Race Problem* (New York: Greenwood Press, 1968); Wilson, 1979.

44. Allison Davis, Burleigh Gardner, and Mary Gardner, *Deep South: A Social Anthropological Study of Caste and Class* (Chicago: University of Chicago Press, 1941); John Dollard, *Caste and Class in a Southern Town* (New Haven: Yale University Press, 1937); Hortense Powdermaker, *After Freedom: A Cultural Study in the Deep South* (New York: Viking Press, 1939); Williams, 1989, 159. The overriding value of the caste school is that it recognized the distinctiveness and resiliency of Southern social relations.

45. E. Franklin Frazier, *The Negro Family in Chicago* (Chicago: University of Chicago Press, 1931), 25–9.

46. E. Franklin Frazier, *The Negro Family in the United States* (Chicago: University of Chicago Press, 1966, orig. 1939), 367, 355.

47. Lemann, 1991, 344; Wilson, 1979; Rainwater, 1967.

48. W. E. B. Du Bois, *Dusk of Dawn* (New York: Schocken, 1968), 180–3; W. E. B. Du Bois "Jim Crow," *Crisis*, 17 (January 1919), 113; and "My Evolving Program for Negro Freedom," in Rayford Logan (ed.), *What the Negro Wants* (Chapel Hill: University of North Carolina Press, 1944), 65; Elliot Rudwick, *W. E. B. Du Bois: Propagandist of Negro Protest* (New York: Atheneum, 1968), 149; Green, 1973, 587–614.

49. Du Bois, 1968, 180–83, 217.

50. Ibid., 197–200; Joseph P. De Marco, "The Rationale and Foundation of Du Bois's Theory of Economic Cooperation," *Phylon* 35 (1), March 1974, 5–14, 8.

51. Green, 1973, 609.

52. Percy, 1941, 299.

53. David Cohn, *Where I was Born and Raised* (Boston: Houghton Mifflin, 1948), 7, 100–1. See *Delta Council News*, March 1946. One of many journalist's and writers engaged

crafting apologias for the plantation system and white supremacy, Cohn prepared his next book at the offices of the Delta Council.

54. Davis *et.al.*, 1941, 46–7.

55. Ibid., 226.

56. Ibid., 47.

57. Ibid., 27.

58. Davis *et al.*, 1941, 265; McMillen, 1990, 154–94, Cobb, 1982, 12; Cobb, 1984, 34. The creation of the BAWI not only raised the curtain on an era of the competitive use of gifts and gimmickry to attract firms, it also suggested a future day when state and local governments would become increasingly preoccupied with establishing and maintaining optimum conditions for attracting new firms. This phenomenon would later be referred to as a form of economic blackmail because it asked workers and communities to remain silent in the face of many types of abuse.

59. Cobb, 1984, 38, 150.

60. *Delta Council News*, "Is there a Need for Negro Education?", February 1946; Dollard, 1937, 196, 195, 203.

61. Delta Council, 1943, 13; Delta Council, *Prospectus, 1944*, 14. In promotional literature the council mentioned the presence of African American health facilities in Greenville, Greenwood, Mound Bayou, Scott, and Yazoo City. The Scott facility was primarily for residents of the massive Delta and Pine Land Company plantation while the Mound Bayou facility was built privately by the African American society the Knights and Daughters of Tabor.

62. Chalmers Archer Jr, *Growing Up Black in Rural Mississippi: Memories of a Family Heritage of a Place* (New York: Walker and Company, 1992), 105.

63. Mary Katherine Aldin and Peter Lee, "B. B. King," *Living Blues* 10–22, 11.

64. Lomax, 1993, 460–1.

65. Lomax, 1981, 119.

66. Ellison, 1989, 5; Al Young, "Toward a Robert Leroy Johnson Memorial Museum," in Pete Welding and Toby Byron (eds.), *Bluesland: Portraits of Twelve Major American Blues Masters* (New York: Dutton Books, 1991), 77. Sheldon Harris, *Blues Who's Who* (New York: Da Capo Press, 1979), 288–9.

67. Palmer, 1981, 173–8, 200–5. Also known as Sonny Boy Williamson II, Aleck "Rice" Miller was born in the Mississippi Delta town of Glendora around 1897. Robert Lockwood was born in the Arkansas Delta town of Marvel before moving to Helena. Lockwood was also known as Robert Jr because of his close personal and musical relationship with Robert Johnson. His mastery of Johnson's style and of various jazz elements, along with his status as the first electric guitarist and lead guitarist regularly heard in the Delta, greatly influenced several visionaries including McKinley Morganfield (Muddy Waters) and Riley "B. B." King. Ibid., 1981, 200–1.

68. Mike Rowe, *Chicago Breakdown* (London: Eddison Press, 1973), 32–9.

69. Langston Hughes, "Here to Yonder: Music at Year's End," *Chicago Defender*, 9 January 1943, cited in Barlow, 1989, 317; Paul and Beth Garon, *Woman with a Guitar: Memphis Minnie's Blues* (New York: Da Capo Press 1992), 13–46.

70. Barlow, 1989, 313.

71. Barlow, 1989, 310. See also Palmer, 1981, 144.

72. Keil, 1966, 54–5.

73. Murray, 1976, 151. See also Ellison, 1989, 29–34.

74. Dan McCall, *The Example of Richard Wright* (New York: Harcourt Brace Jovanovich, 1969), 79.

75. Ibid., 48–9.

76. Ibid., 194.

77. Earl Conrad, "The Blues School of Literature," *Chicago Defender, Weekly Magazine*, 22 December 1945, 11, in Ellison, 1989, 175–86; Phillis R. Klotman, "Langston Hughes, Jess B. Semple and the Blues," *Phylon* 36(1), Spring 1975, 68–77. The poetry,

essays, and other works of Langston Hughes also celebrated the folk and their music. In 1942, Hughes began writing a regular column for the *Chicago Defender* in which the daily experiences of the everyman, blues-loving, rural migrant are chronicled. As developed in the column and in five books between 1950 and 1965, Jess B. Semple emerged as a direct, honest, and humorous sage.

78. Michel Fabre, *The Unfinished Quest of Richard Wright*, 1973; see Chapter 2 for an extended discussion.

79. Margaret Walker, *Richard Wight, Daemonic Genius: A Portrait of the Man, A Critical Look at His Work* (New York: Warner Books, 1988), 65–78, 111.

80. Margaret Walker Alexander, "For My People," in University of Mississippi Press (ed.), *Margaret Walker's "For My People": A Tribute* (Jackson: University of Mississippi Press, 1992), 5.

81. Michael W. Harris, *The Rise of Gospel Blues: The Music of Thomas Andrew Dorsey in the Urban Church* (New York: Oxford University Press, 1992), 189, 198.

82. Ibid., 1992, 98–9.

83. Lomax, 1993, 46–8. According to Professor Lewis Jones of Fisk University, after the incorporation of gospel blues into mainline Baptist services, the songs were standardized and became the model for those Baptist churches that had more in common with the Holiness churches in terms of participatory services. "The preachers are taking charge. It used to be that the sisters and the deacons ran the service. They raised the songs, and kept them going, and those songs brought the mourners through. But they've lost most of that power now ... Now they not even supposed to say amen."

84. H. L. Mitchell, *Roll the Union On: A Pictorial History of the Southern Tenant Farmers' Union* (Chicago: Charles Kerr Publishing, 1987), 83, 87. Two key events were held annually on or near 15 May: the May Cotton Carnival was held in Memphis and the annual meeting of the Delta Council was held in Stoneville, Mississippi.

85. McMillen, 1990, 137.

86. Ibid., 133; Mitchell, 1987, 24.

87. McMillen, 1990, 136.

88. Kennedy, 1946, 279. According to Kennedy, the President's Commission on Farm Tenancy was faced with the following dilemma. "Shall the government aid 3,000,000 farm families to keep growing and expand production on their farms, or shall it allow them to be driven off their farms in order to supply cheap labor for 200,000 big farmers?" The panel proposed to assist both. However, the Delta-based STFU believed that such a policy masked a program of complete monopolization. "We believe that in the cotton South the small homestead visioned in many of the present proposals is an economic anachronism, foredoomed to failure. We strongly dissent from the 'small homestead philosophy' as a solution for the majority of the Southern agricultural workers. It is the more readily accepted by the present landlords because they know it to be relatively ineffective and consequently harmless from their point of view. It runs contrary to generations of experience of croppers and farm workers in the South – experience which, we believe, could be capitalized in co-operative effort under enlightened federal supervision."

89. Letter from H. L. Mitchell to Clyde Johnson, 20 April 1936, File April 20, 1936, STFU Papers, University of North Carolina. See also: Harold A. McDougall, "Land Reform and the Struggle for Black Liberation: From Reconstruction to Remote Claims," in Charles C. Geisler and Frank Popper (eds.), *Land Reform, American Style* (Totowa, New Jersey: Rowman and Allanheld, 1984), 178–80; Kelley, 1987; letter from Clyde Johnson to H. L. Mitchell, n.d.

90. Letter from Dan Franklin to H. L. Mitchell, 1 October 1936; letter from Howard Kester to Lee Hays, 3 October 1936, STFU Papers; H. L. Mitchell, 1981, 35; Richard Couto, *Ain't Gonna Let Nobody Turn Me Around: The Pursuit of Racial Justice in the Rural South* (Philadelphia: Temple University Press, 1991), 184.

91. Letter from H. L. Mitchell to Chester Bowles, 23 February 1946, box 58, STFU Papers. See also McMillen, 1990, 137.

92. Statement of H. L. Mitchell to the USDA State Wage Stabilization Board, Greenville, Mississippi, 6 March 1946, Box 58 STFU Papers.

93. STFU press release, 25 November 1946, STFU Papers. Mitchell made public the minutes of two secret meetings between the American Farm Bureau, the National Council of Farmer Cooperatives, the National Grange, and the Associated Farmers of California which revealed federal involvement in "a conspiracy on the part of large-scale industrialized farm interests to let down immigration bars and to flood the United States with cheap foreign labor ... The permanent program ... will provide for the continued recruitment and transportation of foreign nationals ... for exploitation on the nation's farms, ranches, and plantations." See also letter from H. L. Mitchell to Joseph Duncan, 11 April 1946; STFU press release, Statement of National Farmers Union, 1 October 1946.

94. McMillen, 1990, 137.

95. Cobb, 1992, 204; Lemann, 1991, 49–50.

# 7 The Green Revolution

1. Cobb, 1992, 202; Delta Council, *Proceedings of the Annual Meeting, 1951–1952*, 30. In 1952, the Delta Council announced that it "reaffirms its belief in an All Powerful, Almighty God, The Creator and Supreme Ruler of the Universe, and is unalterably opposed to communism and all of its allied organizations, fronts and sympathizers, which the Council condemn as deadly and treacherous enemies to Godliness."

2. Albert R. Russell, *The First Forty Years: The National Cotton Council, 1939–1979* (Memphis: NCC, 1980), 33–4. US Senator Robert A. Taft of Ohio noted that without "the cotton people, we wouldn't have mustered the two thirds we had to have in both Houses of Congress." Russell, 1980, 8, 37, 38, 54, 59. The NCC viewed the recovery plans for Europe, Japan, and later Korea as opportunities to expand the market for US cotton, cottonseed products, and textiles. Soon after World War Two, Undersecretary of State Will Clayton outlined a direct assistance program to end the "subversive campaigns ... in Europe." An architect of the National Cotton Council, Clayton was also president of Anderson Clayton and Company. With strong foundations in Mississippi, Texas, and California, the firm was the leading cotton merchant in the USA. Clayton's plan for the European Economic Recovery Program was first publicly unveiled by Undersecretary of State Dean Acheson at the Delta Council's annual meeting in 1947. At Clayton's behest the Secretary of State and former army chief of staff George C. Marshall came to the NCC's annual meeting in 1948 to sell the program now known as the Marshall Plan.

3. Cobb, 1992, 202. Senator Eastland later became the leader of the States' Rights Movement, chair of the US Senate Judiciary Committee in 1955, and president pro tempore of the US Senate in 1972. Frank Smith, *Congressman from Mississippi* (New York: Pantheon Books, 1964), 75; Robert Sherrill, *Gothic Politics in the Deep South* (New York: Ballantine Books, 1969), 260. Sherrill caustically noted that "the states that gave their electoral votes to Thurmond ... Alabama. Mississippi, Louisiana, and South Carolina ... are the super South, the nerve strand that has been peeled slick, stretched taut between the poles of Black and White and twanged. They are the hippies of segregation."

4. *Memphis Commercial Appeal*, 24 October 1952.

5. Neil R. McMillen, *The Citizens' Council: Organized Resistance to the Second Reconstruction, 1954–64* (Urbana: University of Illinois Press, 1971), 15–20; Cobb, 1992, 213–17. At the time of the CCA's founding, 68 percent of Sunflower County's residents were African Americans but they were only 0.03 percent of the electorate; *Time*, vol. x, no. 24, 14 June 1954. Others have traced the origins of the Citizens' Council to the formation of a home guard militia after World War Two that was organized to attack returning Black veterans. According to McMillen, only "after securing the support of the

power structure in the rural communities and county seats of the Delta did the Council come out into the open actively to seek mass support."[320]

6. McMillen, 1971, 209; Cobb, 1992, 213–17.

7. McMillen, 1971, 24, 63, 117, 58, 122–4, 332. One Delta legislator suggested that "a few killings would save a lot of bloodshed later on." In attendance at the 1956 founding of the CCA in New Orleans were US senators Eastland and Thurmond, former governors Fielding Wight of Mississippi and Herman Talmadge of Georgia, current governors John Patterson of Alabama and Lester Maddox of Georgia, US Representatives John Bell Williams of Mississippi and Mendel Rivers of South Carolina, Professor Donald Davidson of the Vanderbilt Agrarians, political leader Leander Perez of Louisiana, and future Alabama governor George C. Wallace. William J. Simmons assumed leadership of the national organization and moved its headquarters to a location besides the Governor's mansion in Jackson, Mississippi. The son of an influential Mississippi banker, Simmons was accused by the NAACP of being a Nazi sympathizer when he attended school in Paris during the late 1930s. Simmons's deputy was the great-grandson of Nathan Bedford Forrest, the Ku Klux Klan founder and ancestor of the fictional movie character Forrest Gump.

8. Ibid., 228–31, 179. McMillen noted that the "reverse freedom ride program was attacked by some white Southerners, particularly religious leaders, as an inhuman exercise." Russell was also a mentor of future president Lyndon Johnson.

9. Ibid., 284, 302. The CCA also played a significant role in the Little Rock desegregation crisis. When Central High School was about to reopen in September 1959, a director of the Little Rock Citizens' Council dynamited the school's offices. Governor Faubus pardoned this terrorist after six months in jail and continued working closely with the CCA in establishing segregated White academies.

10. Phillip S. Foner and Ronald Lewis (eds.), *Black Workers: A Documentary History from Colonial Times to the Present*, (Philadelphia: Temple University Press, 1989), 544. McMillen, 1971, 252–5, 236–7, 342. The region's press was no less alarmed. Hodding Carter III of the *Delta Democrat-Times* noted that the CCA had molded opinion against integration and "any deviation from the status quo … to a degree hard to convey to someone who does not live in Mississippi." The publisher of the *Atlanta Constitution*, Ralph McGill, concluded that "Mississippi is ruled by a network of Citizens' Councils. Their political control and their coercive economic power in economic affairs is so vast as to be difficult to comprehend." National reporters were similarly awestruck. James Desmond of the *New York Daily News* warned that "the specter of thought control that the White Citizens' Council brought to Mississippi has become a monstrous cloud blotting out nearly all dissent." A writer for the *New York Post* observed that Mississippi and much of the South was "held captive by a brigade of bigots whose total domination of the populace can be matched only by the Communist Party of Russia."

11. McMillen, 1971, 338, 341, 264–5. The use of state funds by the CCA was attacked in forums throughout the Mississippi; many white residents began to object to the extension of the police state that ruled Black communities to their own. Business organizations objected to the CCA's campaign to get local school boards to forfeit federal funds rather than desegregate. This significant break in the White supremacy alliance operated to weaken the power of the plantation regime in intra-state politics. See Erle Johnston, *Mississippi's Defiant Years: 1953–1973* (Forest, MS: Lake Harbor Publishers, 1990).

12. Smith, 1964, 80. See also *Delta Council News*, January 1948, February 1948, and March 1963; Cash and Lewis, 1986, 42. In 1963, the entire Mid-South area had 8.7 million people and produced 36 percent of the nation's cotton crop, then valued at $800 million.

13. Cleaver, 1975, 61–4, 164.

14. Kirby, 1987, 53, 63–75. Kirby described many manifestations of the neo-plantation: "By the 1960s one might have found row-crop plantations with cotton, soybeans, corn, and peanuts in parts of Georgia and Alabama; with cotton, soybeans, and rice in the deltas of Mississippi, Louisiana, and Arkansas … But many neo-plantations had no row crops at all. Some

specialized in pecans, some were huge dairies, many were enormous livestock plantations with feed grain fields. Most were woodland plantations. Often as large as ten thousand acres, they had small cash-crop fields (such as peanuts) and some pasturage, but most acreage was forested. The woodland neo-planter cut timber for income, but the estate's major function was as hunting preserve."

15. Cobb, 1992, 205.

16. Delta Council, *Science for Better Farming* (Stoneville, MS: Delta Council, 1948); Kirby, 1987, 338. National Cotton Council, *Report of the Proceedings of the Beltwide Cotton Mechanization Conference* (Memphis: NCC, 1947), 46; Russell, 1980, 40–1. The home of the Delta Experiment Station and the Delta Council, the research complex at Stoneville was considered to be among the top three cotton research centers in the world. The other two facilities were located in Pernambuco, Brazil and New Delhi, India. John Rust, "The Origin and Development of the Cotton Picker," 1952, John D. Rust Papers 1933–53, Box 1, Mississippi Valley Collection, Memphis State University; *Memphis Press Scimitar*, 3 May 1949. The first patent for a cotton harvest machine in the United States was granted to two Memphis men in 1850, and most of the 800 patents issued prior to 1930 were for hand-operated devices. In 1928, John Rust filed the first patent for a two-row, tractor-propelled wire spindle cotton picking machine. The farm workers' cooperative at New Llano, Louisiana supported Rust in 1930 in the hope that his machine would empower the cooperative movement of impoverished Southerners. In 1933, the machine made history at the Delta Experiment Station in Stoneville when it picked five bales in a day. Many writers feared that the Rust Cotton Picker would lead to massive labor displacement and community destruction. Excited planters provided Rust with testing land near Clarksdale. Powered by a Ford V-8 truck motor, the machine was picking thirteen bales a day by 1938. The machine eventually mass-produced by Allis Chalmers was based on the Rust patents. Rust used a portion of his wealth to set up an educational foundation which established the predominantly African American Rust College near Oxford, Mississippi, and the University of Mississippi. This was done in part to lessen the devastation wrought by the introduction of his machine.

17. National Cotton Council, *Report of the Proceedings of the Second Annual Beltwide Cotton Mechanization Conference*, (Memphis: National Cotton Council, 1948), 38–40.

18. Russell, 1980; *Delta Council News*, June 1962, April 1965. According to Russell, "Chemical weed control had to be achieved if hand labor input was to be reduced. It was a simple as that." *Memphis Press Scimitar*, 26 January 1956, 29 December 1954. An example of the Fordist integration of planter, bank, oil and manufacturing capital, Woolfolk was the owner of the Woolfolk Farms in Tunica County and served as the Delta Council's president in 1947. He also served as the chairman of the board of both the Mid South Oil and the Farm Equipment Company, and as a director of both the Memphis Chamber of Commerce and the Union Planters Bank of Memphis.

19. *Delta Council News*, July 1959, August 1963, May 1965; Delta Council, *Science for Better Farming*.

20. Cash and Lewis, 1986, 54–6, 70; *Delta Council News*, January 1965; March 1965. Samuel Yette, *The Choice* (New York: Berkeley Medallion Books, 1972), 116–55. In addition to being major cotton states, by the early 1970s the rice cup states represented one of the most powerful blocs in the United States Congress. During the early 1960s the Rice Council focused on both reducing the influence of competing producers and penetrating markets in Europe, South Africa, South Korea, and South Vietnam. Yette argues that this agenda fueled the Vietnam War.

21. *Delta Council News*, May 1965; Cobb, 1992, 207.

22. National Cotton Council, *Report of the Proceedings of the Beltwide Cotton Mechanization Conference*, 1947, 34. See also Grubbs, 1971; Frances Fox Piven and Richard A. Cloward, *Regulating the Poor: The Functions of Public Welfare* (New York: Vintage Books, 1971), 211. According to Piven and Cloward, forced migration combined with

restrictive welfare policies reduced the political threat posed by the "the very gradual breakdown of voting barriers."

23. National Cotton Council, 1947, 22.

24. Ibid., 47. McCaffrey argued that the "first thing we usually hear is that the mechanization of cotton production is going to displace large numbers of people—mainly Negro people—who are now living and producing cotton in the south. This is often discussed as an immediate and impending calamity. We don't think it is, for a number of reasons ... In the first place, many people who discuss the topic do so as if mechanization ... were something just about to begin ... It began in 1924 and has already been carried a long way without calamity having struck ... In 20 years from 1920 to 1940 the number of non-white farms decreased 24.3 percent. Yet there is no social upheaval ... I strongly suspect that many of those who mourn loudest over for the lost job opportunities in cotton growing will be the same individuals who formerly mourned loudest over what they considered the distressful conditions of the Negro cotton laborer."

25. *Delta Council News*, June 1948; Russell, 1980, 45; Cash and Lewis, 1986, 50.

26. Kirby, 1987, 338; Cobb, 1992, 211; Day, 1967, 442.

27. *Delta Council News*, April 1963, April 1965. The Delta Council developed its own version of Manifest Destiny: "According to a statement attributed to the German Chancellor, Prince Otto von Bismark, the warlike tendencies so pronounced in the Prussians, were the result of the abundance of certain minerals coming from the soil ... And by somewhat the same token and related processes of reasoning, we are convinced that the remarkable number, extent, and degree of able leadership to be found in the Delta – birthplace and home of the Delta Council – cannot be related to chance ... [The council is] widely known and highly esteemed here, yonder and even to the uttermost parts of the earth."[1965]

28. *Memphis Press Scimitar*, 13 May 1958. *Delta Council News*, December 1964. Rachel Carson's critique of pesticide use in *Silent Spring* was treated as an attack upon pesticides, machines, African American expulsion, and other pillars of American civilization. Congressman Whitten argued that "the 8 percent of our people on farms feed the 92 percent to provide for us the highest standard of living ever known by man. All this is made possible because intricate and expensive machinery, and chemicals, including chemical pesticides, have been substituted for labor. These enable us to spend 60 percent of our government income on defense. It enables the American consumer to have the finest foods ... We have more than one-half of the world's automobiles and almost two-thirds of the world's paved highways." He concluded that "unless public opinion on chemical pesticides was brought into balance the whole economy could be pulled down."

29. McMillen, 1971, 37, 161–71. For an examination of the social construction of a multi-ethnic white identity after World War Two, see Michael Omi and Howard Winant, *Racial Formation in the United States: From the 1960s to the 1980s* (New York: Routledge and Kegan Paul, 1986). See also Carlton Putnam, *Race and Reason, a Yankee View* (Washington: Public Affairs Press, 1961).

30. McMillen, 1971, 172–88, 246–7.

31. Ibid., 19–20; *Delta Council News*, May 1964, May 1965. Senator John Stennis made the following comments on civil rights legislation. "This bill which I repeat is unconstitutional, was offered by the administration for the politically inspired motive of protecting the alleged civil rights of an organized minority. It would take the basic human and individual rights away from the majority and transfer them to a favored group in the form of special privileges. The truth is that the bill would destroy more civil rights than it could possibly protect and preserve ... I hope those responsible [for cross burnings] are not doing so in the belief that they are helping to defeat the bill."

32. Hodding Carter, *First Person Rural* (Garden City, New York: Doubleday, 1963), 218–25, 242; James Silver, *Mississippi: The Closed Society* (New York: Harcourt, Brace and World, Inc., 1966), xii–xvi; James Silver, *Running Scared: Silver in Mississippi* (Jackson: University of Mississippi Press, 1984), 206–30.

33. Lomax, 1993, 413; Pete Welding, 1991, "Muddy Waters," in Pete Welding and Toby Byron (eds.), *Bluesland: Portraits of Twelve Major American Blues Masters* (New York: Dutton, 1991), 136. See also Palmer, 1981, 101,104.

34. Welding, 1991, 148, 151–2; Michael Bane, *White Boy Singin' the Blues: The Black Roots of White Rock* (New York: Da Capo Press, 1982), 94; Harris, 1979, 390–1.

35. Dixon, 1989, 25, 21.

36. Ibid., 25–30.

37. Ibid., 101.

38. Willie Dixon, "I'm Ready," Hoochie Coochie Music 1954, 1982. See also Dixon, 1989, 23, 6, 41; Dixon, "The Seventh Son," Hoochie Music, 1955, 1983; Dixon, "I'm Your Hoochie Coochie Man," Hoochie Coochie Music, 1957, 1985.

39. Rowe, 1973, 134–9; Elmore James: *The Sky is Crying: The History of Elmore James*, Rhino R2 71190, liner notes by Robert Palmer. Palmer, 1981, 242–45; Dixon, 1990, 99.

40. Ferris, 1978, 29.

41. Stanley Booth, *Rhythm Oil: A Journey through the Music of the American South* (New York: Vintage Books, 1991), 97–9. For a detailed account of King's life, see Charles Sawyer, *B. B. King: The Authorized Biography* (London: Quartet Books 1982), 52–8; Margaret McKee and Fred Chisenhall, *Beale Black and Blue: Life and Music on Black America's Main Street* (Baton Rouge: Louisiana State University Press, 1981), 24–8.

42. Palmer, 1981, 205–7.

43. Mckee and Chisenhall, 1981, 248; Booth, 1991, 101; Giddins, 1981, 41–2.

44. Pete Welding, "B. B. King," in Welding and Byron (eds.), 1991, 179, 176–203. Palmer, 1981, 249–50; Harris, 1979, 293, 223. There are several other key events during the period: the emergence of Duke Records in Houston; the influence of Delta native Eddie "Guitar Slim" Jones and his "back country" gospel-style blues on Ray Charles, Jimmy Hendrix, and soul music; the education of Hendrix during tours with the Flames, B. B. King, Sam Cooke, Little Richard, Ike and Tina Turner, etcetera; and the rise of Clarksdale-born Sam Cooke in first gospel and then the rhythm and blues.

45. Palmer, 1981, 217.

46. Afterwards, Turner issued a number of records and served as a talent scout for several record companies before moving his band to St Louis. Turner, his wife the powerful vocalist Tina Turner, and the band would later become internationally renowned as the Ike and Tina Turner Revue.

47. Palmer, 1981, 224–5. According to Palmer, "a massive shift was taking place in the listening habits of young white Americans, and the shift was felt very early around Memphis … Country and western music was for countrified, lower-class kids. The teenagers who considered themselves sophisticates danced and drank and necked to a soundtrack of 'nigger music.'" Bane, 1982, 121, 125; Harris, 1979, 440–1. In fact, significant blues elements were already entering country music by the late 1920s. Instrumental in this process was Hank Williams of Louisiana and an earlier performer, Mississippian Jimmie Rodgers, known both as "America's Blue Yodeler" and as "the Singing Brakeman."

48. Bane, 1982, 125; Booth, 1991, 49, 202. An eventual friend, Calvin Newborn, recalled that one of Presley's most important talents was the ability quickly to adopt new styles. "One night, probably in late 1952, a teenaged white boy came in there, didn't have on any shoes, barefooted, and asked me if he could play my guitar … In fact, he was the only white somebody in the club … He sang [Big Mama Thornton's] "You Ain't Nothin' But a Hound Dog" and shook his hair—see, at the time I had my hair processed, and I'd shake it down in my face—he tore the house up."

49. Booth, 1991, 47. See also John S. Otto and Augustus M. Burns, "Black and White Cultural Interaction in the Early Twentieth Century South: Race and Hillbilly Music," *Phylon* 35(4), 1974, 407–17.

50. Giddins, 1981, 30, 32–4. "Minstrelsy is said to have died at the hands of vaudeville, but it was a death in form, not spirit … the most influential of modern minstrels

have been Al Jolson, Bing Crosby, and Elvis Presley ... In *Feel Like Going Home*, Jerry Lee Lewis tells Peter Guralnick, 'I loved Al Jolson, I still got all of his records. Even back when I was a kid I listened to him all the time.' Elvis's first record for the Sun label, 'I Love You Because,' was a thinly disguised rewrite of a melody that Jolson never recorded but that rebellious Asa Yoelson sings repeatedly during the first half hour of [the film] *The Jolson Story*, released in 1946."

51. Nelson George, *The Death of Rhythm and Blues* (New York: Pantheon Books, 1988), 52–4, 66–7. African American disc jockey Eddie O'Jay described Freed's approach to popular Black culture. "He didn't copy off any one black deejay, because there weren't any around that I knew of that he could sound like, but anything that was black he would say. Any slogans, he would say them."

52. Ibid., 1981, 261–2. "Rice" Miller (Sonny Boy Williamson II) and Memphis Slim toured Western Europe in 1963 as part of the American folk blues festival and stayed to perform in the new beat clubs. Al Young, "Toward a Robert Leroy Johnson Memorial Museum," in Welding and Byron (eds.), 1991, 73, 78. The "cargo" included a vast array of personal possessions that now serve as the foundation of an international blues trade.

53. Palmer, 1981, 237.

54. Lomax, 1993, 406.

55. James Baldwin, "The Uses of the Blues," in *The Best from Playboy*, (6), 97 in Harrison, 1988, 64–5. See also Singal, 1982, 166; David Leeming, *James Baldwin: A Biography* (New York: Alfred A. Knopf, 1994) 117, 228, 231, 324.

56. Palmer, 1981, 256.

57. Barlow, 1989, 47.

58. Myrlie Evers, *For Us, the Living* (Garden City, New York: Doubleday, 1967), 113–14. This statement was made after the 1954 *Brown v. Board of Education* judgement by Reverend H. H. Humes before ninety "conservative" Black leaders called together by the Governor, Hugh White, and the Speaker of the Mississippi House of Representatives, Walter Sillers. Instead of obtaining support for continued segregation, they were shocked by the group's refusal to go along one more time.

59. McMillen, 1971, 279, 215. For a detailed examination of the entire period see John Dittmer, *Local People: The Struggle for Civil Rights in Mississippi* (Urbana: University of Illinois Press, 1995). Although African American registration quadrupled in the South between the abolition of the white primary in 1944 and the *Brown* decision in 1954, Mississippi was the only state where the number of registrations was declining. US Commission on Civil Rights, *Voting in Mississippi* (Washington, DC: US Government Printing Office, 1965).

60. Cobb, 1992, 221; Stephen J. Whitfield, *A Death in the Delta: The Story of Emmett Till* (Baltimore: Johns Hopkins University Press, 1988).

61. Evers, 1967, 78–9, 84–5, 91–2; Maryanne Vollers, *Ghosts of Mississippi: The Murder of Medgar Evers, the Trials of Byron De La Beckwith and the Haunting of the New South* (Boston: Little, Brown and Company, 1995), 43.

62. Payne, 1995, 31–2, 59, 61, 136–7, 155; Dittmer, 1994, 32–3, 39, 44, 77–8.

63. Civil Rights Documentation and Research Project and Ronald Bailey, *Remembering Medgar Evers ... for a New Generation* (Oxford, MS: Heritage Publications, 1988), 6–17. Evers, 1967. Payne, 1995, 58; Anne Moody, *Coming of Age in Mississippi* (New York: Laurel Books, 1968), 372–4. SNNC activist Anne Moody recounted the how a teenager was beaten to death in 1964, in front of several hundred teenage activists and two Federal Bureau of Investigation agents, for merely mentioning his desire for freedom to two police officers. "'FBI's.' she said. 'They were sitting over there and they saw it all just as we did, and them bastards had the nerve to ask what happened.'"

64. Fannie Lou Hamer, cited in Chana Kai Lee, "A Passionate Pursuit of Justice: The Life and Leadership of Fannie Lou Hamer," PhD thesis, University of California Los Angeles, 1993, 321–2.

65. Payne, 1995, 103.

66. Hanes Walton Jr, *Black Political Parties: An Historical and Political Analysis* (New York: Free Press, 1972), 90.

67. Letter from Walter Sillers to B. F. Smith, 5 June 1961, Walter Sillers Papers Box 2, 1.

68. Letter to Walter Sillers from Edwin Hooker, 8 June 1961, Walter Sillers Papers Box 1. Hooker also expressed concern "about the apparent apathetic and moderate attitude I fear is being engendered in the minds of some of the younger leadership in our area."

69. Walton, 1972, 88, 89. see also Payne, 1995, 107–11.

70. Ibid., 90–1.

71. John Dunson, *Freedom in the Air: Song Movements of the Sixties* (Westport, CT: Greenwood Press, 1965), 61–71, 36. Originally composed of SNCC workers who participated in the "singing army" from Albany, Georgia, beginning in 1962, various groups of the Freedom Singers used the powerful African American song traditions (spirituals, gospels, jazz, and the blues) to mobilize local Blacks while expanding the national constituency for social justice. The members of the original Freedom Singers were Chuck Neblett, Rutha Harris, Bertha Gober, Bernice Johnson Reagon, and Cordell Reagon. The songs developed by the "singing army" of Albany, the sit-in movement in Nashville, and the freedom riders imprisoned in the Delta's Parchman Penitentiary formed the backbone of the repertoire of the Freedom Singers. Another powerful cultural extension was the Free Southern Theater founded by John O'Neal, Doris Derby, and Gilbert Moses in 1963. Charles McLaurin, "Voice of Calm," *Sojourner*, December 1982, Fannie Lou Hamer Papers, Tougaloo College.

72. Walton, 1972, 91–2.

73. Danny Collum, "Stepping Out Into Freedom: The Life of Fannie Lou Hamer," *Sojourners*, December 1982, n.p, Fannie Lou Hamer Papers, Tougaloo College.

74. Edwin King, "A Prophet from the Delta," *Sojourners*, December 1982; Lee, 1993, 270.

75. Nicolaus Mills, *Like a Holy Crusade: Mississippi 1964—The Turning of the Civil Rights Movement in America* (Chicago: Ivan R. Dee, 1992), 163.

76. Collum, 1982, n.p.

77. Cash and Lewis, 1986, 53; *Memphis Press Scimitar*, press release 1962, May 22, 1963. For example, as a planter, Delta Council vice president, and the director of several regional oil, chemical, and implement firms, Aven Whittingon represented the regional bloc's interest on President Kennedy's Cotton Advisory Committee from 1961 until he became the Delta Council's president in 1962. In 1963 he referred to Kennedy's policies as a threat to "the existence of the cotton industry as a major enterprise." *Delta Council News*, January 1964, July 1965. The cotton Green Revolutions generally had five stages. First, the federal government used the PL 480 program to provide countries with reduced-price and free wheat. This created a demand for US grain while undercutting and eliminating local grain production. Third, with financial assistance from the Agency for International Development, the fallow grain fields were planted with cotton. Fourth, the US Export–Import bank provided loans to purchase cotton machinery and chemicals from US manufacturers. Finally, the crop was exported to US textile firms for manufacture, thereby, undercutting the demand for, and the price of, domestic cotton.

# 8  Poor People and the Freedom Blues

1. Martin Luther King Jr, *Where Do We Go From Here: Chaos or Community* (Boston: Beacon Press, 1967), 32–9.

2. Cobb, 1992, 217, 266–7; Calvin Trillin, "US Journal: Resurrection City," *New Yorker*, 15 June 1968; Yette, 1971.

3. Cobb, 1992, 258, 261; *Delta Council News*, n.d., 1966. In an attempt to halt

a COFO voter registration effort, the Leflore County Board of Supervisors voted to suspend commodity distribution in 1962. Under the 1964 food stamp guidelines, planter permission was often required to qualify and planter loans, at interest rates as high as 25 percent, were used to purchase stamps that were then used to purchase food at stores engaged in ruthless price gouging. In response to efforts to reduce the cost of food stamps, Rep. Whitten argued that such a policy would "destroy character more than you might improve nutrition."

4. L. C. Dorsey, *Freedom Came to Mississippi*, n.d., 25–6, Fannie Lou Hamer Papers, Box 1, Folder 14, Tougaloo College; Cobb, 1992, 268–71; Memo to National Council of Churches Staff from Benjamin Payton, 22 March 1966, Delta Ministry Papers Box 1, Folder 2; *Memphis Press Scimitar*, 1 February 1966.

5. Ralph David Abernathy, *And the Walls Came Tumbling Down: An Autobiography* (New York: Harper Perennial, 1990), 412–15.

6. Senator Joseph S. Clark and others to the President, 27 April 1967 in United States Congress, 90th, 1st. Sess. Senate Committee on Labor and Public Welfare, *Poverty: Hunger and Federal Food Programs* (Committee Print), 29–30 in Wayne Rasmussen (ed.), *Agriculture in the United States: A Documentary History*, vols III and IV, (New York: Random House, 1975), 3,097–8.

7. "Contributions to the Delta Ministry Through Interchurch Aid by May 17, 1967," Delta Ministry Papers, Box 1, File 19.

8. David L. Lewis, *King: A Biography* (Urbana: University of Illinois Press, 1978), 359–71; Carl Rowan, "Martin Luther King's Tragic Decision," *Reader's Digest* (September 1967), 37–42; C. Van Woodward, "What Happened to the Civil Rights Movement?" *Harpers*, January 1967.

9. Martin Luther King Jr, "Showdown for Non-violence," *Look* (16 April 1968), 23; Lewis, 1978, 375; Rev. Ralph David Abernathy, address before the National Press Club, 14 June 1968, Southern Christian Leadership Conference Papers Box 177, File 2.

10. Lewis, 1978, 354.

11. Ibid., 373; on Malcolm X see Kay Mills, *This Little Light of Mine: The Life of Fannie Lou Hammer*, (New York: Dutton, 1992), 139–44.

12. Lewis, 1978, 380, 377. King told the striking sanitation workers, "Along with wages and other securities, you're struggling for the right to organize. This is the way to gain power. Don't go back to work until all your demands are met. There is a need to unite beyond class lines. Negro haves must join hands with the Negro have nots."

13. Memo from Hosea Williams to Staff of the SCLC, 8 March 1968, SCLC Papers Box 179, File 4; Lewis, 1978, 385–7.

14. Telegram from Hosea Williams to the 15th Annual Conference on Marketing and Public Relations in the Negro Market, n.d., SCLC Papers Box 177, File 22.

15. Poor People's Campaign 1968 – Memphis Movement to Washington, SCLC Box 177: File 8.

16. Speech of Ralph Abernathy, 19 June 1968, SCLC Papers, Box 77, File 2. A list of a few of the organizations in attendance makes it clear that King and the Mississippi organizers intended the march to be an event designed to shape an entire generation: Alianza de Pueblos Libres, American Negro Labor Council, Americans for Democratic Action, American Friends Service Committee, Appalachian Volunteers Inc., Association of American Indian Affairs, the Center for Manpower Studies, Citizens' Crusade against Poverty, Crusade for Justice, Community Advisors on Equal Employment, Congress of Racial Equality, Council of Jewish Federations and Welfare Funds, Federal Alliance of New Mexico, Federation of Southern Cooperatives, Institute for Policy Studies, Law Center for Constitutional Rights, League of United Latin Americans Councils, Lumbee Citizens Council, Mexican American Legal Defense Fund, Mexican American Political Association, Mexican American Youth Organization, National Indian Youth Council, National Association for Community Development, National Catholic Conference for Interracial Justice, the National Mobilization Committee, National Welfare Rights

Organization, the Peace and Freedom Party, the Ponca Indians of Oklahoma, Pride Inc., Social Service Employees Union, the Southern Student Organizing Committee, Spanish Community Action of the Archdiocese of New York, Students for a Democratic Society, United Church of Christ, United Farm Workers, United Planning Organization, the Urban Coalition, and the Women's Strike for Peace. Several dozen congresspersons and staffers and numerous local state and federal agencies participated. Among the entertainers present were Marlon Brando, Bill Cosby, Robert Culp, Ossie Davis, Tony Franciosa, France Nguyen, and Sidney Poitier.

17. Poor People's Campaign Answer to the Response of the Department of the Interior, 14 June 1968, SCLC Papers 177, File 28; Answer of Poor People's Campaign to the Department of Labor, June 13, 1968, SCLC Papers Box 177, File 30; Abernathy Address, June 19, 1968, SCLC Papers Box 177.

18. *Soul Force*, 19 June 1968, SCLC Papers Box 180, File 3. The daily program of events at the Poor People's University in Resurrection City included lectures by famed scholars and activists: Howard Zinn, professor at Boston University; Charles Hamilton, professor at Roosevelt University and co-author of *Black Power* with Stokely Carmichael (a.k.a. Kwame Toure); editor I. F. Stone; Alex Haley, co-author of *The Autobiography of Malcolm X*, and later to write *Roots*; economist Robert Theobold; and antiwar activist David Dellinger. The chancellor of the university was SNCC leader and current Georgia congressman John Lewis. The courses covered the theory and practice of nonviolence, the economics of poverty, racism as a system, capitalism as a system, restructuring the capitalist system, education, the redevelopment of livable spaces, foreign policy and domestic affairs, Afro-American history, the press, and the Kerner Commission report. The university was modeled on the "Freedom Schools" of Mississippi and Alabama that were designed "to bring a note of relevancy to the standard educational system [and to] bring about ameliorative action by educating and equipping the participants to deal effectively with the established structures of power. Additionally, two-day seminars for the nonpoor were held with speakers such as future Washington, DC, mayor Marion Berry and Democratic Socialists of America founder Michael Harrington.

19. Letter from Orville Freeman, Secretary of Agriculture, to Rev. Ralph D. Abernathy, 23 May 1968, Rasmussen, 1975, 3,099; Orville L. Freeman, "Review of L. R. Browns's Seeds of Change," in United States Agency for International Development, *War on Hunger*, 4 (5), 1970, 6–8, 7. By 1970, Freeman had concluded that "… displacement of large numbers of rural people by mechanization is more responsible for the big city problems which resulted in the burning of cities in the United States in the 1960s than any other factor. For my part, I have no hesitation in confirming this analysis I have visited cotton plantations in the American Southland where in one year labor supported by the plantations dropped from one hundred families to five families." Poor People's Campaign Answers to Department of Agriculture, 12 June 1968, SCLC Papers Box 177: File 26.

20. "Poor Pledge to Step Up Pace of Demonstration," n.d., SCLC Papers Box 179, File 15.

21. Gordon White, n.d., SCLC Papers Box 179, File 31. In response to congressional threats to close down the city, one teenager produced his own flyer. "If Congress attempts to put us out instead of solve the problem we represent there will be a revolution. Wait just one minute! We came here to present Congress and king whitey Johnson with the problem of poverty, racism and genocide, we are not leaving until some changes are made"; Rev. Ralph D. Abernathy, Address to Southern Christian Leadership Conference Solidarity Day March in Support of the Poor People's Campaign, Washington, DC, 19 June 1968, SCLC Papers Box 177: File 2.

22. "Abernathy Speaks," 27 June 1968, SCLC Papers Box: 177: File 2; UPI Bulletin, 17 July 1968, SCLC Papers Box 179, File 28.

23. *Delta Council News*, May 1965, May 1966, May 1967, May 1968, May 1969; Tony Dunbar, *Our Land Too* (New York: Vintage Books, 1971), 73.

24. Cobb, 1992, 272; Johnston, 1990, 325; Cash and Lewis, 1986, 163, 79; *Delta Council News*, September 1968, March 1974.

25. *Delta Council News*, August 1968, April 1974, January 1978; Cash and Lewis, 58–9.

26. *Delta Council News*, March 1966, January 1972; Winston I. Smart, "The Mississippi Christmas Tree," *Choices* (Spring 1990), 28–9; Thomas M. Burton, "Many Farmers Harvest Government Subsidies in Violation of the Law," *Wall Street Journal*, 8 May 1990; Letter of Rep. Silvio Conte (D. MA) to members of the US House of Representatives, "Fair Play in Farm Policy," 13 June 1990. In a 1990 letter requesting co-sponsors for a bipartisan bill to cap farm subsidies, Rep. Conte complained that "cotton is still king under current unenlightened policy. Cotton producers take advantage of the standard deficiency payments of up to $50,000, but also can pick up to $250,000 from Uncle Sam's pocket by repaying government loans at rates below the government loan rate." *Delta Council News*, May 1976. There was powerful bipartisan opposition to such reforms. In his 1976 address to the Delta Council, then chairman of the US House Agricultural Committee and future Speaker of the House of Representatives, Thomas Foley (D. WA), stated, "I simply cannot join with those who would dismantle all program protection and leave the producer to the unpredictable and sometimes capricious forces that do not in any way represent free market forces." Cobb, 1992, 260; Nicholas Von Hoffman, *Mississippi Notebooks* (New York, 1964), 79–81.

27. Lauren Soth, "The Paradox of Hunger and Agricultural Abundance," Farm Policy Committee, National Council of Churches, 1 August 1969, Delta Ministry Papers, Box 1, Folio 23. Press release of US Sen John J. Williams entered into the *Congressional Record*, 23 May 1968, Southern Christian Leadership Conference (SCLC) Papers, Box 177, Folio 42; *Memphis Commercial Appeal*, 17 May 1972.

28. *Delta Council News*, October 1975, May 1974, September 1975, February 1975.

29. Stephen D. Shaffer and Dale Krane, "The Origins and Evolution of a Traditionalistic Society," in Dale Krane and Stephen D. Shaffer (eds.), *Mississippi Government and Politics*, (Lincoln: University of Nebraska Press, 1992), 40, 251; Cobb, 1992, 239–40.

30. J. Earl Williams, *Plantation Politics: The Southern Economic Heritage* (Houston: J. Earl Williams, 1972), 46–56.

31. McMillen, 1971, 354–5.

32. Robert Whitaker, "Southern Nationalism," *Southern Partisan*, Fall 1982, 9–11. In this tract, it was argued that "a liberal Democratic Southerner finds it easier to talk to a conservative Republican Southerner, especially about the interests of his nation, than do politicians from other regions … .The United States was never intended to be a substitute for the cultural identity of its parts. To ask "Americanism" to replace cultural and regional identity is to ask the Constitution to do what it was manifestly not intended to do … For the superpatriot, in short, we have the wrong Constitution." *Southern Libertarian Messenger*, 1982; "God Wills It," *The New Teaching*, mimeo, 1982.

33. John Dittmer, *Local People: The Struggle for Civil Rights in Mississippi* (Urbana: University of Illinois Press, 1995), 363–88; Johnston, 1990, 284–301; Cash and Lewis, 1986, 76, 163; *Delta Council News*, August 1968; Kay Mills, *This Little Light of Mine: The Life of Fannie Lou Hamer*, 1993, 208–9; Confidential Report to the Executive Committee, Commission on the Delta Ministry, 1 October 1965, 5, Delta Ministry Papers Box 2, Folio 3.

34. Johnston, 1990, 91, 303, 338–55. Sovereignty Commission director Johnston traced the origins of the alliance between the commission and moderate Blacks to the conflict over the hiring practices of the CDGM. NAACP field secretary Charles Evers complained that the more moderate NAACP members were not being hired. Evers wanted to extend his power by securing Head Start jobs for NAACP members. According to Johnston, Evers wanted to "get rid of CDGM and thereby weaken the strong base of New York sponsored civil rights workers in the state … The oddest part of it all was that I was trying to figure out a way to get rid of Evers … even though I knew he was

doing the same thing as I – furnishing material against CDGM to OEO in Washington."[291] Johnston goes on to state that Evers and Reverend Kenneth Dean, executive director of the Mississippi Council on Human Relations, regularly provided the commission with sensitive information that was then used to defeat the initiatives of numerous organizations.

35. Dale Krane, "Mississippi and the Federal Union: An 'Approach–Avoidance' Dilemma," in Krane and Shaffer, 1992; Sherill, 1968, 210.

36. Samuel Yette, *The Choice* (New York: Berkeley Medallion Books, 1971), 127–8; Mills, 1993, 122–31, 218–19; *Memphis Press Scimitar*, 23 May 1955, 23 February 1959.

37. Mills, 1993, 229–30, 234, 222–6; Nicholas Van Hoffman "Liberal Dixie Editor Sounds Of", *Chicago Daily News*, 28 July 1965; Delta Ministry Papers Box 1, File 34; Memo to the Commission on the Delta Ministry from Arthur C. Thomas, director, 17 August 1965, Delta Ministry Papers Box 1, File 34. The National Council of Churches provided the Delta Ministry with funds to assist in labor organizing, day care, political education, job training, development projects, educational programs, hunger relief and economic development. One of the board members was Hodding Carter III, who published the *Delta-Democrat Times* in Greenville with his father. Although, he rarely attended Delta Ministry meetings, he tried to deliver a death blow to the organization by red-baiting, black-baiting, and then white-baiting the staff in a 1965 interview: "If those suburban church ladies who pour their thousands of dollars in the ministry could hear Larry talk to farm workers they would drop their teeth ... The truth is that these professionals do not want reform. They want revolutionary change ... We can expect a vigorous trick and persistent effort by the Delta Ministry professionals to block, destroy or otherwise negate any and all attempts at progress which do not include them ... They're now down to Negroes who can be bought out the cheapest. One of their main leaders used to be a fink for the State Sovereignty Commission." Carter's interview sent shock waves through the Delta Ministry and through the National Council of Churches. In response the director of the Delta Ministry, Arthur Thomas, argued that the "significance of the Negro protest movement is that the Negro community is discovering it can speak for itself and achieve its objectives through the democratic process. The Negro community does not need to rely on the beneficence of the white community. This is difficult and painful for white moderates, such as Mr Carter, who have attempted to 'take care' of the Negro community. What is interpreted by some, including Mr Carter, as 'revolutionary change' is in fact the democratizing of an oligarchic paternalistic political and social system."

38. For net migration totals for 1960–1970 see Mississippi Research and Development Center, *Social and Economic Profile of Black Mississippians* (Jackson: Mississippi Research and Development Center, May 1977), 13; US Bureau of the Census, *Census of Population, 1970: General Social and Economic Characteristics, Mississippi*, PC910–C26, (Washington, DC: US Government Printing Office, 1972); Cobb, 1992, 274; Michael J. Piore, "Negro Workers in the Mississippi Delta: Problems of Displacement and Adjustment," *Industrial Relations Research Association Series* (Madison: Industrial Relations Association, 1968), 366–8.

39. Mississippi Research and Development Center, 1977, 10, 25; Vaughn, 1989, 111–19; McBane, 1982, 52, 54–5.

40. Cash and Lewis, 1986, 105; *Memphis Commercial Appeal*, 16 February 1982, 1 March 1983. Cash and Lewis described the heavy federal investment in Stoneville during this period: "The Delta States Research Center for the USDA's Agricultural Research Service was created to assist Arkansas, Louisiana, and Mississippi planters and farmers. Legislation for funding the complex was initiated by Jamie Whitten, chairman of the US House Appropriations Committee ... With the completion of this building, the USDA Center is composed of six major research units housed in three facilities. The Southern Field Crop Insect Management Laboratory, the Cotton Physiology and Genetics Research Unit, and the Southern Weed Science Laboratory are located in the USDA facilities. The Field Crops Mechanization Research Unit and the Soybean Production Research

Unit are housed in the facilities of the Delta Branch Experiment Station. The US Cotton Ginning Laboratory facilities are located on the adjacent campus grounds." A recent addition to the Stoneville complex was the National Warmwater Aquaculture Research Center.

41. Cash and Lewis, 1986, 54–5, 109–16; *Delta Council News*, March 1974, July 1977, February 1978, February 1979, February 1980.

42. Cash and Lewis, 1986, 71, 72; *Delta Council News*, November 1977; "Statement of Marion Berry," in Lower Mississippi Delta Development Commission (LMDDC), *Agricultural Hearing, December 14, 1989*, (Memphis: LMDDC, 1990).

43. Rainbow Whole Foods Co-op, *Alternative Foods and Sustainable Agriculture: Health and Wealth*, (Memphis: LMDDC, March 1990), 3.

44. *Delta Council News*, January 1966; Joel Myers, "'Slip Sliding Away': Pollution Along the River," *New Orleans* (November 1989), 58–65; David Maraniss and Michael Weisskopf, "Jobs and Illness in the Petrochemical Corridor," *Washington Post*, 22 December 1987; Michael H. Brown, "The National Swill," *Science Digest* (June 1986), 56–85.

45. Cobb, 1982, 144–48, 143, 116; Harry S. Ashmore, *An Epitaph for Dixie* (New York: W. W. Norton and Company, 1958), 118.

46. *Delta Council News*, November 1966; April 1967, December 1967, July 1968, February 1969, May 1976; Cash and Lewis, 1986, 73–81. Many of the plant relocations were financed using county-approved BAWI bonds. Major employers were primarily low-value-added operations: paper mills, furniture makers, agricultural chemicals, warehouses, food processors, and tire, glass, carpet, textile, wall board, and plastics manufacturers.

47. Robert Bullard (ed.), *In Search of the New South: The Black Urban Experience in the 1970s and 1980s* (Tuscaloosa, AL: University of Alabama Press, 1989). Stuart Rosenfeld, Edward Bergman and Sarah Rubin, *After the Factories: Changing Employment Patterns in the South* (Research Triangle Park, NC: Southern Growth Policies Board, 1985); James L. Walker, *Economic Development and Black Employment in the Non-metropolitan South* (Austin, TX: Center for the Study of Human Resources, University of Texas, 1977).

48. Charles Campbell, Kathie S. Gilbert, and Paul W. Grimes, "Human Capital Characteristics of the Labor Force," and Phyllis Gray-Ray, "Race Relations in the Delta," in Arthur Cosby, Mitchell Brackin, T. David Mason, and Eunice McCulloch (eds.), *A Social and Economic Portrait of the Mississippi Delta* (Mississippi, MS: Mississippi State University, 1992), 143–8, 29–42; Ken Lawrence and Anne Braden, "The Long Struggle," *Southern Exposure*, XI (6), 85–9.

49. *Delta Council News*, May 1965, May 1968.

50. Ronald S. Borod and W. J. Michael Cody, "The Southern Consciousness: A Source for National Renewal," in H. Brandt Ayers (ed.), *You Can't Eat Magnolias* (New York: McGraw-Hill Books, 1972), 55, 372–9; "Lamar Society Builds a New South," *Anniston Star*, April 22, 1970. Lamar Society members included a number of leading figures in the South: Arkansas's former Republican governor, Winthrop Rockefeller; Mississippi Delta editor and Carter White House official Hodding Carter III; Memphis native, board member of the American Civil Liberties Union, and Lamar Society president W. J. Michael Cody; the African American vice mayor of Atlanta, Maynard Jackson; the Professor of Economics at the University of Texas, Mississippi-born Ray Marshall; the Delta-born editor of *Harpers Magazine*, Willie Morris; former Congressman from the Mississippi Delta, Frank Smith; former governor of North Carolina Terry Sanford; a past director of the Mississippi Economic Council; a Mississippi-born professor of economics at Duke University; the Mississippi-born former president of the University of Alabama; the Chancellor of Vanderbilt University; the president of Southwestern University in Memphis; and a mass of Southern-born Ivy League and Oxford graduates.

51. *Delta Council News*, January 1967; Linda Lear, "Bombshell in Beltsville: The USDA and the Challenge of 'Silent Spring,'" *Agricultural History*, vol. 66, no. 2, Spring

1992, 151–70. *Delta Council News*, December 1966, November 1977. According to Whitten, "Unless our urban population understands agricultural problems ... future generations could go hungry ... The consumer must be convinced that the good health of agriculture is vital to their own health and welfare."[1966] Ten years later an editorial in the *Delta Council News* mourned: "EPA regulations have already cost the loss of important pesticides and threaten the future use of these important materials. What would happen if the use of pesticides were banned? ... The price of farm products would go up at least 50 percent and US consumers would have to spend 25 percent more for food."

52. Lemann, 1991, 344.

53. *Memphis Commercial Appeal*, 15 and 16 June, 1983.

54. Paul Greenberg, *Entirely Personal* (Oxford, MS: University of Mississippi Press, 1992), 133.

55. *The Land Where the Blues Began* (New York: Pantheon Books, 1993) Alan Lomax, 274–5; Michael Haralambos, *Soul Music: The Birth of a Sound in Black America* (New York: Da Capo Press, 1974), 151.

56. Lomax, 1993, 384–5. The veteran performer was eighty-year-old Sam Chatmon, a member of the large and famous Chatmon family which has performed in the Mississippi from the 1850s until the present.

57. Bane, 1982, 234; Paul Garon, *Blues and the Poetic Spirit* ( New York: Da Capo, 1975), 60–1.

58. Ibid., 105, 109.

59. Jim O'Neal, "Interview with Junior Wells," *Living Blues*, 119 (February 1995), 384–5. Wells explained what occurred to him after the State Department-sponsored tour. "I was on tour for the American Folk Blues festival Show [in 1966] ... and I'm in East Berlin playin' and I got over 12,000 people and all they want to hear is 'The Hoodoo Man Blues,' and they want to hear 'Vietcong Blues' ... And they doin' a recordin' on me. So after the tour and I got off the plane in New York and the FBI ... And they say, 'Are you Junior Wells?' I say, 'I don't know. I could be.' 'Yeah you're Junior, I got your picture here. I know who you are.' And he say, 'I got a letter here for you.' I said, 'Well, give it here.' He said, 'No, I have to read this for you.' And it stated that I was never supposed to do 'Vietcong Blues' any more unless I had a release from the State Department. And I haven't got a release from the State Department as of today, and I never sung it anymore."

60. O'Neal, 1995, 384–5.

61. Lomax, 1993, 420–1.

62. Peter Guralnick, *Sweet Soul Music: Rhythm and Blues and the Dream of Southern Freedom* (New York: Harper and Row, 1986).

63. Jim O'Neal, "Modern Chicago Blues: Delta Retentions," in Robert Sacre (ed.), *The Voice of the Delta: Charley Patton and the Mississippi Blues Traditions, Influence and Comparisons: An International Symposium* (Lie` ge: Presses Universitaires de Lie` ge, 1987), 301–8; David Evans, "Mississippi Blues Today and Its Future," in Robert Sacre (ed.), *The Voice of the Delta: Charley Patton and the Mississippi Blues Traditions, Influences and Comparisons: An International Symposium* (Lie` ge: Presses Universitaires de Lie` ge, 1987), 323–7.

64. Robert Pattison, *The Triumph of Vulgarity: Rock Music in the Mirror of Romanticism* (New York: Oxford University Press, 1987), 30–53.

65. Last Poets, "True Blues," *The Legend: The Best of the Last Poets*, Esperanto-ESP8503.

66. Kay Mills, "Interview with Unita Blackwell: MacArthur Genius Award Caps Creative Political Life," *Los Angeles Times*, 2 August 1992. *Jackson Advocate*, 17 January 1970, 6 June 1970, 18 July 1970, 12 December 1970.

67. Judith R. Porter, "What Works and What Doesn't? Perceptions of Economic Development Among Delta Leaders," in Cosby *et al.*, 1992, 305; *Jackson Advocate*, 24 January 1970, 18 July 1970.

68. Frank R. Parker, *Black Votes Count: Political Empowerment in Mississippi after*

*1965* (Chapel Hill: University of North Carolina Press, 1990), 199–203. Cobb, 1992, 247–8; Margaret Edds, *Free at Last* (New York: Adler and Adler, 1987), 165; Theodore J. Davis Jr, "Blacks' Political Representation in Rural Mississippi," in Laurence W. Moreland, Robert P. Steed, and Todd A. Baker, *Blacks in Southern Politics* (New York: Praeger, 1987), 149–60, 150–1. Many of the African American candidates were defeated through the use of at-large elections and second primary runoffs. High rates of out-migration, poverty, and unemployment, threats, and purges of voting rolls also operated to limit the number of victories. These practices were complemented by outright electoral fraud. During the late 1960s, Black voters at one Sunflower County station had to run a hostile gauntlet composed of the sheriff and other Whites intent on intimidating them. By the early 1980s, persistent accusations emerged concerning the election-day practice of demanding mandatory overtime by plantations and firms such Baldwin Piano, Vlassic Pickle and local catfish processors.

69. Letter from Shirley M. Watson to Ms Althea T. L. Simmons, National Office of the NAACP, 13 March 1978. Folio 1107, Box 63, Aaron Henry Papers, Tougaloo College.

70. *Jackson Advocate*, 18 July 1970; *Federation of Southern Cooperatives News*, v.18 (2), July 1990; A. V. Krebs, *The Corporate Reapers: The Book of Agribusiness* (Washington, DC: Essential Books, 1992), 257. Lewis Myers, "Southern Land Project, Southern Mississippi Delta Region," in Robert S. Browne, *Only Six Million Acres: The Decline of Black Owned Land in the Rural South* (New York: Black Economic Research Center, June 1973), Appendix D. Also see United States Civil Rights Commission, *The Decline of Black Farming in America* (Washington, DC: US Government Printing Office, 1982).

71. McDougall, 1984, 183–5.

72. Mills, 1993, 230–1.

73. Fannie Lou Hamer, "If the Name of the Game is Survive, Survive," 27 September 1971, Ruleville, MS, Fannie Lou Hamer Collection, Tougaloo College, Box 1, Folder 1.

74. Ibid., Hamer, 1971, 3.

75. Hamer, "Is it Too Late?" 1971, Fannie Lou Hamer Collection, Box 1, Folder 1.

76. *Delta Democrat-Times*, 16 March 1977; Julian Bond, "Tribute to Fannie Lou Hamer," *Seven Days*, 1/6 (25 April 1977), 37.

## 9  The Crises of Tchula, Tunica, and Delta Pride

1. Malcolm Shepherd, *Minority Business Development in the Lower Mississippi Delta* (Memphis: LMDDC, 1990); *Southern Exposure*, 11/1 (January–February 1983), 10; *Jackson Advocate*, 12 December 1986. After Carthan was freed, the Mississippi office of the US Farmers Home Administration (FmHA) attempted foreclose on his 500-acre farm. The state administrator leading the attack was formerly the supervisor of the Holmes County office. He had been appointed to his new position by the state director of the FmHA, Don Barrett, a member of a major planter family in Holmes County that also held several prominent positions in county law enforcement.

2. Gerald Gabris, "Dynamics of Mississippi Local Government," in Dale Krane and Stephen Shaffer (eds.), *Mississippi Government and Politics*, 1992, 223–48. In a section of his chapter entitled "My Beat is My Kingdom," Gabris explains that under "the beat system supervisors have total control over personnel decisions, contracting, and equipment purchases within their beats and do not usually have to answer to the board as a whole ... Supervisors frequently buy road machinery and equipment for their own beats, even if it duplicates equipment in the neighboring beat." In "The Struggle over Public Policy in a Traditionalistic State," in the same volume, Dale Krane explained the constitutional basis for planter bloc persistence. "The renewal of planter political strength at the end of post-Civil War Reconstruction led to a state constitution that created a

weak governorship and a fragmented state government. Rurality has contributed to the persistence of the justice court judges as a system of informal neighborhood law enforcement. It has also formed the power base for the previously unassailable county supervisors."[210]. *Jackson Advocate*, 10 October 1986; *Memphis Commercial Appeal*, 8 November 1990. In 58 percent African American Tallahatchie County, Johnny Thomas became the first Black on the board of supervisors in 1990 after the Election Commission had to throw out 253 votes for his White opponent. Several precinct officials had failed to record the names of everyone voting and this allowed the ballot boxes to be stuffed.

3. *Jackson Advocate*, 4 April 1985, 1 January 1985, 7 March 1991. Newman was able to maintain his power through seniority, by redistricting out Black voters, and by forming alliances with Black community leaders in his district.

4. *Jackson Advocate*, 24 January 1985, 4 December 1986, 25 December 1986.

5. Charles P. Henry, *Culture and African American Politics* (Bloomington: Indiana University Press, 1990), 88; *Jackson Advocate*, 22 March 1984.

6. Mike Alexander, "A New Culture Struggling to be Born," *Jackson Advocate*, 3 May 1984. At the time, second primaries, or run-off elections, existed in only eleven states: nine Southern states, New York, and New Jersey. The second primary enables a majority-White electorate to be split among several White candidates in the first primary only to be united behind the top White candidate in the second ballot. The requirement that a candidate must have a majority, combined with the refusal of many Whites to vote for Black candidates, usually ensures that a White candidate will be elected and that Blacks will remain excluded from many elected positions.

7. *Jackson Advocate*, 31 May 1984, 2 August 1984, 31 October 1985, 12 December 1985. In his refusal to back the second run of Clark, Tisdale accused him of being responsible for the low Black turnout in 1982, only 24 percent. "Many Blacks were turned off by Clark's funny dealings with some of the better known white racists in the state, particularly Lexington attorney Pat Barrett Sr and legislative leader C. B. 'Buddy' Newman. At the height of the integration crisis, Barrett, as a Holmes County law enforcement officer, arrested and tried voter registration activist Hartman Turnbull after klansmen set Turnbull's house afire; Turnbull was charged with arson. Barrett was allegedly the mastermind behind the scheme which sent former Tchula Mayor Eddie Carthan and Pickens, Mississippi businessman Benjamin Hoover to prison." [May] Right before the 1984 election, Clark's Black campaign manager, Cal Fraley, resigned. He attributed the 1982 loss to the takeover of the campaign by labor leaders and by Democrats who wanted Black votes for the re-election of US Senator John Steniss who had endorsed Clark for that purpose. "When the same thing happened this year—Labor and the Democrats directed their activity toward electing William Winter [US Senator] and Walter Mondale [president]—I could not tolerate it ... oddly enough when labor leaders talk of turning out the vote in Mississippi, they are normally only referring to the Black vote. They seldom, if ever, canvas the white community." [August]

8. *Jackson Advocate*, 13 November 1985. See also issues of 6 November 1985, 19 December 1985; *Essence*, October 1992. Although Espy easily won re-election in 1990, *Essence* reported that African American Republican challenger Dorothy Benford claimed that he had turned his back on Blacks: "His staff is 92 percent white and 73 percent out-of-state. We may be poor, but we're not brain dead." [*Essence*, October 1992].

9. *Jackson Advocate*, 27 September 1984, 10 September 1992; *Daily Helmsman*, Memphis State University, 6 November 1990; *Commonwealth*, 1991. In September 1992, in the same city where three civil right workers were murdered in the early 1960s, eighteen-year-old Andre Jones was found hanging in his jail cell. The Philadelphia, Mississippi, sheriff claimed that it was a simple case of suicide. Jones was the son of Jackson NAACP president Esther Jones-Quinn and the stepson of Nation of Islam minister Charles X. Quinn. *Jackson Advocate*, 11 July 1991, 30 January 1988. One inmate wrote: "the people who run this prison are as uncivilized as the inmates they are supposed to be rehabilitating ... Inmates are still being beaten and sometimes killed for refusing

to work. This article may have an adverse effect on me but I do pray that you publish it …" [30 January]. Manning Marable, "The Paradox of Reform," *Southern Exposure*, 12/1 (February 1984), 20.

10. *Jackson Advocate*, 31 October 1985.

11. *Jackson Advocate*, 25 July 1985.

12. *Jackson Advocate*, 21 February 1985. John Saunders, "Demography in the Delta," in Cosby *et al., A Social and Economic Portrait of the Mississippi Delta*, 1992, 47.

13. *Jackson Advocate*, 25 April 1985.

14. *Jackson Advocate*, 14 March 1985, 18 July 1985, 15 August 1985.

15. *Jackson Advocate*, 12 December 1985, 3 January 1985, 25 October 1984.

16. *Jackson Advocate*, 31 January 1985. A study by the Mississippi State Board of Health found that the state had the highest infant mortality rate in the nation in 1982, 15.4 deaths per thousand compared to a national average of 11.2; the White rate was 11.9 while the Black rate was 21.7. The disparities between White and Black infant death rates in the Delta counties are even more alarming: Sunflower, 11.7 and 23.6; Yazoo, 12.2 and 28.7; Leflore, 19.6 and 31.4; Tunica, 16.2 and 31.6; Coahoma, 11.5 and 31.8; Quitman, 0 and 31.9; Humphreys, 17 and 34.7; and Issaquena, 0 and 41.7. *Memphis Commercial Appeal*, 29 September 1990; *Jackson Clarion-Ledger*, 9 February 1992.

17. *Jackson Advocate*, 24 October 1985: *Memphis Commercial Appeal*, 23 November 1990. According to Harvard study participant and Jackson-based pediatrician Dr Aaron Shirley, the media is ignoring the problem: "if babies were starving, and children were falling in the streets from starvation, the issue would get more coverage … but isn't the death of a child from the secondary cause of chronic malnutrition, just as final as the death of a child from starvation in Africa." [*Jackson advocate*, 24 October 1985] "Troubled Waters," *Newsweek*, 16 April 1990, 73; *Memphis Commercial Appeal*, 27 November 1990.

18. Robert Bullard, *Dumping in Dixie: Race, Class, and Environmental Quality* (Boulder, CO: Westview, 1990); *Jackson Advocate*, 19 December 1985.

19. Krane, 1992, 217; *Memphis Commercial Appeal*, 24 September 1990; *Jackson Advocate*, 14 November 1985.

20. *Jackson Advocate*, 21 November 1985, 16 January 1986, 23 January 1986.

21. *Memphis Commercial Appeal*, 25 September 1990, 21 October 1990.

22. *Jackson Advocate*, 6 October 1986, *Memphis Commercial Appeal*, 26 September 1990.

23. *Memphis Commercial Appeal*, 25 September 1990, 21 November 1990.

24. *Memphis Commercial Appeal*, 13 October 1990, 21 October 1990.

25. *Jackson Advocate*, 18 December 1990; *Jackson Clarion-Ledger*, 14 July 1991.

26. *Memphis Commercial Appeal*, 10 July 1991, 8 October 1990, 4 September 1990.

27. *Memphis Commercial Appeal*, 4 September 1990, 31 October 1990.

28. Stuart Rosenfeld and Edward Bergmen, *Making Connections: After the Factories Revisited* (Research Triangle Park, NC: Southern Growth Policies Board, 1989). MDC, Inc., *Shadows in the Sunbelt: Developing the Rural South in an Era of Economic Consequences* (Chapel Hill: MDC, 1986). The epilogue of this report states that rural and inner-city decay are devastating state fiscal resources. It then proceeds to present a romanticized discussion of the South's higher values squarely situated in Nashville Agrarian tradition. "Much has been written and said in recent years concerning America's reverence for tradition and family. In the South, these ideals are rural. Even those of us a generation or two removed from the farm trace our love of the environment, our concern for thrift, our feelings for our fellow man, our awe of nature, and our sense of place to routines of rural community life and our connections to the land. States in the South must tend to our roots, or in the end risk our values." [16]

29. *Memphis Commercial Appeal*, 10 March 1988. For example, in March 1988, the Economic Development Council of the Memphis Area Chamber of Commerce outlined a development agenda for the more than 100 surrounding counties. *Memphis*

*Commerical Appeal*, 11 March 1989. In 1989, the Mississippi legislature formed a task-force on the agricultural economy in order to unite all of the state's public and private, economic and farming organizations around a single agenda. The Speaker of the House, Tim Ford, stated that the taskforce (which was dominated by the Delta planation bloc) would focus on alternative crops, on marketing, and on establishing textiles mills and soybean processing plants. According to Rep. Steve Holland of Plantersville, change was long overdue. "We pick cotton, we're still King Cotton, and we ship it somewhere else to be woven into textile ... Here it is 1989 and we're yet to have a (modern) cotton processing plant in the state of Mississippi." *Memphis Commercial Appeal*, 30 September 1990; *Jackson Clarion-Ledger*, 20 July 1991. The regional economic downturn also spurred competing utilities to establish industrial stabilization programs. Led by former Mississippi governor William Winter, and partially funded by Mississippi Power and Light (MP&L), the Mid-South Foundation launched several community and industrial development initiatives in Arkansas, Louisiana, and Mississippi beginning in 1990. The Tennessee Valley Authority also became more active in regional affairs.

30. Arthur Cosby, Mitchell Brackin, T. David Mason, and Eunice McCulloch (eds.), *A Social and Economic Portrait of the Mississippi Delta* (Mississippi State, MS: Mississippi State University, 1992), iii, v.

31. *Memphis Commercial Appeal*, 12 May 1988, 14 May 1988.

32. *Memphis Commercial Appeal*, 2 November 1990; *Biographical Directory of the United States Congress, 1774–1999* (Washington, DC: US Government Printing Office, 1989), 1735; Clay Hawthorn, "Down and Out in the Delta," *Nation*, 9 July 1990, 51. A Yale law school graduate, Bill Clinton was elected governor of Arkansas in 1978 and was elected to four additional terms before becoming president in 1992. Clinton was noted for pushing through a controversial educational reform package that included teacher testing. As chair of the National Governors' Association, he helped to craft a welfare policy acceptable to the states and the Reagan administration, namely, the Welfare Reform Act of 1988. In 1989, he chaired President Bush's Governors' Summit on Education. [*Memphis Commercial Appeal*, 2 November 1990] Raymond Mabus Jr graduated from the University of Mississippi and Harvard Law School. He worked on the staff of Governor William Winter between 1980 and 1984 before being elected governor in 1987. Charles Elson (Buddy) Roemer III was born in 1943 and graduated from Harvard in 1967. He became a businessman, farmer, and banker before serving as a congressional representative for four terms. He served one term as the governor of Louisiana from 1988 to 1992.

33. *Arkansas Democrat*, 19 June 1988.

34. *Washington Post*, 17 April 1988.

35. *White River Journal*, Des Arc, Arkansas, 16 March 1990.

36. *Memphis Commercial Appeal*, 21 May 1989, 10 June 1988.

37. *Memphis Commercial Appeal*, 25 October 1988.

38. *Memphis Commercial Appeal*, 3 July 1988.

39. *Memphis Commercial Appeal*, 24 September 1988.

40. *Memphis Commercial Appeal*, 21 May 1989, 2 November 1988; *Biographical Directory of the United States Congress, 1774–1989*, 1989, 1,277, 1024–5; *Memphis Commerical Appeal*, May 1989. Ed Jones represented the Tennessee Delta plantation bloc in Congress between 1969 and 1989. Before entering Congress, Jones was Tennessee's Commissioner of Agriculture and chairman of the United States Agriculture Stabilization and Conservation Service's State Committee for Tennessee. William Webster (Webb) Franklin was born in Greenwood, Mississippi, in 1941. He received his law degree from Mississippi University in 1966 and served as both an assistant district attorney, 1972–78, and as a circuit judge, 1978–82. In 1982, he was elected to Congress as a Republican from Mississippi's second congressional district. Although a commissioner, Franklin attacked the LMDDC from its inception. "Frankly, I don't like the commission way of doing business. I believe Congress is there to do what they are asking

us to do. Fifteen or 20 committees already have the mandate to do what we're doing ..." [May]

41. *Memphis Commercial Appeal*, 11 January 1989, 22 January 1989, 24 January 1989.

42. *Memphis Commercial Appeal*, 30 January 1989, 4 March 1989. Many critics charged that major cities were gerrymandered out of the original LMDDC boundaries. Although the metropolitan areas containing large African American populations were eventually included in the boundaries of the LMDDC, one journalist found that regional leaders were determined that they "will not directly benefit from programs devised by the Commission."

43. *Memphis Commercial Appeal*, 11 February 1990, 12 February 1989, 19 February 1989, 21 February 1989.

44. *Memphis Commercial Appeal*, 1 October 1990. Memphis remains an influential international cotton trading market, the headquarters for the National Cotton Council, and the center of cotton production for the Delta states and for western Tennessee. Consequently, many of the LMDDC's fellow tenants in the Agricenter were key elements within the neo-plantation regime: the USDA's Agricultural Stabilization and Conservation Service, Cotton Extension Office, Farmers Home Administration (FmHA), and Soil Conservation Service; the Pest Control and Plant Certification program of the Tennessee Department of Agriculture; the bio-technology firm Calgene Inc.; farm equipment manufacturer JI Case (successor to International Harvester); Mid-south Farm Equipment; and Southern Aqua-Tech. Larry Lee, "Long Road Lies Ahead for the Delta Commission," *Memphis Commercial Appeal*, 15 March 1989, 14 August 1989, 29 January 1990, 21 May 1989.

45. Lower Mississippi Delta Development Commission, "Agriculture Conference," 14 January 1989 (Memphis: LMDDC, 1990).

46. LMDDC, "Mississippi Public Hearing," 28 November 1989. Clinton-era Arkansas industrial development activities were attacked by African American organizations several times during the late 1980s for deliberate industrial redlining. When it was demanded that the Industrial Development Commission open its files so that documentation could be gathered, the legislature voted to seal the record well into the twenty-first century.

47. LMDDC, "Louisiana Public Hearing," 24 January 1990.

48. *Daily Town Talk*, Alexandria, LA, 24 January 1990; *Economist*, 23 September 1989; *Portageville Missourian*, 4 January 1990.

49. LMDDC, "Agricultural Conference," 14 January 1989, testimony of Tony Parks.

50. LMDDC, "Agricultural Hearing," 14 December 1989 (Memphis: LMDDC, 1990).

51. *Memphis Commercial Appeal*, 4 September 1989, 7 September 1989. According to the latter, although he attended the hearing, Arkansas Rep. Ben McGee (D. Marion) noted that the Blacks at the hearing "aren't really the people who need help, these are basically middle class blacks like myself." One of the leaders of the boycott, Marianna lawyer Bruce Lewellen, stated that the denial of participation in the LMDDC and at all levels was the problem in the region and not just employment. In referring to the boycott which began soon after the all-White panel was appointed, he observed: "They said if they couldn't get our participation, we'll make some new leaders. But that's not going to work ... black people want to see more than just a job. We want to see ownership."

52. LMMDC, "Arkansas Public Hearing," 5 September 1989 (Memphis: LMDDC, 1990).

53. Ibid.

54. LMDDC, "Louisiana Public Hearing," 23 January 1990 (Memphis: LMDDC, 1990).

55. Carson City, Nevada, *Appeal*, 19 May 1990; LMMDC, "Mississippi Public Hearing," 28 November 1989.

56. Ibid.

57. LMDDC, "Louisiana Public Hearing," 24 January 1990 (Memphis: LMDDC, 1990).

58. Ibid.

59. Ibid.

60. Ibid.

61. *Memphis Commercial Appeal*, 6 October 1989.

62. *Memphis Commercial Appeal*, 30 October 1989, 26 August 1990. The assertion of bias against the Delta was part of a much larger regional conflict over federal funding formulas and allocations between the Northeast-Midwest Institute, representing states with a declining industrial and population base, and the seventeen-state Sunbelt Caucus, representing some of the fastest-growing states.

63. *Memphis Commercial Appeal*, 10 May 1990, 10 September 1990.

64. *Memphis Commercial Appeal*, 9 May 1990; LMDDC, *The Delta Initiatives: Realizing the Dream ... Fulfilling the Potential*, 14 May 1990 (Memphis: LMDDC, 1990), 4, 45.

65. *Pine Bluff Commercial*, 11 March 1990; *Little Rock Democrat*, 12 March 1990; *Memphis Commercial Appeal*, 27 July 1990, 26 August 1990, 27 July 1990, 2 November 1990.

66. *Memphis Commercial Appeal*, 1 May 1990, 27 July 1990, 25 September 1990; Paul Greenberg, "Delta Parasites Hang On," *Memphis Commercial Appeal*, October 1990.

67. Paul Greenberg, *Memphis Commercial Appeal*, 14 May 1990, 30 September 1990.

68. *Memphis Commercial Appeal*, 30 September 1990; LMDDC, "Agricultural Hearing," 14 December 1989, testimony of W. A. Percy, (Memphis: LMDDC, 1990).

## 10 Writing the Regional Future

1. Reid Jones, John Thornell, and Gene Hamon, "Educational Development in the Delta," in Arthur Cosby, Mitchell Brackin, T. David Mason, and Eunice McCulloch (eds.), *A Social and Economic Portrait of the Mississippi Delta* (Mississippi State, MS: Social Science Research Center, Mississippi State University, 1992), 90–108, 91. See also Ronald K. House, *The Role of Higher Education in Improving the Economic Climate of the Lower Mississippi Delta Region* (Memphis: LMDDC, 1990).

2. Ibid., 1992, 96, 92, 99.

3. Larry Hailey, "Capacity of the School Systems," in Cosby *et al.* (eds.), 1992, 109–24, 109; LMDDC, *The Delta Initiatives: Realizing The Dream ... Fulfilling the Potential* (Memphis: LMDDC, 1990), 37.

4. Hailey, 1992, 117; Martin Wiseman, "Delta Economy: Local Government Capacity," in Cosby *et al.,* 1992, 214–38, 214.

5. Frank L. Farmer, *Life Chances of Delta Residents in the Lower Mississippi Delta: A Comparison of the Delta Mortality Profile with a National Profile* (Memphis: LMDDC, 1990), 28; Meals for Million/Freedom from Hunger Foundation, *Mississippi Applied Nutrition Program: Innovations in Rural Community Self-Help to Improve Nutrition-Related Health* (Davis, CA: Meals for Millions, April 1987), Appendix F.

6. Farmer, 1990; M. Jocelyn Elders and Jennifer Hui, "Adolescent Health Issues and Policy Implications," in Linda Southward and Charles Washington (eds.), *Strengthening the Family: Policy Imperatives for the Future* (Memphis: LMDDC, 1990), 67–71. Elders later became Solicitor General in the Clinton administration. After repeated attacks by conservative critics for her advocacy of an open discussion of health issues, Clinton asked her to resign.

7. "Panelists' Reactions to Frank Farmer's 'Community Poverty and Community

Health,' in Southward and Washington (eds.), 86–90; LMDDC, *The Delta Initiatives*, 1990, 22.

8. Jaquelyn W. McCray, *Housing Problems and Solutions in the Lower Mississippi Delta Region* (Memphis: LMDDC, 1990), 5.

9. Ibid, 6–8, 20.

10. LMDDC, *Forum on Rural Housing Needs in the Lower Mississippi Delta* (Memphis: LMDDC, 1990), n.p.

11. LMDDC, *The Delta Initiatives*, 1990, 48–55. A major problem with using the Community Reinvestment Act to encourage local corporate responsibility is that rural financial institutions are not required to reveal their community lending practices.

12. LMDCC, *Forum on Rural Housing Needs*, 1990.

13. Frank Farmer, "Community Poverty and Community Health," in Southward and Washington, 1990, 14–35, 28; "Panelists' Reactions," in Southward and Washington, 1990, 80, 101, 105.

14. "Panelists' Reactions," 91–2.

15. R. J. Felix, "Community Health and Community Participation," in Southward and Washington, 1990, 52–66, 58.

16. Farmer, "Community Poverty and Community Health."

17. F. Andrew Deseran and Joachim Singelmann, *Socioeconomic Change in the Labor Markets of the Lower Mississippi Delta, 1975–1986* (Memphis: LMDDC, February 1990).

18. Ibid., 12, A-2, 21–23.

19. Ibid., 1990, 37.

20. Ibid., 1990, 46.

21. T. David Mason, "The Poverty Hurdle as an Impediment to Development in the Mississippi Delta," in Cosby *et al.*, 1992, 279–296, 290–1.

22. Edward Fryar and Wayne P. Miller, *Expanding Export Industry Employment in the Lower Mississippi Delta* (Memphis: LMDDC, 1990), B-3.

23. Ibid., 1.

24. Ibid., 6–7, A-1, A-2, 16, 20. The portfolio method assumes that there is no, and that there could not be, any fundamental debate over the existing complex, and that there could be none. There is no critical examination of the likely portfolio managers or their "proven track record" of creating social, environmental, and economic disasters for the African American communities. Again, new agendas and forms of societal organization are peripheralized by the ordinary operation of this model.

25. Booker T. Washington Foundation, *A Market Study to Define the Prospective Business and Economic Development Benefits Generated by Section 1207, Public Law 99–661* (Memphis: LMDDC, 1990), 23.

26. LMDDC, *Conference on Preserving and Promoting Our Heritage: Final Report and Resource Book* (Memphis: LMDDC, 1990), 23.

27. Ibid., 21.

28. LMDDC, *Louisiana Tourism and Transportation Hearing* (Memphis: LMDDC, 1990), 32, 35–6.

29. LMDDC, *The Delta Initiatives*, 1990, 148–9.

30. Michael Smith, *Behind the Glitter: The Impact of Tourism on Rural Women in the Southeast* (Lexington, KY: Southeast Women's Employment Coalition, 1989), iv, 1–2. "[Tourism] is now one of the top three revenue producers in 46 states and usually ranks among the top five employers ... Outside a narrow tier of male-dominated managers who are drawn to jobs in the tourism industry, tourist employment is predominantly comprised of low-wage jobs which seldom offer the protection of benefits–pension plans, health insurance, even regular, presumably guaranteed breaks on the job ... women who hold these jobs seldom find reason to hope for advancement either in terms of wages or position. It is not uncommon to witness very young men managing older women ... women with years of on-the-job experience which is routinely disregarded and discounted ... While successful development generates much needed local revenue, it also places costly demands

on a community's infrastructure, raises the cost of living, degrades the environment ... dilutes often fragile local cultures, and generates principally marginal seasonal jobs." Additionally, the public sector ends up losing money from having to construct and maintain a new infrastructure.

31. LMDDC, *Agricultural Hearing, December 14, 1989* (Memphis: LMDDC, 1990); statement of Bob Odom, 35.

32. Rainbow Whole Foods Co-op, *Alternative Foods and Sustainable Agriculture: Health and Wealth from Delta Soils* (Memphis: LMDDC, March 1990).

33. LMDDC, *Agricultural Hearing*, 1990, statement of Leroy Percy, n.p.; statement of Cecil Williams, 1–5.

34. Ibid., statement of Calgene vice president Andre Baum, n.p.

35. Ibid., 1990, 8.

36. Magid Dagher, Patrick Ngwolo, Owen Porter, and Gayle Pounds, *Alternative Crop Production and Marketing Strategies for Farmers in the Lower Mississippi Delta Region* (Memphis: LMDDC, 1990), 49. Rainbow Whole Foods Co-op, 1990, 8.

37. Dagher *et al.*, 1990, 49.

38. LMDDC, *Agricultural Hearing December 14, 1989*, 1990, statement of Dan B. Paschall and statement of Bob Odom.

39. Kirby, *Rural Worlds Lost*, 1987, 353; LMDDC, *Agricultural Hearing*, 1990; At the LMDDC's agricultural hearing, the vice president of the 100 year-old Anderson-Tully Company of Memphis stated that his firm's "primary asset is in timberland and its associated resources, with other interests of sawmilling, manufacturing, farming and river transportation, and construction. Anderson-Tully Company is the single largest private landowner within the study area of [the LMDDC], employing 800 people with an annual payroll of $18,000,000." Richard Kluender, *Evaluation of the Timber Resources of the Lower Mississippi Valley Region* (Memphis: LMDDC, 1990), iii.

40. LMDDC, *The Delta Initiatives*, 1990, 80.

41. Ibid., 86–7.

42. LMDDC, *Proceedings of the Conference on Economics, Energy, and the Environment, in the Lower Mississippi Delta* (Memphis: LMDDC, 1990), C7–11, C19–35.

43. Ibid, C29–30.

44. LMDDC, *The Delta Initiatives*, 1990, 80, 77, 84.

45. Noam Chomsky, "Media Control: The Spectacular Achievements of Propaganda" (Westfield, NJ: Open Magazine, 1991) in *Alternative Press Review*, Fall 1993.

46. Ronald K. House and Rhea Harris, *The Labor–Management Cooperation Model and Its Impact on Economic Development and Other Socioeconomic Issues* (Memphis: LMDDC, February 1990), 17.

47. Ibid., 19.

48. Ibid., 1990, 21, 23.

49. Teresa McLendon, *Interstate Cooperation, Regionalism, and Economic Development in the Delta* (Memphis: LMDDC, 1990), 9–10.

50. Paul Purdy, *Report on the Role of the Church in Economic Development* (Memphis: LMDDC, 1990), 19; LMDDC, *Proceedings of the Ecumenical Conference on Economic Issues* (Memphis: LMDDC, 1990), 15.

51. LMDDC, *Proceedings of the Ecumenical Conference*, 1990, 15.

52. Ibid., 18.

53. Clarence Wright, *Race Relations: A Strategy for the Lower Mississippi Delta Region*, (Memphis: LMDDC, 1990), 1, 3.

54. LMDDC, *The Delta Initiatives*, 1990, 61.

55. Arthur Cosby, "Framing the Future: Views on the Future of the Mississippi Delta," in Cosby *et al.*, 1992, 317–25, 320.

56. Judith Porter, "What Works and What Doesn't? Perceptions of Economic Development Among Delta Leaders," in Cosby *et al.*, 1992, 297–310, 304.

57. Ibid., 307.

## 11 The Blues Reconstruction

1. For a discussion of Edwards's leadership in shaping international rice policy see Samuel Yette, *The Choice* (New York: Berkeley Medallion Books, 1971), 139; *Los Angeles Times*, 27 June 1996.

2. *Jackson Clarion Ledger*, 9 February 1992, 13 February 1992, 22 July 1991; *Jackson Advocate*, 7 January 1993, 7 December 1989, 4 July 1991; Thomas Edsall, "Mississippi Turning: GOP Tide Rises on Racial Rift: Gov. Fordice Is in Vanguard of the New South," *Washington Post*, 13 August 1995. John Saunders, "Demography of the Delta," A. Cosby, M. Brackin, T. D. Mason, and E. McCulloch (eds.), *A Social and Economic Portrait of the Mississippi Delta*. (Mississippi: Mississippi State University, 1992), 48–9; *Mississippi Official and Statistical Register*, 1989, 130–78. Before 1980, there was only one Black member of the legislature even though Blacks constituted over one-third of the state's population. After the 1980 census, the federal courts imposed a redistricting plan upon a resistant legislature which resulted in two African Americans entering the 52-member Senate and 20 Blacks entering the 122-seat House after the 1987 state elections. In the Delta, the Delta Council actually had more of its members in the legislature than did African Americans, who represented 60 percent of the total population: four to four in the 22-seat House delegation and two to none in the 10-seat Senate delegation. By 1990, Mississippi's population reached 2,666,287: 36 percent African Americans and 63 percent White, while, minus urbanized De Soto County, the Delta's population was 441,212 persons, 60 percent African American. In 1991, the Department of Justice rejected once again the legislature's redistricting plan because it "unnecessarily fragmented minority populations and submerged urban black population areas with rural ones."

3. Ivory Phillips, "Will Mississippi Ever Change Its Stripes," *Jackson Advocate*, 20 January 1994; *Jackson Clarion Ledger*, 21 and 26 July 1991, 14 and 15 February 1992, 22 July 1991. Some White legislators called the redistricting plan submitted by Black legislators the "Nigger plan." To break the White supremacist resistance, nine African American legislators filed a suit in a federal court that a challenged the legislature's plan. Another forty lawsuits were to be filed challenging county plans that diluted Black voting strength. Whites and Blacks viewed increased Black representation as an opportunity to eliminate the 150-year hold the Delta plantation bloc had had on legislature and on social and economic policy. *Jackson Clarion Ledger* political columnist Bill Minor proclaimed that a new era was dawning. "The once vaunted legislative power of the Delta, where white gentlemen-planter legislators were perpetuated in office to represent counties populated by disenfranchised blacks and held a lion's share of committee chairmanships, is virtually certain to be brought to an end ... Because of the overall decline of population and the increasing black percentages in the Delta, black faces are now expected to replace all but a few white ones from that Northwest region of the state."[22 July].

4. *Memphis Commercial Appeal*, 8 November 1990; Monte Piliawsky, "Racism or Realpolitik?: The Clinton Administration and African-Americans," *Black Scholar*, 24(2) Spring 1994, 2–10, 3; *Jackson Clarion Ledger*, 29 July 1991.

5. *Arkansas Democrat Gazette*, 16 July 1996

6. *Southern Partisan*, Fall 1984, quoted in Peter Applebome, *Dixie Rising: How the South is Shaping American Values, Politics, and Culture* (New York: Times Books, 1996), 121. See also *Washington Post*, 11 August 1994; Ronald Brownstein, "South Rises Again as Region Takes Over GOP Leadership," *Los Angeles Times*, 4 December 1994; *New York Times*, 2 June 1996.

7. *Washington Post*, 22 January 1995. *Wall Street Journal*, 27 September 1994. Occurring simultaneously with the rise of calls from the President and Congress in favor of dismantling federal authority is the rise of calls for regional autonomy. *Los Angeles Times*, 7 June 1996; George F. Will, "They Wish They Were in Dixie," *Baltimore Sun*, 28 December 1995. Founded in Alabama in 1993 by several White professors, the Southern

League is modeled after the Italian separatist Lombard League. According to Will, the goal of the Southern League is "the cultural, social, economic, and political independence and well-being of the Southern people." The antebellum South, the Confederacy and its flag, "cracker culture," Celtic culture, the movies *Braveheart* and *Forest Gump*, plantation balls, states' rights, militias, the Nashville Agrarians, and John C. Calhoun are all celebrated while the New South, carpetbaggers, North-centric professors, the Freedman's Bureau, the Civil Rights and Voting Rights acts, and the "compliant and deadly underclass" are demonized. Among the one thousand attendees at a recent conference were the last living member of the Southern Agrarians and the great grandniece of Nathan Bedford Forrest, the Confederate general who founded the Ku Klux Klan. Christopher Shea, "Defending Dixie,' *Chronicle of Higher Education*, vol. XLII, no. II, 10 November 1995, 9, 17. Several well-known Southern academics have joined the league. Additionally, several critics have claimed that a surprising number of other academics have expressed varying degrees of sympathy for its project, including historian Eugene Genovese. Also see Applebome, 1996, 115–47.

8. William Booth, "Fried Green America: As Mississippi Goes So Goes the Nation," *Washington Post*, 5 February 1995.

9. US Department of Housing and Urban Development and the US Department of Agriculture, *Building Communities Together: The President's Community Enterprise Board* (Washington, DC: US Department of Housing and Urban Development, 1994) 12–14. The announced goal of both programs was to create a partnership in which the federal government would "remove regulatory barriers, simplify program rules, coordinate programs, and invest resources broadly." The requirement of a ten-year strategic plan, regulatory reform, regional targeting, and the delineation of federal, state and local responsibilities was in many ways a duplication of the LMDDC's agenda. The partnership criteria heavily favored applicants representing existing alliances between local chambers of commerce, industry, utilities, universities, banks, and other institutional pillars of the dominant regional blocs.

10. EZ/EC Home Page, US Department of Housing and Urban Development. The Mississippi Delta Empowerment Zone strangely consists of three noncontiguous parcels that cross portions of Bolivar, Sunflower, Leflore, Washington, Humphreys, Holmes. The sixteen municipalities in the three parcels have a population of 29,457 of whom 45.3 percent live in poverty and 79 percent lack a high school diploma. The per capital income is $6,584. The only definite activities are the construction of an adult vocational–technical center, a technical advice center for small businesses, development of a fiber optic telecommunications network around the Delta Council headquarters at the USDA Research Station at Stoneville, and the preservation of the central role of cotton, catfish, and rice.

11. Peter Edelman, "The Worst Thing Bill Clinton Has Done," *Atlantic Monthly*, March 1997, 279(3). 43–58.

12. Ibid.

13. Robert Sheer, "Mississippi Leads the Way in Meanness," *Los Angeles Times*, 24 October 1995. See also Robert Frank, "No quick fix; proposed block grants seem unlikely to cure management problems; Mississippi's recent slip-ups in handling federal aid belie claims of efficiency; but state welfare rolls fall," *Wall Street Journal*, 1 May 1995; Kevin Sack, "In Mississippi, Will Poor Grow Poorer With State Welfare Plan?" *New York Times*, 23 October 1995; William Booth, "School Fearful that 'Johnny Can't Eat,'" *Washington Post*, 7 March 1995; Eric Harrison, "Mississippi Experiment Puts Faith in Religious Groups," *Los Angeles Times*, 29 August 1995. Blurring the line between church and state, "Faith in Families" is another Fordice welfare program. Considered an election-year ploy, its officially stated purpose is the reduction of welfare rolls by encouraging churches to adopt recipients.

14. Edelman, 1997, 43–58. See also Sheer.

15. Alain de Janvry, *The Agrarian Question and Reformism in Latin America* (Baltimore: Johns Hopkins University Press, 1981), 170–1.

16. *Jackson Advocate*, 24 March 1994; *Jet*, 12 May 1997. The institutional rents extracted by the cotton sector and the plantation bloc from the federal government under the Clinton administration are many and varied. For example, while serving as Clinton's Secretary of the USDA, Espy first and foremost, protected the interest of the Delta plantation bloc. Additionally, and often to the detriment of consumers and labor, he supported the interests of large-scale corporate agriculture as a whole. He was also accused of protecting racist practices and individuals. As Secretary, he was sued by several African American farmers from Mississippi for refusing to remedy their complaints about racially discriminatory loan denials and land seizures perpetrated by White employees in the Mississippi office of the USDA. In 1997, Black farmers and employees staged a number of protests against the discriminatory policies and practices of the USDA. Ironically, during one such event at USDA headquarters in Washington, DC, the chairwoman of the Congressional Black Caucus, Maxine Waters, apologized on behalf of the Clinton administration and the Agriculture Department for "years of discrimination."

17. United States Department of Agriculture, "Remarks of Secretary of Agriculture Dan Glickman," Press Release No. 0404.95, 15 May 1995, 1–3.

18. *Los Angeles Times*, 20 January 1996; *New York Times*, 20 January 1996; *Los Angeles Sentinel*, 8 February 1996. All three of the Alabama churches were in a six-mile radius of each other and located in either Greene and Sumter counties, 80 percent and 75 percent African American respectively. The western Tennessee churches attacked were located within one hundred miles of Memphis: Salem Missionary Baptist church, Gibson County, 30 December 1994; Macedonia Missionary Baptist church, Crockett County, and the Johnson Grove Baptist church, Madison County, on 13 January 1995; and the Mount Calvary Baptist church, Hardeman County, 31 January 1995. *New York Times*, 3 January 1994. As reported by Peter Applebome, Bernice Dixon, Rocky Point's clerk, whose uncle was lynched in 1922 and buried in the church graveyard, felt the arson evoked a primal sort of fear. "When this happened it scared people and it still scares them." The initial pace of the investigation also scared people and heightened their fears as word spread that the culprits were known but no arrests were imminent. The three youths were eventually sentenced to three years in jail and ordered to pay $138,000 in restitution. In a widely publicized expression of concern, over 150 volunteers from Black and White churches rebuilt the two sanctuaries. However, according to Francis Lee, an African American leader in Rocky Point, "you hear that Mississippi has moved away from much of the hatred of the past, but beneath the surface the same hatred that was present then is present today." One of the White volunteers observed that some "people, maybe 10 percent, believe that they [the churches] deserve what they got."

19. *New York Times*, 3 January 1994.

20. *Los Angeles Times*, 9, 11, and 20 June 1996. Although two hundred local, state, and federal law enforcement officials investigated the attacks, arrests were slow in coming. Among those arrested in the summer of 1996 were two members of the Ku Klux Klan in South Carolina and a thirteen-year-old White girl in North Carolina. Other federal actions included advising churches on security matters, establishing a toll-free number for tips, and the passage of a bill authored by representatives John Conyers (D.- MI) and Henry Hyde (R.- Il) increasing penalties for the burning of houses of worship.

21. *Jackson Clarion Ledger*, 21 July 1991.

22. Elizabeth Spaid, "Good Times Roll in River Delta and Golden State," *Christian Science Monitor*, 24 November 1995, 3.

23. Ronald Smothers, "Tunica's Wheel of Fortune," *Emerge*, September 1993, 34–7; William Booth, "Casinos Deal Poor Mississippi County a Winning Hand," *Washington Post*, 8 April 1995; Andre Stone, "New dawn in Mississippi Delta," USA Today, May 30, 1997.

24. *Jackson Advocate*, 26 September 1991.

25. Ibid.

26. *Jackson Advoate*, 5 August 1993.

27. J. Clay Smith Jr and Errol D. Brown, "Overview of Supreme Court Opinion in *United States v. Fordice*," paper delivered before a meeting of the National Association for Equal Opportunity in Higher Education, 4 August 1992. *Jackson Clarion Ledger*, 14 July 1991; *Jackson Advocate*, 26 September 1991. Jake Ayers was an important community organizer who was actively involved with the Head Start Program of the Child Development Group of Mississippi, the Mississippi Freedom Democratic Party, the NAACP, Freedom Village, the Delta Blues Festival, and with desegregating secondary education before his death on 26 August 1986, eight months before the trial began.

28. *Jackson Advocate*, 25 March 1993.

29. Ronald Roach and Cheryl D. Fields, "Mississippi Churning," *Black Issues in Higher Education*, 14(6), 15 May 1997, 11–25, 15–19.

30. Jimmie Briggs and Lori S. Robinson, "Black Colleges Under Fire," *Emerge*, (September 1993, 26–31; *New York Times*, 24 April 1996. According to the president of the Grambling State University Alumni Association, Black universities are "being threatened more or less on the level of forced integration. We don't merge. They consolidate or shut it down and you go to the white university." Cheryl D. Fields, "Surveying the Battleground in the Fight for Access," *Black Issues in Higher Education*, 14(6), 15 May 1997, 28–9.

31. *Los Angeles Times*, 26 April 1995; *Jet*, 2 June, 1997, 7.

32. *Daily Bruin News*, 26 September 1994.

33. *Jackson Advocate*, 25 March 1993, 20 January 1994. The members of the commission included Rev. Joseph Lowery, president of the Southern Christian Leadership Conference; Dr Aaron Henry, president of the State Conference of the Mississippi NAACP; Charles Tisdale, publisher of the *Jackson Advocate*; Mississippi representative Jim Evans; Ben Chaney, brother of slain civil rights worker James Chaney; several lawyers; several doctors; and representatives of the National Black Police Officers, the National Council of Churches, the United Methodist Church, and the US Commission on Civil Rights.

34. *Jackson Advocate*, 8 July 1993.

35. Ann Monroe, "Race to the Right," *Mother Jones*, May/June 1997, 34–9, 36; *Jackson Advocate*, 8 March 1990, 24 May 1990, 8 April 1993.

36. Stephen E. Henderson, "Cliche, Monotony, and Touchstone: Folk song composition and the New Black Poetry," in John Oliver Killens and Jerry W. Ward Jr (eds.), *Black Southern Voices: An Anthology of Fiction, Poetry, Drama, Nonfiction, and Critical Essays* (New York: Meridan Books, 1992), 529–49, 530.

37. Mary Ellison, *Extensions of the Blues* (New York: Riverrun Press, 1989), 12.

38. Charles Keil, *Urban Blues* (Chicago: University of Chicago Press, 1970), 189–7; *Jackson Advocate*, 22 April 1993. An example of attempts to limit social vision is the enduring battle over the Confederate battle flag which has occupied the upper lef-hand corner of the Mississippi state flag since 1894. A 1992 bill would have eliminated this symbol from the state flag. After the bill's defeat, the State Conference of the NAACP filed suit to remove it. State Conference president Aaron Henry stated, "[Our] desire is that we don't continue to be subjected to the government's imposing of the Confederate flag on all citizens." Dessie Moore, student body president of Tougaloo College, described the flag as "the symbol of our holocaust." Those adherents of the Confederate-centric civil religion denied that the flag was a celebration of slavery. Fordice argued that the flag was "no segregation symbol in Mississippi. It goes back to our beginning." State senators Mike Gunn and Dean Kirby argued in court that the Civil War was about freedom not slavery and that African American leaders should to be silent on the flag and only speak on approved topics. "Rather than pursue the specter of racism … [p]laintiffs would be infinitely better served by using their energies to wean the poor off welfare, improve health care, and create jobs and improve education for all Mississippians." *Jackson Advocate*, 18 April 1993. Conversely, numerous organizations continue to deny all efforts to silence debates over human rights. For example, the Jackson-based National

Coalition of Blacks for Reparations (N-COBRA) organized the Fourth Annual Holocaust Memorial and Reparations Conference at Southern University in Baton Rouge, Louisiana, in 1993. Reparations of over $6 billion were demanded for the damages caused by slavery, racism, political imprisonment, and miseducation. These funds would be used to establish colleges, immigration programs, development banks, and an autonomous territory. At its Black Nation Day held in Jackson in 1993, a number of national and local organizations conerned with self-determination, rural development, and cultural and human rights assembled to celebrate the twenty-fifth anniversary of the founding of an organization that was nearly destroyed in Jackson two decades earlier, the Republic of New Africa. Among the organizations represented at the Black Nation Day assembly were the New African People's Organization, the Jackson Human Rights Coalition, the city-wide Coalition for Progressive Jackson, the Nation of Islam, the Organization of Black Struggle, the Black United Front, the National Conference of Black Lawyers, the United Afrikan Movement, the Black Consciousness Movement, the Spear and Shield Collective, the Malcolm X Grassroots Movement, the Kwanzaa Coalition, the Afro-American Liberation League, Black Workers for Justice, the Federation of Southern Cooperatives, and representatives from Chicano and Native American organizations.

39. Barlow, 325.

40. Ibid., 326.

41. Ibid., 327–8.

42. Maya Angelou, *I Know Why The Caged Bird Sings* (New York: Random House, 1970), 156.

# Postscript

1. Several firms have taken advantage of MDEZA incentives. A few are using the ten-year, $3000, annual tax write-off for every new employee hired. Some have used new subsidies to expand their operations while others have used them to construct a new catfish processing plant and a new textile mill. Yet some firms have refused to participate because they wanted to hire employees who lived near the zone rather than those African Americans who live in it. Some White religious leaders were also unwilling to participate. "In its application, MDEZA called on local communities to establish race councils, in cooperation with churches, to improve race relations. [Harry] Bowie [the African American president of the Delta Foundation and co-chair of MDEZA] concedes that so far the councils haven't been established. And [African American] Mayor [Karen] Crawford in Isola said churches are reluctant to get involved for fear the government will attempt to interfere with their worship service." Jim Yardley, "The Delta: Growing incentives—Mississippi empowerment program offers hope, points to potential pitfalls," *Atlanta Journal/Constitution*, 13 April 1997.

2. Jason DeParle, "New Welfare Law Weighs Heavy on the Mississippi Delta," *New York Times*, October 16, 1997. DeParle described the impact of welfare reform in the Mississippi Delta in the following manner: "While President Clinton has flatly declared 'the debate is over—we know now that welfare reform works,' the hard luck counties of the Mississippi Delta show the difficulties that can emerge when tough laws collide with a weak economy … with unemployment rates hovering at 10 percent or more, many of those leaving the rolls are failing to find jobs. Indeed, during one recent period, the families dropped for violating the new work rules outnumbered those placed in jobs by a margin of nearly two to one … And the penalties in Mississippi are the nation's toughest. Those who miss appointments or decline work assignments surrender not only their entire cash grant, but all of their family's food stamps and the medical insurance of adults." The per capita federal contribution to AFDC families in Mississippi is the lowest in the nation, $2100 per family as opposed to $7200 per family in Wisconsin. The state's AFDC contribution is also the lowest in the nation, $120 a month for a mother and two

children. Although the welfare rolls declined 26 percent in the previous year in a five-county area surrounding Greenville, one researcher estimated that the economy of this region was only creating one job for every 254 families moved off welfare. Due to the lack of jobs, to meet the work requirement, mothers often have to travel to neighboring counties and states. In September of 1997, nearly half of the women placed on jobs found themselves working for the minimum wage, $5.15 an hour, in an Eudora, Arkansas, catfish processing plant. This plant specializes in hiring poor, young African American mothers who reside in the Deltas of Arkansas, Louisiana, and Mississippi. For the first six months of their employment, Mississippi will pay all but $1 of the worker's hourly wage. In essence, the state is aggressively eliminating destitute families from the welfare and food stamp rolls and then using the monies they need to subsist to subsidize the plantation owners who raise catfish and the plant owners who process them. This allows the latter to pay sub-minimum wages to the former recipients who have been forced to take jobs that are both grueling and crippling. According to DeParle, to "get there, recipients make an hour-long commute on a school bus that leaves Greenville at 6:30 each morning ... Arriving at the plant, they don hairnets, earplugs and steel-lined safety gloves to work along the clattering saws and conveyor belts that process 100,000 catfish a day. Noting that turnover runs to more than 300 percent a year, Donald Taylor, the plant's comptroller, acknowledged the unappealing nature of the minimum-wage work: 'You work in the cold, you work in the wet—and of course you're around guts.'" Faced with a choice between taking a debilitating minimum-wage job with no provisions for childcare on the one hand, and the termination of benefits on the other, many women have chosen termination and all of the hunger, overcrowding, and sickness that flow from it. When asked about the future of the more than eight thousand families on welfare in the Mississippi Delta, the executive director of the Mississippi Department of Human Services responded, "If you've seen *The Grapes of Wrath* that's what it was all about."

3. John Cloud, "The KGB of Mississippi," *Time*, 30 March 1998. Many of the Sovereignty Commission's files were destroyed during the life of the agency. Other files are being withheld from public inspection due to objections raised by those named as informants or terrorists. Overall, the activities described in the newly released documents are likely to reverberate throughout the state and country for many years, in part due to the murders that can now be solved and to the African American leaders whose names are among the list of five thousand informers.

4. "Congressman Thompson Calls for Federal Hate Crime Investigation into Jackson Advocate Bombing," www.house.gov/thompson/012898.html; "Jackson Advocate, Black Weekly Newspaper In Jackson, MS, Firebombed," *Jet Magazine*, 16 February 1998.

# Index